OpenGL
Reference Manual,
Third Edition

The Official Reference Document to OpenGL, Version 1.2

OpenGL Architecture Review Board
Editor: Dave Shreiner

ADDISON-WESLEY

Boston • San Francisco • New York • Toronto • Montreal
London •
Capetown • • Mexico City

Leeds Metropolitan University

17 0357437 9

D1471599

LEEDS METROPOLITAN
UNIVERSITY
LEARNING CENTRE

1703574379
1Q-BV
BP-38453
25.4.03
006.6 OPE

Silicon Graphics, the Silicon Graphics logo, OpenGL, and IRIS are registered trademarks and IRIS Graphics Library is a trademark of SGI. X Window System is a trademark of Massachusetts Institute of Technology.

Many of the designations used by manufacturers and sellers to distinguish their products are claimed as trademarks. Where those designations appear in this book, and Addison-Wesley was aware of a trademark claim, the designations have been printed in initial capital letters or all capital letters.

The authors and publisher have taken care in the preparation of this book, but make no expressed or implied warranty of any kind and assume no responsibility for errors or omissions. No liability is assumed for incidental or consequential damages in connection with or arising out of the use of the information or programs contained herein.

The publisher offers discounts on this book when ordered in quantity for special sales. For more information, please contact:

Pearson Education Corporate Sales Division
201 W. 103rd Street
Indianapolis, IN 46290
(800) 428-5331
corpsales@pearsoned.com

Visit AW on the Web: www.awprofessional.com

Library of Congress Cataloging-in-Publication Data

OpenGL reference manual: the official reference document to OpenGL, version 1.2
OpenGL Architecture Review Board; Dave Shreiner, editor.—3rd ed.
    p. cm.
   Includes bibliographical references.
   ISBN 0-201-65765-1
    1. Computer graphics. 2. OpenGL. I. Shreiner, Dave. II. OpenGL Architecture Review
    Board.

T385.06421999
006.6'6—dc21
                                        99-056697

Copyright © 2000 by Silicon Graphics, Inc.

All rights reserved. No part of this publication may be reproduced, stored in a retrieval system, or transmitted, in any form or by any means, electronic, mechanical, photocopying, recording, or otherwise, without the prior consent of the publisher. Printed in the United States of America. Published simultaneously in Canada.

Text printed on recycled and acid-free paper.

ISBN 0201657651

4 5 6 7 8 9 MA 05 04 03 02

4th Printing July 2002

Contents

Preface

OpenGL is a software interface to graphics hardware (the "GL" stands for Graphics Library). This interface consists of several hundred functions that allow graphics programmers to specify the objects and operations needed to produce high-quality color images of three-dimensional objects. Many of the functions are actually simple variations of each other, so in reality there are only about 180 substantially different functions.

The OpenGL Utility Library (GLU) and the OpenGL Extension to the X Window System (GLX) provide useful supporting features and complement the core OpenGL set of functions. This manual explains what all these functions do. The following list summarizes the contents of each chapter.

- **Chapter 1, Introduction to OpenGL,** provides a conceptual overview of OpenGL. It uses a high-level block diagram to explain all the major stages of processing OpenGL performs.

- **Chapter 2, Overview of Commands and Routines,** describes in more detail how OpenGL processes input data (in the form of vertices specifying a geometric object or of pixels defining an image) and how you can control this processing using OpenGL functions. GLU and GLX functions are also discussed.

- **Chapter 3, Summary of Commands and Routines,** lists the OpenGL commands in groups according to the tasks they perform. The full prototypes provided in this chapter allow you to use it as a quick reference once you understand what the commands accomplish.

- **Chapter 4, Defined Constants and Associated Commands,** lists the constants defined in OpenGL and the commands that use them.

- **Chapter 5, OpenGL Reference Pages**, which forms the bulk of this manual, contains reference pages describing each set of related OpenGL commands. Commands with parameters that differ only in data type are described together. Each reference page describes the parameters, the effect of the commands, and what errors might result from using the commands.

  Additionally, this section contains the reference pages for the OpenGL ARB extensions: multitexture and the imaging subset. Not all OpenGL implementations may include support for the ARB extensions.

- **Chapter 6, GLU Reference Pages**, contains reference pages for all GLU commands.

- **Chapter 7, GLX Reference Pages**, contains reference pages for all GLX commands.

What You Should Know Before Reading This Manual

This manual is intended as the companion reference volume to the third edition of the *OpenGL Programming Guide,* by the OpenGL Architecture Review Board, Mason Woo, Jackie Neider, Tom Davis, and Dave Shreiner (Reading, MA: Addison–Wesley, 1999). Both books assume that you know how to program in C.

While the focus of the *OpenGL Programming Guide* is on how to use OpenGL, the focus of this reference manual is on how OpenGL works. For a complete understanding of OpenGL, you need both types of information. Another difference between the two books is that most of the content of this manual is organized alphabetically, based on the assumption that you know what you don't know and therefore need only to look up a description of a particular command. The *OpenGL Programming Guide* is organized like a tutorial: it explains the simpler OpenGL concepts first and builds up to the more complex ones. Although you don't have to read the *OpenGL Programming Guide* to understand the command descriptions in this manual, your understanding of their intended use will be much more complete if you have read it.

If you don't know much about computer graphics, start with the programming guide rather than this reference manual. In addition, consider these books.

- *Computer Graphics: Principles and Practice* by James D. Foley, Andries van Dam, Steven K. Feiner, and John F. Hughes (Reading, MA:

Addison–Wesley)—This book is an encyclopedic treatment of the subject of computer graphics. It includes a wealth of information but is probably best read after you have some experience with the subject.

- *3D Computer Graphics: A User's Guide for Artists and Designers* by Andrew S. Glassner (New York: Design Press)—This book is a nontechnical, gentle introduction to computer graphics. It focuses on the visual effects that can be achieved rather than on the techniques needed to achieve them.

- *The Way Computer Graphics Work* by Olin Lathrop (New York: John Wiley and Sons, Inc.)—This book is a general introduction to computer graphics directed at the beginner- to intermediate-level computer users. It describes the general principles required for understanding computer graphics.

Style Conventions

This guide uses the following style conventions:

- **Bold**—Command and routine names

- *Italics*—Variables, arguments, parameter names, spatial dimensions, and document names

- Regular—Enumerated types and defined constants

- `Monospace font`—Code examples

Note that this manual uses abbreviations for command names. Many OpenGL commands are just variations of each other. For simplicity, only the base name of the command is used, and an asterisk is included to indicate that there may be more to the actual command name than is being shown. For example, **glVertex*** stands for all variations of the command available to specify vertices.

The commands differ mostly in the data type of arguments. Some commands differ in the number of related arguments and whether those arguments can be specified as a vector or whether they must be specified separately in a list. For example, if you use the **glVertex2f** command, you must supply *x* and *y* coordinates as floating-point numbers; with **glVertex3sv**, you must supply an array of three short integer values for *x*, *y*, and *z*.

Acknowledgments

The original version of this manual owes its existence to many people. Kurt Akeley of Silicon Graphics, Sally Browning of SABL Productions, and Kevin P. Smith of Silicon Graphics wrote most of the material for the first edition, with contributions from Jackie Neider and Mark Segal (both from Silicon Graphics). *The OpenGL Graphics System: A Specification* (coauthored by Mark and Kurt), *The OpenGL Graphics System Utility Library* (written by Kevin), and *OpenGL Graphics with the X Window System* (written by Phil Karlton) served as source documents for the authors. Phil Karlton and Kipp Hickman assisted by helping to define and create OpenGL at Silicon Graphics, with help from Raymond Drewry of Gain Technology, Inc., Fred Fisher of Digital Equipment Corp., and Randi Rost of Kubota Pacific Computer, Inc. The members of the OpenGL Architecture Review Board—Murray Cantor and Linas Vepstas from International Business Machines, Paula Womack and Jeff Lane of Digital Equipment Corporation, Murali Sundaresan of Intel, and Chuck Whitmer of Microsoft—also contributed. Thad Beier, together with Seth Katz and the Inventor team at Silicon Graphics, created the cover image. Kay Maitz of Silicon Graphics, Arthur Evans of Evans Technical Communications, and Susan Blau provided production assistance; Tanya Kucak copyedited the manual. Finally, this book wouldn't exist unless OpenGL did, for which all the members of the OpenGL team at Silicon Graphics need to be thanked for their efforts: Momi Akeley, Allen Akin, Chris Frazier, Bill Glazier, Paul Ho, Simon Hui, Lesley Kalmin, Pierre Tardif, Jim Winget, and especially Wei Yen, in addition to the previously mentioned Kurt, Phil, Mark, Kipp, and Kevin. Many other Silicon Graphics employees, who are too numerous to mention, helped refine the definition and functionality of OpenGL.

For the *OpenGL Reference Manual for OpenGL, Version 1.1*, Renate Kempf of Kempf and Associates and Chris Frazier of Silicon Graphics added all functions that are new in the *OpenGL 1.1 Specification* and edited and checked all other reference pages. The material was then diligently reviewed by Allen Akin, David Blythe, Craig Dunwoody, Chris Frazier, and Paula Womack at Silicon Graphics and by members of the OpenGL Architecture Review Board, including Kurt Akeley at Silicon Graphics, Dave Arns at HP, Bill Armstrong at E&S, Dale Kirkland at Intergraph, and Bimal Poddar at IBM. Simon Hui of Silicon Graphics reviewed the GLX pages, and John Spitzer reviewed the revised foldout graphic.

For the third version, the *OpenGL Reference Manual for OpenGL, Version 1.2*, Dave Shreiner of SGI added most of the manual pages for OpenGL 1.2 and GLX 1.3's new functionality, and updated the poster with the help of

About This Book

David Yu. Norman Chin updated the manual pages for the GLU 1.3. The daunting task of reviewing the manual pages was diligently pursued by Ron Bielaski, Steve Cunningham, Jeffery Galinovsky, Eric Haines, Mark Kilgard, Dale Kirkland, Seth Livingston, Bimal Poddar, David Nishimoto, Mike Schmitt, Scott Thompson, David Yu, and the members of the OpenGL Team at SGI: Craig Dunwoody, Jaya Kanajan, George Kyraizis, Jon Leech, and Ken Nicholson.

Special thanks to Jon Leech, who edited the OpenGL 1.2.1, GLU 1.3, and GLX 1.3 specifications, and the OpenGL ARB for keeping OpenGL alive and thriving, and to Laura Cooper and Dany Galgani for their production assistance in creating this manual.

Chapter 1

Introduction to OpenGL

OpenGL is a software interface for graphics hardware. Its main purpose is to render two- and three-dimensional objects into a frame buffer. The objects are described as sequences of vertices (which define geometric objects) or pixels (which define images). OpenGL performs several processing steps on the data to convert it to pixels to form the final desired image in the frame buffer.

This chapter presents a global view of how OpenGL works; it contains these major sections.

- **OpenGL Fundamentals** briefly explains basic OpenGL concepts, such as what a graphic primitive is and how OpenGL implements a client-server execution model.

- **Basic OpenGL Operation** gives a high-level description of how OpenGL processes data and produces a corresponding image in the frame buffer.

OpenGL Fundamentals

This section explains some of the concepts inherent in OpenGL.

OpenGL Primitives and Commands

OpenGL draws a *primitive*—point, line segment, or polygon—using several selectable modes. You can control each mode independently; that is, setting one mode doesn't affect whether other modes are set (although modes may interact to determine what eventually ends up in the frame buffer). An OpenGL program uses function calls to specify primitives, set modes, and describe other operations.

Primitives are defined by a group of one or more *vertices*. A vertex is a point, an endpoint of a line, or a corner of a polygon. Data (consisting of vertex coordinates, colors, normals, texture coordinates, and edge flags) is associated with a vertex, and each vertex and its associated data are processed independently, in order, and in the same way. The only exception to this rule is if the group of vertices must be *clipped* so that a particular primitive fits within a specified region; in this case, vertex data may be modified and new vertices created. The type of clipping depends on which primitive the group of vertices represents.

Commands are always processed in the order in which they are received, although there may be an indeterminate delay before a command takes effect. This means that each primitive is drawn completely before any subsequent command takes effect. It also means that state-querying commands return data that's consistent with complete execution of all previously issued OpenGL commands.

OpenGL as a Procedural Language

OpenGL is fundamentally procedural rather than descriptive: OpenGL provides fairly direct control over the fundamental operations of two- and three-dimensional graphics. This includes specification of transformation matrices, lighting equation coefficients, antialiasing methods, and pixel update operators. However, OpenGL doesn't let you describe or model complex geometric objects directly.

The OpenGL commands you issue specify how a certain result should be produced (that is, what procedure should be followed) rather than what exactly that result should look like. Because of this procedural nature, it helps to know how OpenGL works—the order in which it carries out its operations, for example—in order to fully understand how to use it.

The OpenGL Execution Model

OpenGL uses a client-server model for interpreting commands. An application (the client) issues commands, which are interpreted and processed by OpenGL (the server). The server may or may not operate on the same computer as the client. In this sense, OpenGL is network-transparent. A server can maintain several GL *contexts*, each of which is an encapsulated GL state. A client can connect to any one of these contexts. The required network protocol can be implemented by augmenting an already existing protocol (such as that of the X Window System) or by using an independent protocol. OpenGL doesn't provide commands for obtaining user input.

The effects of OpenGL commands on the frame buffer are ultimately controlled by the window system that allocates frame buffer resources. The window system determines which portions of the frame buffer OpenGL may access at any given time and communicates to OpenGL how those portions are structured. Therefore, there are no OpenGL commands to configure the frame buffer or initialize OpenGL. Frame buffer configuration takes place outside of OpenGL in conjunction with the window system; OpenGL initialization takes place when the window system allocates a window for OpenGL rendering. (GLX, the X extension of the OpenGL interface, provides these capabilities, as described in "OpenGL Extension to the X Window System.")

Basic OpenGL Operation

Figure 1-1 provides an abstract, high-level block diagram of how OpenGL processes data. In the diagram, commands enter from the left and proceed through what can be thought of as a processing pipeline. Some commands specify geometric objects to be drawn, and others control how the objects are handled during the various processing stages.

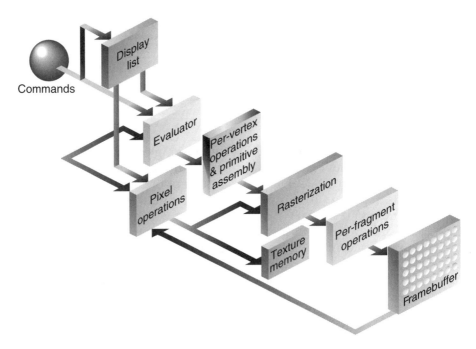

Figure 1-1   How OpenGL Processes Data

When commands enter the pipeline, you can choose to either have all commands proceed immediately through the pipeline or accumulate some of them in a *display list* for processing at a later time.

The *evaluator* stage of processing provides an efficient means for approximating curve and surface geometry by evaluating polynomial commands of input values. During the next stage, *per-vertex operations and primitive assembly*, OpenGL processes geometric primitives—points, line segments, and polygons, all of which are described by vertices. Vertices are transformed and lit, and primitives are clipped to the viewport in preparation for the next stage.

Rasterization produces a series of frame buffer addresses and associated values using a two-dimensional description of a point, line segment, or polygon. Each *fragment* so produced is fed into the last stage, *per-fragment operations*, which performs the final operations on the data before it's stored as pixels in the *frame buffer*. These operations include conditional updates to the frame buffer based on incoming and previously stored depth-values (for depth-buffering). They also include blending of incoming pixel colors with stored colors, as well as masking and other logical operations on pixel values.

Input data can be in the form of pixels rather than vertices. Such data, which might describe an image for use in texture mapping, skips the first stage of processing (just described) and instead is processed as pixels, in the *pixel operations* stage. The result of this stage is either stored as *texture memory*, for use in the rasterization stage, or rasterized. In that case, the resulting fragments are merged into the frame buffer just as if they were generated from geometric data.

An OpenGL application can obtain all elements of OpenGL state, including the contents of the texture memory and even of the frame buffer.

Chapter 2

Overview of Commands and Routines

Many OpenGL commands specifically affect how objects such as points, lines, polygons, and bitmaps are drawn. Other commands, for example those that enable antialiasing or texturing, control how drawing occurs. Still other commands are specifically concerned with frame buffer manipulation.

This chapter briefly describes how all OpenGL commands work together to create the OpenGL processing pipeline. It also gives brief overviews of the commands in the OpenGL Utility Library (GLU) and the OpenGL extensions to the X Window System (GLX).

The chapter has the following main sections.

- **The OpenGL Processing Pipeline** expands on the discussion in Chapter 1 by explaining how specific OpenGL commands control the processing of data.

- **Additional OpenGL Commands** discusses several sets of OpenGL commands not covered in the previous section.

- **OpenGL Utility Library** describes available GLU routines.

- **OpenGL Extension to the X Window System** describes available GLX routines.

The OpenGL Processing Pipeline

While Chapter 1 provided an overview of how OpenGL works, this chapter takes a closer look at the stages in which data is actually processed and ties these stages to OpenGL commands. Figure 2-1 is a more detailed block diagram of the OpenGL processing pipeline.

Through most of the pipeline, you can see three arrows between the major stages. These arrows represent vertices and the two primary types of data that can be associated with vertices: color values and texture coordinates. Note that vertices are assembled into primitives, then to fragments, and finally to pixels in the frame buffer. This progression is discussed in more detail in the following sections.

The effect of an OpenGL command may vary depending on whether certain modes are enabled. For example, the lighting-related commands only have the desired effect of producing a properly lit object if you enable lighting. To enable a particular mode, use the **glEnable** command and supply the appropriate constant to identify the mode (for example, GL_LIGHTING). The following sections don't discuss specific modes, but the reference page for **glEnable** provides a complete list of the modes that can be enabled. To disable a mode, call **glDisable**.

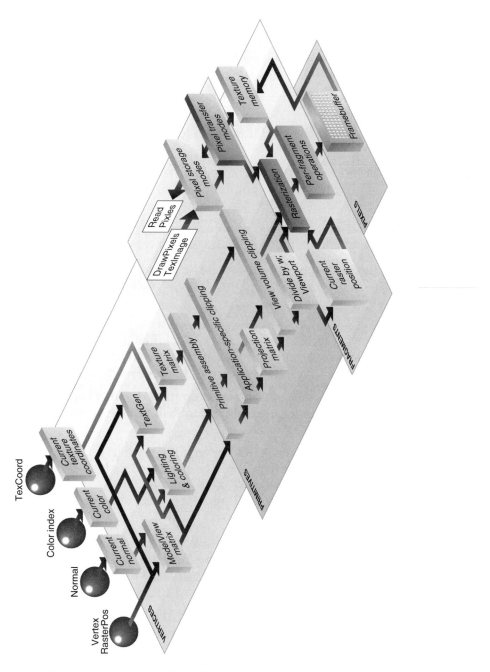

Figure 2-1   Stages of the OpenGL Processing Pipeline

Vertices

This section relates the OpenGL commands that perform per-vertex operations to the processing stages shown in Figure 2-1. It includes information on vertex arrays.

Input Data

You must provide several types of input data to the OpenGL pipeline.

- Vertices—Vertices describe the shape of the desired geometric object. To specify vertices, use **glVertex*** commands in conjunction with **glBegin** and **glEnd** to create a point, line, or polygon. You can also use **glRect*** to describe an entire rectangle at once.

- Edge flag—By default, all edges of polygons are boundary edges. Use the **glEdgeFlag*** command to explicitly set the edge flag.

- Current raster position—The current raster position determines raster coordinates for pixel and bitmap drawing operations. It is specified with **glRasterPos***.

- Current normal—A normal vector associated with a particular vertex determines how a surface at that vertex is oriented in three-dimensional space; this in turn affects how much light that particular vertex receives. Use **glNormal*** to specify a normal vector.

- Current color—The color of a vertex determines the final color of the lit object. Specify color with **glColor*** if in RGBA mode or with **glIndex*** if in color index mode.

- Current texture coordinates—Texture coordinates determine the location in a texture map that should be associated with a vertex of an object. They are specified with **glTexCoord*** and with **glMultiTexCoord*ARB**, if the ARB multitexture extension is supported.

When **glVertex*** is called, the resulting vertex inherits the current edge flag, normal, color, and texture coordinates. Therefore, **glEdgeFlag***, **glNormal***, **glColor***, and **glTexCoord*** must be called before **glVertex*** to affect the resulting vertex.

All of the vertex input data listed above can be specified using "Vertex Arrays," described on page 11, which allow arrays of data values to be passed with a single function call. This may be a more efficient method for specifying vertex data to some OpenGL implementations.

Matrix Transformations

Vertices and normals are each transformed by matrices before they're used to produce an image in the frame buffer. Vertices are transformed by the modelview and projection matrices, while lighting normals are transformed by the modelview matrix. You can use commands such as **glMatrixMode**, **glMultMatrix***, **glRotate***, **glTranslate***, and **glScale*** to compose the desired transformations, or you can directly specify matrices with **glLoadMatrix*** and **glLoadIdentity**. Use **glPushMatrix** and **glPopMatrix** to save and restore modelview and projection matrices on their respective stacks.

Lighting and Coloring

In addition to specifying colors and normal vectors, you may define the desired lighting conditions with **glLight*** and **glLightModel***, and the desired material properties with **glMaterial***. Related commands you might use to control how lighting calculations are performed include **glShadeModel**, **glFrontFace**, and **glColorMaterial**.

Generating Texture Coordinates

Rather than explicitly supplying texture coordinates, you can have OpenGL generate them as a function of other vertex data. This is what the **glTexGen*** command does. After the texture coordinates have been specified or generated, they are transformed by the texture matrix. This matrix is controlled with the same commands mentioned in "Matrix Transformations" above.

Primitive Assembly

Once all these calculations have been performed, vertices are assembled into primitives—points, line segments, or polygons—together with the relevant edge flag, color, and texture information for each vertex.

Vertex Arrays

Vertex arrays let you specify geometric primitives with very few calls. Instead of calling an OpenGL function to pass each individual vertex, normal, or color, you can specify separate arrays of vertices, normals, and colors and use them to define a sequence of primitives (all of the same type) that are drawn when a single call is made to **glDrawArrays**. The functions **glVertexPointer**, **glNormalPointer**, **glColorPointer**, **glIndexPointer**, **glTexCoordPointer**, and **glEdgeFlagPointer** describe the location and organization of the arrays. Use **glEnableClientState** and **glDisableClientState** to specify from which vertex array vertex coordinates and attributes should be accessed.

All of the active data for a single vertex can be specified in a single call to **glArrayElement** which is used in conjunction with **glBegin** and **glEnd**. Additionally, vertex arrays may be randomly accessed using the functions **glDrawElements** and **glDrawRangeElements**.

Primitives

During the next stage of processing, primitives are converted to pixel fragments in several steps: primitives are clipped appropriately, the necessary corresponding adjustments are made to the color and texture data, and the relevant coordinates are transformed to window coordinates. Finally, rasterization converts the clipped primitives to pixel fragments.

Clipping

OpenGL handles points, line segments, and polygons slightly differently if they need to be clipped. Points are either retained in their original state (if they're inside the clip volume) or discarded (if they're outside). If portions of line segments or polygons are outside the clip volume, new vertices are generated at the clip points. For polygons, an entire edge may need to be constructed between such new vertices. For both line segments and polygons that are clipped, the edge flag, color, and texture information is assigned to all new vertices.

Clipping actually happens in two steps.

1. **Application-specific clipping**. Immediately after primitives are assembled, they're clipped in *eye coordinates* as necessary for any arbitrary clipping planes you've defined for your application with **glClipPlane**. (Any OpenGL implementation supports at least six such application-specific clipping planes.)

2. **View volume clipping**. Next, primitives are transformed by the projection matrix (into *clip coordinates*) and clipped by the corresponding viewing volume. You can control this matrix using matrix transformation commands, but it is most typically specified by **glFrustum** or **glOrtho**.

Transforming to Window Coordinates

Before clip coordinates can be converted to *window coordinates*, they are normalized, that is, divided by the value of *w* to yield *normalized device coordinates*. After that, the viewport transformation applied to these normalized coordinates produces window coordinates. You control the viewport, which determines the area of the on-screen window that displays an image, with **glDepthRange** and **glViewport**.

Rasterization

Rasterization is the process by which a primitive is converted to a two-dimensional image. Each point of this image contains such information as color, depth, and texture data. Together, a point and its associated information are called a *fragment*.

The current raster position (as specified with **glRasterPos***) is used in various ways during this stage for pixel drawing and bitmaps. Different issues arise when rasterizing the three different types of primitives; in addition, pixel rectangles and bitmaps need to be rasterized:

- **Primitives.** You control how primitives are rasterized with commands that allow you to choose dimensions and stipple patterns: **glPointSize**, **glLineWidth**, **glLineStipple**, and **glPolygonStipple**. You can also control how the front and back faces of polygons are rasterized with **glCullFace**, **glFrontFace**, and **glPolygonMode**.

- **Pixels.** Several commands control pixel storage and transfer modes. The command **glPixelStore*** controls the encoding of pixels in client memory, and **glPixelTransfer*** and **glPixelMap*** control how pixels are processed before they are placed in the frame buffer. Additional pixel processing is available if the OpenGL implementation you're using supports the "ARB Imaging Subset," described on page 15. A pixel rectangle is specified with **glDrawPixels**; its rasterization is controlled with **glPixelZoom**.

- **Bitmaps.** Bitmaps are rectangles of zeros and ones that specify a particular pattern of fragments to be produced. Each of these fragments has the same associated data. A bitmap is specified using **glBitmap**.

- **Textures.** Texturing maps a portion of a specified texture image onto each primitive when texturing is enabled. To accomplish this mapping, use the color of the texture image at the location indicated by a fragment's texture coordinates to modify the fragment's RGBA color.

To specify a texture image, call **glTexImage1D**, **glTexImage2D**, or **glTexImage3D**. To create a texture image by copying values from the frame buffer, call **glCopyTexImage1D**, **glCopyTexImage2D**. You can also load subimages by calling **glTexSubImage1D**, **glTexSubImage2D**, and **glTexSubImage3D**, or replace parts of a texture image by copying from the frame buffer with **glCopyTexSubImage1D**, **glCopyTexSubImage2D**, or **glCopyTexSubImage3D**. The commands **glTexParameter*** and **glTexEnv*** control how texture values are interpreted and applied to a fragment.

To specify that certain textures are preferentially stored in texture memory, generate the textures as named textures (texture objects) using **glBindTexture**, then call **glPrioritizeTextures** to order them. To delete a texture object, call **glDeleteTexture**.

- **Color Sum.** Adds the color computed from the specular lighting contribution to the fragment after texturing. Use **glLightModel** with an argument of GL_SEPARATE_SPECULAR_COLOR for the GL_LIGHT_MODEL_COLOR_CONTROL parameter to specify that the specular lighting color should be computed separately.

- **Fog.** OpenGL can blend a fog color with a rasterized fragment's post-texturing color using a blending factor that depends on the distance between the eyepoint and the fragment. Use **glFog*** to specify the fog color and blending factor.

- **Polygon Offset.** If you are rendering hidden-line images or applying decals to surfaces, consider calling **glPolygonOffset** to displace the depth values of fragments generated by rendering polygons by a fixed bias plus a variable amount. The amount depends on the change in the polygon's depth values and its screen size. This displacement allows polygons in the same plane to be rendered without interaction. Enable one of the three polygon modes GL_POLYGON_OFFSET_FILL, GL_POLYGON_OFFSET_LINE, or GL_POLYGON_OFFSET_POINT to determine how the displacement takes place.

Applications of polygon offset include rendering hidden-line images, rendering solids with highlighted edges, and applying decals to surfaces.

ARB Imaging Subset

OpenGL implementations may support the optional OpenGL ARB imaging subset, which consists of several additional pixel processing operations. The following functionality is only supported if the string GL_ARB_imaging is returned when **glGetString** is called with GL_EXTENSIONS as an argument.

The functionality included in the ARB imaging subset includes:

- **Color Tables.** Color table lookups provide per-pixel replacement of color components. Color tables are specified using the **glColorTable** routine. To specify a color table based on values in the frame buffer, call **glCopyColorTable**. **glColorSubTable** allows you to replace a portion of a color table, and **glCopyColorSubTable** uses values from the frame buffer to replace the specified portion. Color tables can be scaled and biased when they are specified. Call **glColorTableParameter*** to specify the scale and bias values.

- **Convolution Filters.** Convolutions combine neighboring pixels to compute a resulting pixel value. Convolution filters can be specified using **glConvoltionFilter1D**, **glConvolutionFilter2D**, or **glSeparableFilter2D**. Alternatively, convolution filters can be specified by values in the frame buffer using **glCopyConvolutionFilter1D**, and **glCopyConvolutionFilter2D**. Convolution filters can be scaled and biased when they are specified by calling **glConvolutionParameter*** to specify the scale or bias values.

  After convolution, the resulting pixel values may be scaled and biased. Specify the scale and bias values using **glPixelTransfer***.

- **Color Matrix Transformations.** Matrix transformation can be applied to pixels using the color matrix stack. Call **glMatrixMode** with GL_COLOR to modify the current color matrix with the routines described in "Matrix Transformations."

  After the color matrix transformation, pixel values may be scaled and biased. Call **glPixelTransfer*** to specify the scale and bias values.

- **Histograms.** Histograms determine the distribution of values for a pixel rectangle. Use **glHistogram** to specify which color components are to be counted. Call **glGetHistogram** to retrieve the results of the histogram computation. **glResetHistogram** is called to reset the histogram tables, and **glGetHistogramParameter*** should be called to retrieve values describing the histogram tables.

- **Minmax.** The minimum and maximum pixel values for a pixel rectangle can be computed by calling **glMinmax**. **glGetMinmax** returns the computed minimum and maximums for the selected color components specified with **glMinmax**. The internal minmax tables can be reset by calling **glResetMinmax**, and parameters describing the tables can be obtained by calling **glGetMinmaxParameter***.

- **Blending Equations.** Blending equations allows pixels to be combined in ways other than being summed. **glBlendEquation** specifies how source and destination pixel values should be combined.

- **Constant Blending Colors.** In addition to the standard blending functions, the ARB imaging subset allows constant blending colors to be used as coefficients to source or destination color values. Call **glBlendColor** to specify the constant blending color to be used with the blending coefficients specified with **glBlendFunc**.

Fragments

OpenGL allows a fragment produced by rasterization to modify the corresponding pixel in the frame buffer only if it passes a series of tests. If it does pass, the fragment's data can be used directly to replace the existing frame buffer values, or it can be combined with existing data in the frame buffer, depending on the state of certain modes.

Pixel Ownership Test

The first test determines whether the pixel in the frame buffer corresponding to a particular fragment is owned by the current OpenGL context. If so, the fragment proceeds to the next test. If not, the window system determines whether the fragment is discarded or whether any further fragment operations will be performed with that fragment. This test allows the window system to control OpenGL behavior when, for example, an OpenGL window is obscured.

Scissor Test

The scissor test discards fragments outside an arbitrary screen-aligned rectangle that you specify by calling **glScissor**.

Alpha Test

The alpha test (which is performed only in RGBA mode) discards a fragment depending on the outcome of a comparison between the fragment's alpha value and a constant reference value. The comparison command and reference value are specified with **glAlphaFunc**.

Stencil Test

The stencil test conditionally discards a fragment based on the outcome of a comparison between the value in the stencil buffer and a reference value. The command **glStencilFunc** specifies the comparison command and the reference value. Whether the fragment passes or fails the stencil test, the value in the stencil buffer is modified according to the instructions specified with **glStencilOp**.

Depth Buffer Test

The depth buffer test discards a fragment if a depth comparison fails; **glDepthFunc** specifies the comparison command. The result of the depth comparison also affects the stencil buffer update value if stenciling is enabled.

Blending

Blending combines a fragment's R, G, B, and A values with those stored in the frame buffer at the corresponding location. The blending, which is performed only in RGBA mode, depends on the alpha value of the fragment and that of the corresponding currently stored pixel; it might also depend on the RGB values. To control blending, call **glBlendFunc**, which lets you indicate the source and destination blending factors.

See the "ARB Imaging Subset" section for additional blending functionality provided by OpenGL implementations that support the ARB imaging subset.

Dithering

If dithering is enabled, a dithering algorithm is applied to a fragment's color or color index value. This algorithm depends only on the fragment's value and its *x* and *y* window coordinates.

Logical Operations

A logical operation can be applied between the fragment and the value stored at the corresponding location in the frame buffer; the result replaces the current frame buffer value. You choose the desired logical operation with **glLogicOp**. Logical operations are performed only on color indices, never on RGBA values.

Pixels

During the previous stage of the OpenGL pipeline, fragments are converted to pixels in the frame buffer. The frame buffer is actually organized into a set of logical buffers: the *color, depth, stencil,* and *accumulation* buffers. The color buffer consists of a *front left, front right, back left, back right,* and some number of *auxiliary* buffers. You can issue commands to control these buffers, and you can directly read or copy pixels from them. (Note that the particular OpenGL context you're using may not provide all of these buffers.)

Frame Buffer Operations

You can select the buffer into which color values are written with **glDrawBuffer**. In addition, four different commands are available to mask the writing of bits to each of the logical frame buffers after all per-fragment operations have been performed: **glIndexMask, glColorMask, glDepthMask,** and **glStencilMask**. The operation of the accumulation buffer is controlled with **glAccum**. Finally, **glClear** sets every pixel in a specified subset of the buffers to the value specified with **glClearColor, glClearIndex, glClearDepth, glClearStencil,** or **glClearAccum**.

Reading or Copying Pixels

You can read pixels from the frame buffer into memory, encode them in various ways, and store the encoded result in memory with **glReadPixels**. In addition, you can copy a rectangle of pixel values from one region of the frame buffer to another with **glCopyPixels**. The command **glReadBuffer** controls from which color buffer the pixels are read or copied.

Additional OpenGL Commands

This section briefly describes special groups of commands that aren't explicitly shown as part of the OpenGL processing pipeline in Figure 2-1. These commands accomplish such diverse tasks as evaluating polynomials, using display lists, and obtaining the values of OpenGL state variables.

Using Evaluators

OpenGL evaluator commands let you use a rational polynomial mapping to produce vertices, normals, texture coordinates, and colors. These calculated values are then passed on to the pipeline as if they had been directly specified. The evaluator facility is also used by the NURBS (Non-Uniform Rational B-Spline) commands, which allow you to define curves and surfaces, as described later in this chapter under "OpenGL Utility Library" on page 22 and in Chapter 6 of this book.

To use evaluators, you first have to define the appropriate one- or two-dimensional polynomial mapping using **glMap***. You can then specify and evaluate the domain values for this map in one of two ways.

- Define a series of evenly-spaced domain values to be mapped using **glMapGrid*** and then evaluating a rectangular subset of that grid with **glEvalMesh***. A single point of the grid can be evaluated using **glEvalPoint***.

- Explicitly specify a desired domain value as an argument to **glEvalCoord***, which evaluates the maps at that value.

Performing Selection and Feedback

Selection, feedback, and rendering are mutually exclusive modes of operation. Rendering is the default mode during which fragments are produced by rasterization. In selection and feedback modes, no fragments are produced, and therefore no frame buffer modification occurs. In selection mode, you can determine which primitives would be drawn into some region of a window; in feedback mode, information about primitives that would be rasterized is fed back to the application. You select among these three modes with **glRenderMode**.

Selection

Selection works by returning the current contents of the name stack, which is an array of integer-valued names. You assign the names and build the name stack within the modeling code that specifies the geometry of objects you want to draw.

Whenever a primitive intersects the clip volume, a selection hit occurs. The hit record, which is written into the selection array you've supplied with **glSelectBuffer**, contains information about the contents of the name stack at the time of the hit. (Note that **glSelectBuffer** needs to be called before OpenGL is put into selection mode with **glRenderMode**. Also, the entire contents of the name stack isn't guaranteed to be returned until **glRenderMode** is called to take OpenGL out of selection mode.)

You manipulate the name stack with **glInitNames**, **glLoadName**, **glPushName**, and **glPopName**. For selection, consider using the OpenGL Utility Library (GLU) routine **gluPickMatrix**, which is described later in this chapter ("OpenGL Utility Library" on page 22) and in Chapter 6 of this book.

Feedback

In feedback mode, each primitive that would be rasterized generates a block of values that is copied into the feedback array. You supply this array with **glFeedbackBuffer**, which must be called before OpenGL is put into feedback mode. Each block of values begins with a code indicating the primitive type, followed by values that describe the primitive's vertices and associated data. Entries are also written for bitmaps and pixel rectangles. Values are not guaranteed to be written into the feedback array until **glRenderMode** is called to take OpenGL out of feedback mode. You can use **glPassThrough** to supply a marker that's returned in feedback mode as if it were a primitive.

Using Display Lists

A display list is a group of OpenGL commands that has been stored for subsequent execution. The **glNewList** command begins the creation of a display list, and **glEndList** ends it. With few exceptions, OpenGL commands called between **glNewList** and **glEndList** are appended to the display list and optionally executed. (The reference page for **glNewList** lists all commands that can't be stored and executed from within a display list.) To trigger the execution of a list or set of lists, use **glCallList** or **glCallLists** and supply the identifying number of a particular list or lists. You can manage the indices used to identify display lists with **glGenLists**, **glListBase**, and **glIsList**. You can delete a set of display lists with **glDeleteLists**.

Managing Modes and Execution

The result of many OpenGL commands depends on whether a particular mode is in effect. You use **glEnable** and **glDisable** to set such modes and **glIsEnabled** to determine whether a particular mode is set.

You can control the execution of previously issued OpenGL commands with **glFinish**, which forces all commands to complete, or **glFlush**, which ensures that all such commands are completed in a finite time.

A particular implementation of OpenGL may let you use **glHint** to control certain aspects of rendering with hints. You may be able to control the quality of color and texture coordinate interpolation, the accuracy of fog calculations, and the sampling quality of antialiased points, lines, or polygons.

Obtaining State Information

OpenGL maintains numerous state variables that affect the behavior of many commands. The following variables have specialized query commands:

glGetClipPlane	glGetColorTable[†]	glGetColorTableParameter[†]
glGetConvolutionFilter[†]	glGetConvolutionParameter[†]	glGetHistogram[†]
glGetHistogramParameter[†]	glGetLight	glGetMap
glGetMaterial	glGetMinmax[†]	glGetMinmaxParameter[†]
glGetPixelMap	glGetPointerv	glGetPolygonStipple
glGetSeparableFilter[†]	glGetTexEnv	glGetTexGen
glGetTexImage	glGetTexLevelParameter	glGetTexParameter

Note: [†] Routines are only available if your OpenGL implementation supports the ARB imaging subset.

To obtain the value of other state variables, call **glGetBooleanv**, **glGetDoublev**, **glGetFloatv**, or **glGetIntegerv** as appropriate. The reference page for **glGet*** explains how to use these commands. Other query commands you might want to use are **glGetError**, **glGetString**, and **glIsEnabled**. (See "Handling Errors," later in this chapter for more information about routines related to error handling.) Finally, you can save and restore sets of state variables with **glPushAttrib** and **glPopAttrib**.

OpenGL Utility Library

The OpenGL Utility Library (GLU) contains several groups of commands that complement the core OpenGL interface by providing support for auxiliary features. Since these utility routines make use of core OpenGL commands, any OpenGL implementation is guaranteed to support the utility routines. The prefix for Utility Library routines is *glu* rather than *gl*.

Manipulating Images for Use in Texturing

GLU provides image scaling and automatic mipmapping routines to simplify the specification of texture images. The routine **gluScaleImage** scales a specified image to an accepted texture size; the resulting image can then be passed to OpenGL as a texture. The automatic mipmapping routines **gluBuild1DMipmaps**, **gluBuild2DMipmaps**, and **gluBuild3DMipmaps** create mipmapped texture images from a specified image and pass them to **glTexImage1D**, **glTexImage2D**, and **glTexImage3D**, respectively. Additionally, **gluBuild1DMipmapLevels**, **gluBuild2DMipmapLevels**, and **gluBuild3DMipmapLevels** create a range of mipmap texture images for a specified range of mipmap levels.

Transforming Coordinates

Several commonly-used matrix transformation routines are provided. You can set up a two-dimensional orthographic viewing region with **gluOrtho2D**, a perspective viewing volume with **gluPerspective**, or a viewing volume that's centered on a specified eyepoint with **gluLookAt**. Each routine creates the desired matrix and applies it to the current matrix using **glMultMatrix**.

The **gluPickMatrix** routine simplifies selection by creating a matrix that restricts drawing to a small region of the viewport. If you rerender the scene in selection mode after this matrix has been applied, all objects that would be drawn near the cursor are selected and information about them is stored in the selection buffer. (See "Performing Selection and Feedback" on page 19 for more information about selection mode.)

If you need to determine where in the window an object is being drawn, use **gluProject**, which converts specified coordinates from object coordinates to window coordinates; **gluUnProject** and **gluUnProject4** perform the inverse conversion.

Polygon Tessellation

The polygon tessellation routines triangulate a concave polygon with one or more contours. To use this GLU feature, first create a tessellation object with **gluNewTess**, and define callback routines for processing the triangles generated by the tessellator with **gluTessCallBack**. Then use the commands **gluTessBeginPolygon**, **gluTessVertex**, and **gluTessEndPolygon** to specify the concave polygon to be tessellated. You can also call **gluTessBeginContour** and **gluTessEndContour** to delimit contour descriptions inside a **gluTessBeginPolygon** / **gluTessEndPolygon** pair. To destroy unneeded tessellation objects, call **gluDeleteTess**.

The GLU tessellation routine projects all polygons onto a plane and tessellates that projection. Use **gluTessNormal** to specify a normal to that plane (and as a result the plane itself). If the tessellation plane normal is set to (0, 0, 0)—the initial value—**gluTessNormal** will pick a plane based on the values specified using **gluTessVertex**.

Rendering Spheres, Cylinders, and Disks

You can render spheres, cylinders, and disks using the GLU quadric routines. To do this, create a quadric object with **gluNewQuadric**. Unless you're satisfied with the default values, you can then specify the desired rendering style with one of the following routines.

- **gluQuadricNormals**—determines whether surface normals should be generated, and if so, whether there should be one normal per vertex or one normal per face

- **gluQuadricTexture**—determines whether texture coordinates should be generated

- **gluQuadricOrientation**—determines which side of the quadric should be considered the outside and which the inside

- **gluQuadricDrawStyle**—determines whether the quadric should be drawn as a set of polygons, lines, or points

After you've specified the rendering style, invoke the rendering routine for the desired type of quadric object: **gluSphere**, **gluCylinder**, **gluDisk**, or **gluPartialDisk**. If an error occurs during rendering, the error-handling routine you've specified with **gluQuadricCallBack** is invoked. To destroy a quadric object when you're finished with it, call **gluDeleteQuadric**.

NURBS Curves and Surfaces

The routines described in this section convert NURBS (Non-Uniform Rational B-Spline) curves and surfaces to OpenGL evaluators. You can create and delete a NURBS object with **gluNewNurbsRenderer** and **gluDeleteNurbsRenderer** and establish an error-handling routine with **gluNurbsCallback**.

You specify the desired curves and surfaces with different sets of routines: **gluBeginCurve**, **gluNurbsCurve**, and **gluEndCurve** for curves or **gluBeginSurface**, **gluNurbsSurface**, and **gluEndSurface** for surfaces. You can also specify a trimming region, which defines a subset of the NURBS surface domain to be evaluated, thereby allowing you to create surfaces that have smooth boundaries or that contain holes. The trimming routines are **gluBeginTrim**, **gluPwlCurve**, **gluNurbsCurve**, and **gluEndTrim**.

As with quadric objects, you can control how NURBS curves and surfaces are rendered:

- Whether a curve or surface should be discarded if its control polyhedron lies outside the current viewport

- What the maximum length should be (in pixels) of edges of polygons used to render curves and surfaces

- Whether the projection matrix, modelview matrix, and viewport should be taken from the OpenGL server or whether you'll supply them explicitly with **gluLoadSamplingMatrices**

Use **gluNurbsProperty** to set these properties, or use the default values. To query a NURBS object about its rendering style, call **gluGetNurbsProperty**.

Handling Errors

The routine **gluErrorString** retrieves an error string that corresponds to an OpenGL or GLU error code. The currently defined OpenGL error codes are described in the **glGetError** reference page. The GLU error codes are listed in the **gluErrorString**, **gluTessCallback**, **gluQuadricCallback**, and **gluNurbsCallback** reference pages. Errors generated by GLX routines are listed in the relevant reference pages for those routines.

OpenGL Extension to the X Window System

In the X Window System, OpenGL rendering is made available as an extension to X in the formal X sense: connection and authentication are accomplished with the normal X mechanisms. As with other X extensions, there is a defined network protocol for OpenGL rendering commands encapsulated within the X byte stream. Since performance is critical in three-dimensional rendering, the OpenGL extension to X allows OpenGL to bypass the X server's involvement in data encoding, copying, and interpretation and instead render directly to the graphics pipeline.

This section briefly discusses the routines defined as part of GLX; these routines have the prefix *glX*. You need some knowledge of X to fully understand the following sections and to use GLX successfully.

Initialization

Use **glXQueryExtension** and **glXQueryVersion** to determine whether the GLX extension is defined for an X server and, if so, which version is bound in the server. To determine the capabilities of the GLX implementation, use **glXQueryServerString** and **glXQueryExtensionsString** to query information about extensions that are supported by the X server, and **glXGetClientString** to describe functionality provided the GLX client library.

The **glXChooseFBConfig** routine returns an array of GLXFBConfigs matching the attributes specified. Use **glXGetFBConfigAttrib** to retrieve the value of a particular attribute associated with a particular GLXFBConfig, and choose the GLXFBConfig that best suits your application's needs. A complete listing of all available GLXFBConfigs can be obtained by calling

glXGetFBConfigs. To obtain the XVisualInfo structure associated with a specified GLXFBConfig, call **glXGetVisualFromFBConfig**.

Controlling Rendering

In order to render using OpenGL with GLX, areas to render to and contexts to manage OpenGL state are required. GLX provides several routines for creating, deleting, and managing OpenGL rendering areas and rendering contexts, and associating them together to enable OpenGL rendering.

Additional routines are provided for synchronizing execution between the X and OpenGL streams, swapping front and back buffers, and using an X font.

Managing On-Screen Rendering Areas

To render into an on-screen OpenGL window, first create an X window with a suitable X visual (generally created using the XVisualInfo structure obtained from calling **glXGetVisualFromFBConfig**). To transform that X window into a GLXWindow, call **glXCreateWindow**. To destroy a GLXWindow, call **glXDestroyWindow**.

Managing Off-Screen Rendering Areas

GLX supports two types of off-screen rendering areas: GLXPixmaps and GLXPbuffers. GLXPixmaps are X pixmaps with an associated GLX pixmap resource, and support X rendering as well as OpenGL rendering into the pixmap. GLXPbuffers are a GLX-only resource, and as such, might not be able to be rendered to using X or an X extension other than GLX.

To create a GLXPixmap, first create an X pixmap, and transform it into a GLXPixmap by calling **glXCreatePixmap**. To destroy the GLXPixmap, call **glXDestroyPixmap**, then destroy the original X pixmap.

Since a GLXPbuffer does not have an associated X drawable, one need only call **glXCreatePbuffer** to create a GLXPbuffer resource. Similarly, to destroy a GLXPbuffer, call **glXDestroyPbuffer.**

Managing an OpenGL Rendering Context

An OpenGL rendering context is created with **glXCreateNewContext**. One of the arguments to this routine allows you to request a direct rendering context that bypasses the X server. (Note that in order to do direct rendering, the X server connection must be local and the OpenGL implementation needs to support direct rendering.) You can determine whether a GLX context is direct with **glXIsDirect**. To obtain other attributes of a GLX context, call **glXQueryContext**.

To make a rendering context current (associate a GLX rendering area with a GLX context), use **glXMakeContextCurrent**; **glXGetCurrentContext** returns the current context. You can also obtain the current rendering drawable with **glXGetCurrentDrawable**. Additionally, you can obtain the current read drawable using **glXGetCurrentReadDrawable**. Finally, to obtain the X display associated with the current drawables and context, call **glXGetCurrentDisplay**.

Only one context can be current for any thread at any one time. If you have multiple contexts, you can copy selected groups of OpenGL state variables from one context to another with **glXCopyContext**. When you no longer need a particular context, destroy it with **glXDestroyContext**.

Synchronizing Execution

To prevent X requests from executing until any outstanding OpenGL rendering is completed, call **glXWaitGL**. Any previously issued OpenGL commands are then guaranteed to be executed before any X rendering calls made after **glXWaitGL**. Although calling **glFinish** can achieve the same result, **glXWaitGL** is more efficient in cases where the client and server are on separate machines since the X server waits for the completion of OpenGL rendering, and not the client application, as is the case with **glFlush**.

To prevent an OpenGL command sequence from executing until any outstanding X requests are completed, use **glXWaitX**. This routine guarantees that previously issued X rendering commands are executed before any OpenGL commands made after **glXWaitX**.

Event Processing

In addition to the normal event stream provided by the X server, GLX adds additional events that an application may process. Use **glXSelectEvent** to select which GLX events the application would like to be notified of. Currently, there is only one GLX event that is sent when changes to a GLXPbuffer occur. To retrieve a GLX event, call **glXGetSelectedEvent**.

Swapping Buffers

For double-buffered drawables, the front and back buffers can be exchanged by a call to **glXSwapBuffers**. An implicit **glFlush** is done as part of this function.

Using an X Font

The command **glXUseXFont** provides a shortcut for using X fonts in OpenGL.

Chapter 3

Summary of Commands and Routines

This chapter lists the prototypes for OpenGL, the OpenGL Utility Library, and the OpenGL extension to the X Window System. The prototypes are grouped by functionality, as shown in the following list.

- **OpenGL Commands**

Primitives	Fog
Vertex Arrays	Frame Buffer Operations
Coordinate Transformation	Evaluators
Coloring and Lighting	Selection and Feedback
Clipping	Display Lists
Rasterization	Modes and Execution
Pixel Operations	State Queries
Textures	

- **ARB Extensions**

Multitexture	Imaging Subset

- **GLU Routines**

Texture Images	Quadric Objects
Coordinate Transformation	NURBS Curves and Surfaces
Polygon Tessellation	State Queries

- **GLX Routines**

Initialization	Controlling Rendering

Notation

Some of the OpenGL commands differ from each other only by the data type of the arguments they accept. Certain conventions have therefore been used to refer to these commands in a compact way:

    void **glVertex2{sifd}{v}** (TYPE *x*, TYPE *y*);

In this example, the first set of braces encloses characters identifying the possible data types for the arguments listed as having data type TYPE. (The digit preceding the braces indicates how many arguments the command takes.) The following table lists each possible data type, its corresponding character, and the type definition OpenGL uses for referring to it.

Character	C-Language Type	OpenGL Type Definition
b	signed char	GLbyte
s	short	GLshort
i	int	GLint, GLsizei
f	float	GLfloat, GLclampf
d	double	GLdouble, GLclampd
ub	unsigned char	GLubyte, GLboolean
us	unsigned short	GLushort
ui	unsigned int	GLuint, GLenum, GLbitfield
	void	GLvoid

The second set of braces, if present, contains a **v** for the vector form of the command. If you choose to use the vector form, all the TYPE arguments are collapsed into a single array. For example, here are the nonvector and vector forms of a command, using a floating-point data type:

void **glVertex2f**(GLfloat *x*, GLfloat *y*);

void **glVertex2fv**(GLfloat *v*[2]);

Where the use of the vector form is ambiguous, both the vector and nonvector forms are listed. Note that not all commands with multiple arguments have a vector form and that some commands have only a vector form, in which case the **v** isn't enclosed in braces.

OpenGL Commands

Primitives

Specify vertices or rectangles:

void **glBegin** (GLenum *mode*);
void **glEnd** (void);
void **glVertex2{sifd}{v}** (TYPE *x*, TYPE *y*);
void **glVertex3{sifd}{v}** (TYPE *x*, TYPE *y*, TYPE *z*);
void **glVertex4{sifd}{v}** (TYPE *x*, TYPE *y*, TYPE *z*, TYPE *w*);
void **glRect{sifd}** (TYPE *x1*, TYPE *y1*, TYPE *x2*, TYPE *y2*);
void **glRect{sifd}v** (const TYPE **v1*, const TYPE **v2*);

Specify polygon edge treatment:

void **glEdgeFlag** (GLboolean *flag*);
void **glEdgeFlagv** (const GLboolean **flag*);

Specify polygon offset:

void **glPolygonOffset** (GLfloat *factor*, GLfloat *units*);

Vertex Arrays

Specify vertex arrays:

> void **glVertexPointer** (GLint *size*, GLenum *type*, GLsizei *stride*,
> const GLvoid **pointer*);
> void **glEdgeFlagPointer** (GLsizei *stride*, const GLvoid **pointer*);
> void **glIndexPointer** (GLenum *type*, GLsizei *stride*,
> const GLvoid **pointer*);
> void **glColorPointer** (GLint *size*, GLenum *type*, GLsizei *stride*,
> const GLvoid **pointer*);
> void **glNormalPointer** (GLenum *type*, GLsizei *stride*,
> const GLvoid **pointer*);
> void **glTexCoordPointer** (GLint *size*, GLenum *type*, GLsizei *stride*,
> const GLvoid **pointer*);

Control drawing of vertex arrays and their components:

> void **glInterleavedArrays** (GLenum *format*, GLsizei *stride*,
> const GLvoid **pointer*);
> void **glArrayElement** (GLint *i*);
> void **glDisableClientState** (GLenum *array*);
> void **glEnableClientState** (GLenum *array*);
> void **glDrawElements** (GLenum *mode*, GLsizei *count*, GLenum *type*,
> const GLvoid **indices*);
> void **glDrawRangeElements** (GLenum *mode*, GLuint *start*, GLuint *end*,
> GLsizei *count*, GLenum *type*, const GLvoid **indices*);
> void **glDrawArrays** (GLenum *mode*, GLint *first*, GLsizei *count*);

Save and restore vertex array values:

> void **glPushClientAttrib** (GLbitfield *mask*);
> void **glPopClientAttrib** (void);

Obtain the address of a specified vertex array:

> void **glGetPointerv** (GLenum *pname*, GLvoid ***params*);

Coordinate Transformation

Transform the current matrix:

> void **glRotate{fd}** (TYPE *angle*, TYPE *x*, TYPE *y*, TYPE *z*);
> void **glTranslate{fd}** (TYPE *x*, TYPE *y*, TYPE *z*);
> void **glScale{fd}** (TYPE *x*, TYPE *y*, TYPE *z*);
> void **glMultMatrix{fd}** (const TYPE **m*);
> void **glFrustum** (GLdouble *left*, GLdouble *right*, GLdouble *bottom*,
>   GLdouble *top*, GLdouble *near*, GLdouble *far*);
> void **glOrtho** (GLdouble *left*, GLdouble *right*, GLdouble *bottom*,
>   GLdouble *top*, GLdouble *near*, GLdouble *far*);

Replace the current matrix:

> void **glLoadMatrix{fd}** (const TYPE **m*);
> void **glLoadIdentity** (void);

Manipulate the matrix stack:

> void **glMatrixMode** (GLenum *mode*);
> void **glPushMatrix** (void);
> void **glPopMatrix** (void);

Specify the viewport:

> void **glDepthRange** (GLclampd *near*, GLclampd *far*);
> void **glViewport** (GLint *x*, GLint *y*, GLsizei *width*, GLsizei *height*);

Coloring and Lighting

Set the current color, color index, or normal vector:

> void **glColor3{bsifd ubusui}{v}** (TYPE *red*, TYPE *green*, TYPE *blue*);
> void **glColor4{bsifd ubusui}{v}** (TYPE *red*, TYPE *green*, TYPE *blue*,
>   TYPE *alpha*);
> void **glIndex{sifd ub}{v}** (TYPE *index*);
> void **glNormal3{bsifd}{v}** (TYPE *nx*, TYPE *ny*, TYPE *nz*);

Specify light source, material, or lighting model parameter values:

> void **glLight{if}{v}** (GLenum *light*, GLenum *pname*, TYPE *param*);
> void **glMaterial{if}{v}** (GLenum *face*, GLenum *pname*, TYPE *param*);
> void **glLightModel{if}{v}** (GLenum *pname*, TYPE *param*);

Choose a shading model:

> void **glShadeModel** (GLenum *mode*);

Specify which polygon orientation is front-facing:

> void **glFrontFace** (GLenum *dir*);

Cause a material color to track the current color:

> void **glColorMaterial** (GLenum *face*, GLenum *mode*);

Obtain light source or material parameter values:

> void **glGetLight{if}v** (GLenum *light*, GLenum *pname*, TYPE **params*);
> void **glGetMaterial{if}v** (GLenum *face*, GLenum *pname*, TYPE **params*);

Clipping

Specify a clipping plane:

> void **glClipPlane** (GLenum *plane*, const GLdouble **equation*);

Return clipping plane coefficients:

> void **glGetClipPlane** (GLenum *plane*, GLdouble **equation*);

Rasterization

Set the current raster position:

> void **glRasterPos2{sifd}{v}**(TYPE *x*, TYPE *y*);
> void **glRasterPos3{sifd}{v}**(TYPE *x*, TYPE *y*, TYPE *z*);
> void **glRasterPos4{sifd}{v}**(TYPE *x*, TYPE *y*, TYPE *z*, TYPE *w*);

Specify a bitmap:

> void **glBitmap** (GLsizei *width*, GLsizei *height*, GLfloat *xorig*, GLfloat *yorig*,
> GLfloat *xmove*, GLfloat *ymove*, const GLubyte **bitmap*);

Specify the dimensions of points or lines:

> void **glPointSize** (GLfloat *size*);
> void **glLineWidth** (GLfloat *width*);

Specify or return a stipple pattern for lines or polygons:

> void **glLineStipple** (GLint *factor*, GLushort *pattern*);
> void **glPolygonStipple** (const GLubyte **mask*);
> void **glGetPolygonStipple** (GLubyte **mask*);

Choose how polygons are rasterized:

> void **glCullFace** (GLenum *mode*);
> void **glPolygonMode** (GLenum *face*, GLenum *mode*);

Pixel Operations

Select the source for pixel read or copy operations:

> void **glReadBuffer** (GLenum *mode*);

Read, write, and copy pixels:

> void **glReadPixels** (GLint *x*, GLint *y*, GLsizei *width*, GLsizei *height*,
> GLenum *format*, GLenum *type*, GLvoid **pixels*);
> void **glDrawPixels** (GLsizei *width*, GLsizei *height*, GLenum *format*,
> GLenum *type*, const GLvoid **pixels*);
> void **glCopyPixels** (GLint *x*, GLint *y*, GLsizei *width*, GLsizei *height*,
> GLenum *type*);

Specify or query how pixels are encoded or processed:

> void **glPixelStore{if}** (GLenum *pname*, TYPE *param*);
> void **glPixelTransfer{if}** (GLenum *pname*, TYPE *param*);
> void **glPixelMap{f usui}v** (GLenum *map*, GLint *mapsize*, const TYPE **values*);
> void **glGetPixelMap{f usui}v** (GLenum *map*, TYPE **values*);

Control pixel rasterization:

> void **glPixelZoom** (GLfloat *xfactor*, GLfloat *yfactor*);

Textures

Control how a texture is applied to a fragment:

> void **glTexParameter{if}{v}** (GLenum *target*, GLenum *pname*, TYPE *param*);
> void **glTexEnv{if}{v}** (GLenum *target*, GLenum *pname*, TYPE *param*);

Set the current texture coordinates:

> void **glTexCoord1{sifd}{v}** (TYPE *s*);
> void **glTexCoord2{sifd}{v}** (TYPE *s*, TYPE *t*);
> void **glTexCoord3{sifd}{v}** (TYPE *s*, TYPE *t*, TYPE *r*);
> void **glTexCoord4{sifd}{v}** (TYPE *s*, TYPE *t*, TYPE *r*, TYPE *q*);

Control the generation of texture coordinates:

> void **glTexGen{ifd}{v}** (GLenum *coord*, GLenum *pname*, TYPE *param*);

Specify a one- or two-dimensional texture image or texture subimage:

> void **glTexImage1D** (GLenum *target*, GLint *level*, GLint *internalformat*,
>   GLsizei *width*, GLint *border*, GLenum *format*,
>   GLenum *type*, const GLvoid **pixels*);
> void **glTexImage2D** (GLenum *target*, GLint *level*, GLint *internalformat*,
>   GLsizei *width*, GLsizei *height*, GLint *border*,
>   GLenum *format*, GLenum *type*, const GLvoid **pixels*);

> void **glTexImage3D** (GLenum *target*, GLint *level*, GLenum *internalformat*,
>   GLsizei *width*, GLsizei *height*, GLsizei *depth*, GLint *border*,
>   GLenum *format*, GLenum *type*, const GLvoid **pixels*);
> void **glTexSubImage1D** (GLenum *target*, GLint *level*, GLint *xoffset*,
>   GLsizei *width*, GLenum *format*, GLenum *type*,
>   const GLvoid **pixels*);
> void **glTexSubImage2D** (GLenum *target*, GLint *level*, GLint *xoffset*,
>   GLint *yoffset*, GLsizei *width*, GLsizei *height*,
>   GLenum *format*, GLenum *type*, const GLvoid **pixels*);
> void **glTexSubImage3D** (GLenum *target*, GLint *level*, GLint *xoffset*,
>   GLint *yoffset*, GLint *zoffset*, GLsizei *width*, GLsizei *height*,
>   GLsizei *depth*, GLenum *format*, GLenum *type*,
>   const GLvoid **pixels*);

Test whether a name corresponds to a texture and obtain texture-related parameter values:

> void **glIsTexture** (GLuint *texture*);
> void **glGetTexEnv{if}v** (GLenum *target*, GLenum *pname*, TYPE **params*);
> void **glGetTexGen{ifd}v** (GLenum *coord*, GLenum *pname*, TYPE **params*);
> void **glGetTexImage** (GLenum *target*, GLint *level*, GLenum *format*,
>   GLenum *type*, GLvoid **pixels*);
> void **glGetTexLevelParameter{if}v** (GLenum *target*, GLint *level*,
>   GLenum *pname*, TYPE **params*);
> void **glGetTexParameter{if}v** (GLenum *target*, GLenum *pname*, TYPE **params*);

Copy a texture or part of it:

> void **glCopyTexImage1D** (GLenum *target*, GLint *level*,
> GLenum *internalformat*, GLint *x*, GLint *y*, GLsizei *v*,
> GLint *border*);
> void **glCopyTexImage2D** (GLenum *target*, GLint *level*,
> GLenum *internalformat*, GLint *x*, GLint *y*,
> GLsizei *width*, GLsizei *height*, GLint *border*);
> void **glCopyTexSubImage1D** (GLenum *target*, GLint *level*, GLint *xoffset*,
> GLint *x*, GLint *y*, GLsizei *width*);
> void **glCopyTexSubImage2D** (GLenum *target*, GLint *level*, GLint *xoffset*,
> GLint *yoffset*, GLint *x*, GLint *y*, GLsizei *width*,
> GLsizei *height*);
> void **glCopyTexSubImage3D** (GLenum *target*, GLint *level*, GLint *xoffset*,
> GLint *yoffset*, GLint *zoffset*, GLint *x*, GLint *y*,
> GLsizei *width*, GLsizei *height*);

Create a named texture and prioritize texture memory residence:

> void **glBindTexture** (GLenum *target*, GLuint *texture*);
> void **glDeleteTextures** (GLsizei *n*, const GLuint **textures*);
> GLboolean **glAreTexturesResident** (GLsizei *n*, const GLuint **textures*,
> GLboolean **residences*);
> void **glGenTextures** (GLsizei *n*, GLuint **textures*);
> void **glPrioritizeTextures** (GLsizei *n*, const GLuint **textures*,
> const GLclampf **priorities*);

Fog

Set fog parameters:

> void **glFog{if}{v}** (GLenum *pname*, TYPE *param*);

Frame Buffer Operations

Control per-fragment testing:

> void **glScissor** (GLint *x*, GLint *y*, GLsizei *width*, GLsizei *height*);
> void **glAlphaFunc** (GLenum *func*, GLclampf *ref*);
> void **glStencilFunc** (GLenum *func*, GLint *ref*, GLuint *mask*);
> void **glStencilOp** (GLenum *fail*, GLenum *pass*, GLenum *zpass*);
> void **glDepthFunc** (GLenum *func*);

Combine fragment and frame buffer values:

> void **glBlendFunc** (GLenum *sfactor*, GLenum *dfactor*);
> void **glLogicOp** (GLenum *opcode*);

Clear some or all buffers:

> void **glClear** (GLbitfield *mask*);

Specify color, depth, and stencil values for clear operations:

> void **glClearAccum** (GLfloat *red*, GLfloat *green*, GLfloat *blue*, GLfloat *alpha*);
> void **glClearColor** (GLclampf *red*, GLclampf *green*, GLclampf *blue*,
>   GLclampf *alpha*);
> void **glClearDepth** (GLclampd *depth*);
> void **glClearIndex** (GLfloat *c*);
> void **glClearStencil** (GLint *s*);

Control buffers enabled for writing:

> void **glDrawBuffer** (GLenum *mode*);
> void **glIndexMask** (GLuint *mask*);
> void **glColorMask** (GLboolean *red*, GLboolean *green*, GLboolean *blue*,
>   GLboolean *alpha*);
> void **glDepthMask** (GLboolean *flag*);
> void **glStencilMask** (GLuint *mask*);

Operate on the accumulation buffer:

> void **glAccum** (GLenum *op*, GLfloat *value*);

Evaluators

Define a one- or two-dimensional evaluator:

> void **glMap1{fd}** (GLenum *target*, TYPE *u1*, TYPE *u2*, GLint *stride*,
>   GLint *order*, const TYPE **points*);
> void **glMap2{fd}** (GLenum *target*, TYPE *u1*, TYPE *u2*, GLint *ustride*,
>   GLint *uorder*, TYPE *v1*, TYPE *v2*, GLint *vstride*,
>   GLint *vorder*, const TYPE **points*);

Generate and evaluate a series of map domain values:

> void **glMapGrid1{fd}** (GLint *n*, TYPE *u1*, TYPE *u2*);
> void **glMapGrid2{fd}** (GLint *un*, TYPE *u1*, TYPE *u2*, GLint *vn*, TYPE *v1*,
>   TYPE *v2*);
> void **glEvalMesh1** (GLenum *mode*, GLint *i1*, GLint *i2*);
> void **glEvalMesh2** (GLenum *mode*, GLint *i1*, GLint *i2*, GLint *j1*, GLint *j2*);
> void **glEvalPoint1** (GLint *i*);
> void **glEvalPoint2** (GLint *i*, GLint *j*);

Evaluate one- and two-dimensional maps at a specified domain coordinate:

> void **glEvalCoord1{fd}{v}** (TYPE *u*);
> void **glEvalCoord2{fd}{v}** (TYPE *u*, TYPE *v*);

Obtain evaluator parameter values:

> void **glGetMap{idf}v** (GLenum *target*, GLenum *query*, TYPE **v*);

Selection and Feedback

Control the mode and corresponding buffer:

> GLint **glRenderMode** (GLenum *mode*);
> void **glSelectBuffer** (GLsizei *size*, GLuint **buffer*);
> void **glFeedbackBuffer** (GLsizei *size*, GLenum *type*, GLfloat **buffer*);

Supply a token for feedback mode:

> void **glPassThrough** (GLfloat *token*);

Control the name stack for selection:

> void **glInitNames** (void);
> void **glLoadName** (GLuint *name*);
> void **glPushName** (GLuint *name*);
> void **glPopName** (void);

Display Lists

Create or delete display lists:

> void **glNewList** (GLuint *list*, GLenum *mode*);
> void **glEndList** (void);
> void **glDeleteLists** (GLuint *list*, GLsizei *range*);

Execute a display list or set of lists:

> void **glCallList** (GLuint *list*);
> void **glCallLists** (GLsizei *n*, GLenum *type*, const GLvoid **lists*);

Manage display-list indices:

> GLuint **glGenLists** (GLsizei *range*);
> GLboolean **glIsList** (GLuint *list*);
> void **glListBase** (GLuint *base*);

Modes and Execution

Enable, disable, and query modes:

> void **glEnable** (GLenum *cap*);
> void **glDisable** (GLenum *cap*);
> GLboolean **glIsEnabled** (GLenum *cap*);

Wait until all OpenGL commands have executed completely:

> void **glFinish** (void);

Force all issued OpenGL commands to be executed:

> void **glFlush** (void);

Specify hints for OpenGL operation:

> void **glHint** (GLenum *target*, GLenum *mode*);

State Queries

Obtain information about an error or the current OpenGL connection:

> GLenum **glGetError** (void);
> const GLubyte * **glGetString** (GLenum *name*);

Query state variables:

> void **glGetBooleanv** (GLenum *pname*, GLboolean *params*);
> void **glGetDoublev** (GLenum *pname*, GLdouble *params*);
> void **glGetFloatv** (GLenum *pname*, GLfloat *params*);
> void **glGetIntegerv** (GLenum *pname*, GLint *params*);

Save and restore sets of state variables:

> void **glPushAttrib** (GLbitfield *mask*);
> void **glPopAttrib** (void);

ARB Extensions

Multitexture

Set the current texture coordinates:

> void **glMultiTexCoord1{sifd}{v}ARB** (GLenum *target,* TYPE *s*);
> void **glMultiTexCoord2{sifd}{v}ARB** (GLenum *target,* TYPE *s,* TYPE *t*);
> void **glMultiTexCoord3{sifd}{v}ARB** (GLenum *target,* TYPE *s,* TYPE *t,* TYPE *r*);
> void **glMultiTexCoord4{sifd}{v}ARB** (GLenum *target,* TYPE *s,* TYPE *t,*
> TYPE *r,* TYPE *q*);

Select the active texture unit:

> void **glActiveTextureARB** (GLenum *texture*);

Select the active vertex array:

> void **glClientActiveTextureARB** (GLenum *texture*);

Imaging Subset

Color Tables

Specify a color lookup table or subtable:

> void **glColorTable** (GLenum *target,* GLenum *internalformat,* GLsizei *width,*
> GLenum *format,* GLenum *type,* const GLvoid **table*);
> void **glColorSubTable** (GLenum *target,* GLsizei *start,* GLsizei *count,*
> GLenum *format,* GLenum *type,* const GLvoid **data*);

Copy a color lookup table or subtable:

> void **glCopyColorTable** (GLenum *target,* GLenum *internalformat,* GLint *x,*
> GLint *y,* GLsizei *width*);
> void **glCopyColorSubTable** (GLenum *target,* GLsizei *start,* GLint *x,* GLint *y,*
> GLsizei *width*);

Obtain color table related values:

> void **glGetColorTable** (GLenum *target,* GLenum *format,* GLenum *type,*
> GLvoid **table*);
> void **glGetColorTableParameter{if}v** (GLenum *target,* GLenum *pname,*
> TYPE **params*);

Convolution

Control how a convolution filter is applied to an input image:

>   void **glConvolutionParameter{if}{v}** (GLenum *target*, GLenum *pname*,
>   TYPE *params*);

Specify one- or two-dimensional convolution filters:

>   void **glConvolutionFilter1D** (GLenum *target*, GLenum *internalformat*,
>   GLsizei *width*, GLenum *format*, GLenum *type*,
>   const GLvoid **image*);
>   void **glConvolutionFilter2D** (GLenum *target*, GLenum *internalformat*,
>   GLsizei *width*, GLsizei *height*, GLenum *format*,
>   GLenum *type*, const GLvoid **image*);

Specify two-dimensional separable convolution filters:

>   void **glSeparableFilter2D** (GLenum *target*, GLenum *internalformat*,
>   GLsizei *width*, GLsizei *height*, GLenum *format*,
>   GLenum *type*, const GLvoid **row*, const GLvoid **column*);

Obtain convolution-related parameter values:

>   void **glGetConvolutionFilter** (GLenum *target*, GLenum *format*, GLenum *type*,
>   GLvoid **image*);
>   void **glGetConvolutionParameter{if}v** (GLenum *target*, GLenum *pname*,
>   TYPE **params*);
>   void **glGetSeparableFilter** (GLenum *target*, GLenum *format*, GLenum *type*,
>   GLvoid **row*, GLvoid **column*, GLvoid **span*);

Copy a convolution filter or part of it:

>   void **glCopyConvolutionFilter1D** (GLenum *target*, GLenum *internalformat*,
>   GLint *x*, GLint *y*, GLsizei *width*);
>   void **glCopyConvolutionFilter2D** (GLenum *target*, GLenum *internalformat*,
>   GLint *x*, GLint *y*, GLsizei *width*, GLsizei *height*);

Histogram

Specify histogram format:

>   void **glHistogram** (GLenum *target*, GLsizei *width*, GLenum *internalformat*,
>   GLboolean *sink*);

Obtain histogram values and parameters:

>   void **glGetHistogram** (GLenum *target*, GLboolean *reset*, GLenum *format*,
>   GLenum *type*, GLvoid **values*);
>   void **glGetHistogramParameter{if}v** (GLenum *target*, GLenum *pname*,
>   GLfloat **params*);

Reset internal histogram tables:

> void **glResetHistogram** (GLenum *target*);

Minmax

Specify minmax format:

> void **glMinmax** (GLenum *target*, GLenum *internalformat*, GLboolean *sink*);

Obtain minmax values and parameters:

> void **glGetMinmax** (GLenum *target*, GLboolean *reset*, GLenum *format*,
> > GLenum *type*, GLvoid **values*);
> void **glGetMinmaxParameter{if}v** (GLenum *target*, GLenum *pname*,
> > GLfloat **params*);

Reset internal minmax table:

> void **glResetMinmax** (GLenum *target*);

GLU Routines

Texture Images

Magnify or shrink an image:

> int **gluScaleImage** (GLenum *format*, GLint *widthin*, GLint *heightin*,
> > GLenum *typein*, const void **datain*, GLint *widthout*,
> > GLint *heightout*, GLenum *typeout*, void **dataout*);

Generate mipmaps for an image:

> int **gluBuild1DMipmaps** (GLenum *target*, GLint *internalformat*, GLint *width*,
> > GLenum *format*, GLenum *type*, const void **data*);
> int **gluBuild2DMipmaps** (GLenum *target*, GLint *internalformat*, GLint *width*,
> > GLint *height*, GLenum *format*, GLenum *type*,
> > const void **data*);
> int **gluBuild3DMipmaps** (GLenum *target*, GLint *internalformat*, GLsizei *width*,
> > GLsizei *height*, GLsizei *depth*, GLenum *format*,
> > GLenum *type*, const void **data*);

Generate a range of mipmap levels for an image:

> int **gluBuild1DMipmapLevels** (GLenum *target*, GLint *internalformat*,
>> GLsizei *width*, GLenum *format*, GLenum *type*,
>> GLint *level*, GLint *base*, GLint *max*, const void **data*);

> int **gluBuild2DMipmapLevels** (GLenum *target*, GLint *internalformat*,
>> GLsizei *width*, GLsizei *height*, GLenum *format*,
>> GLenum *type*, GLint *level*, GLint *base*, GLint *max*,
>> const void **data*);

> int **gluBuild3DMipmapLevels** (GLenum *target*, GLint *internalformat*,
>> GLsizei *width*, GLsizei *height*, GLsizei *depth*,
>> GLenum *format*, GLenum *type*, GLint *level*,
>> GLint *base*, GLint *max*, const void **data*);

Coordinate Transformation

Create projection or viewing matrices:

> void **gluOrtho2D** (GLdouble *left*, GLdouble *right*, GLdouble *bottom*,
>> GLdouble *top*);

> void **gluPerspective** (GLdouble *fovy*, GLdouble *aspect*, GLdouble *zNear*,
>> GLdouble *zFar*);

> void **gluPickMatrix** (GLdouble *x*, GLdouble *y*, GLdouble *width*,
>> GLdouble *height*, GLint *viewport*[4]);

> void **gluLookAt** (GLdouble *eyex*, GLdouble *eyey*, GLdouble *eyez*,
>> GLdouble *centerx*, GLdouble *centery*, GLdouble *centerz*,
>> GLdouble *upx*, GLdouble *upy*, GLdouble *upz*);

Convert object coordinates to screen coordinates:

> int **gluProject** (GLdouble *objx*, GLdouble *objy*, GLdouble *objz*,
>> const GLdouble *modelMatrix*[16],
>> const GLdouble *projMatrix*[16],
>> const GLint *viewport*[4], GLdouble **winx*,
>> GLdouble **winy*, GLdouble **winz*);

> int **gluUnProject** (GLdouble *winx*, GLdouble *winy*, GLdouble *winz*,
>> const GLdouble *modelMatrix*[16],
>> const GLdouble *projMatrix*[16],
>> const GLint *viewport*[4], GLdouble **objx*,
>> GLdouble **objy*, GLdouble **objz*);

> int **gluUnProject4** (GLdouble *winx*, GLdouble *winy*, GLdouble *winz*,
>> GLdouble *clipw*, const GLdouble *modelMatrix[16]*,
>> const GLdouble *projMatrix[16]*,
>> const GLint *viewport[4]*, GLdouble *near*,
>> GLdouble *far*, GLdouble* *objx*, GLdouble* *objy*,
>> GLdouble* *objz*, GLdouble **objw*);

Polygon Tessellation

Manage tessellation objects:

GLUtesselator* **gluNewTess** (void);
void **gluTessCallback** (GLUtesselator *tobj, GLenum which, void (*fn)());
void **gluDeleteTess** (GLUtesselator *tobj);
void **gluGetTessProperty** (GLUtesselator* tess, GLenum which,
        GLdouble* data);

Describe the input polygon:

void **gluTessBeginPolygon** (GLUtesselator *tobj);
void **gluTessEndPolygon** (GLUtesselator *tobj);
void **gluTessBeginContour** (GLUtesselator *tess);
void **gluTessEndContour** (GLUtesselator *tess);
void **gluTessVertex** (GLUtesselator *tobj, GLdouble v[3], void *data);
void **gluTessNormal** (GLUtesselator *tess, GLdouble valuex, GLdouble valuey,
        GLdouble valuez);
void **gluTessProperty** (GLUtesselator *tess, GLenum which, GLdouble data);

Quadric Objects

Manage quadric objects:

GLUquadric* **gluNewQuadric** (void);
void **gluDeleteQuadric** (GLUquadric *state);
void **gluQuadricCallback** (GLUquadric *qobj, GLenum which, void (*fn)());

Control the rendering:

void **gluQuadricNormals** (GLUquadric *quadObject, GLenum normals);
void **gluQuadricTexture** (GLUquadric *quadObject,
        GLboolean textureCoords);
void **gluQuadricOrientation** (GLUquadric *quadObject,
        GLenum orientation);
void **gluQuadricDrawStyle** (GLUquadric *quadObject, GLenum drawStyle);

Specify a quadric primitive:

    void **gluCylinder** (GLUquadric **qobj*, GLdouble *baseRadius*,
            GLdouble *topRadius*, GLdouble *height*, GLint *slices*,
            GLint *stacks*);
    void **gluDisk** (GLUquadric **qobj*, GLdouble *innerRadius*,
            GLdouble *outerRadius*, GLint *slices*, GLint *loops*);
    void **gluPartialDisk** (GLUquadric **qobj*, GLdouble *innerRadius*,
            GLdouble *outerRadius*, GLint *slices*, GLint *loops*,
            GLdouble *startAngle*, GLdouble *sweepAngle*);
    void **gluSphere** (GLUquadric **qobj*, GLdouble *radius*, GLint *slices*,
            GLint *stacks*);

NURBS Curves and Surfaces

Manage a NURBS object:

    GLUnurbs* **gluNewNurbsRenderer** (void);
    void **gluDeleteNurbsRenderer** (GLUnurbs **nobj*);
    void **gluNurbsCallback** (GLUnurbs **nobj*, GLenum *which*, void (**fn*)());
    void **gluNurbsCallbackData** (GLUnurbs **nurb*, GLvoid **userData*);

Create a NURBS curve:

    void **gluBeginCurve** (GLUnurbs **nobj*);
    void **gluEndCurve** (GLUnurbs **nobj*);
    void **gluNurbsCurve** (GLUnurbs **nobj*, GLint *nknots*, GLfloat **knot*,
          GLint *stride*, GLfloat **ctlarray*,
          GLint *order*, GLenum *type*);

Create a NURBS surface:

    void **gluBeginSurface** (GLUnurbs **nobj*);
    void **gluEndSurface** (GLUnurbs **nobj*);
    void **gluNurbsSurface** (GLUnurbs **nobj*, GLint *uknot_count*,
          GLfloat **uknot*, GLint *vknot_count*, GLfloat **vknot*,
          GLint *u_stride*, GLint *v_stride*, GLfloat **ctlarray*,
          GLint *sorder*, GLint *torder*, GLenum *type*);

Define a trimming region:

> void **gluBeginTrim** (GLUnurbs *nobj*);
> void **gluEndTrim** (GLUnurbs *nobj*);
> void **gluPwlCurve** (GLUnurbs *nobj*, GLint *count*, GLfloat *array*,
> > GLint *stride*, GLenum *type*);

Control NURBS rendering:

> void **gluLoadSamplingMatrices** (GLUnurbs *nobj*,
> > const GLfloat *modelMatrix*[16],
> > const GLfloat *projMatrix*[16],
> > const GLint *viewport*[4]);
> void **gluNurbsProperty** (GLUnurbs *nobj*, GLenum *property*, GLfloat *value*);
> void **gluGetNurbsProperty** (GLUnurbs *nobj*, GLenum *property*,
> > GLfloat *value*);

State Queries

Produce an error string from an OpenGL error code or describe the GLU version or extension:

> const GLubyte* **gluErrorString** (GLenum *errorCode*);
> const GLubyte* **gluGetString** (GLenum *name*);
> GLboolean **gluCheckExtension** (const GLubyte *extName*,
> > const GLubyte *extString*);

GLX Routines

Initialization

Determine whether the GLX extension is defined on the X server:

> Bool **glXQueryExtension** (Display *dpy*, int *errorBase*, int *eventBase*);
> Bool **glXQueryVersion** (Display *dpy*, int *major*, int *minor*);

Obtain the desired visual:

> XVisualInfo* **glXChooseVisual** (Display *dpy*, int *screen*, int *attribList*);
> int **glXGetConfig** (Display *dpy*, XVisualInfo *vis*, int *attrib*, int *value*);

Query server or client feature support:

const char* **glXQueryExtensionsString** (Display *dpy*, int *screen*);
const char* **glXQueryServerString** (Display *dpy*, int *screen*, int *name*);
const char* **glXGetClientString** (Display *dpy*, int *name*);

Controlling Rendering

Manage or query an OpenGL rendering context:

GLXContext **glXCreateContext** (Display *dpy*, XVisualInfo *vis*,
                    GLXContext *shareList*, Bool *direct*);
void **glXDestroyContext** (Display *dpy*, GLXContext *ctx*);
void **glXCopyContext** (Display *dpy*, GLXContext *src*,
                    GLXContext *dst*, GLuint *mask*);
Bool **glXIsDirect** (Display *dpy*, GLXContext *ctx*);
Bool **glXMakeCurrent** (Display *dpy*, GLXDrawable *draw*, GLXContext *ctx*);
GLXContext **glXGetCurrentContext** (void);
GLXDrawable **glXGetCurrentDrawable** (void);

Perform off-screen rendering:

GLXPixmap **glXCreateGLXPixmap** (Display *dpy*, XVisualInfo *vis*,
                    Pixmap *pixmap*);
void **glXDestroyGLXPixmap** (Display *dpy*, GLXPixmap *pix*);

Synchronize execution:

void **glXWaitGL** (void);
void **glXWaitX** (void);

Exchange front and back buffers:

void **glXSwapBuffers** (Display *dpy*, Window *window*);

Use an X font:

void **glXUseXFont** (Font *font*, int *first*, int *count*, int *listBase*);

Note: For GLX 1.3 implementations, the following commands provide a
super-set of the functionality provided by commands listed
previously.

Query or request frame buffer or visual specifications:

GLXFBConfig* **glXGetFBConfigs** (Display *dpy*, int *screen*, int *nelements*);
GLXFBConfig* **glXChooseFBConfig** (Display *dpy*, int *screen*,
                    const int *attribList*, int *nelements*);
int **glXGetFBConfigAttrib** (Display *dpy*, GLXFBConfig *config*, int *attribute*,
                    int *value*);
XVisualInfo* **glXGetVisualFromFBConfig** (Display *dpy*, GLXFBConfig
config);

Manage GLXDrawables:

GLXWindow **glXCreateWindow** (Display *dpy*, GLXFBConfig *config*,
Window *window*, const int *attribList*);
void **glXDestroyWindow** (Display *dpy*, GLXWindow *window*);
GLXPixmap **glXCreatePixmap** (Display *dpy*, GLXFBConfig *config*,
Pixmap *pixmap*, const int *attribList*);
void **glXDestroyPixmap** (Display *dpy*, GLXPixmap *pixmap*);
GLXPbuffer **glXCreatePbuffer** (Display *dpy*, GLXFBConfig *config*,
const int *attribList*);
void **glXDestroyPbuffer** (Display *dpy*, GLXPbuffer *pbuffer*);
void **glXQueryDrawable** (Display *dpy*, GLXDrawable *drawable*,
int *attribute*, unsigned int *value*);

Manage OpenGL rendering contexts:

GLXContext **glXCreateNewContext** (Display *dpy*, GLXFBConfig *config*,
int *renderType*, GLXContext *shareList*, Bool *direct*);
Bool **glXMakeContextCurrent** (Display *dpy*, GLXDrawable *drawable*,
GLXDrawable *read*, GLXContext *ctx*);
GLXDrawable **glXGetCurrentReadDrawable** (void);
Display* **glXGetCurrentDisplay** (void);
int **glXQueryContext** (Display *dpy*, GLXContext *ctx*, int *attribute*, int *value*);

Select and retrieve GLX Events:

void **glXSelectEvent** (Display *dpy*, GLXDrawable *drawable*,
unsigned long *eventMask*);
void **glXGetSelectedEvent** (Display *dpy*, GLXDrawable *drawable*,
unsigned long *eventMask*);

Chapter 4

Defined Constants and Associated Commands

This chapter lists all the defined constants in OpenGL and their corresponding commands. A constant might indicate a parameter name, a value for a parameter, a mode, a query target, or a return value. Use this table as another index into the reference pages: if you remember the name of a constant, you can use the table to find out which functions use it and then refer to the reference pages for those functions for more information. Note that all the constants listed can be used directly by the corresponding commands; the reference pages list additional, related commands that might be of interest.

Constant	Associated Commands
GL_2D, GL_3D, GL_3D_COLOR, GL_3D_COLOR_TEXTURE, GL_4D_COLOR_TEXTURE	glFeedbackBuffer()
GL_2_BYTES, GL_3_BYTES, GL_4_BYTES	glCallLists()
GL_ACCUM	glAccum()
GL_ACCUM_ALPHA_BITS, GL_ACCUM_BLUE_BITS	glGet*()
GL_ACCUM_BUFFER_BIT	glClear(), glPushAttrib()
GL_ACCUM_CLEAR_VALUE, GL_ACCUM_GREEN_BITS, GL_ACCUM_RED_BITS	glGet*()
GL_ACTIVE_TEXTURE_ARB	glGet*()
GL_ADD	glAccum(), glTexEnv*()
GL_ALIASED_LINE_WIDTH_GRANULARITY, GL_ALIASED_LINE_WIDTH_RANGE, GL_ALIASED_POINT_SIZE_GRANULARITY, GL_ALIASED_POINT_SIZE_RANGE	glGet*()
GL_ALL_ATTRIB_BITS	glPushClientAttrib()

Constant	Associated Commands
GL_ALPHA, GL_ALPHA4, GL_ALPHA8, GL_ALPHA12, GL_ALPHA16	glColorSubTable(), glColorTable(), glConvolutionFilter1D(), glConvolutionFilter2D(), glCopyColorSubTable(), glCopyConvolutionFilter1D(), glCopyConvolutionFilter2D(), glDrawPixels(), glGetColorTable(), glGetConvolutionFilter(), glGetHistogram(), glGetMinmax(), glGetSeparableFilter(), glGetTexImage(), glHistogram(), glMinmax(), glReadPixels(), glResetMinmax(), glSeparableFilter2D(), glTexImage1D(), glTexImage2D(), glTexImage3D(), glTexSubImage1D(), glTexSubImage2D(), glTexSubImage3D()
GL_ALPHA_BIAS	glGet*(), glPixelTransfer*()
GL_ALPHA_BITS	glGet*()
GL_ALPHA_SCALE	glGet*(), glPixelTransfer*()
GL_ALPHA_TEST	glDisable(), glEnable(), glGet*(), glIsEnabled()
GL_ALPHA_TEST_FUNC, GL_ALPHA_TEST_REF	glGet*()
GL_ALWAYS	glAlphaFunc(), glDepthFunc(), glStencilFunc()
GL_AMBIENT	glColorMaterial(), glGetLight*(), glGetMaterial*(), glLight*(), glMaterial*()
GL_AMBIENT_AND_DIFFUSE	glColorMaterial(), glGetMaterial*(), glMaterial*()

Constant	Associated Commands
GL_AND, GL_AND_INVERTED, GL_AND_REVERSE	glLogicOp()
GL_ATTRIB_STACK_DEPTH	glGet*()
GL_AUTO_NORMAL	glDisable(), glEnable(), glGet*(), glIsEnabled()
GL_AUX0 through GL_AUX3	glDrawBuffer(), glReadBuffer()
GL_AUX_BUFFERS	glGet*()
GL_BACK	glColorMaterial(), glCullFace(), glDrawBuffer(), glGetMaterial*(), glMaterial*(), glPolygonMode(), glReadBuffer()
GL_BACK_LEFT, GL_BACK_RIGHT	glDrawBuffer(), glReadBuffer()
GL_BGR, GL_BGRA	glColorSubTable(), glColorTable(), glConvolutionFilter1D(), glConvolutionFilter2D(), glDrawPixels(), glGetColorTable(), glGetConvolutionFilter(), glGetHistogram(), glGetMinmax(), glGetSeparableFilter(), glGetTexImage(), glHistogram(), glReadPixels(), glResetMinmax(), glSeparableFilter2D(), glTexImage1D(), glTexImage2D(), glTexImage3D(), glTexSubImage1D(), glTexSubImage2D(), glTexSubImage3D()
GL_BITMAP	glDrawPixels(), glGetTexImage(), glReadPixels(), glTexImage1D(), glTexImage2D(), glTexSubImage1D(), glTexSubImage2D()
GL_BITMAP_TOKEN	glPassThrough()

Constant	Associated Commands
GL_BLEND	glDisable(), glEnable(), glGet*(), glIsEnabled(), glTexEnv*()
GL_BLEND_COLOR, GL_BLEND_DST, GL_BLEND_EQUATION, GL_BLEND_SRC	glGet*()
GL_BLUE	glColorSubTable(), glColorTable(), glConvolutionFilter1D(), glConvolutionFilter2D(), glDrawPixels(), glGetColorTable(), glGetConvolutionFilter(), glGetHistogram(), glGetMinmax(), glGetSeparableFilter(), glGetTexImage(), glHistogram(), glReadPixels(), glResetMinmax(), glSeparableFilter2D(), glTexImage1D(), glTexImage2D(), glTexImage3D(), glTexSubImage1D(), glTexSubImage2D(), glTexSubImage3D()
GL_BLUE_BIAS	glGet*(), glPixelTransfer*()
GL_BLUE_BITS	glGet*()
GL_BLUE_SCALE	glGet*(), glPixelTransfer*()

Constant	Associated Commands
GL_BYTE	glCallLists(), glColorPointer(), glColorSubTable(), glColorTable(), glConvolutionFilter1D(), glConvolutionFilter2D(), glDrawPixels(), glGetColorTable(), glGetConvolutionFilter(), glGetHistogram(), glGetMinmax(), glGetSeparableFilter(), glGetTexImage(), glHistogram(), glNormalPointer(), glReadPixels(), glResetHistogram(), glResetMinmax(), glSeparableFilter2D(), glTexImage1D(), glTexImage2D(), glTexImage3D(), glTexSubImage1D(), glTexSubImage2D(), glTexSubImage3D()
GL_C3F_V3F, GL_C4F_N3F_V3F, GL_C4UB_V2F, GL_C4UB_V3F	glInterleavedArrays()
GL_CCW	glFrontFace()
GL_CLAMP, GL_CLAMP_TO_EDGE	glTexParameter*()
GL_CLEAR	glLogicOp()
GL_CLIENT_ACTIVE_TEXTURE_ARB	glGet*()
GL_CLIENT_ALL_ATTRIB_BITS	glPushClientAttrib()
GL_CLIENT_ATTRIB_STACK_DEPTH	glGet*()
GL_CLIENT_PIXEL_STORE_BIT, GL_CLIENT_VERTEX_ARRAY_BIT	glPushClientAttrib()
GL_CLIP_PLANE0 through GL_CLIP_PLANE5	glClipPlane(), glDisable(), glEnable(), glGet*(), glGetClipPlane(), glIsEnabled()
GL_COEFF	glGetMap*()

Constant	Associated Commands
GL_COLOR	glCopyPixels(), glMatrixMode()
GL_COLOR_ARRAY	glDisableClientState(), glEnableClientState(), glGet*(), glIsEnabled()
GL_COLOR_ARRAY_POINTER	glGetPointerv()
GL_COLOR_ARRAY_SIZE, GL_COLOR_ARRAY_STRIDE, GL_COLOR_ARRAY_TYPE	glGet*()
GL_COLOR_BUFFER_BIT	glClear(), glPushAttrib()
GL_COLOR_CLEAR_VALUE	glGet*()
GL_COLOR_INDEX	glDrawPixels(), glReadPixels(), glTexImage1D(), glTexImage2D(), glTexImage3D(), glTexSubImage1D(), glTexSubImage2D(), glTexSubImage3D()
GL_COLOR_INDEXES	glGetMaterial*(), glMaterial*()
GL_COLOR_LOGIC_OP, GL_COLOR_MATERIAL	glDisable(), glEnable(), glGet*(), glIsEnabled()
GL_COLOR_MATERIAL_FACE, GL_COLOR_MATERIAL_PARAMETER, GL_COLOR_MATRIX, GL_COLOR_MATRIX_STACK_DEPTH	glGet*()
GL_COLOR_TABLE	glColorSubTable(), glColorTable(), glColorTableParameter*(), glCopyColorSubTable(), glCopyColorTable(), glDisable(), glEnable(), glGet*(), glGetColorTable(), glGetColorTableParameter*(), glIsEnabled()
GL_COLOR_TABLE_ALPHA_SIZE	glGetColorTableParameter*()

Constant	Associated Commands
GL_COLOR_TABLE_BIAS	glColorTableParameter*(), glGetColorTableParameter*()
GL_COLOR_TABLE_BLUE_SIZE, GL_COLOR_TABLE_FORMAT, GL_COLOR_TABLE_GREEN_SIZE, GL_COLOR_TABLE_INTENSITY_SIZE, GL_COLOR_TABLE_LUMINANCE_SIZE, GL_COLOR_TABLE_RED_SIZE	glGetColorTableParameter*()
GL_COLOR_TABLE_SCALE	glColorTableParameter*(), glGetColorTableParameter*()
GL_COLOR_TABLE_WIDTH	glGetColorTableParameter*()
GL_COLOR_WRITEMASK	glGet*()
GL_COMPILE, GL_COMPILE_AND_EXECUTE	glNewList()
GL_CONSTANT_ALPHA	glBlendFunc()
GL_CONSTANT_ATTENUATION	glGetLight*(), glLight*()
GL_CONSTANT_BORDER	glConvolutionParameter*()
GL_CONSTANT_COLOR	glBlendFunc()
GL_CONVOLUTION_1D	glConvolutionFilter1D(), glConvolutionParameter*(), glCopyConvolutionFilter1D(), glDisable(), glEnable(), glGetConvolutionFilter(), glGetConvolutionParameter*(), glIsEnabled()
GL_CONVOLUTION_2D	glConvolutionFilter2D(), glConvolutionParameter*(), glCopyConvolutionFilter2D(), glDisable(), glEnable(), glGetConvolutionFilter(), glGetConvolutionParameter*(), glIsEnabled()
GL_CONVOLUTION_BORDER_COLOR	glConvolutionParameter*(), glGetConvolutionParameter*()

Constant	Associated Commands
GL_CONVOLUTION_BORDER_MODE, GL_CONVOLUTION_FILTER_BIAS, GL_CONVOLUTION_FILTER_SCALE	glConvolutionParameter*(), glGetConvolutionParameter*()
GL_CONVOLUTION_FORMAT, GL_CONVOLUTION_HEIGHT, GL_CONVOLUTION_WIDTH	glGetConvolutionParameter*()
GL_COPY, GL_COPY_INVERTED	glLogicOp()
GL_COPY_PIXEL_TOKEN	glPassThrough()
GL_CULL_FACE	glDisable(), glEnable(), glGet*(), glIsEnabled()
GL_CULL_FACE_MODE	glGet*()
GL_CURRENT_BIT	glPushAttrib()
GL_CURRENT_COLOR, GL_CURRENT_INDEX, GL_CURRENT_NORMAL, GL_CURRENT_RASTER_COLOR, GL_CURRENT_RASTER_DISTANCE, GL_CURRENT_RASTER_INDEX, GL_CURRENT_RASTER_POSITION, GL_CURRENT_RASTER_POSITION_VALID, GL_CURRENT_RASTER_TEXTURE_COORDS, GL_CURRENT_TEXTURE_COORDS	glGet*()
GL_CW	glFrontFace()
GL_DECAL	glTexEnv*()
GL_DECR	glStencilOp()
GL_DEPTH	glCopyPixels()
GL_DEPTH_BIAS	glGet*(), glPixelTransfer*()
GL_DEPTH_BITS	glGet*()
GL_DEPTH_BUFFER_BIT	glClear(), glPushAttrib()
GL_DEPTH_CLEAR_VALUE	glGet*()
GL_DEPTH_COMPONENT	glDrawPixels(), glReadPixels()
GL_DEPTH_FUNC, GL_DEPTH_RANGE	glGet*()

Constant	Associated Commands
GL_DEPTH_SCALE	glGet*(), glPixelTransfer*()
GL_DEPTH_TEST	glDisable(), glEnable(), glGet*(), glIsEnabled()
GL_DEPTH_WRITEMASK	glGet*()
GL_DIFFUSE	glColorMaterial(), glGetLight*(), glGetMaterial*(), glLight*(), glMaterial*()
GL_DITHER	glDisable(), glEnable(), glGet*(), glIsEnabled()
GL_DOMAIN	glGetMap*()
GL_DONT_CARE	glHint()
GL_DOUBLE	glColorPointer(), glIndexPointer(), glNormalPointer(), glTexCoordPointer(), glVertexPointer()
GL_DOUBLEBUFFER, GL_DRAW_BUFFER	glGet*()
GL_DRAW_PIXEL_TOKEN	glPassThrough()
GL_DST_ALPHA, GL_DST_COLOR	glBlendFunc()
GL_EDGE_FLAG	glGet*()
GL_EDGE_FLAG_ARRAY	glDisableClientState(), glEnableClientState(), glGet*(), glIsEnabled()
GL_EDGE_FLAG_ARRAY_POINTER	glGetPointerv()
GL_EDGE_FLAG_ARRAY_STRIDE	glGet*()
GL_EMISSION	glColorMaterial(), glGetMaterial*(), glMaterial*()
GL_ENABLE_BIT	glPushAttrib()
GL_EQUAL	glAlphaFunc(), glDepthFunc(), glStencilFunc()
GL_EQUIV	glLogicOp()

Constant	Associated Commands
GL_EVAL_BIT	glPushAttrib()
GL_EXP, GL_EXP2	glFog*()
GL_EYE_LINEAR	glTexGen*()
GL_EYE_PLANE	glGetTexGen*(), glTexGen*()
GL_FALSE	glAreTexturesResident(), glColorMask(), glEdgeFlag(), glGet*(), glGetHistogram(), glGetMinmax(), glHistogram(), glIsEnabled(), glIsTexture(), glLightModel*(), glPixelStore*()
GL_FASTEST	glHint()
GL_FEEDBACK	glRenderMode()
GL_FEEDBACK_BUFFER_POINTER	glGetPointerv()
GL_FEEDBACK_BUFFER_SIZE, GL_FEEDBACK_BUFFER_TYPE	glGet*()
GL_FILL	glEvalMesh2(), glPolygonMode()
GL_FLAT	glShadeModel()

Constant	Associated Commands
GL_FLOAT	glCallLists(), glColorPointer(), glColorSubTable(), glColorTable(), glConvolutionFilter1D(), glConvolutionFilter2D(), glConvolutionParameterf(), glConvolutionParameterfv(), glDrawPixels(), glGetColorTable(), glGetConvolutionFilter(), glGetConvolutionParameterfv(), glGetHistogram(), glGetHistogramParameterfv(), glGetMinmax(), glGetMinmaxParameterfv(), glGetSeparableFilter(), glGetTexImage(), glHistogram(), glIndexPointer(), glNormalPointer(), glReadPixels(), glResetHistogram(), glResetMinmax(), glSeparableFilter2D(), glTexCoordPointer(), glTexImage1D(), glTexImage2D(), glTexImage3D(), glTexSubImage1D(), glTexSubImage2D(), glTexSubImage3D(), glVertexPointer()
GL_FOG	glDisable(), glEnable(), glGet*(), glIsEnabled()
GL_FOG_BIT	glPushAttrib()
GL_FOG_COLOR, GL_FOG_DENSITY, GL_FOG_END	glFog*(), glGet*()
GL_FOG_HINT	glGet*(), glHint()
GL_FOG_INDEX, GL_FOG_MODE, GL_FOG_START	glFog*(), glGet*()

Constant	Associated Commands
GL_FRONT	glColorMaterial(), glCullFace(), glDrawBuffer(), glGetMaterial*(), glMaterial*(), glPolygonMode(), glReadBuffer()
GL_FRONT_AND_BACK	glColorMaterial(), glCullFace(), glDrawBuffer(), glGetMaterial*(), glMaterial*(), glPolygonMode()
GL_FRONT_FACE	glGet*()
GL_FRONT_LEFT, GL_FRONT_RIGHT	glDrawBuffer(), glReadBuffer()
GL_FUNC_ADD, GL_FUNC_REVERSE_SUBTRACT, GL_FUNC_SUBTRACT	glBlendEquation()
GL_GEQUAL, GL_GREATER	glAlphaFunc(), glDepthFunc(), glStencilFunc()
GL_GREEN	glColorSubTable(), glColorTable(), glConvolutionFilter1D(), glConvolutionFilter2D(), glDrawPixels(), glGetColorTable(), glGetConvolutionFilter(), glGetHistogram(), glGetMinmax(), glGetSeparableFilter(), glGetTexImage(), glHistogram(), glReadPixels(), glResetMinmax(), glSeparableFilter2D(), glTexImage1D(), glTexImage2D(), glTexImage3D(), glTexSubImage1D(), glTexSubImage2D(), glTexSubImage3D()
GL_GREEN_BIAS	glGet*(), glPixelTransfer*()
GL_GREEN_BITS	glGet*()
GL_GREEN_SCALE	glGet*(), glPixelTransfer*()
GL_HINT_BIT	glPushAttrib()

Constant	Associated Commands
GL_HISTOGRAM	glDisable(), glEnable(), glGet*(), glGetHistogram(), glGetHistogramParameter*(), glHistogram(), glIsEnabled(), glResetHistogram()
GL_HISTOGRAM_ALPHA_SIZE, GL_HISTOGRAM_BLUE_SIZE, GL_HISTOGRAM_FORMAT, GL_HISTOGRAM_GREEN_SIZE, GL_HISTOGRAM_LUMINANCE_SIZE, GL_HISTOGRAM_RED_SIZE, GL_HISTOGRAM_SINK, GL_HISTOGRAM_WIDTH	glGetHistogramParameter*()
GL_INCR	glStencilOp()
GL_INDEX_ARRAY	glDisableClientState(), glEnableClientState(), glGet*(), glIsEnabled()
GL_INDEX_ARRAY_POINTER	glGetPointerv()
GL_INDEX_ARRAY_STRIDE, GL_INDEX_ARRAY_TYPE, GL_INDEX_BITS, GL_INDEX_CLEAR_VALUE	glGet*()
GL_INDEX_LOGIC_OP	glDisable(), glEnable(), glGet*(), glIsEnabled()
GL_INDEX_MODE	glGet*()
GL_INDEX_OFFSET, GL_INDEX_SHIFT	glGet*(), glPixelTransfer*()
GL_INDEX_WRITEMASK	glGet*()

Constant	Associated Commands
GL_INT	glCallLists(), glColorPointer(), glColorSubTable(), glColorTable(), glConvolutionFilter1D(), glConvolutionFilter2D(), glConvolutionParameteri(), glConvolutionParameteriv(), glDrawPixels(), glGetColorTable(), glGetConvolutionFilter(), glGetConvolutionParameteriv(), glGetHistogram(), glGetHistogramParameteriv(), glGetMinmax(), glGetMinmaxParameteriv(), glGetSeparableFilter(), glGetTexImage(), glHistogram(), glIndexPointer(), glNormalPointer(), glReadPixels(), glResetHistogram(), glResetMinmax(), glSeparableFilter2D(), glTexCoordPointer(), glTexImage1D(), glTexImage2D(), glTexImage3D(), glTexSubImage1D(), glTexSubImage2D(), glTexSubImage3D(), glVertexPointer()
GL_INTENSITY	glColorTable(), glConvolutionFilter1D(), glConvolutionFilter2D(), glCopyColorSubTable(), glCopyColorTable(), glCopyConvolutionFilter1D(), glCopyConvolutionFilter2D(), glSeparableFilter2D()

Constant	Associated Commands
GL_INTENSITY4, GL_INTENSITY8, GL_INTENSITY12, GL_INTENSITY16	glColorTable(), glConvolutionFilter1D(), glConvolutionFilter2D(), glCopyColorTable(), glCopyConvolutionFilter1D(), glCopyConvolutionFilter2D(), glSeparableFilter2D()
GL_INVALID_ENUM, GL_INVALID_OPERATION, GL_INVALID_VALUE	glGetError()
GL_INVERT	glLogicOp(), glStencilOp()
GL_KEEP	glStencilOp()
GL_LEFT	glDrawBuffer(), glReadBuffer()
GL_LEQUAL, GL_LESS	glAlphaFunc(), glDepthFunc(), glStencilFunc()
GL_LIGHT0 through GL_LIGHT7	glDisable(), glEnable(), glGet*(), glGetLight*(), glIsEnabled(), glLight*()
GL_LIGHTING	glDisable(), glEnable(), glGet*(), glIsEnabled()
GL_LIGHTING_BIT	glPushAttrib()
GL_LIGHT_MODEL_AMBIENT, GL_LIGHT_MODEL_COLOR_CONTROL, GL_LIGHT_MODEL_LOCAL_VIEWER, GL_LIGHT_MODEL_TWO_SIDE	glGet*(), glLightModel*()
GL_LINE	glEvalMesh1(), glEvalMesh2(), glPolygonMode()
GL_LINEAR	glFog*(), glTexParameter*()
GL_LINEAR_ATTENUATION	glGetLight*(), glLight*()
GL_LINEAR_MIPMAP_LINEAR, GL_LINEAR_MIPMAP_NEAREST	glTexParameter*()
GL_LINES	glBegin(), glDrawArrays(), glDrawElements(), glDrawRangeElements()

Constant	Associated Commands
GL_LINE_BIT	glPushAttrib()
GL_LINE_LOOP	glBegin(), glDrawArrays(), glDrawElements(), glDrawRangeElements()
GL_LINE_RESET_TOKEN	glPassThrough()
GL_LINE_SMOOTH	glDisable(), glEnable(), glGet*(), glIsEnabled()
GL_LINE_SMOOTH_HINT	glGet*(), glHint()
GL_LINE_STIPPLE	glDisable(), glEnable(), glGet*(), glIsEnabled()
GL_LINE_STIPPLE_PATTERN, GL_LINE_STIPPLE_REPEAT	glGet*()
GL_LINE_STRIP	glBegin(), glDrawArrays(), glDrawElements(), glDrawRangeElements()
GL_LINE_TOKEN	glPassThrough()
GL_LINE_WIDTH, GL_LINE_WIDTH_GRANULARITY, GL_LINE_WIDTH_RANGE, GL_LIST_BASE	glGet*()
GL_LIST_BIT	glPushAttrib()
GL_LIST_INDEX, GL_LIST_MODE	glGet*()
GL_LOAD	glAccum()
GL_LOGIC_OP_MODE	glGet*()

Constant	Associated Commands
GL_LUMINANCE, GL_LUMINANCE4, GL_LUMINANCE8, GL_LUMINANCE12, GL_LUMINANCE16, GL_LUMINANCE_ALPHA, GL_LUMINANCE4_ALPHA4, GL_LUMINANCE6_ALPHA2, GL_LUMINANCE8_ALPHA8, GL_LUMINANCE12_ALPHA4, GL_LUMINANCE12_ALPHA12, GL_LUMINANCE16_ALPHA16	glColorSubTable(), glColorTable(), glConvolutionFilter1D(), glConvolutionFilter2D(), glCopyColorSubTable(), glCopyConvolutionFilter1D(), glCopyConvolutionFilter2D(), glDrawPixels(), glGetColorTable(), glGetConvolutionFilter(), glGetHistogram(), glGetMinmax(), glGetSeparableFilter(), glGetTexImage(), glHistogram(), glMinmax(), glReadPixels(), glSeparableFilter2D(), glTexImage1D(), glTexImage2D(), glTexImage3D(), glTexSubImage1D(), glTexSubImage2D(), glTexSubImage3D()
GL_MAP1_COLOR_4	glDisable(), glEnable(), glGet*(), glGetMap*(), glIsEnabled(), glMap1*()
GL_MAP1_GRID_DOMAIN, GL_MAP1_GRID_SEGMENTS	glGet*()
GL_MAP1_INDEX, GL_MAP1_NORMAL, GL_MAP1_TEXTURE_COORD_1 throughGL_MAP1_TEXTURE_COORD_4, GL_MAP1_VERTEX_3, GL_MAP1_VERTEX_4	glDisable(), glEnable(), glGet*(), glGetMap*(), glIsEnabled(), glMap1*()
GL_MAP2_COLOR_4	glDisable(), glEnable(), glGet*(), glGetMap*(), glIsEnabled(), glMap2*()
GL_MAP2_GRID_DOMAIN, GL_MAP2_GRID_SEGMENTS	glGet*()
GL_MAP2_INDEX, GL_MAP2_NORMAL, GL_MAP2_TEXTURE_COORD_1, GL_MAP2_TEXTURE_COORD_4, GL_MAP2_VERTEX_3, GL_MAP2_VERTEX_4	glDisable(), glEnable(), glGet*(), glGetMap*(), glIsEnabled(), glMap2*()

Constant	Associated Commands
GL_MAP_COLOR, GL_MAP_STENCIL	glGet*(), glPixelTransfer*()
GL_MATRIX_MODE	glGet*()
GL_MAX	glBlendEquation()
GL_MAX_3D_TEXTURE_SIZE, GL_MAX_ATTRIB_STACK_DEPTH, GL_MAX_CLIENT_ATTRIB_STACK_DEPTH, GL_MAX_CLIP_PLANES, GL_MAX_COLOR_MATRIX_STACK_DEPTH	glGet*()
GL_MAX_CONVOLUTION_HEIGHT, GL_MAX_CONVOLUTION_WIDTH	glGetConvolutionParameter*()
GL_MAX_ELEMENTS_INDICES, GL_MAX_ELEMENTS_VERTICES, GL_MAX_EVAL_ORDER, GL_MAX_LIGHTS, GL_MAX_LIST_NESTING, GL_MAX_MODELVIEW_STACK_DEPTH, GL_MAX_NAME_STACK_DEPTH, GL_MAX_PIXEL_MAP_TABLE, GL_MAX_PROJECTION_STACK_DEPTH, GL_MAX_TEXTURE_SIZE, GL_MAX_TEXTURE_STACK_DEPTH, GL_MAX_TEXTURE_UNITS_ARB, GL_MAX_VIEWPORT_DIMS	glGet*()
GL_MIN	glBlendEquation()
GL_MINMAX	glDisable(), glEnable(), glGet*(), glGetMinmax(), glGetMinmaxParameter*(), glIsEnabled(), glMinmax(), glResetMinmax()
GL_MINMAX_FORMAT, GL_MINMAX_SINK	glGetMinmaxParameter*()
GL_MODELVIEW	glMatrixMode()
GL_MODELVIEW_MATRIX, GL_MODELVIEW_STACK_DEPTH	glGet*()
GL_MODULATE	glTexEnv*()
GL_MULT	glAccum()

Constant	Associated Commands
GL_N3F_V3F	glInterleavedArrays()
GL_NAME_STACK_DEPTH	glGet*()
GL_NAND	glLogicOp()
GL_NEAREST, GL_NEAREST_MIPMAP_LINEAR, GL_NEAREST_MIPMAP_NEAREST	glTexParameter*()
GL_NEVER	glAlphaFunc(), glDepthFunc(), glStencilFunc()
GL_NICEST	glHint()
GL_NONE	glClear(), glDrawBuffer()
GL_NOOP, GL_NOR	glLogicOp()
GL_NORMALIZE	glDisable(), glEnable(), glGet*(), glIsEnabled()
GL_NORMAL_ARRAY	glDisableClientState(), glEnableClientState(), glGet*(), glIsEnabled()
GL_NORMAL_ARRAY_POINTER	glGetPointerv()
GL_NORMAL_ARRAY_STRIDE, GL_NORMAL_ARRAY_TYPE	glGet*()
GL_NOTEQUAL	glAlphaFunc(), glDepthFunc(), glStencilFunc()
GL_NO_ERROR	glGetError()
GL_OBJECT_LINEAR	glTexGen*()
GL_OBJECT_PLANE	glGetTexGen*(), glTexGen*()
GL_ONE, GL_ONE_MINUS_CONSTANT_ALPHA, GL_ONE_MINUS_CONSTANT_COLOR, GL_ONE_MINUS_DST_ALPHA, GL_ONE_MINUS_DST_COLOR, GL_ONE_MINUS_SRC_ALPHA, GL_ONE_MINUS_SRC_COLOR	glBlendFunc()
GL_OR	glLogicOp()

Constant	Associated Commands
GL_ORDER	glGetMap*()
GL_OR_INVERTED, GL_OR_REVERSE	glLogicOp()
GL_OUT_OF_MEMORY	glGetError()
GL_PACK_ALIGNMENT, GL_PACK_IMAGE_HEIGHT, GL_PACK_LSB_FIRST, GL_PACK_ROW_LENGTH, GL_PACK_SKIP_IMAGES, GL_PACK_SKIP_PIXELS, GL_PACK_SKIP_ROWS, GL_PACK_SWAP_BYTES	glGet*(), glPixelStore*()
GL_PASS_THROUGH_TOKEN	glPassThrough()
GL_PERSPECTIVE_CORRECTION_HINT	glGet*(), glHint()
GL_PIXEL_MAP_A_TO_A, GL_PIXEL_MAP_B_TO_B, GL_PIXEL_MAP_G_TO_G, GL_PIXEL_MAP_I_TO_A, GL_PIXEL_MAP_I_TO_B, GL_PIXEL_MAP_I_TO_G, GL_PIXEL_MAP_I_TO_I, GL_PIXEL_MAP_I_TO_R, GL_PIXEL_MAP_R_TO_R, GL_PIXEL_MAP_S_TO_S	glGetPixelMap*(), glPixelMap*()
GL_PIXEL_MAP_A_TO_A_SIZE, GL_PIXEL_MAP_B_TO_B_SIZE, GL_PIXEL_MAP_G_TO_G_SIZE, GL_PIXEL_MAP_I_TO_A_SIZE, GL_PIXEL_MAP_I_TO_B_SIZE, GL_PIXEL_MAP_I_TO_G_SIZE, GL_PIXEL_MAP_I_TO_I_SIZE, GL_PIXEL_MAP_I_TO_R_SIZE, GL_PIXEL_MAP_R_TO_R_SIZE, GL_PIXEL_MAP_S_TO_S_SIZE	glGet*()
GL_PIXEL_MODE_BIT	glPushAttrib()
GL_POINT	glEvalMesh1(), glEvalMesh2(), glPolygonMode()

Constant	Associated Commands
GL_POINTS	glBegin(), glDrawArrays(), glDrawElements(), glDrawRangeElements()
GL_POINT_BIT	glPushAttrib()
GL_POINT_SIZE, GL_POINT_SIZE_GRANULARITY, GL_POINT_SIZE_RANGE	glGet*()
GL_POINT_SMOOTH	glDisable(), glEnable(), glGet*(), glIsEnabled()
GL_POINT_SMOOTH_HINT	glGet*(), glHint()
GL_POINT_TOKEN	glPassThrough()
GL_POLYGON	glBegin(), glDrawArrays(), glDrawElements(), glDrawRangeElements()
GL_POLYGON_BIT	glPushAttrib()
GL_POLYGON_MODE, GL_POLYGON_OFFSET_FACTOR	glGet*()
GL_POLYGON_OFFSET_FILL, GL_POLYGON_OFFSET_LINE, GL_POLYGON_OFFSET_POINT	glDisable(), glEnable(), glGet*(), glIsEnabled()
GL_POLYGON_OFFSET_UNITS	glGet*()
GL_POLYGON_SMOOTH	glDisable(), glEnable(), glGet*(), glIsEnabled()
GL_POLYGON_SMOOTH_HINT	glGet*(), glHint()
GL_POLYGON_STIPPLE	glDisable(), glEnable(), glGet*(), glIsEnabled()
GL_POLYGON_STIPPLE_BIT	glPushAttrib()
GL_POLYGON_TOKEN	glPassThrough()
GL_POSITION	glGetLight*(), glLight*()

Constant	Associated Commands
GL_POST_COLOR_MATRIX_ALPHA_BIAS, GL_POST_COLOR_MATRIX_ALPHA_SCALE, GL_POST_COLOR_MATRIX_BLUE_BIAS, GL_POST_COLOR_MATRIX_BLUE_SCALE	glGet*(), glPixelTransfer*()
GL_POST_COLOR_MATRIX_COLOR_TABLE	glColorSubTable(), glColorTable(), glColorTableParameter*(), glCopyColorSubTable(), glCopyColorTable(), glDisable(), glEnable(), glGet*(), glGetColorTable(), glGetColorTableParameter*(), glIsEnabled()
GL_POST_COLOR_MATRIX_GREEN_BIAS, GL_POST_COLOR_MATRIX_GREEN_SCALE, GL_POST_COLOR_MATRIX_RED_BIAS, GL_POST_COLOR_MATRIX_RED_SCALE, GL_POST_CONVOLUTION_ALPHA_BIAS, GL_POST_CONVOLUTION_ALPHA_SCALE, GL_POST_CONVOLUTION_BLUE_BIAS, GL_POST_CONVOLUTION_BLUE_SCALE	glGet*(), glPixelTransfer*()
GL_POST_CONVOLUTION_COLOR_TABLE	glColorSubTable(), glColorTable(), glColorTableParameter*(), glCopyColorSubTable(), glCopyColorTable(), glDisable(), glEnable(), glGet*(), glGetColorTable(), glGetColorTableParameter*(), glIsEnabled()
GL_POST_CONVOLUTION_GREEN_BIAS, GL_POST_CONVOLUTION_GREEN_SCALE, GL_POST_CONVOLUTION_RED_BIAS, GL_POST_CONVOLUTION_RED_SCALE	glGet*(), glPixelTransfer*()
GL_PROJECTION	glMatrixMode()
GL_PROJECTION_MATRIX, GL_PROJECTION_STACK_DEPTH	glGet*()
GL_PROXY_COLOR_TABLE	glColorSubTable(), glColorTable()

Constant	Associated Commands
GL_PROXY_HISTOGRAM	glHistogram()
GL_PROXY_POST_COLOR_MATRIX_COLOR_TABLE, GL_PROXY_POST_CONVOLUTION_COLOR_TABLE	glColorSubTable(), glColorTable()
GL_PROXY_TEXTURE_1D, GL_PROXY_TEXTURE_2D, GL_PROXY_TEXTURE_3D	glTexImage1D(), glTexImage2D(), glTexImage3D()
GL_Q	glGetTexGen*(), glTexGen*()
GL_QUADRATIC_ATTENUATION	glGetLight*(), glLight*()
GL_QUADS	glBegin(), glDrawArrays(), glDrawElements(), glDrawRangeElements()
GL_QUAD_STRIP	glBegin(), glDrawArrays(), glDrawElements(), glDrawRangeElements()
GL_R	glGetTexGen*(), glTexGen*()
GL_R3_G3_B2	glColorTable(), glConvolutionFilter1D(), glConvolutionFilter2D(), glCopyColorTable(), glCopyConvolutionFilter1D(), glCopyConvolutionFilter2D(), glCopyTexImage1D(), glCopyTexImage2D(), glHistogram(), glMinmax(), glSeparableFilter2D(), glTexImage3D()
GL_READ_BUFFER	glGet*()

Constant	Associated Commands
GL_RED	glColorSubTable(), glColorTable(), glConvolutionFilter1D(), glConvolutionFilter2D(), glDrawPixels(), glGetColorTable(), glGetConvolutionFilter(), glGetHistogram(), glGetMinmax(), glGetSeparableFilter(), glGetTexImage(), glHistogram(), glReadPixels(), glResetMinmax(), glSeparableFilter2D(), glTexImage1D(), glTexImage2D(), glTexImage3D(), glTexSubImage1D(), glTexSubImage2D(), glTexSubImage3D()
GL_REDUCE	glConvolutionParameter*()
GL_RED_BIAS	glGet*(), glPixelTransfer*()
GL_RED_BITS	glGet*()
GL_RED_SCALE	glGet*(), glPixelTransfer*()
GL_RENDER	glRenderMode()
GL_RENDERER	glGetString()
GL_RENDER_MODE	glGet*()
GL_REPEAT	glTexParameter*()
GL_REPLACE	glStencilOp(), glTexEnv*()
GL_REPLICATE_BORDER	glConvolutionParameter*()
GL_RESCALE_NORMAL	glDisable(), glEnable(), glGet*(), glIsEnabled()
GL_RETURN	glAccum()

Constant	Associated Commands
GL_RGB	glColorSubTable(), glColorTable(), glConvolutionFilter1D(), glConvolutionFilter2D(), glCopyColorSubTable(), glCopyConvolutionFilter1D(), glCopyConvolutionFilter2D(), glDrawPixels(), glGetColorTable(), glGetConvolutionFilter(), glGetHistogram(), glGetMinmax(), glGetSeparableFilter(), glGetTexImage(), glHistogram(), glMinmax(), glReadPixels(), glResetMinmax(), glSeparableFilter2D(), glTexImage1D(), glTexImage2D(), glTexImage3D(), glTexSubImage1D(), glTexSubImage2D(), glTexSubImage3D()
GL_RGB4, GL_RGB5, GL_RGB8, GL_RGB10, GL_RGB12, GL_RGB16, GL_RGB5_A1, GL_RGB10_A2	glColorTable(), glConvolutionFilter1D(), glConvolutionFilter2D(), glCopyColorTable(), glCopyConvolutionFilter1D(), glCopyConvolutionFilter2D(), glCopyTexImage1D(), glCopyTexImage2D(), glHistogram(), glMinmax(), glSeparableFilter2D(), glTexImage3D()

Constant	Associated Commands
GL_RGBA	glColorSubTable(), glColorTable(), glConvolutionFilter1D(), glConvolutionFilter2D(), glCopyColorSubTable(), glCopyColorTable(), glCopyConvolutionFilter1D(), glCopyConvolutionFilter2D(), glCopyTexImage1D(), glCopyTexImage2D(), glCopyTexSubImage1D(), glCopyTexSubImage2D(), glCopyTexSubImage3D(), glDrawPixels(), glGetColorTable(), glGetConvolutionFilter(), glGetHistogram(), glGetMinmax(), glGetSeparableFilter(), glGetTexImage(), glHistogram(), glMinmax(), glReadPixels(), glSeparableFilter2D(), glTexImage1D(), glTexImage2D(), glTexImage3D(), glTexSubImage1D(), glTexSubImage2D(), glTexSubImage3D()
GL_RGBA2, GL_RGBA4, GL_RGBA8, GL_RGBA12, GL_RGBA16	glColorTable(), glConvolutionFilter1D(), glConvolutionFilter2D(), glCopyColorTable(), glCopyConvolutionFilter1D(), glCopyConvolutionFilter2D(), glCopyTexImage1D(), glCopyTexImage2D(), glHistogram(), glMinmax(), glSeparableFilter2D(), glTexImage1D(), glTexImage2D(), glTexImage3D()
GL_RGBA_MODE	glGet*()

Constant	Associated Commands
GL_RIGHT	glDrawBuffer(), glReadBuffer()
GL_S	glGetTexGen*(), glTexGen*()
GL_SCISSOR_BIT	glPushAttrib()
GL_SCISSOR_BOX	glGet*()
GL_SCISSOR_TEST	glDisable(), glEnable(), glGet*(), glIsEnabled()
GL_SELECT	glRenderMode()
GL_SELECTION_BUFFER_POINTER	glGetPointerv()
GL_SELECTION_BUFFER_SIZE	glGet*()
GL_SEPARABLE_2D	glDisable(), glEnable(), glGetSeparableFilter(), glIsEnabled(), glSeparableFilter2D()
GL_SEPARATE_SPECULAR_COLOR	glLightModel*()
GL_SET	glLogicOp()
GL_SHADE_MODEL	glGet*()
GL_SHININESS	glGetMaterial*(), glMaterial*()

Constant	Associated Commands
GL_SHORT	glCallLists(), glColorPointer(), glColorSubTable(), glColorTable(), glConvolutionFilter1D(), glConvolutionFilter2D(), glDrawPixels(), glGetColorTable(), glGetConvolutionFilter(), glGetHistogram(), glGetMinmax(), glGetSeparableFilter(), glGetTexImage(), glHistogram(), glIndexPointer(), glNormalPointer(), glReadPixels(), glResetHistogram(), glResetMinmax(), glSeparableFilter2D(), glTexCoordPointer(), glTexImage1D(), glTexImage2D(), glTexImage3D(), glTexSubImage1D(), glTexSubImage2D(), glTexSubImage3D(), glVertexPointer()
GL_SINGLE_COLOR	glLightModel*()
GL_SMOOTH	glShadeModel()
GL_SMOOTH_LINE_WIDTH_GRANULARITY, GL_SMOOTH_LINE_WIDTH_RANGE, GL_SMOOTH_POINT_SIZE_GRANULARITY, GL_SMOOTH_POINT_SIZE_RANGE	glGet*()
GL_SPECULAR	glColorMaterial(), glGetLight*(), glGetMaterial*(), glLight*(), glMaterial*()
GL_SPHERE_MAP	glTexGen*()
GL_SPOT_CUTOFF, GL_SPOT_DIRECTION, GL_SPOT_EXPONENT	glGetLight*(), glLight*()

Constant	Associated Commands
GL_SRC_ALPHA, GL_SRC_ALPHA_SATURATE, GL_SRC_COLOR	glBlendFunc()
GL_STACK_OVERFLOW, GL_STACK_UNDERFLOW	glGetError()
GL_STENCIL	glCopyPixels()
GL_STENCIL_BITS	glGet*()
GL_STENCIL_BUFFER_BIT	glClear(), glPushAttrib()
GL_STENCIL_CLEAR_VALUE, GL_STENCIL_FAIL, GL_STENCIL_FUNC	glGet*()
GL_STENCIL_INDEX	glDrawPixels(), glReadPixels()
GL_STENCIL_PASS_DEPTH_FAIL, GL_STENCIL_PASS_DEPTH_PASS, GL_STENCIL_REF	glGet*()
GL_STENCIL_TEST	glDisable(), glEnable(), glGet*(), glIsEnabled()
GL_STENCIL_VALUE_MASK, GL_STENCIL_WRITEMASK, GL_STEREO, GL_SUBPIXEL_BITS	glGet*()
GL_T	glGetTexGen*(), glTexGen*()
GL_T2F_C3F_V3F, GL_T2F_C4F_N3F_V3F, GL_T2F_C4UB_V3F, GL_T2F_N3F_V3F, GL_T2F_V3F, GL_T4F_C4F_N3F_V4F, GL_T4F_V4F	glInterleavedArrays()
GL_TABLE_TOO_LARGE	glGetError()
GL_TEXTURE	glMatrixMode()
GL_TEXTURE0_ARB through GL_TEXTURE31_ARB	glActiveTextureARB(), glClientActiveTextureARB(), glMultiTexCoord*ARB()

Constant	Associated Commands
GL_TEXTURE_1D	glBindTexture(), glCopyTexImage1D(), glCopyTexSubImage1D(), glDisable(), glEnable(), glGet*(), glGetTexImage(), glGetTexLevelParameter*(), glGetTexParameter*(), glIsEnabled(), glTexImage1D(), glTexParameter*(), glTexSubImage1D()
GL_TEXTURE_2D	glBindTexture(), glCopyTexImage2D(), glCopyTexSubImage2D(), glDisable(), glEnable(), glGet*(), glGetTexImage(), glGetTexLevelParameter*(), glGetTexParameter*(), glIsEnabled(), glTexImage2D(), glTexParameter*(), glTexSubImage2D()
GL_TEXTURE_3D	glBindTexture(), glDisable(), glEnable(), glGet*(), glGetTexImage(), glGetTexLevelParameter*(), glGetTexParameter*(), glIsEnabled(), glTexImage3D(), glTexParameter*(), glTexSubImage3D()
GL_TEXTURE_ALPHA_SIZE	glGetTexLevelParameter*(), glGetTexParameter*()
GL_TEXTURE_BASE_LEVEL	glGetTexLevelParameter*(), glGetTexParameter*(), glTexParameter*()
GL_TEXTURE_BINDING_1D, GL_TEXTURE_BINDING_2D, GL_TEXTURE_BINDING_3D	glGet*()
GL_TEXTURE_BIT	glPushAttrib()
GL_TEXTURE_BLUE_SIZE, GL_TEXTURE_BORDER	glGetTexLevelParameter*(), glGetTexParameter*()

Constant	Associated Commands
GL_TEXTURE_BORDER_COLOR	glGetTexParameter*(), glTexParameter*()
GL_TEXTURE_COORD_ARRAY	glDisableClientState(), glEnableClientState(), glGet*(), glIsEnabled()
GL_TEXTURE_COORD_ARRAY_POINTER	glGetPointerv()
GL_TEXTURE_COORD_ARRAY_SIZE, GL_TEXTURE_COORD_ARRAY_STRIDE, GL_TEXTURE_COORD_ARRAY_TYPE	glGet*()
GL_TEXTURE_DEPTH	glGetTexLevelParameter*(), glGetTexParameter*()
GL_TEXTURE_ENV, GL_TEXTURE_ENV_COLOR, GL_TEXTURE_ENV_MODE	glGetTexEnv*(), glTexEnv*()
GL_TEXTURE_GEN_MODE	glGetTexGen*(), glTexGen*()
GL_TEXTURE_GEN_Q, GL_TEXTURE_GEN_R, GL_TEXTURE_GEN_S, GL_TEXTURE_GEN_T	glDisable(), glEnable(), glGet*(), glIsEnabled()
GL_TEXTURE_GREEN_SIZE, GL_TEXTURE_HEIGHT, GL_TEXTURE_INTENSITY_SIZE, GL_TEXTURE_INTERNAL_FORMAT, GL_TEXTURE_LUMINANCE_SIZE	glGetTexLevelParameter*(), glGetTexParameter*()
GL_TEXTURE_MAG_FILTER	glGetTexParameter*(), glTexParameter*()
GL_TEXTURE_MATRIX	glGet*()
GL_TEXTURE_MAX_LEVEL, GL_TEXTURE_MAX_LOD, GL_TEXTURE_MIN_FILTER, GL_TEXTURE_MIN_LOD, GL_TEXTURE_PRIORITY	glGetTexParameter*(), glTexParameter*()
GL_TEXTURE_RED_SIZE, GL_TEXTURE_RESIDENT	glGetTexLevelParameter*(), glGetTexParameter*()
GL_TEXTURE_STACK_DEPTH	glGet*()

Constant	Associated Commands
GL_TEXTURE_WIDTH	glGetTexLevelParameter*(), glGetTexParameter*()
GL_TEXTURE_WRAP_R, GL_TEXTURE_WRAP_S, GL_TEXTURE_WRAP_T	glGetTexParameter*(), glTexParameter*()
GL_TRANSFORM_BIT	glPushAttrib()
GL_TRIANGLES, GL_TRIANGLE_FAN, GL_TRIANGLE_STRIP	glBegin(), glDrawArrays(), glDrawElements(), glDrawRangeElements()
GL_TRUE	glAreTexturesResident(), glBindTexture(), glCallLists(), glGet*(), glIsTexture(), glPixelStoref(), glPopAttrib(), glPrioritizeTextures()
GL_UNPACK_ALIGNMENT, GL_UNPACK_IMAGE_HEIGHT, GL_UNPACK_LSB_FIRST, GL_UNPACK_ROW_LENGTH, GL_UNPACK_SKIP_IMAGES, GL_UNPACK_SKIP_PIXELS, GL_UNPACK_SKIP_ROWS, GL_UNPACK_SWAP_BYTES	glGet*(), glPixelStore*()

Constant	Associated Commands
GL_UNSIGNED_BYTE	glCallLists(), glColorPointer(), glColorSubTable(), glColorTable(), glConvolutionFilter1D(), glConvolutionFilter2D(), glDrawPixels(), glGetColorTable(), glGetConvolutionFilter(), glGetHistogram(), glGetMinmax(), glGetSeparableFilter(), glGetTexImage(), glHistogram(), glReadPixels(), glSeparableFilter2D(), glTexImage1D(), glTexImage2D(), glTexImage3D(), glTexSubImage1D(), glTexSubImage2D(), glTexSubImage3D()
GL_UNSIGNED_BYTE_2_3_3_REV, GL_UNSIGNED_BYTE_3_3_2	glColorSubTable(), glColorTable(), glConvolutionFilter1D(), glConvolutionFilter2D(), glDrawPixels(), glGetColorTable(), glGetConvolutionFilter(), glGetHistogram(), glGetMinmax(), glGetSeparableFilter(), glGetTexImage(), glHistogram(), glReadPixels(), glSeparableFilter2D(), glTexImage1D(), glTexImage2D(), glTexImage3D(), glTexSubImage1D(), glTexSubImage2D(), glTexSubImage3D()

Constant	Associated Commands
GL_UNSIGNED_INT	glCallLists(), glColorPointer(), glColorSubTable(), glColorTable(), glConvolutionFilter1D(), glConvolutionFilter2D(), glDrawPixels(), glGetColorTable(), glGetConvolutionFilter(), glGetHistogram(), glGetMinmax(), glGetSeparableFilter(), glGetTexImage(), glHistogram(), glReadPixels(), glResetHistogram(), glResetMinmax(), glSeparableFilter2D(), glTexImage1D(), glTexImage2D(), glTexImage3D(), glTexSubImage1D(), glTexSubImage2D(), glTexSubImage3D()
GL_UNSIGNED_INT_8_8_8_8, GL_UNSIGNED_INT_8_8_8_8_REV, GL_UNSIGNED_INT_10_10_10_2, GL_UNSIGNED_INT_2_10_10_10_REV	glColorSubTable(), glColorTable(), glConvolutionFilter1D(), glConvolutionFilter2D(), glDrawPixels(), glGetColorTable(), glGetConvolutionFilter(), glGetHistogram(), glGetMinmax(), glGetSeparableFilter(), glGetTexImage(), glHistogram(), glReadPixels(), glSeparableFilter2D(), glTexImage1D(), glTexImage2D(), glTexImage3D(), glTexSubImage1D(), glTexSubImage2D(), glTexSubImage3D()

Constant	Associated Commands
GL_UNSIGNED_SHORT	glCallLists(), glColorPointer(), glColorSubTable(), glColorTable(), glConvolutionFilter1D(), glConvolutionFilter2D(), glDrawPixels(), glGetColorTable(), glGetConvolutionFilter(), glGetHistogram(), glGetMinmax(), glGetSeparableFilter(), glGetTexImage(), glHistogram(), glReadPixels(), glResetHistogram(), glResetMinmax(), glSeparableFilter2D(), glTexImage1D(), glTexImage2D(), glTexImage3D(), glTexSubImage1D(), glTexSubImage2D(), glTexSubImage3D()
GL_UNSIGNED_SHORT_1_5_5_5_REV, GL_UNSIGNED_SHORT_4_4_4_4, GL_UNSIGNED_SHORT_4_4_4_4_REV, GL_UNSIGNED_SHORT_5_5_5_1, GL_UNSIGNED_SHORT_5_6_5, GL_UNSIGNED_SHORT_5_6_5_REV	glColorSubTable(), glColorTable(), glConvolutionFilter1D(), glConvolutionFilter2D(), glDrawPixels(), glGetColorTable(), glGetConvolutionFilter(), glGetHistogram(), glGetMinmax(), glGetSeparableFilter(), glGetTexImage(), glHistogram(), glReadPixels(), glSeparableFilter2D(), glTexImage1D(), glTexImage2D(), glTexImage3D(), glTexSubImage1D(), glTexSubImage2D(), glTexSubImage3D()
GL_V2F, GL_V3F	glInterleavedArrays()

Constant	Associated Commands
GL_VENDOR, GL_VERSION	glGetString()
GL_VERTEX_ARRAY	glDisableClientState(), glEnableClientState(), glGet*(), glIsEnabled()
GL_VERTEX_ARRAY_POINTER	glGetPointerv()
GL_VERTEX_ARRAY_SIZE, GL_VERTEX_ARRAY_STRIDE, GL_VERTEX_ARRAY_TYPE, GL_VIEWPORT	glGet*()
GL_VIEWPORT_BIT	glPushAttrib()
GL_XOR	glLogicOp()
GL_ZERO	glBlendFunc(), glStencilOp()

Chapter 5

OpenGL Reference Pages

This chapter contains the reference pages for all OpenGL commands in alphabetical order. Each reference page may describe more than one related command. The reference pages for the OpenGL Utility Library (GLU) and for the OpenGL extension to the X Window System (GLX) can be found in the following chapters.

glAccum	glClear	glColorTable
glActiveTextureARB	glClearAccum	glColorTableParameter
glAlphaFunc	glClearColor	glConvolutionFilter1D
glAreTexturesResident	glClearDepth	glConvolutionFilter2D
glArrayElement	glClearIndex	glConvolutionParameter
glBegin, glEnd	glClearStencil	glCopyColorSubTable
glBindTexture	glClientActiveTextureARB	glCopyColorTable
glBitmap	glClipPlane	glCopyConvolutionFilter1D
glBlendColor	glColor	glCopyConvolutionFilter2D
glBlendEquation	glColorMask	glCopyPixels
glBlendFunc	glColorMaterial	glCopyTexImage1D
glCallList	glColorPointer	glCopyTexImage2D
glCallLists	glColorSubTable	glCopyTexSubImage1D

glCopyTexSubImage2D	glFrustum	glGetTexLevelParameter
glCopyTexSubImage3D	glGenLists	glGetTexParameter
glCullFace	glGenTextures	glHint
glDeleteLists	glGet	glHistogram
glDeleteTextures	glGetClipPlane	glIndex
glDepthFunc	glGetColorTable	glIndexMask
glDepthMask	glGetColorTableParameter	glIndexPointer
glDepthRange	glGetConvolutionFilter	glInitNames
glDrawArrays	glGetConvolutionParameter	glInterleavedArrays
glDrawBuffer	glGetError	glIsEnabled
glDrawElements	glGetHistogram	glIsList
glDrawPixels	glGetHistogramParameter	glIsTexture
glDrawRangeElements	glGetLight	glLight
glEdgeFlag	glGetMap	glLightModel
glEdgeFlagPointer	glGetMaterial	glLineStipple
glEnable, glDisable	glGetMinmax	glLineWidth
glEnableClientState, glDisableClientState	glGetMinmaxParameter	glListBase
glEvalCoord	glGetPixelMap	glLoadIdentity
glEvalMesh1, glEvalMesh2	glGetPointerv	glLoadMatrix
glEvalPoint	glGetPolygonStipple	glLoadName
glFeedbackBuffer	glGetSeparableFilter	glLogicOp
glFinish	glGetString	glMap1
glFlush	glGetTexEnv	glMap2
glFog	glGetTexGen	glMapGrid
glFrontFace	glGetTexImage	glMaterial

glMatrixMode	glPushAttrib, glPopAttrib	glStencilMask
glMinmax	glPushClientAttrib, glPopClientAttrib	glStencilOp
glMultiTexCoord	glPushMatrix, glPopMatrix	glTexCoord
glMultMatrix	glPushName, glPopName	glTexCoordPointer
glNewList, glEndList	glRasterPos	glTexEnv
glNormal	glReadBuffer	glTexGen
glNormalPointer	glReadPixels	glTexImage1D
glOrtho	glRect	glTexImage2D
glPassThrough	glRenderMode	glTexImage3D
glPixelMap	glResetHistogram	glTexParameter
glPixelStore	glResetMinmax	glTexSubImage1D
glPixelTransfer	glRotate	glTexSubImage2D
glPixelZoom	glScale	glTexSubImage3D
glPointSize	glScissor	glTranslate
glPolygonMode	glSelectBuffer	glVertex
glPolygonOffset	glSeparableFilter2D	glVertexPointer
glPolygonStipple	glShadeModel	glViewport
glPrioritizeTextures	glStencilFunc	

NAME

glAccum – operate on the accumulation buffer

C SPECIFICATION

void **glAccum**(GLenum *op*,
                 GLfloat *value*)

PARAMETERS

op   Specifies the accumulation buffer operation. Symbolic constants **GL_ACCUM**, **GL_LOAD**, **GL_ADD**, **GL_MULT**, and **GL_RETURN** are accepted.

value Specifies a floating-point value used in the accumulation buffer operation. *op* determines how *value* is used.

DESCRIPTION

The accumulation buffer is an extended-range color buffer. Images are not rendered into it. Rather, images rendered into one of the color buffers are added to the contents of the accumulation buffer after rendering. Effects such as antialiasing (of points, lines, and polygons), motion blur, and depth of field can be created by accumulating images generated with different transformation matrices.

Each pixel in the accumulation buffer consists of red, green, blue, and alpha values. The number of bits per component in the accumulation buffer depends on the implementation. You can examine this number by calling **glGetIntegerv** four times, with arguments **GL_ACCUM_RED_BITS**, **GL_ACCUM_GREEN_BITS**, **GL_ACCUM_BLUE_BITS**, and **GL_ACCUM_ALPHA_BITS**. Regardless of the number of bits per component, the range of values stored by each component is [−1, 1]. The accumulation buffer pixels are mapped one-to-one with frame buffer pixels.

glAccum operates on the accumulation buffer. The first argument, *op*, is a symbolic constant that selects an accumulation buffer operation. The second argument, *value*, is a floating-point value to be used in that operation. Five operations are specified: **GL_ACCUM**, **GL_LOAD**, **GL_ADD**, **GL_MULT**, and **GL_RETURN**.

All accumulation buffer operations are limited to the area of the current scissor box and applied identically to the red, green, blue, and alpha components of each pixel. If a **glAccum** operation results in a value outside the range [−1, 1], the contents of an accumulation buffer pixel component are undefined.

The operations are as follows:

GL_ACCUM   Obtains R, G, B, and A values from the buffer currently selected for reading (see **glReadBuffer**). Each component value is divided by $2^n - 1$, where n is the number of bits allocated to each color component in the currently selected buffer. The result is a floating-point value in the range [0, 1], which is multiplied by *value* and added to the corresponding pixel component in the accumulation buffer, thereby updating the accumulation buffer.

GL_LOAD Similar to **GL_ACCUM**, except that the current value in the accumulation buffer is not used in the calculation of the new value. That is, the R, G, B, and A values from the currently selected buffer are divided by $2^n - 1$, multiplied by *value*, and then stored in the corresponding accumulation buffer cell, overwriting the current value.

GL_ADD Adds *value* to each R, G, B, and A in the accumulation buffer.

GL_MULT Multiplies each R, G, B, and A in the accumulation buffer by *value* and returns the scaled component to its corresponding accumulation buffer location.

GL_RETURN Transfers accumulation buffer values to the color buffer or buffers currently selected for writing. Each R, G, B, and A component is multiplied by *value*, then multiplied by $2^n - 1$, clamped to the range $[0, 2^n - 1]$, and stored in the corresponding display buffer cell. The only fragment operations that are applied to this transfer are pixel ownership, scissor, dithering, and color writemasks.

To clear the accumulation buffer, call **glClearAccum** with R, G, B, and A values to set it to, then call **glClear** with the accumulation buffer enabled.

NOTES

Only pixels within the current scissor box are updated by a **glAccum** operation.

ERRORS

GL_INVALID_ENUM is generated if *op* is not an accepted value.

GL_INVALID_OPERATION is generated if there is no accumulation buffer.

GL_INVALID_OPERATION is generated if **glAccum** is executed between the execution of **glBegin** and the corresponding execution of **glEnd**.

ASSOCIATED GETS

glGet with argument GL_ACCUM_RED_BITS
glGet with argument GL_ACCUM_GREEN_BITS
glGet with argument GL_ACCUM_BLUE_BITS
glGet with argument GL_ACCUM_ALPHA_BITS

SEE ALSO

glClear, glClearAccum, glCopyPixels, glDrawBuffer, glGet, glReadBuffer, glReadPixels, glScissor, glStencilOp

NAME

glActiveTextureARB – select active texture unit

C SPECIFICATION

void **glActiveTextureARB**(GLenum *texture*)

PARAMETERS

texture   Specifies which texture unit to make active. The number of texture units is implementation dependent, but must be at least two. *texture* must be one of **GL_TEXTURE*i*_ARB**, where $0 \leq i <$ **GL_MAX_TEXTURE_UNITS_ARB**, which is an implementation-dependent value. The intial value is **GL_TEXTURE0_ARB**.

DESCRIPTION

glActiveTextureARB selects which texture unit subsequent texture state calls will affect. The number of texture units an implementation supports is implementation dependent, but must be at least 2.

Vertex arrays are client-side GL resources, which are selected by the **glClientActiveTextureARB** routine.

NOTES

glActiveTextureARB is only supported if **GL_ARB_multitexture** is included in the string returned by **glGetString** when called with the argument **GL_EXTENSIONS**.

ERRORS

GL_INVALID_ENUM is generated if *texture* is not one of **GL_TEXTURE*i*_ARB**, where $0 \leq i <$ **GL_MAX_TEXTURE_UNITS_ARB**.

SEE ALSO

glClientActiveTextureARB, **glGetIntegerv**, **glMultiTexCoordARB**, **glTexParameter**

NAME

glAlphaFunc – specify the alpha test function

C SPECIFICATION

void **glAlphaFunc**(GLenum *func*,
GLclampf *ref*)

PARAMETERS

func Specifies the alpha comparison function. Symbolic constants **GL_NEVER**, **GL_LESS**, **GL_EQUAL**, **GL_LEQUAL**, **GL_GREATER**, **GL_NOTEQUAL**, **GL_GEQUAL**, and **GL_ALWAYS** are accepted. The initial value is **GL_ALWAYS**.

ref Specifies the reference value that incoming alpha values are compared to. This value is clamped to the range [0, 1], where 0 represents the lowest possible alpha value and 1 the highest possible value. The initial reference value is 0.

DESCRIPTION

The alpha test discards fragments depending on the outcome of a comparison between an incoming fragment's alpha value and a constant reference value. **glAlphaFunc** specifies the reference value and the comparison function. The comparison is performed only if alpha testing is enabled. By default, it is not enabled. (See **glEnable** and **glDisable** of **GL_ALPHA_TEST**.)

func and *ref* specify the conditions under which the pixel is drawn. The incoming alpha value is compared to *ref* using the function specified by *func*. If the value passes the comparison, the incoming fragment is drawn if it also passes subsequent stencil and depth buffer tests. If the value fails the comparison, no change is made to the frame buffer at that pixel location. The comparison functions are as follows:

GL_NEVER   Never passes.

GL_LESS   Passes if the incoming alpha value is less than the reference value.

GL_EQUAL   Passes if the incoming alpha value is equal to the reference value.

GL_LEQUAL   Passes if the incoming alpha value is less than or equal to the reference value.

GL_GREATER   Passes if the incoming alpha value is greater than the reference value.

GL_NOTEQUAL   Passes if the incoming alpha value is not equal to the reference value.

GL_GEQUAL   Passes if the incoming alpha value is greater than or equal to the reference value.

GL_ALWAYS   Always passes (initial value).

glAlphaFunc operates on all pixel write operations, including those resulting from the scan conversion of points, lines, polygons, and bitmaps, and from pixel draw and copy operations. **glAlphaFunc** does not affect screen clear operations.

NOTES

Alpha testing is performed only in RGBA mode.

ERRORS

GL_INVALID_ENUM is generated if *func* is not an accepted value.

GL_INVALID_OPERATION is generated if **glAlphaFunc** is executed between the execution of **glBegin** and the corresponding execution of **glEnd**.

ASSOCIATED GETS

glGet with argument **GL_ALPHA_TEST_FUNC**
glGet with argument **GL_ALPHA_TEST_REF**
glIsEnabled with argument **GL_ALPHA_TEST**

SEE ALSO

glBlendFunc, **glClear**, **glDepthFunc**, **glEnable**, **glStencilFunc**

NAME

    glAreTexturesResident – determine if textures are loaded in texture memory

C SPECIFICATION

    GLboolean **glAreTexturesResident**(GLsizei *n*,
                                    const GLuint **textures*,
                                    GLboolean **residences*)

PARAMETERS

    n   Specifies the number of textures to be queried.

    textures   Specifies an array containing the names of the textures to be queried.

    residences Specifies an array in which the texture residence status is returned. The residence status of a texture named by an element of *textures* is returned in the corresponding element of *residences*.

DESCRIPTION

    GL establishes a "working set" of textures that are resident in texture memory. These textures can be bound to a texture target much more efficiently than textures that are not resident.

    glAreTexturesResident queries the texture residence status of the *n* textures named by the elements of *textures*. If all the named textures are resident, **glAreTexturesResident** returns **GL_TRUE**, and the contents of *residences* are undisturbed. If not all the named textures are resident, **glAreTexturesResident** returns **GL_FALSE**, and detailed status is returned in the *n* elements of *residences*. If an element of *residences* is **GL_TRUE**, then the texture named by the corresponding element of *textures* is resident.

    The residence status of a single bound texture may also be queried by calling **glGetTexParameter** with the *target* argument set to the target to which the texture is bound, and the *pname* argument set to **GL_TEXTURE_RESIDENT**. This is the only way that the residence status of a default texture can be queried.

NOTES

    glAreTexturesResident is available only if the GL version is 1.1 or greater.

    glAreTexturesResident returns the residency status of the textures at the time of invocation. It does not guarantee that the textures will remain resident at any other time.

    If textures reside in virtual memory (there is no texture memory), they are considered always resident.

Some implementations may not load a texture until the first use of that texture.

ERRORS

GL_INVALID_VALUE is generated if *n* is negative.

GL_INVALID_VALUE is generated if any element in *textures* is 0 or does not name a texture. In that case, the function returns **GL_FALSE** and the contents of *residences* is indeterminate.

GL_INVALID_OPERATION is generated if **glAreTexturesResident** is executed between the execution of **glBegin** and the corresponding execution of **glEnd**.

ASSOCIATED GETS

glGetTexParameter with parameter name **GL_TEXTURE_RESIDENT** retrieves the residence status of a currently bound texture.

SEE ALSO

glBindTexture, **glGetTexParameter**, **glPrioritizeTextures**, **glTexImage1D**, **glTexImage2D**, **glTexImage3D**, **glTexParameter**

NAME

glArrayElement – render a vertex using the specified vertex array element

C SPECIFICATION

void **glArrayElement**(GLint *i*)

PARAMETERS

i Specifies an index into the enabled vertex data arrays.

DESCRIPTION

glArrayElement commands are used within **glBegin/glEnd** pairs to specify vertex and attribute data for point, line, and polygon primitives. If **GL_VERTEX_ARRAY** is enabled when **glArrayElement** is called, a single vertex is drawn, using vertex and attribute data taken from location *i* of the enabled arrays. If **GL_VERTEX_ARRAY** is not enabled, no drawing occurs but the attributes corresponding to the enabled arrays are modified.

Use **glArrayElement** to construct primitives by indexing vertex data, rather than by streaming through arrays of data in first-to-last order. Because each call specifies only a single vertex, it is possible to explicitly specify per-primitive attributes such as a single normal per individual triangle.

Changes made to array data between the execution of **glBegin** and the corresponding execution of **glEnd** may affect calls to **glArrayElement** that are made within the same **glBegin/glEnd** period in non-sequential ways. That is, a call to **glArrayElement** that precedes a change to array data may access the changed data, and a call that follows a change to array data may access original data.

NOTES

glArrayElement is available only if the GL version is 1.1 or greater.

glArrayElement is included in display lists. If **glArrayElement** is entered into a display list, the necessary array data (determined by the array pointers and enables) is also entered into the display list. Because the array pointers and enables are client-side state, their values affect display lists when the lists are created, not when the lists are executed.

SEE ALSO

glClientActiveTextureARB, **glColorPointer**, **glDrawArrays**, **glEdgeFlagPointer**, **glGetPointerv**, **glIndexPointer**, **glInterleavedArrays**, **glNormalPointer**, **glTexCoordPointer**, **glVertexPointer**

NAME

glBegin, glEnd – delimit the vertices of a primitive or a group of like primitives

C SPECIFICATION

void **glBegin**(GLenum *mode*)

PARAMETERS

mode   Specifies the primitive or primitives that will be created from vertices presented between **glBegin** and the subsequent **glEnd**. Ten symbolic constants are accepted: **GL_POINTS, GL_LINES, GL_LINE_STRIP, GL_LINE_LOOP, GL_TRIANGLES, GL_TRIANGLE_STRIP, GL_TRIANGLE_FAN, GL_QUADS, GL_QUAD_STRIP**, and **GL_POLYGON**.

C SPECIFICATION

void **glEnd**(void)

DESCRIPTION

glBegin and **glEnd** delimit the vertices that define a primitive or a group of like primitives. **glBegin** accepts a single argument that specifies in which of ten ways the vertices are interpreted. Taking n as an integer count starting at one, and N as the total number of vertices specified, the interpretations are as follows:

GL_POINTS   Treats each vertex as a single point. Vertex n defines point n. N points are drawn.

GL_LINES   Treats each pair of vertices as an independent line segment. Vertices $2n-1$ and $2n$ define line n. $N/2$ lines are drawn.

GL_LINE_STRIP   Draws a connected group of line segments from the first vertex to the last. Vertices n and $n+1$ define line n. $N-1$ lines are drawn.

GL_LINE_LOOP   Draws a connected group of line segments from the first vertex to the last, then back to the first. Vertices n and $n+1$ define line n. The last line, however, is defined by vertices N and 1. N lines are drawn.

GL_TRIANGLES   Treats each triplet of vertices as an independent triangle. Vertices $3n-2$, $3n-1$, and $3n$ define triangle n. $N/3$ triangles are drawn.

GL_TRIANGLE_STRIP   Draws a connected group of triangles. One triangle is defined for each vertex presented after the first two vertices. For odd n, vertices n, $n+1$, and $n+2$ define triangle n. For even n, vertices $n+1$, n, and $n+2$ define triangle n. $N-2$ triangles are drawn.

GL_TRIANGLE_FAN	Draws a connected group of triangles. One triangle is defined for each vertex presented after the first two vertices. Vertices 1, $n + 1$, and $n + 2$ define triangle n. $N - 2$ triangles are drawn.
GL_QUADS	Treats each group of four vertices as an independent quadrilateral. Vertices $4n - 3$, $4n - 2$, $4n - 1$, and $4n$ define quadrilateral n. $N/4$ quadrilaterals are drawn.
GL_QUAD_STRIP	Draws a connected group of quadrilaterals. One quadrilateral is defined for each pair of vertices presented after the first pair. Vertices $2n - 1$, $2n$, $2n + 2$, and $2n + 1$ define quadrilateral n. $N/2 - 1$ quadrilaterals are drawn. Note that the order in which vertices are used to construct a quadrilateral from strip data is different from that used with independent data.
GL_POLYGON	Draws a single, convex polygon. Vertices 1 through N define this polygon.

Only a subset of GL commands can be used between **glBegin** and **glEnd**. The commands are **glVertex**, **glColor**, **glIndex**, **glNormal**, **glTexCoord**, **glEvalCoord**, **glEvalPoint**, **glArrayElement**, **glMaterial**, and **glEdgeFlag**. Also, it is acceptable to use **glCallList** or **glCallLists** to execute display lists that include only the preceding commands. If any other GL command is executed between **glBegin** and **glEnd**, the error flag is set and the command is ignored.

Regardless of the value chosen for *mode*, there is no limit to the number of vertices that can be defined between **glBegin** and **glEnd**. Lines, triangles, quadrilaterals, and polygons that are incompletely specified are not drawn. Incomplete specification results when either too few vertices are provided to specify even a single primitive or when an incorrect multiple of vertices is specified. The incomplete primitive is ignored; the rest are drawn.

The minimum specification of vertices for each primitive is as follows: 1 for a point, 2 for a line, 3 for a triangle, 4 for a quadrilateral, and 3 for a polygon. Modes that require a certain multiple of vertices are **GL_LINES** (2), **GL_TRIANGLES** (3), **GL_QUADS** (4), and **GL_QUAD_STRIP** (2).

ERRORS

GL_INVALID_ENUM is generated if *mode* is set to an unaccepted value.

GL_INVALID_OPERATION is generated if **glBegin** is executed between a **glBegin** and the corresponding execution of **glEnd**.

GL_INVALID_OPERATION is generated if **glEnd** is executed without being preceded by a **glBegin**.

GL_INVALID_OPERATION is generated if a command other than **glVertex**, **glColor**, **glIndex**, **glNormal**, **glTexCoord**, **glEvalCoord**, **glEvalPoint**, **glArrayElement**, **glMaterial**, **glEdgeFlag**, **glCallList**, or **glCallLists** is executed between the execution of **glBegin** and the corresponding execution **glEnd**.

Execution of **glEnableClientState**, **glDisableClientState**, **glEdgeFlagPointer**, **glTexCoordPointer**, **glColorPointer**, **glIndexPointer**, **glNormalPointer**, **glVertexPointer**, **glInterleavedArrays**, or **glPixelStore** is not allowed after a call to **glBegin** and before the corresponding call to **glEnd**, but an error may or may not be generated.

SEE ALSO

glArrayElement, **glCallList**, **glCallLists**, **glColor**, **glEdgeFlag**, **glEvalCoord**, **glEvalPoint**, **glIndex**, **glMaterial**, **glNormal**, **glTexCoord**, **glVertex**

NAME

    glBindTexture – bind a named texture to a texturing target

C SPECIFICATION

    void **glBindTexture**(GLenum *target*,
                                GLuint *texture*)

PARAMETERS

    target Specifies the target to which the texture is bound. Must be either
             GL_TEXTURE_1D, **GL_TEXTURE_2D**, or **GL_TEXTURE_3D**.

    texture Specifies the name of a texture.

DESCRIPTION

    glBindTexture lets you create or use a named texture. Calling **glBindTexture** with
target set to **GL_TEXTURE_1D**, **GL_TEXTURE_2D**, **GL_TEXTURE_3D** and *texture* set
to the name of the newtexture binds the texture name to the target. When a texture
is bound to a target, the previous binding for that target is automatically broken.

    Texture names are unsigned integers. The value zero is reserved to represent the
default texture for each texture target. Texture names and the corresponding texture contents are local to the shared display-list space (see **glXCreateContext**) of the
current GL rendering context; two rendering contexts share texture names only if
they also share display lists.

    You may use **glGenTextures** to generate a set of new texture names.

    When a texture is first bound, it assumes the dimensionality of its target: A texture
first bound to **GL_TEXTURE_1D** becomes one-dimensional, and a texture first
bound to **GL_TEXTURE_2D** becomes two-dimensional, and a texture first bound to
GL_TEXTURE_3D becomes a three-dimensional texture. The state of a one-
dimensional texture immediately after it is first bound is equivalent to the state of
the default **GL_TEXTURE_1D** at GL initialization, and similarly for two-, and
three-dimensional textures.

    While a texture is bound, GL operations on the target to which it is bound affect the
bound texture, and queries of the target to which it is bound return state from the
bound texture. If texture mapping of the dimensionality of the target to which a
texture is bound is active, the bound texture is used. In effect, the texture targets
become aliases for the textures currently bound to them, and the texture name zero
refers to the default textures that were bound to them at initialization.

    A texture binding created with **glBindTexture** remains active until a different tex-
ture is bound to the same target, or until the bound texture is deleted with
glDeleteTextures.

Once created, a named texture may be re-bound to the target of the matching dimensionality as often as needed. It is usually much faster to use **glBindTexture** to bind an existing named texture to one of the texture targets than it is to reload the texture image using **glTexImage1D**, **glTexImage2D**, or **glTexImage3D**. For additional control over performance, use **glPrioritizeTextures**.

glBindTexture is included in display lists.

NOTES

    glBindTexture is available only if the GL version is 1.1 or greater.

ERRORS

    GL_INVALID_ENUM is generated if *target* is not one of the allowable values.

    GL_INVALID_OPERATION is generated if *texture* has a dimensionality that doesn't match that of *target*.

    GL_INVALID_OPERATION is generated if **glBindTexture** is executed between the execution of **glBegin** and the corresponding execution of **glEnd**.

ASSOCIATED GETS

    glGet with argument **GL_TEXTURE_BINDING_1D**
    glGet with argument **GL_TEXTURE_BINDING_2D**
    glGet with argument **GL_TEXTURE_BINDING_3D**

SEE ALSO

    glAreTexturesResident, **glDeleteTextures**, **glGenTextures**, **glGet**, **glGetTexParameter**, **glIsTexture**, **glPrioritizeTextures**, **glTexImage1D**, **glTexImage2D**, **glTexParameter**

NAME

glBitmap – draw a bitmap

C SPECIFICATION

void **glBitmap**(GLsizei *width*,
              GLsizei *height*,
              GLfloat *xorig*,
              GLfloat *yorig*,
              GLfloat *xmove*,
              GLfloat *ymove*,
              const GLubyte **bitmap*)

PARAMETERS

width, height
> Specify the pixel width and height of the bitmap image.

xorig, yorig Specify the location of the origin in the bitmap image. The origin is measured from the lower left corner of the bitmap, with right and up being the positive axes.

xmove, ymove
> Specify the *x* and *y* offsets to be added to the current raster position after the bitmap is drawn.

bitmap   Specifies the address of the bitmap image.

DESCRIPTION

A bitmap is a binary image. When drawn, the bitmap is positioned relative to the current raster position, and frame buffer pixels corresponding to 1's in the bitmap are written using the current raster color or index. Frame buffer pixels corresponding to 0's in the bitmap are not modified.

glBitmap takes seven arguments. The first pair specifies the width and height of the bitmap image. The second pair specifies the location of the bitmap origin relative to the lower left corner of the bitmap image. The third pair of arguments specifies *x* and *y* offsets to be added to the current raster position after the bitmap has been drawn. The final argument is a pointer to the bitmap image itself.

The bitmap image is interpreted like image data for the **glDrawPixels** command, with *width* and *height* corresponding to the width and height arguments of that command, and with *type* set to **GL_BITMAP** and *format* set to **GL_COLOR_INDEX**. Modes specified using **glPixelStore** affect the interpretation of bitmap image data; modes specified using **glPixelTransfer** do not.

If the current raster position is invalid, **glBitmap** is ignored. Otherwise, the lower left corner of the bitmap image is positioned at the window coordinates

$$x_w = x_r - x_o$$

$$y_w = y_r - y_o$$

where (x_r, y_r) is the raster position and (x_o, y_o) is the bitmap origin. Fragments are then generated for each pixel corresponding to a 1 (one) in the bitmap image. These fragments are generated using the current raster z coordinate, color or color index, and current raster texture coordinates. They are then treated just as if they had been generated by a point, line, or polygon, including texture mapping, fogging, and all per-fragment operations such as alpha and depth testing.

After the bitmap has been drawn, the x and y coordinates of the current raster position are offset by *xmove* and *ymove*. No change is made to the z coordinate of the current raster position, or to the current raster color, texture coordinates, or index.

NOTES

To set a valid raster position outside the viewport, first set a valid raster position inside the viewport, then call **glBitmap** with NULL as the *bitmap* parameter and with *xmove* and *ymove* set to the offsets of the new raster position. This technique is useful when panning an image around the viewport.

ERRORS

GL_INVALID_VALUE is generated if *width* or *height* is negative.

GL_INVALID_OPERATION is generated if **glBitmap** is executed between the execution of **glBegin** and the corresponding execution of **glEnd**.

ASSOCIATED GETS

glGet with argument **GL_CURRENT_RASTER_POSITION**
glGet with argument **GL_CURRENT_RASTER_COLOR**
glGet with argument **GL_CURRENT_RASTER_DISTANCE**
glGet with argument **GL_CURRENT_RASTER_INDEX**
glGet with argument **GL_CURRENT_RASTER_TEXTURE_COORDS**
glGet with argument **GL_CURRENT_RASTER_POSITION_VALID**

SEE ALSO

glDrawPixels, **glPixelStore**, **glPixelTransfer**, **glRasterPos**

NAME

    glBlendColor – set the blend color

C SPECIFICATION

    void **glBlendColor**(GLclampf *red*,
                        GLclampf *green*,
                        GLclampf *blue*,
                        GLclampf *alpha*)

PARAMETERS

    red, green, blue, alpha
                specify the components of **GL_BLEND_COLOR**

DESCRIPTION

    The **GL_BLEND_COLOR** may be used to calculate the source and destination blending factors. The color components are clamped to the range [0, 1] before being stored. See **glBlendFunc** for a complete description of the blending operations. Initially the **GL_BLEND_COLOR** is set to (0, 0, 0, 0).

NOTES

    glBlendColor is part of the **GL_ARB_imaging** subset. **glBlendColor** is present only if **GL_ARB_imaging** is returned when **glGetString** is called with **GL_EXTENSIONS** as its argument.

ERRORS

    GL_INVALID_OPERATION is generated if **glBlendColor** is executed between the execution of **glBegin** and the corresponding execution of **glEnd**.

ASSOCIATED GETS

    glGet with an argument of **GL_BLEND_COLOR**

SEE ALSO

    glBlendEquation, **glBlendFunc**, **glGetString**

NAME

    glBlendEquation – set the blend equation

C SPECIFICATION

    void **glBlendEquation**(GLenum *mode*)

PARAMETERS

    mode specifies how source and destination colors are combined. It must be
        GL_FUNC_ADD, GL_FUNC_SUBTRACT, GL_FUNC_REVERSE_SUBTRACT,
        GL_MIN, GL_MAX.

DESCRIPTION

The blend equation determines how a new pixel (the "source" color) is combined with a pixel already in the framebuffer (the "destination" color).

GL_MIN

    sets the blend equation so that each component of the result color is the minimum of the corresponding components of the source and destination colors.

GL_MAX

    sets the blend equation so that each component of the result color is the maximum of the corresponding components of the source and destination colors.

The remaining blend equations use the source and destination blend factors specified by **glBlendFunc**. See **glBlendFunc** for a description of the various blend factors.

In the equations that follow, source and destination color components are referred to as (R_s, G_s, B_s, A_s) and (R_d, G_d, B_d, A_d), respectively. The result color is referred to as (R_r, G_r, B_r, A_r). The source and destination blend factors are denoted (s_R, s_G, s_B, s_A) and (d_R, d_G, d_B, d_A), respectively. For these equations all color components are understood to have values in the range [0, 1].

GL_FUNC_ADD

    sets the blend equation so that the source and destination data are added. Each component of the source color is multiplied by the corresponding source factor, then each component of the destination color is multiplied by the corresponding destination factor. The result is the componentwise sum of the two products, clamped to the range [0, 1].

$$Rr = \min(1, R_s\, s_R + R_d\, d_R)$$
$$Gr = \min(1, G_s\, s_G + G_d\, d_G)$$
$$Br = \min(1, B_s\, s_B + B_d\, d_B)$$
$$Ar = \min(1, A_s\, s_A + A_d\, d_A)$$

GL_FUNC_SUBTRACT

Is like **GL_FUNC_ADD** except the product of the destination factor and the destination color is componentwise subtracted from the product of the source factor and the source color. The result is clamped to the range [0, 1].

$$Rr = \max(0, R_s\, s_R - R_d\, d_R)$$
$$Gr = \max(0, G_s\, s_G - G_d\, d_G)$$
$$Br = \max(0, B_s\, s_B - B_d\, d_B)$$
$$Ar = \max(0, A_s\, s_A - A_d\, d_A)$$

GL_FUNC_REVERSE_SUBTRACT

Is like **GL_FUNC_ADD** except the product of the source factor and the source color is componentwise subtracted from the product of the destination factor and the destination color. The result is clamped to the range [0, 1].

$$Rr = \max(0, R_d\, d_R - R_s\, s_R)$$
$$Gr = \max(0, G_d\, d_G - G_s\, s_G)$$
$$Br = \max(0, B_d\, d_B - B_s\, s_B)$$
$$Ar = \max(0, A_d\, d_A - A_s\, s_A)$$

The **GL_MIN** and **GL_MAX** equations are useful for applications that analyze image data (image thresholding against a constant color, for example). The **GL_FUNC_ADD** equation is useful for antialiasing and transparency, among other things.

Initially, the blend equation is set to **GL_FUNC_ADD**.

NOTES

glBlendEquation is part of the **GL_ARB_imaging** subset. **glBlendEquation** is present only if **GL_ARB_imaging** is returned when **glGetString** is called with **GL_EXTENSIONS** as its argument.

The **GL_MIN**, and **GL_MAX** equations do not use the source or destination factors, only the source and destination colors.

ERRORS

GL_INVALID_ENUM is generated if *mode* is not one of **GL_FUNC_ADD**, **GL_FUNC_SUBTRACT**, **GL_FUNC_REVERSE_SUBTRACT**, **GL_MAX**, or **GL_MIN**.

GL_INVALID_OPERATION is generated if **glBlendEquation** is executed between the execution of **glBegin** and the corresponding execution of **glEnd**.

ASSOCIATED GETS

>   **glGet** with an argument of **GL_BLEND_EQUATION**

SEE ALSO

>   **glGetString**, **glBlendColor**, **glBlendFunc**

NAME

      glBlendFunc – specify pixel arithmetic

C SPECIFICATION

      void **glBlendFunc**(GLenum *sfactor*,
                        GLenum *dfactor*)

PARAMETERS

    sfactor Specifies how the red, green, blue, and alpha source blending factors are computed. The following symbolic constants are accepted: **GL_ZERO**, **GL_ONE**, **GL_DST_COLOR**, **GL_ONE_MINUS_DST_COLOR**, **GL_SRC_ALPHA**, **GL_ONE_MINUS_SRC_ALPHA**, **GL_DST_ALPHA**, **GL_ONE_MINUS_DST_ALPHA**, and **GL_SRC_ALPHA_SATURATE**. The initial value is **GL_ONE**.

             Additionally, if the **GL_ARB_imaging** extension is supported, the following constants are accepted: **GL_CONSTANT_COLOR**, **GL_ONE_MINUS_CONSTANT_COLOR**, **GL_CONSTANT_ALPHA**, **GL_ONE_MINUS_CONSTANT_ALPHA**.

    dfactor Specifies how the red, green, blue, and alpha destination blending factors are computed. Eight symbolic constants are accepted: **GL_ZERO**, **GL_ONE**, **GL_SRC_COLOR**, **GL_ONE_MINUS_SRC_COLOR**, **GL_SRC_ALPHA**, **GL_ONE_MINUS_SRC_ALPHA**, **GL_DST_ALPHA**, and **GL_ONE_MINUS_DST_ALPHA**. The initial value is **GL_ZERO**.

             Additionally, if the **GL_ARB_imaging** extension is supported, the following constants are accepted: **GL_CONSTANT_COLOR**, **GL_ONE_MINUS_CONSTANT_COLOR**, **GL_CONSTANT_ALPHA**, **GL_ONE_MINUS_CONSTANT_ALPHA**.

DESCRIPTION

      In RGBA mode, pixels can be drawn using a function that blends the incoming (source) RGBA values with the RGBA values that are already in the frame buffer (the destination values). Blending is initially disabled. Use **glEnable** and **glDisable** with argument **GL_BLEND** to enable and disable blending.

      glBlendFunc defines the operation of blending when it is enabled. *sfactor* specifies which of nine methods is used to scale the source color components. *dfactor* specifies which of eight methods is used to scale the destination color components. The eleven possible methods are described in the following table. Each method defines four scale factors, one each for red, green, blue, and alpha.

In the table and in subsequent equations, source and destination color components are referred to as (R_s, G_s, B_s, A_s) and (R_d, G_d, B_d, A_d). The color specified by **glBlendColor** is referred to as (R_c, G_c, B_c, A_c). They are understood to have integer values between 0 and (k_R, k_G, k_B, k_A), where

$$k_c = 2^{m_c} - 1$$

and (m_R, m_G, m_B, m_A) is the number of red, green, blue, and alpha bitplanes.

Source and destination scale factors are referred to as (s_R, s_G, s_B, s_A) and (d_R, d_G, d_B, d_A). The scale factors described in the table, denoted (f_R, f_G, f_B, f_A), represent either source or destination factors. All scale factors have range [0, 1].

Parameter	$(f_R,\ f_G,\ f_B,\ f_A)$
GL_ZERO	$(0, 0, 0, 0)$
GL_ONE	$(1, 1, 1, 1)$
GL_SRC_COLOR	$(R_s/k_R,\ G_s/k_G,\ B_s/k_B,\ A_s/k_A)$
GL_ONE_MINUS_SRC_COLOR	$(1, 1, 1, 1) - (R_s/k_R,\ G_s/k_G,\ B_s/k_B,\ A_s/k_A)$
GL_DST_COLOR	$(R_d/k_R,\ G_d/k_G,\ B_d/k_B,\ A_d/k_A)$
GL_ONE_MINUS_DST_COLOR	$(1, 1, 1, 1) - (R_d/k_R,\ G_d/k_G,\ B_d/k_B,\ A_d/k_A)$
GL_SRC_ALPHA	$(A_s/k_A,\ A_s/k_A,\ A_s/k_A,\ A_s/k_A)$
GL_ONE_MINUS_SRC_ALPHA	$(1, 1, 1, 1) - (A_s/k_A,\ A_s/k_A,\ A_s/k_A,\ A_s/k_A)$
GL_DST_ALPHA	$(A_d/k_A,\ A_d/k_A,\ A_d/k_A,\ A_d/k_A)$
GL_ONE_MINUS_DST_ALPHA	$(1, 1, 1, 1) - (A_d/k_A,\ A_d/k_A,\ A_d/k_A,\ A_d/k_A)$
GL_SRC_ALPHA_SATURATE	$(i,\ i,\ i,\ 1)$
GL_CONSTANT_COLOR	(R_c, G_c, B_c, A_c)
GL_ONE_MINUS_CONSTANT_COLOR	$(1, 1, 1, 1) - (R_c, G_c, B_c, A_c)$
GL_CONSTANT_ALPHA	(A_c, A_c, A_c, A_c)
GL_ONE_MINUS_CONSTANT_ALPHA	$(1, 1, 1, 1) - (A_c, A_c, A_c, A_c)$

In the table,

$$i = \min(A_s,\ k_A - A_d)\ /\ k_A$$

To determine the blended RGBA values of a pixel when drawing in RGBA mode, the system uses the following equations:

$$R_d = \min(k_R,\ R_s\ s_R + R_d\ d_R)$$
$$G_d = \min(k_G,\ G_s\ s_G + G_d\ d_G)$$
$$B_d = \min(k_B,\ B_s\ s_B + B_d\ d_B)$$
$$A_d = \min(k_A,\ A_s\ s_A + A_d\ d_A)$$

Despite the apparent precision of the above equations, blending arithmetic is not exactly specified, because blending operates with imprecise integer color values. However, a blend factor that should be equal to 1 is guaranteed not to modify its multiplicand, and a blend factor equal to 0 reduces its multiplicand to 0. For example, when *sfactor* is **GL_SRC_ALPHA**, *dfactor* is **GL_ONE_MINUS_SRC_ALPHA**, and

A_s is equal to k_A, the equations reduce to simple replacement:

$$R_d = R_s$$
$$G_d = G_s$$
$$B_d = B_s$$
$$A_d = A_s$$

EXAMPLES

Transparency is best implemented using blend function (**GL_SRC_ALPHA, GL_ONE_MINUS_SRC_ALPHA**) with primitives sorted from farthest to nearest. Note that this transparency calculation does not require the presence of alpha bitplanes in the frame buffer.

Blend function (**GL_SRC_ALPHA, GL_ONE_MINUS_SRC_ALPHA**) is also useful for rendering antialiased points and lines in arbitrary order.

Polygon antialiasing is optimized using blend function (**GL_SRC_ALPHA_SATURATE, GL_ONE**) with polygons sorted from nearest to farthest. (See the **glEnable**, **glDisable** reference page and the **GL_POLYGON_SMOOTH** argument for information on polygon antialiasing.) Destination alpha bitplanes, which must be present for this blend function to operate correctly, store the accumulated coverage.

NOTES

Incoming (source) alpha is correctly thought of as a material opacity, ranging from 1.0 (K_A), representing complete opacity, to 0.0 (0), representing complete transparency.

When more than one color buffer is enabled for drawing, the GL performs blending separately for each enabled buffer, using the contents of that buffer for destination color. (See **glDrawBuffer**.)

Blending affects only RGBA rendering. It is ignored by color index renderers.

GL_CONSTANT_COLOR, GL_ONE_MINUS_CONSTANT_COLOR, GL_CONSTANT_ALPHA, GL_ONE_MINUS_CONSTANT_ALPHA are only available if the **GL_ARB_imaging** is supported by your implementation.

ERRORS

GL_INVALID_ENUM is generated if either *sfactor* or *dfactor* is not an accepted value.

GL_INVALID_OPERATION is generated if **glBlendFunc** is executed between the execution of **glBegin** and the corresponding execution of **glEnd**.

ASSOCIATED GETS

glGet with argument **GL_BLEND_SRC**
glGet with argument **GL_BLEND_DST**
glIsEnabled with argument **GL_BLEND**

SEE ALSO

glAlphaFunc, glBlendColor, glBlendEquation, glClear, glDrawBuffer, glEnable, glLogicOp, glStencilFunc

NAME

glCallList – execute a display list

C SPECIFICATION

void **glCallList**(GLuint *list*)

PARAMETERS

list Specifies the integer name of the display list to be executed.

DESCRIPTION

glCallList causes the named display list to be executed. The commands saved in the display list are executed in order, just as if they were called without using a display list. If *list* has not been defined as a display list, **glCallList** is ignored.

glCallList can appear inside a display list. To avoid the possibility of infinite recursion resulting from display lists calling one another, a limit is placed on the nesting level of display lists during display-list execution. This limit is at least 64, and it depends on the implementation.

GL state is not saved and restored across a call to **glCallList**. Thus, changes made to GL state during the execution of a display list remain after execution of the display list is completed. Use **glPushAttrib**, **glPopAttrib**, **glPushMatrix**, and **glPopMatrix** to preserve GL state across **glCallList** calls.

NOTES

Display lists can be executed between a call to **glBegin** and the corresponding call to **glEnd**, as long as the display list includes only commands that are allowed in this interval.

ASSOCIATED GETS

glGet with argument **GL_MAX_LIST_NESTING**
glIsList

SEE ALSO

glCallLists, **glDeleteLists**, **glGenLists**, **glNewList**, **glPushAttrib**, **glPushMatrix**

NAME

glCallLists – execute a list of display lists

C SPECIFICATION

void **glCallLists**(GLsizei *n*,
GLenum *type*,
const GLvoid **lists*)

PARAMETERS

n   Specifies the number of display lists to be executed.

type Specifies the type of values in *lists*. Symbolic constants **GL_BYTE**, **GL_UNSIGNED_BYTE**, **GL_SHORT**, **GL_UNSIGNED_SHORT**, **GL_INT**, **GL_UNSIGNED_INT**, **GL_FLOAT**, **GL_2_BYTES**, **GL_3_BYTES**, and **GL_4_BYTES** are accepted.

lists Specifies the address of an array of name offsets in the display list. The pointer type is void because the offsets can be bytes, shorts, ints, or floats, depending on the value of *type*.

DESCRIPTION

glCallLists causes each display list in the list of names passed as *lists* to be executed. As a result, the commands saved in each display list are executed in order, just as if they were called without using a display list. Names of display lists that have not been defined are ignored.

glCallLists provides an efficient means for executing more than one display list. *type* allows lists with various name formats to be accepted. The formats are as follows:

GL_BYTE	*lists* is treated as an array of signed bytes, each in the range −128 through 127.
GL_UNSIGNED_BYTE	*lists* is treated as an array of unsigned bytes, each in the range 0 through 255.
GL_SHORT	*lists* is treated as an array of signed two-byte integers, each in the range −32768 through 32767.
GL_UNSIGNED_SHORT	*lists* is treated as an array of unsigned two-byte integers, each in the range 0 through 65535.
GL_INT	*lists* is treated as an array of signed four-byte integers.
GL_UNSIGNED_INT	*lists* is treated as an array of unsigned four-byte integers.

GL_FLOAT	*lists* is treated as an array of four-byte floating-point values.
GL_2_BYTES	*lists* is treated as an array of unsigned bytes. Each pair of bytes specifies a single display-list name. The value of the pair is computed as 256 times the unsigned value of the first byte plus the unsigned value of the second byte.
GL_3_BYTES	*lists* is treated as an array of unsigned bytes. Each triplet of bytes specifies a single display-list name. The value of the triplet is computed as 65536 times the unsigned value of the first byte, plus 256 times the unsigned value of the second byte, plus the unsigned value of the third byte.
GL_4_BYTES	*lists* is treated as an array of unsigned bytes. Each quadruplet of bytes specifies a single display-list name. The value of the quadruplet is computed as 16777216 times the unsigned value of the first byte, plus 65536 times the unsigned value of the second byte, plus 256 times the unsigned value of the third byte, plus the unsigned value of the fourth byte.

The list of display-list names is not null-terminated. Rather, *n* specifies how many names are to be taken from *lists*.

An additional level of indirection is made available with the **glListBase** command, which specifies an unsigned offset that is added to each display-list name specified in *lists* before that display list is executed.

glCallLists can appear inside a display list. To avoid the possibility of infinite recursion resulting from display lists calling one another, a limit is placed on the nesting level of display lists during display-list execution. This limit must be at least 64, and it depends on the implementation.

GL state is not saved and restored across a call to **glCallLists**. Thus, changes made to GL state during the execution of the display lists remain after execution is completed. Use **glPushAttrib**, **glPopAttrib**, **glPushMatrix**, and **glPopMatrix** to preserve GL state across **glCallLists** calls.

NOTES

Display lists can be executed between a call to **glBegin** and the corresponding call to **glEnd**, as long as the display list includes only commands that are allowed in this interval.

ERRORS

GL_INVALID_VALUE is generated if *n* is negative.

GL_INVALID_ENUM is generated if *type* is not one of **GL_BYTE**,
GL_UNSIGNED_BYTE, **GL_SHORT**, **GL_UNSIGNED_SHORT**, **GL_INT**,
GL_UNSIGNED_INT, **GL_FLOAT**, **GL_2_BYTES**, **GL_3_BYTES**, **GL_4_BYTES**.

ASSOCIATED GETS

glGet with argument **GL_LIST_BASE**
glGet with argument **GL_MAX_LIST_NESTING**
glIsList

SEE ALSO

glCallList, **glDeleteLists**, **glGenLists**, **glListBase**, **glNewList**, **glPushAttrib**,
glPushMatrix

NAME

glClear – clear buffers to preset values

C SPECIFICATION

void **glClear**(GLbitfield *mask*)

PARAMETERS

mask Bitwise OR of masks that indicate the buffers to be cleared. The four masks are **GL_COLOR_BUFFER_BIT**, **GL_DEPTH_BUFFER_BIT**, **GL_ACCUM_BUFFER_BIT**, and **GL_STENCIL_BUFFER_BIT**.

DESCRIPTION

glClear sets the bitplane area of the window to values previously selected by **glClearColor**, **glClearIndex**, **glClearDepth**, **glClearStencil**, and **glClearAccum**. Multiple color buffers can be cleared simultaneously by selecting more than one buffer at a time using **glDrawBuffer**.

The pixel ownership test, the scissor test, dithering, and the buffer writemasks affect the operation of **glClear**. The scissor box bounds the cleared region. Alpha function, blend function, logical operation, stenciling, texture mapping, and depth-buffering are ignored by **glClear**.

glClear takes a single argument that is the bitwise OR of several values indicating which buffer is to be cleared.

The values are as follows:

GL_COLOR_BUFFER_BIT   Indicates the buffers currently enabled for color writing.

GL_DEPTH_BUFFER_BIT   Indicates the depth buffer.

GL_ACCUM_BUFFER_BIT   Indicates the accumulation buffer.

GL_STENCIL_BUFFER_BIT   Indicates the stencil buffer.

The value to which each buffer is cleared depends on the setting of the clear value for that buffer.

NOTES

If a buffer is not present, then a **glClear** directed at that buffer has no effect.

ERRORS

GL_INVALID_VALUE is generated if any bit other than the four defined bits is set in *mask*.

GL_INVALID_OPERATION is generated if **glClear** is executed between the execution of **glBegin** and the corresponding execution of **glEnd**.

ASSOCIATED GETS

> **glGet** with argument **GL_ACCUM_CLEAR_VALUE**
> **glGet** with argument **GL_DEPTH_CLEAR_VALUE**
> **glGet** with argument **GL_INDEX_CLEAR_VALUE**
> **glGet** with argument **GL_COLOR_CLEAR_VALUE**
> **glGet** with argument **GL_STENCIL_CLEAR_VALUE**

SEE ALSO

> **glClearAccum**, **glClearColor**, **glClearDepth**, **glClearIndex**, **glClearStencil**, **glColorMask**, **glDepthMask**, **glDrawBuffer**, **glScissor**, **glStencilMask**

NAME

glClearAccum – specify clear values for the accumulation buffer

C SPECIFICATION

void **glClearAccum**(GLfloat *red*,
GLfloat *green*,
GLfloat *blue*,
GLfloat *alpha*)

PARAMETERS

red, green, blue, alpha

Specify the red, green, blue, and alpha values used when the accumulation buffer is cleared. The initial values are all 0.

DESCRIPTION

glClearAccum specifies the red, green, blue, and alpha values used by **glClear** to clear the accumulation buffer.

Values specified by **glClearAccum** are clamped to the range [-1, 1].

ERRORS

GL_INVALID_OPERATION is generated if **glClearAccum** is executed between the execution of **glBegin** and the corresponding execution of **glEnd**.

ASSOCIATED GETS

glGet with argument **GL_ACCUM_CLEAR_VALUE**

SEE ALSO

glAccum, glClear

NAME

glClearColor – specify clear values for the color buffers

C SPECIFICATION

void **glClearColor**(GLclampf *red*,
GLclampf *green*,
GLclampf *blue*,
GLclampf *alpha*)

PARAMETERS

red, green, blue, alpha

Specify the red, green, blue, and alpha values used when the color buffers are cleared. The initial values are all 0.

DESCRIPTION

glClearColor specifies the red, green, blue, and alpha values used by **glClear** to clear the color buffers. Values specified by **glClearColor** are clamped to the range [0, 1].

ERRORS

GL_INVALID_OPERATION is generated if **glClearColor** is executed between the execution of **glBegin** and the corresponding execution of **glEnd**.

ASSOCIATED GETS

glGet with argument **GL_COLOR_CLEAR_VALUE**

SEE ALSO

glClear

NAME

glClearDepth – specify the clear value for the depth buffer

C SPECIFICATION

void **glClearDepth**(GLclampd *depth*)

PARAMETERS

depth   Specifies the depth value used when the depth buffer is cleared. The initial value is 1.

DESCRIPTION

glClearDepth specifies the depth value used by **glClear** to clear the depth buffer. Values specified by **glClearDepth** are clamped to the range [0, 1].

ERRORS

GL_INVALID_OPERATION is generated if **glClearDepth** is executed between the execution of **glBegin** and the corresponding execution of **glEnd**.

ASSOCIATED GETS

glGet with argument **GL_DEPTH_CLEAR_VALUE**

SEE ALSO

glClear

NAME

glClearIndex – specify the clear value for the color index buffers

C SPECIFICATION

void **glClearIndex**(GLfloat c)

PARAMETERS

c Specifies the index used when the color index buffers are cleared. The initial value is 0.

DESCRIPTION

glClearIndex specifies the index used by **glClear** to clear the color index buffers. c is not clamped. Rather, c is converted to a fixed-point value with unspecified precision to the right of the binary point. The integer part of this value is then masked with $2^m - 1$, where m is the number of bits in a color index stored in the frame buffer.

ERRORS

GL_INVALID_OPERATION is generated if **glClearIndex** is executed between the execution of **glBegin** and the corresponding execution of **glEnd**.

ASSOCIATED GETS

glGet with argument **GL_INDEX_CLEAR_VALUE**

glGet with argument **GL_INDEX_BITS**

SEE ALSO

glClear

NAME

glClearStencil – specify the clear value for the stencil buffer

C SPECIFICATION

void **glClearStencil**(GLint *s*)

PARAMETERS

s Specifies the index used when the stencil buffer is cleared. The initial value is 0.

DESCRIPTION

glClearStencil specifies the index used by **glClear** to clear the stencil buffer. *s* is masked with $2^m - 1$, where *m* is the number of bits in the stencil buffer.

ERRORS

GL_INVALID_OPERATION is generated if **glClearStencil** is executed between the execution of **glBegin** and the corresponding execution of **glEnd**.

ASSOCIATED GETS

glGet with argument **GL_STENCIL_CLEAR_VALUE**
glGet with argument **GL_STENCIL_BITS**

SEE ALSO

glClear, **glStencilFunc**, **glStencilOp**, **glStencilMask**

NAME

glClientActiveTextureARB – select active texture unit

C SPECIFICATION

void **glClientActiveTextureARB**(GLenum *texture*)

PARAMETERS

texture Specifies which texture unit to make active. The number of texture units is implementation dependent, but must be at least two. *texture* must be one of **GL_TEXTURE*i*_ARB** where $0 \leq i <$ **GL_MAX_TEXTURE_UNITS_ARB**, which is an implementation-dependent value. The initial value is **GL_TEXTURE0_ARB**.

DESCRIPTION

glClientActiveTextureARB selects the vertex array client state parameters to be modified by **glTexCoordPointer**, and enabled or disabled with **glEnableClientState** or **glDisableClientState**, respectively, when called with a parameter of **GL_TEXTURE_COORD_ARRAY**.

NOTES

glClientActiveTextureARB is supported only if **GL_ARB_multitexture** is included in the string returned by **glGetString** when called with the argument **GL_EXTENSIONS**.

glClientActiveTextureARB sets **GL_CLIENT_ACTIVE_TEXTURE_ARB** to the active texture unit.

ERRORS

GL_INVALID_ENUM is generated if *texture* is not one of **GL_TEXTURE*i*_ARB**, where $0 \leq i <$ **GL_MAX_TEXTURE_UNITS_ARB**.

SEE ALSO

glActiveTextureARB, **glDisableClientState**, **glEnableClientState**, **glMultiTexCoordARB**, **glTexCoordPointer**

NAME

glClipPlane – specify a plane against which all geometry is clipped

C SPECIFICATION

void **glClipPlane**(GLenum *plane*,
                       const GLdouble **equation*)

PARAMETERS

plane   Specifies which clipping plane is being positioned. Symbolic names of the
             form **GL_CLIP_PLANE**i, where i is an integer between 0 and
             GL_MAX_CLIP_PLANES – 1, are accepted.

equation Specifies the address of an array of four double-precision floating-point
             values. These values are interpreted as a plane equation.

DESCRIPTION

Geometry is always clipped against the boundaries of a six-plane frustum in x, y, and
z. **glClipPlane** allows the specification of additional planes, not necessarily perpendicular to the x, y, or z axis, against which all geometry is clipped. To determine the
maximum number of additional clipping planes, call **glGetIntegerv** with argument
GL_MAX_CLIP_PLANES. All implementations support at least six such clipping
planes. Because the resulting clipping region is the intersection of the defined half-
spaces, it is always convex.

glClipPlane specifies a half-space using a four-component plane equation. When
glClipPlane is called, *equation* is transformed by the inverse of the modelview
matrix and stored in the resulting eye coordinates. Subsequent changes to the
modelview matrix have no effect on the stored plane-equation components. If the
dot product of the eye coordinates of a vertex with the stored plane equation components is positive or zero, the vertex is *in* with respect to that clipping plane. Otherwise, it is *out*.

To enable and disable clipping planes, call **glEnable** and **glDisable** with the argument **GL_CLIP_PLANE**i, where i is the plane number.

All clipping planes are initially defined as (0, 0, 0, 0) in eye coordinates and are disabled.

NOTES

It is always the case that **GL_CLIP_PLANE**i = **GL_CLIP_PLANE0** + i.

ERRORS

GL_INVALID_ENUM is generated if *plane* is not an accepted value.

GL_INVALID_OPERATION is generated if **glClipPlane** is executed between the execution of **glBegin** and the corresponding execution of **glEnd**.

ASSOCIATED GETS

glGetClipPlane

glIsEnabled with argument **GL_CLIP_PLANE***i*

SEE ALSO

glEnable

NAME

glColor3b, glColor3d, glColor3f, glColor3i, glColor3s, glColor3ub, glColor3ui, glColor3us, glColor4b, glColor4d, glColor4f, glColor4i, glColor4s, glColor4ub, glColor4ui, glColor4us, glColor3bv, glColor3dv, glColor3fv, glColor3iv, glColor3sv, glColor3ubv, glColor3uiv, glColor3usv, glColor4bv, glColor4dv, glColor4fv, glColor4iv, glColor4sv, glColor4ubv, glColor4uiv, glColor4usv – set the current color

C SPECIFICATION

```
void glColor3b( GLbyte red,
                GLbyte green,
                GLbyte blue )
void glColor3d( GLdouble red,
                GLdouble green,
                GLdouble blue )
void glColor3f( GLfloat red,
                GLfloat green,
                GLfloat blue )
void glColor3i( GLint red,
                GLint green,
                GLint blue )
void glColor3s( GLshort red,
                GLshort green,
                GLshort blue )
void glColor3ub( GLubyte red,
                 GLubyte green,
                 GLubyte blue )
void glColor3ui( GLuint red,
                 GLuint green,
                 GLuint blue )
void glColor3us( GLushort red,
                 GLushort green,
                 GLushort blue )
void glColor4b( GLbyte red,
                GLbyte green,
                GLbyte blue,
                GLbyte alpha )
void glColor4d( GLdouble red,
                GLdouble green,
                GLdouble blue,
                GLdouble alpha )
void glColor4f( GLfloat red,
                GLfloat green,
```

GLfloat *blue*,
GLfloat *alpha*)
void **glColor4i**(GLint *red*,
GLint *green*,
GLint *blue*,
GLint *alpha*)
void **glColor4s**(GLshort *red*,
GLshort *green*,
GLshort *blue*,
GLshort *alpha*)
void **glColor4ub**(GLubyte *red*,
GLubyte *green*,
GLubyte *blue*,
GLubyte *alpha*)
void **glColor4ui**(GLuint *red*,
GLuint *green*,
GLuint *blue*,
GLuint *alpha*)
void **glColor4us**(GLushort *red*,
GLushort *green*,
GLushort *blue*,
GLushort *alpha*)

PARAMETERS

red, green, blue
> Specify new red, green, and blue values for the current color.

alpha
> Specifies a new alpha value for the current color. Included only in the four-argument **glColor4** commands.

C SPECIFICATION

void **glColor3bv**(const GLbyte **v*)
void **glColor3dv**(const GLdouble **v*)
void **glColor3fv**(const GLfloat **v*)
void **glColor3iv**(const GLint **v*)
void **glColor3sv**(const GLshort **v*)
void **glColor3ubv**(const GLubyte **v*)
void **glColor3uiv**(const GLuint **v*)
void **glColor3usv**(const GLushort **v*)
void **glColor4bv**(const GLbyte **v*)
void **glColor4dv**(const GLdouble **v*)
void **glColor4fv**(const GLfloat **v*)
void **glColor4iv**(const GLint **v*)
void **glColor4sv**(const GLshort **v*)

void **glColor4ubv**(const GLubyte *v)
void **glColor4uiv**(const GLuint *v)
void **glColor4usv**(const GLushort *v)

PARAMETERS

v   Specifies a pointer to an array that contains red, green, blue, and (some-
times) alpha values.

DESCRIPTION

The GL stores both a current single-valued color index and a current four-valued
RGBA color. **glColor** sets a new four-valued RGBA color. **glColor** has two major
variants: **glColor3** and **glColor4**. **glColor3** variants specify new red, green, and
blue values explicitly and set the current alpha value to 1.0 (full intensity) implicitly. **glColor4** variants specify all four color components explicitly.

glColor3b, **glColor4b**, **glColor3s**, **glColor4s**, **glColor3i**, and **glColor4i** take three or
four signed byte, short, or long integers as arguments. When **v** is appended to the
name, the color commands can take a pointer to an array of such values.

Current color values are stored in floating-point format, with unspecified mantissa
and exponent sizes. Unsigned integer color components, when specified, are
linearly mapped to floating-point values such that the largest representable value
maps to 1.0 (full intensity), and 0 maps to 0.0 (zero intensity). Signed integer color
components, when specified, are linearly mapped to floating-point values such that
the most positive representable value maps to 1.0, and the most negative representable value maps to −1.0. (Note that this mapping does not convert 0 precisely to
0.0.) Floating-point values are mapped directly.

Neither floating-point nor signed integer values are clamped to the range [0,1]
before the current color is updated. However, color components are clamped to this
range before they are interpolated or written into a color buffer.

NOTES

The initial value for the current color is (1, 1, 1, 1).

The current color can be updated at any time. In particular, **glColor** can be called
between a call to **glBegin** and the corresponding call to **glEnd**.

ASSOCIATED GETS

glGet with argument **GL_CURRENT_COLOR**
glGet with argument **GL_RGBA_MODE**

SEE ALSO

glIndex

NAME

glColorMask – enable and disable writing of frame buffer color components

C SPECIFICATION

void **glColorMask**(GLboolean *red*,
                     GLboolean *green*,
                     GLboolean *blue*,
                     GLboolean *alpha*)

PARAMETERS

red, green, blue, alpha

Specify whether red, green, blue, and alpha can or cannot be written into the frame buffer. The initial values are all **GL_TRUE**, indicating that the color components can be written.

DESCRIPTION

glColorMask specifies whether the individual color components in the frame buffer can or cannot be written. If *red* is **GL_FALSE**, for example, no change is made to the red component of any pixel in any of the color buffers, regardless of the drawing operation attempted.

Changes to individual bits of components cannot be controlled. Rather, changes are either enabled or disabled for entire color components.

ERRORS

GL_INVALID_OPERATION is generated if **glColorMask** is executed between the execution of **glBegin** and the corresponding execution of **glEnd**.

ASSOCIATED GETS

glGet with argument **GL_COLOR_WRITEMASK**
glGet with argument **GL_RGBA_MODE**

SEE ALSO

glClear, glColor, glColorPointer, glDepthMask, glIndex, glIndexPointer, glIndexMask, glStencilMask

NAME

glColorMaterial – cause a material color to track the current color

C SPECIFICATION

void **glColorMaterial**(GLenum *face*,
                        GLenum *mode*)

PARAMETERS

face Specifies whether front, back, or both front and back material parameters should track the current color. Accepted values are **GL_FRONT**, **GL_BACK**, and **GL_FRONT_AND_BACK**. The initial value is **GL_FRONT_AND_BACK**.

mode

Specifies which of several material parameters track the current color. Accepted values are **GL_EMISSION**, **GL_AMBIENT**, **GL_DIFFUSE**, **GL_SPECULAR**, and **GL_AMBIENT_AND_DIFFUSE**. The initial value is **GL_AMBIENT_AND_DIFFUSE**.

DESCRIPTION

glColorMaterial specifies which material parameters track the current color. When **GL_COLOR_MATERIAL** is enabled, the material parameter or parameters specified by *mode*, of the material or materials specified by *face*, track the current color at all times.

To enable and disable **GL_COLOR_MATERIAL**, call **glEnable** and **glDisable** with argument **GL_COLOR_MATERIAL**. **GL_COLOR_MATERIAL** is initially disabled.

NOTES

glColorMaterial makes it possible to change a subset of material parameters for each vertex using only the **glColor** command, without calling **glMaterial**. If only such a subset of parameters is to be specified for each vertex, calling **glColorMaterial** is preferable to calling **glMaterial**.

Call **glColorMaterial** before enabling **GL_COLOR_MATERIAL**.

Calling **glDrawElements**, **glDrawArrays**, or **glDrawRangeElements** may leave the current color indeterminate, if the color array is enabled. If **glColorMaterial** is enabled while the current color is indeterminate, the lighting material state specified by *face* and *mode* is also indeterminate.

If the GL version is 1.1 or greater, and **GL_COLOR_MATERIAL** is enabled, evaluated color values affect the results of the lighting equation as if the current color were being modified, but no change is made to the tracking lighting parameter of the current color.

ERRORS

GL_INVALID_ENUM is generated if *face* or *mode* is not an accepted value.

GL_INVALID_OPERATION is generated if **glColorMaterial** is executed between the execution of **glBegin** and the corresponding execution of **glEnd**.

ASSOCIATED GETS

glIsEnabled with argument **GL_COLOR_MATERIAL**
glGet with argument **GL_COLOR_MATERIAL_PARAMETER**
glGet with argument **GL_COLOR_MATERIAL_FACE**

SEE ALSO

glColor, **glColorPointer**, **glDrawArrays**, **glDrawElements**, **glDrawRangeElements**, **glEnable**, **glLight**, **glLightModel**, **glMaterial**

NAME

glColorPointer – define an array of colors

C SPECIFICATION

void **glColorPointer**(GLint *size*,
                       GLenum *type*,
                       GLsizei *stride*,
                       const GLvoid **pointer*)

PARAMETERS

size   Specifies the number of components per color. Must be 3 or 4. The initial
          value is 4.

type   Specifies the data type of each color component in the array. Symbolic con-
          stants **GL_BYTE**, **GL_UNSIGNED_BYTE**, **GL_SHORT**,
          GL_UNSIGNED_SHORT, **GL_INT**, **GL_UNSIGNED_INT**, **GL_FLOAT**, and
          GL_DOUBLE are accepted. The initial value is **GL_FLOAT**.

stride Specifies the byte offset between consecutive colors. If *stride* is 0 (the initial
          value), the colors are understood to be tightly packed in the array. The initial
          value is 0.

pointer Specifies a pointer to the first component of the first color element in the
          array.

DESCRIPTION

glColorPointer specifies the location and data format of an array of color components to use when rendering. *size* specifies the number of components per color,
and must be 3 or 4. *type* specifies the data type of each color component, and *stride*
specifies the byte stride from one color to the next allowing vertices and attributes
to be packed into a single array or stored in separate arrays. (Single-array storage
may be more efficient on some implementations; see **glInterleavedArrays**.)

When a color array is specified, *size*, *type*, *stride*, and *pointer* are saved as client-side
state.

To enable and disable the color array, call **glEnableClientState** and
glDisableClientState with the argument **GL_COLOR_ARRAY**. If enabled, the color
array is used when **glDrawArrays**, **glDrawElements**, **glDrawRangeElements**, or
glArrayElement is called.

NOTES

glColorPointer is available only if the GL version is 1.1 or greater.

The color array is initially disabled and isn't accessed when **glArrayElement**, **glDrawArrays**, **glDrawRangeElements**, or **glDrawElements** is called.

Execution of **glColorPointer** is not allowed between the execution of **glBegin** and the corresponding execution of **glEnd**, but an error may or may not be generated. If no error is generated, the operation is undefined.

glColorPointer is typically implemented on the client side.

Color array parameters are client-side state and are therefore not saved or restored by **glPushAttrib** and **glPopAttrib**. Use **glPushClientAttrib** and **glPopClientAttrib** instead.

ERRORS

GL_INVALID_VALUE is generated if *size* is not 3 or 4.

GL_INVALID_ENUM is generated if *type* is not an accepted value.

GL_INVALID_VALUE is generated if *stride* is negative.

ASSOCIATED GETS

glIsEnabled with argument **GL_COLOR_ARRAY**
glGet with argument **GL_COLOR_ARRAY_SIZE**
glGet with argument **GL_COLOR_ARRAY_TYPE**
glGet with argument **GL_COLOR_ARRAY_STRIDE**
glGetPointerv with argument **GL_COLOR_ARRAY_POINTER**

SEE ALSO

glArrayElement, **glDrawArrays**, **glDrawElements**, **glEdgeFlagPointer**, **glEnable**, **glGetPointerv**, **glIndexPointer**, **glInterleavedArrays**, **glNormalPointer**, **glPopClientAttrib**, **glPushClientAttrib**, **glTexCoordPointer**, **glVertexPointer**

NAME

glColorSubTable – respecify a portion of a color table

C SPECIFICATION

void **glColorSubTable**(GLenum *target*,
                    GLsizei *start*,
                    GLsizei *count*,
                    GLenum *format*,
                    GLenum *type*,
                    const GLvoid **data*)

PARAMETERS

target   Must be one of **GL_COLOR_TABLE**,
        GL_POST_CONVOLUTION_COLOR_TABLE, or
        GL_POST_COLOR_MATRIX_COLOR_TABLE.

start   The starting index of the portion of the color table to be replaced.

count   The number of table entries to replace.

format
        The format of the pixel data in *data*. The allowable values are **GL_RED**,
        GL_GREEN, **GL_BLUE**, **GL_ALPHA**, **GL_LUMINANCE**,
        GL_LUMINANCE_ALPHA, **GL_RGB**, **GL_BGR**, **GL_RGBA**, and **GL_BGRA**.

type   The type of the pixel data in *data*. The allowable values are
        GL_UNSIGNED_BYTE, **GL_BYTE**, **GL_UNSIGNED_SHORT**, **GL_SHORT**,
        GL_UNSIGNED_INT, **GL_INT**, **GL_FLOAT**, **GL_UNSIGNED_BYTE_3_3_2**,
        GL_UNSIGNED_BYTE_2_3_3_REV, **GL_UNSIGNED_SHORT_5_6_5**,
        GL_UNSIGNED_SHORT_5_6_5_REV, **GL_UNSIGNED_SHORT_4_4_4_4**,
        GL_UNSIGNED_SHORT_4_4_4_4_REV, **GL_UNSIGNED_SHORT_5_5_5_1**,
        GL_UNSIGNED_SHORT_1_5_5_5_REV, **GL_UNSIGNED_INT_8_8_8_8**,
        GL_UNSIGNED_INT_8_8_8_8_REV, **GL_UNSIGNED_INT_10_10_10_2**, and
        GL_UNSIGNED_INT_2_10_10_10_REV.

data   Pointer to a one-dimensional array of pixel data that is processed to replace
        the specified region of the color table.

DESCRIPTION

glColorSubTable is used to respecify a contiguous portion of a color table previously
defined using **glColorTable**. The pixels referenced by *data* replace the portion of
the existing table from indices *start* to *start* + *count* − 1, inclusive. This region may
not include any entries outside the range of the color table as it was originally
specified. It is not an error to specify a subtexture with width of 0, but such a
specification has no effect.

NOTES

glColorSubTable is present only if **GL_ARB_imaging** is returned when **glGetString** is called with an argument of **GL_EXTENSIONS**.

ERRORS

GL_INVALID_ENUM is generated if *target* is not one of the allowable values.

GL_INVALID_VALUE is generated if *start* + *count* > *width*.

GL_INVALID_ENUM is generated if *format* is not one of the allowable values.

GL_INVALID_ENUM is generated if *type* is not one of the allowable values.

GL_INVALID_OPERATION is generated if **glColorSubTable** is executed between the execution of **glBegin** and the corresponding execution of **glEnd**.

ASSOCIATED GETS

glGetColorTable, **glGetColorTableParameter**

SEE ALSO

glColorSubTable, **glColorTableParameter**, **glCopyColorTable**, **glCopyColorSubTable**, **glGetColorTable**

NAME

glColorTable – define a color lookup table

C SPECIFICATION

void **glColorTable**(GLenum *target*,
                   GLenum *internalformat*,
                   GLsizei *width*,
                   GLenum *format*,
                   GLenum *type*,
                   const GLvoid **table*)

PARAMETERS

target   Must be one of **GL_COLOR_TABLE**,
GL_POST_CONVOLUTION_COLOR_TABLE,
GL_POST_COLOR_MATRIX_COLOR_TABLE,
GL_PROXY_COLOR_TABLE,
GL_PROXY_POST_CONVOLUTION_COLOR_TABLE, or
GL_PROXY_POST_COLOR_MATRIX_COLOR_TABLE.

internalformat

The internal format of the color table. The allowable values are
GL_ALPHA, **GL_ALPHA4**, **GL_ALPHA8**, **GL_ALPHA12**,
GL_ALPHA16, **GL_LUMINANCE**, **GL_LUMINANCE4**,
GL_LUMINANCE8, **GL_LUMINANCE12**, **GL_LUMINANCE16**,
GL_LUMINANCE_ALPHA, **GL_LUMINANCE4_ALPHA4**,
GL_LUMINANCE6_ALPHA2, **GL_LUMINANCE8_ALPHA8**,
GL_LUMINANCE12_ALPHA4, **GL_LUMINANCE12_ALPHA12**,
GL_LUMINANCE16_ALPHA16, **GL_INTENSITY**, **GL_INTENSITY4**,
GL_INTENSITY8, **GL_INTENSITY12**, **GL_INTENSITY16**,
GL_R3_G3_B2, **GL_RGB**, **GL_RGB4**, **GL_RGB5**, **GL_RGB8**,
GL_RGB10, **GL_RGB12**, **GL_RGB16**, **GL_RGBA**, **GL_RGBA2**,
GL_RGBA4, **GL_RGB5_A1**, **GL_RGBA8**, **GL_RGB10_A2**, **GL_RGBA12**,
and **GL_RGBA16**.

width   The number of entries in the color lookup table specified by *table*.

format   The format of the pixel data in *table*. The allowable values are
GL_RED, **GL_GREEN**, **GL_BLUE**, **GL_ALPHA**, **GL_LUMINANCE**,
GL_LUMINANCE_ALPHA, **GL_RGB**, **GL_BGR**, **GL_RGBA**, and
GL_BGRA.

type   The type of the pixel data in *table*. The allowable values are
GL_UNSIGNED_BYTE, **GL_BYTE**, **GL_UNSIGNED_SHORT**,
GL_SHORT, **GL_UNSIGNED_INT**, **GL_INT**, **GL_FLOAT**,
GL_UNSIGNED_BYTE_3_3_2, **GL_UNSIGNED_BYTE_2_3_3_REV**,

GL_UNSIGNED_SHORT_5_6_5, GL_UNSIGNED_SHORT_5_6_5_REV,
GL_UNSIGNED_SHORT_4_4_4_4,
GL_UNSIGNED_SHORT_4_4_4_4_REV,
GL_UNSIGNED_SHORT_5_5_5_1,
GL_UNSIGNED_SHORT_1_5_5_5_REV,
GL_UNSIGNED_INT_8_8_8_8, GL_UNSIGNED_INT_8_8_8_8_REV,
GL_UNSIGNED_INT_10_10_10_2, and
GL_UNSIGNED_INT_2_10_10_10_REV.

table   Pointer to a one-dimensional array of pixel data that is processed to build the color table.

DESCRIPTION

glColorTable may be used in two ways: to test the actual size and color resolution of a lookup table given a particular set of parameters, or to load the contents of a color lookup table. Use the targets **GL_PROXY_*** for the first case and the other targets for the second case.

If *target* is **GL_COLOR_TABLE**, **GL_POST_CONVOLUTION_COLOR_TABLE**, or **GL_POST_COLOR_MATRIX_COLOR_TABLE**, **glColorTable** builds a color lookup table from an array of pixels. The pixel array specified by *width*, *format*, *type*, and *table* is extracted from memory and processed just as if **glDrawPixels** were called, but processing stops after the final expansion to RGBA is completed.

The four scale parameters and the four bias parameters that are defined for the table are then used to scale and bias the R, G, B, and A components of each pixel. (Use **glColorTableParameter** to set these scale and bias parameters.)

Next, the R, G, B, and A values are clamped to the range [0, 1]. Each pixel is then converted to the internal format specified by *internalformat*. This conversion simply maps the component values of the pixel (R, G, B, and A) to the values included in the internal format (red, green, blue, alpha, luminance, and intensity). The mapping is as follows:

Internal Format	Red	Green	Blue	Alpha	Luminance	Intensity
GL_ALPHA				A		
GL_LUMINANCE					R	
GL_LUMINANCE_ALPHA				A	R	
GL_INTENSITY						R
GL_RGB	R	G	B			
GL_RGBA	R	G	B	A		

Finally, the red, green, blue, alpha, luminance, and/or intensity components of the resulting pixels are stored in the color table. They form a one-dimensional table with indices in the range [0, *width* − 1].

If *target* is **GL_PROXY_***, **glColorTable** recomputes and stores the values of the proxy color table's state variables **GL_COLOR_TABLE_FORMAT**, **GL_COLOR_TABLE_WIDTH**, **GL_COLOR_TABLE_RED_SIZE**, **GL_COLOR_TABLE_GREEN_SIZE**, **GL_COLOR_TABLE_BLUE_SIZE**, **GL_COLOR_TABLE_ALPHA_SIZE**, **GL_COLOR_TABLE_LUMINANCE_SIZE**, and **GL_COLOR_TABLE_INTENSITY_SIZE**. There is no effect on the image or state of any actual color table. If the specified color table is too large to be supported, then all the proxy state variables listed above are set to zero. Otherwise, the color table could be supported by **glColorTable** using the corresponding non-proxy target, and the proxy state variables are set as if that target were being defined.

The proxy state variables can be retrieved by calling **glGetColorTableParameter** with a target of **GL_PROXY_***. This allows the application to decide if a particular **glColorTable** command would succeed, and to determine what the resulting color table attributes would be.

If a color table is enabled, and its width is non-zero, then its contents are used to replace a subset of the components of each RGBA pixel group, based on the internal format of the table.

Each pixel group has color components (R, G, B, A) that are in the range [0.0, 1.0]. The color components are rescaled to the size of the color lookup table to form an index. Then a subset of the components based on the internal format of the table are replaced by the table entry selected by that index. If the color components and contents of the table are represented as follows:

Representation	Meaning
r	Table index computed from R
g	Table index computed from G
b	Table index computed from B
a	Table index computed from A
L[i]	Luminance value at table index i
I[i]	Intensity value at table index i
R[i]	Red value at table index i
G[i]	Green value at table index i
B[i]	Blue value at table index i
A[i]	Alpha value at table index i

then the result of color table lookup is as follows:

Table Internal Format	Resulting Texture Components			
	R	G	B	A
GL_ALPHA	R	G	B	A[a]
GL_LUMINANCE	L[r]	L[g]	L[b]	At
GL_LUMINANCE_ALPHA	L[r]	L[g]	L[b]	A[a]
GL_INTENSITY	I[r]	I[g]	I[b]	I[a]
GL_RGB	R[r]	G[g]	B[b]	A
GL_RGBA	R[r]	G[g]	B[b]	A[a]

When **GL_COLOR_TABLE** is enabled, the colors resulting from the pixel map operation (if it is enabled) are mapped by the color lookup table before being passed to the convolution operation. The colors resulting from the convolution operation are modified by the post convolution color lookup table when **GL_POST_CONVOLUTION_COLOR_TABLE** is enabled. These modified colors are then sent to the color matrix operation. Finally, if **GL_POST_COLOR_MATRIX_COLOR_TABLE** is enabled, the colors resulting from the color matrix operation are mapped by the post color matrix color lookup table before being used by the histogram operation.

NOTES

glColorTable is present only if **GL_ARB_imaging** is returned when **glGetString** is called with an argument of **GL_EXTENSIONS**.

If *target* is set to **GL_COLOR_TABLE**, **GL_POST_CONVOLUTION_COLOR_TABLE**, or **GL_POST_COLOR_MATRIX_COLOR_TABLE**, then *width* must be a power of two or a **GL_INVALID_VALUE** error is generated.

ERRORS

GL_INVALID_ENUM is generated if *target* is not one of the allowable values.

GL_INVALID_ENUM is generated if *internalformat* is not one of the allowable values.

GL_INVALID_VALUE is generated if *width* is less than zero.

GL_INVALID_ENUM is generated if *format* is not one of the allowable values.

GL_INVALID_ENUM is generated if *type* is not one of the allowable values.

GL_TABLE_TOO_LARGE is generated if the requested color table is too large to be supported by the implementation, and *target* is not a **GL_PROXY_*** target.

GL_INVALID_OPERATION is generated if **glColorTable** is executed between the execution of **glBegin** and the corresponding execution of **glEnd**.

ASSOCIATED GETS

glGetColorTableParameter

SEE ALSO

glColorSubTable, glColorTableParameter, glCopyColorTable,
glCopyColorSubTable, glGetColorTable

NAME

glColorTableParameterfv, glColorTableParameteriv – set color lookup table parameters

C SPECIFICATION

void **glColorTableParameterfv**(GLenum *target*,
                                   GLenum *pname*,
                                   const GLfloat **params*)
void **glColorTableParameteriv**(GLenum *target*,
                                   GLenum *pname*,
                                   const GLint **params*)

PARAMETERS

target The target color table. Must be **GL_COLOR_TABLE**, **GL_POST_CONVOLUTION_COLOR_TABLE**, or **GL_POST_COLOR_MATRIX_COLOR_TABLE**.

pname

The symbolic name of a texture color lookup table parameter. Must be one of **GL_COLOR_TABLE_SCALE** or **GL_COLOR_TABLE_BIAS**.

params

A pointer to an array where the values of the parameters are stored.

DESCRIPTION

glColorTableParameter is used to specify the scale factors and bias terms applied to color components when they are loaded into a color table. *target* indicates which color table the scale and bias terms apply to; it must be set to **GL_COLOR_TABLE**, **GL_POST_CONVOLUTION_COLOR_TABLE**, or **GL_POST_COLOR_MATRIX_COLOR_TABLE**.

pname must be **GL_COLOR_TABLE_SCALE** to set the scale factors. In this case, *params* points to an array of four values, which are the scale factors for red, green, blue, and alpha, in that order.

pname must be **GL_COLOR_TABLE_BIAS** to set the bias terms. In this case, *params* points to an array of four values, which are the bias terms for red, green, blue, and alpha, in that order.

The color tables themselves are specified by calling **glColorTable**.

NOTES

glColorTableParameter is available only if **GL_ARB_imaging** is returned from calling **glGetString** with an argument of **GL_EXTENSIONS**.

ERRORS

GL_INVALID_ENUM is generated if *target* or *pname* is not an acceptable value.

GL_INVALID_OPERATION is generated if **glColorTableParameter** is executed between the execution of **glBegin** and the corresponding execution of **glEnd**.

ASSOCIATED GETS

glGetColorTableParameter

SEE ALSO

glColorTable, **glPixelTransfer**

NAME

glConvolutionFilter1D – define a one-dimensional convolution filter

C SPECIFICATION

```
void glConvolutionFilter1D( GLenum target,
                            GLenum internalformat,
                            GLsizei width,
                            GLenum format,
                            GLenum type,
                            const GLvoid *image )
```

PARAMETERS

target   Must be **GL_CONVOLUTION_1D**.

internalformat

The internal format of the convolution filter kernel. The allowable values are **GL_ALPHA**, **GL_LUMINANCE**, **GL_LUMINANCE_ALPHA**, **GL_INTENSITY**, **GL_RGB**, and **GL_RGBA**.

width   The width of the pixel array referenced by *image*.

format   The format of the pixel data in *image*. The allowable values are **GL_ALPHA**, **GL_ALPHA4**, **GL_ALPHA8**, **GL_ALPHA12**, **GL_ALPHA16**, **GL_LUMINANCE**, **GL_LUMINANCE4**, **GL_LUMINANCE8**, **GL_LUMINANCE12**, **GL_LUMINANCE16**, **GL_LUMINANCE_ALPHA**, **GL_LUMINANCE4_ALPHA4**, **GL_LUMINANCE6_ALPHA2**, **GL_LUMINANCE8_ALPHA8**, **GL_LUMINANCE12_ALPHA4**, **GL_LUMINANCE12_ALPHA12**, **GL_LUMINANCE16_ALPHA16**, **GL_INTENSITY**, **GL_INTENSITY4**, **GL_INTENSITY8**, **GL_INTENSITY12**, **GL_INTENSITY16**, **GL_R3_G3_B2**, **GL_RGB**, **GL_RGB4**, **GL_RGB5**, **GL_RGB8**, **GL_RGB10**, **GL_RGB12**, **GL_RGB16**, **GL_RGBA**, **GL_RGBA2**, **GL_RGBA4**, **GL_RGB5_A1**, **GL_RGBA8**, **GL_RGB10_A2**, **GL_RGBA12**, or **GL_RGBA16**.

type   The type of the pixel data in *image*. Symbolic constants **GL_UNSIGNED_BYTE**, **GL_BYTE**, **GL_BITMAP**, **GL_UNSIGNED_SHORT**, **GL_SHORT**, **GL_UNSIGNED_INT**, **GL_INT**, **GL_FLOAT**, **GL_UNSIGNED_BYTE_3_3_2**, **GL_UNSIGNED_BYTE_2_3_3_REV**, **GL_UNSIGNED_SHORT_5_6_5**, **GL_UNSIGNED_SHORT_5_6_5_REV**, **GL_UNSIGNED_SHORT_4_4_4_4**, **GL_UNSIGNED_SHORT_4_4_4_4_REV**, **GL_UNSIGNED_SHORT_5_5_5_1**, **GL_UNSIGNED_SHORT_1_5_5_5_REV**,

GL_UNSIGNED_INT_8_8_8_8, GL_UNSIGNED_INT_8_8_8_8_REV, GL_UNSIGNED_INT_10_10_10_2, and GL_UNSIGNED_INT_2_10_10_10_REV are accepted.

image   Pointer to a one-dimensional array of pixel data that is processed to build the convolution filter kernel.

DESCRIPTION

glConvolutionFilter1D builds a one-dimensional convolution filter kernel from an array of pixels.

The pixel array specified by *width*, *format*, *type*, and *image* is extracted from memory and processed just as if **glDrawPixels** were called, but processing stops after the final expansion to RGBA is completed.

The R, G, B, and A components of each pixel are next scaled by the four 1D GL_CONVOLUTION_FILTER_SCALE parameters and biased by the four 1D GL_CONVOLUTION_FILTER_BIAS parameters. (The scale and bias parameters are set by **glConvolutionParameter** using the GL_CONVOLUTION_1D target and the names GL_CONVOLUTION_FILTER_SCALE and GL_CONVOLUTION_FILTER_BIAS. The parameters themselves are vectors of four values that are applied to red, green, blue, and alpha, in that order.) The R, G, B, and A values are not clamped to [0,1] at any time during this process.

Each pixel is then converted to the internal format specified by *internalformat*. This conversion simply maps the component values of the pixel (R, G, B, and A) to the values included in the internal format (red, green, blue, alpha, luminance, and intensity). The mapping is as follows:

Internal Format	Red	Green	Blue	Alpha	Luminance	Intensity
GL_ALPHA				A		
GL_LUMINANCE					R	
GL_LUMINANCE_ALPHA			A	R		
GL_INTENSITY						R
GL_RGB	R	G	B			
GL_RGBA	R	G	B	A		

The red, green, blue, alpha, luminance, and/or intensity components of the resulting pixels are stored in floating-point rather than integer format. They form a one-dimensional filter kernel image indexed with coordinate *i* such that *i* starts at 0 and increases from left to right. Kernel location *i* is derived from the *i*th pixel, counting from 0.

Note that after a convolution is performed, the resulting color components are also scaled by their corresponding **GL_POST_CONVOLUTION_c_SCALE** parameters and biased by their corresponding **GL_POST_CONVOLUTION_c_BIAS** parameters (where *c* takes on the values **RED**, **GREEN**, **BLUE**, and **ALPHA**). These parameters are set by **glPixelTransfer**.

NOTES

glConvolutionFilter1D is present only if **GL_ARB_imaging** is returned when **glGetString** is called with an argument of **GL_EXTENSIONS**.

ERRORS

GL_INVALID_ENUM is generated if *target* is not **GL_CONVOLUTION_1D**.

GL_INVALID_ENUM is generated if *internalformat* is not one of the allowable values.

GL_INVALID_VALUE is generated if *width* is less than zero or greater than the maximum supported value. This value may be queried with **glGetConvolutionParameter** using target **GL_CONVOLUTION_1D** and name **GL_MAX_CONVOLUTION_WIDTH**.

GL_INVALID_ENUM is generated if *format* is not one of the allowable values.

GL_INVALID_ENUM is generated if *type* is not one of the allowable values.

GL_INVALID_OPERATION is generated if **glConvolutionFilter1D** is executed between the execution of **glBegin** and the corresponding execution of **glEnd**.

GL_INVALID_OPERATION is generated if *format* is one of **GL_UNSIGNED_BYTE_3_3_2**, **GL_UNSIGNED_BYTE_2_3_3_REV**, **GL_UNSIGNED_SHORT_5_6_5**, or **GL_UNSIGNED_SHORT_5_6_5_REV** and *type* is not **GL_RGB**.

GL_INVALID_OPERATION is generated if *format* is one of **GL_UNSIGNED_SHORT_4_4_4_4**, **GL_UNSIGNED_SHORT_4_4_4_4_REV**, **GL_UNSIGNED_SHORT_5_5_5_1**, **GL_UNSIGNED_SHORT_1_5_5_5_REV**, **GL_UNSIGNED_INT_8_8_8_8**, **GL_UNSIGNED_INT_8_8_8_8_REV**, **GL_UNSIGNED_INT_10_10_10_2**, or **GL_UNSIGNED_INT_2_10_10_10_REV** and *type* is neither **GL_RGBA** nor **GL_BGRA**.

ASSOCIATED GETS

glGetConvolutionParameter, **glGetConvolutionFilter**

SEE ALSO

glConvolutionFilter2D, **glSeparableFilter2D**, **glConvolutionParameter**, **glPixelTransfer**

NAME

glConvolutionFilter2D – define a two-dimensional convolution filter

C SPECIFICATION

void **glConvolutionFilter2D**(GLenum *target*,
GLenum *internalformat*,
GLsizei *width*,
GLsizei *height*,
GLenum *format*,
GLenum *type*,
const GLvoid **image*)

PARAMETERS

target   Must be **GL_CONVOLUTION_2D**.

internalformat

The internal format of the convolution filter kernel. The allowable
values are **GL_ALPHA**, **GL_ALPHA4**, **GL_ALPHA8**, **GL_ALPHA12**,
GL_ALPHA16, **GL_LUMINANCE**, **GL_LUMINANCE4**,
GL_LUMINANCE8, **GL_LUMINANCE12**, **GL_LUMINANCE16**,
GL_LUMINANCE_ALPHA, **GL_LUMINANCE4_ALPHA4**,
GL_LUMINANCE6_ALPHA2, **GL_LUMINANCE8_ALPHA8**,
GL_LUMINANCE12_ALPHA4, **GL_LUMINANCE12_ALPHA12**,
GL_LUMINANCE16_ALPHA16, **GL_INTENSITY**, **GL_INTENSITY4**,
GL_INTENSITY8, **GL_INTENSITY12**, **GL_INTENSITY16**,
GL_R3_G3_B2, **GL_RGB**, **GL_RGB4**, **GL_RGB5**, **GL_RGB8**,
GL_RGB10, **GL_RGB12**, **GL_RGB16**, **GL_RGBA**, **GL_RGBA2**,
GL_RGBA4, **GL_RGB5_A1**, **GL_RGBA8**, **GL_RGB10_A2**, **GL_RGBA12**,
or **GL_RGBA16**.

width   The width of the pixel array referenced by *image*.

height   The height of the pixel array referenced by *image*.

format   The format of the pixel data in *image*. The allowable values are
GL_RED, **GL_GREEN**, **GL_BLUE**, **GL_ALPHA**, **GL_RGB**, **GL_BGR**,
GL_RGBA, **GL_BGRA**, **GL_LUMINANCE**, and
GL_LUMINANCE_ALPHA.

type   The type of the pixel data in *image*. Symbolic constants
GL_UNSIGNED_BYTE, **GL_BYTE**, **GL_BITMAP**,
GL_UNSIGNED_SHORT, **GL_SHORT**, **GL_UNSIGNED_INT**, **GL_INT**,
GL_FLOAT, **GL_UNSIGNED_BYTE_3_3_2**,
GL_UNSIGNED_BYTE_2_3_3_REV, **GL_UNSIGNED_SHORT_5_6_5**,
GL_UNSIGNED_SHORT_5_6_5_REV,

GL_UNSIGNED_SHORT_4_4_4_4,
GL_UNSIGNED_SHORT_4_4_4_4_REV,
GL_UNSIGNED_SHORT_5_5_5_1,
GL_UNSIGNED_SHORT_1_5_5_5_REV,
GL_UNSIGNED_INT_8_8_8_8, GL_UNSIGNED_INT_8_8_8_8_REV,
GL_UNSIGNED_INT_10_10_10_2, and
GL_UNSIGNED_INT_2_10_10_10_REV are accepted.

image   Pointer to a two-dimensional array of pixel data that is processed to
               build the convolution filter kernel.

DESCRIPTION

glConvolutionFilter2D builds a two-dimensional convolution filter kernel from an
array of pixels.

The pixel array specified by *width*, *height*, *format*, *type*, and *image* is extracted from
memory and processed just as if **glDrawPixels** were called, but processing stops after
the final expansion to RGBA is completed.

The R, G, B, and A components of each pixel are next scaled by the four 2D
GL_CONVOLUTION_FILTER_SCALE parameters and biased by the four 2D
GL_CONVOLUTION_FILTER_BIAS parameters. (The scale and bias parameters are
set by **glConvolutionParameter** using the **GL_CONVOLUTION_2D** target and the
names **GL_CONVOLUTION_FILTER_SCALE** and
GL_CONVOLUTION_FILTER_BIAS. The parameters themselves are vectors of four
values that are applied to red, green, blue, and alpha, in that order.) The R, G, B,
and A values are not clamped to [0,1] at any time during this process.

Each pixel is then converted to the internal format specified by *internalformat*. This
conversion simply maps the component values of the pixel (R, G, B, and A) to the
values included in the internal format (red, green, blue, alpha, luminance, and
intensity). The mapping is as follows:

Internal Format	Red	Green	Blue	Alpha	Luminance	Intensity
GL_ALPHA				A		
GL_LUMINANCE					R	
GL_LUMINANCE_ALPHA			A	R		
GL_INTENSITY						R
GL_RGB	R	G	B			
GL_RGBA	R	G	B	A		

The red, green, blue, alpha, luminance, and/or intensity components of the resulting pixels are stored in floating-point rather than integer format. They form a two-
dimensional filter kernel image indexed with coordinates i and j such that i starts at

zero and increases from left to right, and *j* starts at zero and increases from bottom to top. Kernel location *i,j* is derived from the *N*th pixel, where *N* is *i+j*width*.

Note that after a convolution is performed, the resulting color components are also scaled by their corresponding **GL_POST_CONVOLUTION_c_SCALE** parameters and biased by their corresponding **GL_POST_CONVOLUTION_c_BIAS** parameters (where *c* takes on the values **RED**, **GREEN**, **BLUE**, and **ALPHA**). These parameters are set by **glPixelTransfer**.

NOTES

glConvolutionFilter2D is present only if **GL_ARB_imaging** is returned when **glGetString** is called with an argument of **GL_EXTENSIONS**.

ERRORS

GL_INVALID_ENUM is generated if *target* is not **GL_CONVOLUTION_2D**.

GL_INVALID_ENUM is generated if *internalformat* is not one of the allowable values.

GL_INVALID_VALUE is generated if *width* is less than zero or greater than the maximum supported value. This value may be queried with **glGetConvolutionParameter** using target **GL_CONVOLUTION_2D** and name **GL_MAX_CONVOLUTION_WIDTH**.

GL_INVALID_VALUE is generated if *height* is less than zero or greater than the maximum supported value. This value may be queried with **glGetConvolutionParameter** using target **GL_CONVOLUTION_2D** and name **GL_MAX_CONVOLUTION_HEIGHT**.

GL_INVALID_ENUM is generated if *format* is not one of the allowable values.

GL_INVALID_ENUM is generated if *type* is not one of the allowable values.

GL_INVALID_OPERATION is generated if **glConvolutionFilter2D** is executed between the execution of **glBegin** and the corresponding execution of **glEnd**.

GL_INVALID_OPERATION is generated if *height* is one of **GL_UNSIGNED_BYTE_3_3_2**, **GL_UNSIGNED_BYTE_2_3_3_REV**, **GL_UNSIGNED_SHORT_5_6_5**, or **GL_UNSIGNED_SHORT_5_6_5_REV** and *format* is not **GL_RGB**.

GL_INVALID_OPERATION is generated if *height* is one of **GL_UNSIGNED_SHORT_4_4_4_4**, **GL_UNSIGNED_SHORT_4_4_4_4_REV**, **GL_UNSIGNED_SHORT_5_5_5_1**, **GL_UNSIGNED_SHORT_1_5_5_5_REV**, **GL_UNSIGNED_INT_8_8_8_8**, **GL_UNSIGNED_INT_8_8_8_8_REV**, **GL_UNSIGNED_INT_10_10_10_2**, or **GL_UNSIGNED_INT_2_10_10_10_REV** and *format* is neither **GL_RGBA** nor **GL_BGRA**.

ASSOCIATED GETS

glGetConvolutionParameter, glGetConvolutionFilter

SEE ALSO

glConvolutionFilter1D, glSeparableFilter2D, glConvolutionParameter, glPixelTransfer

NAME

> **glConvolutionParameterf, glConvolutionParameteri, glConvolution-**
> **Parameterfv, glConvolutionParameteriv** – set convolution parameters

C SPECIFICATION

> void **glConvolutionParameterf**(GLenum *target*,
>   GLenum *pname*,
>   GLfloat *params*)
> void **glConvolutionParameteri**(GLenum *target*,
>   GLenum *pname*,
>   GLint *params*)

PARAMETERS

> *target* The target for the convolution parameter. Must be one of
> **GL_CONVOLUTION_1D**, **GL_CONVOLUTION_2D**, or **GL_SEPARABLE_2D**.
>
> *pname*
> The parameter to be set. Must be **GL_CONVOLUTION_BORDER_MODE**.
>
> *params*
> The parameter value. Must be one of **GL_REDUCE**,
> **GL_CONSTANT_BORDER**, **GL_REPLICATE_BORDER**.

C SPECIFICATION

> void **glConvolutionParameterfv**(GLenum *target*,
>   GLenum *pname*,
>   const GLfloat *params*)
> void **glConvolutionParameteriv**(GLenum *target*,
>   GLenum *pname*,
>   const GLint *params*)

PARAMETERS

> *target* The target for the convolution parameter. Must be one of
> **GL_CONVOLUTION_1D**, **GL_CONVOLUTION_2D**, or
> **GL_SEPARABLE_2D**.
>
> *pname* The parameter to be set. Must be one of
> **GL_CONVOLUTION_BORDER_MODE**,
> **GL_CONVOLUTION_BORDER_COLOR**,
> **GL_CONVOLUTION_FILTER_SCALE**, or
> **GL_CONVOLUTION_FILTER_BIAS**.

params The parameter value. If *pname* is **GL_CONVOLUTION_BORDER_MODE**, *params* must be one of **GL_REDUCE**, **GL_CONSTANT_BORDER**, or **GL_REPLICATE_BORDER**. Otherwise, must be a vector of four values (for red, green, blue, and alpha, respectively) to be used for scaling (when *pname* is **GL_CONVOLUTION_FILTER_SCALE**), or biasing (when *pname* is **GL_CONVOLUTION_FILTER_BIAS**) a convolution filter kernel or setting the constant border color (when *pname* is **GL_CONVOLUTION_BORDER_COLOR**.

DESCRIPTION

glConvolutionParameter sets the value of a convolution parameter.

target selects the convolution filter to be affected: **GL_CONVOLUTION_1D**, **GL_CONVOLUTION_2D**, or **GL_SEPARABLE_2D** for the 1D, 2D, or separable 2D filter, respectively.

pname selects the parameter to be changed. **GL_CONVOLUTION_FILTER_SCALE** and **GL_CONVOLUTION_FILTER_BIAS** affect the definition of the convolution filter kernel; see **glConvolutionFilter1D**, **glConvolutionFilter2D**, and **glSeparableFilter2D** for details. In these cases, *params* is an array of four values to be applied to red, green, blue, and alpha values, respectively. The initial value for **GL_CONVOLUTION_FILTER_SCALE** is (1, 1, 1, 1), and the initial value for **GL_CONVOLUTION_FILTER_BIAS** is (0, 0, 0, 0).

A *pname* value of **GL_CONVOLUTION_BORDER_MODE** controls the convolution border mode. The accepted modes are:

GL_REDUCE

The image resulting from convolution is smaller than the source image. If the filter width is Wf and height is Hf, and the source image width is Ws and height is Hs, then the convolved image width will be $Ws - Wf + 1$ and height will be $Hs - Hf + 1$. (If this reduction would generate an image with zero or negative width and/or height, the output is simply null, with no error generated.) The coordinates of the image resulting from convolution are zero through $Ws - Wf$ in width and zero through $Hs - Hf$ in height.

GL_CONSTANT_BORDER

The image resulting from convolution is the same size as the source image, and processed as if the source image were surrounded by pixels with their color specified by the **GL_CONVOLUTION_BORDER_COLOR**.

GL_REPLICATE_BORDER

The image resulting from convolution is the same size as the source image, and processed as if the outermost pixel on the border of the source image were replicated.

NOTES

glConvolutionParameter is present only if **GL_ARB_imaging** is returned when **glGetString** is called with an argument of **GL_EXTENSIONS**.

In cases where errors can result from the specification of invalid image dimensions, it is the dimensions after convolution that are tested, not the dimensions of the source image. For example, **glTexImage1D** requires power-of-two image size. When **GL_REDUCE** border mode is in effect, the source image must be larger than the final power-of-two size by one less than the size of the 1D filter kernel.

ERRORS

GL_INVALID_ENUM is generated if *target* is not one of the allowable values.

GL_INVALID_ENUM is generated if *pname* is not one of the allowable values.

GL_INVALID_ENUM is generated if *pname* is **GL_CONVOLUTION_BORDER_MODE** and *params* is not one of **GL_REDUCE**, **GL_CONSTANT_BORDER**, or **GL_REPLICATE_BORDER**.

GL_INVALID_OPERATION is generated if **glConvolutionParameter** is executed between the execution of **glBegin** and the corresponding execution of **glEnd**.

ASSOCIATED GETS

glGetConvolutionParameter

SEE ALSO

glConvolutionFilter1D, glConvolutionFilter2D, glSeparableFilter2D, glGetConvolutionParameter

NAME

glCopyColorSubTable – respecify a portion of a color table

C SPECIFICATION

void **glCopyColorSubTable**(GLenum *target*,
GLsizei *start*,
GLint *x*,
GLint *y*,
GLsizei *width*)

PARAMETERS

target Must be one of **GL_COLOR_TABLE**,
GL_POST_CONVOLUTION_COLOR_TABLE, or
GL_POST_COLOR_MATRIX_COLOR_TABLE.

start The starting index of the portion of the color table to be replaced.

x, y The window coordinates of the left corner of the row of pixels to be copied.

width The number of table entries to replace.

DESCRIPTION

glCopyColorSubTable is used to respecify a contiguous portion of a color table pre-viously defined using **glColorTable**. The pixels copied from the framebuffer replace the portion of the existing table from indices *start* to *start* + *x* − 1, inclusive. This region may not include any entries outside the range of the color table, as was origi-nally specified. It is not an error to specify a subtexture with width of 0, but such a specification has no effect.

NOTES

glCopyColorSubTable is present only if **GL_ARB_imaging** is returned when **glGetString** is called with an argument of **GL_EXTENSIONS**.

ERRORS

GL_INVALID_VALUE is generated if *target* is not a previously defined color table.

GL_INVALID_VALUE is generated if *target* is not one of the allowable values.

GL_INVALID_VALUE is generated if *start* + *x* > *width*.

GL_INVALID_OPERATION is generated if **glCopyColorSubTable** is executed between the execution of **glBegin** and the corresponding execution of **glEnd**.

ASSOCIATED GETS

glGetColorTable, glGetColorTableParameter

SEE ALSO

glColorSubTable, glColorTableParameter, glCopyColorTable,
glCopyColorSubTable, glGetColorTable

NAME

glCopyColorTable – copy pixels into a color table

C SPECIFICATION

void **glCopyColorTable**(GLenum *target*,
GLenum *internalformat*,
GLint *x*,
GLint *y*,
GLsizei *width*)

PARAMETERS

target   The color table target. Must be **GL_COLOR_TABLE**,
GL_POST_CONVOLUTION_COLOR_TABLE, or
GL_POST_COLOR_MATRIX_COLOR_TABLE.

internalformat

The internal storage format of the texture image. Must be one of the
following symbolic constants: **GL_ALPHA**, **GL_ALPHA4**,
GL_ALPHA8, **GL_ALPHA12**, **GL_ALPHA16**, **GL_LUMINANCE**,
GL_LUMINANCE4, **GL_LUMINANCE8**, **GL_LUMINANCE12**,
GL_LUMINANCE16, **GL_LUMINANCE_ALPHA**,
GL_LUMINANCE4_ALPHA4, **GL_LUMINANCE6_ALPHA2**,
GL_LUMINANCE8_ALPHA8, **GL_LUMINANCE12_ALPHA4**,
GL_LUMINANCE12_ALPHA12, **GL_LUMINANCE16_ALPHA16**,
GL_INTENSITY, **GL_INTENSITY4**, **GL_INTENSITY8**,
GL_INTENSITY12, **GL_INTENSITY16**, **GL_R3_G3_B2**, **GL_RGB**,
GL_RGB4, **GL_RGB5**, **GL_RGB8**, **GL_RGB10**, **GL_RGB12**, **GL_RGB16**,
GL_RGBA, **GL_RGBA2**, **GL_RGBA4**, **GL_RGB5_A1**, **GL_RGBA8**,
GL_RGB10_A2, **GL_RGBA12**, **GL_RGBA16**.

x   The x coordinate of the lower-left corner of the pixel rectangle to be
transferred to the color table.

y   The y coordinate of the lower-left corner of the pixel rectangle to be
transferred to the color table.

width   The width of the pixel rectangle.

DESCRIPTION

glCopyColorTable loads a color table with pixels from the current
GL_READ_BUFFER (rather than from main memory, as is the case for
glColorTable).

The screen-aligned pixel rectangle with lower-left corner at (x, y) having width *width* and height 1 is loaded into the color table. If any pixels within this region are outside the window that is associated with the GL context, the values obtained for those pixels are undefined.

The pixels in the rectangle are processed just as if **glReadPixels** were called, with *internalformat* set to RGBA, but processing stops after the final conversion to RGBA.

The four scale parameters and the four bias parameters that are defined for the table are then used to scale and bias the R, G, B, and A components of each pixel. The scale and bias parameters are set by calling **glColorTableParameter**.

Next, the R, G, B, and A values are clamped to the range [0,1]. Each pixel is then converted to the internal format specified by *internalformat*. This conversion simply maps the component values of the pixel (R, G, B, and A) to the values included in the internal format (red, green, blue, alpha, luminance, and intensity). The mapping is as follows:

Internal Format	Red	Green	Blue	Alpha	Luminance	Intensity
GL_ALPHA				A		
GL_LUMINANCE					R	
GL_LUMINANCE_ALPHA				A	R	
GL_INTENSITY						R
GL_RGB	R	G	B			
GL_RGBA	R	G	B	A		

Finally, the red, green, blue, alpha, luminance, and/or intensity components of the resulting pixels are stored in the color table. They form a one-dimensional table with indices in the range [0, *width* − 1].

NOTES

glCopyColorTable is available only if **GL_ARB_imaging** is returned from calling **glGetString** with an argument of **GL_EXTENSIONS**.

ERRORS

GL_INVALID_ENUM is generated when *target* is not one of the allowable values.

GL_INVALID_VALUE is generated if *width* is less than zero.

GL_INVALID_VALUE is generated if *internalformat* is not one of the allowable values.

GL_TABLE_TOO_LARGE is generated if the requested color table is too large to be supported by the implementation.

GL_INVALID_OPERATION is generated if **glCopyColorTable** is executed between the execution of **glBegin** and the corresponding execution of **glEnd**.

ASSOCIATED GETS

glGetColorTable, glGetColorTableParameter

SEE ALSO

glColorTable, glColorTableParameter, glReadPixels

NAME

glCopyConvolutionFilter1D – copy pixels into a one-dimensional convolution filter

C SPECIFICATION

void **glCopyConvolutionFilter1D**(GLenum *target*,
GLenum *internalformat*,
GLint *x*,
GLint *y*,
GLsizei *width*)

PARAMETERS

target   Must be **GL_CONVOLUTION_1D**.

internalformat

The internal format of the convolution filter kernel. The allowable values are **GL_ALPHA**, **GL_ALPHA4**, **GL_ALPHA8**, **GL_ALPHA12**, **GL_ALPHA16**, **GL_LUMINANCE**, **GL_LUMINANCE4**, **GL_LUMINANCE8**, **GL_LUMINANCE12**, **GL_LUMINANCE16**, **GL_LUMINANCE_ALPHA**, **GL_LUMINANCE4_ALPHA4**, **GL_LUMINANCE6_ALPHA2**, **GL_LUMINANCE8_ALPHA8**, **GL_LUMINANCE12_ALPHA4**, **GL_LUMINANCE12_ALPHA12**, **GL_LUMINANCE16_ALPHA16**, **GL_INTENSITY**, **GL_INTENSITY4**, **GL_INTENSITY8**, **GL_INTENSITY12**, **GL_INTENSITY16**, **GL_R3_G3_B2**, **GL_RGB**, **GL_RGB4**, **GL_RGB5**, **GL_RGB8**, **GL_RGB10**, **GL_RGB12**, **GL_RGB16**, **GL_RGBA**, **GL_RGBA2**, **GL_RGBA4**, **GL_RGB5_A1**, **GL_RGBA8**, **GL_RGB10_A2**, **GL_RGBA12**, or **GL_RGBA16**.

x, y   The window space coordinates of the lower-left coordinate of the pixel array to copy.

width   The width of the pixel array to copy.

DESCRIPTION

glCopyConvolutionFilter1D defines a one-dimensional convolution filter kernel with pixels from the current **GL_READ_BUFFER** (rather than from main memory, as is the case for **glConvolutionFilter1D**).

The screen-aligned pixel rectangle with lower-left corner at (*x*, *y*), width *width* and height 1 is used to define the convolution filter. If any pixels within this region are outside the window that is associated with the GL context, the values obtained for those pixels are undefined.

The pixels in the rectangle are processed exactly as if **glReadPixels** had been called with *format* set to RGBA, but the process stops just before final conversion. The R, G, B, and A components of each pixel are next scaled by the four 1D **GL_CONVOLUTION_FILTER_SCALE** parameters and biased by the four 1D **GL_CONVOLUTION_FILTER_BIAS** parameters. (The scale and bias parameters are set by **glConvolutionParameter** using the **GL_CONVOLUTION_1D** target and the names **GL_CONVOLUTION_FILTER_SCALE** and **GL_CONVOLUTION_FILTER_BIAS**. The parameters themselves are vectors of four values that are applied to red, green, blue, and alpha, in that order.) The R, G, B, and A values are not clamped to [0,1] at any time during this process.

Each pixel is then converted to the internal format specified by *internalformat*. This conversion simply maps the component values of the pixel (R, G, B, and A) to the values included in the internal format (red, green, blue, alpha, luminance, and intensity). The mapping is as follows:

Internal Format	Red	Green	Blue	Alpha	Luminance	Intensity
GL_ALPHA				A		
GL_LUMINANCE					R	
GL_LUMINANCE_ALPHA			A	R		
GL_INTENSITY						R
GL_RGB	R	G	B			
GL_RGBA	R	G	B	A		

The red, green, blue, alpha, luminance, and/or intensity components of the resulting pixels are stored in floating-point rather than integer format.

Pixel ordering is such that lower x screen coordinates correspond to lower *i* filter image coordinates.

Note that after a convolution is performed, the resulting color components are also scaled by their corresponding **GL_POST_CONVOLUTION_c_SCALE** parameters and biased by their corresponding **GL_POST_CONVOLUTION_c_BIAS** parameters (where *c* takes on the values **RED**, **GREEN**, **BLUE**, and **ALPHA**). These parameters are set by **glPixelTransfer**.

NOTES

glCopyConvolutionFilter1D is present only if **GL_ARB_imaging** is returned when **glGetString** is called with an argument of **GL_EXTENSIONS**.

ERRORS

GL_INVALID_ENUM is generated if *target* is not **GL_CONVOLUTION_1D**.

GL_INVALID_ENUM is generated if *internalformat* is not one of the allowable values.

GL_INVALID_VALUE is generated if *width* is less than zero or greater than the maximum supported value. This value may be queried with **glGetConvolutionParameter** using target **GL_CONVOLUTION_1D** and name **GL_MAX_CONVOLUTION_WIDTH**.

GL_INVALID_OPERATION is generated if **glCopyConvolutionFilter1D** is executed between the execution of **glBegin** and the corresponding execution of **glEnd**.

ASSOCIATED GETS

glGetConvolutionParameter, **glGetConvolutionFilter**

SEE ALSO

glConvolutionFilter1D, **glConvolutionParameter**, **glPixelTransfer**

NAME

glCopyConvolutionFilter2D – copy pixels into a two-dimensional convolution filter

C SPECIFICATION

void **glCopyConvolutionFilter2D**(GLenum *target*,
                                                  GLenum *internalformat*,
                                                  GLint *x*,
                                                  GLint *y*,
                                                  GLsizei *width*,
                                                  GLsizei *height*)

PARAMETERS

target   Must be **GL_CONVOLUTION_2D**.

internalformat

The internal format of the convolution filter kernel. The allowable values are **GL_ALPHA, GL_ALPHA4, GL_ALPHA8, GL_ALPHA12, GL_ALPHA16, GL_LUMINANCE, GL_LUMINANCE4, GL_LUMINANCE8, GL_LUMINANCE12, GL_LUMINANCE16, GL_LUMINANCE_ALPHA, GL_LUMINANCE4_ALPHA4, GL_LUMINANCE6_ALPHA2, GL_LUMINANCE8_ALPHA8, GL_LUMINANCE12_ALPHA4, GL_LUMINANCE12_ALPHA12, GL_LUMINANCE16_ALPHA16, GL_INTENSITY, GL_INTENSITY4, GL_INTENSITY8, GL_INTENSITY12, GL_INTENSITY16, GL_R3_G3_B2, GL_RGB, GL_RGB4, GL_RGB5, GL_RGB8, GL_RGB10, GL_RGB12, GL_RGB16, GL_RGBA, GL_RGBA2, GL_RGBA4, GL_RGB5_A1, GL_RGBA8, GL_RGB10_A2, GL_RGBA12,** or **GL_RGBA16.**

x, *y*   The window space coordinates of the lower-left coordinate of the pixel array to copy.

width   The width of the pixel array to copy.

height   The height of the pixel array to copy.

DESCRIPTION

glCopyConvolutionFilter2D defines a two-dimensional convolution filter kernel with pixels from the current **GL_READ_BUFFER** (rather than from main memory, as is the case for **glConvolutionFilter2D**).

The screen-aligned pixel rectangle with lower-left corner at (*x*, *y*), width *width* and height *height* is used to define the convolution filter. If any pixels within this region are outside the window that is associated with the GL context, the values obtained for those pixels are undefined.

The pixels in the rectangle are processed exactly as if **glReadPixels** had been called with *format* set to RGBA, but the process stops just before final conversion. The R, G, B, and A components of each pixel are next scaled by the four 2D GL_CONVOLUTION_FILTER_SCALE parameters and biased by the four 2D GL_CONVOLUTION_FILTER_BIAS parameters. (The scale and bias parameters are set by **glConvolutionParameter** using the GL_CONVOLUTION_2D target and the names **GL_CONVOLUTION_FILTER_SCALE** and **GL_CONVOLUTION_FILTER_BIAS**. The parameters themselves are vectors of four values that are applied to red, green, blue, and alpha, in that order.) The R, G, B, and A values are not clamped to [0,1] at any time during this process.

Each pixel is then converted to the internal format specified by *internalformat*. This conversion simply maps the component values of the pixel (R, G, B, and A) to the values included in the internal format (red, green, blue, alpha, luminance, and intensity). The mapping is as follows:

Internal Format	Red	Green	Blue	Alpha	Luminance	Intensity
GL_ALPHA				A		
GL_LUMINANCE				R		
GL_LUMINANCE_ALPHA			A	R		
GL_INTENSITY						R
GL_RGB	R	G	B			
GL_RGBA	R	G	B	A		

The red, green, blue, alpha, luminance, and/or intensity components of the resulting pixels are stored in floating-point rather than integer format.

Pixel ordering is such that lower x screen coordinates correspond to lower *i* filter image coordinates, and lower y screen coordinates correspond to lower *j* filter image coordinates.

Note that after a convolution is performed, the resulting color components are also scaled by their corresponding **GL_POST_CONVOLUTION_c_SCALE** parameters and biased by their corresponding **GL_POST_CONVOLUTION_c_BIAS** parameters (where *c* takes on the values **RED**, **GREEN**, **BLUE**, and **ALPHA**). These parameters are set by **glPixelTransfer**.

NOTES

glCopyConvolutionFilter2D is present only if **GL_ARB_imaging** is returned when **glGetString** is called with an argument of **GL_EXTENSIONS**.

ERRORS

GL_INVALID_ENUM is generated if *target* is not GL_CONVOLUTION_2D.

GL_INVALID_ENUM is generated if *internalformat* is not one of the allowable values.

GL_INVALID_VALUE is generated if *width* is less than zero or greater than the maximum supported value. This value may be queried with **glGetConvolutionParameter** using target GL_CONVOLUTION_2D and name GL_MAX_CONVOLUTION_WIDTH.

GL_INVALID_VALUE is generated if *height* is less than zero or greater than the maximum supported value. This value may be queried with **glGetConvolutionParameter** using target GL_CONVOLUTION_2D and name GL_MAX_CONVOLUTION_HEIGHT.

GL_INVALID_OPERATION is generated if **glCopyConvolutionFilter2D** is executed between the execution of **glBegin** and the corresponding execution of **glEnd**.

ASSOCIATED GETS

glGetConvolutionParameter, glGetConvolutionFilter

SEE ALSO

glConvolutionFilter2D, glConvolutionParameter, glPixelTransfer

NAME

glCopyPixels – copy pixels in the frame buffer

C SPECIFICATION

void **glCopyPixels**(GLint *x*,
GLint *y*,
GLsizei *width*,
GLsizei *height*,
GLenum *type*)

PARAMETERS

x, y

Specify the window coordinates of the lower left corner of the rectangular region of pixels to be copied.

width, height

Specify the dimensions of the rectangular region of pixels to be copied. Both must be nonnegative.

type

Specifies whether color values, depth values, or stencil values are to be copied. Symbolic constants **GL_COLOR**, **GL_DEPTH**, and **GL_STENCIL** are accepted.

DESCRIPTION

glCopyPixels copies a screen-aligned rectangle of pixels from the specified frame buffer location to a region relative to the current raster position. Its operation is well defined only if the entire pixel source region is within the exposed portion of the window. Results of copies from outside the window, or from regions of the window that are not exposed, are hardware dependent and undefined.

x and *y* specify the window coordinates of the lower left corner of the rectangular region to be copied. *width* and *height* specify the dimensions of the rectangular region to be copied. Both *width* and *height* must not be negative.

Several parameters control the processing of the pixel data while it is being copied. These parameters are set with three commands: **glPixelTransfer**, **glPixelMap**, and **glPixelZoom**. This reference page describes the effects on **glCopyPixels** of most, but not all, of the parameters specified by these three commands.

glCopyPixels copies values from each pixel with the lower left-hand corner at ($x + i$, $y + j$) for $0 \leq i < width$ and $0 \leq j < height$. This pixel is said to be the *i*th pixel in the *j*th row. Pixels are copied in row order from the lowest to the highest row, left to right in each row.

type specifies whether color, depth, or stencil data is to be copied. The details of the transfer for each data type are as follows:

GL_COLOR   Indices or RGBA colors are read from the buffer currently specified as the read source buffer (see **glReadBuffer**). If the GL is in color index mode, each index that is read from this buffer is converted to a fixed-point format with an unspecified number of bits to the right of the binary point. Each index is then shifted left by **GL_INDEX_SHIFT** bits, and added to **GL_INDEX_OFFSET**. If **GL_INDEX_SHIFT** is negative, the shift is to the right. In either case, zero bits fill otherwise unspecified bit locations in the result. If **GL_MAP_COLOR** is true, the index is replaced with the value that it references in lookup table **GL_PIXEL_MAP_I_TO_I**. Whether the lookup replacement of the index is done or not, the integer part of the index is then ANDed with 2^b-1, where b is the number of bits in a color index buffer.

If the GL is in RGBA mode, the red, green, blue, and alpha components of each pixel that is read are converted to an internal floating-point format with unspecified precision. The conversion maps the largest representable component value to 1.0, and component value 0 to 0.0. The resulting floating-point color values are then multiplied by **GL_c_SCALE** and added to **GL_c_BIAS**, where c is RED, GREEN, BLUE, and ALPHA for the respective color components. The results are clamped to the range [0,1]. If **GL_MAP_COLOR** is true, each color component is scaled by the size of lookup table **GL_PIXEL_MAP_c_TO_c**, then replaced by the value that it references in that table. c is R, G, B, or A.

If the **GL_ARB_imaging** extension is supported, the color values may be additionally processed by color-table lookups, color-matrix transformations, and convolution filters.

The GL then converts the resulting indices or RGBA colors to fragments by attaching the current raster position z coordinate and texture coordinates to each pixel, then assigning window coordinates $(x_r + i, y_r + j)$, where (x_r, y_r) is the current raster position, and the pixel was the ith pixel in the jth row. These pixel fragments are then treated just like the fragments generated by rasterizing points, lines, or polygons. Texture mapping, fog, and all the fragment operations are applied before the fragments are written to the frame buffer.

GL_DEPTH   Depth values are read from the depth buffer and converted directly to an internal floating-point format with unspecified precision. The resulting floating-point depth value is then multiplied by **GL_DEPTH_SCALE** and added to **GL_DEPTH_BIAS**. The result is clamped to the range [0,1].

The GL then converts the resulting depth components to fragments by attaching the current raster position color or color index and texture coordinates to each pixel, then assigning window coordinates $(x_r + i, y_r + j)$, where (x_r, y_r) is the current raster position, and the pixel was the ith pixel in the jth row. These pixel fragments are then treated just like the fragments generated by rasterizing points, lines, or polygons. Texture mapping, fog, and all the fragment operations are applied before the fragments are written to the frame buffer.

GL_STENCIL   Stencil indices are read from the stencil buffer and converted to an internal fixed-point format with an unspecified number of bits to the right of the binary point. Each fixed-point index is then shifted left by **GL_INDEX_SHIFT** bits, and added to **GL_INDEX_OFFSET**. If **GL_INDEX_SHIFT** is negative, the shift is to the right. In either case, zero bits fill otherwise unspecified bit locations in the result. If **GL_MAP_STENCIL** is true, the index is replaced with the value that it references in lookup table **GL_PIXEL_MAP_S_TO_S**. Whether the lookup replacement of the index is done or not, the integer part of the index is then ANDed with $2^b - 1$, where b is the number of bits in the stencil buffer. The resulting stencil indices are then written to the stencil buffer such that the index read from the ith location of the jth row is written to location $(x_r + i, y_r + j)$, where (x_r, y_r) is the current raster position. Only the pixel ownership test, the scissor test, and the stencil writemask affect these write operations.

The rasterization described thus far assumes pixel zoom factors of 1.0. If **glPixelZoom** is used to change the x and y pixel zoom factors, pixels are converted to fragments as follows. If (x_r, y_r) is the current raster position, and a given pixel is in the ith location in the jth row of the source pixel rectangle, then fragments are generated for pixels whose centers are in the rectangle with corners at

$$(x_r + zoom_x\, i,\ y_r + zoom_y\, j)$$

and

$$(x_r + zoom_x\,(i + 1),\ y_r + zoom_y\,(j + 1))$$

where *zoom*$_x$ is the value of **GL_ZOOM_X** and *zoom*$_y$ is the value of **GL_ZOOM_Y**.

EXAMPLES

To copy the color pixel in the lower left corner of the window to the current raster position, use

```
glCopyPixels(0, 0, 1, 1, GL_COLOR);
```

NOTES

Modes specified by **glPixelStore** have no effect on the operation of **glCopyPixels**.

ERRORS

GL_INVALID_ENUM is generated if *type* is not an accepted value.

GL_INVALID_VALUE is generated if either *width* or *height* is negative.

GL_INVALID_OPERATION is generated if *type* is **GL_DEPTH** and there is no depth buffer.

GL_INVALID_OPERATION is generated if *type* is **GL_STENCIL** and there is no stencil buffer.

GL_INVALID_OPERATION is generated if **glCopyPixels** is executed between the execution of **glBegin** and the corresponding execution of **glEnd**.

ASSOCIATED GETS

glGet with argument GL_CURRENT_RASTER_POSITION
glGet with argument GL_CURRENT_RASTER_POSITION_VALID

SEE ALSO

glColorTable, **glConvolutionFilter1D**, **glConvolutionFilter2D**, **glDepthFunc**, **glDrawBuffer**, **glDrawPixels**, **glMatrixMode**, **glPixelMap**, **glPixelTransfer**, **glPixelZoom**, **glRasterPos**, **glReadBuffer**, **glReadPixels**, **glSeparableFilter2D**, **glStencilFunc**

NAME

glCopyTexImage1D – copy pixels into a 1D texture image

C SPECIFICATION

void **glCopyTexImage1D**(GLenum *target*,
                    GLint *level*,
                    GLenum *internalformat*,
                    GLint *x*,
                    GLint *y*,
                    GLsizei *width*,
                    GLint *border*)

PARAMETERS

target   Specifies the target texture. Must be **GL_TEXTURE_1D**.

level   Specifies the level-of-detail number. Level 0 is the base image level.
Level *n* is the *n*th mipmap reduction image.

internalformat

Specifies the internal format of the texture. Must be one of the follow-
ing symbolic constants: **GL_ALPHA, GL_ALPHA4, GL_ALPHA8,
GL_ALPHA12, GL_ALPHA16, GL_LUMINANCE, GL_LUMINANCE4,
GL_LUMINANCE8, GL_LUMINANCE12, GL_LUMINANCE16,
GL_LUMINANCE_ALPHA, GL_LUMINANCE4_ALPHA4,
GL_LUMINANCE6_ALPHA2, GL_LUMINANCE8_ALPHA8,
GL_LUMINANCE12_ALPHA4, GL_LUMINANCE12_ALPHA12,
GL_LUMINANCE16_ALPHA16, GL_INTENSITY, GL_INTENSITY4,
GL_INTENSITY8, GL_INTENSITY12, GL_INTENSITY16, GL_RGB,
GL_R3_G3_B2, GL_RGB4, GL_RGB5, GL_RGB8, GL_RGB10,
GL_RGB12, GL_RGB16, GL_RGBA, GL_RGBA2, GL_RGBA4,
GL_RGB5_A1, GL_RGBA8, GL_RGB10_A2, GL_RGBA12,** or
GL_RGBA16.

x, y   Specify the window coordinates of the left corner of the row of pixels
to be copied.

width   Specifies the width of the texture image. Must be 0 or $2^n + 2 \ast border$ for
some integer *n*. The height of the texture image is 1.

border   Specifies the width of the border. Must be either 0 or 1.

DESCRIPTION

glCopyTexImage1D defines a one-dimensional texture image with pixels from the
current **GL_READ_BUFFER**.

The screen-aligned pixel row with left corner at (x, y) and with a length of *width* + 2 * *border* defines the texture array at the mipmap level specified by *level*. *internalformat* specifies the internal format of the texture array.

The pixels in the row are processed exactly as if **glCopyPixels** had been called, but the process stops just before final conversion. At this point all pixel component values are clamped to the range [0, 1] and then converted to the texture's internal format for storage in the texel array.

Pixel ordering is such that lower x screen coordinates correspond to lower texture coordinates.

If any of the pixels within the specified row of the current **GL_READ_BUFFER** are outside the window associated with the current rendering context, then the values obtained for those pixels are undefined.

NOTES

glCopyTexImage1D is available only if the GL version is 1.1 or greater.

Texturing has no effect in color index mode.

1, 2, 3, and 4 are not accepted values for *internalformat*.

An image with 0 width indicates a NULL texture.

When the **GL_ARB_imaging** extension is supported, the RGBA components copied from the framebuffer may be processed by the imaging pipeline. See **glTexImage1D** for specific details.

ERRORS

GL_INVALID_ENUM is generated if *target* is not one of the allowable values.

GL_INVALID_VALUE is generated if *level* is less than 0.

GL_INVALID_VALUE may be generated if *level* is greater than $\log_2$ max, where max is the returned value of **GL_MAX_TEXTURE_SIZE**.

GL_INVALID_VALUE is generated if *internalformat* is not an allowable value.

GL_INVALID_VALUE is generated if *width* is less than 0 or greater than 2 + **GL_MAX_TEXTURE_SIZE**, or if it cannot be represented as $2^n + 2 *$ (*border*) for some integer value of n.

GL_INVALID_VALUE is generated if *border* is not 0 or 1.

GL_INVALID_OPERATION is generated if **glCopyTexImage1D** is executed between the execution of **glBegin** and the corresponding execution of **glEnd**.

ASSOCIATED GETS

glGetTexImage

glIsEnabled with argument **GL_TEXTURE_1D**

SEE ALSO

glCopyPixels, glCopyTexImage2D, glCopyTexSubImage1D,
glCopyTexSubImage2D, glPixelStore, glPixelTransfer, glTexEnv, glTexGen,
glTexImage1D, glTexImage2D, glTexSubImage1D, glTexSubImage2D,
glTexParameter

NAME

glCopyTexImage2D – copy pixels into a 2D texture image

C SPECIFICATION

void **glCopyTexImage2D**(GLenum *target*,
                          GLint *level*,
                          GLenum *internalformat*,
                          GLint *x*,
                          GLint *y*,
                          GLsizei *width*,
                          GLsizei *height*,
                          GLint *border*)

PARAMETERS

target   Specifies the target texture. Must be **GL_TEXTURE_2D**.

level   Specifies the level-of-detail number. Level 0 is the base image level.
Level *n* is the *n*th mipmap reduction image.

internalformat

Specifies the internal format of the texture. Must be one of the follow-
ing symbolic constants: **GL_ALPHA**, **GL_ALPHA4**, **GL_ALPHA8**,
GL_ALPHA12, **GL_ALPHA16**, **GL_LUMINANCE**, **GL_LUMINANCE4**,
GL_LUMINANCE8, **GL_LUMINANCE12**, **GL_LUMINANCE16**,
GL_LUMINANCE_ALPHA, **GL_LUMINANCE4_ALPHA4**,
GL_LUMINANCE6_ALPHA2, **GL_LUMINANCE8_ALPHA8**,
GL_LUMINANCE12_ALPHA4, **GL_LUMINANCE12_ALPHA12**,
GL_LUMINANCE16_ALPHA16, **GL_INTENSITY**, **GL_INTENSITY4**,
GL_INTENSITY8, **GL_INTENSITY12**, **GL_INTENSITY16**, **GL_RGB**,
GL_R3_G3_B2, **GL_RGB4**, **GL_RGB5**, **GL_RGB8**, **GL_RGB10**,
GL_RGB12, **GL_RGB16**, **GL_RGBA**, **GL_RGBA2**, **GL_RGBA4**,
GL_RGB5_A1, **GL_RGBA8**, **GL_RGB10_A2**, **GL_RGBA12**, or
GL_RGBA16.

x, y   Specify the window coordinates of the lower left corner of the rectangular region of pixels to be copied.

width   Specifies the width of the texture image. Must be 0 or $2^n + 2*border$ for
some integer *n*.

height   Specifies the height of the texture image. Must be 0 or $2^m + 2*border$
for some integer *m*.

border   Specifies the width of the border. Must be either 0 or 1.

DESCRIPTION

glCopyTexImage2D defines a two-dimensional texture image with pixels from the current **GL_READ_BUFFER**.

The screen-aligned pixel rectangle with lower left corner at (x, y) and with a width of *width* + 2 * *border* and a height of *height* + 2 * *border* defines the texture array at the mipmap level specified by *level*. *internalformat* specifies the internal format of the texture array.

The pixels in the rectangle are processed exactly as if **glCopyPixels** had been called, but the process stops just before final conversion. At this point all pixel component values are clamped to the range $[0, 1]$ and then converted to the texture's internal format for storage in the texel array.

Pixel ordering is such that lower x and y screen coordinates correspond to lower s and t texture coordinates.

If any of the pixels within the specified rectangle of the current **GL_READ_BUFFER** are outside the window associated with the current rendering context, then the values obtained for those pixels are undefined.

NOTES

glCopyTexImage2D is available only if the GL version is 1.1 or greater.

Texturing has no effect in color index mode.

1, 2, 3, and 4 are not accepted values for *internalformat*.

An image with height or width of 0 indicates a NULL texture.

When the **GL_ARB_imaging** extension is supported, the RGBA components read from the framebuffer may be processed by the imaging pipeline. See **glTexImage1D** for specific details.

ERRORS

GL_INVALID_ENUM is generated if *target* is not **GL_TEXTURE_2D**.

GL_INVALID_VALUE is generated if *level* is less than 0.

GL_INVALID_VALUE may be generated if *level* is greater than $\log_2$max, where max is the returned value of **GL_MAX_TEXTURE_SIZE**.

GL_INVALID_VALUE is generated if *width* or *height* is less than 0, greater than 2 + **GL_MAX_TEXTURE_SIZE**, or if *width* or *height* cannot be represented as $2^k + 2$ * *border* for some integer k.

GL_INVALID_VALUE is generated if *border* is not 0 or 1.

GL_INVALID_VALUE is generated if *internalformat* is not one of the allowable values.

GL_INVALID_OPERATION is generated if **glCopyTexImage2D** is executed between the execution of **glBegin** and the corresponding execution of **glEnd**.

ASSOCIATED GETS

glGetTexImage
glIsEnabled with argument GL_TEXTURE_2D

SEE ALSO

glCopyPixels, glCopyTexImage1D, glCopyTexSubImage1D, glCopyTexSubImage2D, glPixelStore, glPixelTransfer, glTexEnv, glTexGen, glTexImage1D, glTexImage2D, glTexSubImage1D, glTexSubImage2D, glTexParameter

NAME

      glCopyTexSubImage1D – copy a one-dimensional texture subimage

C SPECIFICATION

      void **glCopyTexSubImage1D**(GLenum *target*,
                            GLint *level*,
                            GLint *xoffset*,
                            GLint *x*,
                            GLint *y*,
                            GLsizei *width*)

PARAMETERS

target   Specifies the target texture. Must be **GL_TEXTURE_1D**.

level   Specifies the level-of-detail number. Level 0 is the base image level. Level *n* is the *n*th mipmap reduction image.

xoffset Specifies the texel offset within the texture array.

x, y   Specify the window coordinates of the left corner of the row of pixels to be copied.

width   Specifies the width of the texture subimage.

DESCRIPTION

glCopyTexSubImage1D replaces a portion of a one-dimensional texture image with pixels from the current **GL_READ_BUFFER** (rather than from main memory, as is the case for **glTexSubImage1D**).

The screen-aligned pixel row with left corner at (*x, y*), and with length *width* replaces the portion of the texture array with x indices *xoffset* through *xoffset* + *width* – 1, inclusive. The destination in the texture array may not include any texels outside the texture array as it was originally specified.

The pixels in the row are processed exactly as if **glCopyPixels** had been called, but the process stops just before final conversion. At this point all pixel component values are clamped to the range [0, 1] and then converted to the texture's internal format for storage in the texel array.

It is not an error to specify a subtexture with zero width, but such a specification has no effect. If any of the pixels within the specified row of the current **GL_READ_BUFFER** are outside the read window associated with the current rendering context, then the values obtained for those pixels are undefined.

No change is made to the *internalformat*, *width*, or *border* parameters of the specified texture array or to texel values outside the specified subregion.

NOTES

glCopyTexSubImage1D is available only if the GL version is 1.1 or greater.

Texturing has no effect in color index mode.

glPixelStore and **glPixelTransfer** modes affect texture images in exactly the way they affect **glDrawPixels**.

When the **GL_ARB_imaging** extension is supported, the RGBA components copied from the framebuffer may be processed by the imaging pipeline. See **glTexImage1D** for specific details.

ERRORS

GL_INVALID_ENUM is generated if *target* is not **GL_TEXTURE_1D**.

GL_INVALID_OPERATION is generated if the texture array has not been defined by a previous **glTexImage1D** or **glCopyTexImage1D** operation.

GL_INVALID_VALUE is generated if *level* is less than 0.

GL_INVALID_VALUE may be generated if $level > \log_2 max$, where *max* is the returned value of **GL_MAX_TEXTURE_SIZE**.

GL_INVALID_VALUE is generated if *xoffset* $< -b$, or (*xoffset* + *width*) $> (w-b)$, where *w* is the **GL_TEXTURE_WIDTH**, and *b* is the **GL_TEXTURE_BORDER** of the texture image being modified. Note that *w* includes twice the border width.

ASSOCIATED GETS

glGetTexImage
glIsEnabled with argument **GL_TEXTURE_1D**

SEE ALSO

glCopyPixels, **glCopyTexImage1D**, **glCopyTexImage2D**, **glCopyTexSubImage2D**, **glCopyTexSubImage3D**, **glPixelStore**, **glPixelTransfer**, **glReadBuffer**, **glTexEnv**, **glTexGen**, **glTexImage1D**, **glTexImage2D**, **glTexImage3D**, **glTexParameter**, **glTexSubImage1D**, **glTexSubImage2D**, **glTexSubImage3D**

NAME

glCopyTexSubImage2D – copy a two-dimensional texture subimage

C SPECIFICATION

void **glCopyTexSubImage2D**(GLenum *target*,
                              GLint *level*,
                              GLint *xoffset*,
                              GLint *yoffset*,
                              GLint *x*,
                              GLint *y*,
                              GLsizei *width*,
                              GLsizei *height*)

PARAMETERS

target Specifies the target texture. Must be **GL_TEXTURE_2D**.

level Specifies the level-of-detail number. Level 0 is the base image level. Level *n* is the *n*th mipmap reduction image.

xoffset Specifies a texel offset in the x direction within the texture array.

yoffset Specifies a texel offset in the y direction within the texture array.

x, y Specify the window coordinates of the lower left corner of the rectangular region of pixels to be copied.

width Specifies the width of the texture subimage.

height Specifies the height of the texture subimage.

DESCRIPTION

glCopyTexSubImage2D replaces a rectangular portion of a two-dimensional texture image with pixels from the current **GL_READ_BUFFER** (rather than from main memory, as is the case for **glTexSubImage2D**).

The screen-aligned pixel rectangle with lower left corner at (*x*, *y*) and with width *width* and height *height* replaces the portion of the texture array with x indices *xoffset* through *xoffset* + *width* − 1, inclusive, and y indices *yoffset* through *yoffset* + *height* − 1, inclusive, at the mipmap level specified by *level*.

The pixels in the rectangle are processed exactly as if **glCopyPixels** had been called, but the process stops just before final conversion. At this point, all pixel component values are clamped to the range [0, 1] and then converted to the texture's internal format for storage in the texel array.

The destination rectangle in the texture array may not include any texels outside the texture array as it was originally specified. It is not an error to specify a subtexture with zero width or height, but such a specification has no effect.

If any of the pixels within the specified rectangle of the current **GL_READ_BUFFER** are outside the read window associated with the current rendering context, then the values obtained for those pixels are undefined.

No change is made to the *internalformat*, *width*, *height*, or *border* parameters of the specified texture array or to texel values outside the specified subregion.

NOTES

glCopyTexSubImage2D is available only if the GL version is 1.1 or greater.

Texturing has no effect in color index mode.

glPixelStore and **glPixelTransfer** modes affect texture images in exactly the way they affect **glDrawPixels**.

When the **GL_ARB_imaging** extension is supported, the RGBA components read from the framebuffer may be processed by the imaging pipeline. See **glTexImage1D** for specific details.

ERRORS

GL_INVALID_ENUM is generated if *target* is not **GL_TEXTURE_2D**.

GL_INVALID_OPERATION is generated if the texture array has not been defined by a previous **glTexImage2D** or **glCopyTexImage2D** operation.

GL_INVALID_VALUE is generated if *level* is less than 0.

GL_INVALID_VALUE may be generated if $level > \log_2 max$, where *max* is the returned value of **GL_MAX_TEXTURE_SIZE**.

GL_INVALID_VALUE is generated if $xoffset < -b$, $(xoffset + width) > (w - b)$, $yoffset < -b$, or $(yoffset + height) > (h - b)$, where *w* is the **GL_TEXTURE_WIDTH**, *h* is the **GL_TEXTURE_HEIGHT**, and *b* is the **GL_TEXTURE_BORDER** of the texture image being modified. Note that *w* and *h* include twice the border width.

GL_INVALID_OPERATION is generated if **glCopyTexSubImage2D** is executed between the execution of **glBegin** and the corresponding execution of **glEnd**.

ASSOCIATED GETS

glGetTexImage
glIsEnabled with argument GL_TEXTURE_2D

SEE ALSO

glCopyPixels, glCopyTexImage1D, glCopyTexImage2D, glCopyTexSubImage1D, glCopyTexSubImage3D, glPixelStore, glPixelTransfer, glReadBuffer, glTexEnv, glTexGen, glTexImage1D, glTexImage2D, glTexImage3D, glTexParameter, glTexSubImage1D, glTexSubImage2D, glTexSubImage3D

SEE ALSO

glCopyPixels, glCopyTexImage1D, glCopyTexImage2D, glCopyTexSubImage1D, glCopyTexSubImage3D, glPixelStore, glPixelTransfer, glReadBuffer, glTexEnv, glTexGen, glTexImage1D, glTexImage2D, glTexImage3D, glTexParameter, glTexSubImage1D, glTexSubImage2D, glTexSubImage3D

NAME

glCopyTexSubImage3D – copy a three-dimensional texture subimage

C SPECIFICATION

void **glCopyTexSubImage3D**(GLenum *target*,
 GLint *level*,
 GLint *xoffset*,
 GLint *yoffset*,
 GLint *zoffset*,
 GLint *x*,
 GLint *y*,
 GLsizei *width*,
 GLsizei *height*)

PARAMETERS

target Specifies the target texture. Must be **GL_TEXTURE_3D**

level Specifies the level-of-detail number. Level 0 is the base image level. Level *n* is the *n*th mipmap reduction image.

xoffset Specifies a texel offset in the x direction within the texture array.

yoffset Specifies a texel offset in the y direction within the texture array.

zoffset Specifies a texel offset in the z direction within the texture array.

x, y Specify the window coordinates of the lower left corner of the rectangular region of pixels to be copied.

width Specifies the width of the texture subimage.

height Specifies the height of the texture subimage.

DESCRIPTION

glCopyTexSubImage3D replaces a rectangular portion of a three-dimensional texture image with pixels from the current **GL_READ_BUFFER** (rather than from main memory, as is the case for **glTexSubImage3D**).

The screen-aligned pixel rectangle with lower left corner at (*x, y*) and with width *width* and height *height* replaces the portion of the texture array with x indices *xoffset* through *xoffset* + *width* − 1, inclusive, and y indices *yoffset* through *yoffset* + *height* − 1, inclusive, at z index *zoffset* and at the mipmap level specified by *level*.

The pixels in the rectangle are processed exactly as if **glCopyPixels** had been called, but the process stops just before final conversion. At this point, all pixel component values are clamped to the range [0, 1] and then converted to the texture's internal format for storage in the texel array.

The destination rectangle in the texture array may not include any texels outside the texture array as it was originally specified. It is not an error to specify a subtexture with zero width or height, but such a specification has no effect.

If any of the pixels within the specified rectangle of the current **GL_READ_BUFFER** are outside the read window associated with the current rendering context, then the values obtained for those pixels are undefined.

No change is made to the *internalformat*, *width*, *height*, *depth*, or *border* parameters of the specified texture array or to texel values outside the specified subregion.

NOTES

glCopyTexSubImage3D is available only if the GL version is 1.2 or greater.

Texturing has no effect in color index mode.

glPixelStore and **glPixelTransfer** modes affect texture images in exactly the way they affect **glDrawPixels**.

When the **GL_ARB_imaging** extension is supported, the RGBA components copied from the framebuffer may be processed by the imaging pipeline, as if they were a two-dimensional texture. See **glTexImage2D** for specific details.

ERRORS

GL_INVALID_ENUM is generated if *target* is not **GL_TEXTURE_3D**.

GL_INVALID_OPERATION is generated if the texture array has not been defined by a previous **glTexImage3D** or **glCopyTexImage3D** operation.

GL_INVALID_VALUE is generated if *level* is less than 0.

GL_INVALID_VALUE may be generated if *level* > $\log_2$ *max* where *max* is the returned value of **GL_MAX_3D_TEXTURE_SIZE**.

GL_INVALID_VALUE is generated if *xoffset* < −*b*, (*xoffset* + *width*) > (*w* − *b*), *yoffset* < −*b*, (*yoffset* + *height*) > (*h* − *b*), *zoffset* < −*b*, or *zoffset* > (*d* − *b*), where *w* is the **GL_TEXTURE_WIDTH**, *h* is the **GL_TEXTURE_HEIGHT**, *d* is the **GL_TEXTURE_DEPTH**, and *b* is the **GL_TEXTURE_BORDER** of the texture image being modified. Note that *w*, *h*, and *d* include twice the border width.

GL_INVALID_OPERATION is generated if **glCopyTexSubImage3D** is executed between the execution of **glBegin** and the corresponding execution of **glEnd**.

ASSOCIATED GETS

glGetTexImage
glIsEnabled with argument GL_TEXTURE_3D

SEE ALSO

glCopyPixels, glCopyTexImage1D, glCopyTexImage2D, glCopyTexSubImage1D, glCopyTexSubImage2D, glPixelStore, glPixelTransfer, glReadBuffer, glTexEnv, glTexGen, glTexImage1D, glTexImage2D, glTexImage3D, glTexParameter.

SEE ALSO

glCopyPixels, glCopyTexImage1D, glCopyTexImage2D, glCopyTexSubImage1D, glCopyTexSubImage2D, glPixelStore, glPixelTransfer, glReadBuffer, glTexEnv, glTexGen, glTexImage1D, glTexImage2D, glTexImage3D, glTexParameter, glTexSubImage1D, glTexSubImage2D, glTexSubImage3D

NAME

glCullFace – specify whether front- or back-facing facets can be culled

C SPECIFICATION

void **glCullFace**(GLenum *mode*)

PARAMETERS

mode   Specifies whether front- or back-facing facets are candidates for culling. Symbolic constants **GL_FRONT**, **GL_BACK**, and **GL_FRONT_AND_BACK** are accepted. The initial value is **GL_BACK**.

DESCRIPTION

glCullFace specifies whether front- or back-facing facets are culled (as specified by *mode*) when facet culling is enabled. Facet culling is initially disabled. To enable and disable facet culling, call the **glEnable** and **glDisable** commands with the argument **GL_CULL_FACE**. Facets include triangles, quadrilaterals, polygons, and rectangles.

glFrontFace specifies which of the clockwise and counterclockwise facets are front-facing and back-facing. See **glFrontFace**.

NOTES

If *mode* is **GL_FRONT_AND_BACK**, no facets are drawn, but other primitives such as points and lines are drawn.

ERRORS

GL_INVALID_ENUM is generated if *mode* is not an accepted value.

GL_INVALID_OPERATION is generated if **glCullFace** is executed between the execution of **glBegin** and the corresponding execution of **glEnd**.

ASSOCIATED GETS

glIsEnabled with argument **GL_CULL_FACE**
glGet with argument **GL_CULL_FACE_MODE**

SEE ALSO

glEnable, **glFrontFace**

NAME

    glDeleteLists – delete a contiguous group of display lists

C SPECIFICATION

    void **glDeleteLists**(GLuint *list*,
                            GLsizei *range*)

PARAMETERS

    list   Specifies the integer name of the first display list to delete.

    range Specifies the number of display lists to delete.

DESCRIPTION

    glDeleteLists causes a contiguous group of display lists to be deleted. *list* is the
    name of the first display list to be deleted, and *range* is the number of display lists to
    delete. All display lists d with $list \leq d \leq list + range - 1$ are deleted.

    All storage locations allocated to the specified display lists are freed, and the names
    are available for reuse at a later time. Names within the range that do not have an
    associated display list are ignored. If *range* is 0, nothing happens.

ERRORS

    GL_INVALID_VALUE is generated if *range* is negative.

    GL_INVALID_OPERATION is generated if **glDeleteLists** is executed between the
    execution of **glBegin** and the corresponding execution of **glEnd**.

SEE ALSO

    glCallList, **glCallLists**, **glGenLists**, **glIsList**, **glNewList**

NAME

glDeleteTextures – delete named textures

C SPECIFICATION

void **glDeleteTextures**(GLsizei *n*,
                                    const GLuint **textures*)

PARAMETERS

n   Specifies the number of textures to be deleted.

textures Specifies an array of textures to be deleted.

DESCRIPTION

glDeleteTextures deletes *n* textures named by the elements of the array *textures*. After a texture is deleted, it has no contents or dimensionality, and its name is free for reuse (for example by **glGenTextures**). If a texture that is currently bound is deleted, the binding reverts to 0 (the default texture).

glDeleteTextures silently ignores 0's and names that do not correspond to existing textures.

NOTES

glDeleteTextures is available only if the GL version is 1.1 or greater.

ERRORS

GL_INVALID_VALUE is generated if *n* is negative.

GL_INVALID_OPERATION is generated if **glDeleteTextures** is executed between the execution of **glBegin** and the corresponding execution of **glEnd**.

ASSOCIATED GETS

glIsTexture

SEE ALSO

glAreTexturesResident, **glBindTexture**, **glCopyTexImage1D**, **glCopyTexImage2D**, **glGenTextures**, **glGet**, **glGetTexParameter**, **glPrioritizeTextures**, **glTexImage1D**, **glTexImage2D**, **glTexParameter**

NAME

glDepthFunc – specify the value used for depth buffer comparisons

C SPECIFICATION

void **glDepthFunc**(GLenum *func*)

PARAMETERS

func Specifies the depth comparison function. Symbolic constants **GL_NEVER**, **GL_LESS**, **GL_EQUAL**, **GL_LEQUAL**, **GL_GREATER**, **GL_NOTEQUAL**, **GL_GEQUAL**, and **GL_ALWAYS** are accepted. The initial value is **GL_LESS**.

DESCRIPTION

glDepthFunc specifies the function used to compare each incoming pixel depth value with the depth value present in the depth buffer. The comparison is performed only if depth testing is enabled. (See **glEnable** and **glDisable** of **GL_DEPTH_TEST**.)

func specifies the conditions under which the pixel will be drawn. The comparison functions are as follows:

GL_NEVER Never passes.

GL_LESS Passes if the incoming depth value is less than the stored depth value.

GL_EQUAL Passes if the incoming depth value is equal to the stored depth value.

GL_LEQUAL Passes if the incoming depth value is less than or equal to the stored depth value.

GL_GREATER Passes if the incoming depth value is greater than the stored depth value.

GL_NOTEQUAL

Passes if the incoming depth value is not equal to the stored depth value.

GL_GEQUAL Passes if the incoming depth value is greater than or equal to the stored depth value.

GL_ALWAYS Always passes.

The initial value of *func* is **GL_LESS**. Initially, depth testing is disabled. Even if the depth buffer exists and the depth mask is non-zero, the depth buffer is not updated if the depth test is disabled.

ERRORS

        GL_INVALID_ENUM is generated if *func* is not an accepted value.

        GL_INVALID_OPERATION is generated if **glDepthFunc** is executed between the execution of **glBegin** and the corresponding execution of **glEnd**.

ASSOCIATED GETS

        glGet with argument **GL_DEPTH_FUNC**
        glIsEnabled with argument **GL_DEPTH_TEST**

SEE ALSO

        glDepthRange, **glEnable**, **glPolygonOffset**

NAME

glDepthMask – enable or disable writing into the depth buffer

C SPECIFICATION

void **glDepthMask**(GLboolean *flag*)

PARAMETERS

flag Specifies whether the depth buffer is enabled for writing. If *flag* is **GL_FALSE**, depth buffer writing is disabled. Otherwise, it is enabled. Initially, depth buffer writing is enabled.

DESCRIPTION

glDepthMask specifies whether the depth buffer is enabled for writing. If *flag* is **GL_FALSE**, depth buffer writing is disabled. Otherwise, it is enabled. Initially, depth buffer writing is enabled.

ERRORS

GL_INVALID_OPERATION is generated if **glDepthMask** is executed between the execution of **glBegin** and the corresponding execution of **glEnd**.

ASSOCIATED GETS

glGet with argument **GL_DEPTH_WRITEMASK**

SEE ALSO

glColorMask, **glDepthFunc**, **glDepthRange**, **glIndexMask**, **glStencilMask**

NAME

glDepthRange – specify mapping of depth values from normalized device coordinates to window coordinates

C SPECIFICATION

void **glDepthRange**(GLclampd *zNear*,
GLclampd *zFar*)

PARAMETERS

zNear Specifies the mapping of the near clipping plane to window coordinates. The initial value is 0.

zFar Specifies the mapping of the far clipping plane to window coordinates. The initial value is 1.

DESCRIPTION

After clipping and division by *w*, depth coordinates range from −1 to 1, corresponding to the near and far clipping planes. **glDepthRange** specifies a linear mapping of the normalized depth coordinates in this range to window depth coordinates. Regardless of the actual depth buffer implementation, window coordinate depth values are treated as though they range from 0 through 1 (like color components). Thus, the values accepted by **glDepthRange** are both clamped to this range before they are accepted.

The setting of (0,1) maps the near plane to 0 and the far plane to 1. With this mapping, the depth buffer range is fully utilized.

NOTES

It is not necessary that *zNear* be less than *zFar*. Reverse mappings such as *zNear* = 1, and *zFar* = 0 are acceptable.

ERRORS

GL_INVALID_OPERATION is generated if **glDepthRange** is executed between the execution of **glBegin** and the corresponding execution of **glEnd**.

ASSOCIATED GETS

glGet with argument **GL_DEPTH_RANGE**

SEE ALSO

glDepthFunc, **glPolygonOffset**, **glViewport**

NAME

glDrawArrays – render primitives from array data

C SPECIFICATION

void **glDrawArrays**(GLenum *mode,*
                     GLint *first,*
                     GLsizei *count*)

PARAMETERS

mode

Specifies what kind of primitives to render. Symbolic constants **GL_POINTS,**
GL_LINE_STRIP, GL_LINE_LOOP, GL_LINES, GL_TRIANGLE_STRIP,
GL_TRIANGLE_FAN, GL_TRIANGLES, GL_QUAD_STRIP, GL_QUADS, and
GL_POLYGON are accepted.

first Specifies the starting index in the enabled arrays.

count

Specifies the number of indices to be rendered.

DESCRIPTION

glDrawArrays specifies multiple geometric primitives with very few subroutine calls.
Instead of calling a GL procedure to pass each individual vertex, normal, texture
coordinate, edge flag, or color, you can prespecify separate arrays of vertices, normals, and colors and use them to construct a sequence of primitives with a single
call to **glDrawArrays.**

When **glDrawArrays** is called, it uses *count* sequential elements from each enabled
array to construct a sequence of geometric primitives, beginning with element *first.*
mode specifies what kind of primitives are constructed, and how the array elements
construct those primitives. If **GL_VERTEX_ARRAY** is not enabled, no geometric
primitives are generated.

Vertex attributes that are modified by **glDrawArrays** have an unspecified value after
glDrawArrays returns. For example, if **GL_COLOR_ARRAY** is enabled, the value of
the current color is undefined after **glDrawArrays** executes. Attributes that aren't
modified remain well defined.

NOTES

glDrawArrays is available only if the GL version is 1.1 or greater.

glDrawArrays is included in display lists. If **glDrawArrays** is entered into a display
list, the necessary array data (determined by the array pointers and enables) is also
entered into the display list. Because the array pointers and enables are client-side
state, their values affect display lists when the lists are created, not when the lists are
executed.

ERRORS

GL_INVALID_ENUM is generated if *mode* is not an accepted value.

GL_INVALID_VALUE is generated if *count* is negative.

GL_INVALID_OPERATION is generated if **glDrawArrays** is executed between the execution of **glBegin** and the corresponding **glEnd**.

SEE ALSO

glArrayElement, **glColorPointer**, **glDrawElements**, **glDrawRangeElements**, **glEdgeFlagPointer**, **glGetPointerv**, **glIndexPointer**, **glInterleavedArrays**, **glNormalPointer**, **glTexCoordPointer**, **glVertexPointer**

NAME

glDrawBuffer – specify which color buffers are to be drawn into

C SPECIFICATION

void **glDrawBuffer**(GLenum *mode*)

PARAMETERS

mode   Specifies up to four color buffers to be drawn into. Symbolic constants **GL_NONE**, **GL_FRONT_LEFT**, **GL_FRONT_RIGHT**, **GL_BACK_LEFT**, **GL_BACK_RIGHT**, **GL_FRONT**, **GL_BACK**, **GL_LEFT**, **GL_RIGHT**, **GL_FRONT_AND_BACK**, and **GL_AUX***i*, where *i* is between 0 and ''**GL_AUX_BUFFERS**'' −1, are accepted (**GL_AUX_BUFFERS** is not the upper limit; use **glGet** to query the number of available aux buffers.) The initial value is **GL_FRONT** for single-buffered contexts, and **GL_BACK** for double-buffered contexts.

DESCRIPTION

When colors are written to the frame buffer, they are written into the color buffers specified by **glDrawBuffer**. The specifications are as follows:

GL_NONE	No color buffers are written.
GL_FRONT_LEFT	Only the front left color buffer is written.
GL_FRONT_RIGHT	Only the front right color buffer is written.
GL_BACK_LEFT	Only the back left color buffer is written.
GL_BACK_RIGHT	Only the back right color buffer is written.
GL_FRONT	Only the front left and front right color buffers are written. If there is no front right color buffer, only the front left color buffer is written.
GL_BACK	Only the back left and back right color buffers are written. If there is no back right color buffer, only the back left color buffer is written.
GL_LEFT	Only the front left and back left color buffers are written. If there is no back left color buffer, only the front left color buffer is written.
GL_RIGHT	Only the front right and back right color buffers are written. If there is no back right color buffer, only the front right color buffer is written.

GL_FRONT_AND_BACK	All the front and back color buffers (front left, front right, back left, back right) are written. If there are no back color buffers, only the front left and front right color buffers are written. If there are no right color buffers, only the front left and back left color buffers are written. If there are no right or back color buffers, only the front left color buffer is written.
GL_AUXi	Only auxiliary color buffer i is written.

If more than one color buffer is selected for drawing, then blending or logical operations are computed and applied independently for each color buffer and can produce different results in each buffer.

Monoscopic contexts include only *left* buffers, and stereoscopic contexts include both *left* and *right* buffers. Likewise, single-buffered contexts include only *front* buffers, and double-buffered contexts include both *front* and *back* buffers. The context is selected at GL initialization.

NOTES

It is always the case that **GL_AUX**i = **GL_AUX0** + i.

ERRORS

GL_INVALID_ENUM is generated if *mode* is not an accepted value.

GL_INVALID_OPERATION is generated if none of the buffers indicated by *mode* exists.

GL_INVALID_OPERATION is generated if **glDrawBuffer** is executed between the execution of **glBegin** and the corresponding execution of **glEnd**.

ASSOCIATED GETS

glGet with argument **GL_DRAW_BUFFER**
glGet with argument **GL_AUX_BUFFERS**

SEE ALSO

glBlendFunc, **glColorMask**, **glIndexMask**, **glLogicOp**, **glReadBuffer**

NAME

        glDrawElements – render primitives from array data

C SPECIFICATION

        void **glDrawElements**(GLenum *mode*,
                              GLsizei *count*,
                              GLenum *type*,
                              const GLvoid **indices*)

PARAMETERS

    mode   Specifies what kind of primitives to render. Symbolic constants **GL_POINTS**, **GL_LINE_STRIP**, **GL_LINE_LOOP**, **GL_LINES**, **GL_TRIANGLE_STRIP**, **GL_TRIANGLE_FAN**, **GL_TRIANGLES**, **GL_QUAD_STRIP**, **GL_QUADS**, and **GL_POLYGON** are accepted.

    count   Specifies the number of elements to be rendered.

    type   Specifies the type of the values in *indices*. Must be one of **GL_UNSIGNED_BYTE**, **GL_UNSIGNED_SHORT**, or **GL_UNSIGNED_INT**.

    indices   Specifies a pointer to the location where the indices are stored.

DESCRIPTION

        glDrawElements specifies multiple geometric primitives with very few subroutine calls. Instead of calling a GL function to pass each individual vertex, normal, texture coordinate, edge flag, or color, you can prespecify separate arrays of vertices, normals, and so on and use them to construct a sequence of primitives with a single call to **glDrawElements**.

        When **glDrawElements** is called, it uses *count* sequential elements from an enabled array, starting at *indices* to construct a sequence of geometric primitives. *mode* specifies what kind of primitives are constructed, and how the array elements construct these primitives. If more than one array is enabled, each is used. If **GL_VERTEX_ARRAY** is not enabled, no geometric primitives are constructed.

        Vertex attributes that are modified by **glDrawElements** have an unspecified value after **glDrawElements** returns. For example, if **GL_COLOR_ARRAY** is enabled, the value of the current color is undefined after **glDrawElements** executes. Attributes that aren't modified maintain their previous values.

NOTES

        glDrawElements is available only if the GL version is 1.1 or greater.

        glDrawElements is included in display lists. If **glDrawElements** is entered into a display list, the necessary array data (determined by the array pointers and enables) is also entered into the display list. Because the array pointers and enables are client-side state, their values affect display lists when the lists are created, not when the lists are executed.

ERRORS

GL_INVALID_ENUM is generated if *mode* is not an accepted value.

GL_INVALID_VALUE is generated if *count* is negative.

GL_INVALID_OPERATION is generated if **glDrawElements** is executed between the execution of **glBegin** and the corresponding **glEnd**.

SEE ALSO

glArrayElement, **glColorPointer**, **glDrawArrays**, **glDrawRangeElements**, **glEdgeFlagPointer**, **glGetPointerv**, **glIndexPointer**, **glInterleavedArrays**, **glNormalPointer**, **glTexCoordPointer**, **glVertexPointer**

NAME

glDrawPixels – write a block of pixels to the frame buffer

C SPECIFICATION

void **glDrawPixels**(GLsizei *width*,
         GLsizei *height*,
         GLenum *format*,
         GLenum *type*,
         const GLvoid **pixels*)

PARAMETERS

width, *height*

Specify the dimensions of the pixel rectangle to be written into the frame buffer.

format Specifies the format of the pixel data. Symbolic constants
GL_COLOR_INDEX, **GL_STENCIL_INDEX**,
GL_DEPTH_COMPONENT, **GL_RGB**, **GL_BGR**, **GL_RGBA**, **GL_BGRA**,
GL_RED, **GL_GREEN**, **GL_BLUE**, **GL_ALPHA**, **GL_LUMINANCE**, and
GL_LUMINANCE_ALPHA are accepted.

type   Specifies the data type for *pixels*. Symbolic constants
GL_UNSIGNED_BYTE, **GL_BYTE**, **GL_BITMAP**,
GL_UNSIGNED_SHORT, **GL_SHORT**, **GL_UNSIGNED_INT**, **GL_INT**,
GL_FLOAT, **GL_UNSIGNED_BYTE_3_3_2**,
GL_UNSIGNED_BYTE_2_3_3_REV, **GL_UNSIGNED_SHORT_5_6_5**,
GL_UNSIGNED_SHORT_5_6_5_REV,
GL_UNSIGNED_SHORT_4_4_4_4,
GL_UNSIGNED_SHORT_4_4_4_4_REV,
GL_UNSIGNED_SHORT_5_5_5_1,
GL_UNSIGNED_SHORT_1_5_5_5_REV, **GL_UNSIGNED_INT_8_8_8_8**,
GL_UNSIGNED_INT_8_8_8_8_REV,
GL_UNSIGNED_INT_10_10_10_2, and
GL_UNSIGNED_INT_2_10_10_10_REV are accepted.

pixels Specifies a pointer to the pixel data.

DESCRIPTION

glDrawPixels reads pixel data from memory and writes it into the frame buffer relative to the current raster position, provided that the raster position is valid. Use **glRasterPos** to set the current raster position; use **glGet** with argument **GL_CURRENT_RASTER_POSITION_VALID** to determine if the specified raster position is valid, and **glGet** with argument **GL_CURRENT_RASTER_POSITION** to query the raster position.

Several parameters define the encoding of pixel data in memory and control the processing of the pixel data before it is placed in the frame buffer. These parameters are set with four commands: **glPixelStore**, **glPixelTransfer**, **glPixelMap**, and **glPixelZoom**. This reference page describes the effects on **glDrawPixels** of many, but not all, of the parameters specified by these four commands.

Data is read from *pixels* as a sequence of signed or unsigned bytes, signed or unsigned shorts, signed or unsigned integers, or single-precision floating-point values, depending on *type*. When *type* is one of GL_UNSIGNED_BYTE, GL_BYTE, GL_UNSIGNED_SHORT, GL_SHORT, GL_UNSIGNED_INT, GL_INT, or GL_FLOAT each of these bytes, shorts, integers, or floating-point values is interpreted as one color or depth component, or one index, depending on *format*. When *type* is one of GL_UNSIGNED_BYTE_3_3_2, GL_UNSIGNED_SHORT_5_6_5, GL_UNSIGNED_SHORT_4_4_4_4, GL_UNSIGNED_SHORT_5_5_5_1, GL_UNSIGNED_INT_8_8_8_8, GL_UNSIGNED_INT_10_10_10_2, each unsigned value is interpreted as containing all the components for a single pixel, with the color components arranged according to *format*. When *type* is one of GL_UNSIGNED_BYTE_2_3_3_REV, GL_UNSIGNED_SHORT_5_6_5_REV, GL_UNSIGNED_SHORT_4_4_4_4_REV, GL_UNSIGNED_SHORT_1_5_5_5_REV, GL_UNSIGNED_INT_8_8_8_8_REV, GL_UNSIGNED_INT_2_10_10_10_REV, each unsigned value is interpreted as containing all color components, specified by *format*, for a single pixel in a reversed order. Indices are always treated individually. Color components are treated as groups of one, two, three, or four values, again based on *format*. Both individual indices and groups of components are referred to as pixels. If *type* is GL_BITMAP, the data must be unsigned bytes, and *format* must be either GL_COLOR_INDEX or GL_STENCIL_INDEX. Each unsigned byte is treated as eight 1-bit pixels, with bit ordering determined by GL_UNPACK_LSB_FIRST (see **glPixelStore**).

width × *height* pixels are read from memory, starting at location *pixels*. By default, these pixels are taken from adjacent memory locations, except that after all *width* pixels are read, the read pointer is advanced to the next four-byte boundary. The four-byte row alignment is specified by **glPixelStore** with argument GL_UNPACK_ALIGNMENT, and it can be set to one, two, four, or eight bytes. Other pixel store parameters specify different read pointer advancements, both before the first pixel is read and after all *width* pixels are read. See the **glPixelStore** reference page for details on these options.

The *width* × *height* pixels that are read from memory are each operated on in the same way, based on the values of several parameters specified by **glPixelTransfer** and **glPixelMap**. The details of these operations, as well as the target buffer into which the pixels are drawn, are specific to the format of the pixels, as specified by *format*. *format* can assume one of 13 symbolic values:

GL_COLOR_INDEX

Each pixel is a single value, a color index. It is converted to fixed-point format, with an unspecified number of bits to the right of the binary point, regardless of the memory data type. Floating-point values convert to true fixed-point values. Signed and unsigned integer data is converted with all fraction bits set to 0. Bitmap data convert to either 0 or 1.

Each fixed-point index is then shifted left by **GL_INDEX_SHIFT** bits and added to **GL_INDEX_OFFSET**. If **GL_INDEX_SHIFT** is negative, the shift is to the right. In either case, zero bits fill otherwise unspecified bit locations in the result.

If the GL is in RGBA mode, the resulting index is converted to an RGBA pixel with the help of the **GL_PIXEL_MAP_I_TO_R**, **GL_PIXEL_MAP_I_TO_G**, **GL_PIXEL_MAP_I_TO_B**, and **GL_PIXEL_MAP_I_TO_A** tables. If the GL is in color index mode, and if **GL_MAP_COLOR** is true, the index is replaced with the value that it references in lookup table **GL_PIXEL_MAP_I_TO_I**. Whether the lookup replacement of the index is done or not, the integer part of the index is then ANDed with 2^b-1, where b is the number of bits in a color index buffer.

The GL then converts the resulting indices or RGBA colors to fragments by attaching the current raster position z coordinate and texture coordinates to each pixel, then assigning x and y window coordinates to the nth fragment such that

$$x_n = x_r + n \bmod \textit{width}$$

$$y_n = y_r + \lfloor n / \textit{width} \rfloor$$

where (x_r, y_r) is the current raster position. These pixel fragments are then treated just like the fragments generated by rasterizing points, lines, or polygons. Texture mapping, fog, and all the fragment operations are applied before the fragments are written to the frame buffer.

GL_STENCIL_INDEX

Each pixel is a single value, a stencil index. It is converted to fixed-point format, with an unspecified number of bits to the right of the binary point, regardless of the memory data type. Floating-point values convert to true fixed-point values. Signed and unsigned integer data is converted with all fraction bits set to 0. Bitmap data convert to either 0 or 1.

Each fixed-point index is then shifted left by **GL_INDEX_SHIFT** bits, and added to **GL_INDEX_OFFSET**. If **GL_INDEX_SHIFT** is negative, the shift is to the right. In either case, zero bits fill otherwise unspecified bit locations in the result. If **GL_MAP_STENCIL** is true, the index is replaced with the value that it references in lookup table **GL_PIXEL_MAP_S_TO_S**. Whether the lookup replacement of the index is done or not, the integer part of the index is then ANDed with $2^b - 1$, where b is the number of bits in the stencil buffer. The resulting stencil indices are then written to the stencil buffer such that the nth index is written to location

$$x_n = x_r + n \bmod width$$

$$y_n = y_r + \lfloor n/width \rfloor$$

where (x_r, y_r) is the current raster position. Only the pixel ownership test, the scissor test, and the stencil writemask affect these write operations.

GL_DEPTH_COMPONENT

Each pixel is a single-depth component. Floating-point data is converted directly to an internal floating-point format with unspecified precision. Signed integer data is mapped linearly to the internal floating-point format such that the most positive representable integer value maps to 1.0, and the most negative representable value maps to –1.0. Unsigned integer data is mapped similarly: the largest integer value maps to 1.0, and 0 maps to 0.0. The resulting floating-point depth value is then multiplied by **GL_DEPTH_SCALE** and added to **GL_DEPTH_BIAS**. The result is clamped to the range [0,1].

The GL then converts the resulting depth components to fragments by attaching the current raster position color or color index and texture coordinates to each pixel, then assigning x and y window coordinates to the nth fragment such that

$$x_n = x_r + n \bmod width$$

$$y_n = y_r + \lfloor n/width \rfloor$$

where (x_r, y_r) is the current raster position. These pixel fragments are then treated just like the fragments generated by rasterizing points, lines, or polygons. Texture mapping, fog, and all the fragment operations are applied before the fragments are written to the frame buffer.

GL_RGBA

GL_BGRA

Each pixel is a four-component group: for **GL_RGBA**, the red component is first, followed by green, followed by blue, followed by alpha; for **GL_BGRA** the order is blue, green, red and then alpha. Floating-point values are converted directly to an internal floating-point format with unspecified precision. Signed integer values are mapped linearly to the internal floating-point format such that the most positive representable integer value maps to 1.0, and the most negative representable value maps to −1.0. (Note that this mapping does not convert 0 precisely to 0.0.) Unsigned integer data is mapped similarly: the largest integer value maps to 1.0, and 0 maps to 0.0. The resulting floating-point color values are then multiplied by **GL_c_SCALE** and added to **GL_c_BIAS**, where c is RED, GREEN, BLUE, and ALPHA for the respective color components. The results are clamped to the range [0,1].

If **GL_MAP_COLOR** is true, each color component is scaled by the size of lookup table **GL_PIXEL_MAP_c_TO_c**, then replaced by the value that it references in that table. c is R, G, B, or A respectively.

The GL then converts the resulting RGBA colors to fragments by attaching the current raster position z coordinate and texture coordinates to each pixel, then assigning x and y window coordinates to the nth fragment such that

$$x_n = x_r + n \bmod \mathit{width}$$

$$y_n = y_r + \lfloor n/\mathit{width} \rfloor$$

where (x_r, y_r) is the current raster position. These pixel fragments are then treated just like the fragments generated by rasterizing points, lines, or polygons. Texture mapping, fog, and all the fragment operations are applied before the fragments are written to the frame buffer.

GL_RED

Each pixel is a single red component. This component is converted to the internal floating-point format in the same way the red component of an RGBA pixel is. It is then converted to an RGBA pixel with green and blue set to 0, and alpha set to 1. After this conversion, the pixel is treated as if it had been read as an RGBA pixel.

GL_GREEN

Each pixel is a single green component. This component is converted to the internal floating-point format in the same way the green component of an RGBA pixel is. It is then converted to an RGBA pixel with red and blue set to 0, and alpha set to 1. After this conversion, the pixel is treated as if it had been read as an RGBA pixel.

GL_BLUE

Each pixel is a single blue component. This component is converted to the internal floating-point format in the same way the blue component of an RGBA pixel is. It is then converted to an RGBA pixel with red and green set to 0, and alpha set to 1. After this conversion, the pixel is treated as if it had been read as an RGBA pixel.

GL_ALPHA

Each pixel is a single alpha component. This component is converted to the internal floating-point format in the same way the alpha component of an RGBA pixel is. It is then converted to an RGBA pixel with red, green, and blue set to 0. After this conversion, the pixel is treated as if it had been read as an RGBA pixel.

GL_RGB

GL_BGR

Each pixel is a three-component group: red first, followed by green, followed by blue; for **GL_BGR**, the first component is blue, followed by green and then red. Each component is converted to the internal floating-point format in the same way the red, green, and blue components of an RGBA pixel are. The color triple is converted to an RGBA pixel with alpha set to 1. After this conversion, the pixel is treated as if it had been read as an RGBA pixel.

GL_LUMINANCE

Each pixel is a single luminance component. This component is converted to the internal floating-point format in the same way the red component of an RGBA pixel is. It is then converted to an RGBA pixel with red, green, and blue set to the converted luminance value, and alpha set to 1. After this conversion, the pixel is treated as if it had been read as an RGBA pixel.

GL_LUMINANCE_ALPHA

Each pixel is a two-component group: luminance first, followed by alpha. The two components are converted to the internal floating-point format in the same way the red component of an RGBA pixel is. They are then converted to an RGBA pixel with red, green, and blue set to the converted luminance value, and alpha set to the converted alpha value. After this conversion, the pixel is treated as if it had been read as an RGBA pixel.

The following table summarizes the meaning of the valid constants for the *type* parameter:

Type	Corresponding Type
GL_UNSIGNED_BYTE	unsigned 8-bit integer
GL_BYTE	signed 8-bit integer
GL_BITMAP	single bits in unsigned 8-bit integers
GL_UNSIGNED_SHORT	unsigned 16-bit integer
GL_SHORT	signed 16-bit integer
GL_UNSIGNED_INT	unsigned 32-bit integer
GL_INT	32-bit integer
GL_FLOAT	single-precision floating-point
GL_UNSIGNED_BYTE_3_3_2	unsigned 8-bit integer
GL_UNSIGNED_BYTE_2_3_3_REV	unsigned 8-bit integer with reversed component ordering
GL_UNSIGNED_SHORT_5_6_5	unsigned 16-bit integer
GL_UNSIGNED_SHORT_5_6_5_REV	unsigned 16-bit integer with reversed component ordering
GL_UNSIGNED_SHORT_4_4_4_4	unsigned 16-bit integer
GL_UNSIGNED_SHORT_4_4_4_4_REV	unsigned 16-bit integer with reversed component ordering
GL_UNSIGNED_SHORT_5_5_5_1	unsigned 16-bit integer
GL_UNSIGNED_SHORT_1_5_5_5_REV	unsigned 16-bit integer with reversed component ordering
GL_UNSIGNED_INT_8_8_8_8	unsigned 32-bit integer
GL_UNSIGNED_INT_8_8_8_8_REV	unsigned 32-bit integer with reversed component ordering
GL_UNSIGNED_INT_10_10_10_2	unsigned 32-bit integer
GL_UNSIGNED_INT_2_10_10_10_REV	unsigned 32-bit integer with reversed component ordering

The rasterization described so far assumes pixel zoom factors of 1. If **glPixelZoom** is used to change the x and y pixel zoom factors, pixels are converted to fragments as follows. If (x_r, y_r) is the current raster position, and a given pixel is in the nth column and mth row of the pixel rectangle, then fragments are generated for pixels whose centers are in the rectangle with corners at

$$(x_r + zoom_x\, n,\ y_r + zoom_y\, m)$$

$$(x_r + zoom_x\, (n + 1),\ y_r + zoom_y\, (m + 1))$$

where $zoom_x$ is the value of **GL_ZOOM_X** and $zoom_y$ is the value of **GL_ZOOM_Y**.

NOTES

GL_BGR and GL_BGRA are only valid for *format* if the GL version is 1.2 or greater.

GL_UNSIGNED_BYTE_3_3_2, GL_UNSIGNED_BYTE_2_3_3_REV,
GL_UNSIGNED_SHORT_5_6_5, GL_UNSIGNED_SHORT_5_6_5_REV,
GL_UNSIGNED_SHORT_4_4_4_4, GL_UNSIGNED_SHORT_4_4_4_4_REV,
GL_UNSIGNED_SHORT_5_5_5_1, GL_UNSIGNED_SHORT_1_5_5_5_REV,

GL_UNSIGNED_INT_8_8_8_8, GL_UNSIGNED_INT_8_8_8_8_REV, GL_UNSIGNED_INT_10_10_10_2, and GL_UNSIGNED_INT_2_10_10_10_REV are only valid for *type* if the GL version is 1.2 or greater.

ERRORS

GL_INVALID_VALUE is generated if either *width* or *height* is negative.

GL_INVALID_ENUM is generated if *format* or *type* is not one of the accepted values.

GL_INVALID_OPERATION is generated if *format* is **GL_RED**, **GL_GREEN**, **GL_BLUE**, **GL_ALPHA**, **GL_RGB**, **GL_RGBA**, **GL_BGR**, **GL_BGRA**, **GL_LUMINANCE**, or **GL_LUMINANCE_ALPHA**, and the GL is in color index mode.

GL_INVALID_ENUM is generated if *type* is **GL_BITMAP** and *format* is not either **GL_COLOR_INDEX** or **GL_STENCIL_INDEX**.

GL_INVALID_OPERATION is generated if *format* is **GL_STENCIL_INDEX** and there is no stencil buffer.

GL_INVALID_OPERATION is generated if **glDrawPixels** is executed between the execution of **glBegin** and the corresponding execution of **glEnd**.

GL_INVALID_OPERATION is generated if *format* is one **GL_UNSIGNED_BYTE_3_3_2**, **GL_UNSIGNED_BYTE_2_3_3_REV**, **GL_UNSIGNED_SHORT_5_6_5**, of **GL_UNSIGNED_SHORT_5_6_5_REV** and *format* is not **GL_RGB**.

GL_INVALID_OPERATION is generated if *format* is one of **GL_UNSIGNED_SHORT_4_4_4_4**, **GL_UNSIGNED_SHORT_4_4_4_4_REV**, **GL_UNSIGNED_SHORT_5_5_5_1**, **GL_UNSIGNED_SHORT_1_5_5_5_REV**, **GL_UNSIGNED_INT_8_8_8_8**, **GL_UNSIGNED_INT_8_8_8_8_REV**, **GL_UNSIGNED_INT_10_10_10_2**, or **GL_UNSIGNED_INT_2_10_10_10_REV** and *format* is neither **GL_RGBA** nor **GL_BGRA**.

ASSOCIATED GETS

glGet with argument GL_CURRENT_RASTER_POSITION
glGet with argument GL_CURRENT_RASTER_POSITION_VALID

SEE ALSO

glAlphaFunc, glBlendFunc, glCopyPixels, glDepthFunc, glLogicOp, glPixelMap, glPixelStore, glPixelTransfer, glPixelZoom, glRasterPos, glReadPixels, glScissor, glStencilFunc

NAME

glDrawRangeElements – render primitives from array data

C SPECIFICATION

void **glDrawRangeElements**(GLenum *mode*,
                        GLuint *start*,
                        GLuint *end*,
                        GLsizei *count*,
                        GLenum *type*,
                        const GLvoid **indices*)

PARAMETERS

mode   Specifies what kind of primitives to render. Symbolic constants **GL_POINTS**,
            GL_LINE_STRIP, **GL_LINE_LOOP**, **GL_LINES**, **GL_TRIANGLE_STRIP**,
            GL_TRIANGLE_FAN, **GL_TRIANGLES**, **GL_QUAD_STRIP**, **GL_QUADS**, and
            GL_POLYGON are accepted.

start   Specifies the minimum array index contained in *indices*.

end   Specifies the maximum array index contained in *indices*.

count   Specifies the number of elements to be rendered.

type   Specifies the type of the values in *count*. Must be one of
            GL_UNSIGNED_BYTE, **GL_UNSIGNED_SHORT**, or **GL_UNSIGNED_INT**.

indices   Specifies a pointer to the location where the indices are stored.

DESCRIPTION

glDrawRangeElements is a restricted form of **glDrawElements**. *mode*, *start*, *end*, and
count match the corresponding arguments to **glDrawElements**, with the additional
constraint that all values in the arrays *count* must lie between *start* and *end*,
inclusive.

Implementations denote recommended maximum amounts of vertex and
index data, which may be queried by calling **glGet** with argument
GL_MAX_ELEMENTS_VERTICES and **GL_MAX_ELEMENTS_INDICES**. If
end − *start* + 1 is greater than the value of **GL_MAX_ELEMENTS_VERTICES**, or if
count is greater than the value of **GL_MAX_ELEMENTS_INDICES**, then the call may
operate at reduced performance. There is no requirement that all vertices in the
range [*start*, *end*] be referenced. However, the implementation may partially process
unused vertices, reducing performance from what could be achieved with an
optimal index set.

When **glDrawRangeElements** is called, it uses *count* sequential elements from an enabled array, starting at *start* to construct a sequence of geometric primitives. *mode* specifies what kind of primitives are constructed, and how the array elements construct these primitives. If more than one array is enabled, each is used. If **GL_VERTEX_ARRAY** is not enabled, no geometric primitives are constructed.

Vertex attributes that are modified by **glDrawRangeElements** have an unspecified value after **glDrawRangeElements** returns. For example, if **GL_COLOR_ARRAY** is enabled, the value of the current color is undefined after **glDrawRangeElements** executes. Attributes that aren't modified maintain their previous values.

NOTES

glDrawRangeElements is available only if the GL version is 1.2 or greater.

glDrawRangeElements is included in display lists. If **glDrawRangeElements** is entered into a display list, the necessary array data (determined by the array pointers and enables) is also entered into the display list. Because the array pointers and enables are client-side state, their values affect display lists when the lists are created, not when the lists are executed.

ERRORS

It is an error for indices to lie outside the range [*start*, *end*], but implementations may not check for this situation. Such indices cause implementation-dependent behavior.

GL_INVALID_ENUM is generated if *mode* is not an accepted value.

GL_INVALID_VALUE is generated if *count* is negative.

GL_INVALID_VALUE is generated if *end* < *start*.

GL_INVALID_OPERATION is generated if **glDrawRangeElements** is executed between the execution of **glBegin** and the corresponding **glEnd**.

ASSOCIATED GETS

glGet with argument GL_MAX_ELEMENTS_VERTICES

glGet with argument GL_MAX_ELEMENTS_INDICES

SEE ALSO

glArrayElement, glColorPointer, glDrawArrays, glDrawElements, glEdgeFlagPointer, glGetPointerv, glIndexPointer, glInterleavedArrays, glNormalPointer, glTexCoordPointer, glVertexPointer

NAME

glEdgeFlag, glEdgeFlagv – flag edges as either boundary or nonboundary

C SPECIFICATION

void **glEdgeFlag**(GLboolean *flag*)

PARAMETERS

flag Specifies the current edge flag value, either **GL_TRUE** or **GL_FALSE**. The initial value is **GL_TRUE**.

C SPECIFICATION

void **glEdgeFlagv**(const GLboolean **flag*)

PARAMETERS

flag Specifies a pointer to an array that contains a single boolean element, which replaces the current edge flag value.

DESCRIPTION

Each vertex of a polygon, separate triangle, or separate quadrilateral specified between a **glBegin/glEnd** pair is marked as the start of either a boundary or nonboundary edge. If the current edge flag is true when the vertex is specified, the vertex is marked as the start of a boundary edge. Otherwise, the vertex is marked as the start of a nonboundary edge. **glEdgeFlag** sets the edge flag bit to **GL_TRUE** if *flag* is **GL_TRUE**, and to **GL_FALSE** otherwise.

The vertices of connected triangles and connected quadrilaterals are always marked as boundary, regardless of the value of the edge flag.

Boundary and nonboundary edge flags on vertices are significant only if **GL_POLYGON_MODE** is set to **GL_POINT** or **GL_LINE**. See **glPolygonMode**.

NOTES

The current edge flag can be updated at any time. In particular, **glEdgeFlag** can be called between a call to **glBegin** and the corresponding call to **glEnd**.

ASSOCIATED GETS

glGet with argument **GL_EDGE_FLAG**

SEE ALSO

glBegin, glEdgeFlagPointer, glPolygonMode

NAME

glEdgeFlagPointer – define an array of edge flags

C SPECIFICATION

void **glEdgeFlagPointer**(GLsizei *stride*,
　　　　　　　　　　　const GLboolean **pointer*)

PARAMETERS

stride　Specifies the byte offset between consecutive edge flags. If *stride* is 0 (the initial value), the edge flags are understood to be tightly packed in the array. The initial value is 0.

pointer　Specifies a pointer to the first edge flag in the array. The initial value is zero.

DESCRIPTION

glEdgeFlagPointer specifies the location and data format of an array of boolean edge flags to use when rendering. *stride* specifies the byte stride from one edge flag to the next allowing vertices and attributes to be packed into a single array or stored in separate arrays. (Single-array storage may be more efficient on some implementations; see **glInterleavedArrays**.)

When an edge flag array is specified, *stride* and *pointer* are saved as client-side state.

To enable and disable the edge flag array, call **glEnableClientState** and **glDisableClientState** with the argument GL_EDGE_FLAG_ARRAY. If enabled, the edge flag array is used when **glDrawArrays**, **glDrawElements**, or **glArrayElement** is called.

Use **glDrawArrays** to construct a sequence of primitives (all of the same type) from prespecified vertex and vertex attribute arrays. Use **glArrayElement** to specify primitives by indexing vertices and vertex attributes and **glDrawElements** to construct a sequence of primitives by indexing vertices and vertex attributes.

NOTES

glEdgeFlagPointer is available only if the GL version is 1.1 or greater.

The edge flag array is initially disabled and it won't be accessed when **glArrayElement**, **glDrawElements** or **glDrawArrays** is called.

Execution of **glEdgeFlagPointer** is not allowed between the execution of **glBegin** and the corresponding execution of **glEnd**, but an error may or may not be generated. If no error is generated, the operation is undefined.

glEdgeFlagPointer is typically implemented on the client side.

Edge flag array parameters are client-side state and are therefore not saved or restored by **glPushAttrib** and **glPopAttrib**. Use **glPushClientAttrib** and **glPopClientAttrib** instead.

ERRORS

GL_INVALID_ENUM is generated if *stride* is negative.

ASSOCIATED GETS

glIsEnabled with argument **GL_EDGE_FLAG_ARRAY**
glGet with argument **GL_EDGE_FLAG_ARRAY_STRIDE**
glGetPointerv with argument **GL_EDGE_FLAG_ARRAY_POINTER**

SEE ALSO

glArrayElement, **glColorPointer**, **glDrawArrays**, **glDrawElements**, **glEnable**, **glGetPointerv**, **glIndexPointer**, **glNormalPointer**, **glPopClientAttrib**, **glPushClientAttrib**, **glTexCoordPointer**, **glVertexPointer**

NAME

glEnable, **glDisable** – enable or disable server-side GL capabilities

C SPECIFICATION

void **glEnable**(GLenum *cap*)

PARAMETERS

cap Specifies a symbolic constant indicating a GL capability.

C SPECIFICATION

void **glDisable**(GLenum *cap*)

PARAMETERS

cap   Specifies a symbolic constant indicating a GL capability.

DESCRIPTION

glEnable and **glDisable** enable and disable various capabilities. Use **glIsEnabled** or **glGet** to determine the current setting of any capability. The initial value for each capability with the exception of **GL_DITHER** is **GL_FALSE**. The initial value for **GL_DITHER** is **GL_TRUE**.

Both **glEnable** and **glDisable** take a single argument, *cap*, which can assume one of the following values:

GL_ALPHA_TEST	If enabled, do alpha testing. See **glAlphaFunc**.
GL_AUTO_NORMAL	If enabled, generate normal vectors when either **GL_MAP2_VERTEX_3** or **GL_MAP2_VERTEX_4** is used to generate vertices. See **glMap2**.
GL_BLEND	If enabled, blend the incoming RGBA color values with the values in the color buffers. See **glBlendFunc**.
GL_CLIP_PLANE*i*	If enabled, clip geometry against user-defined clipping plane *i*. See **glClipPlane**.
GL_COLOR_LOGIC_OP	If enabled, apply the currently selected logical operation to the incoming RGBA color and color buffer values. See **glLogicOp**.
GL_COLOR_MATERIAL	If enabled, have one or more material parameters track the current color. See **glColorMaterial**.
GL_COLOR_TABLE	If enabled, preform a color table lookup on the incoming RGBA color values. See **glColorTable**.

GL_CONVOLUTION_1D If enabled, perform a 1D convolution operation on incoming RGBA color values. See **glConvolutionFilter1D**.

GL_CONVOLUTION_2D If enabled, perform a 2D convolution operation on incoming RGBA color values. See **glConvolutionFilter2D**.

GL_CULL_FACE If enabled, cull polygons based on their winding in window coordinates. See **glCullFace**.

GL_DEPTH_TEST If enabled, do depth comparisons and update the depth buffer. Note that even if the depth buffer exists and the depth mask is non-zero, the depth buffer is not updated if the depth test is disabled. See **glDepthFunc** and **glDepthRange**.

GL_DITHER If enabled, dither color components or indices before they are written to the color buffer.

GL_FOG If enabled, blend a fog color into the posttexturing color. See **glFog**.

GL_HISTOGRAM If enabled, histogram incoming RGBA color values. See **glHistogram**.

GL_INDEX_LOGIC_OP If enabled, apply the currently selected logical operation to the incoming index and color buffer indices. See **glLogicOp**.

GL_LIGHT*i* If enabled, include light *i* in the evaluation of the lighting equation. See **glLightModel** and **glLight**.

GL_LIGHTING If enabled, use the current lighting parameters to compute the vertex color or index. Otherwise, simply associate the current color or index with each vertex. See **glMaterial**, **glLightModel**, and **glLight**.

GL_LINE_SMOOTH If enabled, draw lines with correct filtering. Otherwise, draw aliased lines. See **glLineWidth**.

GL_LINE_STIPPLE If enabled, use the current line stipple pattern when drawing lines. See **glLineStipple**.

GL_MAP1_COLOR_4 If enabled, calls to **glEvalCoord1**, **glEvalMesh1**, and **glEvalPoint1** generate RGBA values. See **glMap1**.

GL_MAP1_INDEX If enabled, calls to **glEvalCoord1**, **glEvalMesh1**, and **glEvalPoint1** generate color indices. See **glMap1**.

GL_MAP1_NORMAL   If enabled, calls to **glEvalCoord1**, **glEvalMesh1**, and **glEvalPoint1** generate normals. See **glMap1**.

GL_MAP1_TEXTURE_COORD_1
If enabled, calls to **glEvalCoord1**, **glEvalMesh1**, and **glEvalPoint1** generate s texture coordinates. See **glMap1**.

GL_MAP1_TEXTURE_COORD_2
If enabled, calls to **glEvalCoord1**, **glEvalMesh1**, and **glEvalPoint1** generate s and t texture coordinates. See **glMap1**.

GL_MAP1_TEXTURE_COORD_3
If enabled, calls to **glEvalCoord1**, **glEvalMesh1**, and **glEvalPoint1** generate s, t, and r texture coordinates. See **glMap1**.

GL_MAP1_TEXTURE_COORD_4
If enabled, calls to **glEvalCoord1**, **glEvalMesh1**, and **glEvalPoint1** generate s, t, r, and q texture coordinates. See **glMap1**.

GL_MAP1_VERTEX_3   If enabled, calls to **glEvalCoord1**, **glEvalMesh1**, and **glEvalPoint1** generate x, y, and z vertex coordinates. See **glMap1**.

GL_MAP1_VERTEX_4   If enabled, calls to **glEvalCoord1**, **glEvalMesh1**, and **glEvalPoint1** generate homogeneous x, y, z, and w vertex coordinates. See **glMap1**.

GL_MAP2_COLOR_4   If enabled, calls to **glEvalCoord2**, **glEvalMesh2**, and **glEvalPoint2** generate RGBA values. See **glMap2**.

GL_MAP2_INDEX   If enabled, calls to **glEvalCoord2**, **glEvalMesh2**, and **glEvalPoint2** generate color indices. See **glMap2**.

GL_MAP2_NORMAL   If enabled, calls to **glEvalCoord2**, **glEvalMesh2**, and **glEvalPoint2** generate normals. See **glMap2**.

GL_MAP2_TEXTURE_COORD_1
If enabled, calls to **glEvalCoord2**, **glEvalMesh2**, and **glEvalPoint2** generate s texture coordinates. See **glMap2**.

GL_MAP2_TEXTURE_COORD_2
If enabled, calls to **glEvalCoord2**, **glEvalMesh2**, and **glEvalPoint2** generate s and t texture coordinates. See **glMap2**.

GL_MAP2_TEXTURE_COORD_3

If enabled, calls to **glEvalCoord2**, **glEvalMesh2**, and **glEvalPoint2** generate *s*, *t*, and *r* texture coordinates. See **glMap2**.

GL_MAP2_TEXTURE_COORD_4

If enabled, calls to **glEvalCoord2**, **glEvalMesh2**, and **glEvalPoint2** generate *s*, *t*, *r*, and *q* texture coordinates. See **glMap2**.

GL_MAP2_VERTEX_3   If enabled, calls to **glEvalCoord2**, **glEvalMesh2**, and **glEvalPoint2** generate *x*, *y*, and *z* vertex coordinates. See **glMap2**.

GL_MAP2_VERTEX_4   If enabled, calls to **glEvalCoord2**, **glEvalMesh2**, and **glEvalPoint2** generate homogeneous *x*, *y*, *z*, and *w* vertex coordinates. See **glMap2**.

GL_MINMAX   If enabled, compute the minimum and maximum values of incoming RGBA color values. See **glMinmax**.

GL_NORMALIZE   If enabled, normal vectors specified with **glNormal** are scaled to unit length after transformation. See **glNormal**.

GL_POINT_SMOOTH   If enabled, draw points with proper filtering. Otherwise, draw aliased points. See **glPointSize**.

GL_POLYGON_OFFSET_FILL

If enabled, and if the polygon is rendered in **GL_FILL** mode, an offset is added to depth values of a polygon's fragments before the depth comparison is performed. See **glPolygonOffset**.

GL_POLYGON_OFFSET_LINE

If enabled, and if the polygon is rendered in **GL_LINE** mode, an offset is added to depth values of a polygon's fragments before the depth comparison is performed. See **glPolygonOffset**.

GL_POLYGON_OFFSET_POINT

If enabled, an offset is added to depth values of a polygon's fragments before the depth comparison is performed, if the polygon is rendered in **GL_POINT** mode. See **glPolygonOffset**.

GL_POLYGON_SMOOTH

If enabled, draw polygons with proper filtering. Otherwise, draw aliased polygons. For correct anti-aliased polygons, an alpha buffer is needed and the polygons must be sorted front to back.

GL_POLYGON_STIPPLE If enabled, use the current polygon stipple pattern when rendering polygons. See **glPolygonStipple**.

GL_POST_COLOR_MATRIX_COLOR_TABLE
If enabled, preform a color table lookup on RGBA color values after color matrix transformation. See **glColorTable**.

GL_POST_CONVOLUTION_COLOR_TABLE
If enabled, preform a color table lookup on RGBA color values after convolution. See **glColorTable**.

GL_RESCALE_NORMAL If enabled, normal vectors specified with **glNormal** are scaled to unit length after transformation. See **glNormal**.

GL_SEPARABLE_2D If enabled, perform a two-dimensional convolution operation using a separable convolution filter on incoming RGBA color values. See **glSeparableFilter2D**.

GL_SCISSOR_TEST If enabled, discard fragments that are outside the scissor rectangle. See **glScissor**.

GL_STENCIL_TEST If enabled, do stencil testing and update the stencil buffer. See **glStencilFunc** and **glStencilOp**.

GL_TEXTURE_1D If enabled, one-dimensional texturing is performed (unless two- or three-dimensional texturing is also enabled). See **glTexImage1D**.

GL_TEXTURE_2D If enabled, two-dimensional texturing is performed (unless three-dimensional texturing is also enabled). See **glTexImage2D**.

GL_TEXTURE_3D If enabled, three-dimensional texturing is performed. See **glTexImage3D**.

GL_TEXTURE_GEN_Q If enabled, the q texture coordinate is computed using the texture generation function defined with **glTexGen**. Otherwise, the current q texture coordinate is used. See **glTexGen**.

GL_TEXTURE_GEN_R If enabled, the r texture coordinate is computed using the texture generation function defined with **glTexGen**. Otherwise, the current r texture coordinate is used. See **glTexGen**.

GL_TEXTURE_GEN_S   If enabled, the *s* texture coordinate is computed using the texture generation function defined with **glTexGen**. Otherwise, the current *s* texture coordinate is used. See **glTexGen**.

GL_TEXTURE_GEN_T   If enabled, the *t* texture coordinate is computed using the texture generation function defined with **glTexGen**. Otherwise, the current *t* texture coordinate is used. See **glTexGen**.

NOTES

GL_POLYGON_OFFSET_FILL, GL_POLYGON_OFFSET_LINE, GL_POLYGON_OFFSET_POINT, GL_COLOR_LOGIC_OP, and GL_INDEX_LOGIC_OP are available only if the GL version is 1.1 or greater.

GL_RESCALE_NORMAL, and GL_TEXTURE_3D are available only if the GL version is 1.2 or greater.

GL_COLOR_TABLE, GL_CONVOLUTION_1D, GL_CONVOLUTION_2D, GL_HISTOGRAM, GL_MINMAX, GL_POST_COLOR_MATRIX_COLOR_TABLE, GL_POST_CONVOLUTION_COLOR_TABLE, and GL_SEPARABLE_2D are available only if **GL_ARB_imaging** is returned from **glGet** with an argument of GL_EXTENSIONS.

If **GL_ARB_multitexture** is supported, GL_TEXTURE_1D, GL_TEXTURE_2D, GL_TEXTURE_3D, GL_TEXTURE_GEN_S, GL_TEXTURE_GEN_T, GL_TEXTURE_GEN_R, and GL_TEXTURE_GEN_Q enable or disable the respective state for the active texture unit specified with **glActiveTextureARB**.

ERRORS

GL_INVALID_ENUM is generated if *cap* is not one of the values listed previously.

GL_INVALID_OPERATION is generated if **glEnable** or **glDisable** is executed between the execution of **glBegin** and the corresponding execution of **glEnd**.

SEE ALSO

glActiveTextureARB, glAlphaFunc, glBlendFunc, glClipPlane, glColorMaterial, glCullFace, glDepthFunc, glDepthRange, glEnableClientState, glFog, glGet, glIsEnabled, glLight, glLightModel, glLineWidth, glLineStipple, glLogicOp, glMap1, glMap2, glMaterial, glNormal, glPointSize, glPolygonMode, glPolygonOffset, glPolygonStipple, glScissor, glStencilFunc, glStencilOp, glTexGen, glTexImage1D, glTexImage2D, glTexImage3D

NAME

glEnableClientState, **glDisableClientState** – enable or disable client-side capability

C SPECIFICATION

void **glEnableClientState**(GLenum *array*)

PARAMETERS

array Specifies the capability to enable. Symbolic constants **GL_COLOR_ARRAY**, **GL_EDGE_FLAG_ARRAY**, **GL_INDEX_ARRAY**, **GL_NORMAL_ARRAY**, **GL_TEXTURE_COORD_ARRAY**, and **GL_VERTEX_ARRAY** are accepted.

C SPECIFICATION

void **glDisableClientState**(GLenum *array*)

PARAMETERS

array   Specifies the capability to disable.

DESCRIPTION

glEnableClientState and **glDisableClientState** enable or disable individual client-side capabilities. By default, all client-side capabilities are disabled. Both **glEnableClientState** and **glDisableClientState** take a single argument, *array*, which can assume one of the following values:

GL_COLOR_ARRAY   If enabled, the color array is enabled for writing and used during rendering when **glArrayElement**, **glDrawArrays**, **glDrawElement**, or **glDrawRangeElements** is called. See **glColorPointer**.

GL_EDGE_FLAG_ARRAY If enabled, the edge flag array is enabled for writing and used during rendering when **glArrayElement**, **glDrawArrays**, **glDrawElement**, or **glDrawRangeElements** is called. See **glEdgeFlagPointer**.

GL_INDEX_ARRAY   If enabled, the index array is enabled for writing and used during rendering when **glArrayElement**, **glDrawArrays**, **glDrawElement**, or **glDrawRangeElements** is called. See **glIndexPointer**.

GL_NORMAL_ARRAY   If enabled, the normal array is enabled for writing and used during rendering when **glArrayElement**, **glDrawArrays**, **glDrawElement**, or **glDrawRangeElements** is called. See **glNormalPointer**.

GL_TEXTURE_COORD_ARRAY
If enabled, the texture coordinate array is enabled for writing and used during rendering when **glArrayElement, glDrawArrays, glDrawElement**, or **glDrawRangeElements** is called. See **glTexCoordPointer**.

GL_VERTEX_ARRAY
If enabled, the vertex array is enabled for writing and used during rendering when **glArrayElement, glDrawArrays, glDrawElement**, or **glDrawRangeElements** is called. See **glVertexPointer**.

NOTES

glEnableClientState is available only if the GL version is 1.1 or greater.

If **GL_ARB_multitexture** is supported, enabling and disabling **GL_TEXTURE_COORD_ARRAY** affects the active client texture unit. The active client texture unit is controlled with **glClientActiveTextureARB**.

ERRORS

GL_INVALID_ENUM is generated if *array* is not an accepted value.

glEnableClientState is not allowed between the execution of **glBegin** and the corresponding **glEnd**, but an error may or may not be generated. If no error is generated, the behavior is undefined.

SEE ALSO

glArrayElement, glClientActiveTextureARB, glColorPointer, glDrawArrays, glDrawElements, glEdgeFlagPointer, glEnable, glGetPointerv, glIndexPointer, glInterleavedArrays, glNormalPointer, glTexCoordPointer, glVertexPointer

NAME

glEvalCoord1d, **glEvalCoord1f**, **glEvalCoord2d**, **glEvalCoord2f**, **glEvalCoord1dv**, **glEvalCoord1fv**, **glEvalCoord2dv**, **glEvalCoord2fv** – evaluate enabled one- and two-dimensional maps

C SPECIFICATION

void **glEvalCoord1d**(GLdouble *u*)
void **glEvalCoord1f**(GLfloat *u*)
void **glEvalCoord2d**(GLdouble *u*,
                 GLdouble *v*)
void **glEvalCoord2f**(GLfloat *u*,
                 GLfloat *v*)

PARAMETERS

u Specifies a value that is the domain coordinate *u* to the basis function defined in a previous **glMap1** or **glMap2** command.

v Specifies a value that is the domain coordinate *v* to the basis function defined in a previous **glMap2** command. This argument is not present in a **glEvalCoord1** command.

C SPECIFICATION

void **glEvalCoord1dv**(const GLdouble **u*)
void **glEvalCoord1fv**(const GLfloat **u*)
void **glEvalCoord2dv**(const GLdouble **u*)
void **glEvalCoord2fv**(const GLfloat **u*)

PARAMETERS

u Specifies a pointer to an array containing either one or two domain coordinates. The first coordinate is *u*. The second coordinate is *v*, which is present only in **glEvalCoord2** versions.

DESCRIPTION

glEvalCoord1 evaluates enabled one-dimensional maps at argument *u*. **glEvalCoord2** does the same for two-dimensional maps using two domain values, *u* and *v*. To define a map, call **glMap1** and **glMap2**; to enable and disable it, call **glEnable** and **glDisable**.

When one of the **glEvalCoord** commands is issued, all currently enabled maps of the indicated dimension are evaluated. Then, for each enabled map, it is as if the corresponding GL command had been issued with the computed value. That is, if **GL_MAP1_INDEX** or **GL_MAP2_INDEX** is enabled, a **glIndex** command is simulated. If **GL_MAP1_COLOR_4** or **GL_MAP2_COLOR_4** is enabled, a **glColor** command is simulated. If **GL_MAP1_NORMAL** or **GL_MAP2_NORMAL** is enabled, a normal vector is produced, and if any of **GL_MAP1_TEXTURE_COORD_1**, **GL_MAP1_TEXTURE_COORD_2**, **GL_MAP1_TEXTURE_COORD_3**, **GL_MAP1_TEXTURE_COORD_4**, **GL_MAP2_TEXTURE_COORD_1**, **GL_MAP2_TEXTURE_COORD_2**, **GL_MAP2_TEXTURE_COORD_3**, or **GL_MAP2_TEXTURE_COORD_4** is enabled, then an appropriate **glTexCoord** command is simulated.

For color, color index, normal, and texture coordinates the GL uses evaluated values instead of current values for those evaluations that are enabled, and current values otherwise, However, the evaluated values do not update the current values. Thus, if **glVertex** commands are interspersed with **glEvalCoord** commands, the color, normal, and texture coordinates associated with the **glVertex** commands are not affected by the values generated by the **glEvalCoord** commands, but only by the most recent **glColor**, **glIndex**, **glNormal**, and **glTexCoord** commands.

No commands are issued for maps that are not enabled. If more than one texture evaluation is enabled for a particular dimension (for example, **GL_MAP2_TEXTURE_COORD_1** and **GL_MAP2_TEXTURE_COORD_2**), then only the evaluation of the map that produces the larger number of coordinates (in this case, **GL_MAP2_TEXTURE_COORD_2**) is carried out. **GL_MAP1_VERTEX_4** overrides **GL_MAP1_VERTEX_3**, and **GL_MAP2_VERTEX_4** overrides **GL_MAP2_VERTEX_3**, in the same manner. If neither a three- nor a four-component vertex map is enabled for the specified dimension, the **glEvalCoord** command is ignored.

If you have enabled automatic normal generation, by calling **glEnable** with argument **GL_AUTO_NORMAL**, **glEvalCoord2** generates surface normals analytically, regardless of the contents or enabling of the **GL_MAP2_NORMAL** map. Let

$$\mathbf{m} = \frac{\partial \mathbf{p}}{\partial u} \times \frac{\partial \mathbf{p}}{\partial v}$$

Then the generated normal **n** is

$$\mathbf{n} = \frac{\mathbf{m}}{||\mathbf{m}||}$$

If automatic normal generation is disabled, the corresponding normal map **GL_MAP2_NORMAL**, if enabled, is used to produce a normal. If neither automatic normal generation nor a normal map is enabled, no normal is generated for **glEvalCoord2** commands.

ASSOCIATED GETS

glIsEnabled with argument **GL_MAP1_VERTEX_3**
glIsEnabled with argument **GL_MAP1_VERTEX_4**
glIsEnabled with argument **GL_MAP1_INDEX**
glIsEnabled with argument **GL_MAP1_COLOR_4**

glIsEnabled with argument GL_MAP1_NORMAL
glIsEnabled with argument GL_MAP1_TEXTURE_COORD_1
glIsEnabled with argument GL_MAP1_TEXTURE_COORD_2
glIsEnabled with argument GL_MAP1_TEXTURE_COORD_3
glIsEnabled with argument GL_MAP1_TEXTURE_COORD_4
glIsEnabled with argument GL_MAP2_VERTEX_3
glIsEnabled with argument GL_MAP2_VERTEX_4
glIsEnabled with argument GL_MAP2_INDEX
glIsEnabled with argument GL_MAP2_COLOR_4
glIsEnabled with argument GL_MAP2_NORMAL
glIsEnabled with argument GL_MAP2_TEXTURE_COORD_1
glIsEnabled with argument GL_MAP2_TEXTURE_COORD_2
glIsEnabled with argument GL_MAP2_TEXTURE_COORD_3
glIsEnabled with argument GL_MAP2_TEXTURE_COORD_4
glIsEnabled with argument GL_AUTO_NORMAL
glGetMap

SEE ALSO

glBegin, **glColor**, **glEnable**, **glEvalMesh**, **glEvalPoint**, **glIndex**, **glMap1**, **glMap2**, **glMapGrid**, **glNormal**, **glTexCoord**, **glVertex**

NAME

glEvalMesh1, glEvalMesh2 – compute a one- or two-dimensional grid of points or lines

C SPECIFICATION

```
void glEvalMesh1( GLenum mode,
                  GLint i1,
                  GLint i2 )
```

PARAMETERS

mode In **glEvalMesh1**, specifies whether to compute a one-dimensional mesh of points or lines. Symbolic constants **GL_POINT** and **GL_LINE** are accepted.

i1, i2 Specify the first and last integer values for grid domain variable i.

C SPECIFICATION

```
void glEvalMesh2( GLenum mode,
                  GLint i1,
                  GLint i2,
                  GLint j1,
                  GLint j2 )
```

PARAMETERS

mode In **glEvalMesh2**, specifies whether to compute a two-dimensional mesh of points, lines, or polygons. Symbolic constants **GL_POINT**, **GL_LINE**, and **GL_FILL** are accepted.

i1, i2 Specify the first and last integer values for grid domain variable i.

j1, j2 Specify the first and last integer values for grid domain variable j.

DESCRIPTION

glMapGrid and **glEvalMesh** are used in tandem to efficiently generate and evaluate a series of evenly-spaced map domain values. **glEvalMesh** steps through the integer domain of a one- or two-dimensional grid, whose range is the domain of the evaluation maps specified by **glMap1** and **glMap2**. *mode* determines whether the resulting vertices are connected as points, lines, or filled polygons.

In the one-dimensional case, **glEvalMesh1**, the mesh is generated as if the following code fragment were executed:

```
glBegin( type );
for ( i = i1; i <= i2; i += 1 )
    glEvalCoord1( i · Δu + u₁ );
glEnd();
```

223

where

$$\Delta u = (u_2 - u_1) / n$$

and n, u_1, and u_2 are the arguments to the most recent **glMapGrid1** command. *type* is **GL_POINTS** if *mode* is **GL_POINT**, or **GL_LINES** if *mode* is **GL_LINE**.

The one absolute numeric requirement is that if $i = n$, then the value computed from $i \cdot \Delta u + u_1$ is exactly u_2.

In the two-dimensional case, **glEvalMesh2**, let

$$\Delta u = (u_2 - u_1) / n$$

$$\Delta v = (v_2 - v_1) / m,$$

where n, u_1, u_2, m, v_1, and v_2 are the arguments to the most recent **glMapGrid2** command. Then, if *mode* is **GL_FILL**, the **glEvalMesh2** command is equivalent to:

```
for ( j = j1; j < j2; j += 1 ) {
   glBegin( GL_QUAD_STRIP );
   for ( i = i1; i <= i2; i += 1 ) {
      glEvalCoord2( i · Δu + u₁, j · Δv + v₁ );
      glEvalCoord2( i · Δu + u₁, (j+1) · Δv + v₁ );
   }
   glEnd();
}
```

If *mode* is **GL_LINE**, then a call to **glEvalMesh2** is equivalent to:

```
for ( j = j1; j <= j2; j += 1 ) {
   glBegin( GL_LINE_STRIP );
   for ( i = i1; i <= i2; i += 1 )
      glEvalCoord2( i · Δu + u₁, j · Δv + v₁ );
   glEnd();
}

for ( i = i1;  i <= i2; i += 1 ) {
   glBegin( GL_LINE_STRIP );
   for ( j = j1; j <= j1; j += 1 )
      glEvalCoord2( i · Δu + u₁, j · Δv + v₁ );
   glEnd();
}
```

And finally, if *mode* is **GL_POINT**, then a call to **glEvalMesh2** is equivalent to:

```
glBegin( GL_POINTS );
for ( j = j1; j <= j2; j += 1 )
    for ( i = i1; i <= i2; i += 1 )
        glEvalCoord2( i · Δu + u₁, j · Δv + v₁ );
glEnd();
```

In all three cases, the only absolute numeric requirements are that if $i = n$, then the value computed from $i \cdot \Delta u + u_1$ is exactly u_2, and if $j = m$, then the value computed from $j \cdot \Delta v + v_1$ is exactly v_2.

ERRORS

GL_INVALID_ENUM is generated if *mode* is not an accepted value.

GL_INVALID_OPERATION is generated if **glEvalMesh** is executed between the execution of **glBegin** and the corresponding execution of **glEnd**.

ASSOCIATED GETS

glGet with argument **GL_MAP1_GRID_DOMAIN**
glGet with argument **GL_MAP2_GRID_DOMAIN**
glGet with argument **GL_MAP1_GRID_SEGMENTS**
glGet with argument **GL_MAP2_GRID_SEGMENTS**

SEE ALSO

glBegin, **glEvalCoord**, **glEvalPoint**, **glMap1**, **glMap2**, **glMapGrid**

NAME

      glEvalPoint1, **glEvalPoint2** – generate and evaluate a single point in a mesh

C SPECIFICATION

      void **glEvalPoint1** (GLint i)
      void **glEvalPoint2** (GLint i,
                        GLint j)

PARAMETERS

      i Specifies the integer value for grid domain variable i.

      j Specifies the integer value for grid domain variable j (**glEvalPoint2** only).

DESCRIPTION

      glMapGrid and **glEvalMesh** are used in tandem to efficiently generate and evaluate a series of evenly spaced map domain values. **glEvalPoint** can be used to evaluate a single grid point in the same gridspace that is traversed by **glEvalMesh**. Calling **glEvalPoint1** is equivalent to calling

```
glEvalCoord1 ( i · Δu + u₁ );
```

      where

$$\Delta u = (u_2 - u_1)/n$$

      and n, u_1, and u_2 are the arguments to the most recent **glMapGrid1** command. The one absolute numeric requirement is that if $i = n$, then the value computed from $i \cdot \Delta u + u_1$ is exactly u_2.

      In the two-dimensional case, **glEvalPoint2**, let

$$\Delta u = (u_2 - u_1)/n$$

$$\Delta v = (v_2 - v_1)/m,$$

      where n, u_1, u_2, m, v_1, and v_2 are the arguments to the most recent **glMapGrid2** command. Then the **glEvalPoint2** command is equivalent to calling

```
glEvalCoord2 ( i · Δu + u₁,  j · Δv + v₁ );
```

      The only absolute numeric requirements are that if $i = n$, then the value computed from $i \cdot \Delta u + u_1$ is exactly u_2, and if $j = m$, then the value computed from $i \cdot \Delta v + v_1$ is exactly v_2.

ASSOCIATED GETS

>**glGet** with argument **GL_MAP1_GRID_DOMAIN**
>**glGet** with argument **GL_MAP2_GRID_DOMAIN**
>**glGet** with argument **GL_MAP1_GRID_SEGMENTS**
>**glGet** with argument **GL_MAP2_GRID_SEGMENTS**

SEE ALSO

>**glEvalCoord**, **glEvalMesh**, **glMap1**, **glMap2**, **glMapGrid**

NAME

glFeedbackBuffer – controls feedback mode

C SPECIFICATION

void **glFeedbackBuffer**(GLsizei *size*,
                          GLenum *type*,
                          GLfloat **buffer*)

PARAMETERS

size   Specifies the maximum number of values that can be written into *buffer*.

type   Specifies a symbolic constant that describes the information that will be
         returned for each vertex. **GL_2D**, **GL_3D**, **GL_3D_COLOR**,
         GL_3D_COLOR_TEXTURE, and **GL_4D_COLOR_TEXTURE** are accepted.

buffer Returns the feedback data.

DESCRIPTION

The **glFeedbackBuffer** function controls feedback. Feedback, like selection, is a GL
mode. The mode is selected by calling **glRenderMode** with **GL_FEEDBACK**. When
the GL is in feedback mode, no pixels are produced by rasterization. Instead, information about primitives that would have been rasterized is fed back to the application using the GL.

glFeedbackBuffer has three arguments: *buffer* is a pointer to an array of floating-
point values into which feedback information is placed. *size* indicates the size of the
array. *type* is a symbolic constant describing the information that is fed back for
each vertex. **glFeedbackBuffer** must be issued before feedback mode is enabled (by
calling **glRenderMode** with argument **GL_FEEDBACK**). Setting **GL_FEEDBACK**
without establishing the feedback buffer, or calling **glFeedbackBuffer** while the GL
is in feedback mode, is an error.

When **glRenderMode** is called while in feedback mode, it returns the number of
entries placed in the feedback array, and resets the feedback array pointer to the
base of the feedback buffer. The returned value never exceeds *size*. If the feedback
data required more room than was available in *buffer*, **glRenderMode** returns a
negative value. To take the GL out of feedback mode, call **glRenderMode** with a
parameter value other than **GL_FEEDBACK**.

While in feedback mode, each primitive, bitmap, or pixel rectangle that would be
rasterized generates a block of values that are copied into the feedback array. If
doing so would cause the number of entries to exceed the maximum, the block is
partially written so as to fill the array (if there is any room left at all), and an
overflow flag is set. Each block begins with a code indicating the primitive type, followed by values that describe the primitive's vertices and associated data. Entries
are also written for bitmaps and pixel rectangles. Feedback occurs after polygon

culling and **glPolygonMode** interpretation of polygons has taken place, so polygons that are culled are not returned in the feedback buffer. It can also occur after polygons with more than three edges are broken up into triangles, if the GL implementation renders polygons by performing this decomposition.

The **glPassThrough** command can be used to insert a marker into the feedback buffer. See **glPassThrough**.

Following is the grammar for the blocks of values written into the feedback buffer. Each primitive is indicated with a unique identifying value followed by some number of vertices. Polygon entries include an integer value indicating how many vertices follow. A vertex is fed back as some number of floating-point values, as determined by *type*. Colors are fed back as four values in RGBA mode and one value in color index mode.

feedbackList ← feedbackItem feedbackList | feedbackItem

feedbackItem ← point | lineSegment | polygon | bitmap | pixelRectangle | passThru

point ← **GL_POINT_TOKEN** vertex

lineSegment ← **GL_LINE_TOKEN** vertex vertex | **GL_LINE_RESET_TOKEN** vertex vertex

polygon ← **GL_POLYGON_TOKEN** n polySpec

polySpec ← polySpec vertex | vertex vertex vertex

bitmap ← **GL_BITMAP_TOKEN** vertex

pixelRectangle ← **GL_DRAW_PIXEL_TOKEN** vertex | **GL_COPY_PIXEL_TOKEN** vertex

passThru ← **GL_PASS_THROUGH_TOKEN** value

vertex ← 2d | 3d | 3dColor | 3dColorTexture | 4dColorTexture

2d ← value value

3d ← value value value

3dColor ← value value value color

3dColorTexture ← value value value color tex

4dColorTexture ← value value value value color tex

color ← rgba | index

rgba ← value value value value

index ← value

tex ← value value value value

value is a floating-point number, and *n* is a floating-point integer giving the number of vertices in the polygon. GL_POINT_TOKEN, GL_LINE_TOKEN, GL_LINE_RESET_TOKEN, GL_POLYGON_TOKEN, GL_BITMAP_TOKEN, GL_DRAW_PIXEL_TOKEN, GL_COPY_PIXEL_TOKEN and GL_PASS_THROUGH_TOKEN are symbolic floating-point constants. GL_LINE_RESET_TOKEN is returned whenever the line stipple pattern is reset. The data returned as a vertex depends on the feedback *type*.

The following table gives the correspondence between *type* and the number of values per vertex. *k* is 1 in color index mode and 4 in RGBA mode.

Type	Coordinates	Color	Texture	Total Number of Values
GL_2D	x, y			2
GL_3D	x, y, z			3
GL_3D_COLOR	x, y, z	k		$3 + k$
GL_3D_COLOR_TEXTURE	$x, y, z,$	k	4	$7 + k$
GL_4D_COLOR_TEXTURE	x, y, z, w	k	4	$8 + k$

Feedback vertex coordinates are in window coordinates, except *w*, which is in clip coordinates. Feedback colors are lighted, if lighting is enabled. Feedback texture coordinates are generated, if texture coordinate generation is enabled. They are always transformed by the texture matrix.

NOTES

glFeedbackBuffer, when used in a display list, is not compiled into the display list but is executed immediately.

When the **GL_ARB_multitexture** extension is supported, **glFeedbackBuffer** returns only the texture coordinates of texture unit **GL_TEXTURE0_ARB**.

ERRORS

GL_INVALID_ENUM is generated if *type* is not an accepted value.

GL_INVALID_VALUE is generated if *size* is negative.

GL_INVALID_OPERATION is generated if **glFeedbackBuffer** is called while the render mode is **GL_FEEDBACK**, or if **glRenderMode** is called with argument **GL_FEEDBACK** before **glFeedbackBuffer** is called at least once.

GL_INVALID_OPERATION is generated if **glFeedbackBuffer** is executed between the execution of **glBegin** and the corresponding execution of **glEnd**.

ASSOCIATED GETS

glGet with argument GL_RENDER_MODE
glGet with argument GL_FEEDBACK_BUFFER_POINTER
glGet with argument GL_FEEDBACK_BUFFER_SIZE
glGet with argument GL_FEEDBACK_BUFFER_TYPE

SEE ALSO

glBegin, **glLineStipple**, **glPassThrough**, **glPolygonMode**, **glRenderMode**, **glSelectBuffer**

NAME

glFinish – block until all GL execution is complete

C SPECIFICATION

void **glFinish**(void)

DESCRIPTION

glFinish does not return until the effects of all previously called GL commands are complete. Such effects include all changes to GL state, all changes to connection state, and all changes to the frame buffer contents.

NOTES

glFinish requires a round trip to the server.

ERRORS

GL_INVALID_OPERATION is generated if **glFinish** is executed between the execution of **glBegin** and the corresponding execution of **glEnd**.

SEE ALSO

glFlush

NAME

glFlush – force execution of GL commands in finite time

C SPECIFICATION

void **glFlush**(void)

DESCRIPTION

Different GL implementations buffer commands in several different locations, including network buffers and the graphics accelerator itself. **glFlush** empties all of these buffers, causing all issued commands to be executed as quickly as they are accepted by the actual rendering engine. Though this execution may not be completed in any particular time period, it does complete in finite time.

Because any GL program might be executed over a network, or on an accelerator that buffers commands, all programs should call **glFlush** whenever they count on having all of their previously issued commands completed. For example, call **glFlush** before waiting for user input that depends on the generated image.

NOTES

glFlush can return at any time. It does not wait until the execution of all previously issued GL commands is complete.

ERRORS

GL_INVALID_OPERATION is generated if **glFlush** is executed between the execution of **glBegin** and the corresponding execution of **glEnd**.

SEE ALSO

glFinish

NAME

glFogf, glFogi, glFogfv, glFogiv – specify fog parameters

C SPECIFICATION

void **glFogf**(GLenum *pname*,
         GLfloat *param*)
void **glFogi**(GLenum *pname*,
         GLint *param*)

PARAMETERS

pname Specifies a single-valued fog parameter. **GL_FOG_MODE**, **GL_FOG_DENSITY**, **GL_FOG_START**, **GL_FOG_END**, and **GL_FOG_INDEX** are accepted.

param Specifies the value that *pname* will be set to.

C SPECIFICATION

void **glFogfv**(GLenum *pname*,
         const GLfloat **params*)
void **glFogiv**(GLenum *pname*,
         const GLint **params*)

PARAMETERS

pname Specifies a fog parameter. **GL_FOG_MODE**, **GL_FOG_DENSITY**, **GL_FOG_START**, **GL_FOG_END**, **GL_FOG_INDEX**, and **GL_FOG_COLOR** are accepted.

params Specifies the value or values to be assigned to *pname*. **GL_FOG_COLOR** requires an array of four values. All other parameters accept an array containing only a single value.

DESCRIPTION

Fog is initially disabled. While enabled, fog affects rasterized geometry, bitmaps, and pixel blocks, but not buffer clear operations. To enable and disable fog, call **glEnable** and **glDisable** with argument **GL_FOG**.

glFog assigns the value or values in *params* to the fog parameter specified by *pname*. The following values are accepted for *pname*:

GL_FOG_MODE   *params* is a single integer or floating-point value that specifies the equation to be used to compute the fog blend factor, *f*. Three symbolic constants are accepted: **GL_LINEAR**, **GL_EXP**, and **GL_EXP2**. The equations corresponding to these symbolic constants are defined below. The initial fog mode is **GL_EXP**.

GL_FOG_DENSITY	*params* is a single integer or floating-point value that specifies *density*, the fog density used in both exponential fog equations. Only nonnegative densities are accepted. The initial fog density is 1.
GL_FOG_START	*params* is a single integer or floating-point value that specifies *start*, the near distance used in the linear fog equation. The initial near distance is 0.
GL_FOG_END	*params* is a single integer or floating-point value that specifies *end*, the far distance used in the linear fog equation. The initial far distance is 1.
GL_FOG_INDEX	*params* is a single integer or floating-point value that specifies i_f, the fog color index. The initial fog index is 0.
GL_FOG_COLOR	*params* contains four integer or floating-point values that specify C_f, the fog color. Integer values are mapped linearly such that the most positive representable value maps to 1.0, and the most negative representable value maps to –1.0. Floating-point values are mapped directly. After conversion, all color components are clamped to the range [0,1]. The initial fog color is (0, 0, 0, 0).

Fog blends a fog color with each rasterized pixel fragment's posttexturing color using a blending factor *f*. Factor *f* is computed in one of three ways, depending on the fog mode. Let *z* be the distance in eye coordinates from the origin to the fragment being fogged. The equation for **GL_LINEAR** fog is

$$f = \frac{end - z}{end - start}$$

The equation for **GL_EXP** fog is

$$f = e^{-(density \cdot z)}$$

The equation for **GL_EXP2** fog is

$$f = e^{-(density \cdot z)^2}$$

Regardless of the fog mode, *f* is clamped to the range [0, 1] after it is computed. Then, if the GL is in RGBA color mode, the fragment's red, green, and blue colors, represented by C_r, are replaced by

$$C_r' = f C_r + (1-f) C_f$$

Fog does not affect a fragment's alpha component.

In color index mode, the fragment's color index i_r is replaced by

$$i_r' = i_r + (1-f) i_f$$

ERRORS

GL_INVALID_ENUM is generated if *pname* is not an accepted value, or if *pname* is **GL_FOG_MODE** and *params* is not an accepted value.

GL_INVALID_VALUE is generated if *pname* is **GL_FOG_DENSITY**, and *params* is negative.

GL_INVALID_OPERATION is generated if **glFog** is executed between the execution of **glBegin** and the corresponding execution of **glEnd**.

ASSOCIATED GETS

glIsEnabled with argument **GL_FOG**
glGet with argument **GL_FOG_COLOR**
glGet with argument **GL_FOG_INDEX**
glGet with argument **GL_FOG_DENSITY**
glGet with argument **GL_FOG_START**
glGet with argument **GL_FOG_END**
glGet with argument **GL_FOG_MODE**

SEE ALSO

glEnable

NAME

glFrontFace – define front- and back-facing polygons

C SPECIFICATION

void **glFrontFace**(GLenum *mode*)

PARAMETERS

mode　Specifies the orientation of front-facing polygons. **GL_CW** and **GL_CCW** are accepted. The initial value is **GL_CCW**.

DESCRIPTION

In a scene composed entirely of opaque closed surfaces, back-facing polygons are never visible. Eliminating these invisible polygons has the obvious benefit of speeding up the rendering of the image. To enable and disable elimination of back-facing polygons, call **glEnable** and **glDisable** with argument **GL_CULL_FACE**.

The projection of a polygon to window coordinates is said to have clockwise winding if an imaginary object following the path from its first vertex, its second vertex, and so on, to its last vertex, and finally back to its first vertex, moves in a clockwise direction about the interior of the polygon. The polygon's winding is said to be counterclockwise if the imaginary object following the same path moves in a counterclockwise direction about the interior of the polygon. **glFrontFace** specifies whether polygons with clockwise winding in window coordinates, or counterclockwise winding in window coordinates, are taken to be front-facing. Passing **GL_CCW** to *mode* selects counterclockwise polygons as front-facing; **GL_CW** selects clockwise polygons as front-facing. By default, counterclockwise polygons are taken to be front-facing.

ERRORS

GL_INVALID_ENUM is generated if *mode* is not an accepted value.

GL_INVALID_OPERATION is generated if **glFrontFace** is executed between the execution of **glBegin** and the corresponding execution of **glEnd**.

ASSOCIATED GETS

glGet with argument **GL_FRONT_FACE**

SEE ALSO

glCullFace, **glLightModel**

NAME

glFrustum – multiply the current matrix by a perspective matrix

C SPECIFICATION

void **glFrustum**(GLdouble *left*,
GLdouble *right*,
GLdouble *bottom*,
GLdouble *top*,
GLdouble *zNear*,
GLdouble *zFar*)

PARAMETERS

left, right

Specify the coordinates for the left and right vertical clipping planes.

bottom, top

Specify the coordinates for the bottom and top horizontal clipping planes.

zNear, zFar

Specify the distances to the near and far depth clipping planes. Both distances must be positive.

DESCRIPTION

glFrustum describes a perspective matrix that produces a perspective projection. The current matrix (see **glMatrixMode**) is multiplied by this matrix and the result replaces the current matrix, as if **glMultMatrix** were called with the following matrix as its argument:

$$
\begin{bmatrix}
\dfrac{2\,zNear}{right - left} & 0 & A & 0 \\[2ex]
0 & \dfrac{2\,zNear}{top - bottom} & B & 0 \\[2ex]
0 & 0 & C & D \\[1ex]
0 & 0 & -1 & 0
\end{bmatrix}
$$

$$ A = \frac{right + left}{right - left} $$

$$ B = \frac{top + bottom}{top - bottom} $$

$$ C = -\frac{zFar + zNear}{zFar - zNear} $$

$$D = -\frac{2\ zFar\ zNear}{zFar - zNear}$$

Typically, the matrix mode is **GL_PROJECTION**, and (*left*, *bottom*, *−zNear*) and (*right*, *top*, *−zNear*) specify the points on the near clipping plane that are mapped to the lower left and upper right corners of the window, assuming that the eye is located at (0, 0, 0). *−zFar* specifies the location of the far clipping plane. Both *zNear* and *zFar* must be positive.

Use **glPushMatrix** and **glPopMatrix** to save and restore the current matrix stack.

NOTES

Depth buffer precision is affected by the values specified for *zNear* and *zFar*. The greater the ratio of *zFar* to *zNear* is, the less effective the depth buffer will be at distinguishing between surfaces that are near each other. If

$$r = \frac{zFar}{zNear}$$

roughly $\log_2(r)$ bits of depth buffer precision are lost. Because *r* approaches infinity as *zNear* approaches 0, *zNear* must never be set to 0.

ERRORS

GL_INVALID_VALUE is generated if *zNear* or *zFar* is not positive, or if *left* = *right*, or *bottom* = *top*.

GL_INVALID_OPERATION is generated if **glFrustum** is executed between the execution of **glBegin** and the corresponding execution of **glEnd**.

ASSOCIATED GETS

glGet with argument **GL_MATRIX_MODE**
glGet with argument **GL_MODELVIEW_MATRIX**
glGet with argument **GL_PROJECTION_MATRIX**
glGet with argument **GL_TEXTURE_MATRIX**
glGet with argument **GL_COLOR_MATRIX**

SEE ALSO

glOrtho, **glMatrixMode**, **glMultMatrix**, **glPushMatrix**, **glViewport**

NAME

glGenLists – generate a contiguous set of empty display lists

C SPECIFICATION

GLuint **glGenLists**(GLsizei *range*)

PARAMETERS

range   Specifies the number of contiguous empty display lists to be generated.

DESCRIPTION

glGenLists has one argument, *range*. It returns an integer n such that *range* contiguous empty display lists, named n, $n+1$, ..., $n+range-1$, are created. If *range* is 0, if there is no group of *range* contiguous names available, or if any error is generated, no display lists are generated, and 0 is returned.

ERRORS

GL_INVALID_VALUE is generated if *range* is negative.

GL_INVALID_OPERATION is generated if **glGenLists** is executed between the execution of **glBegin** and the corresponding execution of **glEnd**.

ASSOCIATED GETS

glIsList

SEE ALSO

glCallList, **glCallLists**, **glDeleteLists**, **glNewList**

NAME

glGenTextures – generate texture names

C SPECIFICATION

void **glGenTextures**(GLsizei *n*,
                       GLuint *textures*)

PARAMETERS

n   Specifies the number of texture names to be generated.

textures Specifies an array in which the generated texture names are stored.

DESCRIPTION

glGenTextures returns *n* texture names in *textures*. There is no guarantee that the names form a contiguous set of integers; however, it is guaranteed that none of the returned names was in use immediately before the call to **glGenTextures**.

The generated textures have no dimensionality; they assume the dimensionality of the texture target to which they are first bound (see **glBindTexture**).

Texture names returned by a call to **glGenTextures** are not returned by subsequent calls, unless they are first deleted with **glDeleteTextures**.

NOTES

glGenTextures is available only if the GL version is 1.1 or greater.

ERRORS

GL_INVALID_VALUE is generated if *n* is negative.

GL_INVALID_OPERATION is generated if **glGenTextures** is executed between the execution of **glBegin** and the corresponding execution of **glEnd**.

ASSOCIATED GETS

glIsTexture

SEE ALSO

glBindTexture, **glCopyTexImage1D**, **glCopyTexImage2D**, **glDeleteTextures**, **glGet**, **glGetTexParameter**, **glTexImage1D**, **glTexImage2D**, **glTexImage3D**, **glTexParameter**

NAME

glGetBooleanv, glGetDoublev, glGetFloatv, glGetIntegerv – return the value or values of a selected parameter

C SPECIFICATION

void **glGetBooleanv**(GLenum *pname*,
                        GLboolean **params*)

C SPECIFICATION

void **glGetDoublev**(GLenum *pname*,
                        GLdouble **params*)

C SPECIFICATION

void **glGetFloatv**(GLenum *pname*,
                       GLfloat **params*)

C SPECIFICATION

void **glGetIntegerv**(GLenum *pname*,
                         GLint **params*)

PARAMETERS

pname   Specifies the parameter value to be returned. The symbolic constants in the list below are accepted.

params Returns the value or values of the specified parameter.

DESCRIPTION

These four commands return values for simple state variables in GL. *pname* is a symbolic constant indicating the state variable to be returned, and *params* is a pointer to an array of the indicated type in which to place the returned data.

Type conversion is performed if *params* has a different type than the state variable value being requested. If **glGetBooleanv** is called, a floating-point (or integer) value is converted to **GL_FALSE** if and only if it is 0.0 (or 0). Otherwise, it is converted to **GL_TRUE**. If **glGetIntegerv** is called, boolean values are returned as **GL_TRUE** or **GL_FALSE**, and most floating-point values are rounded to the nearest integer value. Floating-point colors and normals, however, are returned with a linear mapping that maps 1.0 to the most positive representable integer value, and −1.0 to the most negative representable integer value. If **glGetFloatv** or **glGetDoublev** is called, boolean values are returned as **GL_TRUE** or **GL_FALSE**, and integer values are converted to floating-point values.

The following symbolic constants are accepted by *pname*:

GL_ACCUM_ALPHA_BITS

> *params* returns one value, the number of alpha bitplanes in the accumulation buffer.

GL_ACCUM_BLUE_BITS   *params* returns one value, the number of blue bitplanes in the accumulation buffer.

GL_ACCUM_CLEAR_VALUE

> *params* returns four values: the red, green, blue, and alpha values used to clear the accumulation buffer. Integer values, if requested, are linearly mapped from the internal floating-point representation such that 1.0 returns the most positive representable integer value, and −1.0 returns the most negative representable integer value. The initial value is (0, 0, 0, 0). See **glClearAccum**.

GL_ACCUM_GREEN_BITS

> *params* returns one value, the number of green bitplanes in the accumulation buffer.

GL_ACCUM_RED_BITS   *params* returns one value, the number of red bitplanes in the accumulation buffer.

GL_ACTIVE_TEXTURE_ARB

> *params* returns a single value indicating the active multitexture unit. The initial value is **GL_TEXTURE0_ARB**. See **glActiveTextureARB**.

GL_ALIASED_POINT_SIZE_RANGE

> *params* returns two values, the smallest and largest supported sizes for aliased points.

GL_ALIASED_LINE_WIDTH_RANGE

> *params* returns two values, the smallest and largest supported widths for aliased lines.

GL_ALPHA_BIAS   *params* returns one value, the alpha bias factor used during pixel transfers. The initial value is 0. See **glPixelTransfer**.

GL_ALPHA_BITS   *params* returns one value, the number of alpha bitplanes in each color buffer.

GL_ALPHA_SCALE   *params* returns one value, the alpha scale factor used during pixel transfers. The initial value is 1. See **glPixelTransfer**.

GL_ALPHA_TEST *params* returns a single boolean value indicating whether alpha testing of fragments is enabled. The initial value is **GL_FALSE**. See **glAlphaFunc**.

GL_ALPHA_TEST_FUNC *params* returns one value, the symbolic name of the alpha test function. The initial value is **GL_ALWAYS**. See **glAlphaFunc**.

GL_ALPHA_TEST_REF *params* returns one value, the reference value for the alpha test. The initial value is 0. See **glAlphaFunc**. An integer value, if requested, is linearly mapped from the internal floating-point representation such that 1.0 returns the most positive representable integer value, and −1.0 returns the most negative representable integer value.

GL_ATTRIB_STACK_DEPTH

params returns one value, the depth of the attribute stack. If the stack is empty, 0 is returned. The initial value is 0. See **glPushAttrib**.

GL_AUTO_NORMAL *params* returns a single boolean value indicating whether 2D map evaluation automatically generates surface normals. The initial value is **GL_FALSE**. See **glMap2**.

GL_AUX_BUFFERS *params* returns one value, the number of auxiliary color buffers. The initial value is 0.

GL_BLEND *params* returns a single boolean value indicating whether blending is enabled. The initial value is **GL_FALSE**. See **glBlendFunc**.

GL_BLEND_COLOR *params* returns four values, the red, green, blue, and alpha values which are the components of the blend color. See **glBlendColor**.

GL_BLEND_DST *params* returns one value, the symbolic constant identifying the destination blend function. The initial value is **GL_ZERO**. See **glBlendFunc**.

GL_BLEND_EQUATION *params* returns one value, a symbolic constant indicating whether the blend equation is **GL_FUNC_ADD**, **GL_MIN** or **GL_MAX**. See **glBlendEquation**.

GL_BLEND_SRC *params* returns one value, the symbolic constant identifying the source blend function. The initial value is **GL_ONE**. See **glBlendFunc**.

GL_BLUE_BIAS *params* returns one value, the blue bias factor used during pixel transfers. The initial value is 0. See **glPixelTransfer**.

GL_BLUE_BITS *params* returns one value, the number of blue bitplanes in each color buffer.

GL_BLUE_SCALE *params* returns one value, the blue scale factor used during pixel transfers. The initial value is 1. See **glPixelTransfer**.

GL_CLIENT_ACTIVE_TEXTURE_ARB
params returns a single integer value indicating the current client active multitexture unit. The initial value is **GL_TEXTURE0_ARB**. See **glClientActiveTextureARB**.

GL_CLIENT_ATTRIB_STACK_DEPTH
params returns one value indicating the depth of the attribute stack. The initial value is 0. See **glPushClientAttrib**.

GL_CLIP_PLANE*i* *params* returns a single boolean value indicating whether the specified clipping plane is enabled. The initial value is **GL_FALSE**. See **glClipPlane**.

GL_COLOR_ARRAY *params* returns a single boolean value indicating whether the color array is enabled. The initial value is **GL_FALSE**. See **glColorPointer**.

GL_COLOR_ARRAY_SIZE
params returns one value, the number of components per color in the color array. The initial value is 4. See **glColorPointer**.

GL_COLOR_ARRAY_STRIDE
params returns one value, the byte offset between consecutive colors in the color array. The initial value is 0. See **glColorPointer**.

GL_COLOR_ARRAY_TYPE
params returns one value, the data type of each component in the color array. The initial value is **GL_FLOAT**. See **glColorPointer**.

GL_COLOR_CLEAR_VALUE
params returns four values: the red, green, blue, and alpha values used to clear the color buffers. Integer values, if requested, are linearly mapped from the internal floating-point representation such that 1.0 returns the most positive representable integer value, and −1.0

returns the most negative representable integer value. The initial value is (0, 0, 0, 0). See **glClearColor**.

GL_COLOR_LOGIC_OP *params* returns a single boolean value indicating whether a fragment's RGBA color values are merged into the framebuffer using a logical operation. The initial value is **GL_FALSE**. See **glLogicOp**.

GL_COLOR_MATERIAL *params* returns a single boolean value indicating whether one or more material parameters are tracking the current color. The initial value is **GL_FALSE**. See **glColorMaterial**.

GL_COLOR_MATERIAL_FACE

params returns one value, a symbolic constant indicating which materials have a parameter that is tracking the current color. The initial value is **GL_FRONT_AND_BACK**. See **glColorMaterial**.

GL_COLOR_MATERIAL_PARAMETER

params returns one value, a symbolic constant indicating which material parameters are tracking the current color. The initial value is **GL_AMBIENT_AND_DIFFUSE**. See **glColorMaterial**.

GL_COLOR_MATRIX *params* returns sixteen values: the color matrix on the top of the color matrix stack. Initially this matrix is the identity matrix. See **glPushMatrix**.

GL_COLOR_MATRIX_STACK_DEPTH

params returns one value, the maximum supported depth of the projection matrix stack. The value must be at least 2. See **glPushMatrix**.

GL_COLOR_TABLE *params* returns a single boolean value indicating whether the color table lookup is enabled. See **glColorTable**.

GL_COLOR_WRITEMASK

params returns four boolean values: the red, green, blue, and alpha write enables for the color buffers. The initial value is (**GL_TRUE**, **GL_TRUE**, **GL_TRUE**, **GL_TRUE**). See **glColorMask**.

GL_CONVOLUTION_1D *params* returns a single boolean value indicating whether 1D convolution is enabled. The initial value is **GL_FALSE**. See **glConvolutionFilter1D**.

GL_CONVOLUTION_2D   *params* returns a single boolean value indicating whether 2D convolution is enabled. The initial value is **GL_FALSE**. See **glConvolutionFilter2D**.

GL_CULL_FACE   *params* returns a single boolean value indicating whether polygon culling is enabled. The initial value is **GL_FALSE**. See **glCullFace**.

GL_CULL_FACE_MODE   *params* returns one value, a symbolic constant indicating which polygon faces are to be culled. The initial value is **GL_BACK**. See **glCullFace**.

GL_CURRENT_COLOR   *params* returns four values: the red, green, blue, and alpha values of the current color. Integer values, if requested, are linearly mapped from the internal floating-point representation such that 1.0 returns the most positive representable integer value, and −1.0 returns the most negative representable integer value. See **glColor**. The initial value is (1, 1, 1, 1).

GL_CURRENT_INDEX   *params* returns one value, the current color index. The initial value is 1. See **glIndex**.

GL_CURRENT_NORMAL   *params* returns three values: the x, y, and z values of the current normal. Integer values, if requested, are linearly mapped from the internal floating-point representation such that 1.0 returns the most positive representable integer value, and −1.0 returns the most negative representable integer value. The initial value is (0, 0, 1). See **glNormal**.

GL_CURRENT_RASTER_COLOR

params returns four values: the red, green, blue, and alpha values of the current raster position. Integer values, if requested, are linearly mapped from the internal floating-point representation such that 1.0 returns the most positive representable integer value, and −1.0 returns the most negative representable integer value. The initial value is (1, 1, 1, 1). See **glRasterPos**.

GL_CURRENT_RASTER_DISTANCE

params returns one value, the distance from the eye to the current raster position. The initial value is 0. See **glRasterPos**.

GL_CURRENT_RASTER_INDEX

> *params* returns one value, the color index of the current raster position. The initial value is 1. See **glRasterPos**.

GL_CURRENT_RASTER_POSITION

> *params* returns four values: the x, y, z, and w components of the current raster position. x, y, and z are in window coordinates, and w is in clip coordinates. The initial value is (0, 0, 0, 1). See **glRasterPos**.

GL_CURRENT_RASTER_POSITION_VALID

> *params* returns a single boolean value indicating whether the current raster position is valid. The initial value is **GL_TRUE**. See **glRasterPos**.

GL_CURRENT_RASTER_TEXTURE_COORDS

> *params* returns four values: the s, t, r, and q current raster texture coordinates. The initial value is (0, 0, 0, 1). See **glRasterPos** and **glTexCoord**.

GL_CURRENT_TEXTURE_COORDS

> *params* returns four values: the s, t, r, and q current texture coordinates. The initial value is (0, 0, 0, 1). See **glTexCoord**.

GL_DEPTH_BIAS

> *params* returns one value, the depth bias factor used during pixel transfers. The initial value is 0. See **glPixelTransfer**.

GL_DEPTH_BITS

> *params* returns one value, the number of bitplanes in the depth buffer.

GL_DEPTH_CLEAR_VALUE

> *params* returns one value, the value that is used to clear the depth buffer. Integer values, if requested, are linearly mapped from the internal floating-point representation such that 1.0 returns the most positive representable integer value, and −1.0 returns the most negative representable integer value. The initial value is 1. See **glClearDepth**.

GL_DEPTH_FUNC

> *params* returns one value, the symbolic constant that indicates the depth comparison function. The initial value is **GL_LESS**. See **glDepthFunc**.

GL_DEPTH_RANGE *params* returns two values: the near and far mapping limits for the depth buffer. Integer values, if requested, are linearly mapped from the internal floating-point representation such that 1.0 returns the most positive representable integer value, and −1.0 returns the most negative representable integer value. The initial value is (0, 1). See **glDepthRange**.

GL_DEPTH_SCALE *params* returns one value, the depth scale factor used during pixel transfers. The initial value is 1. See **glPixelTransfer**.

GL_DEPTH_TEST *params* returns a single boolean value indicating whether depth testing of fragments is enabled. The initial value is **GL_FALSE**. See **glDepthFunc** and **glDepthRange**.

GL_DEPTH_WRITEMASK
params returns a single boolean value indicating if the depth buffer is enabled for writing. The initial value is **GL_TRUE**. See **glDepthMask**.

GL_DITHER *params* returns a single boolean value indicating whether dithering of fragment colors and indices is enabled. The initial value is **GL_TRUE**.

GL_DOUBLEBUFFER *params* returns a single boolean value indicating whether double buffering is supported.

GL_DRAW_BUFFER *params* returns one value, a symbolic constant indicating which buffers are being drawn to. See **glDrawBuffer**. The initial value is **GL_BACK** if there are back buffers, otherwise it is **GL_FRONT**.

GL_EDGE_FLAG *params* returns a single boolean value indicating whether the current edge flag is **GL_TRUE** or **GL_FALSE**. The initial value is **GL_TRUE**. See **glEdgeFlag**.

GL_EDGE_FLAG_ARRAY *params* returns a single boolean value indicating whether the edge flag array is enabled. The initial value is **GL_FALSE**. See **glEdgeFlagPointer**.

GL_EDGE_FLAG_ARRAY_STRIDE
params returns one value, the byte offset between consecutive edge flags in the edge flag array. The initial value is 0. See **glEdgeFlagPointer**.

GL_FEEDBACK_BUFFER_SIZE

params returns one value, the size of the feedback buffer. See **glFeedbackBuffer**.

GL_FEEDBACK_BUFFER_TYPE

params returns one value, the type of the feedback buffer. See **glFeedbackBuffer**.

GL_FOG

params returns a single boolean value indicating whether fogging is enabled. The initial value is **GL_FALSE**. See **glFog**.

GL_FOG_COLOR

params returns four values: the red, green, blue, and alpha components of the fog color. Integer values, if requested, are linearly mapped from the internal floating-point representation such that 1.0 returns the most positive representable integer value, and −1.0 returns the most negative representable integer value. The initial value is (0, 0, 0, 0). See **glFog**.

GL_FOG_DENSITY

params returns one value, the fog density parameter. The initial value is 1. See **glFog**.

GL_FOG_END

params returns one value, the end factor for the linear fog equation. The initial value is 1. See **glFog**.

GL_FOG_HINT

params returns one value, a symbolic constant indicating the mode of the fog hint. The initial value is **GL_DONT_CARE**. See **glHint**.

GL_FOG_INDEX

params returns one value, the fog color index. The initial value is 0. See **glFog**.

GL_FOG_MODE

params returns one value, a symbolic constant indicating which fog equation is selected. The initial value is **GL_EXP**. See **glFog**.

GL_FOG_START

params returns one value, the start factor for the linear fog equation. The initial value is 0. See **glFog**.

GL_FRONT_FACE

params returns one value, a symbolic constant indicating whether clockwise or counterclockwise polygon winding is treated as front-facing. The initial value is **GL_CCW**. See **glFrontFace**.

GL_GREEN_BIAS

params returns one value, the green bias factor used during pixel transfers. The initial value is 0.

GL_GREEN_BITS	*params* returns one value, the number of green bitplanes in each color buffer.
GL_GREEN_SCALE	*params* returns one value, the green scale factor used during pixel transfers. The initial value is 1. See **glPixelTransfer**.
GL_HISTOGRAM	*params* returns a single boolean value indicating whether histogram is enabled. The initial value is **GL_FALSE**. See **glHistogram**.
GL_INDEX_ARRAY	*params* returns a single boolean value indicating whether the color index array is enabled. The initial value is **GL_FALSE**. See **glIndexPointer**.

GL_INDEX_ARRAY_STRIDE

params returns one value, the byte offset between consecutive color indexes in the color index array. The initial value is 0. See **glIndexPointer**.

GL_INDEX_ARRAY_TYPE

params returns one value, the data type of indexes in the color index array. The initial value is **GL_FLOAT**. See **glIndexPointer**.

GL_INDEX_BITS	*params* returns one value, the number of bitplanes in each color index buffer.

GL_INDEX_CLEAR_VALUE

params returns one value, the color index used to clear the color index buffers. The initial value is 0. See **glClearIndex**.

GL_INDEX_LOGIC_OP	*params* returns a single boolean value indicating whether a fragment's index values are merged into the framebuffer using a logical operation. The initial value is **GL_FALSE**. See **glLogicOp**.
GL_INDEX_MODE	*params* returns a single boolean value indicating whether the GL is in color index mode (**GL_TRUE**) or RGBA mode (**GL_FALSE**).
GL_INDEX_OFFSET	*params* returns one value, the offset added to color and stencil indices during pixel transfers. The initial value is 0. See **glPixelTransfer**.
GL_INDEX_SHIFT	*params* returns one value, the amount that color and stencil indices are shifted during pixel transfers. The initial value is 0. See **glPixelTransfer**.

GL_INDEX_WRITEMASK *params* returns one value, a mask indicating which bit-planes of each color index buffer can be written. The initial value is all 1's. See **glIndexMask**.

GL_LIGHT*i* *params* returns a single boolean value indicating whether the specified light is enabled. The initial value is **GL_FALSE**. See **glLight** and **glLightModel**.

GL_LIGHTING *params* returns a single boolean value indicating whether lighting is enabled. The initial value is **GL_FALSE**. See **glLightModel**.

GL_LIGHT_MODEL_AMBIENT
params returns four values: the red, green, blue, and alpha components of the ambient intensity of the entire scene. Integer values, if requested, are linearly mapped from the internal floating-point representation such that 1.0 returns the most positive representable integer value, and −1.0 returns the most negative representable integer value. The initial value is (0.2, 0.2, 0.2, 1.0). See **glLightModel**.

GL_LIGHT_MODEL_COLOR_CONTROL
params returns single enumerated value indicating whether specular reflection calculations are separated from normal lighting computations. The initial value is **GL_SINGLE_COLOR**.

GL_LIGHT_MODEL_LOCAL_VIEWER
params returns a single boolean value indicating whether specular reflection calculations treat the viewer as being local to the scene. The initial value is **GL_FALSE**. See **glLightModel**.

GL_LIGHT_MODEL_TWO_SIDE
params returns a single boolean value indicating whether separate materials are used to compute lighting for front- and back-facing polygons. The initial value is **GL_FALSE**. See **glLightModel**.

GL_LINE_SMOOTH *params* returns a single boolean value indicating whether antialiasing of lines is enabled. The initial value is **GL_FALSE**. See **glLineWidth**.

GL_LINE_SMOOTH_HINT
params returns one value, a symbolic constant indicating the mode of the line antialiasing hint. The initial value is **GL_DONT_CARE**. See **glHint**.

GL_LINE_STIPPLE	*params* returns a single boolean value indicating whether stippling of lines is enabled. The initial value is **GL_FALSE**. See **glLineStipple**.

GL_LINE_STIPPLE_PATTERN
params returns one value, the 16-bit line stipple pattern. The initial value is all 1's. See **glLineStipple**.

GL_LINE_STIPPLE_REPEAT
params returns one value, the line stipple repeat factor. The initial value is 1. See **glLineStipple**.

GL_LINE_WIDTH	*params* returns one value, the line width as specified with **glLineWidth**. The initial value is 1.

GL_LINE_WIDTH_GRANULARITY
params returns one value, the width difference between adjacent supported widths for antialiased lines. See **glLineWidth**.

GL_LINE_WIDTH_RANGE
params returns two values: the smallest and largest supported widths for antialiased lines. See **glLineWidth**.

GL_LIST_BASE	*params* returns one value, the base offset added to all names in arrays presented to **glCallLists**. The initial value is 0. See **glListBase**.

GL_LIST_INDEX	*params* returns one value, the name of the display list currently under construction. 0 is returned if no display list is currently under construction. The initial value is 0. See **glNewList**.

GL_LIST_MODE	*params* returns one value, a symbolic constant indicating the construction mode of the display list currently under construction. The initial value is 0. See **glNewList**.

GL_LOGIC_OP_MODE	*params* returns one value, a symbolic constant indicating the selected logic operation mode. The initial value is **GL_COPY**. See **glLogicOp**.

GL_MAP1_COLOR_4	*params* returns a single boolean value indicating whether 1D evaluation generates colors. The initial value is **GL_FALSE**. See **glMap1**.

GL_MAP1_GRID_DOMAIN
params returns two values: the endpoints of the 1D map's grid domain. The initial value is (0, 1). See **glMapGrid**.

GL_MAP1_GRID_SEGMENTS

params returns one value, the number of partitions in the 1D map's grid domain. The initial value is 1. See **glMapGrid**.

GL_MAP1_INDEX *params* returns a single boolean value indicating whether 1D evaluation generates color indices. The initial value is **GL_FALSE**. See **glMap1**.

GL_MAP1_NORMAL *params* returns a single boolean value indicating whether 1D evaluation generates normals. The initial value is **GL_FALSE**. See **glMap1**.

GL_MAP1_TEXTURE_COORD_1

params returns a single boolean value indicating whether 1D evaluation generates 1D texture coordinates. The initial value is **GL_FALSE**. See **glMap1**.

GL_MAP1_TEXTURE_COORD_2

params returns a single boolean value indicating whether 1D evaluation generates 2D texture coordinates. The initial value is **GL_FALSE**. See **glMap1**.

GL_MAP1_TEXTURE_COORD_3

params returns a single boolean value indicating whether 1D evaluation generates 3D texture coordinates. The initial value is **GL_FALSE**. See **glMap1**.

GL_MAP1_TEXTURE_COORD_4

params returns a single boolean value indicating whether 1D evaluation generates 4D texture coordinates. The initial value is **GL_FALSE**. See **glMap1**.

GL_MAP1_VERTEX_3 *params* returns a single boolean value indicating whether 1D evaluation generates 3D vertex coordinates. The initial value is **GL_FALSE**. See **glMap1**.

GL_MAP1_VERTEX_4 *params* returns a single boolean value indicating whether 1D evaluation generates 4D vertex coordinates. The initial value is **GL_FALSE**. See **glMap1**.

GL_MAP2_COLOR_4 *params* returns a single boolean value indicating whether 2D evaluation generates colors. The initial value is **GL_FALSE**. See **glMap2**.

GL_MAP2_GRID_DOMAIN

params returns four values: the endpoints of the 2D map's *i* and *j* grid domains. The initial value is (0,1; 0,1). See **glMapGrid**.

GL_MAP2_GRID_SEGMENTS

> *params* returns two values: the number of partitions in the 2D map's *i* and *j* grid domains. The initial value is (1,1). See **glMapGrid**.

GL_MAP2_INDEX
> *params* returns a single boolean value indicating whether 2D evaluation generates color indices. The initial value is **GL_FALSE**. See **glMap2**.

GL_MAP2_NORMAL
> *params* returns a single boolean value indicating whether 2D evaluation generates normals. The initial value is **GL_FALSE**. See **glMap2**.

GL_MAP2_TEXTURE_COORD_1

> *params* returns a single boolean value indicating whether 2D evaluation generates 1D texture coordinates. The initial value is **GL_FALSE**. See **glMap2**.

GL_MAP2_TEXTURE_COORD_2

> *params* returns a single boolean value indicating whether 2D evaluation generates 2D texture coordinates. The initial value is **GL_FALSE**. See **glMap2**.

GL_MAP2_TEXTURE_COORD_3

> *params* returns a single boolean value indicating whether 2D evaluation generates 3D texture coordinates. The initial value is **GL_FALSE**. See **glMap2**.

GL_MAP2_TEXTURE_COORD_4

> *params* returns a single boolean value indicating whether 2D evaluation generates 4D texture coordinates. The initial value is **GL_FALSE**. See **glMap2**.

GL_MAP2_VERTEX_3
> *params* returns a single boolean value indicating whether 2D evaluation generates 3D vertex coordinates. The initial value is **GL_FALSE**. See **glMap2**.

GL_MAP2_VERTEX_4
> *params* returns a single boolean value indicating whether 2D evaluation generates 4D vertex coordinates. The initial value is **GL_FALSE**. See **glMap2**.

GL_MAP_COLOR
> *params* returns a single boolean value indicating if colors and color indices are to be replaced by table lookup during pixel transfers. The initial value is **GL_FALSE**. See **glPixelTransfer**.

GL_MAP_STENCIL   *params* returns a single boolean value indicating if stencil indices are to be replaced by table lookup during pixel transfers. The initial value is **GL_FALSE**. See **glPixelTransfer**.

GL_MATRIX_MODE   *params* returns one value, a symbolic constant indicating which matrix stack is currently the target of all matrix operations. The initial value is **GL_MODELVIEW**. See **glMatrixMode**.

GL_MAX_3D_TEXTURE_SIZE

params returns one value, a rough estimate of the largest 3D texture that the GL can handle. If the GL version is 1.2 or greater, use **GL_PROXY_TEXTURE_3D** to determine if a texture is too large. See **glTexImage3D**.

GL_MAX_CLIENT_ATTRIB_STACK_DEPTH

params returns one value indicating the maximum supported depth of the client attribute stack. See **glPushClientAttrib**.

GL_MAX_ATTRIB_STACK_DEPTH

params returns one value, the maximum supported depth of the attribute stack. The value must be at least 16. See **glPushAttrib**.

GL_MAX_CLIP_PLANES   *params* returns one value, the maximum number of application-defined clipping planes. The value must be at least 6. See **glClipPlane**.

GL_MAX_COLOR_MATRIX_STACK_DEPTH

params returns one value, the maximum supported depth of the color matrix stack. The value must be at least 2. See **glPushMatrix**.

GL_MAX_ELEMENTS_INDICES

params returns one value, the recommended maximum number of vertex array indices. See **glDrawRangeElements**.

GL_MAX_ELEMENTS_VERTICES

params returns one value, the recommended maximum number of vertex array vertices. See **glDrawRangeElements**.

GL_MAX_EVAL_ORDER   *params* returns one value, the maximum equation order supported by 1D and 2D evaluators. The value must be at least 8. See **glMap1** and **glMap2**.

GL_MAX_LIGHTS   *params* returns one value, the maximum number of lights. The value must be at least 8. See **glLight**.

GL_MAX_LIST_NESTING

params returns one value, the maximum recursion depth allowed during display-list traversal. The value must be at least 64. See **glCallList**.

GL_MAX_MODELVIEW_STACK_DEPTH

params returns one value, the maximum supported depth of the modelview matrix stack. The value must be at least 32. See **glPushMatrix**.

GL_MAX_NAME_STACK_DEPTH

params returns one value, the maximum supported depth of the selection name stack. The value must be at least 64. See **glPushName**.

GL_MAX_PIXEL_MAP_TABLE

params returns one value, the maximum supported size of a **glPixelMap** lookup table. The value must be at least 32. See **glPixelMap**.

GL_MAX_PROJECTION_STACK_DEPTH

params returns one value, the maximum supported depth of the projection matrix stack. The value must be at least 2. See **glPushMatrix**.

GL_MAX_TEXTURE_SIZE

params returns one value. The value gives a rough estimate of the largest texture that the GL can handle. If the GL version is 1.1 or greater, use **GL_PROXY_TEXTURE_1D** or **GL_PROXY_TEXTURE_2D** to determine if a texture is too large. See **glTexImage1D** and **glTexImage2D**.

GL_MAX_TEXTURE_STACK_DEPTH

params returns one value, the maximum supported depth of the texture matrix stack. The value must be at least 2. See **glPushMatrix**.

GL_MAX_TEXTURE_UNITS_ARB
params returns a single value indicating the number of texture units supported. The value must be at least 1. See **glActiveTextureARB**.

GL_MAX_VIEWPORT_DIMS
params returns two values: the maximum supported width and height of the viewport. These must be at least as large as the visible dimensions of the display being rendered to. See **glViewport**.

GL_MINMAX
params returns a single boolean value indicating whether pixel minmax values are computed. The initial value is **GL_FALSE**. See **glMinmax**.

GL_MODELVIEW_MATRIX
params returns sixteen values: the modelview matrix on the top of the modelview matrix stack. Initially this matrix is the identity matrix. See **glPushMatrix**.

GL_MODELVIEW_STACK_DEPTH
params returns one value, the number of matrices on the modelview matrix stack. The initial value is 1. See **glPushMatrix**.

GL_NAME_STACK_DEPTH
params returns one value, the number of names on the selection name stack. The initial value is 0. See **glPushName**.

GL_NORMAL_ARRAY
params returns a single boolean value, indicating whether the normal array is enabled. The initial value is **GL_FALSE**. See **glNormalPointer**.

GL_NORMAL_ARRAY_STRIDE
params returns one value, the byte offset between consecutive normals in the normal array. The initial value is 0. See **glNormalPointer**.

GL_NORMAL_ARRAY_TYPE
params returns one value, the data type of each coordinate in the normal array. The initial value is **GL_FLOAT**. See **glNormalPointer**.

GL_NORMALIZE
params returns a single boolean value indicating whether normals are automatically scaled to unit length after they have been transformed to eye coordinates. The initial value is **GL_FALSE**. See **glNormal**.

GL_PACK_ALIGNMENT   *params* returns one value, the byte alignment used for writing pixel data to memory. The initial value is 4. See **glPixelStore**.

GL_PACK_IMAGE_HEIGHT

params returns one value, the image height used for writing pixel data to memory. The initial value is 0. See **glPixelStore**.

GL_PACK_LSB_FIRST   *params* returns a single boolean value indicating whether single-bit pixels being written to memory are written first to the least significant bit of each unsigned byte. The initial value is **GL_FALSE**. See **glPixelStore**.

GL_PACK_ROW_LENGTH

params returns one value, the row length used for writing pixel data to memory. The initial value is 0. See **glPixelStore**.

GL_PACK_SKIP_IMAGES *params* returns one value, the number of pixel images skipped before the first pixel is written into memory. The initial value is 0. See **glPixelStore**.

GL_PACK_SKIP_PIXELS   *params* returns one value, the number of pixel locations skipped before the first pixel is written into memory. The initial value is 0. See **glPixelStore**.

GL_PACK_SKIP_ROWS   *params* returns one value, the number of rows of pixel locations skipped before the first pixel is written into memory. The initial value is 0. See **glPixelStore**.

GL_PACK_SWAP_BYTES *params* returns a single boolean value indicating whether the bytes of two-byte and four-byte pixel indices and components are swapped before being written to memory. The initial value is **GL_FALSE**. See **glPixelStore**.

GL_PERSPECTIVE_CORRECTION_HINT

params returns one value, a symbolic constant indicating the mode of the perspective correction hint. The initial value is **GL_DONT_CARE**. See **glHint**.

GL_PIXEL_MAP_A_TO_A_SIZE

params returns one value, the size of the alpha-to-alpha pixel translation table. The initial value is 1. See **glPixelMap**.

GL_PIXEL_MAP_B_TO_B_SIZE

> *params* returns one value, the size of the blue-to-blue pixel translation table. The initial value is 1. See **glPixelMap**.

GL_PIXEL_MAP_G_TO_G_SIZE

> *params* returns one value, the size of the green-to-green pixel translation table. The initial value is 1. See **glPixelMap**.

GL_PIXEL_MAP_I_TO_A_SIZE

> *params* returns one value, the size of the index-to-alpha pixel translation table. The initial value is 1. See **glPixelMap**.

GL_PIXEL_MAP_I_TO_B_SIZE

> *params* returns one value, the size of the index-to-blue pixel translation table. The initial value is 1. See **glPixelMap**.

GL_PIXEL_MAP_I_TO_G_SIZE

> *params* returns one value, the size of the index-to-green pixel translation table. The initial value is 1. See **glPixelMap**.

GL_PIXEL_MAP_I_TO_I_SIZE

> *params* returns one value, the size of the index-to-index pixel translation table. The initial value is 1. See **glPixelMap**.

GL_PIXEL_MAP_I_TO_R_SIZE

> *params* returns one value, the size of the index-to-red pixel translation table. The initial value is 1. See **glPixelMap**.

GL_PIXEL_MAP_R_TO_R_SIZE

> *params* returns one value, the size of the red-to-red pixel translation table. The initial value is 1. See **glPixelMap**.

GL_PIXEL_MAP_S_TO_S_SIZE

> *params* returns one value, the size of the stencil-to-stencil pixel translation table. The initial value is 1. See **glPixelMap**.

GL_POINT_SIZE

> *params* returns one value, the point size as specified by **glPointSize**. The initial value is 1.

GL_POINT_SIZE_GRANULARITY

params returns one value, the size difference between adjacent supported sizes for antialiased points. See **glPointSize**.

GL_POINT_SIZE_RANGE *params* returns two values: the smallest and largest supported sizes for antialiased points. The smallest size must be at most 1, and the largest size must be at least 1. See **glPointSize**.

GL_POINT_SMOOTH *params* returns a single boolean value indicating whether antialiasing of points is enabled. The initial value is **GL_FALSE**. See **glPointSize**.

GL_POINT_SMOOTH_HINT

params returns one value, a symbolic constant indicating the mode of the point antialiasing hint. The initial value is **GL_DONT_CARE**. See **glHint**.

GL_POLYGON_MODE *params* returns two values: symbolic constants indicating whether front-facing and back-facing polygons are rasterized as points, lines, or filled polygons. The initial value is **GL_FILL**. See **glPolygonMode**.

GL_POLYGON_OFFSET_FACTOR

params returns one value, the scaling factor used to determine the variable offset that is added to the depth value of each fragment generated when a polygon is rasterized. The initial value is 0. See **glPolygonOffset**.

GL_POLYGON_OFFSET_UNITS

params returns one value. This value is multiplied by an implementation-specific value and then added to the depth value of each fragment generated when a polygon is rasterized. The initial value is 0. See **glPolygonOffset**.

GL_POLYGON_OFFSET_FILL

params returns a single boolean value indicating whether polygon offset is enabled for polygons in fill mode. The initial value is **GL_FALSE**. See **glPolygonOffset**.

GL_POLYGON_OFFSET_LINE

params returns a single boolean value indicating whether polygon offset is enabled for polygons in line mode. The initial value is **GL_FALSE**. See **glPolygonOffset**.

GL_POLYGON_OFFSET_POINT

> *params* returns a single boolean value indicating whether polygon offset is enabled for polygons in point mode. The initial value is **GL_FALSE**. See **glPolygonOffset**.

GL_POLYGON_SMOOTH

> *params* returns a single boolean value indicating whether antialiasing of polygons is enabled. The initial value is **GL_FALSE**. See **glPolygonMode**.

GL_POLYGON_SMOOTH_HINT

> *params* returns one value, a symbolic constant indicating the mode of the polygon antialiasing hint. The initial value is **GL_DONT_CARE**. See **glHint**.

GL_POLYGON_STIPPLE *params* returns a single boolean value indicating whether polygon stippling is enabled. The initial value is **GL_FALSE**. See **glPolygonStipple**.

GL_POST_COLOR_MATRIX_COLOR_TABLE

> *params* returns a single boolean value indicating whether post color matrix transformation lookup is enabled. The initial value is **GL_FALSE**. See **glColorTable**.

GL_POST_COLOR_MATRIX_RED_BIAS

> *params* returns one value, the red bias factor applied to RGBA fragments after color matrix transformations. The initial value is 0. See **glPixelTransfer**.

GL_POST_COLOR_MATRIX_GREEN_BIAS

> *params* returns one value, the green bias factor applied to RGBA fragments after color matrix transformations. The initial value is 0. See **glPixelTransfer**

GL_POST_COLOR_MATRIX_BLUE_BIAS

> *params* returns one value, the blue bias factor applied to RGBA fragments after color matrix transformations. The initial value is 0. See **glPixelTransfer**.

GL_POST_COLOR_MATRIX_ALPHA_BIAS

> *params* returns one value, the alpha bias factor applied to RGBA fragments after color matrix transformations. The initial value is 0. See **glPixelTransfer**.

GL_POST_COLOR_MATRIX_RED_SCALE

> *params* returns one value, the red scale factor applied to RGBA fragments after color matrix transformations. The initial value is 1. See **glPixelTransfer**.

GL_POST_COLOR_MATRIX_GREEN_SCALE

params returns one value, the green scale factor applied to RGBA fragments after color matrix transformations. The initial value is 1. See **glPixelTransfer**.

GL_POST_COLOR_MATRIX_BLUE_SCALE

params returns one value, the blue scale factor applied to RGBA fragments after color matrix transformations. The initial value is 1. See **glPixelTransfer**.

GL_POST_COLOR_MATRIX_ALPHA_SCALE

params returns one value, the alpha scale factor applied to RGBA fragments after color matrix transformations. The initial value is 1. See **glPixelTransfer**.

GL_POST_CONVOLUTION_COLOR_TABLE

params returns a single boolean value indicating whether post convolution lookup is enabled. The initial value is **GL_FALSE**. See **glColorTable**.

GL_POST_CONVOLUTION_RED_BIAS

params returns one value, the red bias factor applied to RGBA fragments after convolution. The initial value is 0. See **glPixelTransfer**.

GL_POST_CONVOLUTION_GREEN_BIAS

params returns one value, the green bias factor applied to RGBA fragments after convolution. The initial value is 0. See **glPixelTransfer**.

GL_POST_CONVOLUTION_BLUE_BIAS

params returns one value, the blue bias factor applied to RGBA fragments after convolution. The initial value is 0. See **glPixelTransfer**.

GL_POST_CONVOLUTION_ALPHA_BIAS

params returns one value, the alpha bias factor applied to RGBA fragments after convolution. The initial value is 0. See **glPixelTransfer**.

GL_POST_CONVOLUTION_RED_SCALE

params returns one value, the red scale factor applied to RGBA fragments after convolution. The initial value is 1. See **glPixelTransfer**.

GL_POST_CONVOLUTION_GREEN_SCALE

> *params* returns one value, the green scale factor applied to RGBA fragments after convolution. The initial value is 1. See **glPixelTransfer**.

GL_POST_CONVOLUTION_BLUE_SCALE

> *params* returns one value, the blue scale factor applied to RGBA fragments after convolution. The initial value is 1. See **glPixelTransfer**.

GL_POST_CONVOLUTION_ALPHA_SCALE

> *params* returns one value, the alpha scale factor applied to RGBA fragments after convolution. The initial value is 1. See **glPixelTransfer**.

GL_PROJECTION_MATRIX

> *params* returns sixteen values: the projection matrix on the top of the projection matrix stack. Initially this matrix is the identity matrix. See **glPushMatrix**.

GL_PROJECTION_STACK_DEPTH

> *params* returns one value, the number of matrices on the projection matrix stack. The initial value is 1. See **glPushMatrix**.

GL_READ_BUFFER   *params* returns one value, a symbolic constant indicating which color buffer is selected for reading. The initial value is **GL_BACK** if there is a back buffer, otherwise it is **GL_FRONT**. See **glReadPixels** and **glAccum**.

GL_RED_BIAS   *params* returns one value, the red bias factor used during pixel transfers. The initial value is 0.

GL_RED_BITS   *params* returns one value, the number of red bitplanes in each color buffer.

GL_RED_SCALE   *params* returns one value, the red scale factor used during pixel transfers. The initial value is 1. See **glPixelTransfer**.

GL_RENDER_MODE   *params* returns one value, a symbolic constant indicating whether the GL is in render, select, or feedback mode. The initial value is **GL_RENDER**. See **glRenderMode**.

GL_RESCALE_NORMAL   *params* returns single boolean value indicating whether normal rescaling is enabled. See **glEnable**.

GL_RGBA_MODE   *params* returns a single boolean value indicating whether the GL is in RGBA mode (true) or color index mode (false). See **glColor**.

GL_SCISSOR_BOX   *params* returns four values: the *x* and *y* window coordinates of the scissor box, followed by its width and height. Initially the *x* and *y* window coordinates are both 0 and the width and height are set to the size of the window. See **glScissor**.

GL_SCISSOR_TEST   *params* returns a single boolean value indicating whether scissoring is enabled. The initial value is **GL_FALSE**. See **glScissor**.

GL_SELECTION_BUFFER_SIZE
params return one value, the size of the selection buffer. See **glSelectBuffer**.

GL_SEPARABLE_2D   *params* returns a single boolean value indicating whether 2D separable convolution is enabled. The initial value is **GL_FALSE**. See **glSeparableFilter2D**.

GL_SHADE_MODEL   *params* returns one value, a symbolic constant indicating whether the shading mode is flat or smooth. The initial value is **GL_SMOOTH**. See **glShadeModel**.

GL_SMOOTH_LINE_WIDTH_RANGE
params returns two values, the smallest and largest supported widths for antialiased lines. See **glLineWidth**.

GL_SMOOTH_LINE_WIDTH_GRANULARITY
params returns one value, the granularity of widths for antialiased lines. See **glLineWidth**.

GL_SMOOTH_POINT_SIZE_RANGE
params returns two values, the smallest and largest supported widths for antialiased points. See **glPointSize**.

GL_SMOOTH_POINT_SIZE_GRANULARITY
params returns one value, the granularity of sizes for antialiased points. See **glPointSize**.

GL_STENCIL_BITS   *params* returns one value, the number of bitplanes in the stencil buffer.

GL_STENCIL_CLEAR_VALUE
params returns one value, the index to which the stencil bitplanes are cleared. The initial value is 0. See **glClearStencil**.

GL_STENCIL_FAIL   *params* returns one value, a symbolic constant indicating what action is taken when the stencil test fails. The initial value is **GL_KEEP**. See **glStencilOp**.

GL_STENCIL_FUNC   *params* returns one value, a symbolic constant indicating what function is used to compare the stencil reference value with the stencil buffer value. The initial value is **GL_ALWAYS**. See **glStencilFunc**.

GL_STENCIL_PASS_DEPTH_FAIL

params returns one value, a symbolic constant indicating what action is taken when the stencil test passes, but the depth test fails. The initial value is **GL_KEEP**. See **glStencilOp**.

GL_STENCIL_PASS_DEPTH_PASS

params returns one value, a symbolic constant indicating what action is taken when the stencil test passes and the depth test passes. The initial value is **GL_KEEP**. See **glStencilOp**.

GL_STENCIL_REF   *params* returns one value, the reference value that is compared with the contents of the stencil buffer. The initial value is 0. See **glStencilFunc**.

GL_STENCIL_TEST   *params* returns a single boolean value indicating whether stencil testing of fragments is enabled. The initial value is **GL_FALSE**. See **glStencilFunc** and **glStencilOp**.

GL_STENCIL_VALUE_MASK

params returns one value, the mask that is used to mask both the stencil reference value and the stencil buffer value before they are compared. The initial value is all 1's. See **glStencilFunc**.

GL_STENCIL_WRITEMASK

params returns one value, the mask that controls writing of the stencil bitplanes. The initial value is all 1's. See **glStencilMask**.

GL_STEREO   *params* returns a single boolean value indicating whether stereo buffers (left and right) are supported.

GL_SUBPIXEL_BITS   *params* returns one value, an estimate of the number of bits of subpixel resolution that are used to position rasterized geometry in window coordinates. The initial value is 4.

GL_TEXTURE_1D   *params* returns a single boolean value indicating whether 1D texture mapping is enabled. The initial value is **GL_FALSE**. See **glTexImage1D**.

GL_TEXTURE_BINDING_1D
params returns a single value, the name of the texture currently bound to the target **GL_TEXTURE_1D**. The initial value is 0. See **glBindTexture**.

GL_TEXTURE_2D
params returns a single boolean value indicating whether 2D texture mapping is enabled. The initial value is **GL_FALSE**. See **glTexImage2D**.

GL_TEXTURE_BINDING_2D
params returns a single value, the name of the texture currently bound to the target **GL_TEXTURE_2D**. The initial value is 0. See **glBindTexture**.

GL_TEXTURE_3D
params returns a single boolean value indicating whether 3D texture mapping is enabled. The initial value is **GL_FALSE**. See **glTexImage3D**.

GL_TEXTURE_BINDING_3D
params returns a single value, the name of the texture currently bound to the target **GL_TEXTURE_3D**. The initial value is 0. See **glBindTexture**.

GL_TEXTURE_COORD_ARRAY
params returns a single boolean value indicating whether the texture coordinate array is enabled. The initial value is **GL_FALSE**. See **glTexCoordPointer**.

GL_TEXTURE_COORD_ARRAY_SIZE
params returns one value, the number of coordinates per element in the texture coordinate array. The initial value is 4. See **glTexCoordPointer**.

GL_TEXTURE_COORD_ARRAY_STRIDE
params returns one value, the byte offset between consecutive elements in the texture coordinate array. The initial value is 0. See **glTexCoordPointer**.

GL_TEXTURE_COORD_ARRAY_TYPE
params returns one value, the data type of the coordinates in the texture coordinate array. The initial value is **GL_FLOAT**. See **glTexCoordPointer**.

GL_TEXTURE_GEN_Q
params returns a single boolean value indicating whether automatic generation of the *q* texture coordinate is enabled. The initial value is **GL_FALSE**. See **glTexGen**.

GL_TEXTURE_GEN_R   *params* returns a single boolean value indicating whether automatic generation of the *r* texture coordinate is enabled. The initial value is **GL_FALSE**. See **glTexGen**.

GL_TEXTURE_GEN_S   *params* returns a single boolean value indicating whether automatic generation of the *S* texture coordinate is enabled. The initial value is **GL_FALSE**. See **glTexGen**.

GL_TEXTURE_GEN_T   *params* returns a single boolean value indicating whether automatic generation of the T texture coordinate is enabled. The initial value is **GL_FALSE**. See **glTexGen**.

GL_TEXTURE_MATRIX   *params* returns sixteen values: the texture matrix on the top of the texture matrix stack. Initially this matrix is the identity matrix. See **glPushMatrix**.

GL_TEXTURE_STACK_DEPTH

params returns one value, the number of matrices on the texture matrix stack. The initial value is 1. See **glPushMatrix**.

GL_UNPACK_ALIGNMENT

params returns one value, the byte alignment used for reading pixel data from memory. The initial value is 4. See **glPixelStore**.

GL_UNPACK_IMAGE_HEIGHT

params returns one value, the image height used for reading pixel data from memory. The initial is 0. See **glPixelStore**.

GL_UNPACK_LSB_FIRST   *params* returns a single boolean value indicating whether single-bit pixels being read from memory are read first from the least significant bit of each unsigned byte. The initial value is **GL_FALSE**. See **glPixelStore**.

GL_UNPACK_ROW_LENGTH

params returns one value, the row length used for reading pixel data from memory. The initial value is 0. See **glPixelStore**.

GL_UNPACK_SKIP_IMAGES

params returns one value, the number of pixel images skipped before the first pixel is read from memory. The initial value is 0. See **glPixelStore**.

GL_UNPACK_SKIP_PIXELS

params returns one value, the number of pixel locations skipped before the first pixel is read from memory. The initial value is 0. See **glPixelStore**.

GL_UNPACK_SKIP_ROWS

params returns one value, the number of rows of pixel locations skipped before the first pixel is read from memory. The initial value is 0. See **glPixelStore**.

GL_UNPACK_SWAP_BYTES

params returns a single boolean value indicating whether the bytes of two-byte and four-byte pixel indices and components are swapped after being read from memory. The initial value is **GL_FALSE**. See **glPixelStore**.

GL_VERTEX_ARRAY

params returns a single boolean value indicating whether the vertex array is enabled. The initial value is **GL_FALSE**. See **glVertexPointer**.

GL_VERTEX_ARRAY_SIZE

params returns one value, the number of coordinates per vertex in the vertex array. The initial value is 4. See **glVertexPointer**.

GL_VERTEX_ARRAY_STRIDE

params returns one value, the byte offset between consecutive vertices in the vertex array. The initial value is 0. See **glVertexPointer**.

GL_VERTEX_ARRAY_TYPE

params returns one value, the data type of each coordinate in the vertex array. The initial value is **GL_FLOAT**. See **glVertexPointer**.

GL_VIEWPORT

params returns four values: the x and y window coordinates of the viewport, followed by its width and height. Initially the x and y window coordinates are both set to 0, and the width and height are set to the width and height of the window into which the GL will do its rendering. See **glViewport**.

GL_ZOOM_X

params returns one value, the x pixel zoom factor. The initial value is 1. See **glPixelZoom**.

GL_ZOOM_Y
　　　　　　　params returns one value, the *y* pixel zoom factor. The initial value is 1. See **glPixelZoom**.

Many of the boolean parameters can also be queried more easily using **glIsEnabled**.

NOTES
GL_COLOR_LOGIC_OP, GL_COLOR_ARRAY, GL_COLOR_ARRAY_SIZE, GL_COLOR_ARRAY_STRIDE, GL_COLOR_ARRAY_TYPE, GL_EDGE_FLAG_ARRAY, GL_EDGE_FLAG_ARRAY_STRIDE, GL_INDEX_ARRAY, GL_INDEX_ARRAY_STRIDE, GL_INDEX_ARRAY_TYPE, GL_INDEX_LOGIC_OP, GL_NORMAL_ARRAY, GL_NORMAL_ARRAY_STRIDE, GL_NORMAL_ARRAY_TYPE, GL_POLYGON_OFFSET_UNITS, GL_POLYGON_OFFSET_FACTOR, GL_POLYGON_OFFSET_FILL, GL_POLYGON_OFFSET_LINE, GL_POLYGON_OFFSET_POINT, GL_TEXTURE_COORD_ARRAY, GL_TEXTURE_COORD_ARRAY_SIZE, GL_TEXTURE_COORD_ARRAY_STRIDE, GL_TEXTURE_COORD_ARRAY_TYPE, GL_VERTEX_ARRAY, GL_VERTEX_ARRAY_SIZE, GL_VERTEX_ARRAY_STRIDE, and **GL_VERTEX_ARRAY_TYPE** are available only if the GL version is 1.1 or greater.

GL_ALIASED_POINT_SIZE_RANGE, GL_ALIASED_POINT_SIZE_GRANULARITY, GL_FEEDBACK_BUFFER_SIZE, GL_FEEDBACK_BUFFER_TYPE, GL_LIGHT_MODEL_AMBIENT, GL_LIGHT_MODEL_COLOR_CONTROL, GL_MAX_3D_TEXTURE_SIZE, GL_MAX_ELEMENTS_INDICES, GL_MAX_ELEMENTS_VERTICES, GL_PACK_IMAGE_HEIGHT, GL_PACK_SKIP_IMAGES, GL_RESCALE_NORMAL, GL_SELECTION_BUFFER_SIZE, GL_SMOOTH_LINE_WIDTH_GRANULARITY, GL_SMOOTH_LINE_WIDTH_RANGE, GL_SMOOTH_POINT_SIZE_GRANULARITY, GL_SMOOTH_POINT_SIZE_RANGE, GL_TEXTURE_3D, GL_TEXTURE_BINDING_3D, GL_UNPACK_IMAGE_HEIGHT, and **GL_UNPACK_SKIP_IMAGES** are available only if the GL version is 1.2 or greater.

GL_LINE_WIDTH_GRANULARITY was deprecated in GL version 1.2. Its functionality was replaced by **GL_SMOOTH_LINE_WIDTH_GRANULARITY**.

GL_LINE_WIDTH_RANGE was deprecated in GL version 1.2. Its functionality was replaced by **GL_SMOOTH_LINE_WIDTH_RANGE**.

GL_POINT_SIZE_GRANULARITY was deprecated in GL version 1.2. Its functionality was replaced by **GL_SMOOTH_POINT_SIZE_GRANULARITY**.

GL_POINT_SIZE_RANGE was deprecated in GL version 1.2. Its functionality was replaced by **GL_SMOOTH_POINT_SIZE_RANGE**.

GL_BLEND_COLOR, GL_BLEND_EQUATION, GL_COLOR_MATRIX, GL_COLOR_MATRIX_STACK_DEPTH, GL_COLOR_TABLE, GL_CONVOLUTION_1D, GL_CONVOLUTION_2D, GL_HISTOGRAM, GL_MAX_COLOR_MATRIX_STACK_DEPTH, GL_MINMAX,

GL_POST_COLOR_MATRIX_COLOR_TABLE,
GL_POST_COLOR_MATRIX_RED_BIAS,
GL_POST_COLOR_MATRIX_GREEN_BIAS,
GL_POST_COLOR_MATRIX_BLUE_BIAS,
GL_POST_COLOR_MATRIX_ALPHA_BIAS,
GL_POST_COLOR_MATRIX_RED_SCALE,
GL_POST_COLOR_MATRIX_GREEN_SCALE,
GL_POST_COLOR_MATRIX_BLUE_SCALE,
GL_POST_COLOR_MATRIX_ALPHA_SCALE,
GL_POST_CONVOLUTION_COLOR_TABLE,
GL_POST_CONVOLUTION_RED_BIAS, GL_POST_CONVOLUTION_GREEN_BIAS,
GL_POST_CONVOLUTION_BLUE_BIAS,
GL_POST_CONVOLUTION_ALPHA_BIAS,
GL_POST_CONVOLUTION_RED_SCALE,
GL_POST_CONVOLUTION_GREEN_SCALE,
GL_POST_CONVOLUTION_BLUE_SCALE,
GL_POST_CONVOLUTION_ALPHA_SCALE, and **GL_SEPARABLE_2D** are available
only if **GL_ARB_imaging** is returned from **glGet** when called with the argument
GL_EXTENSIONS.

GL_ACTIVE_TEXTURE_ARB, GL_CLIENT_ACTIVE_TEXTURE_ARB, and
GL_MAX_TEXTURE_UNITS_ARB are available only if **GL_ARB_multitexture** is
returned from **glGet** when called with the argument **GL_EXTENSIONS**.

When the **GL_ARB_multitexture** extension is supported, the following parameters
return the associated value for the active texture unit:
GL_CURRENT_RASTER_TEXTURE_COORDS, GL_TEXTURE_1D,
GL_TEXTURE_BINDING_1D, GL_TEXTURE_2D, GL_TEXTURE_BINDING_2D,
GL_TEXTURE_3D, GL_TEXTURE_BINDING_3D, GL_TEXTURE_GEN_S,
GL_TEXTURE_GEN_T, GL_TEXTURE_GEN_R, GL_TEXTURE_GEN_Q,
GL_TEXTURE_MATRIX, and **GL_TEXTURE_STACK_DEPTH.** Likewise, the follow-
ing parameters return the associated value for the active client texture unit:
GL_TEXTURE_COORD_ARRAY, GL_TEXTURE_COORD_ARRAY_SIZE,
GL_TEXTURE_COORD_ARRAY_STRIDE, GL_TEXTURE_COORD_ARRAY_TYPE.

ERRORS

GL_INVALID_ENUM is generated if *pname* is not an accepted value.

GL_INVALID_OPERATION is generated if **glGet** is executed between the execution
of **glBegin** and the corresponding execution of **glEnd**.

SEE ALSO

glGetClipPlane, glGetColorTable, glGetColorTableParameter,
glGetConvolutionFilter, glGetConvolutionParameter, glGetError,
glGetHistogram, glGetHistogramParameter, glGetLight, glGetMap,
glGetMaterial, glGetMinmax, glGetMinmaxParameter, glGetPixelMap,

glGetPointerv, glGetPolygonStipple, glGetSeparableFilter, glGetString, glGetTexEnv, glGetTexGen, glGetTexImage, glGetTexLevelParameter, glGetTexParameter, glIsEnabled

NAME

      glGetClipPlane – return the coefficients of the specified clipping plane

C SPECIFICATION

      void **glGetClipPlane**(GLenum *plane*,
                              GLdouble **equation*)

PARAMETERS

      plane   Specifies a clipping plane. The number of clipping planes depends on the implementation, but at least six clipping planes are supported. They are identified by symbolic names of the form **GL_CLIP_PLANE***i* where $0 \le i <$ **GL_MAX_CLIP_PLANES**.

      equation Returns four double-precision values that are the coefficients of the plane equation of *plane* in eye coordinates. The initial value is (0, 0, 0, 0).

DESCRIPTION

      glGetClipPlane returns in *equation* the four coefficients of the plane equation for *plane*.

NOTES

      It is always the case that **GL_CLIP_PLANE***i* = **GL_CLIP_PLANE0** + *i*.

      If an error is generated, no change is made to the contents of *equation*.

ERRORS

      GL_INVALID_ENUM is generated if *plane* is not an accepted value.

      GL_INVALID_OPERATION is generated if **glGetClipPlane** is executed between the execution of **glBegin** and the corresponding execution of **glEnd**.

SEE ALSO

      glClipPlane

NAME

glGetColorTable – retrieve contents of a color lookup table

C SPECIFICATION

void **glGetColorTable**(GLenum *target*,
GLenum *format*,
GLenum *type*,
GLvoid **table*)

PARAMETERS

target Must be **GL_COLOR_TABLE**, **GL_POST_CONVOLUTION_COLOR_TABLE**, or **GL_POST_COLOR_MATRIX_COLOR_TABLE**.

format
The format of the pixel data in *table*. The possible values are **GL_RED**, **GL_GREEN**, **GL_BLUE**, **GL_ALPHA**, **GL_LUMINANCE**, **GL_LUMINANCE_ALPHA**, **GL_RGB**, **GL_BGR**, **GL_RGBA**, and **GL_BGRA**.

type The type of the pixel data in *table*. Symbolic constants **GL_UNSIGNED_BYTE**, **GL_BYTE**, **GL_BITMAP**, **GL_UNSIGNED_SHORT**, **GL_SHORT**, **GL_UNSIGNED_INT**, **GL_INT**, **GL_FLOAT**, **GL_UNSIGNED_BYTE_3_3_2**, **GL_UNSIGNED_BYTE_2_3_3_REV**, **GL_UNSIGNED_SHORT_5_6_5**, **GL_UNSIGNED_SHORT_5_6_5_REV**, **GL_UNSIGNED_SHORT_4_4_4_4**, **GL_UNSIGNED_SHORT_4_4_4_4_REV**, **GL_UNSIGNED_SHORT_5_5_5_1**, **GL_UNSIGNED_SHORT_1_5_5_5_REV**, **GL_UNSIGNED_INT_8_8_8_8**, **GL_UNSIGNED_INT_8_8_8_8_REV**, **GL_UNSIGNED_INT_10_10_10_2**, and **GL_UNSIGNED_INT_2_10_10_10_REV** are accepted.

table Pointer to a one-dimensional array of pixel data containing the contents of the color table.

DESCRIPTION

glGetColorTable returns in *table* the contents of the color table specified by *target*. No pixel transfer operations are performed, but pixel storage modes that are applicable to **glReadPixels** are performed.

Color components that are requested in the specified *format*, but which are not included in the internal format of the color lookup table, are returned as zero. The assignments of internal color components to the components requested by *format* are

Internal Component   Resulting Component

red	red
green	green
blue	blue
alpha	alpha
luminance	red
intensity	red

NOTES

glGetColorTable is present only if **GL_ARB_imaging** is returned when **glGetString** is called with an argument of **GL_EXTENSIONS**.

ERRORS

GL_INVALID_ENUM is generated if *target* is not one of the allowable values.

GL_INVALID_ENUM is generated if *format* is not one of the allowable values.

GL_INVALID_ENUM is generated if *type* is not one of the allowable values.

GL_INVALID_OPERATION is generated if *type* is one of **GL_UNSIGNED_BYTE_3_3_2**, **GL_UNSIGNED_BYTE_2_3_3_REV**, **GL_UNSIGNED_SHORT_5_6_5**, or **GL_UNSIGNED_SHORT_5_6_5_REV** and *format* is not **GL_RGB**.

GL_INVALID_OPERATION is generated if *type* is one of **GL_UNSIGNED_SHORT_4_4_4_4**, **GL_UNSIGNED_SHORT_4_4_4_4_REV**, **GL_UNSIGNED_SHORT_5_5_5_1**, **GL_UNSIGNED_SHORT_1_5_5_5_REV**, **GL_UNSIGNED_INT_8_8_8_8**, **GL_UNSIGNED_INT_8_8_8_8_REV**, **GL_UNSIGNED_INT_10_10_10_2**, or **GL_UNSIGNED_INT_2_10_10_10_REV** and *format* is neither **GL_RGBA** nor **GL_BGRA**.

GL_INVALID_OPERATION is generated if **glGetColorTable** is executed between the execution of **glBegin** and the corresponding execution of **glEnd**.

SEE ALSO

glColorTable, **glColorTableParameter**, **glGetColorTableParameter**

glGetColorTableParameterfv, **glGetColorTableParameteriv** – get color lookup table parameters

C SPECIFICATION

void **glGetColorTableParameterfv**(GLenum *target*,
                                   GLenum *pname*,
                                   GLfloat **params*)
void **glGetColorTableParameteriv**(GLenum *target*,
                                  GLenum *pname*,
                                  GLint **params*)

PARAMETERS

target   The target color table. Must be **GL_COLOR_TABLE**, **GL_POST_CONVOLUTION_COLOR_TABLE**, **GL_POST_COLOR_MATRIX_COLOR_TABLE**, **GL_PROXY_COLOR_TABLE**, **GL_PROXY_POST_CONVOLUTION_COLOR_TABLE**, **GL_PROXY_POST_COLOR_MATRIX_COLOR_TABLE**.

pname
    The symbolic name of a color lookup table parameter. Must be one of **GL_COLOR_TABLE_BIAS**, **GL_COLOR_TABLE_SCALE**, **GL_COLOR_TABLE_FORMAT**, **GL_COLOR_TABLE_WIDTH**, **GL_COLOR_TABLE_RED_SIZE**, **GL_COLOR_TABLE_GREEN_SIZE**, **GL_COLOR_TABLE_BLUE_SIZE**, **GL_COLOR_TABLE_ALPHA_SIZE**, **GL_COLOR_TABLE_LUMINANCE_SIZE**, or **GL_COLOR_TABLE_INTENSITY_SIZE**.

params
    A pointer to an array where the values of the parameter will be stored.

DESCRIPTION

Returns parameters specific to color table *target*.

When *pname* is set to **GL_COLOR_TABLE_SCALE** or **GL_COLOR_TABLE_BIAS**, **glGetColorTableParameter** returns the color table scale or bias parameters for the table specified by *target*. For these queries, *target* must be set to **GL_COLOR_TABLE**, **GL_POST_CONVOLUTION_COLOR_TABLE**, or **GL_POST_COLOR_MATRIX_COLOR_TABLE** and *params* points to an array of four elements, which receive the scale or bias factors for red, green, blue, and alpha, in that order.

glGetColorTableParameter can also be used to retrieve the format and size parameters for a color table. For these queries, set *target* to either the color table target or the proxy color table target. The format and size parameters are set by **glColorTable**.

The following table lists the format and size parameters that may be queried. For each symbolic constant listed below for *pname*, *params* must point to an array of the given length, and receive the values indicated.

Parameter	N	Meaning
GL_COLOR_TABLE_FORMAT	1	Internal format (e.g. **GL_RGBA**)
GL_COLOR_TABLE_WIDTH	1	Number of elements in table
GL_COLOR_TABLE_RED_SIZE	1	Size of red component, in bits
GL_COLOR_TABLE_GREEN_SIZE	1	Size of green component
GL_COLOR_TABLE_BLUE_SIZE	1	Size of blue component
GL_COLOR_TABLE_ALPHA_SIZE	1	Size of alpha component
GL_COLOR_TABLE_LUMINANCE_SIZE	1	Size of luminance component
GL_COLOR_TABLE_INTENSITY_SIZE	1	Size of intensity component

NOTES

glGetColorTableParameter is present only if **GL_ARB_imaging** is returned when **glGetString** is called with an argument of **GL_EXTENSIONS**.

ERRORS

GL_INVALID_ENUM is generated if *target* or *pname* is not an acceptable value.

GL_INVALID_OPERATION is generated if **glGetColorTableParameter** is executed between the execution of **glBegin** and the corresponding execution of **glEnd**.

SEE ALSO

glColorTable, **glTexParameter**, **glColorTableParameter**

NAME

glGetConvolutionFilter – get current 1D or 2D convolution filter kernel

C SPECIFICATION

void **glGetConvolutionFilter**(GLenum *target*,
GLenum *format*,
GLenum *type*,
GLvoid **image*)

PARAMETERS

target　The filter to be retrieved. Must be one of **GL_CONVOLUTION_1D** or **GL_CONVOLUTION_2D**.

format

Format of the output image. Must be one of **GL_RED**, **GL_GREEN**, **GL_BLUE**, **GL_ALPHA**, **GL_RGB**, **GL_BGR**, **GL_RGBA**, **GL_BGRA**, **GL_LUMINANCE**, or **GL_LUMINANCE_ALPHA**.

type　Data type of components in the output image. Symbolic constants **GL_UNSIGNED_BYTE**, **GL_BYTE**, **GL_BITMAP**, **GL_UNSIGNED_SHORT**, **GL_SHORT**, **GL_UNSIGNED_INT**, **GL_INT**, **GL_FLOAT**, **GL_UNSIGNED_BYTE_3_3_2**, **GL_UNSIGNED_BYTE_2_3_3_REV**, **GL_UNSIGNED_SHORT_5_6_5**, **GL_UNSIGNED_SHORT_5_6_5_REV**, **GL_UNSIGNED_SHORT_4_4_4_4**, **GL_UNSIGNED_SHORT_4_4_4_4_REV**, **GL_UNSIGNED_SHORT_5_5_5_1**, **GL_UNSIGNED_SHORT_1_5_5_5_REV**, **GL_UNSIGNED_INT_8_8_8_8**, **GL_UNSIGNED_INT_8_8_8_8_REV**, **GL_UNSIGNED_INT_10_10_10_2**, and **GL_UNSIGNED_INT_2_10_10_10_REV** are accepted.

image　Pointer to storage for the output image.

DESCRIPTION

glGetConvolutionFilter returns the current 1D or 2D convolution filter kernel as an image. The one- or two-dimensional image is placed in *image* according to the specifications in *format* and *type*. No pixel transfer operations are performed on this image, but the relevant pixel storage modes are applied.

Color components that are present in *format* but not included in the internal format of the filter are returned as zero. The assignments of internal color components to the components of *format* are as follows.

Internal Component	Resulting Component
Red	Red
Green	Green
Blue	Blue
Alpha	Alpha
Luminance	Red
Intensity	Red

NOTES

glGetConvolutionFilter is present only if **GL_ARB_imaging** is returned when **glGetString** is called with an argument of **GL_EXTENSIONS**.

The current separable 2D filter must be retrieved with **glGetSeparableFilter** rather than **glGetConvolutionFilter**.

ERRORS

GL_INVALID_ENUM is generated if *target* is not one of the allowable values.

GL_INVALID_ENUM is generated if *format* is not one of the allowable values.

GL_INVALID_ENUM is generated if *type* is not one of the allowable values.

GL_INVALID_OPERATION is generated if **glGetConvolutionFilter** is executed between the execution of **glBegin** and the corresponding execution of **glEnd**.

GL_INVALID_OPERATION is generated if *type* is one of GL_UNSIGNED_BYTE_3_3_2, GL_UNSIGNED_BYTE_2_3_3_REV, GL_UNSIGNED_SHORT_5_6_5, or GL_UNSIGNED_SHORT_5_6_5_REV and *format* is not **GL_RGB**.

GL_INVALID_OPERATION is generated if *type* is one of GL_UNSIGNED_SHORT_4_4_4_4, GL_UNSIGNED_SHORT_4_4_4_4_REV, GL_UNSIGNED_SHORT_5_5_5_1, GL_UNSIGNED_SHORT_1_5_5_5_REV, GL_UNSIGNED_INT_8_8_8_8, GL_UNSIGNED_INT_8_8_8_8_REV, GL_UNSIGNED_INT_10_10_10_2, or GL_UNSIGNED_INT_2_10_10_10_REV and *format* is neither **GL_RGBA** nor **GL_BGRA**.

ASSOCIATED GETS

glGetConvolutionParameter

SEE ALSO

glGetSeparableFilter, glConvolutionParameter, glConvolutionFilter1D, glConvolutionFilter2D

NAME

glGetConvolutionParameterfv, glGetConvolutionParameteriv – get convolution parameters

C SPECIFICATION

void **glGetConvolutionParameterfv**(GLenum *target*,
            GLenum *pname*,
            GLfloat **params*)
void **glGetConvolutionParameteriv**(GLenum *target*,
            GLenum *pname*,
            GLint **params*)

PARAMETERS

target The filter whose parameters are to be retrieved. Must be one of **GL_CONVOLUTION_1D**, **GL_CONVOLUTION_2D**, or **GL_SEPARABLE_2D**.

pname

The parameter to be retrieved. Must be one of **GL_CONVOLUTION_BORDER_MODE**, **GL_CONVOLUTION_BORDER_COLOR**, **GL_CONVOLUTION_FILTER_SCALE**, **GL_CONVOLUTION_FILTER_BIAS**, **GL_CONVOLUTION_FORMAT**, **GL_CONVOLUTION_WIDTH**, **GL_CONVOLUTION_HEIGHT**, **GL_MAX_CONVOLUTION_WIDTH**, or **GL_MAX_CONVOLUTION_HEIGHT**.

params

Pointer to storage for the parameters to be retrieved.

DESCRIPTION

glGetConvolutionParameter retrieves convolution parameters. *target* determines which convolution filter is queried. *pname* determines which parameter is returned:

GL_CONVOLUTION_BORDER_MODE

The convolution border mode. See **glConvolutionParameter** for a list of border modes.

GL_CONVOLUTION_BORDER_COLOR

The current convolution border color. *params* must be a pointer to an array of four elements, which will receive the red, green, blue, and alpha border colors.

GL_CONVOLUTION_FILTER_SCALE

The current filter scale factors. *params* must be a pointer to an array of four elements, which will receive the red, green, blue, and alpha filter scale factors in that order.

GL_CONVOLUTION_FILTER_BIAS

The current filter bias factors. *params* must be a pointer to an array of four elements, which will receive the red, green, blue, and alpha filter bias terms in that order.

GL_CONVOLUTION_FORMAT

The current internal format. See **glConvolutionFilter1D**, **glConvolutionFilter2D**, and **glSeparableFilter2D** for lists of allowable formats.

GL_CONVOLUTION_WIDTH

The current filter image width.

GL_CONVOLUTION_HEIGHT

The current filter image height.

GL_MAX_CONVOLUTION_WIDTH

The maximum acceptable filter image width.

GL_MAX_CONVOLUTION_HEIGHT

The maximum acceptable filter image height.

ERRORS

GL_INVALID_ENUM is generated if *target* is not one of the allowable values.

GL_INVALID_ENUM is generated if *pname* is not one of the allowable values.

GL_INVALID_ENUM is generated if *target* is **GL_CONVOLUTION_1D** and *pname* is **GL_CONVOLUTION_HEIGHT** or **GL_MAX_CONVOLUTION_HEIGHT**.

GL_INVALID_OPERATION is generated if **glGetConvolutionParameter** is executed between the execution of **glBegin** and the corresponding execution of **glEnd**.

SEE ALSO

glGetConvolutionFilter, **glGetSeparableFilter2D**, **glConvolutionParameter**

NAME

    glGetError – return error information

C SPECIFICATION

    GLenum **glGetError**(void)

DESCRIPTION

    glGetError returns the value of the error flag. Each detectable error is assigned a numeric code and symbolic name. When an error occurs, the error flag is set to the appropriate error code value. No other errors are recorded until **glGetError** is called, the error code is returned, and the flag is reset to **GL_NO_ERROR**. If a call to **glGetError** returns **GL_NO_ERROR**, there has been no detectable error since the last call to **glGetError**, or since the GL was initialized.

    To allow for distributed implementations, there may be several error flags. If any single error flag has recorded an error, the value of that flag is returned and that flag is reset to **GL_NO_ERROR** when **glGetError** is called. If more than one flag has recorded an error, **glGetError** returns and clears an arbitrary error flag value. Thus, **glGetError** should always be called in a loop, until it returns **GL_NO_ERROR**, if all error flags are to be reset.

    Initially, all error flags are set to **GL_NO_ERROR**.

    The following errors are currently defined:

GL_NO_ERROR	No error has been recorded. The value of this symbolic constant is guaranteed to be 0.
GL_INVALID_ENUM	An unacceptable value is specified for an enumerated argument. The offending command is ignored, and has no other side effect than to set the error flag.
GL_INVALID_VALUE	A numeric argument is out of range. The offending command is ignored, and has no other side effect than to set the error flag.
GL_INVALID_OPERATION	The specified operation is not allowed in the current state. The offending command is ignored, and has no other side effect than to set the error flag.
GL_STACK_OVERFLOW	This command would cause a stack overflow. The offending command is ignored, and has no other side effect than to set the error flag.

GL_STACK_UNDERFLOW	This command would cause a stack underflow. The offending command is ignored, and has no other side effect than to set the error flag.
GL_OUT_OF_MEMORY	There is not enough memory left to execute the command. The state of the GL is undefined, except for the state of the error flags, after this error is recorded.
GL_TABLE_TOO_LARGE	The specified table exceeds the implementation's maximum supported table size. The offending command is ignored, and has no other side effect than to set the error flag.

When an error flag is set, results of a GL operation are undefined only if **GL_OUT_OF_MEMORY** has occurred. In all other cases, the command generating the error is ignored and has no effect on the GL state or frame buffer contents. If the generating command returns a value, it returns 0. If **glGetError** itself generates an error, it returns 0.

NOTES

GL_TABLE_TOO_LARGE was introduced in GL version 1.2.

ERRORS

GL_INVALID_OPERATION is generated if **glGetError** is executed between the execution of **glBegin** and the corresponding execution of **glEnd**. In this case **glGetError** returns 0.

NAME

    glGetHistogram – get histogram table

C SPECIFICATION

    void **glGetHistogram**(GLenum *target*,
                           GLboolean *reset*,
                           GLenum *format*,
                           GLenum *type*,
                           GLvoid **values*)

PARAMETERS

    target Must be **GL_HISTOGRAM**.

    reset If **GL_TRUE**, each component counter that is actually returned is reset to zero. (Other counters are unaffected.) If **GL_FALSE**, none of the counters in the histogram table is modified.

    format

        The format of values to be returned in *values*. Must be one of **GL_RED**, **GL_GREEN**, **GL_BLUE**, **GL_ALPHA**, **GL_RGB**, **GL_BGR**, **GL_RGBA**, **GL_BGRA**, **GL_LUMINANCE**, or **GL_LUMINANCE_ALPHA**.

    type The type of values to be returned in *values*. Symbolic constants **GL_UNSIGNED_BYTE**, **GL_BYTE**, **GL_BITMAP**, **GL_UNSIGNED_SHORT**, **GL_SHORT**, **GL_UNSIGNED_INT**, **GL_INT**, **GL_FLOAT**, **GL_UNSIGNED_BYTE_3_3_2**, **GL_UNSIGNED_BYTE_2_3_3_REV**, **GL_UNSIGNED_SHORT_5_6_5**, **GL_UNSIGNED_SHORT_5_6_5_REV**, **GL_UNSIGNED_SHORT_4_4_4_4**, **GL_UNSIGNED_SHORT_4_4_4_4_REV**, **GL_UNSIGNED_SHORT_5_5_5_1**, **GL_UNSIGNED_SHORT_1_5_5_5_REV**, **GL_UNSIGNED_INT_8_8_8_8**, **GL_UNSIGNED_INT_8_8_8_8_REV**, **GL_UNSIGNED_INT_10_10_10_2**, and **GL_UNSIGNED_INT_2_10_10_10_REV** are accepted.

    values A pointer to storage for the returned histogram table.

DESCRIPTION

    glGetHistogram returns the current histogram table as a one-dimensional image with the same width as the histogram. No pixel transfer operations are performed on this image, but pixel storage modes that are applicable to 1D images are honored.

    Color components that are requested in the specified *format*, but which are not included in the internal format of the histogram, are returned as zero.

The assignments of internal color components to the components requested by *format* are:

Internal Component	Resulting Component
Red	Red
Green	Green
Blue	Blue
Alpha	Alpha
Luminance	Red

NOTES

glGetHistogram is present only if **GL_ARB_imaging** is returned when **glGetString** is called with an argument of **GL_EXTENSIONS**.

ERRORS

GL_INVALID_ENUM is generated if *target* is not **GL_HISTOGRAM**.

GL_INVALID_ENUM is generated if *format* is not one of the allowable values.

GL_INVALID_ENUM is generated if *type* is not one of the allowable values.

GL_INVALID_OPERATION is generated if **glGetHistogram** is executed between the execution of **glBegin** and the corresponding execution of **glEnd**.

GL_INVALID_OPERATION is generated if *type* is one of GL_UNSIGNED_BYTE_3_3_2, GL_UNSIGNED_BYTE_2_3_3_REV, GL_UNSIGNED_SHORT_5_6_5, or GL_UNSIGNED_SHORT_5_6_5_REV and *format* is not **GL_RGB**.

GL_INVALID_OPERATION is generated if *type* is one of GL_UNSIGNED_SHORT_4_4_4_4, GL_UNSIGNED_SHORT_4_4_4_4_REV, GL_UNSIGNED_SHORT_5_5_5_1, GL_UNSIGNED_SHORT_1_5_5_5_REV, GL_UNSIGNED_INT_8_8_8_8, GL_UNSIGNED_INT_8_8_8_8_REV, GL_UNSIGNED_INT_10_10_10_2, or GL_UNSIGNED_INT_2_10_10_10_REV and *format* is neither **GL_RGBA** nor **GL_BGRA**.

SEE ALSO

glHistogram, **glResetHistogram**, **glGetHistogramParameter**

NAME

glGetHistogramParameterfv, **glGetHistogramParameteriv** – get histogram parameters

C SPECIFICATION

void **glGetHistogramParameterfv**(GLenum *target*,
                                     GLenum *pname*,
                                     GLfloat **params*)
void **glGetHistogramParameteriv**(GLenum *target*,
                                     GLenum *pname*,
                                     GLint **params*)

PARAMETERS

target Must be one of **GL_HISTOGRAM** or **GL_PROXY_HISTOGRAM**.

pname
The name of the parameter to be retrieved. Must be one of
GL_HISTOGRAM_WIDTH, **GL_HISTOGRAM_FORMAT**,
GL_HISTOGRAM_RED_SIZE, **GL_HISTOGRAM_GREEN_SIZE**,
GL_HISTOGRAM_BLUE_SIZE, **GL_HISTOGRAM_ALPHA_SIZE**,
GL_HISTOGRAM_LUMINANCE_SIZE, or **GL_HISTOGRAM_SINK**.

params
Pointer to storage for the returned values.

DESCRIPTION

glGetHistogramParameter is used to query parameter values for the current histogram or for a proxy. The histogram state information may be queried by calling **glGetHistogramParameter** with a *target* of **GL_HISTOGRAM** (to obtain information for the current histogram table) or **GL_PROXY_HISTOGRAM** (to obtain information from the most recent proxy request) and one of the following values for the *pname* argument:

Parameter	Description
GL_HISTOGRAM_WIDTH	Histogram table width
GL_HISTOGRAM_FORMAT	Internal format
GL_HISTOGRAM_RED_SIZE	Red component counter size, in bits
GL_HISTOGRAM_GREEN_SIZE	Green component counter size, in bits

Parameter	Description
GL_HISTOGRAM_BLUE_SIZE	Blue component counter size, in bits
GL_HISTOGRAM_ALPHA_SIZE	Alpha component counter size, in bits
GL_HISTOGRAM_LUMINANCE_SIZE	Luminance component counter size, in bits
GL_HISTOGRAM_SINK	Value of the *sink* parameter

NOTES

glGetHistogramParameter is present only if **GL_ARB_imaging** is returned when **glGetString** is called with an argument of **GL_EXTENSIONS**.

ERRORS

GL_INVALID_ENUM is generated if *target* is not one of the allowable values.

GL_INVALID_ENUM is generated if *pname* is not one of the allowable values.

GL_INVALID_OPERATION is generated if **glGetHistogramParameter** is executed between the execution of **glBegin** and the corresponding execution of **glEnd**.

SEE ALSO

glGetHistogram, **glHistogram**

NAME

glGetLightfv, glGetLightiv – return light source parameter values

C SPECIFICATION

void **glGetLightfv**(GLenum *light*,
                        GLenum *pname*,
                        GLfloat **params*)
void **glGetLightiv**(GLenum *light*,
                        GLenum *pname*,
                        GLint **params*)

PARAMETERS

light   Specifies a light source. The number of possible lights depends on the imple-
            mentation, but at least eight lights are supported. They are identified by
            symbolic names of the form **GL_LIGHT***i* where $0 \leq i <$ **GL_MAX_LIGHTS**.

pname   Specifies a light source parameter for *light*. Accepted symbolic names are
            GL_AMBIENT, GL_DIFFUSE, GL_SPECULAR, GL_POSITION,
            GL_SPOT_DIRECTION, GL_SPOT_EXPONENT, GL_SPOT_CUTOFF,
            GL_CONSTANT_ATTENUATION, GL_LINEAR_ATTENUATION, and
            GL_QUADRATIC_ATTENUATION.

params Returns the requested data.

DESCRIPTION

glGetLight returns in *params* the value or values of a light source parameter. *light*
names the light and is a symbolic name of the form **GL_LIGHT***i* for $0 \leq i <$
GL_MAX_LIGHTS, where **GL_MAX_LIGHTS** is an implementation dependent constant that is greater than or equal to eight. *pname* specifies one of ten light source
parameters, again by symbolic name.

The following parameters are defined:

GL_AMBIENT   *params* returns four integer or floating-point values represent-
                    ing the ambient intensity of the light source. Integer values,
                    when requested, are linearly mapped from the internal
                    floating-point representation such that 1.0 maps to the most
                    positive representable integer value, and –1.0 maps to the most
                    negative representable integer value. If the internal value is
                    outside the range [–1, 1], the corresponding integer return
                    value is undefined. The initial value is (0, 0, 0, 1).

GL_DIFFUSE   *params* returns four integer or floating-point values represent-
                    ing the diffuse intensity of the light source. Integer values,
                    when requested, are linearly mapped from the internal
                    floating-point representation such that 1.0 maps to the most

positive representable integer value, and −1.0 maps to the most negative representable integer value. If the internal value is outside the range [−1, 1], the corresponding integer return value is undefined. The initial value for **GL_LIGHT0** is (1, 1, 1, 1); for other lights, the initial value is (0, 0, 0, 0).

GL_SPECULAR   *params* returns four integer or floating-point values representing the specular intensity of the light source. Integer values, when requested, are linearly mapped from the internal floating-point representation such that 1.0 maps to the most positive representable integer value, and −1.0 maps to the most negative representable integer value. If the internal value is outside the range [−1, 1], the corresponding integer return value is undefined. The initial value for **GL_LIGHT0** is (1, 1, 1, 1); for other lights, the initial value is (0, 0, 0, 0).

GL_POSITION   *params* returns four integer or floating-point values representing the position of the light source. Integer values, when requested, are computed by rounding the internal floating-point values to the nearest integer value. The returned values are those maintained in eye coordinates. They will not be equal to the values specified using **glLight**, unless the model-view matrix was identity at the time **glLight** was called. The initial value is (0, 0, 1, 0).

GL_SPOT_DIRECTION
params returns three integer or floating-point values representing the direction of the light source. Integer values, when requested, are computed by rounding the internal floating-point values to the nearest integer value. The returned values are those maintained in eye coordinates. They will not be equal to the values specified using **glLight**, unless the model-view matrix was identity at the time **glLight** was called. Although spot direction is normalized before being used in the lighting equation, the returned values are the transformed versions of the specified values prior to normalization. The initial value is (0, 0, −1).

GL_SPOT_EXPONENT
params returns a single integer or floating-point value representing the spot exponent of the light. An integer value, when requested, is computed by rounding the internal floating-point representation to the nearest integer. The initial value is 0.

GL_SPOT_CUTOFF *params* returns a single integer or floating-point value representing the spot cutoff angle of the light. An integer value, when requested, is computed by rounding the internal floating-point representation to the nearest integer. The initial value is 180.

GL_CONSTANT_ATTENUATION

params returns a single integer or floating-point value representing the constant (not distance-related) attenuation of the light. An integer value, when requested, is computed by rounding the internal floating-point representation to the nearest integer. The initial value is 1.

GL_LINEAR_ATTENUATION

params returns a single integer or floating-point value representing the linear attenuation of the light. An integer value, when requested, is computed by rounding the internal floating-point representation to the nearest integer. The initial value is 0.

GL_QUADRATIC_ATTENUATION

params returns a single integer or floating-point value representing the quadratic attenuation of the light. An integer value, when requested, is computed by rounding the internal floating-point representation to the nearest integer. The initial value is 0.

NOTES

It is always the case that **GL_LIGHT**i = **GL_LIGHT0** + i.

If an error is generated, no change is made to the contents of *params*.

ERRORS

GL_INVALID_ENUM is generated if *light* or *pname* is not an accepted value.

GL_INVALID_OPERATION is generated if **glGetLight** is executed between the execution of **glBegin** and the corresponding execution of **glEnd**.

SEE ALSO

glLight

NAME

glGetMapdv, **glGetMapfv**, **glGetMapiv** – return evaluator parameters

C SPECIFICATION

void **glGetMapdv**(GLenum *target*,
                            GLenum *query*,
                            GLdouble **v*)
void **glGetMapfv**(GLenum *target*,
                            GLenum *query*,
                            GLfloat **v*)
void **glGetMapiv**(GLenum *target*,
                            GLenum *query*,
                            GLint **v*)

PARAMETERS

target   Specifies the symbolic name of a map. Accepted values are
           GL_MAP1_COLOR_4, **GL_MAP1_INDEX**, **GL_MAP1_NORMAL**,
           GL_MAP1_TEXTURE_COORD_1, **GL_MAP1_TEXTURE_COORD_2**,
           GL_MAP1_TEXTURE_COORD_3, **GL_MAP1_TEXTURE_COORD_4**,
           GL_MAP1_VERTEX_3, **GL_MAP1_VERTEX_4**, **GL_MAP2_COLOR_4**,
           GL_MAP2_INDEX, **GL_MAP2_NORMAL**, **GL_MAP2_TEXTURE_COORD_1**,
           GL_MAP2_TEXTURE_COORD_2, **GL_MAP2_TEXTURE_COORD_3**,
           GL_MAP2_TEXTURE_COORD_4, **GL_MAP2_VERTEX_3**, and
           GL_MAP2_VERTEX_4.

query   Specifies which parameter to return. Symbolic names **GL_COEFF**,
           GL_ORDER, and **GL_DOMAIN** are accepted.

v   Returns the requested data.

DESCRIPTION

glMap1 and **glMap2** define evaluators. **glGetMap** returns evaluator parameters.
target chooses a map, *query* selects a specific parameter, and *v* points to storage where
the values will be returned.

The acceptable values for the *target* parameter are described in the **glMap1** and
glMap2 reference pages.

query can assume the following values:

GL_COEFF   *v* returns the control points for the evaluator function. One-
                   dimensional evaluators return *order* control points, and two-
                   dimensional evaluators return *uorder* × *vorder* control points. Each
                   control point consists of one, two, three, or four integer, single-
                   precision floating-point, or double-precision floating-point values,
                   depending on the type of the evaluator. The GL returns two-

dimensional control points in row-major order, incrementing the *uorder* index quickly and the *vorder* index after each row. Integer values, when requested, are computed by rounding the internal floating-point values to the nearest integer values.

GL_ORDER   *v* returns the order of the evaluator function. One-dimensional evaluators return a single value, *order*. The initial value is 1. Two-dimensional evaluators return two values, *uorder* and *vorder*. The initial value is 1,1.

GL_DOMAIN   *v* returns the linear *u* and *v* mapping parameters. One-dimensional evaluators return two values, *u*1 and *u*2, as specified by **glMap1**. Two-dimensional evaluators return four values (*u*1, *u*2, *v*1, and *v*2) as specified by **glMap2**. Integer values, when requested, are computed by rounding the internal floating-point values to the nearest integer values.

NOTES

If an error is generated, no change is made to the contents of *v*.

ERRORS

GL_INVALID_ENUM is generated if either *target* or *query* is not an accepted value.

GL_INVALID_OPERATION is generated if **glGetMap** is executed between the execution of **glBegin** and the corresponding execution of **glEnd**.

SEE ALSO

glEvalCoord, **glMap1**, **glMap2**

NAME

glGetMaterialfv, **glGetMaterialiv** – return material parameters

C SPECIFICATION

void **glGetMaterialfv**(GLenum *face*,
                              GLenum *pname*,
                              GLfloat *params*)
void **glGetMaterialiv**(GLenum *face*,
                              GLenum *pname*,
                              GLint *params*)

PARAMETERS

face   Specifies which of the two materials is being queried. **GL_FRONT** or **GL_BACK** are accepted, representing the front and back materials, respectively.

pname Specifies the material parameter to return. **GL_AMBIENT**, **GL_DIFFUSE**, **GL_SPECULAR**, **GL_EMISSION**, **GL_SHININESS**, and **GL_COLOR_INDEXES** are accepted.

params Returns the requested data.

DESCRIPTION

glGetMaterial returns in *params* the value or values of parameter *pname* of material *face*. Six parameters are defined:

GL_AMBIENT   *params* returns four integer or floating-point values representing the ambient reflectance of the material. Integer values, when requested, are linearly mapped from the internal floating-point representation such that 1.0 maps to the most positive representable integer value, and −1.0 maps to the most negative representable integer value. If the internal value is outside the range [−1, 1], the corresponding integer return value is undefined. The initial value is (0.2, 0.2, 0.2, 1.0)

GL_DIFFUSE   *params* returns four integer or floating-point values representing the diffuse reflectance of the material. Integer values, when requested, are linearly mapped from the internal floating-point representation such that 1.0 maps to the most positive representable integer value, and −1.0 maps to the most negative representable integer value. If the internal value is outside the range [−1, 1], the corresponding integer return value is undefined. The initial value is (0.8, 0.8, 0.8, 1.0).

GL_SPECULAR   *params* returns four integer or floating-point values representing the specular reflectance of the material. Integer values, when requested, are linearly mapped from the internal floating-point representation such that 1.0 maps to the most positive representable integer value, and −1.0 maps to the most negative representable integer value. If the internal value is outside the range [−1, 1], the corresponding integer return value is undefined. The initial value is (0, 0, 0, 1).

GL_EMISSION   *params* returns four integer or floating-point values representing the emitted light intensity of the material. Integer values, when requested, are linearly mapped from the internal floating-point representation such that 1.0 maps to the most positive representable integer value, and −1.0 maps to the most negative representable integer value. If the internal value is outside the range [−1, 1.0], the corresponding integer return value is undefined. The initial value is (0, 0, 0, 1).

GL_SHININESS   *params* returns one integer or floating-point value representing the specular exponent of the material. Integer values, when requested, are computed by rounding the internal floating-point value to the nearest integer value. The initial value is 0.

GL_COLOR_INDEXES *params* returns three integer or floating-point values representing the ambient, diffuse, and specular indices of the material. These indices are used only for color index lighting. (All the other parameters are used only for RGBA lighting.) Integer values, when requested, are computed by rounding the internal floating-point values to the nearest integer values.

NOTES

If an error is generated, no change is made to the contents of *params*.

ERRORS

GL_INVALID_ENUM is generated if *face* or *pname* is not an accepted value.

GL_INVALID_OPERATION is generated if **glGetMaterial** is executed between the execution of **glBegin** and the corresponding execution of **glEnd**.

SEE ALSO

glMaterial

NAME

glGetMinmax – get minimum and maximum pixel values

C SPECIFICATION

void **glGetMinmax**(GLenum *target*,
                     GLboolean *reset*,
                     GLenum *format*,
                     GLenum *type*,
                     GLvoid **values*)

PARAMETERS

target Must be **GL_MINMAX**.

reset If **GL_TRUE**, all entries in the minmax table that are actually returned are reset to their initial values. (Other entries are unaltered.) If **GL_FALSE**, the minmax table is unaltered.

format
The format of the data to be returned in *values*. Must be one of **GL_RED**, **GL_GREEN**, **GL_BLUE**, **GL_ALPHA**, **GL_RGB**, **GL_BGR**, **GL_RGBA**, **GL_BGRA**, **GL_LUMINANCE**, or **GL_LUMINANCE_ALPHA**.

type The type of the data to be returned in *values*. Symbolic constants **GL_UNSIGNED_BYTE**, **GL_BYTE**, **GL_BITMAP**, **GL_UNSIGNED_SHORT**, **GL_SHORT**, **GL_UNSIGNED_INT**, **GL_INT**, **GL_FLOAT**, **GL_UNSIGNED_BYTE_3_3_2**, **GL_UNSIGNED_BYTE_2_3_3_REV**, **GL_UNSIGNED_SHORT_5_6_5**, **GL_UNSIGNED_SHORT_5_6_5_REV**, **GL_UNSIGNED_SHORT_4_4_4_4**, **GL_UNSIGNED_SHORT_4_4_4_4_REV**, **GL_UNSIGNED_SHORT_5_5_5_1**, **GL_UNSIGNED_SHORT_1_5_5_5_REV**, **GL_UNSIGNED_INT_8_8_8_8**, **GL_UNSIGNED_INT_8_8_8_8_REV**, **GL_UNSIGNED_INT_10_10_10_2**, and **GL_UNSIGNED_INT_2_10_10_10_REV** are accepted.

values A pointer to storage for the returned values.

DESCRIPTION

glGetMinmax returns the accumulated minimum and maximum pixel values (computed on a per-component basis) in a one-dimensional image of width 2. The first set of return values are the minima, and the second set of return values are the maxima. The format of the return values is determined by *format*, and their type is determined by *type*.

No pixel transfer operations are performed on the return values, but pixel storage modes that are applicable to 1-dimensional images are performed. Color components that are requested in the specified *format*, but that are not included in the internal format of the minmax table, are returned as zero. The assignment of internal color components to the components requested by *format* are as follows:

Internal Component	Resulting Component
Red	Red
Green	Green
Blue	Blue
Alpha	Alpha
Luminance	Red

If *reset* is **GL_TRUE**, the minmax table entries corresponding to the return values are reset to their initial values. Minimum and maximum values that are not returned are not modified, even if *reset* is **GL_TRUE**.

NOTES

glGetMinmax is present only if **GL_ARB_imaging** is returned when **glGetString** is called with an argument of **GL_EXTENSIONS**.

ERRORS

GL_INVALID_ENUM is generated if *target* is not **GL_MINMAX**.

GL_INVALID_ENUM is generated if *format* is not one of the allowable values.

GL_INVALID_ENUM is generated if *type* is not one of the allowable values.

GL_INVALID_OPERATION is generated if **glGetMinmax** is executed between the execution of **glBegin** and the corresponding execution of **glEnd**.

GL_INVALID_OPERATION is generated if *type* is one of **GL_UNSIGNED_BYTE_3_3_2**, **GL_UNSIGNED_BYTE_2_3_3_REV**, **GL_UNSIGNED_SHORT_5_6_5**, or **GL_UNSIGNED_SHORT_5_6_5_REV** and *format* is not **GL_RGB**.

GL_INVALID_OPERATION is generated if *type* is one of **GL_UNSIGNED_SHORT_4_4_4_4**, **GL_UNSIGNED_SHORT_4_4_4_4_REV**, **GL_UNSIGNED_SHORT_5_5_5_1**, **GL_UNSIGNED_SHORT_1_5_5_5_REV**, **GL_UNSIGNED_INT_8_8_8_8**, **GL_UNSIGNED_INT_8_8_8_8_REV**, **GL_UNSIGNED_INT_10_10_10_2**, or **GL_UNSIGNED_INT_2_10_10_10_REV** and *format* is neither **GL_RGBA** nor **GL_BGRA**.

SEE ALSO

glMinmax, **glResetMinmax**, **glGetMinmaxParameter**

NAME

glGetMinmaxParameterfv, **glGetMinmaxParameteriv** – get minmax parameters

C SPECIFICATION

void **glGetMinmaxParameterfv**(GLenum *target*,
                               GLenum *pname*,
                               GLfloat **params*)
void **glGetMinmaxParameteriv**(GLenum *target*,
                               GLenum *pname*,
                               GLint **params*)

PARAMETERS

target Must be **GL_MINMAX**.

pname
> The parameter to be retrieved. Must be one of **GL_MINMAX_FORMAT** or **GL_MINMAX_SINK**.

params
> A pointer to storage for the retrieved parameters.

DESCRIPTION

glGetMinmaxParameter retrieves parameters for the current minmax table by setting *pname* to one of the following values:

Parameter	Description
GL_MINMAX_FORMAT	Internal format of minmax table
GL_MINMAX_SINK	Value of the *sink* parameter

NOTES

glGetMinmaxParameter is present only if **GL_ARB_imaging** is returned when **glGetString** is called with an argument of **GL_EXTENSIONS**.

ERRORS

GL_INVALID_ENUM is generated if *target* is not **GL_MINMAX**.

GL_INVALID_ENUM is generated if *pname* is not one of the allowable values.

GL_INVALID_OPERATION is generated if **glGetMinmaxParameter** is executed between the execution of **glBegin** and the corresponding execution of **glEnd**.

SEE ALSO

glMinmax, glGetMinmax

NAME

glGetPixelMapfv, **glGetPixelMapuiv**, **glGetPixelMapusv** – return the specified pixel map

C SPECIFICATION

void **glGetPixelMapfv**(GLenum *map*,
                    GLfloat **values*)
void **glGetPixelMapuiv**(GLenum *map*,
                    GLuint **values*)
void **glGetPixelMapusv**(GLenum *map*,
                    GLushort **values*)

PARAMETERS

map   Specifies the name of the pixel map to return. Accepted values are
          GL_PIXEL_MAP_I_TO_I, GL_PIXEL_MAP_S_TO_S,
          GL_PIXEL_MAP_I_TO_R, GL_PIXEL_MAP_I_TO_G,
          GL_PIXEL_MAP_I_TO_B, GL_PIXEL_MAP_I_TO_A,
          GL_PIXEL_MAP_R_TO_R, GL_PIXEL_MAP_G_TO_G,
          GL_PIXEL_MAP_B_TO_B, and GL_PIXEL_MAP_A_TO_A.

values Returns the pixel map contents.

DESCRIPTION

See the **glPixelMap** reference page for a description of the acceptable values for the *map* parameter. **glGetPixelMap** returns in *values* the contents of the pixel map specified in *map*. Pixel maps are used during the execution of **glReadPixels**, **glDrawPixels**, **glCopyPixels**, **glTexImage1D**, **glTexImage2D**, **glTexImage3D**, **glTexSubImage1D**, **glTexSubImage2D**, **glTexSubImage3D**, **glCopyTexImage1D**, **glCopyTexImage2D**, **glCopyTexSubImage1D**, **glCopyTexSubImage2D**, **glCopyTexSubImage3D**, **glColorTable**, **glColorSubTable**, **glCopyColorTable**, **glCopyColorSubTable**, **glConvolutionFilter1D**, **glConvolutionFilter2D**, **glSeparableFilter2D**, **glGetHistogram**, **glGetMinmax**, and **glGetTexImage** to map color indices, stencil indices, color components, and depth components to other values.

Unsigned integer values, if requested, are linearly mapped from the internal fixed or floating-point representation such that 1.0 maps to the largest representable integer value, and 0.0 maps to 0. Return unsigned integer values are undefined if the map value was not in the range [0,1].

To determine the required size of *map*, call **glGet** with the appropriate symbolic constant.

NOTES

If an error is generated, no change is made to the contents of *values*.

ERRORS

GL_INVALID_ENUM is generated if *map* is not an accepted value.

GL_INVALID_OPERATION is generated if **glGetPixelMap** is executed between the execution of **glBegin** and the corresponding execution of **glEnd**.

ASSOCIATED GETS

glGet with argument **GL_PIXEL_MAP_I_TO_I_SIZE**
glGet with argument **GL_PIXEL_MAP_S_TO_S_SIZE**
glGet with argument **GL_PIXEL_MAP_I_TO_R_SIZE**
glGet with argument **GL_PIXEL_MAP_I_TO_G_SIZE**
glGet with argument **GL_PIXEL_MAP_I_TO_B_SIZE**
glGet with argument **GL_PIXEL_MAP_I_TO_A_SIZE**
glGet with argument **GL_PIXEL_MAP_R_TO_R_SIZE**
glGet with argument **GL_PIXEL_MAP_G_TO_G_SIZE**
glGet with argument **GL_PIXEL_MAP_B_TO_B_SIZE**
glGet with argument **GL_PIXEL_MAP_A_TO_A_SIZE**
glGet with argument **GL_MAX_PIXEL_MAP_TABLE**

SEE ALSO

glColorSubTable, **glColorTable**, **glConvolutionFilter1D**, **glConvolutionFilter2D**, **glCopyColorSubTable**, **glCopyColorTable**, **glCopyPixels**, **glCopyTexImage1D**, **glCopyTexImage2D**, **glCopyTexSubImage1D**, **glCopyTexSubImage2D**, **glCopyTexSubImage3D**, **glDrawPixels**, **glGetHistogram**, **glGetMinmax**, **glGetTexImage**, **glPixelMap**, **glPixelTransfer**, **glReadPixels**, **glSeparableFilter2D**, **glTexImage1D**, **glTexImage1D**, **glTexImage2D** **glTexImage2D**, **glTexImage3D**, **glTexSubImage1D**, **glTexSubImage2D**, **glTexSubImage3D**

NAME

glGetPointerv – return the address of the specified pointer

C SPECIFICATION

void **glGetPointerv**(GLenum *pname*,
                       GLvoid* **params*)

PARAMETERS

pname   Specifies the array or buffer pointer to be returned. Symbolic constants **GL_COLOR_ARRAY_POINTER**, **GL_EDGE_FLAG_ARRAY_POINTER**, **GL_FEEDBACK_BUFFER_POINTER**, **GL_INDEX_ARRAY_POINTER**, **GL_NORMAL_ARRAY_POINTER**, **GL_TEXTURE_COORD_ARRAY_POINTER**, **GL_SELECTION_BUFFER_POINTER**, and **GL_VERTEX_ARRAY_POINTER** are accepted.

params Returns the pointer value specified by *pname*.

DESCRIPTION

glGetPointerv returns pointer information. *pname* is a symbolic constant indicating the pointer to be returned, and *params* is a pointer to a location in which to place the returned data.

NOTES

glGetPointerv is available only if the GL version is 1.1 or greater.

The pointers are all client-side state.

The initial value for each pointer is 0.

When the **GL_ARB_multitexture** extension is supported, querying the **GL_TEXTURE_COORD_ARRAY_POINTER** returns the value for the active client texture unit.

ERRORS

GL_INVALID_ENUM is generated if *pname* is not an accepted value.

SEE ALSO

glArrayElement, **glClientActiveTextureARB**, **glColorPointer**, **glDrawArrays**, **glEdgeFlagPointer**, **glFeedbackBuffer**, **glIndexPointer**, **glInterleavedArrays**, **glNormalPointer**, **glSelectBuffer**, **glTexCoordPointer**, **glVertexPointer**

NAME

glGetPolygonStipple – return the polygon stipple pattern

C SPECIFICATION

void **glGetPolygonStipple**(GLubyte *mask*)

PARAMETERS

mask Returns the stipple pattern. The initial value is all 1's.

DESCRIPTION

glGetPolygonStipple returns to *mask* a 32 × 32 polygon stipple pattern. The pattern is packed into memory as if **glReadPixels** with both *height* and *width* of 32, *type* of **GL_BITMAP**, and *format* of **GL_COLOR_INDEX** were called, and the stipple pattern were stored in an internal 32 × 32 color index buffer. Unlike **glReadPixels**, however, pixel transfer operations (shift, offset, pixel map) are not applied to the returned stipple image.

NOTES

If an error is generated, no change is made to the contents of *mask*.

ERRORS

GL_INVALID_OPERATION is generated if **glGetPolygonStipple** is executed between the execution of **glBegin** and the corresponding execution of **glEnd**.

SEE ALSO

glPixelStore, **glPixelTransfer**, **glPolygonStipple**, **glReadPixels**

NAME

glGetSeparableFilter – get separable convolution filter kernel images

C SPECIFICATION

void **glGetSeparableFilter**(GLenum *target*,
GLenum *format*,
GLenum *type*,
GLvoid **row*,
GLvoid **column*,
GLvoid **span*)

PARAMETERS

target The separable filter to be retrieved. Must be **GL_SEPARABLE_2D**.

format
Format of the output images. Must be one of **GL_RED**, **GL_GREEN**,
GL_BLUE, **GL_ALPHA**, **GL_RGB**, **GL_BGR GL_RGBA**, **GL_BGRA**,
GL_LUMINANCE, or **GL_LUMINANCE_ALPHA**.

type Data type of components in the output images. Symbolic constants
GL_UNSIGNED_BYTE, **GL_BYTE**, **GL_BITMAP**, **GL_UNSIGNED_SHORT**,
GL_SHORT, **GL_UNSIGNED_INT**, **GL_INT**, **GL_FLOAT**,
GL_UNSIGNED_BYTE_3_3_2, **GL_UNSIGNED_BYTE_2_3_3_REV**,
GL_UNSIGNED_SHORT_5_6_5, **GL_UNSIGNED_SHORT_5_6_5_REV**,
GL_UNSIGNED_SHORT_4_4_4_4, **GL_UNSIGNED_SHORT_4_4_4_4_REV**,
GL_UNSIGNED_SHORT_5_5_5_1, **GL_UNSIGNED_SHORT_1_5_5_5_REV**,
GL_UNSIGNED_INT_8_8_8_8, **GL_UNSIGNED_INT_8_8_8_8_REV**,
GL_UNSIGNED_INT_10_10_10_2, and
GL_UNSIGNED_INT_2_10_10_10_REV are accepted.

row Pointer to storage for the row filter image.

column
Pointer to storage for the column filter image.

span Pointer to storage for the span filter image (currently unused).

DESCRIPTION

glGetSeparableFilter returns the two one-dimensional filter kernel images for the
current separable 2D convolution filter. The row image is placed in *row* and the
column image is placed in *column* according to the specifications in *format* and *type*.
(In the current implementation, *span* is not affected in any way.) No pixel transfer
operations are performed on the images, but the relevant pixel storage modes are
applied.

Color components that are present in *format* but not included in the internal format of the filters are returned as zero. The assignments of internal color components to the components of *format* are as follows:

Internal Component	Resulting Component
Red	Red
Green	Green
Blue	Blue
Alpha	Alpha
Luminance	Red
Intensity	Red

NOTES

glGetSeparableFilter is present only if **GL_ARB_imaging** is returned when **glGetString** is called with an argument of **GL_EXTENSIONS**.

Non-separable 2D filters must be retrieved with **glGetConvolutionFilter**.

ERRORS

GL_INVALID_ENUM is generated if *target* is not **GL_SEPARABLE_2D**.

GL_INVALID_ENUM is generated if *format* is not one of the allowable values.

GL_INVALID_ENUM is generated if *type* is not one of the allowable values.

GL_INVALID_OPERATION is generated if **glGetSeparableFilter** is executed between the execution of **glBegin** and the corresponding execution of **glEnd**.

GL_INVALID_OPERATION is generated if *type* is one of **GL_UNSIGNED_BYTE_3_3_2**, **GL_UNSIGNED_BYTE_2_3_3_REV**, **GL_UNSIGNED_SHORT_5_6_5**, or **GL_UNSIGNED_SHORT_5_6_5_REV** and *format* is not **GL_RGB**.

GL_INVALID_OPERATION is generated if *type* is one of **GL_UNSIGNED_SHORT_4_4_4_4**, **GL_UNSIGNED_SHORT_4_4_4_4_REV**, **GL_UNSIGNED_SHORT_5_5_5_1**, **GL_UNSIGNED_SHORT_1_5_5_5_REV**, **GL_UNSIGNED_INT_8_8_8_8**, **GL_UNSIGNED_INT_8_8_8_8_REV**, **GL_UNSIGNED_INT_10_10_10_2**, or **GL_UNSIGNED_INT_2_10_10_10_REV** and *format* is neither **GL_RGBA** nor **GL_BGRA**.

ASSOCIATED GETS

glGetConvolutionParameter

SEE ALSO

glGetConvolutionFilter, **glConvolutionParameter**, **glSeparableFilter2D**

NAME

glGetString – return a string describing the current GL connection

C SPECIFICATION

const GLubyte * **glGetString**(GLenum *name*)

PARAMETERS

name   Specifies a symbolic constant, one of **GL_VENDOR**, **GL_RENDERER**, **GL_VERSION**, or **GL_EXTENSIONS**.

DESCRIPTION

glGetString returns a pointer to a static string describing some aspect of the current GL connection. *name* can be one of the following:

GL_VENDOR   Returns the company responsible for this GL implementation. This name does not change from release to release.

GL_RENDERER   Returns the name of the renderer. This name is typically specific to a particular configuration of a hardware platform. It does not change from release to release.

GL_VERSION   Returns a version or release number.

GL_EXTENSIONS   Returns a space-separated list of supported extensions to GL.

Because the GL does not include queries for the performance characteristics of an implementation, some applications are written to recognize known platforms and modify their GL usage based on known performance characteristics of these platforms. Strings **GL_VENDOR** and **GL_RENDERER** together uniquely specify a platform. They do not change from release to release and should be used by platform-recognition algorithms.

Some applications want to make use of features that are not part of the standard GL. These features may be implemented as extensions to the standard GL. The **GL_EXTENSIONS** string is a space-separated list of supported GL extensions. (Extension names never contain a space character.)

The **GL_VERSION** string begins with a version number. The version number uses one of these forms:

major_number.minor_number
major_number.minor_number.release_number

Vendor-specific information may follow the version number. Its format depends on the implementation, but a space always separates the version number and the vendor-specific information.

All strings are null-terminated.

NOTES

If an error is generated, **glGetString** returns 0.

The client and server may support different versions or extensions. **glGetString** always returns a compatible version number or list of extensions. The release number always describes the server.

ERRORS

GL_INVALID_ENUM is generated if *name* is not an accepted value.

GL_INVALID_OPERATION is generated if **glGetString** is executed between the execution of **glBegin** and the corresponding execution of **glEnd**.

NAME

glGetTexEnvfv, **glGetTexEnviv** – return texture environment parameters

C SPECIFICATION

void **glGetTexEnvfv**(GLenum *target*,
                         GLenum *pname*,
                         GLfloat **params*)
void **glGetTexEnviv**(GLenum *target*,
                         GLenum *pname*,
                         GLint **params*)

PARAMETERS

target Specifies a texture environment. Must be **GL_TEXTURE_ENV**.

pname
Specifies the symbolic name of a texture environment parameter. Accepted values are **GL_TEXTURE_ENV_MODE** and **GL_TEXTURE_ENV_COLOR**.

params
Returns the requested data.

DESCRIPTION

glGetTexEnv returns in *params* selected values of a texture environment that was specified with **glTexEnv**. *target* specifies a texture environment. Currently, only one texture environment is defined and supported: **GL_TEXTURE_ENV**.

pname names a specific texture environment parameter, as follows:

GL_TEXTURE_ENV_MODE
params returns the single-valued texture environment mode, a symbolic constant. The initial value is **GL_MODULATE**.

GL_TEXTURE_ENV_COLOR
params returns four integer or floating-point values that are the texture environment color. Integer values, when requested, are linearly mapped from the internal floating-point representation such that 1.0 maps to the most positive representable integer, and –1.0 maps to the most negative representable integer. The initial value is (0, 0, 0, 0).

NOTES

If an error is generated, no change is made to the contents of *params*.

When the **GL_ARB_multitexture** extension is supported, **glGetTexEnv** returns the texture environment parameters for the active texture unit.

ERRORS

GL_INVALID_ENUM is generated if *target* or *pname* is not an accepted value.

GL_INVALID_OPERATION is generated if **glGetTexEnv** is executed between the execution of **glBegin** and the corresponding execution of **glEnd**.

SEE ALSO

glActiveTextureARB, **glTexEnv**

NAME

   glGetTexGendv, glGetTexGenfv, glGetTexGeniv – return texture coordinate generation parameters

C SPECIFICATION

   void **glGetTexGendv**(GLenum *coord*,
                          GLenum *pname*,
                          GLdouble **params*)
   void **glGetTexGenfv**(GLenum *coord*,
                          GLenum *pname*,
                          GLfloat **params*)
   void **glGetTexGeniv**(GLenum *coord*,
                          GLenum *pname*,
                          GLint **params*)

PARAMETERS

   coord   Specifies a texture coordinate. Must be **GL_S**, **GL_T**, **GL_R**, or **GL_Q**.

   pname   Specifies the symbolic name of the value(s) to be returned. Must be either **GL_TEXTURE_GEN_MODE** or the name of one of the texture generation plane equations: **GL_OBJECT_PLANE** or **GL_EYE_PLANE**.

   params Returns the requested data.

DESCRIPTION

   glGetTexGen returns in *params* selected parameters of a texture coordinate generation function that was specified using **glTexGen**. *coord* names one of the (*s, t, r, q*) texture coordinates, using the symbolic constant **GL_S**, **GL_T**, **GL_R**, or **GL_Q**.

   pname specifies one of three symbolic names:

   GL_TEXTURE_GEN_MODE   *params* returns the single-valued texture generation function, a symbolic constant. The initial value is **GL_EYE_LINEAR**.

   GL_OBJECT_PLANE   *params* returns the four plane equation coefficients that specify object linear-coordinate generation. Integer values, when requested, are mapped directly from the internal floating-point representation.

   GL_EYE_PLANE   *params* returns the four plane equation coefficients that specify eye linear-coordinate generation. Integer values, when requested, are mapped directly from the internal floating-point representation. The returned values are those maintained in eye coordinates. They are not equal to the values specified using **glTexGen**, unless the modelview matrix was identity when **glTexGen** was called.

NOTES

If an error is generated, no change is made to the contents of *params*.

When the **GL_ARB_multitexture** extension is supported, **glGetTexGen** returns the texture coordinate generation parameters for the active texture unit.

ERRORS

GL_INVALID_ENUM is generated if *coord* or *pname* is not an accepted value.

GL_INVALID_OPERATION is generated if **glGetTexGen** is executed between the execution of **glBegin** and the corresponding execution of **glEnd**.

SEE ALSO

glActiveTextureARB, **glTexGen**

NAME

glGetTexImage – return a texture image

C SPECIFICATION

void **glGetTexImage**(GLenum *target*,
GLint *level*,
GLenum *format*,
GLenum *type*,
GLvoid **pixels*)

PARAMETERS

target Specifies which texture is to be obtained. **GL_TEXTURE_1D**, **GL_TEXTURE_2D**, and **GL_TEXTURE_3D** are accepted.

level Specifies the level-of-detail number of the desired image. Level 0 is the base image level. Level *n* is the *n*th mipmap reduction image.

format
Specifies a pixel format for the returned data. The supported formats are **GL_RED**, **GL_GREEN**, **GL_BLUE**, **GL_ALPHA**, **GL_RGB**, **GL_BGR**, **GL_RGBA**, **GL_BGRA**, **GL_LUMINANCE**, and **GL_LUMINANCE_ALPHA**.

type Specifies a pixel type for the returned data. The supported types are **GL_UNSIGNED_BYTE**, **GL_BYTE**, **GL_UNSIGNED_SHORT**, **GL_SHORT**, **GL_UNSIGNED_INT**, **GL_INT**, **GL_FLOAT**, **GL_UNSIGNED_BYTE_3_3_2**, **GL_UNSIGNED_BYTE_2_3_3_REV**, **GL_UNSIGNED_SHORT_5_6_5**, **GL_UNSIGNED_SHORT_5_6_5_REV**, **GL_UNSIGNED_SHORT_4_4_4_4**, **GL_UNSIGNED_SHORT_4_4_4_4_REV**, **GL_UNSIGNED_SHORT_5_5_5_1**, **GL_UNSIGNED_SHORT_1_5_5_5_REV**, **GL_UNSIGNED_INT_8_8_8_8**, **GL_UNSIGNED_INT_8_8_8_8_REV**, **GL_UNSIGNED_INT_10_10_10_2**, and **GL_UNSIGNED_INT_2_10_10_10_REV**.

pixels Returns the texture image. Should be a pointer to an array of the type specified by *type*.

DESCRIPTION

glGetTexImage returns a texture image into *pixels*. *target* specifies whether the desired texture image is one specified by **glTexImage1D** (**GL_TEXTURE_1D**), **glTexImage2D** (**GL_TEXTURE_2D**), or **glTexImage3D** (**GL_TEXTURE_3D**). *level* specifies the level-of-detail number of the desired image. *format* and *type* specify the format and type of the desired image array. See the reference pages **glTexImage1D** and **glDrawPixels** for a description of the acceptable values for the *format* and *type* parameters, respectively.

To understand the operation of **glGetTexImage**, consider the selected internal four-component texture image to be an RGBA color buffer the size of the image. The semantics of **glGetTexImage** are then identical to those of **glReadPixels**, with the exception that no pixel transfer operations are performed, when called with the same *format* and *type*, with *x* and *y* set to 0, *width* set to the width of the texture image (including border if one was specified), and *height* set to 1 for 1D images, or to the height of the texture image (including border if one was specified) for 2D images. Because the internal texture image is an RGBA image, pixel formats **GL_COLOR_INDEX**, **GL_STENCIL_INDEX**, and **GL_DEPTH_COMPONENT** are not accepted, and pixel type **GL_BITMAP** is not accepted.

If the selected texture image does not contain four components, the following mappings are applied. Single-component textures are treated as RGBA buffers with red set to the single-component value, green set to 0, blue set to 0, and alpha set to 1. Two-component textures are treated as RGBA buffers with red set to the value of component zero, alpha set to the value of component one, and green and blue set to 0. Finally, three-component textures are treated as RGBA buffers with red set to component zero, green set to component one, blue set to component two, and alpha set to 1.

To determine the required size of *pixels*, use **glGetTexLevelParameter** to determine the dimensions of the internal texture image, then scale the required number of pixels by the storage required for each pixel, based on *format* and *type*. Be sure to take the pixel storage parameters into account, especially **GL_PACK_ALIGNMENT**.

NOTES

If an error is generated, no change is made to the contents of *pixels*.

When the **GL_ARB_multitexture** extension is supported, **glGetTexImage** returns the texture image for the active texture unit.

The types **GL_UNSIGNED_BYTE_3_3_2**, **GL_UNSIGNED_BYTE_2_3_3_REV**, **GL_UNSIGNED_SHORT_5_6_5**, **GL_UNSIGNED_SHORT_5_6_5_REV**, **GL_UNSIGNED_SHORT_4_4_4_4**, **GL_UNSIGNED_SHORT_4_4_4_4_REV**, **GL_UNSIGNED_SHORT_5_5_5_1**, **GL_UNSIGNED_SHORT_1_5_5_5_REV**, **GL_UNSIGNED_INT_8_8_8_8**, **GL_UNSIGNED_INT_8_8_8_8_REV**, **GL_UNSIGNED_INT_10_10_10_2**, **GL_UNSIGNED_INT_2_10_10_10_REV**, and the formats **GL_BGR**, and **GL_BGRA** are available only if the GL version is 1.2 or greater.

ERRORS

GL_INVALID_ENUM is generated if *target*, *format*, or *type* is not an accepted value.

GL_INVALID_VALUE is generated if *level* is less than 0.

GL_INVALID_VALUE may be generated if *level* is greater than $\log_2$ max, where max is the returned value of **GL_MAX_TEXTURE_SIZE**.

GL_INVALID_OPERATION is generated if **glGetTexImage** is executed between the execution of **glBegin** and the corresponding execution of **glEnd**.

GL_INVALID_OPERATION is returned if *type* is one of GL_UNSIGNED_BYTE_3_3_2, GL_UNSIGNED_BYTE_2_3_3_REV, GL_UNSIGNED_SHORT_5_6_5, or GL_UNSIGNED_SHORT_5_6_5_REV and *format* is not **GL_RGB**.

GL_INVALID_OPERATION is returned if *type* is one of GL_UNSIGNED_SHORT_4_4_4_4, GL_UNSIGNED_SHORT_4_4_4_4_REV, GL_UNSIGNED_SHORT_5_5_5_1, GL_UNSIGNED_SHORT_1_5_5_5_REV, GL_UNSIGNED_INT_8_8_8_8, GL_UNSIGNED_INT_8_8_8_8_REV, GL_UNSIGNED_INT_10_10_10_2, or GL_UNSIGNED_INT_2_10_10_10_REV, and *format* is neither **GL_RGBA** or **GL_BGRA**.

ASSOCIATED GETS

glGetTexLevelParameter with argument **GL_TEXTURE_WIDTH**
glGetTexLevelParameter with argument **GL_TEXTURE_HEIGHT**
glGetTexLevelParameter with argument **GL_TEXTURE_BORDER**
glGetTexLevelParameter with argument **GL_TEXTURE_INTERNALFORMAT**
glGet with arguments **GL_PACK_ALIGNMENT** and others

SEE ALSO

glActiveTextureARB, **glDrawPixels**, **glReadPixels**, **glTexEnv**, **glTexGen**, **glTexImage1D**, **glTexImage2D**, **glTexImage3D**, **glTexSubImage1D**, **glTexSubImage2D**, **glTexSubImage3D**, **glTexParameter**

NAME

glGetTexLevelParameterfv, glGetTexLevelParameteriv – return texture parameter values for a specific level of detail

C SPECIFICATION

void **glGetTexLevelParameterfv**(GLenum *target*,
GLint *level*,
GLenum *pname*,
GLfloat **params*)

void **glGetTexLevelParameteriv**(GLenum *target*,
GLint *level*,
GLenum *pname*,
GLint **params*)

PARAMETERS

target Specifies the symbolic name of the target texture, either **GL_TEXTURE_1D**, **GL_TEXTURE_2D**, **GL_TEXTURE_3D**, **GL_PROXY_TEXTURE_1D**, **GL_PROXY_TEXTURE_2D**, or **GL_PROXY_TEXTURE_3D**.

level Specifies the level-of-detail number of the desired image. Level 0 is the base image level. Level *n* is the *n*th mipmap reduction image.

pname
Specifies the symbolic name of a texture parameter. **GL_TEXTURE_WIDTH**, **GL_TEXTURE_HEIGHT**, **GL_TEXTURE_DEPTH**, **GL_TEXTURE_INTERNAL_FORMAT**, **GL_TEXTURE_BORDER**, **GL_TEXTURE_RED_SIZE**, **GL_TEXTURE_GREEN_SIZE**, **GL_TEXTURE_BLUE_SIZE**, **GL_TEXTURE_ALPHA_SIZE**, **GL_TEXTURE_LUMINANCE_SIZE**, and **GL_TEXTURE_INTENSITY_SIZE** are accepted.

params
Returns the requested data.

DESCRIPTION

glGetTexLevelParameter returns in *params* texture parameter values for a specific level-of-detail value, specified as *level*. *target* defines the target texture, either **GL_TEXTURE_1D**, **GL_TEXTURE_2D**, **GL_TEXTURE_3D**, **GL_PROXY_TEXTURE_1D**, **GL_PROXY_TEXTURE_2D**, or **GL_PROXY_TEXTURE_3D**.

GL_MAX_TEXTURE_SIZE, and **GL_MAX_3D_TEXTURE_SIZE** are not really descriptive enough. It has to report the largest square texture image that can be accommodated with mipmaps and borders, but a long skinny texture, or a texture without mipmaps and borders, may easily fit in texture memory. The proxy targets allow the user to more accurately query whether the GL can accommodate a texture of a given configuration. If the texture cannot be accommodated, the texture state variables, which may be queried with **glGetTexLevelParameter**, are set to 0. If the texture can be accommodated, the texture state values will be set as they would be set for a non-proxy target.

pname specifies the texture parameter whose value or values will be returned.

The accepted parameter names are as follows:

GL_TEXTURE_WIDTH

> *params* returns a single value, the width of the texture image. This value includes the border of the texture image. The initial value is 0.

GL_TEXTURE_HEIGHT

> *params* returns a single value, the height of the texture image. This value includes the border of the texture image. The initial value is 0.

GL_TEXTURE_DEPTH

> *params* returns a single value, the depth of the texture image. This value includes the border of the texture image. The initial value is 0.

GL_TEXTURE_INTERNAL_FORMAT

> *params* returns a single value, the internal format of the texture image.

GL_TEXTURE_BORDER

> *params* returns a single value, the width in pixels of the border of the texture image. The initial value is 0.

GL_TEXTURE_RED_SIZE,

GL_TEXTURE_GREEN_SIZE,

GL_TEXTURE_BLUE_SIZE,

GL_TEXTURE_ALPHA_SIZE,

GL_TEXTURE_LUMINANCE_SIZE,

GL_TEXTURE_INTENSITY_SIZE

> The internal storage resolution of an individual component. The resolution chosen by the GL will be a close match for the resolution requested by the user with the component argument of **glTexImage1D**, **glTexImage2D**, **glTexImage3D**, **glCopyTexImage1D**, and **glCopyTexImage2D**. The initial value is 0.

NOTES

If an error is generated, no change is made to the contents of *params*.

GL_TEXTURE_INTERNAL_FORMAT is available only if the GL version is 1.1 or greater. In version 1.0, use **GL_TEXTURE_COMPONENTS** instead.

GL_PROXY_TEXTURE_1D and **GL_PROXY_TEXTURE_2D** are available only if the GL version is 1.1 or greater.

GL_TEXTURE_3D, **GL_PROXY_TEXTURE_3D**, and **GL_TEXTURE_DEPTH** are available only if the GL version is 1.2 or greater.

When the **GL_ARB_multitexture** extension is supported, **glGetTexLevelParameter** returns the texture level parameters for the active texture unit.

ERRORS

GL_INVALID_ENUM is generated if *target* or *pname* is not an accepted value.

GL_INVALID_VALUE is generated if *level* is less than 0.

GL_INVALID_VALUE may be generated if *level* is greater than $\log_2 max$, where *max* is the returned value of **GL_MAX_TEXTURE_SIZE**.

GL_INVALID_OPERATION is generated if **glGetTexLevelParameter** is executed between the execution of **glBegin** and the corresponding execution of **glEnd**.

SEE ALSO

glActiveTextureARB, glGetTexParameter, glCopyTexImage1D, glCopyTexImage2D, glCopyTexSubImage1D, glCopyTexSubImage2D, glCopyTexSubImage3D, glTexEnv, glTexGen, glTexImage1D, glTexImage2D, glTexImage3D, glTexSubImage1D, glTexSubImage2D, glTexSubImage3D, glTexParameter

NAME

glGetTexParameterfv, glGetTexParameteriv – return texture parameter values

C SPECIFICATION

void **glGetTexParameterfv**(GLenum *target*,
                             GLenum *pname*,
                             GLfloat **params*)
void **glGetTexParameteriv**(GLenum *target*,
                             GLenum *pname*,
                             GLint **params*)

PARAMETERS

target Specifies the symbolic name of the target texture.
         GL_TEXTURE_1D,**GL_TEXTURE_2D**, and **GL_TEXTURE_3D** are accepted.

pname
         Specifies the symbolic name of a texture parameter.
         GL_TEXTURE_MAG_FILTER, GL_TEXTURE_MIN_FILTER,
         GL_TEXTURE_MIN_LOD, GL_TEXTURE_MAX_LOD,
         GL_TEXTURE_BASE_LEVEL, GL_TEXTURE_MAX_LEVEL,
         GL_TEXTURE_WRAP_S, GL_TEXTURE_WRAP_T, GL_TEXTURE_WRAP_R,
         GL_TEXTURE_BORDER_COLOR, GL_TEXTURE_PRIORITY, and
         GL_TEXTURE_RESIDENT are accepted.

params
         Returns the texture parameters.

DESCRIPTION

glGetTexParameter returns in *params* the value or values of the texture parameter
specified as *pname*. *target* defines the target texture, either **GL_TEXTURE_1D**,
GL_TEXTURE_2D, or **GL_TEXTURE_3D** to specify one-, two-, or three-dimensional
texturing. *pname* accepts the same symbols as **glTexParameter**, with the same
interpretations:

GL_TEXTURE_MAG_FILTER   Returns the single-valued texture
                                magnification filter, a symbolic constant. The
                                initial value is **GL_LINEAR**.

GL_TEXTURE_MIN_FILTER   Returns the single-valued texture minification
                                filter, a symbolic constant. The initial value is
                                GL_NEAREST_MIPMAP_LINEAR.

GL_TEXTURE_MIN_LOD   Returns the single-valued texture minimum
                                level-of-detail value. The initial value is −1000.

GL_TEXTURE_MAX_LOD	Returns the single-valued texture maximum level-of-detail value. The initial value is 1000.
GL_TEXTURE_BASE_LEVEL	Returns the single-valued base texture mipmap level. The initial value is 0.
GL_TEXTURE_MAX_LEVEL	Returns the single-valued maximum texture mipmap array level. The initial value is 1000.
GL_TEXTURE_WRAP_S	Returns the single-valued wrapping function for texture coordinate *s*, a symbolic constant. The initial value is **GL_REPEAT**.
GL_TEXTURE_WRAP_T	Returns the single-valued wrapping function for texture coordinate *t*, a symbolic constant. The initial value is **GL_REPEAT**.
GL_TEXTURE_WRAP_R	Returns the single-valued wrapping function for texture coordinate *r*, a symbolic constant. The initial value is **GL_REPEAT**.
GL_TEXTURE_BORDER_COLOR	Returns four integer or floating-point numbers that comprise the RGBA color of the texture border. Floating-point values are returned in the range [0, 1]. Integer values are returned as a linear mapping of the internal floating-point representation such that 1.0 maps to the most positive representable integer and −1.0 maps to the most negative representable integer. The initial value is (0, 0, 0, 0).
GL_TEXTURE_PRIORITY	Returns the residence priority of the target texture (or the named texture bound to it). The initial value is 1. See **glPrioritizeTextures**.
GL_TEXTURE_RESIDENT	Returns the residence status of the target texture. If the value returned in *params* is **GL_TRUE**, the texture is resident in texture memory. See **glAreTexturesResident**.

NOTES

GL_TEXTURE_PRIORITY and **GL_TEXTURE_RESIDENT** are available only if the GL version is 1.1 or greater.

GL_TEXTURE_3D, **GL_TEXTURE_MIN_LOD**, **GL_TEXTURE_MAX_LOD**, **GL_TEXTURE_BASE_LEVEL**, **GL_TEXTURE_MAX_LEVEL**, and **GL_TEXTURE_WRAP_R** are available only if the GL version is 1.2 or greater.

If an error is generated, no change is made to the contents of *params*.

ERRORS

GL_INVALID_ENUM is generated if *target* or *pname* is not an accepted value.

GL_INVALID_OPERATION is generated if **glGetTexParameter** is executed between the execution of **glBegin** and the corresponding execution of **glEnd**.

SEE ALSO

glAreTexturesResident, **glPrioritizeTextures**, **glTexParameter**

NAME

glHint – specify implementation-specific hints

C SPECIFICATION

void **glHint**(GLenum *target*,
                GLenum *mode*)

PARAMETERS

target Specifies a symbolic constant indicating the behavior to be controlled.
GL_FOG_HINT, **GL_LINE_SMOOTH_HINT**,
GL_PERSPECTIVE_CORRECTION_HINT, **GL_POINT_SMOOTH_HINT**, and
GL_POLYGON_SMOOTH_HINT are accepted.

mode Specifies a symbolic constant indicating the desired behavior. **GL_FASTEST**,
GL_NICEST, and **GL_DONT_CARE** are accepted.

DESCRIPTION

Certain aspects of GL behavior, when there is room for interpretation, can be controlled with hints. A hint is specified with two arguments. *target* is a symbolic constant indicating the behavior to be controlled, and *mode* is another symbolic constant indicating the desired behavior. The initial value for each *target* is
GL_DONT_CARE. *mode* can be one of the following:

GL_FASTEST   The most efficient option should be chosen.

GL_NICEST   The most correct, or highest quality, option should be chosen.

GL_DONT_CARE   No preference.

Though the implementation aspects that can be hinted are well defined, the interpretation of the hints depends on the implementation. The hint aspects that can be specified with *target*, along with suggested semantics, are as follows:

GL_FOG_HINT   Indicates the accuracy of fog calculation. If per-pixel fog calculation is not efficiently supported by the GL implementation, hinting **GL_DONT_CARE** or **GL_FASTEST** can result in per-vertex calculation of fog effects.

GL_LINE_SMOOTH_HINT
        Indicates the sampling quality of antialiased lines. If a larger filter function is applied, hinting **GL_NICEST** can result in more pixel fragments being generated during rasterization,

GL_PERSPECTIVE_CORRECTION_HINT
        Indicates the quality of color and texture coordinate interpolation. If perspective-corrected parameter interpolation is not efficiently supported by the GL implementation, hinting **GL_DONT_CARE** or **GL_FASTEST** can result in simple linear

interpolation of colors and/or texture coordinates.

GL_POINT_SMOOTH_HINT

Indicates the sampling quality of antialiased points. If a larger filter function is applied, hinting **GL_NICEST** can result in more pixel fragments being generated during rasterization,

GL_POLYGON_SMOOTH_HINT

Indicates the sampling quality of antialiased polygons. Hinting **GL_NICEST** can result in more pixel fragments being generated during rasterization, if a larger filter function is applied.

NOTES

The interpretation of hints depends on the implementation. Some implementations ignore **glHint** settings.

ERRORS

GL_INVALID_ENUM is generated if either *target* or *mode* is not an accepted value.

GL_INVALID_OPERATION is generated if **glHint** is executed between the execution of **glBegin** and the corresponding execution of **glEnd**.

NAME

glHistogram – define histogram table

C SPECIFICATION

void **glHistogram**(GLenum *target*,
GLsizei *width*,
GLenum *internalformat*,
GLboolean *sink*)

PARAMETERS

target The histogram whose parameters are to be set. Must be one of **GL_HISTOGRAM** or **GL_PROXY_HISTOGRAM**.

width The number of entries in the histogram table. Must be a power of 2.

internalformat

The format of entries in the histogram table. Must be one of **GL_ALPHA**, **GL_ALPHA4**, **GL_ALPHA8**, **GL_ALPHA12**, **GL_ALPHA16**, **GL_LUMINANCE**, **GL_LUMINANCE4**, **GL_LUMINANCE8**, **GL_LUMINANCE12**, **GL_LUMINANCE16**, **GL_LUMINANCE_ALPHA**, **GL_LUMINANCE4_ALPHA4**, **GL_LUMINANCE6_ALPHA2**, **GL_LUMINANCE8_ALPHA8**, **GL_LUMINANCE12_ALPHA4**, **GL_LUMINANCE12_ALPHA12**, **GL_LUMINANCE16_ALPHA16**, **GL_R3_G3_B2**, **GL_RGB**, **GL_RGB4**, **GL_RGB5**, **GL_RGB8**, **GL_RGB10**, **GL_RGB12**, **GL_RGB16**, **GL_RGBA**, **GL_RGBA2**, **GL_RGBA4**, **GL_RGB5_A1**, **GL_RGBA8**, **GL_RGB10_A2**, **GL_RGBA12**, or **GL_RGBA16**.

sink If **GL_TRUE**, pixels will be consumed by the histogramming process and no drawing or texture loading will take place. If **GL_FALSE**, pixels will proceed to the minmax process after histogramming.

DESCRIPTION

When **GL_HISTOGRAM** is enabled, RGBA color components are converted to histogram table indices by clamping to the range [0,1], multiplying by the width of the histogram table, and rounding to the nearest integer. The table entries selected by the RGBA indices are then incremented. (If the internal format of the histogram table includes luminance, then the index derived from the R color component determines the luminance table entry to be incremented.) If a histogram table entry is incremented beyond its maximum value, then its value becomes undefined. (This is not an error.)

Histogramming is performed only for RGBA pixels (though these may be specified originally as color indices and converted to RGBA by index table lookup). Histogramming is enabled with **glEnable** and disabled with **glDisable**.

When *target* is **GL_HISTOGRAM**, **glHistogram** redefines the current histogram table to have *width* entries of the format specified by *internalformat*. The entries are indexed 0 through *width* – 1, and all entries are initialized to zero. The values in the previous histogram table, if any, are lost. If *sink* is **GL_TRUE**, then pixels are discarded after histogramming; no further processing of the pixels takes place, and no drawing, texture loading, or pixel readback will result.

When *target* is **GL_PROXY_HISTOGRAM**, **glHistogram** computes all state information as if the histogram table were to be redefined, but does not actually define the new table. If the requested histogram table is too large to be supported, then the state information will be set to zero. This provides a way to determine if a histogram table with the given parameters can be supported.

NOTES

glHistogram is present only if **GL_ARB_imaging** is returned when **glGetString** is called with an argument of **GL_EXTENSIONS**.

ERRORS

GL_INVALID_ENUM is generated if *target* is not one of the allowable values.

GL_INVALID_VALUE is generated if *width* is less than zero or is not a power of 2.

GL_INVALID_ENUM is generated if *internalformat* is not one of the allowable values.

GL_TABLE_TOO_LARGE is generated if *target* is **GL_HISTOGRAM** and the histogram table specified is too large for the implementation.

GL_INVALID_OPERATION is generated if **glHistogram** is executed between the execution of **glBegin** and the corresponding execution of **glEnd**.

ASSOCIATED GETS

glGetHistogramParameter

SEE ALSO

glGetHistogram, glResetHistogram

NAME

glIndexd, glIndexf, glIndexi, glIndexs, glIndexub, glIndexdv, glIndexfv, glIndexiv, glIndexsv, glIndexubv – set the current color index

C SPECIFICATION

void **glIndexd**(GLdouble *c*)
void **glIndexf**(GLfloat *c*)
void **glIndexi**(GLint *c*)
void **glIndexs**(GLshort *c*)
void **glIndexub**(GLubyte *c*)

PARAMETERS

c Specifies the new value for the current color index.

C SPECIFICATION

void **glIndexdv**(const GLdouble *c)
void **glIndexfv**(const GLfloat *c)
void **glIndexiv**(const GLint *c)
void **glIndexsv**(const GLshort *c)
void **glIndexubv**(const GLubyte *c)

PARAMETERS

c   Specifies a pointer to a one-element array that contains the new value for the current color index.

DESCRIPTION

glIndex updates the current (single-valued) color index. It takes one argument, the new value for the current color index.

The current index is stored as a floating-point value. Integer values are converted directly to floating-point values, with no special mapping. The initial value is 1.

Index values outside the representable range of the color index buffer are not clamped. However, before an index is dithered (if enabled) and written to the frame buffer, it is converted to fixed-point format. Any bits in the integer portion of the resulting fixed-point value that do not correspond to bits in the frame buffer are masked out.

NOTES

glIndexub and **glIndexubv** are available only if the GL version is 1.1 or greater.

The current index can be updated at any time. In particular, **glIndex** can be called between a call to **glBegin** and the corresponding call to **glEnd**.

ASSOCIATED GETS

glGet with argument **GL_CURRENT_INDEX**

SEE ALSO

glColor, glIndexPointer

NAME

glIndexMask – control the writing of individual bits in the color index buffers

C SPECIFICATION

void **glIndexMask**(GLuint *mask*)

PARAMETERS

mask Specifies a bit mask to enable and disable the writing of individual bits in the color index buffers. Initially, the mask is all 1's.

DESCRIPTION

glIndexMask controls the writing of individual bits in the color index buffers. The least significant n bits of *mask*, where n is the number of bits in a color index buffer, specify a mask. Where a 1 (one) appears in the mask, it's possible to write to the corresponding bit in the color index buffer (or buffers). Where a 0 (zero) appears, the corresponding bit is write-protected.

This mask is used only in color index mode, and it affects only the buffers currently selected for writing (see **glDrawBuffer**). Initially, all bits are enabled for writing.

ERRORS

GL_INVALID_OPERATION is generated if **glIndexMask** is executed between the execution of **glBegin** and the corresponding execution of **glEnd**.

ASSOCIATED GETS

glGet with argument GL_INDEX_WRITEMASK

SEE ALSO

glColorMask, **glDepthMask**, **glDrawBuffer**, **glIndex**, **glIndexPointer**, **glStencilMask**

NAME

glIndexPointer – define an array of color indexes

C SPECIFICATION

void **glIndexPointer**(GLenum *type*,
                        GLsizei *stride*,
                        const GLvoid **pointer*)

PARAMETERS

type   Specifies the data type of each color index in the array. Symbolic constants **GL_UNSIGNED_BYTE**, **GL_SHORT**, **GL_INT**, **GL_FLOAT**, and **GL_DOUBLE** are accepted. The initial value is **GL_FLOAT**.

stride   Specifies the byte offset between consecutive color indexes. If *stride* is 0 (the initial value), the color indexes are understood to be tightly packed in the array. The initial value is 0.

pointer Specifies a pointer to the first index in the array. The initial value is 0.

DESCRIPTION

glIndexPointer specifies the location and data format of an array of color indexes to use when rendering. *type* specifies the data type of each color index and *stride* gives the byte stride from one color index to the next allowing vertices and attributes to be packed into a single array or stored in separate arrays. (Single-array storage may be more efficient on some implementations; see **glInterleavedArrays**.)

type, *stride*, and *pointer* are saved as client-side state.

The color index array is initially disabled. To enable and disable the array, call **glEnableClientState** and **glDisableClientState** with the argument **GL_INDEX_ARRAY**. If enabled, the color index array is used when **glDrawArrays**, **glDrawElements** or **glArrayElement** is called.

Use **glDrawArrays** to construct a sequence of primitives (all of the same type) from prespecified vertex and vertex attribute arrays. Use **glArrayElement** to specify primitives by indexing vertices and vertex attributes and **glDrawElements** to construct a sequence of primitives by indexing vertices and vertex attributes.

NOTES

glIndexPointer is available only if the GL version is 1.1 or greater.

The color index array is initially disabled, and it isn't accessed when **glArrayElement**, **glDrawElements**, or **glDrawArrays** is called.

Execution of **glIndexPointer** is not allowed between **glBegin** and the corresponding **glEnd**, but an error may or may not be generated. If an error is not generated, the operation is undefined.

glIndexPointer is typically implemented on the client side.

Since the color index array parameters are client-side state, they are not saved or restored by **glPushAttrib** and **glPopAttrib**. Use **glPushClientAttrib** and **glPopClientAttrib** instead.

ERRORS

GL_INVALID_ENUM is generated if *type* is not an accepted value.

GL_INVALID_VALUE is generated if *stride* is negative.

ASSOCIATED GETS

glIsEnabled with argument **GL_INDEX_ARRAY**
glGet with argument **GL_INDEX_ARRAY_TYPE**
glGet with argument **GL_INDEX_ARRAY_STRIDE**
glGetPointerv with argument **GL_INDEX_ARRAY_POINTER**

SEE ALSO

glArrayElement, **glColorPointer**, **glDrawArrays**, **glDrawElements**, **glEdgeFlagPointer**, **glEnable**, **glGetPointerv**, **glInterleavedArrays**, **glNormalPointer**, **glPopClientAttrib**, **glPushClientAttrib**, **glTexCoordPointer**, **glVertexPointer**

NAME

glInitNames – initialize the name stack

C SPECIFICATION

void **glInitNames**(void)

DESCRIPTION

The name stack is used during selection mode to allow sets of rendering commands to be uniquely identified. It consists of an ordered set of unsigned integers. **glInitNames** causes the name stack to be initialized to its default empty state.

The name stack is always empty while the render mode is not **GL_SELECT**. Calls to **glInitNames** while the render mode is not **GL_SELECT** are ignored.

ERRORS

GL_INVALID_OPERATION is generated if **glInitNames** is executed between the execution of **glBegin** and the corresponding execution of **glEnd**.

ASSOCIATED GETS

glGet with argument **GL_NAME_STACK_DEPTH**
glGet with argument **GL_MAX_NAME_STACK_DEPTH**

SEE ALSO

glLoadName, **glPushName**, **glRenderMode**, **glSelectBuffer**

NAME

glInterleavedArrays – simultaneously specify and enable several interleaved arrays

C SPECIFICATION

void **glInterleavedArrays**(GLenum *format*,
GLsizei *stride*,
const GLvoid **pointer*)

PARAMETERS

format Specifies the type of array to enable. Symbolic constants **GL_V2F**, **GL_V3F**, **GL_C4UB_V2F**, **GL_C4UB_V3F**, **GL_C3F_V3F**, **GL_N3F_V3F**, **GL_C4F_N3F_V3F**, **GL_T2F_V3F**, **GL_T4F_V4F**, **GL_T2F_C4UB_V3F**, **GL_T2F_C3F_V3F**, **GL_T2F_N3F_V3F**, **GL_T2F_C4F_N3F_V3F**, and **GL_T4F_C4F_N3F_V4F** are accepted.

stride Specifies the offset in bytes between each aggregate array element.

DESCRIPTION

glInterleavedArrays lets you specify and enable individual color, normal, texture and vertex arrays whose elements are part of a larger aggregate array element. For some implementations, this is more efficient than specifying the arrays separately.

If *stride* is 0, the aggregate elements are stored consecutively. Otherwise, *stride* bytes occur between the beginning of one aggregate array element and the beginning of the next aggregate array element.

format serves as a "key" describing the extraction of individual arrays from the aggregate array. If *format* contains a T, then texture coordinates are extracted from the interleaved array. If C is present, color values are extracted. If N is present, normal coordinates are extracted. Vertex coordinates are always extracted.

The digits 2, 3, and 4 denote how many values are extracted. F indicates that values are extracted as floating-point values. Colors may also be extracted as 4 unsigned bytes if 4UB follows the C. If a color is extracted as 4 unsigned bytes, the vertex array element which follows is located at the first possible floating-point aligned address.

NOTES

glInterleavedArrays is available only if the GL version is 1.1 or greater.

If **glInterleavedArrays** is called while compiling a display list, it is not compiled into the list, and it is executed immediately.

Execution of **glInterleavedArrays** is not allowed between the execution of **glBegin** and the corresponding execution of **glEnd**, but an error may or may not be generated. If no error is generated, the operation is undefined.

glInterleavedArrays is typically implemented on the client side.

Vertex array parameters are client-side state and are therefore not saved or restored by **glPushAttrib** and **glPopAttrib**. Use **glPushClientAttrib** and **glPopClientAttrib** instead.

When the **GL_ARB_multitexture** extension is supported, **glInterleavedArrays** only updates the texture coordinate array for the active texture unit. The texture coordinate state for other client texture units is not updated, regardless of whether the client texture unit is enabled or not.

ERRORS

GL_INVALID_ENUM is generated if *format* is not an accepted value.

GL_INVALID_VALUE is generated if *stride* is negative.

SEE ALSO

glArrayElement, glClientActiveTextureARB, glColorPointer, glDrawArrays, glDrawElements, glEdgeFlagPointer, glEnableClientState, glGetPointer, glIndexPointer, glNormalPointer, glTexCoordPointer, glVertexPointer

NAME

glIsEnabled – test whether a capability is enabled

C SPECIFICATION

GLboolean **glIsEnabled**(GLenum *cap*)

PARAMETERS

cap   Specifies a symbolic constant indicating a GL capability.

DESCRIPTION

glIsEnabled returns **GL_TRUE** if *cap* is an enabled capability and returns **GL_FALSE** otherwise. Initially all capabilities except **GL_DITHER** are disabled; **GL_DITHER** is initially enabled.

The following capabilities are accepted for *cap*:

Constant	See
GL_ALPHA_TEST	glAlphaFunc
GL_AUTO_NORMAL	glEvalCoord
GL_BLEND	glBlendFunc, glLogicOp
GL_CLIP_PLANE*i*	glClipPlane
GL_COLOR_ARRAY	glColorPointer
GL_COLOR_LOGIC_OP	glLogicOp
GL_COLOR_MATERIAL	glColorMaterial
GL_COLOR_TABLE	glColorTable
GL_CONVOLUTION_1D	glConvolutionFilter1D
GL_CONVOLUTION_2D	glConvolutionFilter2D
GL_CULL_FACE	glCullFace
GL_DEPTH_TEST	glDepthFunc, glDepthRange
GL_DITHER	glEnable
GL_EDGE_FLAG_ARRAY	glEdgeFlagPointer
GL_FOG	glFog
GL_HISTOGRAM	glHistogram
GL_INDEX_ARRAY	glIndexPointer
GL_INDEX_LOGIC_OP	glLogicOp
GL_LIGHT*i*	glLightModel, glLight
GL_LIGHTING	glMaterial, glLightModel, glLight
GL_LINE_SMOOTH	glLineWidth
GL_LINE_STIPPLE	glLineStipple
GL_MAP1_COLOR_4	glMap1
GL_MAP1_INDEX	glMap1
GL_MAP1_NORMAL	glMap1

GL_MAP1_TEXTURE_COORD_1	glMap1
GL_MAP1_TEXTURE_COORD_2	glMap1
GL_MAP1_TEXTURE_COORD_3	glMap1
GL_MAP1_TEXTURE_COORD_4	glMap1
GL_MAP2_COLOR_4	glMap2
GL_MAP2_INDEX	glMap2
GL_MAP2_NORMAL	glMap2
GL_MAP2_TEXTURE_COORD_1	glMap2
GL_MAP2_TEXTURE_COORD_2	glMap2
GL_MAP2_TEXTURE_COORD_3	glMap2
GL_MAP2_TEXTURE_COORD_4	glMap2
GL_MAP2_VERTEX_3	glMap2
GL_MAP2_VERTEX_4	glMap2
GL_MINMAX	glMinmax
GL_NORMAL_ARRAY	glNormalPointer
GL_NORMALIZE	glNormal
GL_POINT_SMOOTH	glPointSize
GL_POLYGON_SMOOTH	glPolygonMode
GL_POLYGON_OFFSET_FILL	glPolygonOffset
GL_POLYGON_OFFSET_LINE	glPolygonOffset
GL_POLYGON_OFFSET_POINT	glPolygonOffset
GL_POLYGON_STIPPLE	glPolygonStipple
GL_POST_COLOR_MATRIX_COLOR_TABLE	glColorTable
GL_POST_CONVOLUTION_COLOR_TABLE	glColorTable
GL_RESCALE_NORMAL	glNormal
GL_SCISSOR_TEST	glScissor
GL_SEPARABLE_2D	glSeparableFilter2D
GL_STENCIL_TEST	glStencilFunc, glStencilOp
GL_TEXTURE_1D	glTexImage1D
GL_TEXTURE_2D	glTexImage2D
GL_TEXTURE_3D	glTexImage3D
GL_TEXTURE_COORD_ARRAY	glTexCoordPointer
GL_TEXTURE_GEN_Q	glTexGen
GL_TEXTURE_GEN_R	glTexGen
GL_TEXTURE_GEN_S	glTexGen
GL_TEXTURE_GEN_T	glTexGen
GL_VERTEX_ARRAY	glVertexPointer

NOTES

If an error is generated, **glIsEnabled** returns 0.

GL_COLOR_LOGIC_OP, GL_COLOR_ARRAY, GL_EDGE_FLAG_ARRAY, GL_INDEX_ARRAY, GL_INDEX_LOGIC_OP, GL_NORMAL_ARRAY, GL_POLYGON_OFFSET_FILL, GL_POLYGON_OFFSET_LINE, GL_POLYGON_OFFSET_POINT, GL_TEXTURE_COORD_ARRAY, and GL_VERTEX_ARRAY are available only if the GL version is 1.1 or greater

GL_RESCALE_NORMAL, and GL_TEXTURE_3D are available only if the GL version is 1.2 or greater.

GL_COLOR_TABLE, GL_CONVOLUTION_1D, GL_CONVOLUTION_2D, GL_HISTOGRAM, GL_MINMAX, GL_POST_COLOR_MATRIX_COLOR_TABLE, GL_POST_CONVOLUTION_COLOR_TABLE, and GL_SEPARABLE_2D are available only if **GL_ARB_imaging** is returned when **glGet** is called with GL_EXTENSIONS.

When the **GL_ARB_multitexture** extension is supported, the following parameters return the associated value for the active texture unit. GL_TEXTURE_1D, GL_TEXTURE_BINDING_1D, GL_TEXTURE_2D, GL_TEXTURE_BINDING_2D, GL_TEXTURE_3D, GL_TEXTURE_BINDING_3D, GL_TEXTURE_GEN_S, GL_TEXTURE_GEN_T, GL_TEXTURE_GEN_R, GL_TEXTURE_GEN_Q, GL_TEXTURE_MATRIX, and GL_TEXTURE_STACK_DEPTH. Likewise, the following parameters return the associated value for the active client texture unit: GL_TEXTURE_COORD_ARRAY, GL_TEXTURE_COORD_ARRAY_SIZE, GL_TEXTURE_COORD_ARRAY_STRIDE, GL_TEXTURE_COORD_ARRAY_TYPE.

ERRORS

GL_INVALID_ENUM is generated if *cap* is not an accepted value.

GL_INVALID_OPERATION is generated if **glIsEnabled** is executed between the execution of **glBegin** and the corresponding execution of **glEnd**.

SEE ALSO

glEnable, **glEnableClientState**, **glGet**

NAME

glIsList – determine if a name corresponds to a display-list

C SPECIFICATION

GLboolean **glIsList**(GLuint *list*)

PARAMETERS

list Specifies a potential display-list name.

DESCRIPTION

glIsList returns **GL_TRUE** if *list* is the name of a display list and returns **GL_FALSE** otherwise.

ERRORS

GL_INVALID_OPERATION is generated if **glIsList** is executed between the execution of **glBegin** and the corresponding execution of **glEnd**.

SEE ALSO

glCallList, **glCallLists**, **glDeleteLists**, **glGenLists**, **glNewList**

NAME

glIsTexture – determine if a name corresponds to a texture

C SPECIFICATION

GLboolean **glIsTexture**(GLuint *texture*)

PARAMETERS

texture Specifies a value that may be the name of a texture.

DESCRIPTION

glIsTexture returns **GL_TRUE** if *texture* is currently the name of a texture. If *texture* is zero, or is a non-zero value that is not currently the name of a texture, or if an error occurs, **glIsTexture** returns **GL_FALSE**.

NOTES

glIsTexture is available only if the GL version is 1.1 or greater.

ERRORS

GL_INVALID_OPERATION is generated if **glIsTexture** is executed between the execution of **glBegin** and the corresponding execution of **glEnd**.

SEE ALSO

glBindTexture, **glCopyTexImage1D**, **glCopyTexImage2D**, **glDeleteTextures**, **glGenTextures**, **glGet**, **glGetTexParameter**, **glTexImage1D**, **glTexImage2D**, **glTexImage3D**, **glTexParameter**

NAME

    glLightf, glLighti, glLightfv, glLightiv – set light source parameters

C SPECIFICATION

    void **glLightf**(GLenum *light*,
                    GLenum *pname*,
                    GLfloat *param*)
    void **glLighti**(GLenum *light*,
                    GLenum *pname*,
                    GLint *param*)

PARAMETERS

    light   Specifies a light. The number of lights depends on the implementation, but at least eight lights are supported. They are identified by symbolic names of the form **GL_LIGHT**i where $0 \leq i <$ **GL_MAX_LIGHTS**.

    pname Specifies a single-valued light source parameter for *light*. **GL_SPOT_EXPONENT**, **GL_SPOT_CUTOFF**, **GL_CONSTANT_ATTENUATION**, **GL_LINEAR_ATTENUATION**, and **GL_QUADRATIC_ATTENUATION** are accepted.

    param Specifies the value that parameter *pname* of light source *light* will be set to.

C SPECIFICATION

    void **glLightfv**(GLenum *light*,
                    GLenum *pname*,
                    const GLfloat **params*)
    void **glLightiv**(GLenum *light*,
                    GLenum *pname*,
                    const GLint **params*)

PARAMETERS

    light   Specifies a light. The number of lights depends on the implementation, but at least eight lights are supported. They are identified by symbolic names of the form **GL_LIGHT**i where $0 \leq i <$ **GL_MAX_LIGHTS**.

    pname Specifies a light source parameter for *light*. **GL_AMBIENT**, **GL_DIFFUSE**, **GL_SPECULAR**, **GL_POSITION**, **GL_SPOT_CUTOFF**, **GL_SPOT_DIRECTION**, **GL_SPOT_EXPONENT**, **GL_CONSTANT_ATTENUATION**, **GL_LINEAR_ATTENUATION**, and **GL_QUADRATIC_ATTENUATION** are accepted.

params Specifies a pointer to the value or values that parameter *pname* of light source *light* will be set to.

DESCRIPTION

glLight sets the values of individual light source parameters. *light* names the light and is a symbolic name of the form **GL_LIGHT***i*, where $0 \le i < $ **GL_MAX_LIGHTS**. *pname* specifies one of ten light source parameters, again by symbolic name. *params* is either a single value or a pointer to an array that contains the new values.

To enable and disable lighting calculation, call **glEnable** and **glDisable** with argument **GL_LIGHTING**. Lighting is initially disabled. When it is enabled, light sources that are enabled contribute to the lighting calculation. Light source *i* is enabled and disabled using **glEnable** and **glDisable** with argument **GL_LIGHT***i*.

The ten light parameters are as follows:

GL_AMBIENT *params* contains four integer or floating-point values that specify the ambient RGBA intensity of the light. Integer values are mapped linearly such that the most positive representable value maps to 1.0, and the most negative representable value maps to −1.0. Floating-point values are mapped directly. Neither integer nor floating-point values are clamped. The initial ambient light intensity is (0, 0, 0, 1).

GL_DIFFUSE *params* contains four integer or floating-point values that specify the diffuse RGBA intensity of the light. Integer values are mapped linearly such that the most positive representable value maps to 1.0, and the most negative representable value maps to −1.0. Floating-point values are mapped directly. Neither integer nor floating-point values are clamped. The initial value for **GL_LIGHT0** is (1, 1, 1, 1); for other lights, the initial value is (0, 0, 0, 0).

GL_SPECULAR *params* contains four integer or floating-point values that specify the specular RGBA intensity of the light. Integer values are mapped linearly such that the most positive representable value maps to 1.0, and the most negative representable value maps to −1.0. Floating-point values are mapped directly. Neither integer nor floating-point values are clamped. The initial value for **GL_LIGHT0** is (1, 1, 1, 1); for other lights, the initial value is (0, 0, 0, 0).

GL_POSITION *params* contains four integer or floating-point values that specify the position of the light in homogeneous object coordinates. Both integer and floating-point values are mapped directly. Neither integer nor floating-point values are clamped.

The position is transformed by the modelview matrix when **glLight** is called (just as if it were a point), and it is stored in eye coordinates. If the *w* component of the position is 0, the light is treated as a directional source. Diffuse and specular lighting calculations take the light's direction, but not its actual position, into account, and attenuation is disabled. Otherwise, diffuse and specular lighting calculations are based on the actual location of the light in eye coordinates, and attenuation is enabled. The initial position is (0, 0, 1, 0); thus, the initial light source is directional, parallel to, and in the direction of the −*z* axis.

GL_SPOT_DIRECTION

params contains three integer or floating-point values that specify the direction of the light in homogeneous object coordinates. Both integer and floating-point values are mapped directly. Neither integer nor floating-point values are clamped.

The spot direction is transformed by the inverse of the modelview matrix when **glLight** is called (just as if it were a normal), and it is stored in eye coordinates. It is significant only when **GL_SPOT_CUTOFF** is not 180, which it is initially. The initial direction is (0, 0, −1).

GL_SPOT_EXPONENT

params is a single integer or floating-point value that specifies the intensity distribution of the light. Integer and floating-point values are mapped directly. Only values in the range [0,128] are accepted.

Effective light intensity is attenuated by the cosine of the angle between the direction of the light and the direction from the light to the vertex being lighted, raised to the power of the spot exponent. Thus, higher spot exponents result in a more focused light source, regardless of the spot cutoff angle (see **GL_SPOT_CUTOFF**, next paragraph). The initial spot exponent is 0, resulting in uniform light distribution.

GL_SPOT_CUTOFF *params* is a single integer or floating-point value that specifies the maximum spread angle of a light source. Integer and floating-point values are mapped directly. Only values in the range [0,90] and the special value 180 are accepted. If the angle between the direction of the light and the direction from the light to the vertex being lighted is greater than the spot cutoff angle, the light is completely masked. Otherwise, its intensity is controlled by the spot exponent and the attenuation factors. The initial spot cutoff is 180, resulting in uniform light distribution.

GL_CONSTANT_ATTENUATION

GL_LINEAR_ATTENUATION

GL_QUADRATIC_ATTENUATION

params is a single integer or floating-point value that specifies one of the three light attenuation factors. Integer and floating-point values are mapped directly. Only nonnegative values are accepted. If the light is positional, rather than directional, its intensity is attenuated by the reciprocal of the sum of the constant factor, the linear factor times the distance between the light and the vertex being lighted, and the quadratic factor times the square of the same distance. The initial attenuation factors are (1, 0, 0), resulting in no attenuation.

NOTES

It is always the case that **GL_LIGHT***i* = **GL_LIGHT0** + *i*.

ERRORS

GL_INVALID_ENUM is generated if either *light* or *pname* is not an accepted value.

GL_INVALID_VALUE is generated if a spot exponent value is specified outside the range [0,128], or if spot cutoff is specified outside the range [0,90] (except for the special value 180), or if a negative attenuation factor is specified.

GL_INVALID_OPERATION is generated if **glLight** is executed between the execution of **glBegin** and the corresponding execution of **glEnd**.

ASSOCIATED GETS

glGetLight

glIsEnabled with argument GL_LIGHTING

SEE ALSO

glColorMaterial, **glLightModel**, **glMaterial**

NAME

glLightModelf, glLightModeli, glLightModelfv, glLightModeliv – set the lighting model parameters

C SPECIFICATION

void **glLightModelf**(GLenum *pname*,
                        GLfloat *param*)
void **glLightModeli**(GLenum *pname*,
                        GLint *param*)

PARAMETERS

pname   Specifies a single-valued lighting model parameter.
GL_LIGHT_MODEL_LOCAL_VIEWER,
GL_LIGHT_MODEL_COLOR_CONTROL, and
GL_LIGHT_MODEL_TWO_SIDE are accepted.

param   Specifies the value that *param* will be set to.

C SPECIFICATION

void **glLightModelfv**(GLenum *pname*,
                        const GLfloat **params*)
void **glLightModeliv**(GLenum *pname*,
                        const GLint **params*)

PARAMETERS

pname   Specifies a lighting model parameter. **GL_LIGHT_MODEL_AMBIENT**,
GL_LIGHT_MODEL_COLOR_CONTROL,
GL_LIGHT_MODEL_LOCAL_VIEWER, and
GL_LIGHT_MODEL_TWO_SIDE are accepted.

params   Specifies a pointer to the value or values that *params* will be set to.

DESCRIPTION

glLightModel sets the lighting model parameter. *pname* names a parameter and *params* gives the new value. There are three lighting model parameters:

GL_LIGHT_MODEL_AMBIENT

params contains four integer or floating-point values that specify the ambient RGBA intensity of the entire scene. Integer values are mapped linearly such that the most positive representable value maps to 1.0, and the most negative representable value maps to –1.0. Floating-point values are mapped directly. Neither integer nor floating-point values are clamped. The initial ambient scene intensity is (0.2, 0.2, 0.2, 1.0).

GL_LIGHT_MODEL_COLOR_CONTROL
> *params* must be either **GL_SEPARATE_SPECULAR_COLOR** or **GL_SINGLE_COLOR**. **GL_SINGLE_COLOR** specifies that a single color is generated from the lighting computation for a vertex. **GL_SEPARATE_SPECULAR_COLOR** specifies that the specular color computation of lighting be stored separately from the remainder of the lighting computation. The specular color is summed into the generated fragment's color after the application of texture mapping (if enabled). The initial value is **GL_SINGLE_COLOR**.

GL_LIGHT_MODEL_LOCAL_VIEWER
> *params* is a single integer or floating-point value that specifies how specular reflection angles are computed. If *params* is 0 (or 0.0), specular reflection angles take the view direction to be parallel to and in the direction of the -z axis, regardless of the location of the vertex in eye coordinates. Otherwise, specular reflections are computed from the origin of the eye coordinate system. The initial value is 0.

GL_LIGHT_MODEL_TWO_SIDE
> *params* is a single integer or floating-point value that specifies whether one- or two-sided lighting calculations are done for polygons. It has no effect on the lighting calculations for points, lines, or bitmaps. If *params* is 0 (or 0.0), one-sided lighting is specified, and only the *front* material parameters are used in the lighting equation. Otherwise, two-sided lighting is specified. In this case, vertices of back-facing polygons are lighted using the *back* material parameters, and have their normals reversed before the lighting equation is evaluated. Vertices of front-facing polygons are always lighted using the *front* material parameters, with no change to their normals. The initial value is 0.

In RGBA mode, the lighted color of a vertex is the sum of the material emission intensity, the product of the material ambient reflectance and the lighting model full-scene ambient intensity, and the contribution of each enabled light source. Each light source contributes the sum of three terms: ambient, diffuse, and specular. The ambient light source contribution is the product of the material ambient reflectance and the light's ambient intensity. The diffuse light source contribution is the product of the material diffuse reflectance, the light's diffuse intensity, and the dot product of the vertex's normal with the normalized vector from the vertex to the light source. The specular light source contribution is the product of the material specular reflectance, the light's specular intensity, and the dot product of the normalized vertex-to-eye and vertex-to-light vectors, raised to the power of the shininess of the material. All three light source contributions are attenuated equally based on the distance from the vertex to the light source and on light source direction, spread exponent, and spread cutoff angle. All dot products are replaced with 0 if they evaluate to a negative value.

The alpha component of the resulting lighted color is set to the alpha value of the material diffuse reflectance.

In color index mode, the value of the lighted index of a vertex ranges from the ambient to the specular values passed to **glMaterial** using **GL_COLOR_INDEXES**. Diffuse and specular coefficients, computed with a (.30, .59, .11) weighting of the lights' colors, the shininess of the material, and the same reflection and attenuation equations as in the RGBA case, determine how much above ambient the resulting index is.

NOTES

GL_LIGHT_MODEL_COLOR_CONTROL is available only if the GL version is 1.2 or greater.

ERRORS

GL_INVALID_ENUM is generated if *pname* is not an accepted value.

GL_INVALID_ENUM is generated if *pname* is GL_LIGHT_MODEL_COLOR_CONTROL and *params* is not one of GL_SINGLE_COLOR or GL_SEPARATE_SPECULAR_COLOR.

GL_INVALID_OPERATION is generated if **glLightModel** is executed between the execution of **glBegin** and the corresponding execution of **glEnd**.

ASSOCIATED GETS

glGet with argument **GL_LIGHT_MODEL_AMBIENT**
glGet with argument **GL_LIGHT_MODEL_COLOR_CONTROL**
glGet with argument **GL_LIGHT_MODEL_LOCAL_VIEWER**
glGet with argument **GL_LIGHT_MODEL_TWO_SIDE**
glIsEnabled with argument **GL_LIGHTING**

SEE ALSO

glLight, **glMaterial**

NAME

glLineStipple – specify the line stipple pattern

C SPECIFICATION

void **glLineStipple**(GLint *factor*,
  GLushort *pattern*)

PARAMETERS

factor   Specifies a multiplier for each bit in the line stipple pattern. If *factor* is 3, for example, each bit in the pattern is used three times before the next bit in the pattern is used. *factor* is clamped to the range [1, 256] and defaults to 1.

pattern Specifies a 16-bit integer whose bit pattern determines which fragments of a line will be drawn when the line is rasterized. Bit zero is used first; the default pattern is all 1's.

DESCRIPTION

Line stippling masks out certain fragments produced by rasterization; those fragments will not be drawn. The masking is achieved by using three parameters: the 16-bit line stipple pattern *pattern*, the repeat count *factor*, and an integer stipple counter *s*.

Counter *s* is reset to 0 whenever **glBegin** is called, and before each line segment of a **glBegin**(GL_LINES)/**glEnd** sequence is generated. It is incremented after each fragment of a unit width aliased line segment is generated, or after each *i* fragments of an *i* width line segment are generated. The *i* fragments associated with count *s* are masked out if

$$pattern \text{ bit } (s \text{ / } factor) \text{ mod } 16$$

is 0, otherwise these fragments are sent to the frame buffer. Bit zero of *pattern* is the least significant bit.

Antialiased lines are treated as a sequence of 1×*width* rectangles for purposes of stippling. Whether rectagle *s* is rasterized or not depends on the fragment rule described for aliased lines, counting rectangles rather than groups of fragments.

To enable and disable line stippling, call **glEnable** and **glDisable** with argument **GL_LINE_STIPPLE**. When enabled, the line stipple pattern is applied as described above. When disabled, it is as if the pattern were all 1's. Initially, line stippling is disabled.

ERRORS

GL_INVALID_OPERATION is generated if **glLineStipple** is executed between the execution of **glBegin** and the corresponding execution of **glEnd**.

ASSOCIATED GETS

glGet with argument **GL_LINE_STIPPLE_PATTERN**
glGet with argument **GL_LINE_STIPPLE_REPEAT**
glIsEnabled with argument **GL_LINE_STIPPLE**

SEE ALSO

glLineWidth, **glPolygonStipple**

NAME

glLineWidth – specify the width of rasterized lines

C SPECIFICATION

void **glLineWidth**(GLfloat *width*)

PARAMETERS

width Specifies the width of rasterized lines. The initial value is 1.

DESCRIPTION

glLineWidth specifies the rasterized width of both aliased and antialiased lines. Using a line width other than 1 has different effects, depending on whether line antialiasing is enabled. To enable and disable line antialiasing, call **glEnable** and **glDisable** with argument **GL_LINE_SMOOTH**. Line antialiasing is initially disabled.

If line antialiasing is disabled, the actual width is determined by rounding the supplied width to the nearest integer. (If the rounding results in the value 0, it is as if the line width were 1.) If $|\Delta x| \geq |\Delta y|$, i pixels are filled in each column that is rasterized, where i is the rounded value of *width*. Otherwise, i pixels are filled in each row that is rasterized.

If antialiasing is enabled, line rasterization produces a fragment for each pixel square that intersects the region lying within the rectangle having width equal to the current line width, length equal to the actual length of the line, and centered on the mathematical line segment. The coverage value for each fragment is the window coordinate area of the intersection of the rectangular region with the corresponding pixel square. This value is saved and used in the final rasterization step.

Not all widths can be supported when line antialiasing is enabled. If an unsupported width is requested, the nearest supported width is used. Only width 1 is guaranteed to be supported; others depend on the implementation. Likewise, there is a range for aliased line widths as well. To query the range of supported widths and the size difference between supported widths within the range, call **glGet** with arguments **GL_ALIASED_LINE_WIDTH_RANGE**, **GL_SMOOTH_LINE_WIDTH_RANGE**, **GL_SMOOTH_LINE_WIDTH_GRANULARITY**.

NOTES

The line width specified by **glLineWidth** is always returned when **GL_LINE_WIDTH** is queried. Clamping and rounding for aliased and antialiased lines have no effect on the specified value.

Nonantialiased line width may be clamped to an implementation-dependent maximum. Call **glGet** with **GL_ALIASED_LINE_WIDTH_RANGE** to determine the maximum width.

ERRORS

GL_INVALID_VALUE is generated if *width* is less than or equal to 0.

GL_INVALID_OPERATION is generated if **glLineWidth** is executed between the execution of **glBegin** and the corresponding execution of **glEnd**.

ASSOCIATED GETS

glGet with argument **GL_LINE_WIDTH**
glGet with argument **GL_ALIASED_LINE_WIDTH_RANGE**
glGet with argument **GL_SMOOTH_LINE_WIDTH_RANGE**
glGet with argument **GL_SMOOTH_LINE_WIDTH_GRANULARITY**
glIsEnabled with argument **GL_LINE_SMOOTH**

SEE ALSO

glEnable

NAME

glListBase – set the display-list base for **glCallLists**

C SPECIFICATION

void **glListBase**(GLuint *base*)

PARAMETERS

base Specifies an integer offset that will be added to **glCallLists** offsets to generate display-list names. The initial value is 0.

DESCRIPTION

glCallLists specifies an array of offsets. Display-list names are generated by adding *base* to each offset. Names that reference valid display lists are executed; the others are ignored.

ERRORS

GL_INVALID_OPERATION is generated if **glListBase** is executed between the execution of **glBegin** and the corresponding execution of **glEnd**.

ASSOCIATED GETS

glGet with argument **GL_LIST_BASE**

SEE ALSO

glCallLists

NAME

    glLoadIdentity – replace the current matrix with the identity matrix

C SPECIFICATION

    void **glLoadIdentity**(void)

DESCRIPTION

    glLoadIdentity replaces the current matrix with the identity matrix. It is semantically equivalent to calling **glLoadMatrix** with the identity matrix

$$\begin{matrix} 1 & 0 & 0 & 0 \\ 0 & 1 & 0 & 0 \\ 0 & 0 & 1 & 0 \\ 0 & 0 & 0 & 1 \end{matrix}$$

    but in some cases it is more efficient.

ERRORS

    GL_INVALID_OPERATION is generated if **glLoadIdentity** is executed between the execution of **glBegin** and the corresponding execution of **glEnd**.

ASSOCIATED GETS

    glGet with argument **GL_MATRIX_MODE**
    glGet with argument **GL_COLOR_MATRIX**
    glGet with argument **GL_MODELVIEW_MATRIX**
    glGet with argument **GL_PROJECTION_MATRIX**
    glGet with argument **GL_TEXTURE_MATRIX**

SEE ALSO

    glLoadMatrix, **glMatrixMode**, **glMultMatrix**, **glPushMatrix**

NAME

glLoadMatrixd, glLoadMatrixf – replace the current matrix with the specified matrix

C SPECIFICATION

void **glLoadMatrixd**(const GLdouble *m*)
void **glLoadMatrixf**(const GLfloat *m*)

PARAMETERS

m Specifies a pointer to 16 consecutive values, which are used as the elements of a 4 × 4 column-major matrix.

DESCRIPTION

glLoadMatrix replaces the current matrix with the one whose elements are specified by *m*. The current matrix is the projection matrix, modelview matrix, or texture matrix, depending on the current matrix mode (see **glMatrixMode**).

The current matrix, M, defines a transformation of coordinates. For instance, assume M refers to the modelview matrix. If $v = (v[0], v[1], v[2], v[3])$ is the set of object coordinates of a vertex, and *m* points to an array of 16 single- or double-precision floating-point values $m[0], m[1], ..., m[15]$, then the modelview transformation $M(v)$ does the following:

$$M(v) = \begin{matrix} m[0] & m[4] & m[8] & m[12] \\ m[1] & m[5] & m[9] & m[13] \\ m[2] & m[6] & m[10] & m[14] \\ m[3] & m[7] & m[11] & m[15] \end{matrix} \times \begin{matrix} v[0] \\ v[1] \\ v[2] \\ v[3] \end{matrix}$$

Where "×" denotes matrix multiplication.

Projection and texture transformations are similarly defined.

NOTES

While the elements of the matrix may be specified with single or double precision, the GL implementation may store or operate on these values in less than single precision.

ERRORS

GL_INVALID_OPERATION is generated if **glLoadMatrix** is executed between the execution of **glBegin** and the corresponding execution of **glEnd**.

ASSOCIATED GETS

      glGet with argument **GL_MATRIX_MODE**

      glGet with argument **GL_COLOR_MATRIX**

      glGet with argument **GL_MODELVIEW_MATRIX**

      glGet with argument **GL_PROJECTION_MATRIX**

      glGet with argument **GL_TEXTURE_MATRIX**

SEE ALSO

      glLoadIdentity, **glMatrixMode**, **glMultMatrix**, **glPushMatrix**

NAME

glLoadName – load a name onto the name stack

C SPECIFICATION

void **glLoadName**(GLuint *name*)

PARAMETERS

name Specifies a name that will replace the top value on the name stack.

DESCRIPTION

The name stack is used during selection mode to allow sets of rendering commands to be uniquely identified. It consists of an ordered set of unsigned integers. **glLoadName** causes *name* to replace the value on the top of the name stack, which is initially empty.

The name stack is always empty while the render mode is not **GL_SELECT**. Calls to **glLoadName** while the render mode is not **GL_SELECT** are ignored.

ERRORS

GL_INVALID_OPERATION is generated if **glLoadName** is called while the name stack is empty.

GL_INVALID_OPERATION is generated if **glLoadName** is executed between the execution of **glBegin** and the corresponding execution of **glEnd**.

ASSOCIATED GETS

glGet with argument **GL_NAME_STACK_DEPTH**
glGet with argument **GL_MAX_NAME_STACK_DEPTH**

SEE ALSO

glInitNames, **glPushName**, **glRenderMode**, **glSelectBuffer**

NAME

glLogicOp – specify a logical pixel operation for color index rendering

C SPECIFICATION

void **glLogicOp**(GLenum *opcode*)

PARAMETERS

opcode Specifies a symbolic constant that selects a logical operation. The following symbols are accepted: **GL_CLEAR**, **GL_SET**, **GL_COPY**, **GL_COPY_INVERTED**, **GL_NOOP**, **GL_INVERT**, **GL_AND**, **GL_NAND**, **GL_OR**, **GL_NOR**, **GL_XOR**, **GL_EQUIV**, **GL_AND_REVERSE**, **GL_AND_INVERTED**, **GL_OR_REVERSE**, and **GL_OR_INVERTED**. The initial value is **GL_COPY**.

DESCRIPTION

glLogicOp specifies a logical operation that, when enabled, is applied between the incoming color index or RGBA color and the color index or RGBA color at the corresponding location in the frame buffer. To enable or disable the logical operation, call **glEnable** and **glDisable** using the symbolic constant **GL_COLOR_LOGIC_OP** for RGBA mode or **GL_INDEX_LOGIC_OP** for color index mode. The initial value is disabled for both operations.

Opcode	Resulting Operation
GL_CLEAR	0
GL_SET	1
GL_COPY	s
GL_COPY_INVERTED	~s
GL_NOOP	d
GL_INVERT	~d
GL_AND	s & d
GL_NAND	~(s & d)
GL_OR	s | d
GL_NOR	~(s | d)
GL_XOR	s ^ d
GL_EQUIV	~(s ^ d)
GL_AND_REVERSE	s & ~d
GL_AND_INVERTED	~s & d
GL_OR_REVERSE	s | ~d
GL_OR_INVERTED	~s | d

opcode is a symbolic constant chosen from the list above. In the explanation of the logical operations, *s* represents the incoming color index and *d* represents the index in the frame buffer. Standard C-language operators are used. As these bitwise operators suggest, the logical operation is applied independently to each bit pair of the source and destination indices or colors.

NOTES

Color index logical operations are always supported. RGBA logical operations are supported only if the GL version is 1.1 or greater.

When more than one RGBA color or index buffer is enabled for drawing, logical operations are performed separately for each enabled buffer, using for the destination value the contents of that buffer (see **glDrawBuffer**).

ERRORS

GL_INVALID_ENUM is generated if *opcode* is not an accepted value.

GL_INVALID_OPERATION is generated if **glLogicOp** is executed between the execution of **glBegin** and the corresponding execution of **glEnd**.

ASSOCIATED GETS

glGet with argument **GL_LOGIC_OP_MODE**.
glIsEnabled with argument **GL_COLOR_LOGIC_OP** or **GL_INDEX_LOGIC_OP**.

SEE ALSO

glAlphaFunc, **glBlendFunc**, **glDrawBuffer**, **glEnable**, **glStencilOp**

NAME

glMap1d, **glMap1f** – define a one-dimensional evaluator

C SPECIFICATION

```
void glMap1d( GLenum target,
              GLdouble u1,
              GLdouble u2,
              GLint stride,
              GLint order,
              const GLdouble *points )
void glMap1f( GLenum target,
              GLfloat u1,
              GLfloat u2,
              GLint stride,
              GLint order,
              const GLfloat *points )
```

PARAMETERS

target Specifies the kind of values that are generated by the evaluator. Symbolic constants **GL_MAP1_VERTEX_3**, **GL_MAP1_VERTEX_4**, **GL_MAP1_INDEX**, **GL_MAP1_COLOR_4**, **GL_MAP1_NORMAL**, **GL_MAP1_TEXTURE_COORD_1**, **GL_MAP1_TEXTURE_COORD_2**, **GL_MAP1_TEXTURE_COORD_3**, and **GL_MAP1_TEXTURE_COORD_4** are accepted.

u1, u2

Specify a linear mapping of u, as presented to **glEvalCoord1**, to $\hat{u}$, the variable that is evaluated by the equations specified by this command.

stride Specifies the number of floats or doubles between the beginning of one control point and the beginning of the next one in the data structure referenced in *points*. This allows control points to be embedded in arbitrary data structures. The only constraint is that the values for a particular control point must occupy contiguous memory locations.

order Specifies the number of control points. Must be positive.

points Specifies a pointer to the array of control points.

DESCRIPTION

Evaluators provide a way to use polynomial or rational polynomial mapping to produce vertices, normals, texture coordinates, and colors. The values produced by an evaluator are sent to further stages of GL processing just as if they had been presented using **glVertex**, **glNormal**, **glTexCoord**, and **glColor** commands, except that the generated values do not update the current normal, texture coordinates, or color.

All polynomial or rational polynomial splines of any degree (up to the maximum degree supported by the GL implementation) can be described using evaluators. These include almost all splines used in computer graphics: B-splines, Bezier curves, Hermite splines, and so on.

Evaluators define curves based on Bernstein polynomials. Define $p(\hat{u})$ as

$$p(\hat{u}) \; = \; \sum_{i=0}^{n} B_i^n(\hat{u}) R_i$$

where R_i is a control point and $B_i^n(\hat{u})$ is the ith Bernstein polynomial of degree n ($order = n + 1$):

$$B_i^n(\hat{u}) \; = \; \binom{n}{i} \hat{u}^i (1-\hat{u})^{n-i}$$

Recall that

$$0^0 \equiv 1 \text{ and } \binom{n}{0} \equiv 1$$

glMap1 is used to define the basis and to specify what kind of values are produced. Once defined, a map can be enabled and disabled by calling **glEnable** and **glDisable** with the map name, one of the nine predefined values for *target* described below. **glEvalCoord1** evaluates the one-dimensional maps that are enabled. When **glEvalCoord1** presents a value u, the Bernstein functions are evaluated using $\hat{u}$, where

$$\hat{u} \; = \; \frac{u - u1}{u2 - u1}$$

target is a symbolic constant that indicates what kind of control points are provided in *points*, and what output is generated when the map is evaluated. It can assume one of nine predefined values:

GL_MAP1_VERTEX_3   Each control point is three floating-point values representing x, y, and z. Internal **glVertex3** commands are generated when the map is evaluated.

GL_MAP1_VERTEX_4   Each control point is four floating-point values representing *x*, *y*, *z*, and *w*. Internal **glVertex4** commands are generated when the map is evaluated.

GL_MAP1_INDEX   Each control point is a single floating-point value representing a color index. Internal **glIndex** commands are generated when the map is evaluated but the current index is not updated with the value of these **glIndex** commands.

GL_MAP1_COLOR_4   Each control point is four floating-point values representing red, green, blue, and alpha. Internal **glColor4** commands are generated when the map is evaluated but the current color is not updated with the value of these **glColor4** commands.

GL_MAP1_NORMAL   Each control point is three floating-point values representing the *x*, *y*, and *z* components of a normal vector. Internal **glNormal** commands are generated when the map is evaluated but the current normal is not updated with the value of these **glNormal** commands.

GL_MAP1_TEXTURE_COORD_1

Each control point is a single floating-point value representing the *s* texture coordinate. Internal **glTexCoord1** commands are generated when the map is evaluated but the current texture coordinates are not updated with the value of these **glTexCoord** commands.

GL_MAP1_TEXTURE_COORD_2

Each control point is two floating-point values representing the *s* and *t* texture coordinates. Internal **glTexCoord2** commands are generated when the map is evaluated but the current texture coordinates are not updated with the value of these **glTexCoord** commands.

GL_MAP1_TEXTURE_COORD_3

Each control point is three floating-point values representing the *s*, *t*, and *r* texture coordinates. Internal **glTexCoord3** commands are generated when the map is evaluated but the current texture coordinates are not updated with the value of these **glTexCoord** commands.

GL_MAP1_TEXTURE_COORD_4

Each control point is four floating-point values representing the *s*, *t*, *r*, and *q* texture coordinates. Internal **glTexCoord4** commands are generated when the map is evaluated but the current texture coordinates are not updated with the value of these **glTexCoord** commands.

stride, *order*, and *points* define the array addressing for accessing the control points. *points* is the location of the first control point, which occupies one, two, three, or four contiguous memory locations, depending on which map is being defined. *order* is the number of control points in the array. *stride* specifies how many float or double locations to advance the internal memory pointer to reach the next control point.

NOTES

As is the case with all GL commands that accept pointers to data, it is as if the contents of *points* were copied by **glMap1** before **glMap1** returns. Changes to the contents of *points* have no effect after **glMap1** is called.

ERRORS

GL_INVALID_ENUM is generated if *target* is not an accepted value.

GL_INVALID_VALUE is generated if *u1* is equal to *u2*.

GL_INVALID_VALUE is generated if *stride* is less than the number of values in a control point.

GL_INVALID_VALUE is generated if *order* is less than 1 or greater than the return value of **GL_MAX_EVAL_ORDER**.

GL_INVALID_OPERATION is generated if **glMap1** is executed between the execution of **glBegin** and the corresponding execution of **glEnd**.

When the **GL_ARB_multitexture** extension is supported, GL_INVALID_OPERATION is generated if **glMap1** is called and the value of **GL_ACTIVE_TEXTURE_ARB** is not **GL_TEXTURE0_ARB**.

ASSOCIATED GETS

glGetMap
glGet with argument **GL_MAX_EVAL_ORDER**
glIsEnabled with argument **GL_MAP1_VERTEX_3**
glIsEnabled with argument **GL_MAP1_VERTEX_4**
glIsEnabled with argument **GL_MAP1_INDEX**
glIsEnabled with argument **GL_MAP1_COLOR_4**
glIsEnabled with argument **GL_MAP1_NORMAL**
glIsEnabled with argument **GL_MAP1_TEXTURE_COORD_1**
glIsEnabled with argument **GL_MAP1_TEXTURE_COORD_2**
glIsEnabled with argument **GL_MAP1_TEXTURE_COORD_3**
glIsEnabled with argument **GL_MAP1_TEXTURE_COORD_4**

SEE ALSO

glBegin, glColor, glEnable, glEvalCoord, glEvalMesh, glEvalPoint, glMap2, glMapGrid, glNormal, glTexCoord, glVertex

NAME

    glMap2d, **glMap2f** – define a two-dimensional evaluator

C SPECIFICATION

    void **glMap2d**(GLenum *target*,
                      GLdouble *u1*,
                      GLdouble *u2*,
                      GLint *ustride*,
                      GLint *uorder*,
                      GLdouble *v1*,
                      GLdouble *v2*,
                      GLint *vstride*,
                      GLint *vorder*,
                      const GLdouble **points*)
    void **glMap2f**(GLenum *target*,
                      GLfloat *u1*,
                      GLfloat *u2*,
                      GLint *ustride*,
                      GLint *uorder*,
                      GLfloat *v1*,
                      GLfloat *v2*,
                      GLint *vstride*,
                      GLint *vorder*,
                      const GLfloat **points*)

PARAMETERS

    target Specifies the kind of values that are generated by the evaluator. Symbolic constants **GL_MAP2_VERTEX_3**, **GL_MAP2_VERTEX_4**, **GL_MAP2_INDEX**, **GL_MAP2_COLOR_4**, **GL_MAP2_NORMAL**, **GL_MAP2_TEXTURE_COORD_1**, **GL_MAP2_TEXTURE_COORD_2**, **GL_MAP2_TEXTURE_COORD_3**, and **GL_MAP2_TEXTURE_COORD_4** are accepted.

    u1, *u2* Specify a linear mapping of *u*, as presented to **glEvalCoord2**, to $\hat{u}$, one of the two variables that are evaluated by the equations specified by this command. Initially, *u1* is 0 and *u2* is 1.

    ustride Specifies the number of floats or doubles between the beginning of control point R_{ij} and the beginning of control point $R_{(i+1)j}$, where *i* and *j* are the *u* and *v* control point indices, respectively. This allows control points to be embedded in arbitrary data structures. The only constraint is that the values for a particular control point must occupy contiguous memory locations. The initial value of *ustride* is 0.

uorder   Specifies the dimension of the control point array in the *u* axis. Must be positive. The initial value is 1.

v1, v2   Specify a linear mapping of *v*, as presented to **glEvalCoord2**, to $\hat{v}$, one of the two variables that are evaluated by the equations specified by this command. Initially, *v1* is 0 and *v2* is 1.

vstride   Specifies the number of floats or doubles between the beginning of control point R_{ij} and the beginning of control point $R_{i(j+1)}$, where *i* and *j* are the *u* and *v* control point indices, respectively. This allows control points to be embedded in arbitrary data structures. The only constraint is that the values for a particular control point must occupy contiguous memory locations. The initial value of *vstride* is 0.

vorder   Specifies the dimension of the control point array in the *v* axis. Must be positive. The initial value is 1.

points   Specifies a pointer to the array of control points.

DESCRIPTION

Evaluators provide a way to use polynomial or rational polynomial mapping to produce vertices, normals, texture coordinates, and colors. The values produced by an evaluator are sent on to further stages of GL processing just as if they had been presented using **glVertex**, **glNormal**, **glTexCoord**, and **glColor** commands, except that the generated values do not update the current normal, texture coordinates, or color.

All polynomial or rational polynomial splines of any degree (up to the maximum degree supported by the GL implementation) can be described using evaluators. These include almost all surfaces used in computer graphics, including B-spline surfaces, NURBS surfaces, Bezier surfaces, and so on.

Evaluators define surfaces based on bivariate Bernstein polynomials. Define $p(\hat{u}, \hat{v})$ as

$$p(\hat{u}, \hat{v}) = \sum_{i=0}^{n} \sum_{j=0}^{m} B_i^n(\hat{u}) \, B_j^m(\hat{v}) \, R_{ij}$$

where R_{ij} is a control point, $B_i^n(\hat{u})$ is the *i*th Bernstein polynomial of degree *n* (*uorder* = *n* + 1)

$$B_i^n(\hat{u}) = \binom{n}{i} \hat{u}^i (1-\hat{u})^{n-i}$$

and $B_j^m(\hat{v})$ is the *j*th Bernstein polynomial of degree *m* (*vorder* = *m* + 1)

$$B_j^m(\hat{v}) = \begin{pmatrix} m \\ j \end{pmatrix} \hat{v}^j(1-\hat{v})^{m-j}$$

Recall that

$$0^0 \equiv 1 \text{ and } \begin{pmatrix} n \\ 0 \end{pmatrix} \equiv 1$$

glMap2 is used to define the basis and to specify what kind of values are produced. Once defined, a map can be enabled and disabled by calling **glEnable** and **glDisable** with the map name, one of the nine predefined values for *target*, described below. When **glEvalCoord2** presents values u and v, the bivariate Bernstein polynomials are evaluated using $\hat{u}$ and $\hat{v}$, where

$$\hat{u} = \frac{u - u1}{u2 - u1}$$

$$\hat{v} = \frac{v - v1}{v2 - v1}$$

target is a symbolic constant that indicates what kind of control points are provided in *points*, and what output is generated when the map is evaluated. It can assume one of nine predefined values:

GL_MAP2_VERTEX_3 Each control point is three floating-point values representing x, y, and z. Internal **glVertex3** commands are generated when the map is evaluated.

GL_MAP2_VERTEX_4 Each control point is four floating-point values representing x, y, z, and w. Internal **glVertex4** commands are generated when the map is evaluated.

GL_MAP2_INDEX Each control point is a single floating-point value representing a color index. Internal **glIndex** commands are generated when the map is evaluated but the current index is not updated with the value of these **glIndex** commands.

GL_MAP2_COLOR_4 Each control point is four floating-point values representing red, green, blue, and alpha. Internal **glColor4** commands are generated when the map is evaluated but the current color is not updated with the value of these **glColor4** commands.

GL_MAP2_NORMAL — Each control point is three floating-point values representing the *x*, *y*, and *z* components of a normal vector. Internal **glNormal** commands are generated when the map is evaluated but the current normal is not updated with the value of these **glNormal** commands.

GL_MAP2_TEXTURE_COORD_1

Each control point is a single floating-point value representing the *s* texture coordinate. Internal **glTexCoord1** commands are generated when the map is evaluated but the current texture coordinates are not updated with the value of these **glTexCoord** commands.

GL_MAP2_TEXTURE_COORD_2

Each control point is two floating-point values representing the *s* and *t* texture coordinates. Internal **glTexCoord2** commands are generated when the map is evaluated but the current texture coordinates are not updated with the value of these **glTexCoord** commands.

GL_MAP2_TEXTURE_COORD_3

Each control point is three floating-point values representing the *s*, *t*, and *r* texture coordinates. Internal **glTexCoord3** commands are generated when the map is evaluated but the current texture coordinates are not updated with the value of these **glTexCoord** commands.

GL_MAP2_TEXTURE_COORD_4

Each control point is four floating-point values representing the *s*, *t*, *r*, and *q* texture coordinates. Internal **glTexCoord4** commands are generated when the map is evaluated but the current texture coordinates are not updated with the value of these **glTexCoord** commands.

ustride, *uorder*, *vstride*, *vorder*, and *points* define the array addressing for accessing the control points. *points* is the location of the first control point, which occupies one, two, three, or four contiguous memory locations, depending on which map is being defined. There are *uorder* × *vorder* control points in the array. *ustride* specifies how many float or double locations are skipped to advance the internal memory pointer from control point R_{ij} to control point $R_{(i+1)j}$. *vstride* specifies how many float or double locations are skipped to advance the internal memory pointer from control point R_{ij} to control point $R_{i(j+1)}$.

NOTES

As is the case with all GL commands that accept pointers to data, it is as if the contents of *points* were copied by **glMap2** before **glMap2** returns. Changes to the contents of *points* have no effect after **glMap2** is called.

Initially, **GL_AUTO_NORMAL** is enabled. If **GL_AUTO_NORMAL** is enabled, normal vectors are generated when either **GL_MAP2_VERTEX_3** or **GL_MAP2_VERTEX_4** is used to generate vertices.

ERRORS

GL_INVALID_ENUM is generated if *target* is not an accepted value.

GL_INVALID_VALUE is generated if *u1* is equal to *u2*, or if *v1* is equal to *v2*.

GL_INVALID_VALUE is generated if either *ustride* or *vstride* is less than the number of values in a control point.

GL_INVALID_VALUE is generated if either *uorder* or *vorder* is less than 1 or greater than the return value of **GL_MAX_EVAL_ORDER**.

GL_INVALID_OPERATION is generated if **glMap2** is executed between the execution of **glBegin** and the corresponding execution of **glEnd**.

When the **GL_ARB_multitexture** extension is supported, **GL_INVALID_OPERATION** is generated if **glMap2** is called and the value of **GL_ACTIVE_TEXTURE_ARB** is not **GL_TEXTURE0_ARB**.

ASSOCIATED GETS

glGetMap
glGet with argument **GL_MAX_EVAL_ORDER**
glIsEnabled with argument **GL_MAP2_VERTEX_3**
glIsEnabled with argument **GL_MAP2_VERTEX_4**
glIsEnabled with argument **GL_MAP2_INDEX**
glIsEnabled with argument **GL_MAP2_COLOR_4**
glIsEnabled with argument **GL_MAP2_NORMAL**
glIsEnabled with argument **GL_MAP2_TEXTURE_COORD_1**
glIsEnabled with argument **GL_MAP2_TEXTURE_COORD_2**
glIsEnabled with argument **GL_MAP2_TEXTURE_COORD_3**
glIsEnabled with argument **GL_MAP2_TEXTURE_COORD_4**

SEE ALSO

glBegin, **glColor**, **glEnable**, **glEvalCoord**, **glEvalMesh**, **glEvalPoint**, **glMap1**, **glMapGrid**, **glNormal**, **glTexCoord**, **glVertex**

NAME

glMapGrid1d, glMapGrid1f, glMapGrid2d, glMapGrid2f – define a one- or two-dimensional mesh

C SPECIFICATION

```
void glMapGrid1d( GLint un,
                  GLdouble u1,
                  GLdouble u2 )
void glMapGrid1f( GLint un,
                  GLfloat u1,
                  GLfloat u2 )
void glMapGrid2d( GLint un,
                  GLdouble u1,
                  GLdouble u2,
                  GLint vn,
                  GLdouble v1,
                  GLdouble v2 )
void glMapGrid2f( GLint un,
                  GLfloat u1,
                  GLfloat u2,
                  GLint vn,
                  GLfloat v1,
                  GLfloat v2 )
```

PARAMETERS

un Specifies the number of partitions in the grid range interval [*u1*, *u2*]. Must be positive.

u1, u2
Specify the mappings for integer grid domain values $i = 0$ and $i = un$.

vn Specifies the number of partitions in the grid range interval [*v1*, *v2*] (**glMapGrid2** only).

v1, v2
Specify the mappings for integer grid domain values $j = 0$ and $j = vn$ (**glMapGrid2** only).

DESCRIPTION

glMapGrid and **glEvalMesh** are used together to efficiently generate and evaluate a series of evenly-spaced map domain values. **glEvalMesh** steps through the integer domain of a one- or two-dimensional grid, whose range is the domain of the evaluation maps specified by **glMap1** and **glMap2**.

glMapGrid1 and **glMapGrid2** specify the linear grid mappings between the *i* (or *i* and *j*) integer grid coordinates, to the *u* (or *u* and *v*) floating-point evaluation map coordinates. See **glMap1** and **glMap2** for details of how *u* and *v* coordinates are evaluated.

glMapGrid1 specifies a single linear mapping such that integer grid coordinate 0 maps exactly to *u1*, and integer grid coordinate *un* maps exactly to *u2*. All other integer grid coordinates *i* are mapped so that

$$u = i(u2-u1)/un + u1$$

glMapGrid2 specifies two such linear mappings. One maps integer grid coordinate *i* = 0 exactly to *u1*, and integer grid coordinate *i* = *un* exactly to *u2*. The other maps integer grid coordinate *j* = 0 exactly to *v1*, and integer grid coordinate *j* = *vn* exactly to *v2*. Other integer grid coordinates *i* and *j* are mapped such that

$$u = i(u2-u1)/un + u1$$

$$v = j(v2-v1)/vn + v1$$

The mappings specified by **glMapGrid** are used identically by **glEvalMesh** and **glEvalPoint**.

ERRORS

GL_INVALID_VALUE is generated if either *un* or *vn* is not positive.

GL_INVALID_OPERATION is generated if **glMapGrid** is executed between the execution of **glBegin** and the corresponding execution of **glEnd**.

ASSOCIATED GETS

glGet with argument **GL_MAP1_GRID_DOMAIN**
glGet with argument **GL_MAP2_GRID_DOMAIN**
glGet with argument **GL_MAP1_GRID_SEGMENTS**
glGet with argument **GL_MAP2_GRID_SEGMENTS**

SEE ALSO

glEvalCoord, **glEvalMesh**, **glEvalPoint**, **glMap1**, **glMap2**

NAME

glMaterialf, **glMateriali**, **glMaterialfv**, **glMaterialiv** – specify material parameters for the lighting model

C SPECIFICATION

void **glMaterialf**(GLenum *face*,
                     GLenum *pname*,
                     GLfloat *param*)
void **glMateriali**(GLenum *face*,
                     GLenum *pname*,
                     GLint *param*)

PARAMETERS

face   Specifies which face or faces are being updated. Must be one of **GL_FRONT**, **GL_BACK**, or **GL_FRONT_AND_BACK**.

pname   Specifies the single-valued material parameter of the face or faces that is being updated. Must be **GL_SHININESS**.

param   Specifies the value that parameter **GL_SHININESS** will be set to.

C SPECIFICATION

void **glMaterialfv**(GLenum *face*,
                      GLenum *pname*,
                      const GLfloat **params*)
void **glMaterialiv**(GLenum *face*,
                      GLenum *pname*,
                      const GLint **params*)

PARAMETERS

face   Specifies which face or faces are being updated. Must be one of **GL_FRONT**, **GL_BACK**, or **GL_FRONT_AND_BACK**.

pname   Specifies the material parameter of the face or faces that is being updated. Must be one of **GL_AMBIENT**, **GL_DIFFUSE**, **GL_SPECULAR**, **GL_EMISSION**, **GL_SHININESS**, **GL_AMBIENT_AND_DIFFUSE**, or **GL_COLOR_INDEXES**.

params Specifies a pointer to the value or values that *pname* will be set to.

DESCRIPTION

glMaterial assigns values to material parameters. There are two matched sets of material parameters. One, the *front-facing* set, is used to shade points, lines, bitmaps, and all polygons (when two-sided lighting is disabled), or just front-facing polygons (when two-sided lighting is enabled). The other set, *back-facing*, is used to shade back-facing polygons only when two-sided lighting is enabled. Refer to the **glLightModel** reference page for details concerning one- and two-sided lighting calculations.

glMaterial takes three arguments. The first, *face*, specifies whether the **GL_FRONT** materials, the **GL_BACK** materials, or both **GL_FRONT_AND_BACK** materials will be modified. The second, *pname*, specifies which of several parameters in one or both sets will be modified. The third, *params*, specifies what value or values will be assigned to the specified parameter.

Material parameters are used in the lighting equation that is optionally applied to each vertex. The equation is discussed in the **glLightModel** reference page. The parameters that can be specified using **glMaterial**, and their interpretations by the lighting equation, are as follows:

GL_AMBIENT   *params* contains four integer or floating-point values that specify the ambient RGBA reflectance of the material. Integer values are mapped linearly such that the most positive representable value maps to 1.0, and the most negative representable value maps to −1.0. Floating-point values are mapped directly. Neither integer nor floating-point values are clamped. The initial ambient reflectance for both front- and back-facing materials is (0.2, 0.2, 0.2, 1.0).

GL_DIFFUSE   *params* contains four integer or floating-point values that specify the diffuse RGBA reflectance of the material. Integer values are mapped linearly such that the most positive representable value maps to 1.0, and the most negative representable value maps to −1.0. Floating-point values are mapped directly. Neither integer nor floating-point values are clamped. The initial diffuse reflectance for both front- and back-facing materials is (0.8, 0.8, 0.8, 1.0).

GL_SPECULAR   *params* contains four integer or floating-point values that specify the specular RGBA reflectance of the material. Integer values are mapped linearly such that the most positive representable value maps to 1.0, and the most negative representable value maps to −1.0. Floating-point values are mapped directly. Neither integer nor floating-point values are clamped. The initial specular reflectance for both front- and back-facing materials is (0, 0, 0, 1).

GL_EMISSION   *params* contains four integer or floating-point values that specify the RGBA emitted light intensity of the material. Integer values are mapped linearly such that the most positive representable value maps to 1.0, and the most negative representable value maps to −1.0. Floating-point values are mapped directly. Neither integer nor floating-point values are clamped. The initial emission intensity for both front- and back-facing materials is (0, 0, 0, 1).

GL_SHININESS   *params* is a single integer or floating-point value that specifies the RGBA specular exponent of the material. Integer and floating-point values are mapped directly. Only values in the range [0,128] are accepted. The initial specular exponent for both front- and back-facing materials is 0.

GL_AMBIENT_AND_DIFFUSE

Equivalent to calling **glMaterial** twice with the same parameter values, once with **GL_AMBIENT** and once with **GL_DIFFUSE**.

GL_COLOR_INDEXES

params contains three integer or floating-point values specifying the color indices for ambient, diffuse, and specular lighting. These three values, and **GL_SHININESS**, are the only material values used by the color index mode lighting equation. Refer to the **glLightModel** reference page for a discussion of color index lighting.

NOTES

The material parameters can be updated at any time. In particular, **glMaterial** can be called between a call to **glBegin** and the corresponding call to **glEnd**. If only a single material parameter is to be changed per vertex, however, **glColorMaterial** is preferred over **glMaterial** (see **glColorMaterial**).

While the ambient, diffuse, specular and emission material parameters all have alpha components, only the diffuse alpha component is used in the lighting computation.

ERRORS

GL_INVALID_ENUM is generated if either *face* or *pname* is not an accepted value.

GL_INVALID_VALUE is generated if a specular exponent outside the range [0,128] is specified.

ASSOCIATED GETS
glGetMaterial

SEE ALSO
glColorMaterial, glLight, glLightModel

NAME

glMatrixMode – specify which matrix is the current matrix

C SPECIFICATION

void **glMatrixMode**(GLenum *mode*)

PARAMETERS

mode Specifies which matrix stack is the target for subsequent matrix operations. Three values are accepted: **GL_MODELVIEW**, **GL_PROJECTION**, and **GL_TEXTURE**. The initial value is **GL_MODELVIEW**.

Additionally, if the **GL_ARB_imaging** extension is supported, **GL_COLOR** is also accepted.

DESCRIPTION

glMatrixMode sets the current matrix mode. *mode* can assume one of four values:

GL_MODELVIEW Applies subsequent matrix operations to the modelview matrix stack.

GL_PROJECTION Applies subsequent matrix operations to the projection matrix stack.

GL_TEXTURE Applies subsequent matrix operations to the texture matrix stack.

GL_COLOR Applies subsequent matrix operations to the color matrix stack.

To find out which matrix stack is currently the target of all matrix operations, call **glGet** with argument **GL_MATRIX_MODE**. The initial value is **GL_MODELVIEW**.

ERRORS

GL_INVALID_ENUM is generated if *mode* is not an accepted value.

GL_INVALID_OPERATION is generated if **glMatrixMode** is executed between the execution of **glBegin** and the corresponding execution of **glEnd**.

ASSOCIATED GETS

glGet with argument **GL_MATRIX_MODE**

SEE ALSO

glLoadMatrix, **glPushMatrix**

NAME

glMinmax – define minmax table

C SPECIFICATION

void **glMinmax**(GLenum *target*,
                 GLenum *internalformat*,
                 GLboolean *sink*)

PARAMETERS

target   The minmax table whose parameters are to be set. Must be
                    GL_MINMAX.

internalformat
                    The format of entries in the minmax table. Must be one of
                    GL_ALPHA, **GL_ALPHA4**, **GL_ALPHA8**, **GL_ALPHA12**,
                    GL_ALPHA16, **GL_LUMINANCE**, **GL_LUMINANCE4**,
                    GL_LUMINANCE8, **GL_LUMINANCE12**, **GL_LUMINANCE16**,
                    GL_LUMINANCE_ALPHA, **GL_LUMINANCE4_ALPHA4**,
                    GL_LUMINANCE6_ALPHA2, **GL_LUMINANCE8_ALPHA8**,
                    GL_LUMINANCE12_ALPHA4, **GL_LUMINANCE12_ALPHA12**,
                    GL_LUMINANCE16_ALPHA16, **GL_R3_G3_B2**, **GL_RGB**, **GL_RGB4**,
                    GL_RGB5, **GL_RGB8**, **GL_RGB10**, **GL_RGB12**, **GL_RGB16**,
                    GL_RGBA, **GL_RGBA2**, **GL_RGBA4**, **GL_RGB5_A1**, **GL_RGBA8**,
                    GL_RGB10_A2, **GL_RGBA12**, or **GL_RGBA16**.

sink   If **GL_TRUE**, pixels will be consumed by the minmax process and no
                    drawing or texture loading will take place. If **GL_FALSE**, pixels will
                    proceed to the final conversion process after minmax.

DESCRIPTION

When **GL_MINMAX** is enabled, the RGBA components of incoming pixels are compared to the minimum and maximum values for each component, which are stored
in the 2-element minmax table. (The first element stores the minima, and the
second element stores the maxima.) If a pixel component is greater than the
corresponding component in the maximum element, then the maximum element is
updated with the pixel component value. If a pixel component is less than the
corresponding component in the minimum element, then the minimum element is
updated with the pixel component value. (In both cases, if the internal format of
the minmax table includes luminance, then the R color component of incoming
pixels is used for comparison.) The contents of the minmax table may be retrieved
at a later time by calling **glGetMinmax**. The minmax operation is enabled or disabled by calling **glEnable** or **glDisable**, respectively, with an argument of
GL_MINMAX.

glMinmax redefines the current minmax table to have entries of the format specified by *internalformat*. The maximum element is initialized with the smallest possible component values, and the minimum element is initialized with the largest possible component values. The values in the previous minmax table, if any, are lost. If *sink* is **GL_TRUE**, then pixels are discarded after minmax; no further processing of the pixels takes place, and no drawing, texture loading, or pixel readback will result.

NOTES

glMinmax is present only if **GL_ARB_imaging** is returned when **glGetString** is called with an argument of **GL_EXTENSIONS**.

ERRORS

GL_INVALID_ENUM is generated if *target* is not one of the allowable values.

GL_INVALID_ENUM is generated if *internalformat* is not one of the allowable values.

GL_INVALID_OPERATION is generated if **glMinmax** is executed between the execution of **glBegin** and the corresponding execution of **glEnd**.

ASSOCIATED GETS

glGetMinmaxParameter

SEE ALSO

glGetMinmax, **glResetMinmax**

NAME

glMultiTexCoord1dARB, glMultiTexCoord1fARB, glMultiTexCoord1iARB, glMultiTexCoord1sARB, glMultiTexCoord2dARB, glMultiTexCoord2fARB, glMultiTexCoord2iARB, glMultiTexCoord2sARB, glMultiTexCoord3dARB, glMultiTexCoord3fARB, glMultiTexCoord3iARB, glMultiTexCoord3sARB, glMultiTexCoord4dARB, glMultiTexCoord4fARB, glMultiTexCoord4iARB, glMultiTexCoord4sARB, glMultiTexCoord1dvARB, glMultiTexCoord1fvARB, glMultiTexCoord1ivARB, glMultiTexCoord1svARB, glMultiTexCoord2dvARB, glMultiTexCoord2fvARB, glMultiTexCoord2ivARB, glMultiTexCoord2svARB, glMultiTexCoord3dvARB, glMultiTexCoord3fvARB, glMultiTexCoord3ivARB, glMultiTexCoord3svARB, glMultiTexCoord4dvARB, glMultiTexCoord4fvARB, glMultiTexCoord4ivARB, glMultiTexCoord4svARB – set the current texture coordinates

C SPECIFICATION

void **glMultiTexCoord1dARB**(GLenum *target*,
            GLdouble *s*)
void **glMultiTexCoord1fARB**(GLenum *target*,
            GLfloat *s*)
void **glMultiTexCoord1iARB**(GLenum *target*,
            GLint *s*)
void **glMultiTexCoord1sARB**(GLenum *target*,
            GLshort *s*)
void **glMultiTexCoord2dARB**(GLenum *target*,
            GLdouble *s*,
            GLdouble *t*)
void **glMultiTexCoord2fARB**(GLenum *target*,
            GLfloat *s*,
            GLfloat *t*)
void **glMultiTexCoord2iARB**(GLenum *target*,
            GLint *s*,
            GLint *t*)
void **glMultiTexCoord2sARB**(GLenum *target*,
            GLshort *s*,
            GLshort *t*)
void **glMultiTexCoord3dARB**(GLenum *target*,
            GLdouble *s*,
            GLdouble *t*,
            GLdouble *r*)
void **glMultiTexCoord3fARB**(GLenum *target*,
            GLfloat *s*,
            GLfloat *t*,
            GLfloat *r*)

> void **glMultiTexCoord3iARB**(GLenum *target*,
>   GLint *s*,
>   GLint *t*,
>   GLint *r*)
> void **glMultiTexCoord3sARB**(GLenum *target*,
>   GLshort *s*,
>   GLshort *t*,
>   GLshort *r*)
> void **glMultiTexCoord4dARB**(GLenum *target*,
>   GLdouble *s*,
>   GLdouble *t*,
>   GLdouble *r*,
>   GLdouble *q*)
> void **glMultiTexCoord4fARB**(GLenum *target*,
>   GLfloat *s*,
>   GLfloat *t*,
>   GLfloat *r*,
>   GLfloat *q*)
> void **glMultiTexCoord4iARB**(GLenum *target*,
>   GLint *s*,
>   GLint *t*,
>   GLint *r*,
>   GLint *q*)
> void **glMultiTexCoord4sARB**(GLenum *target*,
>   GLshort *s*,
>   GLshort *t*,
>   GLshort *r*,
>   GLshort *q*)

PARAMETERS

target Specifies texture unit whose coordinates should be modified. The number of texture units is implementation dependent, but must be at least two. Must be one of **GL_TEXTURE*i*_ARB** where $0 \le i <$ **GL_MAX_TEXTURE_UNITS_ARB**, which is an implementation-dependent value.

s, t, r, q
Specify *s*, *t*, *r*, and *q* texture coordinates for *target* texture unit. Not all parameters are present in all forms of the command.

C SPECIFICATION

> void **glMultiTexCoord1dvARB**(GLenum *target*,
>   const GLdouble **v*)
> void **glMultiTexCoord1fvARB**(GLenum *target*,
>   const GLfloat **v*)

void **glMultiTexCoord1ivARB**(GLenum *target*,
　　　　　　　　　　const GLint **v*)
void **glMultiTexCoord1svARB**(GLenum *target*,
　　　　　　　　　　const GLshort **v*)
void **glMultiTexCoord2dvARB**(GLenum *target*,
　　　　　　　　　　const GLdouble **v*)
void **glMultiTexCoord2fvARB**(GLenum *target*,
　　　　　　　　　　const GLfloat **v*)
void **glMultiTexCoord2ivARB**(GLenum *target*,
　　　　　　　　　　const GLint **v*)
void **glMultiTexCoord2svARB**(GLenum *target*,
　　　　　　　　　　const GLshort **v*)
void **glMultiTexCoord3dvARB**(GLenum *target*,
　　　　　　　　　　const GLdouble **v*)
void **glMultiTexCoord3fvARB**(GLenum *target*,
　　　　　　　　　　const GLfloat **v*)
void **glMultiTexCoord3ivARB**(GLenum *target*,
　　　　　　　　　　const GLint **v*)
void **glMultiTexCoord3svARB**(GLenum *target*,
　　　　　　　　　　const GLshort **v*)
void **glMultiTexCoord4dvARB**(GLenum *target*,
　　　　　　　　　　const GLdouble **v*)
void **glMultiTexCoord4fvARB**(GLenum *target*,
　　　　　　　　　　const GLfloat **v*)
void **glMultiTexCoord4ivARB**(GLenum *target*,
　　　　　　　　　　const GLint **v*)
void **glMultiTexCoord4svARB**(GLenum *target*,
　　　　　　　　　　const GLshort **v*)

PARAMETERS

target　Specifies texture unit whose coordinates should be modified. The number of texture units is implementation dependent, but must be at least two. Must be one of **GL_TEXTURE*i*_ARB**, where $0 \leq i <$ the implementation-dependent value of **GL_MAX_TEXTURE_UNITS_ARB**.

v　Specifies a pointer to an array of one, two, three, or four elements, which in turn specify the *s*, *t*, *r*, and *q* texture coordinates.

DESCRIPTION

glMultiTexCoordARB specifies texture coordinates in one, two, three, or four dimensions. **glMultiTexCoord1ARB** sets the current texture coordinates to (s, 0, 0, 1); a call to **glMultiTexCoord2ARB** sets them to (s, t, 0, 1). Similarly, **glMultiTexCoord3ARB** specifies the texture coordinates as (s, t, r, 1), and **glMultiTexCoord4ARB** defines all four components explicitly as (s, t, r, q).

The current texture coordinates are part of the data that is associated with each vertex and with the current raster position. Initially, the values for s, t, r, q are $(0, 0, 0, 1)$.

NOTES

glMultiTexCoordARB is only supported if **GL_ARB_multitexture** is included in the string returned by **glGetString** when called with the argument **GL_EXTENSIONS**.

The current texture coordinates can be updated at any time. In particular, **glMultiTexCoordARB** can be called between a call to **glBegin** and the corresponding call to **glEnd**.

It is always the case that **GL_TEXTUREi_ARB** = **GL_TEXTURE0_ARB** + i.

ASSOCIATED GETS

glGet with argument **GL_CURRENT_TEXTURE_COORDS** with appropriate texture unit selected.

SEE ALSO

glActiveTextureARB, **glClientActiveTextureARB**, **glTexCoord**, **glTexCoordPointer**, **glVertex**

NAME

glMultMatrixd, glMultMatrixf – multiply the current matrix with the specified matrix

C SPECIFICATION

void **glMultMatrixd**(const GLdouble *m*)
void **glMultMatrixf**(const GLfloat *m*)

PARAMETERS

m Points to 16 consecutive values that are used as the elements of a 4×4 column-major matrix.

DESCRIPTION

glMultMatrix multiplies the current matrix with the one specified using m, and replaces the current matrix with the product.

The current matrix is determined by the current matrix mode (see **glMatrixMode**). It is either the projection matrix, modelview matrix, or the texture matrix.

EXAMPLES

If the current matrix is C, and the coordinates to be transformed are, $v = (v[0], v[1], v[2], v[3])$. Then the current transformation is $C \times v$, or

$$
\begin{bmatrix}
c[0] & c[4] & c[8] & c[12] \\
c[1] & c[5] & c[9] & c[13] \\
c[2] & c[6] & c[10] & c[14] \\
c[3] & c[7] & c[11] & c[15]
\end{bmatrix}
\times
\begin{bmatrix}
v[0] \\
v[1] \\
v[2] \\
v[3]
\end{bmatrix}
$$

Calling **glMultMatrix** with an argument of $m = m[0], m[1], ..., m[15]$ replaces the current transformation with $(C \times M) \times v$, or

$$
\begin{bmatrix}
c[0] & c[4] & c[8] & c[12] \\
c[1] & c[5] & c[9] & c[13] \\
c[2] & c[6] & c[10] & c[14] \\
c[3] & c[7] & c[11] & c[15]
\end{bmatrix}
\times
\begin{bmatrix}
m[0] & m[4] & m[8] & m[12] \\
m[1] & m[5] & m[9] & m[13] \\
m[2] & m[6] & m[10] & m[14] \\
m[3] & m[7] & m[11] & m[15]
\end{bmatrix}
\times
\begin{bmatrix}
v[0] \\
v[1] \\
v[2] \\
v[3]
\end{bmatrix}
$$

Where 'x' denotes matrix multiplication, and v is represented as a 4×1 matrix.

NOTES

While the elements of the matrix may be specified with single or double precision, the GL may store or operate on these values in less than single precision.

In many computer languages 4×4 arrays are represented in row-major order. The transformations just described represent these matrices in column-major order. The order of the multiplication is important. For example, if the current transformation is a rotation, and **glMultMatrix** is called with a translation matrix, the translation is done directly on the coordinates to be transformed, while the rotation is done on the results of that translation.

ERRORS

GL_INVALID_OPERATION is generated if **glMultMatrix** is executed between the execution of **glBegin** and the corresponding execution of **glEnd**.

ASSOCIATED GETS

glGet with argument **GL_MATRIX_MODE**
glGet with argument **GL_COLOR_MATRIX**
glGet with argument **GL_MODELVIEW_MATRIX**
glGet with argument **GL_PROJECTION_MATRIX**
glGet with argument **GL_TEXTURE_MATRIX**

SEE ALSO

glLoadIdentity, **glLoadMatrix**, **glMatrixMode**, **glPushMatrix**

NAME

glNewList, glEndList – create or replace a display list

C SPECIFICATION

void **glNewList**(GLuint *list*,
                            GLenum *mode*)

PARAMETERS

list Specifies the display-list name.

mode

Specifies the compilation mode, which can be **GL_COMPILE** or
GL_COMPILE_AND_EXECUTE.

C SPECIFICATION

void **glEndList**(void)

DESCRIPTION

Display lists are groups of GL commands that have been stored for subsequent execution. Display lists are created with **glNewList**. All subsequent commands are placed in the display list, in the order issued, until **glEndList** is called.

glNewList has two arguments. The first argument, *list*, is a positive integer that becomes the unique name for the display list. Names can be created and reserved with **glGenLists** and tested for uniqueness with **glIsList**. The second argument, *mode*, is a symbolic constant that can assume one of two values:

GL_COMPILE   Commands are merely compiled.

GL_COMPILE_AND_EXECUTE

Commands are executed as they are compiled into the display list.

Certain commands are not compiled into the display list but are executed immediately, regardless of the display-list mode. These commands are **glAreTexturesResident**, **glColorPointer**, **glDeleteLists**, **glDeleteTextures**, **glDisableClientState**, **glEdgeFlagPointer**, **glEnableClientState**, **glFeedbackBuffer**, **glFinish**, **glFlush**, **glGenLists**, **glGenTextures**, **glIndexPointer**, **glInterleavedArrays**, **glIsEnabled**, **glIsList**, **glIsTexture**, **glNormalPointer**, **glPopClientAttrib**, **glPixelStore**, **glPushClientAttrib**, **glReadPixels**, **glRenderMode**, **glSelectBuffer**, **glTexCoordPointer**, **glVertexPointer**, and all of the **glGet** commands.

Similarly, **glTexImage1D**, **glTexImage2D**, and **glTexImage3D** are executed immediately and not compiled into the display list when their first argument is **GL_PROXY_TEXTURE_1D**, **GL_PROXY_TEXTURE_1D**, or **GL_PROXY_TEXTURE_3D**, respectively.

When the **GL_ARB_imaging** extension is supported, **glHistogram** executes immediately when its argument is **GL_PROXY_HISTOGRAM**. Similarly, **glColorTable** executes immediately when its first argument is **glPROXY_COLOR_TABLE**, **glPROXY_POST_CONVOLUTION_COLOR_TABLE**, or **glPROXY_POST_COLOR_MATRIX_COLOR_TABLE**.

When the **GL_ARB_multitexture** extension is supported, **glClientActiveTextureARB** is not compiled into display lists, but executed immediately.

When **glEndList** is encountered, the display-list definition is completed by associating the list with the unique name *list* (specified in the **glNewList** command). If a display list with name *list* already exists, it is replaced only when **glEndList** is called.

NOTES

glCallList and **glCallLists** can be entered into display lists. Commands in the display list or lists executed by **glCallList** or **glCallLists** are not included in the display list being created, even if the list creation mode is **GL_COMPILE_AND_EXECUTE**.

A display list is just a group of commands and arguments, so errors generated by commands in a display list must be generated when the list is executed. If the list is created in **GL_COMPILE** mode, errors are not generated until the list is executed.

ERRORS

GL_INVALID_VALUE is generated if *list* is 0.

GL_INVALID_ENUM is generated if *mode* is not an accepted value.

GL_INVALID_OPERATION is generated if **glEndList** is called without a preceding **glNewList**, or if **glNewList** is called while a display list is being defined.

GL_INVALID_OPERATION is generated if **glNewList** or **glEndList** is executed between the execution of **glBegin** and the corresponding execution of **glEnd**.

GL_OUT_OF_MEMORY is generated if there is insufficient memory to compile the display list. If the GL version is 1.1 or greater, no change is made to the previous contents of the display list, if any, and no other change is made to the GL state. (It is as if no attempt had been made to create the new display list.)

ASSOCIATED GETS

glIsList
glGet with argument **GL_LIST_INDEX**
glGet with argument **GL_LIST_MODE**

SEE ALSO

glCallList, glCallLists, glDeleteLists, glGenLists

NAME

glNormal3b, glNormal3d, glNormal3f, glNormal3i, glNormal3s, glNormal3bv, glNormal3dv, glNormal3fv, glNormal3iv, glNormal3sv – set the current normal vector

C SPECIFICATION

```
void glNormal3b( GLbyte nx,
                 GLbyte ny,
                 GLbyte nz )
void glNormal3d( GLdouble nx,
                 GLdouble ny,
                 GLdouble nz )
void glNormal3f( GLfloat nx,
                 GLfloat ny,
                 GLfloat nz )
void glNormal3i( GLint nx,
                 GLint ny,
                 GLint nz )
void glNormal3s( GLshort nx,
                 GLshort ny,
                 GLshort nz )
```

PARAMETERS

nx, ny, nz

Specify the *x*, *y*, and *z* coordinates of the new current normal. The initial value of the current normal is the unit vector, (0, 0, 1).

C SPECIFICATION

```
void glNormal3bv( const GLbyte *v )
void glNormal3dv( const GLdouble *v )
void glNormal3fv( const GLfloat *v )
void glNormal3iv( const GLint *v )
void glNormal3sv( const GLshort *v )
```

PARAMETERS

v   Specifies a pointer to an array of three elements: the *x*, *y*, and *z* coordinates of the new current normal.

DESCRIPTION

The current normal is set to the given coordinates whenever **glNormal** is issued. Byte, short, or integer arguments are converted to floating-point format with a linear mapping that maps the most positive representable integer value to 1.0, and the most negative representable integer value to −1.0.

Normals specified with **glNormal** need not have unit length. If **GL_NORMALIZE** is enabled, then normals of any length specified with **glNormal** are normalized after transformation. If **GL_RESCALE_NORMAL** is enabled, normals are scaled by a scaling factor derived from the modelview matrix. **GL_RESCALE_NORMAL** requires that the originally specified normals were of unit length, and that the modelview matrix contain only uniform scales for proper results. To enable and disable normalization, call **glEnable** and **glDisable** with either **GL_NORMALIZE** or **GL_RESCALE_NORMAL**. Normalization is initially disabled.

NOTES

The current normal can be updated at any time. In particular, **glNormal** can be called between a call to **glBegin** and the corresponding call to **glEnd**.

ASSOCIATED GETS

glGet with argument **GL_CURRENT_NORMAL**
glIsEnabled with argument **GL_NORMALIZE**
glIsEnabled with argument **GL_RESCALE_NORMAL**

SEE ALSO

glBegin, **glColor**, **glIndex**, **glNormalPointer**, **glTexCoord**, **glVertex**

NAME

glNormalPointer – define an array of normals

C SPECIFICATION

void **glNormalPointer**(GLenum *type*,
                        GLsizei *stride*,
                        const GLvoid **pointer*)

PARAMETERS

type   Specifies the data type of each coordinate in the array. Symbolic constants **GL_BYTE**, **GL_SHORT**, **GL_INT**, **GL_FLOAT**, and **GL_DOUBLE** are accepted. The initial value is **GL_FLOAT**.

stride Specifies the byte offset between consecutive normals. If *stride* is 0– the initial value–the normals are understood to be tightly packed in the array. The initial value is 0.

pointer Specifies a pointer to the first coordinate of the first normal in the array. The initial value is 0.

DESCRIPTION

glNormalPointer specifies the location and data format of an array of normals to use when rendering. *type* specifies the data type of the normal coordinates and *stride* gives the byte stride from one normal to the next, allowing vertices and attributes to be packed into a single array or stored in separate arrays. (Single-array storage may be more efficient on some implementations; see **glInterleavedArrays**.) When a normal array is specified, *type*, *stride*, and *pointer* are saved as client-side state.

To enable and disable the normal array, call **glEnableClientState** and **glDisableClientState** with the argument **GL_NORMAL_ARRAY**. If enabled, the normal array is used when **glDrawArrays**, **glDrawElements**, or **glArrayElement** is called.

Use **glDrawArrays** to construct a sequence of primitives (all of the same type) from prespecified vertex and vertex attribute arrays. Use **glArrayElement** to specify primitives by indexing vertices and vertex attributes and **glDrawElements** to construct a sequence of primitives by indexing vertices and vertex attributes.

NOTES

glNormalPointer is available only if the GL version is 1.1 or greater.

The normal array is initially disabled and isn't accessed when **glArrayElement**, **glDrawElements**, or **glDrawArrays** is called.

Execution of **glNormalPointer** is not allowed between **glBegin** and the corresponding **glEnd**, but an error may or may not be generated. If an error is not generated, the operation is undefined.

glNormalPointer is typically implemented on the client side.

Since the normal array parameters are client-side state, they are not saved or restored by **glPushAttrib** and **glPopAttrib**. Use **glPushClientAttrib** and **glPopClientAttrib** instead.

ERRORS

GL_INVALID_ENUM is generated if *type* is not an accepted value.

GL_INVALID_VALUE is generated if *stride* is negative.

ASSOCIATED GETS

glIsEnabled with argument **GL_NORMAL_ARRAY**
glGet with argument **GL_NORMAL_ARRAY_TYPE**
glGet with argument **GL_NORMAL_ARRAY_STRIDE**
glGetPointerv with argument **GL_NORMAL_ARRAY_POINTER**

SEE ALSO

glArrayElement, **glColorPointer**, **glDrawArrays**, **glDrawElements**, **glEdgeFlagPointer**, **glEnable**, **glGetPointerv**, **glIndexPointer**, **glInterleavedArrays**, **glPopClientAttrib**, **glPushClientAttrib**, **glTexCoordPointer**, **glVertexPointer**

NAME

glOrtho – multiply the current matrix with an orthographic matrix

C SPECIFICATION

void **glOrtho**(GLdouble *left*,
GLdouble *right*,
GLdouble *bottom*,
GLdouble *top*,
GLdouble *zNear*,
GLdouble *zFar*)

PARAMETERS

left, right

Specify the coordinates for the left and right vertical clipping planes.

bottom, top

Specify the coordinates for the bottom and top horizontal clipping planes.

zNear, zFar

Specify the distances to the nearer and farther depth clipping planes.
These values are negative if the plane is to be behind the viewer.

DESCRIPTION

glOrtho describes a transformation that produces a parallel projection. The current matrix (see **glMatrixMode**) is multiplied by this matrix and the result replaces the current matrix, as if **glMultMatrix** were called with the following matrix as its argument:

$$\begin{bmatrix} \dfrac{2}{right-left} & 0 & 0 & t_x \\[2ex] 0 & \dfrac{2}{top-bottom} & 0 & t_y \\[2ex] 0 & 0 & \dfrac{-2}{zFar-zNear} & t_z \\[2ex] 0 & 0 & 0 & 1 \end{bmatrix}$$

where

$$t_x = -\frac{right + left}{right - left}$$

$$t_y = -\frac{top + bottom}{top - bottom}$$

$$t_z = -\frac{zFar + zNear}{zFar - zNear}$$

Typically, the matrix mode is **GL_PROJECTION**, and (*left, bottom, −zNear*) and (*right, top, −zNear*) specify the points on the near clipping plane that are mapped to the lower left and upper right corners of the window, respectively, assuming that the eye is located at (0, 0, 0). *−zFar* specifies the location of the far clipping plane. Both *zNear* and *zFar* can be either positive or negative.

Use **glPushMatrix** and **glPopMatrix** to save and restore the current matrix stack.

ERRORS

GL_INVALID_OPERATION is generated if **glOrtho** is executed between the execution of **glBegin** and the corresponding execution of **glEnd**.

ASSOCIATED GETS

glGet with argument **GL_MATRIX_MODE**
glGet with argument **GL_COLOR_MATRIX**
glGet with argument **GL_MODELVIEW_MATRIX**
glGet with argument **GL_PROJECTION_MATRIX**
glGet with argument **GL_TEXTURE_MATRIX**

SEE ALSO

glFrustum, **glMatrixMode**, **glMultMatrix**, **glPushMatrix**, **glViewport**

NAME

glPassThrough – place a marker in the feedback buffer

C SPECIFICATION

void **glPassThrough**(GLfloat *token*)

PARAMETERS

token   Specifies a marker value to be placed in the feedback buffer following a **GL_PASS_THROUGH_TOKEN**.

DESCRIPTION

Feedback is a GL render mode. The mode is selected by calling **glRenderMode** with **GL_FEEDBACK**. When the GL is in feedback mode, no pixels are produced by rasterization. Instead, information about primitives that would have been rasterized is fed back to the application using the GL. See the **glFeedbackBuffer** reference page for a description of the feedback buffer and the values in it.

glPassThrough inserts a user-defined marker in the feedback buffer when it is executed in feedback mode. *token* is returned as if it were a primitive; it is indicated with its own unique identifying value: **GL_PASS_THROUGH_TOKEN**. The order of **glPassThrough** commands with respect to the specification of graphics primitives is maintained.

NOTES

glPassThrough is ignored if the GL is not in feedback mode.

ERRORS

GL_INVALID_OPERATION is generated if **glPassThrough** is executed between the execution of **glBegin** and the corresponding execution of **glEnd**.

ASSOCIATED GETS

glGet with argument **GL_RENDER_MODE**

SEE ALSO

glFeedbackBuffer, **glRenderMode**

NAME

    glPixelMapfv, glPixelMapuiv, glPixelMapusv – set up pixel transfer maps

C SPECIFICATION

    void **glPixelMapfv**(GLenum *map*,
                          GLint *mapsize*,
                          const GLfloat **values*)
    void **glPixelMapuiv**(GLenum *map*,
                          GLint *mapsize*,
                          const GLuint **values*)
    void **glPixelMapusv**(GLenum *map*,
                          GLint *mapsize*,
                          const GLushort **values*)

PARAMETERS

    map   Specifies a symbolic map name. Must be one of the following:
                GL_PIXEL_MAP_I_TO_I, GL_PIXEL_MAP_S_TO_S,
                GL_PIXEL_MAP_I_TO_R, GL_PIXEL_MAP_I_TO_G,
                GL_PIXEL_MAP_I_TO_B, GL_PIXEL_MAP_I_TO_A,
                GL_PIXEL_MAP_R_TO_R, GL_PIXEL_MAP_G_TO_G,
                GL_PIXEL_MAP_B_TO_B, or GL_PIXEL_MAP_A_TO_A.

    mapsize
                Specifies the size of the map being defined.

    values   Specifies an array of *mapsize* values.

DESCRIPTION

    glPixelMap sets up translation tables, or *maps*, used by **glCopyPixels**, **glCopyTexImage1D**, **glCopyTexImage2D**, **glCopyTexSubImage1D**, **glCopyTexSubImage2D**, **glCopyTexSubImage3D**, **glDrawPixels**, **glReadPixels**, **glTexImage1D**, **glTexImage2D**, **glTexImage3D**, **glTexSubImage1D**, **glTexSubImage2D**, and **glTexSubImage3D**. Additionally, if the **GL_ARB_imaging** subset is supported, the routines **glColorTable**, **glColorSubTable**, **glConvolutionFilter1D**, **glConvolutionFilter2D**, **glHistogram**, **glMinmax**, and **glSeparableFilter2D**. Use of these maps is described completely in the **glPixelTransfer** reference page, and partly in the reference pages for the pixel and texture image commands. Only the specification of the maps is described in this reference page.

    map is a symbolic map name, indicating one of ten maps to set. *mapsize* specifies the number of entries in the map, and *values* is a pointer to an array of *mapsize* map values.

The ten maps are as follows:

GL_PIXEL_MAP_I_TO_I	Maps color indices to color indices.
GL_PIXEL_MAP_S_TO_S	Maps stencil indices to stencil indices.
GL_PIXEL_MAP_I_TO_R	Maps color indices to red components.
GL_PIXEL_MAP_I_TO_G	Maps color indices to green components.
GL_PIXEL_MAP_I_TO_B	Maps color indices to blue components.
GL_PIXEL_MAP_I_TO_A	Maps color indices to alpha components.
GL_PIXEL_MAP_R_TO_R	Maps red components to red components.
GL_PIXEL_MAP_G_TO_G	Maps green components to green components.
GL_PIXEL_MAP_B_TO_B	Maps blue components to blue components.
GL_PIXEL_MAP_A_TO_A	Maps alpha components to alpha components.

The entries in a map can be specified as single-precision floating-point numbers, unsigned short integers, or unsigned long integers. Maps that store color component values (all but **GL_PIXEL_MAP_I_TO_I** and **GL_PIXEL_MAP_S_TO_S**) retain their values in floating-point format, with unspecified mantissa and exponent sizes. Floating-point values specified by **glPixelMapfv** are converted directly to the internal floating-point format of these maps, then clamped to the range [0,1]. Unsigned integer values specified by **glPixelMapusv** and **glPixelMapuiv** are converted linearly such that the largest representable integer maps to 1.0, and 0 maps to 0.0.

Maps that store indices, **GL_PIXEL_MAP_I_TO_I** and **GL_PIXEL_MAP_S_TO_S**, retain their values in fixed-point format, with an unspecified number of bits to the right of the binary point. Floating-point values specified by **glPixelMapfv** are converted directly to the internal fixed-point format of these maps. Unsigned integer values specified by **glPixelMapusv** and **glPixelMapuiv** specify integer values, with all 0's to the right of the binary point.

The following table shows the initial sizes and values for each of the maps. Maps that are indexed by either color or stencil indices must have *mapsize* = 2^n for some n or the results are undefined. The maximum allowable size for each map depends on the implementation and can be determined by calling **glGet** with argument **GL_MAX_PIXEL_MAP_TABLE**. The single maximum applies to all maps; it is at least 32.

map	Lookup Index	Lookup Value	Initial Size	Initial Value
GL_PIXEL_MAP_I_TO_I	color index	color index	1	0
GL_PIXEL_MAP_S_TO_S	stencil index	stencil index	1	0
GL_PIXEL_MAP_I_TO_R	color index	R	1	0
GL_PIXEL_MAP_I_TO_G	color index	G	1	0
GL_PIXEL_MAP_I_TO_B	color index	B	1	0
GL_PIXEL_MAP_I_TO_A	color index	A	1	0
GL_PIXEL_MAP_R_TO_R	R	R	1	0
GL_PIXEL_MAP_G_TO_G	G	G	1	0
GL_PIXEL_MAP_B_TO_B	B	B	1	0
GL_PIXEL_MAP_A_TO_A	A	A	1	0

ERRORS

GL_INVALID_ENUM is generated if *map* is not an accepted value.

GL_INVALID_VALUE is generated if *mapsize* is less than one or larger than GL_MAX_PIXEL_MAP_TABLE.

GL_INVALID_VALUE is generated if *map* is GL_PIXEL_MAP_I_TO_I, GL_PIXEL_MAP_S_TO_S, GL_PIXEL_MAP_I_TO_R, GL_PIXEL_MAP_I_TO_G, GL_PIXEL_MAP_I_TO_B, or GL_PIXEL_MAP_I_TO_A, and *mapsize* is not a power of two.

GL_INVALID_OPERATION is generated if **glPixelMap** is executed between the execution of **glBegin** and the corresponding execution of **glEnd**.

ASSOCIATED GETS

glGetPixelMap
glGet with argument GL_PIXEL_MAP_I_TO_I_SIZE
glGet with argument GL_PIXEL_MAP_S_TO_S_SIZE
glGet with argument GL_PIXEL_MAP_I_TO_R_SIZE
glGet with argument GL_PIXEL_MAP_I_TO_G_SIZE
glGet with argument GL_PIXEL_MAP_I_TO_B_SIZE
glGet with argument GL_PIXEL_MAP_I_TO_A_SIZE
glGet with argument GL_PIXEL_MAP_R_TO_R_SIZE
glGet with argument GL_PIXEL_MAP_G_TO_G_SIZE
glGet with argument GL_PIXEL_MAP_B_TO_B_SIZE
glGet with argument GL_PIXEL_MAP_A_TO_A_SIZE
glGet with argument GL_MAX_PIXEL_MAP_TABLE

SEE ALSO

glColorTable, glColorSubTable, glConvolutionFilter1D, glConvolutionFilter2D, glCopyPixels, glCopyTexImage1D, glCopyTexImage2D, glCopyTexSubImage1D, glCopyTexSubImage2D, glDrawPixels, glHistogram, glMinmax, glPixelStore, glPixelTransfer, glReadPixels, glSeparableFilter2D, glTexImage1D, glTexImage2D, glTexImage3D, glTexSubImage1D, glTexSubImage2D, glTexSubImage3D

NAME

glPixelStoref, **glPixelStorei** – set pixel storage modes

C SPECIFICATION

void **glPixelStoref**(GLenum *pname*,
                       GLfloat *param*)
void **glPixelStorei**(GLenum *pname*,
                       GLint *param*)

PARAMETERS

pname   Specifies the symbolic name of the parameter to be set. Six values affect the packing of pixel data into memory: **GL_PACK_SWAP_BYTES**, **GL_PACK_LSB_FIRST**, **GL_PACK_ROW_LENGTH**, **GL_PACK_IMAGE_HEIGHT**, **GL_PACK_SKIP_PIXELS**, **GL_PACK_SKIP_ROWS**, **GL_PACK_SKIP_IMAGES**, and **GL_PACK_ALIGNMENT**. Six more affect the unpacking of pixel data *from* memory: **GL_UNPACK_SWAP_BYTES**, **GL_UNPACK_LSB_FIRST**, **GL_UNPACK_ROW_LENGTH**, **GL_UNPACK_IMAGE_HEIGHT**, **GL_UNPACK_SKIP_PIXELS**, **GL_UNPACK_SKIP_ROWS**, **GL_UNPACK_SKIP_IMAGES**, and **GL_UNPACK_ALIGNMENT**.

param   Specifies the value that *pname* is set to.

DESCRIPTION

glPixelStore sets pixel storage modes that affect the operation of subsequent **glDrawPixels** and **glReadPixels** as well as the unpacking of polygon stipple patterns (see **glPolygonStipple**), bitmaps (see **glBitmap**), texture patterns (see **glTexImage1D**, **glTexImage2D**, **glTexImage3D**, **glTexSubImage1D**, **glTexSubImage2D**, **glTexSubImage3D**). Additionally, if the **GL_ARB_imaging** extension is supported, pixle storage modes affect convlution filters (see **glConvolutionFilter1D**, **glConvolutionFilter2D**, and **glSeparableFilter2D**, color table (see **glColorTable**, and **glColorSubTable**, and unpacking histogram (See **glHistogram**), and minmax (See **glMinmax**) data.

pname is a symbolic constant indicating the parameter to be set, and *param* is the new value. Six of the twelve storage parameters affect how pixel data is returned to client memory. They are as follows:

GL_PACK_SWAP_BYTES

If true, byte ordering for multibyte color components, depth components, color indices, or stencil indices is reversed. That is, if a four-byte component consists of bytes b_0, b_1, b_2, b_3, it is stored in memory as b_3, b_2, b_1, b_0 if **GL_PACK_SWAP_BYTES** is true. **GL_PACK_SWAP_BYTES** has no effect on the memory order of components within a pixel, only on the order of bytes within components or indices. For example, the three components of a **GL_RGB** format pixel are always stored with red first, green second, and blue third, regardless of the value of **GL_PACK_SWAP_BYTES**.

GL_PACK_LSB_FIRST

If true, bits are ordered within a byte from least significant to most significant; otherwise, the first bit in each byte is the most significant one. This parameter is significant for bitmap data only.

GL_PACK_ROW_LENGTH

If greater than 0, **GL_PACK_ROW_LENGTH** defines the number of pixels in a row. If the first pixel of a row is placed at location p in memory, then the location of the first pixel of the next row is obtained by skipping

$$k = \begin{array}{ll} nl & s \geq a \\ \dfrac{a}{s} \left\lceil \dfrac{snl}{a} \right\rceil & s < a \end{array}$$

components or indices, where n is the number of components or indices in a pixel, l is the number of pixels in a row (**GL_PACK_ROW_LENGTH** if it is greater than 0, the *width* argument to the pixel routine otherwise), a is the value of **GL_PACK_ALIGNMENT**, and s is the size, in bytes, of a single component (if $a<s$, then it is as if $a = s$). In the case of 1-bit values, the location of the next row is obtained by skipping

$$k = 8a \left\lceil \dfrac{nl}{8a} \right\rceil$$

components or indices.

The word *component* in this description refers to the nonindex values red, green, blue, alpha, and depth. Storage format **GL_RGB**, for example, has three components per pixel: first red, then green, and finally blue.

GL_PACK_IMAGE_HEIGHT

If greater than 0, **GL_PACK_IMAGE_HEIGHT** defines the number of pixels in an image three-dimensional texture volume. Where "image" is defined by all pixels sharing the same third dimension index. If the first pixel of a row is placed at location p in memory, then the location of the first pixel of the next row is obtained by skipping

$$k = \begin{array}{ll} nlh & s \geq a \\ \dfrac{a}{s} \left\lceil \dfrac{snlh}{a} \right\rceil & s < a \end{array}$$

components or indices, where n is the number of components or indices in a pixel, l is the number of pixels in a row (**GL_PACK_ROW_LENGTH** if it is greater than 0, the *width* argument to **glTexImage3d** otherwise), h is the number of rows in a pixel image (**GL_PACK_IMAGE_HEIGHT** if it is greater than 0, the *height* arguemnt to the **glTexImage3D** routine otherwise), a is the value of **GL_PACK_ALIGNMENT**, and s is the size, in bytes, of a single component (if $a<s$, then it is as if $a=s$).

The word *component* in this description refers to the nonindex values red, green, blue, alpha, and depth. Storage format **GL_RGB**, for example, has three components per pixel: first red, then green, and finally blue.

GL_PACK_SKIP_PIXELS, **GL_PACK_SKIP_ROWS**, and **GL_PACK_SKIP_IMAGES**

These values are provided as a convenience to the programmer; they provide no functionality that cannot be duplicated simply by incrementing the pointer passed to **glReadPixels**. Setting **GL_PACK_SKIP_PIXELS** to i is equivalent to incrementing the pointer by in components or indices, where n is the number of components or indices in each pixel. Setting **GL_PACK_SKIP_ROWS** to j is equivalent to incrementing the pointer by jm components or indices, where m is the number of components or indices per row, as just computed in the **GL_PACK_ROW_LENGTH** section. Setting **GL_PACK_SKIP_IMAGES** to k is equivalent to incrementing the pointer by kp, where p is the number of components or indices per image, as computed in the **GL_PACK_IMAGE_HEIGHT** section.

GL_PACK_ALIGNMENT

Specifies the alignment requirements for the start of each pixel row in memory. The allowable values are 1 (byte-alignment), 2 (rows aligned to even-numbered bytes), 4 (word-alignment), and 8 (rows start on double-word boundaries).

The other six of the twelve storage parameters affect how pixel data is read from client memory. These values are significant for **glDrawPixels**, **glTexImage1D**, **glTexImage2D**, **glTexImage3D**, **glTexSubImage1D**, **glTexSubImage2D**, **glTexSubImage3D**, **glBitmap**, and **glPolygonStipple**.

Additionally, if the **GL_ARB_imaging** extension is supported, **glColorTable**, **glColorSubTable**, **glConvolutionFilter1D**, **glConvolutionFilter2D**, and **glSeparableFilter2D**. They are as follows:

GL_UNPACK_SWAP_BYTES

If true, byte ordering for multibyte color components, depth components, color indices, or stencil indices is reversed. That is, if a four-byte component consists of bytes b_0, b_1, b_2, b_3, it is taken from memory as b_3, b_2, b_1, b_0 if **GL_UNPACK_SWAP_BYTES** is true. **GL_UNPACK_SWAP_BYTES** has no effect on the memory order of components within a pixel, only on the order of bytes within components or indices. For example, the three components of a **GL_RGB** format pixel are always stored with red first, green second, and blue third, regardless of the value of **GL_UNPACK_SWAP_BYTES**.

GL_UNPACK_LSB_FIRST

If true, bits are ordered within a byte from least significant to most significant; otherwise, the first bit in each byte is the most significant one. This is relevant only for bitmap data.

GL_UNPACK_ROW_LENGTH

If greater than 0, **GL_UNPACK_ROW_LENGTH** defines the number of pixels in a row. If the first pixel of a row is placed at location p in memory, then the location of the first pixel of the next row is obtained by skipping

$$k = \begin{cases} nl & s \geq a \\ \dfrac{a}{s} \left\lceil \dfrac{snl}{a} \right\rceil & s < a \end{cases}$$

components or indices, where n is the number of components or indices in a pixel, l is the number of pixels in a row (**GL_UNPACK_ROW_LENGTH** if it is greater than 0, the *width* argument to the pixel routine otherwise), a is the value of **GL_UNPACK_ALIGNMENT**, and s is the size, in bytes, of a single component (if $a<s$, then it is as if $a=s$). In the case of 1-bit values, the location of the next row is obtained by skipping

$$k = 8a \left\lceil \frac{nl}{8a} \right\rceil$$

components or indices.

The word *component* in this description refers to the nonindex values red, green, blue, alpha, and depth. Storage format **GL_RGB**, for example, has three components per pixel: first red, then green, and finally blue.

GL_UNPACK_IMAGE_HEIGHT

If greater than 0, **GL_UNPACK_IMAGE_HEIGHT** defines the number of pixels in an image of a three-dimensional texture volume. Where "image" is defined by all pixel sharing the same third dimension index. If the first pixel of a row is placed at location p in memory, then the location of the first pixel of the next row is obtained by skipping

$$k = \begin{cases} nlh & s \geq a \\ \dfrac{a}{s} \left\lceil \dfrac{snlh}{a} \right\rceil & s < a \end{cases}$$

components or indices, where n is the number of components or indices in a pixel, l is the number of pixels in a row (**GL_UNPACK_ROW_LENGTH** if it is greater than 0, the *width* argument to **glTexImage3D** otherwise), h is the number of rows in an image (**GL_UNPACK_IMAGE_HEIGHT** if it is greater than 0, the *height* argument to **glTexImage3D** otherwise), a is the value of **GL_UNPACK_ALIGNMENT**, and s is the size, in bytes, of a single component (if $a<s$, then it is as if $a = s$).

The word *component* in this description refers to the nonindex values red, green, blue, alpha, and depth. Storage format **GL_RGB**, for example, has three components per pixel: first red, then green, and finally blue.

GL_UNPACK_SKIP_PIXELS and **GL_UNPACK_SKIP_ROWS**

These values are provided as a convenience to the programmer; they provide no functionality that cannot be duplicated by incrementing the pointer passed to **glDrawPixels**, **glTexImage1D**, **glTexImage2D**, **glTexSubImage1D**, **glTexSubImage2D**, **glBitmap**, or **glPolygonStipple**. Setting **GL_UNPACK_SKIP_PIXELS** to i is equivalent to incrementing the pointer by in components or indices, where n is the number of components or indices in each pixel. Setting **GL_UNPACK_SKIP_ROWS** to j is equivalent to incrementing the pointer by jk components or indices, where k is the number of components or indices per row, as just computed in the **GL_UNPACK_ROW_LENGTH** section.

GL_UNPACK_ALIGNMENT

Specifies the alignment requirements for the start of each pixel row in memory. The allowable values are 1 (byte-alignment), 2 (rows aligned to even-numbered bytes), 4 (word-alignment), and 8 (rows start on double-word boundaries).

The following table gives the type, initial value, and range of valid values for each storage parameter that can be set with **glPixelStore**.

pname	Type	Initial Value	Valid Range
GL_PACK_SWAP_BYTES	boolean	false	true or false
GL_PACK_LSB_FIRST	boolean	false	true or false
GL_PACK_ROW_LENGTH	integer	0	$[0,\infty)$
GL_PACK_IMAGE_HEIGHT	integer	0	$[0, \infty)$
GL_PACK_SKIP_ROWS	integer	0	$[0,\infty)$
GL_PACK_SKIP_PIXELS	integer	0	$[0,\infty)$
GL_PACK_SKIP_IMAGES	integer	0	$[0,\infty)$
GL_PACK_ALIGNMENT	integer	4	1, 2, 4, or 8

GL_UNPACK_SWAP_BYTES	boolean	false	true or false
GL_UNPACK_LSB_FIRST	boolean	false	true or false
GL_UNPACK_ROW_LENGTH	integer	0	$[0,\infty)$
GL_UNPACK_IMAGE_HEIGHT	integer	0	$[0,\infty)$
GL_UNPACK_SKIP_ROWS	integer	0	$[0,\infty)$
GL_UNPACK_SKIP_PIXELS	integer	0	$[0,\infty)$
GL_UNPACK_SKIP_IMAGES	integer	0	$[0,\infty)$
GL_UNPACK_ALIGNMENT	integer	4	1, 2, 4, or 8

glPixelStoref can be used to set any pixel store parameter. If the parameter type is boolean, then if *param* is 0, the parameter is false; otherwise it is set to true. If *pname* is a integer type parameter, *param* is rounded to the nearest integer.

Likewise, **glPixelStorei** can also be used to set any of the pixel store parameters. Boolean parameters are set to false if *param* is 0 and true otherwise.

NOTES

The pixel storage modes in effect when **glDrawPixels**, **glReadPixels**, **glTexImage1D**, **glTexImage2D**, **glTexImage3D**, **glTexSubImage1D**, **glTexSubImage2D**, **glTexSubImage3D**, **glBitmap**, or **glPolygonStipple** is placed in a display list control the interpretation of memory data. Likewise, if the **GL_ARB_imaging** extension is supported, the pixel storage modes in effect when **glColorTable**, **glColorSubTable**, **glConvolutionFilter1D**, **glConvolutionFilter2D**, of **glSeparableFilter2D** is placed in a display list control the intrepretation of memory data. The pixel storage modes in effect when a display list is executed are not significant.

Pixel storage modes are client state and must be pushed and restored using **glPushClientAttrib** and **glPopClientAttrib**.

ERRORS

GL_INVALID_ENUM is generated if *pname* is not an accepted value.

GL_INVALID_VALUE is generated if a negative row length, pixel skip, or row skip value is specified, or if alignment is specified as other than 1, 2, 4, or 8.

GL_INVALID_OPERATION is generated if **glPixelStore** is executed between the execution of **glBegin** and the corresponding execution of **glEnd**.

ASSOCIATED GETS

glGet with argument **GL_PACK_SWAP_BYTES**
glGet with argument **GL_PACK_LSB_FIRST**
glGet with argument **GL_PACK_ROW_LENGTH**
glGet with argument **GL_PACK_IMAGE_HEIGHT**
glGet with argument **GL_PACK_SKIP_ROWS**
glGet with argument **GL_PACK_SKIP_PIXELS**

glGet with argument **GL_PACK_SKIP_IMAGES**
glGet with argument **GL_PACK_ALIGNMENT**
glGet with argument **GL_UNPACK_SWAP_BYTES**
glGet with argument **GL_UNPACK_LSB_FIRST**
glGet with argument **GL_UNPACK_ROW_LENGTH**
glGet with argument **GL_UNPACK_IMAGE_HEIGHT**
glGet with argument **GL_UNPACK_SKIP_ROWS**
glGet with argument **GL_UNPACK_SKIP_PIXELS**
glGet with argument **GL_UNPACK_SKIP_IMAGES**
glGet with argument **GL_UNPACK_ALIGNMENT**

SEE ALSO

glBitmap, **glColorTable**, **glColorSubTable**, **glConvolutionFilter1D**, **glConvolutionFilter2D**, **glSeparableFilter2D**, **glDrawPixels**, **glHistogram**, **glMinmax**, **glPixelMap**, **glPixelTransfer**, **glPixelZoom**, **glPolygonStipple**, **glPushClientAttrib**, **glReadPixels**, **glTexImage1D**, **glTexImage2D**, **glTexImage3D**, **glTexSubImage1D**, **glTexSubImage2D**, **glTexSubImage3D**

NAME

glPixelTransferf, glPixelTransferi – set pixel transfer modes

C SPECIFICATION

void **glPixelTransferf**(GLenum *pname*,
                              GLfloat *param*)
void **glPixelTransferi**(GLenum *pname*,
                              GLint *param*)

PARAMETERS

pname　Specifies the symbolic name of the pixel transfer parameter to be set. Must
be one of the following: **GL_MAP_COLOR**, **GL_MAP_STENCIL**,
GL_INDEX_SHIFT, **GL_INDEX_OFFSET**, **GL_RED_SCALE**, **GL_RED_BIAS**,
GL_GREEN_SCALE, **GL_GREEN_BIAS**, **GL_BLUE_SCALE**, **GL_BLUE_BIAS**,
GL_ALPHA_SCALE, **GL_ALPHA_BIAS**, **GL_DEPTH_SCALE**, or
GL_DEPTH_BIAS.

Additionally, if the **GL_ARB_imaging** extension is supported, the following
symbolic names are accepted: **GL_POST_COLOR_MATRIX_RED_SCALE**,
GL_POST_COLOR_MATRIX_GREEN_SCALE,
GL_POST_COLOR_MATRIX_BLUE_SCALE,
GL_POST_COLOR_MATRIX_ALPHA_SCALE,
GL_POST_COLOR_MATRIX_RED_BIAS,
GL_POST_COLOR_MATRIX_GREEN_BIAS,
GL_POST_COLOR_MATRIX_BLUE_BIAS,
GL_POST_COLOR_MATRIX_ALPHA_BIAS,
GL_POST_CONVOLUTION_RED_SCALE,
GL_POST_CONVOLUTION_GREEN_SCALE,
GL_POST_CONVOLUTION_BLUE_SCALE,
GL_POST_CONVOLUTION_ALPHA_SCALE,
GL_POST_CONVOLUTION_RED_BIAS,
GL_POST_CONVOLUTION_GREEN_BIAS,
GL_POST_CONVOLUTION_BLUE_BIAS, and
GL_POST_CONVOLUTION_ALPHA_BIAS.

param　Specifies the value that *pname* is set to.

DESCRIPTION

glPixelTransfer sets pixel transfer modes that affect the operation of subsequent
glCopyPixels, **glCopyTexImage1D**, **glCopyTexImage2D**, **glCopyTexSubImage1D**,
glCopyTexSubImage2D, **glCopyTexSubImage3D**, **glDrawPixels**, **glReadPixels**,
glTexImage1D, **glTexImage2D**, **glTexImage3D**, **glTexSubImage1D**,
glTexSubImage2D, and **glTexSubImage3D** commands. Additionally, if the
GL_ARB_imaging subset is supported, the routines **glColorTable**,

glColorSubTable, **glConvolutionFilter1D**, **glConvolutionFilter2D**, **glHistogram**, **glMinmax**, and **glSeparableFilter2D** are also affected. The algorithms that are specified by pixel transfer modes operate on pixels after they are read from the frame buffer (**glCopyPixels glCopyTexImage1D**, **glCopyTexImage2D**, **glCopyTexSubImage1D**, **glCopyTexSubImage2D**, **glCopyTexSubImage3D**, and **glReadPixels**), or unpacked from client memory (**glDrawPixels**, **glTexImage1D**, **glTexImage2D**, **glTexImage3D**, **glTexSubImage1D**, **glTexSubImage2D**, and **glTexSubImage3D**). Pixel transfer operations happen in the same order, and in the same manner, regardless of the command that resulted in the pixel operation. Pixel storage modes (see **glPixelStore**) control the unpacking of pixels being read from client memory, and the packing of pixels being written back into client memory.

Pixel transfer operations handle four fundamental pixel types: *color, color index, depth,* and *stencil. Color* pixels consist of four floating-point values with unspecified mantissa and exponent sizes, scaled such that 0 represents zero intensity and 1 represents full intensity. *Color indices* comprise a single fixed-point value, with unspecified precision to the right of the binary point. *Depth* pixels comprise a single floating-point value, with unspecified mantissa and exponent sizes, scaled such that 0.0 represents the minimum depth buffer value, and 1.0 represents the maximum depth buffer value. Finally, *stencil* pixels comprise a single fixed-point value, with unspecified precision to the right of the binary point.

The pixel transfer operations performed on the four basic pixel types are as follows:

Color   Each of the four color components is multiplied by a scale factor, then added to a bias factor. That is, the red component is multiplied by **GL_RED_SCALE**, then added to **GL_RED_BIAS**; the green component is multiplied by **GL_GREEN_SCALE**, then added to **GL_GREEN_BIAS**; the blue component is multiplied by **GL_BLUE_SCALE**, then added to **GL_BLUE_BIAS**; and the alpha component is multiplied by **GL_ALPHA_SCALE**, then added to **GL_ALPHA_BIAS**. After all four color components are scaled and biased, each is clamped to the range [0,1]. All color, scale, and bias values are specified with **glPixelTransfer**.

If **GL_MAP_COLOR** is true, each color component is scaled by the size of the corresponding color-to-color map, then replaced by the contents of that map indexed by the scaled component. That is, the red component is scaled by **GL_PIXEL_MAP_R_TO_R_SIZE**, then replaced by the contents of **GL_PIXEL_MAP_R_TO_R** indexed by itself. The green component is scaled by **GL_PIXEL_MAP_G_TO_G_SIZE**, then replaced by the contents of **GL_PIXEL_MAP_G_TO_G** indexed by itself. The blue component is scaled by **GL_PIXEL_MAP_B_TO_B_SIZE**, then replaced by the contents of **GL_PIXEL_MAP_B_TO_B** indexed by itself. And the alpha component is scaled by **GL_PIXEL_MAP_A_TO_A_SIZE**, then replaced by the contents of **GL_PIXEL_MAP_A_TO_A** indexed by itself. All components taken from the maps are then clamped to the range [0,1]. **GL_MAP_COLOR** is specified with **glPixelTransfer**. The contents of the various maps are specified with **glPixelMap**.

If the **GL_ARB_imaging** extension is supported, each of the four color components may be scaled and biased after tranformation by the color matrix. That is, the red component is multiplied by **GL_POST_COLOR_MATRIX_RED_SCALE**, then added to **GL_POST_COLOR_MATRIX_RED_BIAS**; the green component is multiplied by **GL_POST_COLOR_MATRIX_GREEN_SCALE**, then added to **GL_POST_COLOR_MATRIX_GREEN_BIAS**; the blue component is multiplied by **GL_POST_COLOR_MATRIX_BLUE_SCALE**, then added to **GL_POST_COLOR_MATRIX_BLUE_BIAS**; and the alpha component is multiplied by **GL_POST_COLOR_MATRIX_ALPHA_SCALE**, then added to **GL_POST_COLOR_MATRIX_ALPHA_BIAS**. After all four color components are scaled and biased, each is clamped to the range [0,1].

Similarly, if the **GL_ARB_imaging** extension is supported, each of the four color components may be scaled and biased after processing by the enabled convolution filter. That is, the red component is multiplied by **GL_POST_CONVOLUTION_RED_SCALE**, then added to **GL_POST_CONVOLUTION_RED_BIAS**; the green component is multiplied by **GL_POST_CONVOLUTION_GREEN_SCALE**, then added to **GL_POST_CONVOLUTION_GREEN_BIAS**; the blue component is multiplied by **GL_POST_CONVOLUTION_BLUE_SCALE**, then added to **GL_POST_CONVOLUTION_BLUE_BIAS**; and the alpha component is multiplied by **GL_POST_CONVOLUTION_ALPHA_SCALE**, then added to **GL_POST_CONVOLUTION_ALPHA_BIAS**. After all four color components are scaled and biased, each is clamped to the range [0,1].

Color index Each color index is shifted left by **GL_INDEX_SHIFT** bits; any bits beyond the number of fraction bits carried by the fixed-point index are filled with zeros. If **GL_INDEX_SHIFT** is negative, the shift is to the right, again zero filled. Then **GL_INDEX_OFFSET** is added to the index. **GL_INDEX_SHIFT** and **GL_INDEX_OFFSET** are specified with **glPixelTransfer**.

From this point, operation diverges depending on the required format of the resulting pixels. If the resulting pixels are to be written to a color index buffer, or if they are being read back to client memory in **GL_COLOR_INDEX** format, the pixels continue to be treated as indices. If **GL_MAP_COLOR** is true, each index is masked by $2^n - 1$, where n is **GL_PIXEL_MAP_I_TO_I_SIZE**, then replaced by the contents of **GL_PIXEL_MAP_I_TO_I** indexed by the masked value. **GL_MAP_COLOR** is specified with **glPixelTransfer**. The contents of the index map is specified with **glPixelMap**.

If the resulting pixels are to be written to an RGBA color buffer, or if they are read back to client memory in a format other than **GL_COLOR_INDEX**, the pixels are converted from indices to colors by referencing the four maps **GL_PIXEL_MAP_I_TO_R**, **GL_PIXEL_MAP_I_TO_G**, **GL_PIXEL_MAP_I_TO_B**, and **GL_PIXEL_MAP_I_TO_A**. Before being dereferenced, the index is masked by $2^n - 1$, where n is **GL_PIXEL_MAP_I_TO_R_SIZE** for the red map, **GL_PIXEL_MAP_I_TO_G_SIZE** for the green map, **GL_PIXEL_MAP_I_TO_B_SIZE** for the blue map, and **GL_PIXEL_MAP_I_TO_A_SIZE** for the alpha map. All components taken from the maps are then clamped to the range [0,1]. The contents of the four maps is specified with **glPixelMap**.

Depth   Each depth value is multiplied by **GL_DEPTH_SCALE**, added to **GL_DEPTH_BIAS**, then clamped to the range [0,1].

Stencil   Each index is shifted **GL_INDEX_SHIFT** bits just as a color index is, then added to **GL_INDEX_OFFSET**. If **GL_MAP_STENCIL** is true, each index is masked by $2^n - 1$, where n is **GL_PIXEL_MAP_S_TO_S_SIZE**, then replaced by the contents of **GL_PIXEL_MAP_S_TO_S** indexed by the masked value.

The following table gives the type, initial value, and range of valid values for each of the pixel transfer parameters that are set with **glPixelTransfer**.

pname	Type	Initial Value	Valid Range
GL_MAP_COLOR	boolean	false	true/false
GL_MAP_STENCIL	boolean	false	true/false
GL_INDEX_SHIFT	integer	0	$(-\infty,\infty)$
GL_INDEX_OFFSET	integer	0	$(-\infty,\infty)$
GL_RED_SCALE	float	1	$(-\infty,\infty)$
GL_GREEN_SCALE	float	1	$(-\infty,\infty)$
GL_BLUE_SCALE	float	1	$(-\infty,\infty)$
GL_ALPHA_SCALE	float	1	$(-\infty,\infty)$
GL_DEPTH_SCALE	float	1	$(-\infty,\infty)$
GL_RED_BIAS	float	0	$(-\infty,\infty)$
GL_GREEN_BIAS	float	0	$(-\infty,\infty)$
GL_BLUE_BIAS	float	0	$(-\infty,\infty)$

GL_ALPHA_BIAS	float	0	$(-\infty,\infty)$
GL_DEPTH_BIAS	float	0	$(-\infty,\infty)$
GL_POST_COLOR_MATRIX_RED_SCALE	float	1	$(-\infty,\infty)$
GL_POST_COLOR_MATRIX_GREEN_SCALE	float	1	$(-\infty,\infty)$
GL_POST_COLOR_MATRIX_BLUE_SCALE	float	1	$(-\infty,\infty)$
GL_POST_COLOR_MATRIX_ALPHA_SCALE	float	1	$(-\infty,\infty)$
GL_POST_COLOR_MATRIX_RED_BIAS	float	0	$(-\infty,\infty)$
GL_POST_COLOR_MATRIX_GREEN_BIAS	float	0	$(-\infty,\infty)$
GL_POST_COLOR_MATRIX_BLUE_BIAS	float	0	$(-\infty,\infty)$
GL_POST_COLOR_MATRIX_ALPHA_BIAS	float	0	$(-\infty,\infty)$
GL_POST_CONVOLUTION_RED_SCALE	float	1	$(-\infty,\infty)$
GL_POST_CONVOLUTION_GREEN_SCALE	float	1	$(-\infty,\infty)$
GL_POST_CONVOLUTION_BLUE_SCALE	float	1	$(-\infty,\infty)$
GL_POST_CONVOLUTION_ALPHA_SCALE	float	1	$(-\infty,\infty)$
GL_POST_CONVOLUTION_RED_BIAS	float	0	$(-\infty,\infty)$
GL_POST_CONVOLUTION_GREEN_BIAS	float	0	$(-\infty,\infty)$
GL_POST_CONVOLUTION_BLUE_BIAS	float	0	$(-\infty,\infty)$
GL_POST_CONVOLUTION_ALPHA_BIAS	float	0	$(-\infty,\infty)$

glPixelTransferf can be used to set any pixel transfer parameter. If the parameter type is boolean, 0 implies false and any other value implies true. If *pname* is an integer parameter, *param* is rounded to the nearest integer.

Likewise, **glPixelTransferi** can be used to set any of the pixel transfer parameters. Boolean parameters are set to false if *param* is 0 and to true otherwise. *param* is converted to floating point before being assigned to real-valued parameters.

NOTES

If a **glColorTable**, **glColorSubTable**, **glConvolutionFilter1D**, **glConvolutionFilter2D**, **glCopyPixels**, **glCopyTexImage1D**, **glCopyTexImage2D**, **glCopyTexSubImage1D**, **glCopyTexSubImage2D**, **glCopyTexSubImage3D**, **glDrawPixels**, **glReadPixels**, **glSeparableFilter2D**, **glTexImage1D**, **glTexImage2D**, **glTexImage3D**, **glTexSubImage1D**, **glTexSubImage2D**, or **glTexSubImage3D**. command is placed in a display list (see **glNewList** and **glCallList**), the pixel transfer mode settings in effect when the display list is *executed* are the ones that are used. They may be different from the settings when the command was compiled into the display list.

ERRORS

GL_INVALID_ENUM is generated if *pname* is not an accepted value.

GL_INVALID_OPERATION is generated if **glPixelTransfer** is executed between the execution of **glBegin** and the corresponding execution of **glEnd**.

ASSOCIATED GETS

glGet with argument GL_MAP_COLOR
glGet with argument GL_MAP_STENCIL
glGet with argument GL_INDEX_SHIFT
glGet with argument GL_INDEX_OFFSET
glGet with argument GL_RED_SCALE
glGet with argument GL_RED_BIAS
glGet with argument GL_GREEN_SCALE
glGet with argument GL_GREEN_BIAS
glGet with argument GL_BLUE_SCALE
glGet with argument GL_BLUE_BIAS
glGet with argument GL_ALPHA_SCALE
glGet with argument GL_ALPHA_BIAS
glGet with argument GL_DEPTH_SCALE
glGet with argument GL_DEPTH_BIAS
glGet with argument GL_POST_COLOR_MATRIX_RED_SCALE
glGet with argument GL_POST_COLOR_MATRIX_RED_BIAS
glGet with argument GL_POST_COLOR_MATRIX_GREEN_SCALE
glGet with argument GL_POST_COLOR_MATRIX_GREEN_BIAS
glGet with argument GL_POST_COLOR_MATRIX_BLUE_SCALE
glGet with argument GL_POST_COLOR_MATRIX_BLUE_BIAS
glGet with argument GL_POST_COLOR_MATRIX_ALPHA_SCALE
glGet with argument GL_POST_COLOR_MATRIX_ALPHA_BIAS
glGet with argument GL_POST_CONVOLUTION_RED_SCALE
glGet with argument GL_POST_CONVOLUTION_RED_BIAS
glGet with argument GL_POST_CONVOLUTION_GREEN_SCALE
glGet with argument GL_POST_CONVOLUTION_GREEN_BIAS
glGet with argument GL_POST_CONVOLUTION_BLUE_SCALE
glGet with argument GL_POST_CONVOLUTION_BLUE_BIAS
glGet with argument GL_POST_CONVOLUTION_ALPHA_SCALE
glGet with argument GL_POST_CONVOLUTION_ALPHA_BIAS

SEE ALSO

glCallList, **glColorTable**, **glColorSubTable**, **glConvolutionFilter1D**, **glConvolutionFilter2D**, **glCopyPixels**, **glCopyTexImage1D**, **glCopyTexImage2D**, **glCopyTexSubImage1D**, **glCopyTexSubImage2D**, **glCopyTexSubImage3D**, **glDrawPixels**, **glNewList**, **glPixelMap**, **glPixelStore**, **glPixelZoom**, **glReadPixels**, **glTexImage1D**, **glTexImage2D**, **glTexImage3D**, **glTexSubImage1D**, **glTexSubImage2D**, **glTexSubImage3D**

NAME

glPixelZoom – specify the pixel zoom factors

C SPECIFICATION

void **glPixelZoom**(GLfloat *xfactor*,
                     GLfloat *yfactor*)

PARAMETERS

xfactor, yfactor

Specify the *x* and *y* zoom factors for pixel write operations.

DESCRIPTION

glPixelZoom specifies values for the *x* and *y* zoom factors. During the execution of **glDrawPixels** or **glCopyPixels**, if (x_r, y_r) is the current raster position, and a given element is in the *m*th row and *n*th column of the pixel rectangle, then pixels whose centers are in the rectangle with corners at

$$(x_r + n \cdot xfactor, \; y_r + m \cdot yfactor)$$

$$(x_r + (n+1) \cdot xfactor, \; y_r + (m+1) \cdot yfactor)$$

are candidates for replacement. Any pixel whose center lies on the bottom or left edge of this rectangular region is also modified.

Pixel zoom factors are not limited to positive values. Negative zoom factors reflect the resulting image about the current raster position.

ERRORS

GL_INVALID_OPERATION is generated if **glPixelZoom** is executed between the execution of **glBegin** and the corresponding execution of **glEnd**.

ASSOCIATED GETS

glGet with argument **GL_ZOOM_X**
glGet with argument **GL_ZOOM_Y**

SEE ALSO

glCopyPixels, **glDrawPixels**

NAME

glPointSize – specify the diameter of rasterized points

C SPECIFICATION

void **glPointSize**(GLfloat *size*)

PARAMETERS

size Specifies the diameter of rasterized points. The initial value is 1.

DESCRIPTION

glPointSize specifies the rasterized diameter of both aliased and antialiased points. Using a point size other than 1 has different effects, depending on whether point antialiasing is enabled. To enable and disable point antialiasing, call **glEnable** and **glDisable** with argument **GL_POINT_SMOOTH**. Point antialiasing is initially disabled.

If point antialiasing is disabled, the actual size is determined by rounding the supplied size to the nearest integer. (If the rounding results in the value 0, it is as if the point size were 1.) If the rounded size is odd, then the center point (x, y) of the pixel fragment that represents the point is computed as

$$(\ x_w \ + .5, \ y_w \ + .5)$$

where w subscripts indicate window coordinates. All pixels that lie within the square grid of the rounded size centered at (x, y) make up the fragment. If the size is even, the center point is

$$(\ x_w + .5 \ , \ y_w + .5 \ )$$

and the rasterized fragment's centers are the half-integer window coordinates within the square of the rounded size centered at (x, y). All pixel fragments produced in rasterizing a nonantialiased point are assigned the same associated data, that of the vertex corresponding to the point.

If antialiasing is enabled, then point rasterization produces a fragment for each pixel square that intersects the region lying within the circle having diameter equal to the current point size and centered at the point's (x_w, y_w). The coverage value for each fragment is the window coordinate area of the intersection of the circular region with the corresponding pixel square. This value is saved and used in the final rasterization step. The data associated with each fragment is the data associated with the point being rasterized.

Not all sizes are supported when point antialiasing is enabled. If an unsupported size is requested, the nearest supported size is used. Only size 1 is guaranteed to be supported; others depend on the implementation. To query the range of supported sizes and the size difference between supported sizes within the range, call **glGet** with arguments **GL_SMOOTH_POINT_SIZE_RANGE** and **GL_SMOOTH_POINT_SIZE_GRANULARITY**. For aliased points, query the supported ranges and granularity with **glGet** with arguments **GL_ALIASED_POINT_SIZE_RANGE** and **GL_ALIASED_POINT_SIZE_GRANULARITY**.

NOTES

The point size specified by **glPointSize** is always returned when **GL_POINT_SIZE** is queried. Clamping and rounding for aliased and antialiased points have no effect on the specified value.

A non-antialiased point size may be clamped to an implementation-dependent maximum. Although this maximum cannot be queried, it must be no less than the maximum value for antialiased points, rounded to the nearest integer value.

GL_POINT_SIZE_RANGE and **GL_POINT_SIZE_GRANULARITY** are deprecated in GL versions 1.2 and greater. Their functionality has been replaced by **GL_SMOOTH_POINT_SIZE_RANGE** and **GL_SMOOTH_POINT_SIZE_GRANULARITY**.

ERRORS

GL_INVALID_VALUE is generated if *size* is less than or equal to 0.

GL_INVALID_OPERATION is generated if **glPointSize** is executed between the execution of **glBegin** and the corresponding execution of **glEnd**.

ASSOCIATED GETS

glGet with argument **GL_POINT_SIZE**
glGet with argument **GL_ALIASED_POINT_SIZE_RANGE**
glGet with argument **GL_ALIASED_POINT_SIZE_GRANULARITY**
glGet with argument **GL_SMOOTH_POINT_SIZE_RANGE**
glGet with argument **GL_SMOOTH_POINT_SIZE_GRANULARITY**
glIsEnabled with argument **GL_POINT_SMOOTH**

SEE ALSO

glEnable

NAME

　　glPolygonMode – select a polygon rasterization mode

C SPECIFICATION

　　void **glPolygonMode**(GLenum *face*,
　　　　　　　　　　　　GLenum *mode*)

PARAMETERS

　　face Specifies the polygons that *mode* applies to. Must be **GL_FRONT** for front-facing polygons, **GL_BACK** for back-facing polygons, or **GL_FRONT_AND_BACK** for front- and back-facing polygons.

　　mode
　　　　Specifies how polygons will be rasterized. Accepted values are **GL_POINT**, **GL_LINE**, and **GL_FILL**. The initial value is **GL_FILL** for both front- and back-facing polygons.

DESCRIPTION

　　glPolygonMode controls the interpretation of polygons for rasterization. *face* describes which polygons *mode* applies to: front-facing polygons (**GL_FRONT**), back-facing polygons (**GL_BACK**), or both (**GL_FRONT_AND_BACK**). The polygon mode affects only the final rasterization of polygons. In particular, a polygon's vertices are lit and the polygon is clipped and possibly culled before these modes are applied.

　　Three modes are defined and can be specified in *mode*:

　　GL_POINT　　Polygon vertices that are marked as the start of a boundary edge are drawn as points. Point attributes such as **GL_POINT_SIZE** and **GL_POINT_SMOOTH** control the rasterization of the points. Polygon rasterization attributes other than **GL_POLYGON_MODE** have no effect.

　　GL_LINE　　Boundary edges of the polygon are drawn as line segments. They are treated as connected line segments for line stippling; the line stipple counter and pattern are not reset between segments (see **glLineStipple**). Line attributes such as **GL_LINE_WIDTH** and **GL_LINE_SMOOTH** control the rasterization of the lines. Polygon rasterization attributes other than **GL_POLYGON_MODE** have no effect.

　　GL_FILL　　The interior of the polygon is filled. Polygon attributes such as **GL_POLYGON_STIPPLE** and **GL_POLYGON_SMOOTH** control the rasterization of the polygon.

EXAMPLES

To draw a surface with filled back-facing polygons and outlined front-facing polygons, call

```
glPolygonMode(GL_FRONT, GL_LINE);
```

NOTES

Vertices are marked as boundary or nonboundary with an edge flag. Edge flags are generated internally by the GL when it decomposes polygons; they can be set explicitly using **glEdgeFlag**.

ERRORS

GL_INVALID_ENUM is generated if either *face* or *mode* is not an accepted value.

GL_INVALID_OPERATION is generated if **glPolygonMode** is executed between the execution of **glBegin** and the corresponding execution of **glEnd**.

ASSOCIATED GETS

glGet with argument **GL_POLYGON_MODE**

SEE ALSO

glBegin, **glEdgeFlag**, **glLineStipple**, **glLineWidth**, **glPointSize**, **glPolygonStipple**

NAME

glPolygonOffset – set the scale and units used to calculate depth values

C SPECIFICATION

void **glPolygonOffset**(GLfloat *factor*,
                                        GLfloat *units*)

PARAMETERS

factor Specifies a scale factor that is used to create a variable depth offset for each polygon. The initial value is 0.

units Is multiplied by an implementation-specific value to create a constant depth offset. The initial value is 0.

DESCRIPTION

When **GL_POLYGON_OFFSET_FILL**, **GL_POLYGON_OFFSET_LINE**, or **GL_POLYGON_OFFSET_POINT** is enabled, each fragment's *depth* value will be offset after it is interpolated from the *depth* values of the appropriate vertices. The value of the offset is *factor * DZ + r * units*, where *DZ* is a measurement of the change in depth relative to the screen area of the polygon, and *r* is the smallest value that is guaranteed to produce a resolvable offset for a given implementation. The offset is added before the depth test is performed and before the value is written into the depth buffer.

glPolygonOffset is useful for rendering hidden-line images, for applying decals to surfaces, and for rendering solids with highlighted edges.

NOTES

glPolygonOffset is available only if the GL version is 1.1 or greater.

glPolygonOffset has no effect on depth coordinates placed in the feedback buffer.

glPolygonOffset has no effect on selection.

ERRORS

GL_INVALID_OPERATION is generated if **glPolygonOffset** is executed between the execution of **glBegin** and the corresponding execution of **glEnd**.

ASSOCIATED GETS

glIsEnabled with argument **GL_POLYGON_OFFSET_FILL**, **GL_POLYGON_OFFSET_LINE**, or **GL_POLYGON_OFFSET_POINT**.

glGet with argument **GL_POLYGON_OFFSET_FACTOR** or **GL_POLYGON_OFFSET_UNITS**.

SEE ALSO

glDepthFunc, **glEnable**, **glGet**, **glIsEnabled**

NAME

glPolygonStipple – set the polygon stippling pattern

C SPECIFICATION

void **glPolygonStipple**(const GLubyte *mask*)

PARAMETERS

mask Specifies a pointer to a 32 × 32 stipple pattern that will be unpacked from memory in the same way that **glDrawPixels** unpacks pixels.

DESCRIPTION

Polygon stippling, like line stippling (see **glLineStipple**), masks out certain fragments produced by rasterization, creating a pattern. Stippling is independent of polygon antialiasing.

mask is a pointer to a 32 × 32 stipple pattern that is stored in memory just like the pixel data supplied to a **glDrawPixels** call with *height* and *width* both equal to 32, a pixel format of **GL_COLOR_INDEX**, and data type of **GL_BITMAP**. That is, the stipple pattern is represented as a 32 × 32 array of 1-bit color indices packed in unsigned bytes. **glPixelStore** parameters like **GL_UNPACK_SWAP_BYTES** and **GL_UNPACK_LSB_FIRST** affect the assembling of the bits into a stipple pattern. Pixel transfer operations (shift, offset, pixel map) are not applied to the stipple image, however.

To enable and disable polygon stippling, call **glEnable** and **glDisable** with argument **GL_POLYGON_STIPPLE**. Polygon stippling is initially disabled. If it's enabled, a rasterized polygon fragment with window coordinates x_w and y_w is sent to the next stage of the GL if and only if the (x_w mod 32)th bit in the (y_w mod 32)th row of the stipple pattern is 1 (one). When polygon stippling is disabled, it is as if the stipple pattern consists of all 1's.

ERRORS

GL_INVALID_OPERATION is generated if **glPolygonStipple** is executed between the execution of **glBegin** and the corresponding execution of **glEnd**.

ASSOCIATED GETS

glGetPolygonStipple
glIsEnabled with argument **GL_POLYGON_STIPPLE**

SEE ALSO

glDrawPixels, **glLineStipple**, **glPixelStore**, **glPixelTransfer**

NAME

glPrioritizeTextures – set texture residence priority

C SPECIFICATION

void **glPrioritizeTextures**(GLsizei *n*,
                               const GLuint **textures*,
                               const GLclampf **priorities*)

PARAMETERS

n   Specifies the number of textures to be prioritized.

textures   Specifies an array containing the names of the textures to be prioritized.

priorities Specifies an array containing the texture priorities. A priority given in an element of *priorities* applies to the texture named by the corresponding element of *textures*.

DESCRIPTION

glPrioritizeTextures assigns the *n* texture priorities given in *priorities* to the *n* textures named in *textures*.

The GL establishes a "working set" of textures that are resident in texture memory. These textures may be bound to a texture target much more efficiently than textures that are not resident. By specifying a priority for each texture, **glPrioritizeTextures** allows applications to guide the GL implementation in determining which textures should be resident.

The priorities given in *priorities* are clamped to the range [0,1] before they are assigned. 0 indicates the lowest priority; textures with priority 0 are least likely to be resident. 1 indicates the highest priority; textures with priority 1 are most likely to be resident. However, textures are not guaranteed to be resident until they are used.

glPrioritizeTextures silently ignores attempts to prioritize texture 0, or any texture name that does not correspond to an existing texture.

glPrioritizeTextures does not require that any of the textures named by *textures* be bound to a texture target. **glTexParameter** may also be used to set a texture's priority, but only if the texture is currently bound. This is the only way to set the priority of a default texture.

NOTES

glPrioritizeTextures is available only if the GL version is 1.1 or greater.

ERRORS

GL_INVALID_VALUE is generated if *n* is negative.

GL_INVALID_OPERATION is generated if **glPrioritizeTextures** is executed between the execution of **glBegin** and the corresponding execution of **glEnd**.

ASSOCIATED GETS

glGetTexParameter with parameter name **GL_TEXTURE_PRIORITY** retrieves the priority of a currently bound texture.

SEE ALSO

glAreTexturesResident, **glBindTexture**, **glCopyTexImage1D**, **glCopyTexImage2D**, **glTexImage1D**, **glTexImage2D**, **glTexImage3D**, **glTexParameter**

NAME

glPushAttrib, glPopAttrib – push and pop the server attribute stack

C SPECIFICATION

void **glPushAttrib**(GLbitfield *mask*)

PARAMETERS

mask Specifies a mask that indicates which attributes to save. Values for *mask* are listed below.

C SPECIFICATION

void **glPopAttrib**(void)

DESCRIPTION

glPushAttrib takes one argument, a mask that indicates which groups of state variables to save on the attribute stack. Symbolic constants are used to set bits in the mask. *mask* is typically constructed by ORing several of these constants together. The special mask **GL_ALL_ATTRIB_BITS** can be used to save all stackable states.

The symbolic mask constants and their associated GL state are as follows (the second column lists which attributes are saved):

GL_ACCUM_BUFFER_BIT	Accumulation buffer clear value
GL_COLOR_BUFFER_BIT	**GL_ALPHA_TEST** enable bit Alpha test function and reference value **GL_BLEND** enable bit Blending source and destination functions Constant blend color Blending equation **GL_DITHER** enable bit **GL_DRAW_BUFFER** setting **GL_COLOR_LOGIC_OP** enable bit **GL_INDEX_LOGIC_OP** enable bit Logic op function Color mode and index mode clear values Color mode and index mode writemasks
GL_CURRENT_BIT	Current RGBA color Current color index Current normal vector Current texture coordinates

	Current raster position
	GL_CURRENT_RASTER_POSITION_VALID flag
	RGBA color associated with current raster position
	Color index associated with current raster position
	Texture coordinates associated with current raster positi◼
	GL_EDGE_FLAG flag
GL_DEPTH_BUFFER_BIT	**GL_DEPTH_TEST** enable bit
	Depth buffer test function
	Depth buffer clear value
	GL_DEPTH_WRITEMASK enable bit
GL_ENABLE_BIT	**GL_ALPHA_TEST** flag
	GL_AUTO_NORMAL flag
	GL_BLEND flag
	Enable bits for the user-definable clipping planes
	GL_COLOR_MATERIAL
	GL_CULL_FACE flag
	GL_DEPTH_TEST flag
	GL_DITHER flag
	GL_FOG flag
	GL_LIGHTi where $0 <= i <$**GL_MAX_LIGHTS**
	GL_LIGHTING flag
	GL_LINE_SMOOTH flag
	GL_LINE_STIPPLE flag
	GL_COLOR_LOGIC_OP flag
	GL_INDEX_LOGIC_OP flag
	GL_MAP1_x where x is a map type
	GL_MAP2_x where x is a map type
	GL_NORMALIZE flag
	GL_POINT_SMOOTH flag
	GL_POLYGON_OFFSET_LINE flag
	GL_POLYGON_OFFSET_FILL flag
	GL_POLYGON_OFFSET_POINT flag
	GL_POLYGON_SMOOTH flag
	GL_POLYGON_STIPPLE flag
	GL_SCISSOR_TEST flag
	GL_STENCIL_TEST flag
	GL_TEXTURE_1D flag
	GL_TEXTURE_2D flag
	GL_TEXTURE_3D flag

Flags **GL_TEXTURE_GEN_***x* where *x* is S, T, R, or Q

GL_EVAL_BIT	**GL_MAP1_***x* enable bits, where *x* is a map type
	GL_MAP2_*x* enable bits, where *x* is a map type
	1D grid endpoints and divisions
	2D grid endpoints and divisions
	GL_AUTO_NORMAL enable bit
GL_FOG_BIT	**GL_FOG** enable bit
	Fog color
	Fog density
	Linear fog start
	Linear fog end
	Fog index
	GL_FOG_MODE value
GL_HINT_BIT	**GL_PERSPECTIVE_CORRECTION_HINT** setting
	GL_POINT_SMOOTH_HINT setting
	GL_LINE_SMOOTH_HINT setting
	GL_POLYGON_SMOOTH_HINT setting
	GL_FOG_HINT setting
GL_LIGHTING_BIT	**GL_COLOR_MATERIAL** enable bit
	GL_COLOR_MATERIAL_FACE value
	Color material parameters that are tracking the current color
	Ambient scene color
	GL_LIGHT_MODEL_LOCAL_VIEWER value
	GL_LIGHT_MODEL_TWO_SIDE setting
	GL_LIGHTING enable bit
	Enable bit for each light
	Ambient, diffuse, and specular intensity for each light
	Direction, position, exponent, and cutoff angle for each light
	Constant, linear, and quadratic attenuation factors for each light
	Ambient, diffuse, specular, and emissive color for each material
	Ambient, diffuse, and specular color indices for each material
	Specular exponent for each material
	GL_SHADE_MODEL setting
GL_LINE_BIT	**GL_LINE_SMOOTH** flag
	GL_LINE_STIPPLE enable bit
	Line stipple pattern and repeat counter

	Line width
GL_LIST_BIT	**GL_LIST_BASE** setting
GL_PIXEL_MODE_BIT	**GL_RED_BIAS** and **GL_RED_SCALE** settings **GL_GREEN_BIAS** and **GL_GREEN_SCALE** values **GL_BLUE_BIAS** and **GL_BLUE_SCALE** **GL_ALPHA_BIAS** and **GL_ALPHA_SCALE** **GL_DEPTH_BIAS** and **GL_DEPTH_SCALE** **GL_INDEX_OFFSET** and **GL_INDEX_SHIFT** values **GL_MAP_COLOR** and **GL_MAP_STENCIL** flags **GL_ZOOM_X** and **GL_ZOOM_Y** factors **GL_READ_BUFFER** setting
GL_POINT_BIT	**GL_POINT_SMOOTH** flag Point size
GL_POLYGON_BIT	**GL_CULL_FACE** enable bit **GL_CULL_FACE_MODE** value **GL_FRONT_FACE** indicator **GL_POLYGON_MODE** setting **GL_POLYGON_SMOOTH** flag **GL_POLYGON_STIPPLE** enable bit **GL_POLYGON_OFFSET_FILL** flag **GL_POLYGON_OFFSET_LINE** flag **GL_POLYGON_OFFSET_POINT** flag **GL_POLYGON_OFFSET_FACTOR** **GL_POLYGON_OFFSET_UNITS**
GL_POLYGON_STIPPLE_BIT	Polygon stipple image
GL_SCISSOR_BIT	**GL_SCISSOR_TEST** flag Scissor box
GL_STENCIL_BUFFER_BIT	**GL_STENCIL_TEST** enable bit Stencil function and reference value Stencil value mask Stencil fail, pass, and depth buffer pass actions Stencil buffer clear value Stencil buffer writemask

GL_TEXTURE_BIT	Enable bits for the four texture coordinates
	Border color for each texture image
	Minification function for each texture image
	Magnification function for each texture image
	Texture coordinates and wrap mode for each texture image
	Color and mode for each texture environment
	Enable bits **GL_TEXTURE_GEN_**_x_, _x_ is S, T, R, and Q
	GL_TEXTURE_GEN_MODE setting for S, T, R, and Q
	glTexGen plane equations for S, T, R, and Q
	Current texture bindings (for example, **GL_TEXTURE_BINDING_2D**)
GL_TRANSFORM_BIT	Coefficients of the six clipping planes
	Enable bits for the user-definable clipping planes
	GL_MATRIX_MODE value
	GL_NORMALIZE flag
	GL_RESCALE_NORMAL flag
GL_VIEWPORT_BIT	Depth range (near and far)
	Viewport origin and extent

glPopAttrib restores the values of the state variables saved with the last **glPushAttrib** command. Those not saved are left unchanged.

It is an error to push attributes onto a full stack, or to pop attributes off an empty stack. In either case, the error flag is set and no other change is made to GL state.

Initially, the attribute stack is empty.

NOTES

Not all values for GL state can be saved on the attribute stack. For example, render mode state, and select and feedback state cannot be saved. Client state must be saved with **glPushClientAttrib**.

The depth of the attribute stack depends on the implementation, but it must be at least 16.

When the **GL_ARB_multitexture** extension is supported, pushing and popping texture state apples to all supported texture units.

ERRORS

GL_STACK_OVERFLOW is generated if **glPushAttrib** is called while the attribute stack is full.

GL_STACK_UNDERFLOW is generated if **glPopAttrib** is called while the attribute stack is empty.

GL_INVALID_OPERATION is generated if **glPushAttrib** or **glPopAttrib** is executed between the execution of **glBegin** and the corresponding execution of **glEnd**.

ASSOCIATED GETS

glGet with argument **GL_ATTRIB_STACK_DEPTH**

glGet with argument **GL_MAX_ATTRIB_STACK_DEPTH**

SEE ALSO

glGet, glGetClipPlane, glGetError, glGetLight, glGetMap, glGetMaterial, glGetPixelMap, glGetPolygonStipple, glGetString, glGetTexEnv, glGetTexGen, glGetTexImage, glGetTexLevelParameter, glGetTexParameter, glIsEnabled, glPushClientAttrib

NAME

glPushClientAttrib, glPopClientAttrib – push and pop the client attribute stack

C SPECIFICATION

void **glPushClientAttrib**(GLbitfield *mask*)

PARAMETERS

mask Specifies a mask that indicates which attributes to save. Values for *mask* are listed below.

C SPECIFICATION

void **glPopClientAttrib**(void)

DESCRIPTION

glPushClientAttrib takes one argument, a mask that indicates which groups of client-state variables to save on the client attribute stack. Symbolic constants are used to set bits in the mask. *mask* is typically constructed by OR'ing several of these constants together. The special mask **GL_CLIENT_ALL_ATTRIB_BITS** can be used to save all stackable client state.

The symbolic mask constants and their associated GL client state are as follows (the second column lists which attributes are saved):

GL_CLIENT_PIXEL_STORE_BIT   Pixel storage modes
GL_CLIENT_VERTEX_ARRAY_BIT   Vertex arrays (and enables)

glPopClientAttrib restores the values of the client-state variables saved with the last **glPushClientAttrib**. Those not saved are left unchanged.

It is an error to push attributes onto a full client attribute stack, or to pop attributes off an empty stack. In either case, the error flag is set, and no other change is made to GL state.

Initially, the client attribute stack is empty.

NOTES

glPushClientAttrib is available only if the GL version is 1.1 or greater.

Not all values for GL client state can be saved on the attribute stack. For example, select and feedback state cannot be saved.

The depth of the attribute stack depends on the implementation, but it must be at least 16.

Use **glPushAttrib** and **glPopAttrib** to push and restore state which is kept on the server. Only pixel storage modes and vertex array state may be pushed and popped with **glPushClientAttrib** and **glPopClientAttrib**.

When the **GL_ARB_multitexture** extension is supported, pushing and popping client vertex array state apples to all supported texture units, and the active client texture state.

ERRORS

GL_STACK_OVERFLOW is generated if **glPushClientAttrib** is called while the attribute stack is full.

GL_STACK_UNDERFLOW is generated if **glPopClientAttrib** is called while the attribute stack is empty.

ASSOCIATED GETS

glGet with argument **GL_ATTRIB_STACK_DEPTH**
glGet with argument **GL_MAX_CLIENT_ATTRIB_STACK_DEPTH**

SEE ALSO

glColorPointer, **glDisableClientState**, **glEdgeFlagPointer**, **glEnableClientState**, **glGet**, **glGetError**, **glIndexPointer**, **glNormalPointer**, **glNewList**, **glPixelStore**, **glPushAttrib**, **glTexCoordPointer**, **glVertexPointer**

NAME

glPushMatrix, glPopMatrix – push and pop the current matrix stack

C SPECIFICATION

void **glPushMatrix**(void)

C SPECIFICATION

void **glPopMatrix**(void)

DESCRIPTION

There is a stack of matrices for each of the matrix modes. In **GL_MODELVIEW** mode, the stack depth is at least 32. In the other modes, **GL_COLOR**, const(PROJECTION), and **GL_TEXTURE**, the depth is at least 2. The current matrix in any mode is the matrix on the top of the stack for that mode.

glPushMatrix pushes the current matrix stack down by one, duplicating the current matrix. That is, after a **glPushMatrix** call, the matrix on top of the stack is identical to the one below it.

glPopMatrix pops the current matrix stack, replacing the current matrix with the one below it on the stack.

Initially, each of the stacks contains one matrix, an identity matrix.

It is an error to push a full matrix stack, or to pop a matrix stack that contains only a single matrix. In either case, the error flag is set and no other change is made to GL state.

ERRORS

GL_STACK_OVERFLOW is generated if **glPushMatrix** is called while the current matrix stack is full.

GL_STACK_UNDERFLOW is generated if **glPopMatrix** is called while the current matrix stack contains only a single matrix.

GL_INVALID_OPERATION is generated if **glPushMatrix** or **glPopMatrix** is executed between the execution of **glBegin** and the corresponding execution of **glEnd**.

ASSOCIATED GETS

glGet with argument **GL_MATRIX_MODE**
glGet with argument **GL_COLOR_MATRIX**
glGet with argument **GL_MODELVIEW_MATRIX**
glGet with argument **GL_PROJECTION_MATRIX**
glGet with argument **GL_TEXTURE_MATRIX**
glGet with argument **GL_COLOR_STACK_DEPTH**
glGet with argument **GL_MODELVIEW_STACK_DEPTH**
glGet with argument **GL_PROJECTION_STACK_DEPTH**

glGet with argument **GL_TEXTURE_STACK_DEPTH**
glGet with argument **GL_MAX_MODELVIEW_STACK_DEPTH**
glGet with argument **GL_MAX_PROJECTION_STACK_DEPTH**
glGet with argument **GL_MAX_TEXTURE_STACK_DEPTH**

SEE ALSO

glFrustum, **glLoadIdentity**, **glLoadMatrix**, **glMatrixMode**, **glMultMatrix**, **glOrtho**, **glRotate**, **glScale**, **glTranslate**, **glViewport**

NAME

glPushName, **glPopName** – push and pop the name stack

C SPECIFICATION

void **glPushName**(GLuint *name*)

PARAMETERS

name   Specifies a name that will be pushed onto the name stack.

C SPECIFICATION

void **glPopName**(void)

DESCRIPTION

The name stack is used during selection mode to allow sets of rendering commands to be uniquely identified. It consists of an ordered set of unsigned integers and is initially empty.

glPushName causes *name* to be pushed onto the name stack. **glPopName** pops one name off the top of the stack.

The maximum name stack depth is implementation-dependent; call **GL_MAX_NAME_STACK_DEPTH** to find out the value for a particular implementation. It is an error to push a name onto a full stack, or to pop a name off an empty stack. It is also an error to manipulate the name stack between the execution of **glBegin** and the corresponding execution of **glEnd**. In any of these cases, the error flag is set and no other change is made to GL state.

The name stack is always empty while the render mode is not **GL_SELECT**. Calls to **glPushName** or **glPopName** while the render mode is not **GL_SELECT** are ignored.

ERRORS

GL_STACK_OVERFLOW is generated if **glPushName** is called while the name stack is full.

GL_STACK_UNDERFLOW is generated if **glPopName** is called while the name stack is empty.

GL_INVALID_OPERATION is generated if **glPushName** or **glPopName** is executed between a call to **glBegin** and the corresponding call to **glEnd**.

ASSOCIATED GETS

glGet with argument **GL_NAME_STACK_DEPTH**

glGet with argument **GL_MAX_NAME_STACK_DEPTH**

SEE ALSO

glInitNames, glLoadName, glRenderMode, glSelectBuffer

NAME

glRasterPos2d, **glRasterPos2f**, **glRasterPos2i**, **glRasterPos2s**, **glRasterPos3d**, **glRasterPos3f**, **glRasterPos3i**, **glRasterPos3s**, **glRasterPos4d**, **glRasterPos4f**, **glRasterPos4i**, **glRasterPos4s**, **glRasterPos2dv**, **glRasterPos2fv**, **glRasterPos2iv**, **glRasterPos2sv**, **glRasterPos3dv**, **glRasterPos3fv**, **glRasterPos3iv**, **glRasterPos3sv**, **glRasterPos4dv**, **glRasterPos4fv**, **glRasterPos4iv**, **glRasterPos4sv** – specify the raster position for pixel operations

C SPECIFICATION

void **glRasterPos2d**(GLdouble *x*,
                GLdouble *y*)

void **glRasterPos2f**(GLfloat *x*,
                GLfloat *y*)

void **glRasterPos2i**(GLint *x*,
                GLint *y*)

void **glRasterPos2s**(GLshort *x*,
                GLshort *y*)

void **glRasterPos3d**(GLdouble *x*,
                GLdouble *y*,
                GLdouble *z*)

void **glRasterPos3f**(GLfloat *x*,
                GLfloat *y*,
                GLfloat *z*)

void **glRasterPos3i**(GLint *x*,
                GLint *y*,
                GLint *z*)

void **glRasterPos3s**(GLshort *x*,
                GLshort *y*,
                GLshort *z*)

void **glRasterPos4d**(GLdouble *x*,
                GLdouble *y*,
                GLdouble *z*,
                GLdouble *w*)

void **glRasterPos4f**(GLfloat *x*,
                GLfloat *y*,
                GLfloat *z*,
                GLfloat *w*)

void **glRasterPos4i**(GLint *x*,
                GLint *y*,
                GLint *z*,
                GLint *w*)

void **glRasterPos4s**(GLshort *x*,
                GLshort *y*,

GLshort *z*,
GLshort *w*)

PARAMETERS

x, y, z, w

Specify the *x*, *y*, *z*, and *w* object coordinates (if present) for the raster position.

C SPECIFICATION

void **glRasterPos2dv**(const GLdouble **v*)
void **glRasterPos2fv**(const GLfloat **v*)
void **glRasterPos2iv**(const GLint **v*)
void **glRasterPos2sv**(const GLshort **v*)
void **glRasterPos3dv**(const GLdouble **v*)
void **glRasterPos3fv**(const GLfloat **v*)
void **glRasterPos3iv**(const GLint **v*)
void **glRasterPos3sv**(const GLshort **v*)
void **glRasterPos4dv**(const GLdouble **v*)
void **glRasterPos4fv**(const GLfloat **v*)
void **glRasterPos4iv**(const GLint **v*)
void **glRasterPos4sv**(const GLshort **v*)

PARAMETERS

v   Specifies a pointer to an array of two, three, or four elements, specifying *x*, *y*, *z*, and *w* coordinates, respectively.

DESCRIPTION

The GL maintains a 3D position in window coordinates. This position, called the raster position, is used to position pixel and bitmap write operations. It is maintained with subpixel accuracy. See **glBitmap**, **glDrawPixels**, and **glCopyPixels**.

The current raster position consists of three window coordinates (*x*, *y*, *z*), a clip coordinate value (*w*), an eye coordinate distance, a valid bit, and associated color data and texture coordinates. The *w* coordinate is a clip coordinate, because *w* is not projected to window coordinates. **glRasterPos4** specifies object coordinates *x*, *y*, *z*, and *w* explicitly. **glRasterPos3** specifies object coordinate *x*, *y*, and *z* explicitly, while *w* is implicitly set to 1. **glRasterPos2** uses the argument values for *x* and *y* while implicitly setting *z* and *w* to 0 and 1.

The object coordinates presented by **glRasterPos** are treated just like those of a **glVertex** command: They are transformed by the current modelview and projection matrices and passed to the clipping stage. If the vertex is not culled, then it is projected and scaled to window coordinates, which become the new current raster position, and the **GL_CURRENT_RASTER_POSITION_VALID** flag is set. If the vertex *is* culled, then the valid bit is cleared and the current raster position and associated color and texture coordinates are undefined.

The current raster position also includes some associated color data and texture coordinates. If lighting is enabled, then GL_CURRENT_RASTER_COLOR (in RGBA mode) or GL_CURRENT_RASTER_INDEX (in color index mode) is set to the color produced by the lighting calculation (see **glLight**, **glLightModel**, and **glShadeModel**). If lighting is disabled, current color (in RGBA mode, state variable GL_CURRENT_COLOR) or color index (in color index mode, state variable GL_CURRENT_INDEX) is used to update the current raster color.

Likewise, GL_CURRENT_RASTER_TEXTURE_COORDS is updated as a function of GL_CURRENT_TEXTURE_COORDS, based on the texture matrix and the texture generation functions (see **glTexGen**). Finally, the distance from the origin of the eye coordinate system to the vertex as transformed by only the modelview matrix replaces GL_CURRENT_RASTER_DISTANCE.

Initially, the current raster position is (0, 0, 0, 1), the current raster distance is 0, the valid bit is set, the associated RGBA color is (1, 1, 1, 1), the associated color index is 1, and the associated texture coordinates are (0, 0, 0, 1). In RGBA mode, GL_CURRENT_RASTER_INDEX is always 1; in color index mode, the current raster RGBA color always maintains its initial value.

NOTES

The raster position is modified both by **glRasterPos** and by **glBitmap**.

When the raster position coordinates are invalid, drawing commands that are based on the raster position are ignored (that is, they do not result in changes to GL state).

Calling **glDrawElements**, or **glDrawRangeElements** may leave the current color or index indeterminate. If **glRasterPos** is executed while the current color or index is indeterminate, the current raster color or current raster index remains indeterminate.

To set a valid raster position outside the viewport, first set a valid raster position, then call **glBitmap** with NULL as the *bitmap* parameter.

When the **GL_ARB_imaging** extension is supported, there are distinct raster texture coordinates for each texture unit. Each texture unit's current ratster texture coordinates are updated by **glRasterPos**.

ERRORS

GL_INVALID_OPERATION is generated if **glRasterPos** is executed between the execution of **glBegin** and the corresponding execution of **glEnd**.

ASSOCIATED GETS

glGet with argument GL_CURRENT_RASTER_POSITION
glGet with argument GL_CURRENT_RASTER_POSITION_VALID
glGet with argument GL_CURRENT_RASTER_DISTANCE
glGet with argument GL_CURRENT_RASTER_COLOR

glGet with argument **GL_CURRENT_RASTER_INDEX**

glGet with argument **GL_CURRENT_RASTER_TEXTURE_COORDS**

SEE ALSO

glBitmap, **glCopyPixels**, **glDrawArrays**, **glDrawElements**, **glDrawRangeElements**, **glDrawPixels**, **glTexCoord**, **glTexGen**, **glVertex**

NAME

glReadBuffer – select a color buffer source for pixels

C SPECIFICATION

void **glReadBuffer**(GLenum *mode*)

PARAMETERS

mode Specifies a color buffer. Accepted values are **GL_FRONT_LEFT**, **GL_FRONT_RIGHT**, **GL_BACK_LEFT**, **GL_BACK_RIGHT**, **GL_FRONT**, **GL_BACK**, **GL_LEFT**, **GL_RIGHT**, and **GL_AUX***i*, where *i* is between 0 and **GL_AUX_BUFFERS** −1.

DESCRIPTION

glReadBuffer specifies a color buffer as the source for subsequent **glReadPixels**, **glCopyTexImage1D**, **glCopyTexImage2D**, **glCopyTexSubImage1D**, **glCopyTexSubImage2D**, **glCopyTexSubImage3D**, and **glCopyPixels** commands. *mode* accepts one of twelve or more predefined values. (**GL_AUX0** through **GL_AUX3** are always defined.) In a fully configured system, **GL_FRONT**, **GL_LEFT**, and **GL_FRONT_LEFT** all name the front left buffer, **GL_FRONT_RIGHT** and **GL_RIGHT** name the front right buffer, and **GL_BACK_LEFT** and **GL_BACK** name the back left buffer.

Nonstereo double-buffered configurations have only a front left and a back left buffer. Single-buffered configurations have a front left and a front right buffer if stereo, and only a front left buffer if nonstereo. It is an error to specify a nonexistent buffer to **glReadBuffer**.

mode is initially **GL_FRONT** in single-buffered configurations, and **GL_BACK** in double-buffered configurations.

ERRORS

GL_INVALID_ENUM is generated if *mode* is not one of the twelve (or more) accepted values.

GL_INVALID_OPERATION is generated if *mode* specifies a buffer that does not exist.

GL_INVALID_OPERATION is generated if **glReadBuffer** is executed between the execution of **glBegin** and the corresponding execution of **glEnd**.

ASSOCIATED GETS

glGet with argument **GL_READ_BUFFER**

SEE ALSO

glCopyPixels, **glCopyTexImage1D**, **glCopyTexImage2D**, **glCopyTexSubImage1D**, **glCopyTexSubImage2D**, **glCopyTexSubImage3D**, **glDrawBuffer**, **glReadPixels**

NAME

glReadPixels – read a block of pixels from the frame buffer

C SPECIFICATION

void **glReadPixels**(GLint *x*,
                        GLint *y*,
                        GLsizei *width*,
                        GLsizei *height*,
                        GLenum *format*,
                        GLenum *type*,
                        GLvoid **pixels*)

PARAMETERS

x, y

> Specify the window coordinates of the first pixel that is read from the frame buffer. This location is the lower left corner of a rectangular block of pixels.

width, height

> Specify the dimensions of the pixel rectangle. *width* and *height* of one correspond to a single pixel.

format

> Specifies the format of the pixel data. The following symbolic values are accepted: **GL_COLOR_INDEX**, **GL_STENCIL_INDEX**, **GL_DEPTH_COMPONENT**, **GL_RED**, **GL_GREEN**, **GL_BLUE**, **GL_ALPHA**, **GL_RGB**, **GL_BGR**, **GL_RGBA**, **GL_BGRA**, **GL_LUMINANCE**, and **GL_LUMINANCE_ALPHA**.

type

> Specifies the data type of the pixel data. Must be one of **GL_UNSIGNED_BYTE**, **GL_BYTE**, **GL_BITMAP**, **GL_UNSIGNED_SHORT**, **GL_SHORT**, **GL_UNSIGNED_INT**, **GL_INT**, **GL_FLOAT**, **GL_UNSIGNED_BYTE_3_3_2**, **GL_UNSIGNED_BYTE_2_3_3_REV**, **GL_UNSIGNED_SHORT_5_6_5**, **GL_UNSIGNED_SHORT_5_6_5_REV**, **GL_UNSIGNED_SHORT_4_4_4_4**, **GL_UNSIGNED_SHORT_4_4_4_4_REV**, **GL_UNSIGNED_SHORT_5_5_5_1**, **GL_UNSIGNED_SHORT_1_5_5_5_REV**, **GL_UNSIGNED_INT_8_8_8_8**, **GL_UNSIGNED_INT_8_8_8_8_REV**, **GL_UNSIGNED_INT_10_10_10_2**, or **GL_UNSIGNED_INT_2_10_10_10_REV**.

pixels

> Returns the pixel data.

DESCRIPTION

glReadPixels returns pixel data from the frame buffer, starting with the pixel whose lower left corner is at location (x, y), into client memory starting at location *pixels*. Several parameters control the processing of the pixel data before it is placed into client memory. These parameters are set with three commands: **glPixelStore**, **glPixelTransfer**, and **glPixelMap**. This reference page describes the effects on **glReadPixels** of most, but not all of the parameters specified by these three commands.

When the **GL_ARB_imaging** extension is supported, the pixel data may be processed by additional operations including color table lookup, color matrix tranformations, convolutions, histograms and minimum and maximun pixel value computations.

glReadPixels returns values from each pixel with lower left corner at ($x + i$, $y + j$) for $0 \le i < width$ and $0 \le j < height$. This pixel is said to be the ith pixel in the jth row. Pixels are returned in row order from the lowest to the highest row, left to right in each row.

format specifies the format for the returned pixel values; accepted values are:

GL_COLOR_INDEX

Color indices are read from the color buffer selected by **glReadBuffer**. Each index is converted to fixed point, shifted left or right depending on the value and sign of **GL_INDEX_SHIFT**, and added to **GL_INDEX_OFFSET**. If **GL_MAP_COLOR** is **GL_TRUE**, indices are replaced by their mappings in the table **GL_PIXEL_MAP_I_TO_I**.

GL_STENCIL_INDEX

Stencil values are read from the stencil buffer. Each index is converted to fixed point, shifted left or right depending on the value and sign of **GL_INDEX_SHIFT**, and added to **GL_INDEX_OFFSET**. If **GL_MAP_STENCIL** is **GL_TRUE**, indices are replaced by their mappings in the table **GL_PIXEL_MAP_S_TO_S**.

GL_DEPTH_COMPONENT

Depth values are read from the depth buffer. Each component is converted to floating point such that the minimum depth value maps to 0 and the maximum value maps to 1. Each component is then multiplied by **GL_DEPTH_SCALE**, added to **GL_DEPTH_BIAS**, and finally clamped to the range [0,1].

GL_RED

GL_GREEN

GL_BLUE

GL_ALPHA

GL_RGB

GL_BGR

GL_RGBA

GL_BGRA

GL_LUMINANCE

GL_LUMINANCE_ALPHA

Processing differs depending on whether color buffers store color indices or RGBA color components. If color indices are stored, they are read from the color buffer selected by **glReadBuffer**. Each index is converted to fixed point, shifted left or right depending on the value and sign of **GL_INDEX_SHIFT**, and added to **GL_INDEX_OFFSET**. Indices are then replaced by the red, green, blue, and alpha values obtained by indexing the tables **GL_PIXEL_MAP_I_TO_R**, **GL_PIXEL_MAP_I_TO_G**, **GL_PIXEL_MAP_I_TO_B**, and **GL_PIXEL_MAP_I_TO_A**. Each table must be of size 2^n, but n may be different for different tables. Before an index is used to look up a value in a table of size 2^n, it must be masked against 2^n-1.

If RGBA color components are stored in the color buffers, they are read from the color buffer selected by **glReadBuffer**. Each color component is converted to floating point such that zero intensity maps to 0.0 and full intensity maps to 1.0. Each component is then multiplied by **GL_c_SCALE** and added to **GL_c_BIAS**, where c is RED, GREEN, BLUE, or ALPHA. Finally, if **GL_MAP_COLOR** is **GL_TRUE**, each component is clamped to the range [0, 1], scaled to the size of its corresponding table, and is then replaced by its mapping in the table **GL_PIXEL_MAP_c_TO_c**, where c is R, G, B, or A.

Unneeded data is then discarded. For example, **GL_RED** discards the green, blue, and alpha components, while **GL_RGB** discards only the alpha component. **GL_LUMINANCE** computes a single-component value as the sum of the red, green, and blue components, and **GL_LUMINANCE_ALPHA** does the same, while keeping alpha as a second value. The final values are clamped to the range [0, 1].

The shift, scale, bias, and lookup factors just described are all specified by **glPixelTransfer**. The lookup table contents themselves are specified by **glPixelMap**.

Finally, the indices or components are converted to the proper format, as specified by *type*. If *format* is **GL_COLOR_INDEX** or **GL_STENCIL_INDEX** and *type* is not **GL_FLOAT**, each index is masked with the mask value given in the following table. If *type* is **GL_FLOAT**, then each integer index is converted to single-precision floating-point format.

If *format* is **GL_RED**, **GL_GREEN**, **GL_BLUE**, **GL_ALPHA**, **GL_RGB**, **GL_BGR**, **GL_RGBA**, **GL_BGRA**, **GL_LUMINANCE**, or **GL_LUMINANCE_ALPHA** and *type* is not **GL_FLOAT**, each component is multiplied by the multiplier shown in the following table. If type is **GL_FLOAT**, then each component is passed as is (or converted to the client's single-precision floating-point format if it is different from the one used by the GL).

type	index mask	component conversion
GL_UNSIGNED_BYTE	2^8-1	$(2^8-1)c$
GL_BYTE	2^7-1	$[(2^8-1)c-1]/2$
GL_BITMAP	1	1
GL_UNSIGNED_SHORT	$2^{16}-1$	$(2^{16}-1)c$
GL_SHORT	$2^{15}-1$	$[(2^{16}-1)c-1]/2$
GL_UNSIGNED_INT	$2^{32}-1$	$(2^{32}-1)c$
GL_INT	$2^{31}-1$	$[(2^{32}-1)c-1]/2$
GL_FLOAT	none	c

Return values are placed in memory as follows. If *format* is **GL_COLOR_INDEX**, **GL_STENCIL_INDEX**, **GL_DEPTH_COMPONENT**, **GL_RED**, **GL_GREEN**, **GL_BLUE**, **GL_ALPHA**, or **GL_LUMINANCE**, a single value is returned and the data for the ith pixel in the jth row is placed in location (j) *width* $+ i$. **GL_RGB** and **GL_BGR** return three values, **GL_RGBA** and **GL_BGRA** return four values, and **GL_LUMINANCE_ALPHA** returns two values for each pixel, with all values corresponding to a single pixel occupying contiguous space in *pixels*. Storage parameters set by **glPixelStore**, such as **GL_PACK_LSB_FIRST** and **GL_PACK_SWAP_BYTES**, affect the way that data is written into memory. See **glPixelStore** for a description.

NOTES

Values for pixels that lie outside the window connected to the current GL context are undefined.

If an error is generated, no change is made to the contents of *pixels*.

ERRORS

GL_INVALID_ENUM is generated if *format* or *type* is not an accepted value.

GL_INVALID_ENUM is generated if *type* is **GL_BITMAP** and *format* is not **GL_COLOR_INDEX** or **GL_STENCIL_INDEX**.

GL_INVALID_VALUE is generated if either *width* or *height* is negative.

GL_INVALID_OPERATION is generated if *format* is **GL_COLOR_INDEX** and the color buffers store RGBA color components.

GL_INVALID_OPERATION is generated if *format* is **GL_STENCIL_INDEX** and there is no stencil buffer.

GL_INVALID_OPERATION is generated if *format* is **GL_DEPTH_COMPONENT** and there is no depth buffer.

GL_INVALID_OPERATION is generated if **glReadPixels** is executed between the execution of **glBegin** and the corresponding execution of **glEnd**.

GL_INVALID_OPERATION is generated if *type* is one of **GL_UNSIGNED_BYTE_3_3_2**, **GL_UNSIGNED_BYTE_2_3_3_REV**, **GL_UNSIGNED_SHORT_5_6_5**, or **GL_UNSIGNED_SHORT_5_6_5_REV** and *format* is not **GL_RGB**.

GL_INVALID_OPERATION is generated if *type* is one of **GL_UNSIGNED_SHORT_4_4_4_4**, **GL_UNSIGNED_SHORT_4_4_4_4_REV**, **GL_UNSIGNED_SHORT_5_5_5_1**, **GL_UNSIGNED_SHORT_1_5_5_5_REV**, **GL_UNSIGNED_INT_8_8_8_8**, **GL_UNSIGNED_INT_8_8_8_8_REV**, **GL_UNSIGNED_INT_10_10_10_2**, or **GL_UNSIGNED_INT_2_10_10_10_REV** and *format* is neither **GL_RGBA** nor **GL_BGRA**.

The formats **GL_BGR**, and **GL_BGRA** and types **GL_UNSIGNED_BYTE_3_3_2**, **GL_UNSIGNED_BYTE_2_3_3_REV**, **GL_UNSIGNED_SHORT_5_6_5**, **GL_UNSIGNED_SHORT_5_6_5_REV**, **GL_UNSIGNED_SHORT_4_4_4_4**, **GL_UNSIGNED_SHORT_4_4_4_4_REV**, **GL_UNSIGNED_SHORT_5_5_5_1**, **GL_UNSIGNED_SHORT_1_5_5_5_REV**, **GL_UNSIGNED_INT_8_8_8_8**, **GL_UNSIGNED_INT_8_8_8_8_REV**, **GL_UNSIGNED_INT_10_10_10_2**, and **GL_UNSIGNED_INT_2_10_10_10_REV** are available only if the GL version is 1.2 or greater.

ASSOCIATED GETS

glGet with argument **GL_INDEX_MODE**

SEE ALSO

glCopyPixels, **glDrawPixels**, **glPixelMap**, **glPixelStore**, **glPixelTransfer**, **glReadBuffer**

NAME

glRectd, **glRectf**, **glRecti**, **glRects**, **glRectdv**, **glRectfv**, **glRectiv**, **glRectsv** – draw a rectangle

C SPECIFICATION

```
void glRectd( GLdouble x1,
              GLdouble y1,
              GLdouble x2,
              GLdouble y2 )
void glRectf( GLfloat x1,
              GLfloat y1,
              GLfloat x2,
              GLfloat y2 )
void glRecti( GLint x1,
              GLint y1,
              GLint x2,
              GLint y2 )
void glRects( GLshort x1,
              GLshort y1,
              GLshort x2,
              GLshort y2 )
```

PARAMETERS

x1, *y1*

> Specify one vertex of a rectangle.

x2, *y2*

> Specify the opposite vertex of the rectangle.

C SPECIFICATION

```
void glRectdv( const GLdouble *v1,
               const GLdouble *v2 )
void glRectfv( const GLfloat *v1,
               const GLfloat *v2 )
void glRectiv( const GLint *v1,
               const GLint *v2 )
void glRectsv( const GLshort *v1,
               const GLshort *v2 )
```

PARAMETERS

v1   Specifies a pointer to one vertex of a rectangle.

v2   Specifies a pointer to the opposite vertex of the rectangle.

DESCRIPTION

glRect supports efficient specification of rectangles as two corner points. Each rectangle command takes four arguments, organized either as two consecutive pairs of (x,y) coordinates, or as two pointers to arrays, each containing an (x,y) pair. The resulting rectangle is defined in the $z = 0$ plane.

glRect(*x1, y1, x2, y2*) is exactly equivalent to the following sequence:

```
glBegin(GL_POLYGON);
glVertex2(x1, y1);
glVertex2(x2, y1);
glVertex2(x2, y2);
glVertex2(x1, y2);
glEnd();
```

Note that if the second vertex is above and to the right of the first vertex, the rectangle is constructed with a counterclockwise winding.

ERRORS

GL_INVALID_OPERATION is generated if **glRect** is executed between the execution of **glBegin** and the corresponding execution of **glEnd**.

SEE ALSO

glBegin, **glVertex**

NAME

glRenderMode – set rasterization mode

C SPECIFICATION

GLint **glRenderMode**(GLenum *mode*)

PARAMETERS

mode Specifies the rasterization mode. Three values are accepted: **GL_RENDER**, **GL_SELECT**, and **GL_FEEDBACK**. The initial value is **GL_RENDER**.

DESCRIPTION

glRenderMode sets the rasterization mode. It takes one argument, *mode*, which can assume one of three predefined values:

GL_RENDER Render mode. Primitives are rasterized, producing pixel fragments, which are written into the frame buffer. This is the normal mode and also the default mode.

GL_SELECT Selection mode. No pixel fragments are produced, and no change to the frame buffer contents is made. Instead, a record of the names of primitives that would have been drawn if the render mode had been **GL_RENDER** is returned in a select buffer, which must be created (see **glSelectBuffer**) before selection mode is entered.

GL_FEEDBACK Feedback mode. No pixel fragments are produced, and no change to the frame buffer contents is made. Instead, the coordinates and attributes of vertices that would have been drawn if the render mode had been **GL_RENDER** is returned in a feedback buffer, which must be created (see **glFeedbackBuffer**) before feedback mode is entered.

The return value of **glRenderMode** is determined by the render mode at the time **glRenderMode** is called, rather than by *mode*. The values returned for the three render modes are as follows:

GL_RENDER 0.

GL_SELECT The number of hit records transferred to the select buffer.

GL_FEEDBACK The number of values (not vertices) transferred to the feedback buffer.

See the **glSelectBuffer** and **glFeedbackBuffer** reference pages for more details concerning selection and feedback operation.

NOTES

If an error is generated, **glRenderMode** returns 0 regardless of the current render mode.

ERRORS

GL_INVALID_ENUM is generated if *mode* is not one of the three accepted values.

GL_INVALID_OPERATION is generated if **glSelectBuffer** is called while the render mode is **GL_SELECT**, or if **glRenderMode** is called with argument **GL_SELECT** before **glSelectBuffer** is called at least once.

GL_INVALID_OPERATION is generated if **glFeedbackBuffer** is called while the render mode is **GL_FEEDBACK**, or if **glRenderMode** is called with argument **GL_FEEDBACK** before **glFeedbackBuffer** is called at least once.

GL_INVALID_OPERATION is generated if **glRenderMode** is executed between the execution of **glBegin** and the corresponding execution of **glEnd**.

ASSOCIATED GETS

glGet with argument **GL_RENDER_MODE**

SEE ALSO

glFeedbackBuffer, **glInitNames**, **glLoadName**, **glPassThrough**, **glPushName**, **glSelectBuffer**

NAME

glResetHistogram – reset histogram table entries to zero

C SPECIFICATION

void **glResetHistogram**(GLenum *target*)

PARAMETERS

target Must be **GL_HISTOGRAM**.

DESCRIPTION

glResetHistogram resets all the elements of the current histogram table to zero.

NOTES

glResetHistogram is present only if **GL_ARB_imaging** is returned when **glGetString** is called with an argument of **GL_EXTENSIONS**.

ERRORS

GL_INVALID_ENUM is generated if *target* is not **GL_HISTOGRAM**.

GL_INVALID_OPERATION is generated if **glResetHistogram** is executed between the execution of **glBegin** and the corresponding execution of **glEnd**.

SEE ALSO

glHistogram

NAME

glResetMinmax – reset minmax table entries to initial values

C SPECIFICATION

void **glResetMinmax**(GLenum *target*)

PARAMETERS

target Must be **GL_MINMAX**.

DESCRIPTION

glResetMinmax resets the elements of the current minmax table to their initial values: the "maximum" element receives the minimum possible component values, and the "minimum" element receives the maximum possible component values.

NOTES

glResetMinmax is present only if **GL_ARB_imaging** is returned when **glGetString** is called with an argument of **GL_EXTENSIONS**.

ERRORS

GL_INVALID_ENUM is generated if *target* is not **GL_MINMAX**.

GL_INVALID_OPERATION is generated if **glResetMinmax** is executed between the execution of **glBegin** and the corresponding execution of **glEnd**.

SEE ALSO

glMinmax

NAME

      glRotated, glRotatef – multiply the current matrix by a rotation matrix

C SPECIFICATION

      void **glRotated**(GLdouble *angle*,
                     GLdouble *x*,
                     GLdouble *y*,
                     GLdouble *z*)
      void **glRotatef**(GLfloat *angle*,
                    GLfloat *x*,
                    GLfloat *y*,
                    GLfloat *z*)

PARAMETERS

      angle Specifies the angle of rotation, in degrees.

      x, y, z
            Specify the *x*, *y*, and *z* coordinates of a vector, respectively.

DESCRIPTION

      glRotate produces a rotation of *angle* degrees around the vector (x, y, z). The current matrix (see **glMatrixMode**) is multiplied by a rotation matrix with the product replacing the current matrix, as if **glMultMatrix** were called with the following matrix as its argument:

$$\begin{matrix} x^2(1-c)+c & xy(1-c)-zs & xz(1-c)+ys & 0 \\ yx(1-c)+zs & y^2(1-c)+c & yz(1-c)-xs & 0 \\ xz(1-c)-ys & yz(1-c)+xs & z^2(1-c)+c & 0 \\ 0 & 0 & 0 & 1 \end{matrix}$$

Where $c = \cos(angle)$, $s = \sin(angle)$, and $||(x,y,z)|| = 1$ (if not, the GL will normalize this vector).

If the matrix mode is either **GL_MODELVIEW** or **GL_PROJECTION**, all objects drawn after **glRotate** is called are rotated. Use **glPushMatrix** and **glPopMatrix** to save and restore the unrotated coordinate system.

NOTES

      This rotation follows the right-hand rule, so if the vector (x, y, z) points toward the user, the rotation will be counterclockwise.

ERRORS

GL_INVALID_OPERATION is generated if **glRotate** is executed between the execution of **glBegin** and the corresponding execution of **glEnd**.

ASSOCIATED GETS

glGet with argument **GL_MATRIX_MODE**
glGet with argument **GL_COLOR_MATRIX**
glGet with argument **GL_MODELVIEW_MATRIX**
glGet with argument **GL_PROJECTION_MATRIX**
glGet with argument **GL_TEXTURE_MATRIX**

SEE ALSO

glMatrixMode, **glMultMatrix**, **glPushMatrix**, **glScale**, **glTranslate**

NAME

glScaled, glScalef – multiply the current matrix by a general scaling matrix

C SPECIFICATION

```
void glScaled( GLdouble x,
               GLdouble y,
               GLdouble z )
void glScalef( GLfloat x,
               GLfloat y,
               GLfloat z )
```

PARAMETERS

x, y, z
    Specify scale factors along the *x*, *y*, and *z* axes, respectively.

DESCRIPTION

glScale produces a nonuniform scaling along the *x*, *y*, and *z* axes. The three parameters indicate the desired scale factor along each of the three axes.

The current matrix (see **glMatrixMode**) is multiplied by this scale matrix, and the product replaces the current matrix as if **glScale** were called with the following matrix as its argument:

$$
\begin{matrix}
x & 0 & 0 & 0 \\
0 & y & 0 & 0 \\
0 & 0 & z & 0 \\
0 & 0 & 0 & 1
\end{matrix}
$$

If the matrix mode is either **GL_MODELVIEW** or **GL_PROJECTION**, all objects drawn after **glScale** is called are scaled.

Use **glPushMatrix** and **glPopMatrix** to save and restore the unscaled coordinate system.

NOTES

If scale factors other than 1 are applied to the modelview matrix and lighting is enabled, lighting often appears wrong. In that case, enable automatic normalization of normals by calling **glEnable** with the argument **GL_NORMALIZE**.

ERRORS

GL_INVALID_OPERATION is generated if **glScale** is executed between the execution of **glBegin** and the corresponding execution of **glEnd**.

ASSOCIATED GETS

glGet with argument **GL_MATRIX_MODE**
glGet with argument **GL_COLOR_MATRIX**
glGet with argument **GL_MODELVIEW_MATRIX**
glGet with argument **GL_PROJECTION_MATRIX**
glGet with argument **GL_TEXTURE_MATRIX**

SEE ALSO

glMatrixMode, **glMultMatrix**, **glPushMatrix**, **glRotate**, **glTranslate**

NAME

glScissor – define the scissor box

C SPECIFICATION

void **glScissor**(GLint *x*,
    GLint *y*,
    GLsizei *width*,
    GLsizei *height*)

PARAMETERS

x, *y*
    Specify the lower left corner of the scissor box. Initially (0, 0).

width, *height*
    Specify the width and height of the scissor box. When a GL context is first attached to a window, *width* and *height* are set to the dimensions of that window.

DESCRIPTION

glScissor defines a rectangle, called the scissor box, in window coordinates. The first two arguments, *x* and *y*, specify the lower left corner of the box. *width* and *height* specify the width and height of the box.

To enable and disable the scissor test, call **glEnable** and **glDisable** with argument **GL_SCISSOR_TEST**. The test is initially disabled. While the test is enabled, only pixels that lie within the scissor box can be modified by drawing commands. Window coordinates have integer values at the shared corners of frame buffer pixels. glScissor(0,0,1,1) allows modification of only the lower left pixel in the window, and glScissor(0,0,0,0) doesn't allow modification of any pixels in the window.

When the scissor test is disabled, it is as though the scissor box includes the entire window.

ERRORS

GL_INVALID_VALUE is generated if either *width* or *height* is negative.

GL_INVALID_OPERATION is generated if **glScissor** is executed between the execution of **glBegin** and the corresponding execution of **glEnd**.

ASSOCIATED GETS

glGet with argument **GL_SCISSOR_BOX**
glIsEnabled with argument **GL_SCISSOR_TEST**

SEE ALSO

glEnable, **glViewport**

NAME

glSelectBuffer – establish a buffer for selection mode values

C SPECIFICATION

void **glSelectBuffer**(GLsizei *size*,
                        GLuint **buffer*)

PARAMETERS

size   Specifies the size of *buffer*.

buffer Returns the selection data.

DESCRIPTION

glSelectBuffer has two arguments: *buffer* is a pointer to an array of unsigned integers, and *size* indicates the size of the array. *buffer* returns values from the name stack (see **glInitNames**, **glLoadName**, **glPushName**) when the rendering mode is **GL_SELECT** (see **glRenderMode**). **glSelectBuffer** must be issued before selection mode is enabled, and it must not be issued while the rendering mode is **GL_SELECT**.

A programmer can use selection to determine which primitives are drawn into some region of a window. The region is defined by the current modelview and perspective matrices.

In selection mode, no pixel fragments are produced from rasterization. Instead, if a primitive or a raster position intersects the clipping volume defined by the viewing frustum and the user-defined clipping planes, this primitive causes a selection hit. (With polygons, no hit occurs if the polygon is culled.) When a change is made to the name stack, or when **glRenderMode** is called, a hit record is copied to *buffer* if any hits have occurred since the last such event (name stack change or **glRenderMode** call). The hit record consists of the number of names in the name stack at the time of the event, followed by the minimum and maximum depth values of all vertices that hit since the previous event, followed by the name stack contents, bottom name first.

Depth values (which are in the range [0,1]) are multiplied by $2^{32} - 1$, before being placed in the hit record.

An internal index into *buffer* is reset to 0 whenever selection mode is entered. Each time a hit record is copied into *buffer*, the index is incremented to point to the cell just past the end of the block of names – that is, to the next available cell. If the hit record is larger than the number of remaining locations in *buffer*, as much data as can fit is copied, and the overflow flag is set. If the name stack is empty when a hit record is copied, that record consists of 0 followed by the minimum and maximum depth values.

To exit selection mode, call **glRenderMode** with an argument other than
GL_SELECT. Whenever **glRenderMode** is called while the render mode is
GL_SELECT, it returns the number of hit records copied to *buffer*, resets the
overflow flag and the selection buffer pointer, and initializes the name stack to be
empty. If the overflow bit was set when **glRenderMode** was called, a negative hit
record count is returned.

NOTES

The contents of *buffer* is undefined until **glRenderMode** is called with an argument
other than **GL_SELECT**.

glBegin/glEnd primitives and calls to **glRasterPos** can result in hits.

ERRORS

GL_INVALID_VALUE is generated if *size* is negative.

GL_INVALID_OPERATION is generated if **glSelectBuffer** is called while the render
mode is **GL_SELECT**, or if **glRenderMode** is called with argument **GL_SELECT**
before **glSelectBuffer** is called at least once.

GL_INVALID_OPERATION is generated if **glSelectBuffer** is executed between the
execution of **glBegin** and the corresponding execution of **glEnd**.

ASSOCIATED GETS

glGet with argument **GL_NAME_STACK_DEPTH**
glGet with argument **GL_SELECTION_BUFFER_SIZE**
glGetPointerv with argument **GL_SELECTION_BUFFER_POINTER**

SEE ALSO

glFeedbackBuffer, glInitNames, glLoadName, glPushName, glRenderMode

NAME

glSeparableFilter2D – define a separable two-dimensional convolution filter

C SPECIFICATION

void **glSeparableFilter2D**(GLenum *target*,
                    GLenum *internalformat*,
                    GLsizei *width*,
                    GLsizei *height*,
                    GLenum *format*,
                    GLenum *type*,
                    const GLvoid **row*,
                    const GLvoid **column*)

PARAMETERS

target Must be **GL_SEPARABLE_2D**.

internalformat

The internal format of the convolution filter kernel. The allowable values are **GL_ALPHA**, **GL_ALPHA4**, **GL_ALPHA8**, **GL_ALPHA12**, **GL_ALPHA16**, **GL_LUMINANCE**, **GL_LUMINANCE4**, **GL_LUMINANCE8**, **GL_LUMINANCE12**, **GL_LUMINANCE16**, **GL_LUMINANCE_ALPHA**, **GL_LUMINANCE4_ALPHA4**, **GL_LUMINANCE6_ALPHA2**, **GL_LUMINANCE8_ALPHA8**, **GL_LUMINANCE12_ALPHA4**, **GL_LUMINANCE12_ALPHA12**, **GL_LUMINANCE16_ALPHA16**, **GL_INTENSITY**, **GL_INTENSITY4**, **GL_INTENSITY8**, **GL_INTENSITY12**, **GL_INTENSITY16**, **GL_R3_G3_B2**, **GL_RGB**, **GL_RGB4**, **GL_RGB5**, **GL_RGB8**, **GL_RGB10**, **GL_RGB12**, **GL_RGB16**, **GL_RGBA**, **GL_RGBA2**, **GL_RGBA4**, **GL_RGB5_A1**, **GL_RGBA8**, **GL_RGB10_A2**, **GL_RGBA12**, or **GL_RGBA16**.

width The number of elements in the pixel array referenced by *row*. (This is the width of the separable filter kernel.)

height The number of elements in the pixel array referenced by *column*. (This is the height of the separable filter kernel.)

format The format of the pixel data in *row* and *column*. The allowable values are **GL_RED**, **GL_GREEN**, **GL_BLUE**, **GL_ALPHA**, **GL_RGB**, **GL_BGR**, **GL_RGBA**, **GL_BGRA**, **GL_INTENSITY**, **GL_LUMINANCE**, and **GL_LUMINANCE_ALPHA**.

type	The type of the pixel data in *row* and *column*. Symbolic constants **GL_UNSIGNED_BYTE**, **GL_BYTE**, **GL_BITMAP**, **GL_UNSIGNED_SHORT**, **GL_SHORT**, **GL_UNSIGNED_INT**, **GL_INT**, **GL_FLOAT**, **GL_UNSIGNED_BYTE_3_3_2**, **GL_UNSIGNED_BYTE_2_3_3_REV**, **GL_UNSIGNED_SHORT_5_6_5**, **GL_UNSIGNED_SHORT_5_6_5_REV**, **GL_UNSIGNED_SHORT_4_4_4_4**, **GL_UNSIGNED_SHORT_4_4_4_4_REV**, **GL_UNSIGNED_SHORT_5_5_5_1**, **GL_UNSIGNED_SHORT_1_5_5_5_REV**, **GL_UNSIGNED_INT_8_8_8_8**, **GL_UNSIGNED_INT_8_8_8_8_REV**, **GL_UNSIGNED_INT_10_10_10_2**, and **GL_UNSIGNED_INT_2_10_10_10_REV** are accepted.
row	Pointer to a one-dimensional array of pixel data that is processed to build the row filter kernel.
column	Pointer to a one-dimensional array of pixel data that is processed to build the column filter kernel.

DESCRIPTION

glSeparableFilter2D builds a two-dimensional separable convolution filter kernel from two arrays of pixels.

The pixel arrays specified by (*width, format, type, row*) and (*height, format, type, column*) are processed just as if they had been passed to **glDrawPixels**, but processing stops after the final expansion to RGBA is completed.

Next, the R, G, B, and A components of all pixels in both arrays are scaled by the four separable 2D **GL_CONVOLUTION_FILTER_SCALE** parameters and biased by the four separable 2D **GL_CONVOLUTION_FILTER_BIAS** parameters. (The scale and bias parameters are set by **glConvolutionParameter** using the **GL_SEPARABLE_2D** target and the names **GL_CONVOLUTION_FILTER_SCALE** and **GL_CONVOLUTION_FILTER_BIAS**. The parameters themselves are vectors of four values that are applied to red, green, blue, and alpha, in that order.) The R, G, B, and A values are not clamped to [0,1] at any time during this process.

Each pixel is then converted to the internal format specified by *internalformat*. This conversion simply maps the component values of the pixel (R, G, B, and A) to the values included in the internal format (red, green, blue, alpha, luminance, and intensity). The mapping is as follows:

Internal Format	Red	Green	Blue	Alpha	Luminance	Intensity
GL_LUMINANCE					R	
GL_LUMINANCE_ALPHA				A	R	
GL_INTENSITY						R
GL_RGB	R	G	B			
GL_RGBA	R	G	B	A		

The red, green, blue, alpha, luminance, and/or intensity components of the resulting pixels are stored in floating-point rather than integer format. They form two one-dimensional filter kernel images. The row image is indexed by coordinate i starting at zero and increasing from left to right. Each location in the row image is derived from element i of *row*. The column image is indexed by coordinate j starting at zero and increasing from bottom to top. Each location in the column image is derived from element j of *column*.

Note that after a convolution is performed, the resulting color components are also scaled by their corresponding **GL_POST_CONVOLUTION_c_SCALE** parameters and biased by their corresponding **GL_POST_CONVOLUTION_c_BIAS** parameters (where c takes on the values **RED**, **GREEN**, **BLUE**, and **ALPHA**). These parameters are set by **glPixelTransfer**.

NOTES

glSeparableFilter2D is present only if **GL_ARB_imaging** is returned when **glGetString** is called with an argument of **GL_EXTENSIONS**.

ERRORS

GL_INVALID_ENUM is generated if *target* is not **GL_SEPARABLE_2D**.

GL_INVALID_ENUM is generated if *internalformat* is not one of the allowable values.

GL_INVALID_VALUE is generated if *width* is less than zero or greater than the maximum supported value. This value may be queried with **glGetConvolutionParameter** using target **GL_SEPARABLE_2D** and name **GL_MAX_CONVOLUTION_WIDTH**.

GL_INVALID_VALUE is generated if *height* is less than zero or greater than the maximum supported value. This value may be queried with **glGetConvolutionParameter** using target **GL_SEPARABLE_2D** and name **GL_MAX_CONVOLUTION_HEIGHT**.

GL_INVALID_ENUM is generated if *format* is not one of the allowable values.

GL_INVALID_ENUM is generated if *type* is not one of the allowable values.

GL_INVALID_OPERATION is generated if **glSeparableFilter2D** is executed between the execution of **glBegin** and the corresponding execution of **glEnd**.

GL_INVALID_OPERATION is generated if *height* is one of GL_UNSIGNED_BYTE_3_3_2, GL_UNSIGNED_BYTE_2_3_3_REV, GL_UNSIGNED_SHORT_5_6_5, or GL_UNSIGNED_SHORT_5_6_5_REV and *format* is not **GL_RGB**.

GL_INVALID_OPERATION is generated if *height* is one of GL_UNSIGNED_SHORT_4_4_4_4, GL_UNSIGNED_SHORT_4_4_4_4_REV, GL_UNSIGNED_SHORT_5_5_5_1, GL_UNSIGNED_SHORT_1_5_5_5_REV, GL_UNSIGNED_INT_8_8_8_8, GL_UNSIGNED_INT_8_8_8_8_REV, GL_UNSIGNED_INT_10_10_10_2, or GL_UNSIGNED_INT_2_10_10_10_REV and *format* is neither **GL_RGBA** nor **GL_BGRA**.

ASSOCIATED GETS

glGetConvolutionParameter, glGetSeparableFilter

SEE ALSO

glConvolutionFilter1D, glConvolutionFilter2D, glConvolutionParameter, glPixelTransfer

NAME

glShadeModel – select flat or smooth shading

C SPECIFICATION

void **glShadeModel**(GLenum *mode*)

PARAMETERS

mode Specifies a symbolic value representing a shading technique. Accepted values are **GL_FLAT** and **GL_SMOOTH**. The initial value is **GL_SMOOTH**.

DESCRIPTION

GL primitives can have either flat or smooth shading. Smooth shading, the default, causes the computed colors of vertices to be interpolated as the primitive is rasterized, typically assigning different colors to each resulting pixel fragment. Flat shading selects the computed color of just one vertex and assigns it to all the pixel fragments generated by rasterizing a single primitive. In either case, the computed color of a vertex is the result of lighting if lighting is enabled, or it is the current color at the time the vertex was specified if lighting is disabled.

Flat and smooth shading are indistinguishable for points. Starting when **glBegin** is issued and counting vertices and primitives from 1, the GL gives each flat-shaded line segment i the computed color of vertex $i + 1$, its second vertex. Counting similarly from 1, the GL gives each flat-shaded polygon the computed color of the vertex listed in the following table. This is the last vertex to specify the polygon in all cases except single polygons, where the first vertex specifies the flat-shaded color.

Primitive Type of Polygon i	Vertex
Single polygon ($i \equiv 1$)	1
Triangle strip	$i + 2$
Triangle fan	$i + 2$
Independent triangle	$3i$
Quad strip	$2i + 2$
Independent quad	$4i$

Flat and smooth shading are specified by **glShadeModel** with *mode* set to **GL_FLAT** and **GL_SMOOTH**, respectively.

ERRORS

GL_INVALID_ENUM is generated if *mode* is any value other than **GL_FLAT** or **GL_SMOOTH**.

GL_INVALID_OPERATION is generated if **glShadeModel** is executed between the execution of **glBegin** and the corresponding execution of **glEnd**.

ASSOCIATED GETS

glGet with argument **GL_SHADE_MODEL**

SEE ALSO

glBegin, **glColor**, **glLight**, **glLightModel**

NAME

glStencilFunc – set function and reference value for stencil testing

C SPECIFICATION

void **glStencilFunc**(GLenum *func*,
GLint *ref*,
GLuint *mask*)

PARAMETERS

func Specifies the test function. Eight tokens are valid: **GL_NEVER**, **GL_LESS**, **GL_LEQUAL**, **GL_GREATER**, **GL_GEQUAL**, **GL_EQUAL**, **GL_NOTEQUAL**, and **GL_ALWAYS**. The initial value is **GL_ALWAYS**.

ref Specifies the reference value for the stencil test. *ref* is clamped to the range $[0, 2^n-1]$, where n is the number of bitplanes in the stencil buffer. The initial value is 0.

mask
   Specifies a mask that is ANDed with both the reference value and the stored stencil value when the test is done. The initial value is all 1's.

DESCRIPTION

Stenciling, like depth-buffering, enables and disables drawing on a per-pixel basis. You draw into the stencil planes using GL drawing primitives, then render geometry and images, using the stencil planes to mask out portions of the screen. Stenciling is typically used in multipass rendering algorithms to achieve special effects, such as decals, outlining, and constructive solid geometry rendering.

The stencil test conditionally eliminates a pixel based on the outcome of a comparison between the reference value and the value in the stencil buffer. To enable and disable the test, call **glEnable** and **glDisable** with argument **GL_STENCIL_TEST**. To specify actions based on the outcome of the stencil test, call **glStencilOp**.

func is a symbolic constant that determines the stencil comparison function. It accepts one of eight values, shown in the following list. *ref* is an integer reference value that is used in the stencil comparison. It is clamped to the range $[0, 2^n-1]$, where n is the number of bitplanes in the stencil buffer. *mask* is bitwise ANDed with both the reference value and the stored stencil value, with the ANDed values participating in the comparison.

If *stencil* represents the value stored in the corresponding stencil buffer location, the following list shows the effect of each comparison function that can be specified by *func*. Only if the comparison succeeds is the pixel passed through to the next stage in the rasterization process (see **glStencilOp**). All tests treat *stencil* values as unsigned integers in the range $[0, 2^n-1]$, where n is the number of bitplanes in the stencil buffer.

The following values are accepted by *func*:

GL_NEVER	Always fails.
GL_LESS	Passes if (*ref* & *mask*) < (*stencil* & *mask*).
GL_LEQUAL	Passes if (*ref* & *mask*) ≤ (*stencil* & *mask*).
GL_GREATER	Passes if (*ref* & *mask*) > (*stencil* & *mask*).
GL_GEQUAL	Passes if (*ref* & *mask*) ≥ (*stencil* & *mask*).
GL_EQUAL	Passes if (*ref* & *mask*) = (*stencil* & *mask*).
GL_NOTEQUAL	Passes if (*ref* & *mask*) ≠ (*stencil* & *mask*).
GL_ALWAYS	Always passes.

NOTES

Initially, the stencil test is disabled. If there is no stencil buffer, no stencil modification can occur and it is as if the stencil test always passes.

ERRORS

GL_INVALID_ENUM is generated if *func* is not one of the eight accepted values.

GL_INVALID_OPERATION is generated if **glStencilFunc** is executed between the execution of **glBegin** and the corresponding execution of **glEnd**.

ASSOCIATED GETS

glGet with argument **GL_STENCIL_FUNC**
glGet with argument **GL_STENCIL_VALUE_MASK**
glGet with argument **GL_STENCIL_REF**
glGet with argument **GL_STENCIL_BITS**
glIsEnabled with argument **GL_STENCIL_TEST**

SEE ALSO

glAlphaFunc, **glBlendFunc**, **glDepthFunc**, **glEnable**, **glIsEnabled**, **glLogicOp**, **glStencilOp**

NAME

glStencilMask – control the writing of individual bits in the stencil planes

C SPECIFICATION

void **glStencilMask**(GLuint *mask*)

PARAMETERS

mask Specifies a bit mask to enable and disable writing of individual bits in the
stencil planes. Initially, the mask is all 1's.

DESCRIPTION

glStencilMask controls the writing of individual bits in the stencil planes. The least
significant *n* bits of *mask*, where *n* is the number of bits in the stencil buffer, specify
a mask. Where a 1 appears in the mask, it's possible to write to the corresponding
bit in the stencil buffer. Where a 0 appears, the corresponding bit is write-protected.
Initially, all bits are enabled for writing.

ERRORS

GL_INVALID_OPERATION is generated if **glStencilMask** is executed between the
execution of **glBegin** and the corresponding execution of **glEnd**.

ASSOCIATED GETS

glGet with argument **GL_STENCIL_WRITEMASK**
glGet with argument **GL_STENCIL_BITS**

SEE ALSO

glColorMask, **glDepthMask**, **glIndexMask**, **glStencilFunc**, **glStencilOp**

NAME

glStencilOp – set stencil test actions

C SPECIFICATION

void **glStencilOp**(GLenum *fail*,
GLenum *zfail*,
GLenum *zpass*)

PARAMETERS

fail Specifies the action to take when the stencil test fails. Six symbolic constants are accepted: **GL_KEEP**, **GL_ZERO**, **GL_REPLACE**, **GL_INCR**, **GL_DECR**, and **GL_INVERT**. The initial value is **GL_KEEP**.

zfail Specifies the stencil action when the stencil test passes, but the depth test fails. *zfail* accepts the same symbolic constants as *fail*. The initial value is **GL_KEEP**.

zpass

Specifies the stencil action when both the stencil test and the depth test pass, or when the stencil test passes and either there is no depth buffer or depth testing is not enabled. *zpass* accepts the same symbolic constants as *fail*. The initial value is **GL_KEEP**.

DESCRIPTION

Stenciling, like depth-buffering, enables and disables drawing on a per-pixel basis. You draw into the stencil planes using GL drawing primitives, then render geometry and images, using the stencil planes to mask out portions of the screen. Stenciling is typically used in multipass rendering algorithms to achieve special effects, such as decals, outlining, and constructive solid geometry rendering.

The stencil test conditionally eliminates a pixel based on the outcome of a comparison between the value in the stencil buffer and a reference value. To enable and disable the test, call **glEnable** and **glDisable** with argument **GL_STENCIL_TEST**; to control it, call **glStencilFunc**.

glStencilOp takes three arguments that indicate what happens to the stored stencil value while stenciling is enabled. If the stencil test fails, no change is made to the pixel's color or depth buffers, and *fail* specifies what happens to the stencil buffer contents. The following six actions are possible.

GL_KEEP	Keeps the current value.
GL_ZERO	Sets the stencil buffer value to 0.
GL_REPLACE	Sets the stencil buffer value to *ref*, as specified by **glStencilFunc**.

GL_INCR	Increments the current stencil buffer value. Clamps to the maximum representable unsigned value.
GL_DECR	Decrements the current stencil buffer value. Clamps to 0.
GL_INVERT	Bitwise inverts the current stencil buffer value.

Stencil buffer values are treated as unsigned integers. When incremented and decremented, values are clamped to 0 and 2^n-1, where n is the value returned by querying **GL_STENCIL_BITS**.

The other two arguments to **glStencilOp** specify stencil buffer actions that depend on whether subsequent depth buffer tests succeed (*zpass*) or fail (*zfail*) (see **glDepthFunc**). The actions are specified using the same six symbolic constants as *fail*. Note that *zfail* is ignored when there is no depth buffer, or when the depth buffer is not enabled. In these cases, *fail* and *zpass* specify stencil action when the stencil test fails and passes, respectively.

NOTES

Initially the stencil test is disabled. If there is no stencil buffer, no stencil modification can occur and it is as if the stencil tests always pass, regardless of any call to **glStencilOp**.

ERRORS

GL_INVALID_ENUM is generated if *fail*, *zfail*, or *zpass* is any value other than the six defined constant values.

GL_INVALID_OPERATION is generated if **glStencilOp** is executed between the execution of **glBegin** and the corresponding execution of **glEnd**.

ASSOCIATED GETS

glGet with argument GL_STENCIL_FAIL
glGet with argument GL_STENCIL_PASS_DEPTH_PASS
glGet with argument GL_STENCIL_PASS_DEPTH_FAIL
glGet with argument GL_STENCIL_BITS
glIsEnabled with argument GL_STENCIL_TEST

SEE ALSO

glAlphaFunc, glBlendFunc, glDepthFunc, glEnable, glLogicOp, glStencilFunc

NAME

glTexCoord1d, glTexCoord1f, glTexCoord1i, glTexCoord1s, glTexCoord2d, glTexCoord2f, glTexCoord2i, glTexCoord2s, glTexCoord3d, glTexCoord3f, glTexCoord3i, glTexCoord3s, glTexCoord4d, glTexCoord4f, glTexCoord4i, glTexCoord4s, glTexCoord1dv, glTexCoord1fv, glTexCoord1iv, glTexCoord1sv, glTexCoord2dv, glTexCoord2fv, glTexCoord2iv, glTexCoord2sv, glTexCoord3dv, glTexCoord3fv, glTexCoord3iv, glTexCoord3sv, glTexCoord4dv, glTexCoord4fv, glTexCoord4iv, glTexCoord4sv – set the current texture coordinates

C SPECIFICATION

void **glTexCoord1d**(GLdouble *s*)

void **glTexCoord1f**(GLfloat *s*)

void **glTexCoord1i**(GLint *s*)

void **glTexCoord1s**(GLshort *s*)

void **glTexCoord2d**(GLdouble *s*,
                        GLdouble *t*)

void **glTexCoord2f**(GLfloat *s*,
                        GLfloat *t*)

void **glTexCoord2i**(GLint *s*,
                        GLint *t*)

void **glTexCoord2s**(GLshort *s*,
                        GLshort *t*)

void **glTexCoord3d**(GLdouble *s*,
                        GLdouble *t*,
                        GLdouble *r*)

void **glTexCoord3f**(GLfloat *s*,
                        GLfloat *t*,
                        GLfloat *r*)

void **glTexCoord3i**(GLint *s*,
                        GLint *t*,
                        GLint *r*)

void **glTexCoord3s**(GLshort *s*,
                        GLshort *t*,
                        GLshort *r*)

void **glTexCoord4d**(GLdouble *s*,
                        GLdouble *t*,
                        GLdouble *r*,
                        GLdouble *q*)

void **glTexCoord4f**(GLfloat *s*,
                        GLfloat *t*,
                        GLfloat *r*,
                        GLfloat *q*)

```
       void glTexCoord4i( GLint s,
                          GLint t,
                          GLint r,
                          GLint q )
       void glTexCoord4s( GLshort s,
                          GLshort t,
                          GLshort r,
                          GLshort q )
```

PARAMETERS

s, t, r, q

Specify s, t, r, and q texture coordinates. Not all parameters are present in all forms of the command.

C SPECIFICATION

```
       void glTexCoord1dv( const GLdouble *v )
       void glTexCoord1fv( const GLfloat *v )
       void glTexCoord1iv( const GLint *v )
       void glTexCoord1sv( const GLshort *v )
       void glTexCoord2dv( const GLdouble *v )
       void glTexCoord2fv( const GLfloat *v )
       void glTexCoord2iv( const GLint *v )
       void glTexCoord2sv( const GLshort *v )
       void glTexCoord3dv( const GLdouble *v )
       void glTexCoord3fv( const GLfloat *v )
       void glTexCoord3iv( const GLint *v )
       void glTexCoord3sv( const GLshort *v )
       void glTexCoord4dv( const GLdouble *v )
       void glTexCoord4fv( const GLfloat *v )
       void glTexCoord4iv( const GLint *v )
       void glTexCoord4sv( const GLshort *v )
```

PARAMETERS

v   Specifies a pointer to an array of one, two, three, or four elements, which in turn specify the s, t, r, and q texture coordinates.

DESCRIPTION

glTexCoord specifies texture coordinates in one, two, three, or four dimensions. **glTexCoord1** sets the current texture coordinates to $(s, 0, 0, 1)$; a call to **glTexCoord2** sets them to $(s, t, 0, 1)$. Similarly, **glTexCoord3** specifies the texture coordinates as $(s, t, r, 1)$, and **glTexCoord4** defines all four components explicitly as (s, t, r, q).

The current texture coordinates are part of the data that is associated with each vertex and with the current raster position. Initially, the values for *s, t, r,* and *q* are (0, 0, 0, 1).

NOTES

The current texture coordinates can be updated at any time. In particular, **glTexCoord** can be called between a call to **glBegin** and the corresponding call to **glEnd**.

When the **GL_ARB_imaging** extension is supported, **glTexCoord** always updates texture unit **GL_TEXTURE0_ARB**.

ASSOCIATED GETS

glGet with argument **GL_CURRENT_TEXTURE_COORDS**

SEE ALSO

glTexCoordPointer, **glVertex**

NAME

glTexCoordPointer – define an array of texture coordinates

C SPECIFICATION

void **glTexCoordPointer**(GLint *size*,
GLenum *type*,
GLsizei *stride*,
const GLvoid **pointer*)

PARAMETERS

size   Specifies the number of coordinates per array element. Must be 1, 2, 3 or 4. The initial value is 4.

type   Specifies the data type of each texture coordinate. Symbolic constants **GL_SHORT**, **GL_INT**, **GL_FLOAT**, or **GL_DOUBLE** are accepted. The initial value is **GL_FLOAT**.

stride   Specifies the byte offset between consecutive array elements. If *stride* is 0, the array elements are understood to be tightly packed. The initial value is 0.

pointer Specifies a pointer to the first coordinate of the first element in the array. The initial value is 0.

DESCRIPTION

glTexCoordPointer specifies the location and data format of an array of texture coordinates to use when rendering. *size* specifies the number of coordinates per element, and must be 1, 2, 3, or 4. *type* specifies the data type of each texture coordinate and *stride* specifies the byte stride from one array element to the next allowing vertices and attributes to be packed into a single array or stored in separate arrays. (Single-array storage may be more efficient on some implementations; see **glInterleavedArrays**.) When a texture coordinate array is specified, *size*, *type*, *stride*, and *pointer* are saved client-side state.

To enable and disable the texture coordinate array, call **glEnableClientState** and **glDisableClientState** with the argument GL_TEXTURE_COORD_ARRAY. If enabled, the texture coordinate array is used when **glDrawArrays**, **glDrawElements**, **glDrawRangeElements** or **glArrayElement** is called.

Use **glDrawArrays** to construct a sequence of primitives (all of the same type) from prespecified vertex and vertex attribute arrays. Use **glArrayElement** to specify primitives by indexing vertices and vertex attributes and **glDrawElements** to construct a sequence of primitives by indexing vertices and vertex attributes.

NOTES

glTexCoordPointer is available only if the GL version is 1.1 or greater.

The texture coordinate array is initially disabled and it won't be accessed when **glArrayElement**, **glDrawElements**, **glDrawRangeElements**, or **glDrawArrays** is called.

Execution of **glTexCoordPointer** is not allowed between the execution of **glBegin** and the corresponding execution of **glEnd**, but an error may or may not be generated. If no error is generated, the operation is undefined.

glTexCoordPointer is typically implemented on the client side with no protocol.

The texture coordinate array parameters are client-side state and are therefore not saved or restored by **glPushAttrib** and **glPopAttrib**. Use **glPushClientAttrib** and **glPopClientAttrib** instead.

When the **GL_ARB_imaging** extension is supported, **glTexCoordPointer** updates the texture coordinate array state of the active client texture unit, specified with **glClientActiveTextureARB**.

ERRORS

GL_INVALID_VALUE is generated if *size* is not 1, 2, 3, or 4.

GL_INVALID_ENUM is generated if *type* is not an accepted value.

GL_INVALID_VALUE is generated if *stride* is negative.

ASSOCIATED GETS

glIsEnabled with argument **GL_TEXTURE_COORD_ARRAY**
glGet with argument **GL_TEXTURE_COORD_ARRAY_SIZE**
glGet with argument **GL_TEXTURE_COORD_ARRAY_TYPE**
glGetPointerv with argument **GL_TEXTURE_COORD_ARRAY_POINTER**

SEE ALSO

glArrayElement, **glClientActiveTextureARB**, **glColorPointer**, **glDrawArrays**, **glDrawElements**, **glDrawRangeElements**, **glEdgeFlagPointer**, **glEnable**, **glGetPointerv**, **glIndexPointer**, **glNormalPointer**, **glPopClientAttrib**, **glPushClientAttrib**, **glTexCoord**, **glVertexPointer**

NAME

glTexEnvf, glTexEnvi, glTexEnvfv, glTexEnviv – set texture environment parameters

C SPECIFICATION

void **glTexEnvf**(GLenum *target*,
　　　　　　　GLenum *pname*,
　　　　　　　GLfloat *param*)
void **glTexEnvi**(GLenum *target*,
　　　　　　　GLenum *pname*,
　　　　　　　GLint *param*)

PARAMETERS

target　Specifies a texture environment. Must be **GL_TEXTURE_ENV**.

pname

Specifies the symbolic name of a single-valued texture environment parameter. Must be **GL_TEXTURE_ENV_MODE**.

param

Specifies a single symbolic constant, one of **GL_MODULATE**, **GL_DECAL**, **GL_BLEND**, or **GL_REPLACE**.

C SPECIFICATION

void **glTexEnvfv**(GLenum *target*,
　　　　　　　GLenum *pname*,
　　　　　　　const GLfloat **params*)
void **glTexEnviv**(GLenum *target*,
　　　　　　　GLenum *pname*,
　　　　　　　const GLint **params*)

PARAMETERS

target　Specifies a texture environment. Must be **GL_TEXTURE_ENV**.

pname　Specifies the symbolic name of a texture environment parameter. Accepted values are **GL_TEXTURE_ENV_MODE** and **GL_TEXTURE_ENV_COLOR**.

params　Specifies a pointer to a parameter array that contains either a single symbolic constant or an RGBA color.

DESCRIPTION

A texture environment specifies how texture values are interpreted when a fragment is textured. *target* must be **GL_TEXTURE_ENV**. *pname* can be either **GL_TEXTURE_ENV_MODE** or **GL_TEXTURE_ENV_COLOR**.

If *pname* is **GL_TEXTURE_ENV_MODE**, then *params* is (or points to) the symbolic name of a texture function. Four texture functions may be specified: **GL_MODULATE**, **GL_DECAL**, **GL_BLEND**, and **GL_REPLACE**.

A texture function acts on the fragment to be textured using the texture image value that applies to the fragment (see **glTexParameter**) and produces an RGBA color for that fragment. The following table shows how the RGBA color is produced for each of the three texture functions that can be chosen. C is a triple of color values (RGB) and A is the associated alpha value. RGBA values extracted from a texture image are in the range [0,1]. The subscript f refers to the incoming fragment, the subscript t to the texture image, the subscript c to the texture environment color, and subscript v indicates a value produced by the texture function.

A texture image can have up to four components per texture element (see **glTexImage1D**, **glTexImage2D**, **glTexImage3D**, **glCopyTexImage1D**, and **glCopyTexImage2D**). In a one-component image, L_t indicates that single component. A two-component image uses L_t and A_t. A three-component image has only a color value, C_t. A four-component image has both a color value C_t and an alpha value A_t.

Base internal format	**Texture functions**			
	GL_MODULATE	**GL_DECAL**	**GL_BLEND**	**GL_REPLACE**
GL_ALPHA	$C_v = C_f$ $A_v = A_f A_t$	undefined	$C_v = C_f$ $A_v = A_t A_f$	$C_v = C_f$ $A_v = A_t$
GL_LUMINANCE (or 1)	$C_v = L_t C_f$ $A_v = A_f$	undefined	$C_v = (1{-}L_t)C_f$ $+L_t C_c$ $A_v = A_f$	$C_v = L_t$ $A_v = A_f$
GL_LUMINANCE _ALPHA (or 2)	$C_v = L_t C_f$ $A_v = A_t A_f$	undefined	$C_v = (1{-}L_t)C_f$ $+L_t C_c$ $A_v = A_t A_f$	$C_v = L_t$ $A_v = A_t$
GL_INTENSITY	$C_v = C_f I_t$ $A_v = A_f I_t$	undefined	$C_v = (1{-}I_t)C_f$ $+I_t C_c$ $A_v = (1{-}I_t)A_f$ $+I_t A_c$	$C_v = I_t$ $A_v = I_t$
GL_RGB (or 3)	$C_v = C_t C_f$ $A_v = A_f$	$C_v = C_t$ $A_v = A_f$	$C_v = (1{-}C_t)C_f$ $+C_t C_c$ $A_v = A_f$	$C_v = C_t$ $A_v = A_f$
GL_RGBA (or 4)	$C_v = C_t C_f$ $A_v = A_t A_f$	$C_v = (1{-}A_t)C_f$ $+A_t C_t$ $A_v = A_f$	$C_v = (1{-}C_t)C_f$ $+C_t C_c$ $A_v = A_t A_f$	$C_v = C_t$ $A_v = A_t$

If *pname* is **GL_TEXTURE_ENV_COLOR**, *params* is a pointer to an array that holds an RGBA color consisting of four values. Integer color components are interpreted linearly such that the most positive integer maps to 1.0, and the most negative integer maps to -1.0. The values are clamped to the range [0,1] when they are specified. C_c takes these four values.

GL_TEXTURE_ENV_MODE defaults to **GL_MODULATE** and **GL_TEXTURE_ENV_COLOR** defaults to (0, 0, 0, 0).

NOTES

GL_REPLACE may only be used if the GL version is 1.1 or greater.

Internal formats other than 1, 2, 3, or 4 may only be used if the GL version is 1.1 or greater.

When the **GL_ARB_multitexture** extension is supported, **glTexEnv** controls the texture environment for the current active texture unit, selected by **glActiveTextureARB**. **GL_INVALID_ENUM** is generated when *target* or *pname* is not one of the accepted defined values, or when *params* should have a defined constant value (based on the value of *pname*) and does not.

GL_INVALID_OPERATION is generated if **glTexEnv** is executed between the execution of **glBegin** and the corresponding execution of **glEnd**.

ASSOCIATED GETS
glGetTexEnv

SEE ALSO
glActiveTextureARB, glCopyPixels, glCopyTexImage1D, glCopyTexImage2D, glCopyTexSubImage1D, glCopyTexSubImage2D, glCopyTexSubImage3D, glTexImage1D, glTexImage2D, glTexImage3D, glTexParameter, glTexSubImage1D, glTexSubImage2D, glTexSubImage3D

NAME

glTexGend, glTexGenf, glTexGeni, glTexGendv, glTexGenfv, glTexGeniv – control the generation of texture coordinates

C SPECIFICATION

void **glTexGend**(GLenum *coord*,
     GLenum *pname*,
     GLdouble *param*)
void **glTexGenf**(GLenum *coord*,
     GLenum *pname*,
     GLfloat *param*)
void **glTexGeni**(GLenum *coord*,
     GLenum *pname*,
     GLint *param*)

PARAMETERS

coord Specifies a texture coordinate. Must be one of **GL_S**, **GL_T**, **GL_R**, or **GL_Q**.

pname Specifies the symbolic name of the texture-coordinate generation function. Must be **GL_TEXTURE_GEN_MODE**.

param Specifies a single-valued texture generation parameter, one of **GL_OBJECT_LINEAR**, **GL_EYE_LINEAR**, or **GL_SPHERE_MAP**.

C SPECIFICATION

void **glTexGendv**(GLenum *coord*,
     GLenum *pname*,
     const GLdouble **params*)
void **glTexGenfv**(GLenum *coord*,
     GLenum *pname*,
     const GLfloat **params*)
void **glTexGeniv**(GLenum *coord*,
     GLenum *pname*,
     const GLint **params*)

PARAMETERS

coord Specifies a texture coordinate. Must be one of **GL_S**, **GL_T**, **GL_R**, or **GL_Q**.

pname Specifies the symbolic name of the texture-coordinate generation function or function parameters. Must be **GL_TEXTURE_GEN_MODE**, **GL_OBJECT_PLANE**, or **GL_EYE_PLANE**.

params Specifies a pointer to an array of texture generation parameters. If *pname* is **GL_TEXTURE_GEN_MODE**, then the array must contain a single symbolic constant, one of **GL_OBJECT_LINEAR**, **GL_EYE_LINEAR**, or **GL_SPHERE_MAP**. Otherwise, *params* holds the coefficients for the texture-coordinate generation function specified by *pname*.

DESCRIPTION

glTexGen selects a texture-coordinate generation function or supplies coefficients for one of the functions. *coord* names one of the (s, t, r, q) texture coordinates; it must be one of the symbols **GL_S**, **GL_T**, **GL_R**, or **GL_Q**. *pname* must be one of three symbolic constants: **GL_TEXTURE_GEN_MODE**, **GL_OBJECT_PLANE**, or **GL_EYE_PLANE**. If *pname* is GL_TEXTURE_GEN_MODE, then *params* chooses a mode, one of **GL_OBJECT_LINEAR**, **GL_EYE_LINEAR**, or **GL_SPHERE_MAP**. If *pname* is either **GL_OBJECT_PLANE** or **GL_EYE_PLANE**, *params* contains coefficients for the corresponding texture generation function.

If the texture generation function is **GL_OBJECT_LINEAR**, the function

$$g = p_1 x_o + p_2 y_o + p_3 z_o + p_4 w_o$$

is used, where g is the value computed for the coordinate named in *coord*, p_1, p_2, p_3, and p_4 are the four values supplied in *params*, and x_o, y_o, z_o, and w_o are the object coordinates of the vertex. This function can be used, for example, to texture-map terrain using sea level as a reference plane (defined by p_1, p_2, p_3, and p_4). The altitude of a terrain vertex is computed by the **GL_OBJECT_LINEAR** coordinate generation function as its distance from sea level; that altitude can then be used to index the texture image to map white snow onto peaks and green grass onto foothills.

If the texture generation function is **GL_EYE_LINEAR**, the function

$$g = p_1' x_e + p_2' y_e + p_3' z_e + p_4' w_e$$

is used, where

$$(p_1' \quad p_2' \quad p_3' \quad p_4') = (p_1 \quad p_2 \quad p_3 \quad p_4) \, M^{-1}$$

and x_e, y_e, z_e, and w_e are the eye coordinates of the vertex, p_1, p_2, p_3, and p_4 are the values supplied in *params*, and M is the modelview matrix when **glTexGen** is invoked. If M is poorly conditioned or singular, texture coordinates generated by the resulting function may be inaccurate or undefined.

Note that the values in *params* define a reference plane in eye coordinates. The modelview matrix that is applied to them may not be the same one in effect when the polygon vertices are transformed. This function establishes a field of texture coordinates that can produce dynamic contour lines on moving objects.

If *pname* is **GL_SPHERE_MAP** and *coord* is either **GL_S** or **GL_T**, s and t texture coordinates are generated as follows. Let u be the unit vector pointing from the origin to the polygon vertex (in eye coordinates). Let n sup prime be the current normal, after transformation to eye coordinates. Let be the reflection vector such that

$$f = (f_x \ f_y \ f_z)^T$$

$$f = u - 2n'n'^T u$$

Finally, let $m = 2\sqrt{f_x^2 + f_y^2 + (f_z + 1)^2}$. Then the values assigned to the s and t texture coordinates are

$$s = \frac{f_x}{m} + \frac{1}{2}$$

$$t = \frac{f_y}{m} + \frac{1}{2}$$

To enable or disable a texture-coordinate generation function, call **glEnable** or **glDisable** with one of the symbolic texture-coordinate names (-**GL_TEXTURE_GEN_S**, **GL_TEXTURE_GEN_T**, **GL_TEXTURE_GEN_R**, or **GL_TEXTURE_GEN_Q**) as the argument. When enabled, the specified texture coordinate is computed according to the generating function associated with that coordinate. When disabled, subsequent vertices take the specified texture coordinate from the current set of texture coordinates. Initially, all texture generation functions are set to **GL_EYE_LINEAR** and are disabled. Both s plane equations are (1, 0, 0, 0), both t plane equations are (0, 1, 0, 0), and all r and q plane equations are (0, 0, 0, 0).

When the **GL_ARB_multitexture** extension is supported, **glTexGen** set the texture generation parameters for the currently active texture unit, selected with **glActiveTextureARB**.

ERRORS

GL_INVALID_ENUM is generated when *coord* or *pname* is not an accepted defined value, or when *pname* is **GL_TEXTURE_GEN_MODE** and *params* is not an accepted defined value.

GL_INVALID_ENUM is generated when *pname* is **GL_TEXTURE_GEN_MODE**, *params* is **GL_SPHERE_MAP**, and *coord* is either **GL_R** or **GL_Q**.

GL_INVALID_OPERATION is generated if **glTexGen** is executed between the execution of **glBegin** and the corresponding execution of **glEnd**.

ASSOCIATED GETS

glGetTexGen
glIsEnabled with argument **GL_TEXTURE_GEN_S**
glIsEnabled with argument **GL_TEXTURE_GEN_T**
glIsEnabled with argument **GL_TEXTURE_GEN_R**
glIsEnabled with argument **GL_TEXTURE_GEN_Q**

SEE ALSO

glActiveTextureARB, glCopyPixels, glCopyTexImage2D,
glCopyTexSubImage1D, glCopyTexSubImage2D, glCopyTexSubImage3D,
glTexEnv, glTexImage1D, glTexImage2D, glTexImage3D, glTexParameter,
glTexSubImage1D, glTexSubImage2D, glTexSubImage3D

NAME

glTexImage1D – specify a one-dimensional texture image

C SPECIFICATION

void **glTexImage1D**(GLenum *target*,
                    GLint *level*,
                    GLint *internalformat*,
                    GLsizei *width*,
                    GLint *border*,
                    GLenum *format*,
                    GLenum *type*,
                    const GLvoid **pixels*)

PARAMETERS

target   Specifies the target texture. Must be **GL_TEXTURE_1D** or **GL_PROXY_TEXTURE_1D**.

level   Specifies the level-of-detail number. Level 0 is the base image level. Level *n* is the *n*th mipmap reduction image.

internalformat

Specifies the number of color components in the texture. Must be 1, 2, 3, or 4, or one of the following symbolic constants: **GL_ALPHA**, **GL_ALPHA4**, **GL_ALPHA8**, **GL_ALPHA12**, **GL_ALPHA16**, **GL_LUMINANCE**, **GL_LUMINANCE4**, **GL_LUMINANCE8**, **GL_LUMINANCE12**, **GL_LUMINANCE16**, **GL_LUMINANCE_ALPHA**, **GL_LUMINANCE4_ALPHA4**, **GL_LUMINANCE6_ALPHA2**, **GL_LUMINANCE8_ALPHA8**, **GL_LUMINANCE12_ALPHA4**, **GL_LUMINANCE12_ALPHA12**, **GL_LUMINANCE16_ALPHA16**, **GL_INTENSITY**, **GL_INTENSITY4**, **GL_INTENSITY8**, **GL_INTENSITY12**, **GL_INTENSITY16**, **GL_RGB**, **GL_R3_G3_B2**, **GL_RGB4**, **GL_RGB5**, **GL_RGB8**, **GL_RGB10**, **GL_RGB12**, **GL_RGB16**, **GL_RGBA**, **GL_RGBA2**, **GL_RGBA4**, **GL_RGB5_A1**, **GL_RGBA8**, **GL_RGB10_A2**, **GL_RGBA12**, or **GL_RGBA16**.

width   Specifies the width of the texture image. Must be $2^n+2(border)$ for some integer *n*. All implementations support texture images that are at least 64 texels wide. The height of the 1D texture image is 1.

border   Specifies the width of the border. Must be either 0 or 1.

format   Specifies the format of the pixel data. The following symbolic values are accepted: **GL_COLOR_INDEX**, **GL_RED**, **GL_GREEN**, **GL_BLUE**, **GL_ALPHA**, **GL_RGB**, **GL_BGR**, **GL_RGBA**, **GL_BGRA**, **GL_LUMINANCE**, and **GL_LUMINANCE_ALPHA**.

type	Specifies the data type of the pixel data. The following symbolic values are accepted: **GL_UNSIGNED_BYTE**, **GL_BYTE**, **GL_BITMAP**, **GL_UNSIGNED_SHORT**, **GL_SHORT**, **GL_UNSIGNED_INT**, **GL_INT**, **GL_FLOAT**, **GL_UNSIGNED_BYTE_3_3_2**, **GL_UNSIGNED_BYTE_2_3_3_REV**, **GL_UNSIGNED_SHORT_5_6_5**, **GL_UNSIGNED_SHORT_5_6_5_REV**, **GL_UNSIGNED_SHORT_4_4_4_4**, **GL_UNSIGNED_SHORT_4_4_4_4_REV**, **GL_UNSIGNED_SHORT_5_5_5_1**, **GL_UNSIGNED_SHORT_1_5_5_5_REV**, **GL_UNSIGNED_INT_8_8_8_8**, **GL_UNSIGNED_INT_8_8_8_8_REV**, **GL_UNSIGNED_INT_10_10_10_2**, and **GL_UNSIGNED_INT_2_10_10_10_REV**.
pixels	Specifies a pointer to the image data in memory.

DESCRIPTION

Texturing maps a portion of a specified texture image onto each graphical primitive for which texturing is enabled. To enable and disable one-dimensional texturing, call **glEnable** and **glDisable** with argument **GL_TEXTURE_1D**.

Texture images are defined with **glTexImage1D**. The arguments describe the parameters of the texture image, such as width, width of the border, level-of-detail number (see **glTexParameter**), and the internal resolution and format used to store the image. The last three arguments describe how the image is represented in memory; they are identical to the pixel formats used for **glDrawPixels**.

If *target* is **GL_PROXY_TEXTURE_1D**, no data is read from *pixels*, but all of the texture image state is recalculated, checked for consistency, and checked against the implementation's capabilities. If the implementation cannot handle a texture of the requested texture size, it sets all of the image state to 0, but does not generate an error (see **glGetError**). To query for an entire mipmap array, use an image array level greater than or equal to 1.

If *target* is **GL_TEXTURE_1D**, data is read from *pixels* as a sequence of signed or unsigned bytes, shorts, or longs, or single-precision floating-point values, depending on *type*. These values are grouped into sets of one, two, three, or four values, depending on *format*, to form elements. If *type* is **GL_BITMAP**, the data is considered as a string of unsigned bytes (and *format* must be **GL_COLOR_INDEX**). Each data byte is treated as eight 1-bit elements, with bit ordering determined by **GL_UNPACK_LSB_FIRST** (see **glPixelStore**).

The first element corresponds to the left end of the texture array. Subsequent elements progress left-to-right through the remaining texels in the texture array. The final element corresponds to the right end of the texture array.

format determines the composition of each element in *pixels*. It can assume one of eleven symbolic values:

GL_COLOR_INDEX

Each element is a single value, a color index. The GL converts it to fixed point (with an unspecified number of zero bits to the right of the binary point), shifted left or right depending on the value and sign of **GL_INDEX_SHIFT**, and added to **GL_INDEX_OFFSET** (see **glPixelTransfer**). The resulting index is converted to a set of color components using the **GL_PIXEL_MAP_I_TO_R**, **GL_PIXEL_MAP_I_TO_G**, **GL_PIXEL_MAP_I_TO_B**, and **GL_PIXEL_MAP_I_TO_A** tables, and clamped to the range [0,1].

GL_RED Each element is a single red component. The GL converts it to floating point and assembles it into an RGBA element by attaching 0 for green and blue, and 1 for alpha. Each component is then multiplied by the signed scale factor **GL_c_SCALE**, added to the signed bias **GL_c_BIAS**. and clamped to the range [0,1] (see **glPixelTransfer**).

GL_GREEN

Each element is a single green component. The GL converts it to floating point and assembles it into an RGBA element by attaching 0 for red and blue, and 1 for alpha. Each component is then multiplied by the signed scale factor **GL_c_SCALE**, added to the signed bias **GL_c_BIAS**, and clamped to the range [0,1] (see **glPixelTransfer**).

GL_BLUE Each element is a single blue component. The GL converts it to floating point and assembles it into an RGBA element by attaching 0 for red and green, and 1 for alpha. Each component is then multiplied by the signed scale factor **GL_c_SCALE**, added to the signed bias **GL_c_BIAS**, and clamped to the range [0,1] (see **glPixelTransfer**).

GL_ALPHA

Each element is a single alpha component. The GL converts it to floating point and assembles it into an RGBA element by attaching 0 for red, green, and blue. Each component is then multiplied by the signed scale factor **GL_c_SCALE**, added to the signed bias **GL_c_BIAS**, and clamped to the range [0,1] (see **glPixelTransfer**).

GL_RGB

GL_BGR Each element is an RGB triple. The GL converts it to floating point and assembles it into an RGBA element by attaching 1 for alpha. Each component is then multiplied by the signed scale factor **GL_c_SCALE**, added to the signed bias **GL_c_BIAS**, and clamped to the range [0,1] (see **glPixelTransfer**).

GL_RGBA

GL_BGRA

Each element contains all four components. Each component is then multiplied by the signed scale factor **GL_c_SCALE**, added to the signed bias **GL_c_BIAS**, and clamped to the range [0,1] (see **glPixelTransfer**).

GL_LUMINANCE

Each element is a single luminance value. The GL converts it to floating point, then assembles it into an RGBA element by replicating the luminance value three times for red, green, and blue and attaching 1 for alpha. Each component is then multiplied by the signed scale factor **GL_c_SCALE**, added to the signed bias **GL_c_BIAS**, and clamped to the range [0,1] (see **glPixelTransfer**).

GL_LUMINANCE_ALPHA

Each element is a luminance/alpha pair. The GL converts it to floating point, then assembles it into an RGBA element by replicating the luminance value three times for red, green, and blue. Each component is then multiplied by the signed scale factor **GL_c_SCALE**, added to the signed bias **GL_c_BIAS**, and clamped to the range [0,1] (see **glPixelTransfer**).

If an application wants to store the texture at a certain resolution or in a certain format, it can request the resolution and format with *internalformat*. The GL will choose an internal representation that closely approximates that requested by *internalformat*, but it may not match exactly. (The representations specified by **GL_LUMINANCE**, **GL_LUMINANCE_ALPHA**, **GL_RGB**, and **GL_RGBA** must match exactly. The numeric values 1, 2, 3, and 4 may also be used to specify the preceding representations.)

Use the **GL_PROXY_TEXTURE_1D** target to try out a resolution and format. The implementation will update and recompute its best match for the requested storage resolution and format. To query this state, call **glGetTexLevelParameter**. If the texture cannot be accommodated, texture state is set to 0.

A one-component texture image uses only the red component of the RGBA color from *pixels*. A two-component image uses the R and A values. A three-component image uses the R, G, and B values. A four-component image uses all of the RGBA components.

NOTES

Texturing has no effect in color index mode.

If the **GL_ARB_imaging** extension is supported, RGBA elements may also be processed by the imaging pipeline. The following stages may be applied to an RGBA color before color component clamping to the range [0, 1]:

1. Color component replacement by the color table specified for
   GL_COLOR_TABLE, if enabled. See **glColorTable**.

2. One-dimensional convolution filtering, if enabled. See
   glConvolutionFilter1D.

   If a convolution filter changes the __width of the texture (by processing with a
   GL_CONVOLUTION_BORDER_MODE of **GL_REDUCE**, for example), the *width*
   must $2^n+2(border)$, for some integer n, after filtering.

3. RGBA components may be multiplied by **GL_POST_CONVOLUTION_c_SCALE**,
   and added to **GL_POST_CONVOLUTION_c_BIAS**, if enabled. See
   glPixelTransfer.

4. Color component replacement by the color table specified for
   GL_POST_CONVOLUTION_COLOR_TABLE, if enabled. See **glColorTable**.

5. Transformation by the color matrix. See **glMatrixMode**.

6. RGBA components may be multiplied by **GL_POST_COLOR_MATRIX_c_SCALE**,
   and added to **GL_POST_COLOR_MATRIX_c_BIAS**, if enabled. See
   glPixelTransfer.

7. Color component replacement by the color table specified for
   GL_POST_COLOR_MATRIX_COLOR_TABLE, if enabled. See **glColorTable**.

The texture image can be represented by the same data formats as the pixels in a
glDrawPixels command, except that **GL_STENCIL_INDEX** and
GL_DEPTH_COMPONENT cannot be used. **glPixelStore** and **glPixelTransfer**
modes affect texture images in exactly the way they affect **glDrawPixels**.

GL_PROXY_TEXTURE_1D may be used only if the GL version is 1.1 or greater.

Internal formats other than 1, 2, 3, or 4 may be used only if the GL version is 1.1 or
greater.

In GL version 1.1 or greater, *pixels* may be a null pointer. In this case texture
memory is allocated to accommodate a texture of width *width*. You can then download subtextures to initialize the texture memory. The image is undefined if the program tries to apply an uninitialized portion of the texture image to a primitive.

Formats **GL_BGR**, and **GL_BGRA** and types **GL_UNSIGNED_BYTE_3_3_2**,
GL_UNSIGNED_BYTE_2_3_3_REV, **GL_UNSIGNED_SHORT_5_6_5**,
GL_UNSIGNED_SHORT_5_6_5_REV, **GL_UNSIGNED_SHORT_4_4_4_4**,
GL_UNSIGNED_SHORT_4_4_4_4_REV, **GL_UNSIGNED_SHORT_5_5_5_1**,
GL_UNSIGNED_SHORT_1_5_5_5_REV, **GL_UNSIGNED_INT_8_8_8_8**,
GL_UNSIGNED_INT_8_8_8_8_REV, **GL_UNSIGNED_INT_10_10_10_2**, and
GL_UNSIGNED_INT_2_10_10_10_REV are available only if the GL version is 1.2 or
greater.

When the **GL_ARB_multitexture** extension is supported, **glTexImage1D** specifies the one-dimensional texture for the current texture unit, specified with **glActiveTextureARB**.

ERRORS

GL_INVALID_ENUM is generated if *target* is not **GL_TEXTURE_1D** or **GL_PROXY_TEXTURE_1D**.

GL_INVALID_ENUM is generated if *format* is not an accepted format constant. Format constants other than **GL_STENCIL_INDEX** and **GL_DEPTH_COMPONENT** are accepted.

GL_INVALID_ENUM is generated if *type* is not a type constant.

GL_INVALID_ENUM is generated if *type* is **GL_BITMAP** and *format* is not **GL_COLOR_INDEX**.

GL_INVALID_VALUE is generated if *level* is less than 0.

GL_INVALID_VALUE may be generated if *level* is greater than $\log_2 max$, where *max* is the returned value of **GL_MAX_TEXTURE_SIZE**.

GL_INVALID_VALUE is generated if *internalformat* is not 1, 2, 3, 4, or one of the accepted resolution and format symbolic constants.

GL_INVALID_VALUE is generated if *width* is less than 0 or greater than 2 + **GL_MAX_TEXTURE_SIZE**, or if it cannot be represented as $2^n + 2(border)$ for some integer value of *n*.

GL_INVALID_VALUE is generated if *border* is not 0 or 1.

GL_INVALID_OPERATION is generated if **glTexImage1D** is executed between the execution of **glBegin** and the corresponding execution of **glEnd**.

GL_INVALID_OPERATION is generated if *type* is one of **GL_UNSIGNED_BYTE_3_3_2**, **GL_UNSIGNED_BYTE_2_3_3_REV**, **GL_UNSIGNED_SHORT_5_6_5**, or **GL_UNSIGNED_SHORT_5_6_5_REV** and *format* is not **GL_RGB**.

GL_INVALID_OPERATION is generated if *type* is one of **GL_UNSIGNED_SHORT_4_4_4_4**, **GL_UNSIGNED_SHORT_4_4_4_4_REV**, **GL_UNSIGNED_SHORT_5_5_5_1**, **GL_UNSIGNED_SHORT_1_5_5_5_REV**, **GL_UNSIGNED_INT_8_8_8_8**, **GL_UNSIGNED_INT_8_8_8_8_REV**, **GL_UNSIGNED_INT_10_10_10_2**, or **GL_UNSIGNED_INT_2_10_10_10_REV** and *format* is neither **GL_RGBA** nor **GL_BGRA**.

ASSOCIATED GETS

glGetTexImage
glIsEnabled with argument **GL_TEXTURE_1D**

SEE ALSO

glActiveTextureARB, glColorTable, glConvolutionFilter1D, glCopyPixels,
glCopyTexImage1D, glCopyTexImage2D, glCopyTexSubImage1D,
glCopyTexSubImage2D, glCopyTexSubImage3D, glDrawPixels, glMatrixMode,
glPixelStore, glPixelTransfer, glTexEnv, glTexGen, glTexImage2D,
glTexImage3D, glTexSubImage1D, glTexSubImage2D, glTexSubImage3D,
glTexParameter

NAME

  glTexImage2D – specify a two-dimensional texture image

C SPECIFICATION

  void **glTexImage2D**(GLenum *target*,
            GLint *level*,
            GLint *internalformat*,
            GLsizei *width*,
            GLsizei *height*,
            GLint *border*,
            GLenum *format*,
            GLenum *type*,
            const GLvoid **pixels*)

PARAMETERS

  target   Specifies the target texture. Must be **GL_TEXTURE_2D** or **GL_PROXY_TEXTURE_2D**.

  level   Specifies the level-of-detail number. Level 0 is the base image level. Level *n* is the *n*th mipmap reduction image.

  internalformat

        Specifies the number of color components in the texture. Must be 1, 2, 3, or 4, or one of the following symbolic constants: **GL_ALPHA**, **GL_ALPHA4**, **GL_ALPHA8**, **GL_ALPHA12**, **GL_ALPHA16**, **GL_LUMINANCE**, **GL_LUMINANCE4**, **GL_LUMINANCE8**, **GL_LUMINANCE12**, **GL_LUMINANCE16**, **GL_LUMINANCE_ALPHA**, **GL_LUMINANCE4_ALPHA4**, **GL_LUMINANCE6_ALPHA2**, **GL_LUMINANCE8_ALPHA8**, **GL_LUMINANCE12_ALPHA4**, **GL_LUMINANCE12_ALPHA12**, **GL_LUMINANCE16_ALPHA16**, **GL_INTENSITY**, **GL_INTENSITY4**, **GL_INTENSITY8**, **GL_INTENSITY12**, **GL_INTENSITY16**, **GL_R3_G3_B2**, **GL_RGB**, **GL_RGB4**, **GL_RGB5**, **GL_RGB8**, **GL_RGB10**, **GL_RGB12**, **GL_RGB16**, **GL_RGBA**, **GL_RGBA2**, **GL_RGBA4**, **GL_RGB5_A1**, **GL_RGBA8**, **GL_RGB10_A2**, **GL_RGBA12**, or **GL_RGBA16**.

  width   Specifies the width of the texture image. Must be $2^n + 2(border)$ for some integer *n*. All implementations support texture images that are at least 64 texels wide.

  height   Specifies the height of the texture image. Must be $2^m + 2(border)$ for some integer *m*. All implementations support texture images that are at least 64 texels high.

border	Specifies the width of the border. Must be either 0 or 1.
format	Specifies the format of the pixel data. The following symbolic values are accepted: **GL_COLOR_INDEX, GL_RED, GL_GREEN, GL_BLUE, GL_ALPHA, GL_RGB, GL_BGR GL_RGBA, GL_BGRA, GL_LUMINANCE**, and **GL_LUMINANCE_ALPHA**.
type	Specifies the data type of the pixel data. The following symbolic values are accepted: **GL_UNSIGNED_BYTE, GL_BYTE, GL_BITMAP, GL_UNSIGNED_SHORT, GL_SHORT, GL_UNSIGNED_INT, GL_INT, GL_FLOAT, GL_UNSIGNED_BYTE_3_3_2, GL_UNSIGNED_BYTE_2_3_3_REV, GL_UNSIGNED_SHORT_5_6_5, GL_UNSIGNED_SHORT_5_6_5_REV, GL_UNSIGNED_SHORT_4_4_4_4, GL_UNSIGNED_SHORT_4_4_4_4_REV, GL_UNSIGNED_SHORT_5_5_5_1, GL_UNSIGNED_SHORT_1_5_5_5_REV, GL_UNSIGNED_INT_8_8_8_8, GL_UNSIGNED_INT_8_8_8_8_REV, GL_UNSIGNED_INT_10_10_10_2**, and **GL_UNSIGNED_INT_2_10_10_10_REV**.
pixels	Specifies a pointer to the image data in memory.

DESCRIPTION

Texturing maps a portion of a specified texture image onto each graphical primitive for which texturing is enabled. To enable and disable two-dimensional texturing, call **glEnable** and **glDisable** with argument **GL_TEXTURE_2D**.

To define texture images, call **glTexImage2D**. The arguments describe the parameters of the texture image, such as height, width, width of the border, level-of-detail number (see **glTexParameter**), and number of color components provided. The last three arguments describe how the image is represented in memory; they are identical to the pixel formats used for **glDrawPixels**.

If *target* is **GL_PROXY_TEXTURE_2D**, no data is read from *pixels*, but all of the texture image state is recalculated, checked for consistency, and checked against the implementation's capabilities. If the implementation cannot handle a texture of the requested texture size, it sets all of the image state to 0, but does not generate an error (see **glGetError**). To query for an entire mipmap array, use an image array level greater than or equal to 1.

If *target* is **GL_TEXTURE_2D**, data is read from *pixels* as a sequence of signed or unsigned bytes, shorts, or longs, or single-precision floating-point values, depending on *type*. These values are grouped into sets of one, two, three, or four values, depending on *format*, to form elements. If *type* is **GL_BITMAP**, the data is considered as a string of unsigned bytes (and *format* must be **GL_COLOR_INDEX**).

Each data byte is treated as eight 1-bit elements, with bit ordering determined by GL_UNPACK_LSB_FIRST (see **glPixelStore**).

The first element corresponds to the lower left corner of the texture image. Subsequent elements progress left-to-right through the remaining texels in the lowest row of the texture image, and then in successively higher rows of the texture image. The final element corresponds to the upper right corner of the texture image.

format determines the composition of each element in *pixels*. It can assume one of eleven symbolic values:

GL_COLOR_INDEX

Each element is a single value, a color index. The GL converts it to fixed point (with an unspecified number of zero bits to the right of the binary point), shifted left or right depending on the value and sign of **GL_INDEX_SHIFT**, and added to **GL_INDEX_OFFSET** (see **glPixelTransfer**). The resulting index is converted to a set of color components using the **GL_PIXEL_MAP_I_TO_R**, **GL_PIXEL_MAP_I_TO_G**, **GL_PIXEL_MAP_I_TO_B**, and **GL_PIXEL_MAP_I_TO_A** tables, and clamped to the range [0,1].

GL_RED Each element is a single red component. The GL converts it to floating point and assembles it into an RGBA element by attaching 0 for green and blue, and 1 for alpha. Each component is then multiplied by the signed scale factor **GL_c_SCALE**, added to the signed bias **GL_c_BIAS**, and clamped to the range [0,1] (see **glPixelTransfer**).

GL_GREEN

Each element is a single green component. The GL converts it to floating point and assembles it into an RGBA element by attaching 0 for red and blue, and 1 for alpha. Each component is then multiplied by the signed scale factor **GL_c_SCALE**, added to the signed bias **GL_c_BIAS**, and clamped to the range [0,1] (see **glPixelTransfer**).

GL_BLUE Each element is a single blue component. The GL converts it to floating point and assembles it into an RGBA element by attaching 0 for red and green, and 1 for alpha. Each component is then multiplied by the signed scale factor **GL_c_SCALE**, added to the signed bias **GL_c_BIAS**, and clamped to the range [0,1] (see **glPixelTransfer**).

GL_ALPHA

Each element is a single alpha component. The GL converts it to floating point and assembles it into an RGBA element by attaching 0 for red, green, and blue. Each component is then multiplied by the signed scale factor **GL_c_SCALE**, added to the signed bias **GL_c_BIAS**, and clamped to the range [0,1] (see **glPixelTransfer**).

GL_RGB

GL_BGR Each element is an RGB triple. The GL converts it to floating point and assembles it into an RGBA element by attaching 1 for alpha. Each component is then multiplied by the signed scale factor **GL_c_SCALE**, added to the signed bias **GL_c_BIAS**, and clamped to the range [0,1] (see **glPixelTransfer**).

GL_RGBA

GL_BGRA

Each element contains all four components. Each component is multiplied by the signed scale factor **GL_c_SCALE**, added to the signed bias **GL_c_BIAS**, and clamped to the range [0,1] (see **glPixelTransfer**).

GL_LUMINANCE

Each element is a single luminance value. The GL converts it to floating point, then assembles it into an RGBA element by replicating the luminance value three times for red, green, and blue and attaching 1 for alpha. Each component is then multiplied by the signed scale factor **GL_c_SCALE**, added to the signed bias **GL_c_BIAS**, and clamped to the range [0,1] (see **glPixelTransfer**).

GL_LUMINANCE_ALPHA

Each element is a luminance/alpha pair. The GL converts it to floating point, then assembles it into an RGBA element by replicating the luminance value three times for red, green, and blue. Each component is then multiplied by the signed scale factor **GL_c_SCALE**, added to the signed bias **GL_c_BIAS**, and clamped to the range [0,1] (see **glPixelTransfer**).

Refer to the **glDrawPixels** reference page for a description of the acceptable values for the *type* parameter.

If an application wants to store the texture at a certain resolution or in a certain format, it can request the resolution and format with *internalformat*. The GL will choose an internal representation that closely approximates that requested by *internalformat*, but it may not match exactly. (The representations specified by **GL_LUMINANCE**, **GL_LUMINANCE_ALPHA**, **GL_RGB**, and **GL_RGBA** must match exactly. The numeric values 1, 2, 3, and 4 may also be used to specify the above representations.)

Use the **GL_PROXY_TEXTURE_2D** target to try out a resolution and format. The implementation will update and recompute its best match for the requested storage resolution and format. To then query this state, call **glGetTexLevelParameter**. If the texture cannot be accommodated, texture state is set to 0.

A one-component texture image uses only the red component of the RGBA color extracted from *pixels*. A two-component image uses the R and A values. A three-component image uses the R, G, and B values. A four-component image uses all of the RGBA components.

NOTES

Texturing has no effect in color index mode.

If the **GL_ARB_imaging** extension is supported, RGBA elements may also be processed by the imaging pipeline. The following stages may be applied to an RGBA color before color component clamping to the range [0, 1]:

1. Color component replacement by the color table specified for **GL_COLOR_TABLE**, if enabled. See **glColorTable**.

2. Two-dimensional Convolution filtering, if enabled. See **glConvolutionFilter1D**.

   If a convolution filter changes the __width of the texture (by processing with a **GL_CONVOLUTION_BORDER_MODE** of **GL_REDUCE**, for example), the *width* must 2^n+2(*height*), for some integer n, and *height* must be 2^m+(*border*), for some integer m, after filtering.

3. RGBA components may be multiplied by **GL_POST_CONVOLUTION_c_SCALE**, and added to **GL_POST_CONVOLUTION_c_BIAS**, if enabled. See **glPixelTransfer**.

4. Color component replacement by the color table specified for **GL_POST_CONVOLUTION_COLOR_TABLE**, if enabled. See **glColorTable**.

5. Transformation by the color matrix. See **glMatrixMode**.

6. RGBA components may be multiplied by **GL_POST_COLOR_MATRIX_c_SCALE**, and added to **GL_POST_COLOR_MATRIX_c_BIAS**, if enabled. See **glPixelTransfer**.

7. Color component replacement by the color table specified for **GL_POST_COLOR_MATRIX_COLOR_TABLE**, if enabled. See **glColorTable**.

The texture image can be represented by the same data formats as the pixels in a **glDrawPixels** command, except that **GL_STENCIL_INDEX** and **GL_DEPTH_COMPONENT** cannot be used. **glPixelStore** and **glPixelTransfer** modes affect texture images in exactly the way they affect **glDrawPixels**.

glTexImage2D and **GL_PROXY_TEXTURE_2D** are available only if the GL version is 1.1 or greater.

Internal formats other than 1, 2, 3, or 4 may be used only if the GL version is 1.1 or greater.

In GL version 1.1 or greater, *pixels* may be a null pointer. In this case texture memory is allocated to accommodate a texture of width *width* and height *height*. You can then download subtextures to initialize this texture memory. The image is undefined if the user tries to apply an uninitialized portion of the texture image to a primitive.

Formats **GL_BGR**, and **GL_BGRA** and types **GL_UNSIGNED_BYTE_3_3_2**, **GL_UNSIGNED_BYTE_2_3_3_REV**, **GL_UNSIGNED_SHORT_5_6_5**, **GL_UNSIGNED_SHORT_5_6_5_REV**, **GL_UNSIGNED_SHORT_4_4_4_4**, **GL_UNSIGNED_SHORT_4_4_4_4_REV**, **GL_UNSIGNED_SHORT_5_5_5_1**, **GL_UNSIGNED_SHORT_1_5_5_5_REV**, **GL_UNSIGNED_INT_8_8_8_8**, **GL_UNSIGNED_INT_8_8_8_8_REV**, **GL_UNSIGNED_INT_10_10_10_2**, and **GL_UNSIGNED_INT_2_10_10_10_REV** are available only if the GL version is 1.2 or greater.

When the **GL_ARB_multitexture** extension is supported, **glTexImage2D** specifies the two-dimensional texture for the current texture unit, specified with **glActiveTextureARB**.

ERRORS

GL_INVALID_ENUM is generated if *target* is not **GL_TEXTURE_2D** or **GL_PROXY_TEXTURE_2D**.

GL_INVALID_ENUM is generated if *format* is not an accepted format constant. Format constants other than **GL_STENCIL_INDEX** and **GL_DEPTH_COMPONENT** are accepted.

GL_INVALID_ENUM is generated if *type* is not a type constant.

GL_INVALID_ENUM is generated if *type* is **GL_BITMAP** and *format* is not **GL_COLOR_INDEX**.

GL_INVALID_VALUE is generated if *level* is less than 0.

GL_INVALID_VALUE may be generated if *level* is greater than $\log_2 max$, where *max* is the returned value of **GL_MAX_TEXTURE_SIZE**.

GL_INVALID_VALUE is generated if *internalformat* is not 1, 2, 3, 4, or one of the accepted resolution and format symbolic constants.

GL_INVALID_VALUE is generated if *width* or *height* is less than 0 or greater than 2 + **GL_MAX_TEXTURE_SIZE**, or if either cannot be represented as $2^k + 2(border)$ for some integer value of *k*.

GL_INVALID_VALUE is generated if *border* is not 0 or 1.

GL_INVALID_OPERATION is generated if **glTexImage2D** is executed between the execution of **glBegin** and the corresponding execution of **glEnd**.

GL_INVALID_OPERATION is generated if *type* is one of
GL_UNSIGNED_BYTE_3_3_2, GL_UNSIGNED_BYTE_2_3_3_REV,
GL_UNSIGNED_SHORT_5_6_5, or GL_UNSIGNED_SHORT_5_6_5_REV and *format*
is not **GL_RGB**.

GL_INVALID_OPERATION is generated if *type* is one of
GL_UNSIGNED_SHORT_4_4_4_4, GL_UNSIGNED_SHORT_4_4_4_4_REV,
GL_UNSIGNED_SHORT_5_5_5_1, GL_UNSIGNED_SHORT_1_5_5_5_REV,
GL_UNSIGNED_INT_8_8_8_8, GL_UNSIGNED_INT_8_8_8_8_REV,
GL_UNSIGNED_INT_10_10_10_2, or GL_UNSIGNED_INT_2_10_10_10_REV and
format is neither **GL_RGBA** nor **GL_BGRA**.

ASSOCIATED GETS

glGetTexImage
glIsEnabled with argument **GL_TEXTURE_2D**

SEE ALSO

glColorTable, **glConvolutionFilter2D**, **glCopyPixels**, **glCopyTexImage1D**,
glCopyTexImage2D, **glCopyTexSubImage1D**, **glCopyTexSubImage2D**,
glCopyTexSubImage3D, **glDrawPixels**, **glMatrixMode**, **glPixelStore**,
glPixelTransfer, **glSeparableFilter2D**, **glTexEnv**, **glTexGen**, **glTexImage1D**,
glTexImage3D, **glTexSubImage1D**, **glTexSubImage2D**, **glTexSubImage3D**,
glTexParameter

NAME

glTexImage3D – specify a three-dimensional texture image

C SPECIFICATION

void **glTexImage3D**(GLenum *target,*
                  GLint *level,*
                  GLenum *internalformat,*
                  GLsizei *width,*
                  GLsizei *height,*
                  GLsizei *depth,*
                  GLint *border,*
                  GLenum *format,*
                  GLenum *type,*
                  const GLvoid **pixels*)

PARAMETERS

target   Specifies the target texture. Must be **GL_TEXTURE_3D** or
                  GL_PROXY_TEXTURE_3D.

level   Specifies the level-of-detail number. Level 0 is the base image level.
                  Level *n* is the nth mipmap reduction image.

internalformat

                  Specifies the number of color components in the texture. Must be 1,
                  2, 3, or 4, or one of the following symbolic constants: **GL_ALPHA,
                  GL_ALPHA4, GL_ALPHA8, GL_ALPHA12, GL_ALPHA16,
                  GL_LUMINANCE, GL_LUMINANCE4, GL_LUMINANCE8,
                  GL_LUMINANCE12, GL_LUMINANCE16, GL_LUMINANCE_ALPHA,
                  GL_LUMINANCE4_ALPHA4, GL_LUMINANCE6_ALPHA2,
                  GL_LUMINANCE8_ALPHA8, GL_LUMINANCE12_ALPHA4,
                  GL_LUMINANCE12_ALPHA12, GL_LUMINANCE16_ALPHA16,
                  GL_INTENSITY, GL_INTENSITY4, GL_INTENSITY8,
                  GL_INTENSITY12, GL_INTENSITY16, GL_R3_G3_B2, GL_RGB,
                  GL_RGB4, GL_RGB5, GL_RGB8, GL_RGB10, GL_RGB12, GL_RGB16,
                  GL_RGBA, GL_RGBA2, GL_RGBA4, GL_RGB5_A1, GL_RGBA8,
                  GL_RGB10_A2, GL_RGBA12,** or **GL_RGBA16.**

width   Specifies the width of the texture image. Must be $2^n + 2(border)$ for
                  some integer *n*. All implementations support texture images that are at
                  least 64 texels wide.

height   Specifies the height of the texture image. Must be $2^m + 2(border)$ for
                  some integer *m*. All implementations support texture images that
                  are at least 64 texels high.

depth	Specifies the depth of the texture image. Must be $2^k + 2(border)$ for some integer k. All implementations support texture images that are at least 64 texels deep.
border	Specifies the width of the border. Must be either 0 or 1.
format	Specifies the format of the pixel data. The following symbolic values are accepted: **GL_COLOR_INDEX**, **GL_RED**, **GL_GREEN**, **GL_BLUE**, **GL_ALPHA**, **GL_RGB**, **GL_BGR**, **GL_RGBA**, **GL_BGRA**, **GL_LUMINANCE**, and **GL_LUMINANCE_ALPHA**.
type	Specifies the data type of the pixel data. The following symbolic values are accepted: **GL_UNSIGNED_BYTE**, **GL_BYTE**, **GL_BITMAP**, **GL_UNSIGNED_SHORT**, **GL_SHORT**, **GL_UNSIGNED_INT**, **GL_INT**, **GL_FLOAT GL_UNSIGNED_BYTE_3_3_2**, **GL_UNSIGNED_BYTE_2_3_3_REV**, **GL_UNSIGNED_SHORT_5_6_5**, **GL_UNSIGNED_SHORT_5_6_5_REV**, **GL_UNSIGNED_SHORT_4_4_4_4**, **GL_UNSIGNED_SHORT_4_4_4_4_REV**, **GL_UNSIGNED_SHORT_5_5_5_1**, **GL_UNSIGNED_SHORT_1_5_5_5_REV**, **GL_UNSIGNED_INT_8_8_8_8**, **GL_UNSIGNED_INT_8_8_8_8_REV**, **GL_UNSIGNED_INT_10_10_10_2**, and **GL_UNSIGNED_INT_2_10_10_10_REV**.
pixels	Specifies a pointer to the image data in memory.

DESCRIPTION

Texturing maps a portion of a specified texture image onto each graphical primitive for which texturing is enabled. To enable and disable three-dimensional texturing, call **glEnable** and **glDisable** with argument **GL_TEXTURE_3D**.

To define texture images, call **glTexImage3D**. The arguments describe the parameters of the texture image, such as height, width, depth, width of the border, level-of-detail number (see **glTexParameter**), and number of color components provided. The last three arguments describe how the image is represented in memory; they are identical to the pixel formats used for **glDrawPixels**.

If *target* is **GL_PROXY_TEXTURE_3D**, no data is read from *pixels*, but all of the texture image state is recalculated, checked for consistency, and checked against the implementation's capabilities. If the implementation cannot handle a texture of the requested texture size, it sets all of the image state to 0, but does not generate an error (see **glGetError**). To query for an entire mipmap array, use an image array level greater than or equal to 1.

If *target* is **GL_TEXTURE_3D**, data is read from *pixels* as a sequence of signed or unsigned bytes, shorts, or longs, or single-precision floating-point values, depending on *type*. These values are grouped into sets of one, two, three, or four values, depending on *format*, to form elements. If *type* is **GL_BITMAP**, the data is considered as a string of unsigned bytes (and *format* must be **GL_COLOR_INDEX**). Each data byte is treated as eight 1-bit elements, with bit ordering determined by **GL_UNPACK_LSB_FIRST** (see **glPixelStore**).

The first element corresponds to the lower left corner of the texture image. Subsequent elements progress left-to-right through the remaining texels in the lowest row of the texture image, and then in successively higher rows of the texture image. The final element corresponds to the upper right corner of the texture image.

format determines the composition of each element in *pixels*. It can assume one of eleven symbolic values:

GL_COLOR_INDEX
Each element is a single value, a color index. The GL converts it to fixed point (with an unspecified number of zero bits to the right of the binary point), shifted left or right depending on the value and sign of **GL_INDEX_SHIFT**, and added to **GL_INDEX_OFFSET** (see **glPixelTransfer**). The resulting index is converted to a set of color components using the **GL_PIXEL_MAP_I_TO_R**, **GL_PIXEL_MAP_I_TO_G**, **GL_PIXEL_MAP_I_TO_B**, and **GL_PIXEL_MAP_I_TO_A** tables, and clamped to the range [0,1].

GL_RED Each element is a single red component. The GL converts it to floating point and assembles it into an RGBA element by attaching 0 for green and blue, and 1 for alpha. Each component is then multiplied by the signed scale factor **GL_c_SCALE**, added to the signed bias **GL_c_BIAS**, and clamped to the range [0,1] (see **glPixelTransfer**).

GL_GREEN
Each element is a single green component. The GL converts it to floating point and assembles it into an RGBA element by attaching 0 for red and blue, and 1 for alpha. Each component is then multiplied by the signed scale factor **GL_c_SCALE**, added to the signed bias **GL_c_BIAS**, and clamped to the range [0,1] (see **glPixelTransfer**).

GL_BLUE Each element is a single blue component. The GL converts it to floating point and assembles it into an RGBA element by attaching 0 for red and green, and 1 for alpha. Each component is then multiplied by the signed scale factor **GL_c_SCALE**, added to the signed bias **GL_c_BIAS**, and clamped to the range [0,1] (see **glPixelTransfer**).

GL_ALPHA

Each element is a single alpha component. The GL converts it to floating point and assembles it into an RGBA element by attaching 0 for red, green, and blue. Each component is then multiplied by the signed scale factor **GL_c_SCALE**, added to the signed bias **GL_c_BIAS**, and clamped to the range [0,1] (see **glPixelTransfer**).

GL_RGB

GL_BGR Each element is an RGB triple. The GL converts it to floating point and assembles it into an RGBA element by attaching 1 for alpha. Each component is then multiplied by the signed scale factor **GL_c_SCALE**, added to the signed bias **GL_c_BIAS**, and clamped to the range [0,1] (see **glPixelTransfer**).

GL_RGBA

GL_BGRA

Each element contains all four components. Each component is multiplied by the signed scale factor **GL_c_SCALE**, added to the signed bias **GL_c_BIAS**, and clamped to the range [0,1] (see **glPixelTransfer**).

GL_LUMINANCE

Each element is a single luminance value. The GL converts it to floating point, then assembles it into an RGBA element by replicating the luminance value three times for red, green, and blue and attaching 1 for alpha. Each component is then multiplied by the signed scale factor **GL_c_SCALE**, added to the signed bias **GL_c_BIAS**, and clamped to the range [0,1] (see **glPixelTransfer**).

GL_LUMINANCE_ALPHA

Each element is a luminance/alpha pair. The GL converts it to floating point, then assembles it into an RGBA element by replicating the luminance value three times for red, green, and blue. Each component is then multiplied by the signed scale factor **GL_c_SCALE**, added to the signed bias **GL_c_BIAS**, and clamped to the range [0,1] (see **glPixelTransfer**).

Refer to the **glDrawPixels** reference page for a description of the acceptable values for the *type* parameter.

If an application wants to store the texture at a certain resolution or in a certain format, it can request the resolution and format with *internalformat*. The GL will choose an internal representation that closely approximates that requested by *internalformat*, but it may not match exactly. (The representations specified by **GL_LUMINANCE, GL_LUMINANCE_ALPHA, GL_RGB**, and **GL_RGBA** must match exactly. The numeric values 1, 2, 3, and 4 may also be used to specify the above representations.)

Use the **GL_PROXY_TEXTURE_3D** target to try out a resolution and format. The implementation will update and recompute its best match for the requested storage resolution and format. To then query this state, call **glGetTexLevelParameter**. If the texture cannot be accommodated, texture state is set to 0.

A one-component texture image uses only the red component of the RGBA color extracted from *pixels*. A two-component image uses the R and A values. A three-component image uses the R, G, and B values. A four-component image uses all of the RGBA components.

NOTES

Texturing has no effect in color index mode.

The texture image can be represented by the same data formats as the pixels in a **glDrawPixels** command, except that **GL_STENCIL_INDEX** and **GL_DEPTH_COMPONENT** cannot be used. **glPixelStore** and **glPixelTransfer** modes affect texture images in exactly the way they affect **glDrawPixels**.

glTexImage3D is available only if the GL version is 1.2 or greater.

Internal formats other than 1, 2, 3, or 4 may be used only if the GL version is 1.1 or greater.

pixels may be a null pointer. In this case texture memory is allocated to accommodate a texture of width *width*, height *height*, and depth *depth*. You can then download subtextures to initialize this texture memory. The image is undefined if the user tries to apply an uninitialized portion of the texture image to a primitive.

Formats **GL_BGR**, and **GL_BGRA** and types **GL_UNSIGNED_BYTE_3_3_2**, **GL_UNSIGNED_BYTE_2_3_3_REV**, **GL_UNSIGNED_SHORT_5_6_5**, **GL_UNSIGNED_SHORT_5_6_5_REV**, **GL_UNSIGNED_SHORT_4_4_4_4**, **GL_UNSIGNED_SHORT_4_4_4_4_REV**, **GL_UNSIGNED_SHORT_5_5_5_1**, **GL_UNSIGNED_SHORT_1_5_5_5_REV**, **GL_UNSIGNED_INT_8_8_8_8**, **GL_UNSIGNED_INT_8_8_8_8_REV**, **GL_UNSIGNED_INT_10_10_10_2**, and **GL_UNSIGNED_INT_2_10_10_10_REV** are available only if the GL version is 1.2 or greater.

When the **GL_ARB_multitexture** extension is supported, **glTexImage3D** specifies the three-dimensional texture for the current texture unit, specified with **glActiveTextureARB**.

If the **GL_ARB_imaging** extension is supported, RGBA elements may also be processed by the imaging pipeline. The following stages may be applied to an RGBA color before color component clamping to the range [0, 1]:

1. Color component replacement by the color table specified for **GL_COLOR_TABLE**, if enabled. See **glColorTable**.

2. Color component replacement by the color table specified for
GL_POST_CONVOLUTION_COLOR_TABLE, if enabled. See **glColorTable**.

3. Transformation by the color matrix. See **glMatrixMode**.

4. RGBA components may be multiplied by **GL_POST_COLOR_MATRIX_c_SCALE**,
and added to **GL_POST_COLOR_MATRIX_c_BIAS**, if enabled. See
glPixelTransfer.

5. Color component replacement by the color table specified for
GL_POST_COLOR_MATRIX_COLOR_TABLE, if enabled. See **glColorTable**.

ERRORS

GL_INVALID_ENUM is generated if *target* is not **GL_TEXTURE_3D** or
GL_PROXY_TEXTURE_3D.

GL_INVALID_ENUM is generated if *format* is not an accepted format constant. Format constants other than **GL_STENCIL_INDEX** and **GL_DEPTH_COMPONENT** are
accepted.

GL_INVALID_ENUM is generated if *type* is not a type constant.

GL_INVALID_ENUM is generated if *type* is **GL_BITMAP** and *format* is not
GL_COLOR_INDEX.

GL_INVALID_VALUE is generated if *level* is less than 0.

GL_INVALID_VALUE may be generated if *level* is greater than $\log_2 max$, where *max*
is the returned value of **GL_MAX_TEXTURE_SIZE**.

GL_INVALID_VALUE is generated if *internalformat* is not 1, 2, 3, 4, or one of the
accepted resolution and format symbolic constants.

GL_INVALID_VALUE is generated if *width*, *height*, or *depth* is less than 0 or greater
than 2 + **GL_MAX_TEXTURE_SIZE**, or if either cannot be represented as
$2^k + 2(border)$ for some integer value of *k*.

GL_INVALID_VALUE is generated if *border* is not 0 or 1.

GL_INVALID_OPERATION is generated if **glTexImage3D** is executed between the
execution of **glBegin** and the corresponding execution of **glEnd**.

GL_INVALID_OPERATION is generated if *type* is one of
GL_UNSIGNED_BYTE_3_3_2, **GL_UNSIGNED_BYTE_2_3_3_REV**,
GL_UNSIGNED_SHORT_5_6_5, or **GL_UNSIGNED_SHORT_5_6_5_REV** and *format*
is not **GL_RGB**.

GL_INVALID_OPERATION is generated if *type* is one of
GL_UNSIGNED_SHORT_4_4_4_4, **GL_UNSIGNED_SHORT_4_4_4_4_REV**,
GL_UNSIGNED_SHORT_5_5_5_1, **GL_UNSIGNED_SHORT_1_5_5_5_REV**,
GL_UNSIGNED_INT_8_8_8_8, **GL_UNSIGNED_INT_8_8_8_8_REV**,
GL_UNSIGNED_INT_10_10_10_2, or **GL_UNSIGNED_INT_2_10_10_10_REV** and

format is neither **GL_RGBA** nor **GL_BGRA**.

ASSOCIATED GETS

glGetTexImage

glIsEnabled with argument **GL_TEXTURE_3D**

SEE ALSO

glActiveTextureARB, glCopyPixels, glCopyTexImage1D, glCopyTexImage2D, glCopyTexSubImage1D, glCopyTexSubImage2D, glCopyTexSubImage3D, glDrawPixels, glPixelStore, glPixelTransfer, glTexEnv, glTexGen, glTexImage1D, glTexImage2D, glTexSubImage1D, glTexSubImage2D, glTexSubImage3D, glTexParameter

NAME

glTexParameterf, glTexParameteri, glTexParameterfv, glTexParameteriv – set texture parameters

C SPECIFICATION

void **glTexParameterf**(GLenum *target*,
                         GLenum *pname*,
                         GLfloat *param*)
void **glTexParameteri**(GLenum *target*,
                         GLenum *pname*,
                         GLint *param*)

PARAMETERS

target   Specifies the target texture, which must be either GL_TEXTURE_1D, GL_TEXTURE_2D, or GL_TEXTURE_3D.

pname

Specifies the symbolic name of a single-valued texture parameter. *pname* can be one of the following: GL_TEXTURE_MIN_FILTER, GL_TEXTURE_MAG_FILTER, GL_TEXTURE_MIN_LOD, GL_TEXTURE_MAX_LOD, GL_TEXTURE_BASE_LEVEL, GL_TEXTURE_MAX_LEVEL, GL_TEXTURE_WRAP_S, GL_TEXTURE_WRAP_T, GL_TEXTURE_WRAP_R, or GL_TEXTURE_PRIORITY.

param

Specifies the value of *pname*.

C SPECIFICATION

void **glTexParameterfv**(GLenum *target*,
                          GLenum *pname*,
                          const GLfloat **params*)
void **glTexParameteriv**(GLenum *target*,
                          GLenum *pname*,
                          const GLint **params*)

PARAMETERS

target   Specifies the target texture, which must be either GL_TEXTURE_1D, GL_TEXTURE_2D or GL_TEXTURE_3D.

pname   Specifies the symbolic name of a texture parameter. *pname* can be one of the following: GL_TEXTURE_MIN_FILTER, GL_TEXTURE_MAG_FILTER, GL_TEXTURE_MIN_LOD, GL_TEXTURE_MAX_LOD, GL_TEXTURE_BASE_LEVEL, GL_TEXTURE_MAX_LEVEL,

> GL_TEXTURE_WRAP_S, GL_TEXTURE_WRAP_T, GL_TEXTURE_WRAP_R, GL_TEXTURE_BORDER_COLOR, or GL_TEXTURE_PRIORITY.

params Specifies a pointer to an array where the value or values of *pname* are stored.

DESCRIPTION

Texture mapping is a technique that applies an image onto an object's surface as if the image were a decal or cellophane shrink-wrap. The image is created in texture space, with an (*s*, *t*) coordinate system. A texture is a one- or two-dimensional image and a set of parameters that determine how samples are derived from the image.

glTexParameter assigns the value or values in *params* to the texture parameter specified as *pname*. *target* defines the target texture, either **GL_TEXTURE_1D**, **GL_TEXTURE_2D**, or **GL_TEXTURE_3D**. The following symbols are accepted in *pname*:

GL_TEXTURE_MIN_FILTER

The texture minifying function is used whenever the pixel being textured maps to an area greater than one texture element. There are six defined minifying functions. Two of them use the nearest one or nearest four texture elements to compute the texture value. The other four use mipmaps.

A mipmap is an ordered set of arrays representing the same image at progressively lower resolutions. If the texture has dimensions $2^n \times 2^m$, there are $\max(n,m)+1$ mipmaps. The first mipmap is the original texture, with dimensions $2^n \times 2^m$. Each subsequent mipmap has dimensions $2^{k-1} \times 2^{l-1}$, where $2^k \times 2^l$ are the dimensions of the previous mipmap, until either $k = 0$ or $l = 0$. At that point, subsequent mipmaps have dimension $1 \times 2^{l-1}$ or $2^{k-1} \times 1$ until the final mipmap, which has dimension 1×1. To define the mipmaps, call **glTexImage1D**, **glTexImage2D**, **glTexImage3D**, **glCopyTexImage1D**, or **glCopyTexImage2D** with the *level* argument indicating the order of the mipmaps. Level 0 is the original texture; level $\max(n,m)$ is the final 1×1 mipmap.

params supplies a function for minifying the texture as one of the following:

GL_NEAREST

Returns the value of the texture element that is nearest (in Manhattan distance) to the center of the pixel being textured.

GL_LINEAR

Returns the weighted average of the four texture elements that are closest to the center of the pixel being textured. These can include border texture elements, depending on the values of **GL_TEXTURE_WRAP_S** and **GL_TEXTURE_WRAP_T**, and on the exact mapping.

GL_NEAREST_MIPMAP_NEAREST

> Chooses the mipmap that most closely matches the size of the pixel being textured and uses the **GL_NEAREST** criterion (the texture element nearest to the center of the pixel) to produce a texture value.

GL_LINEAR_MIPMAP_NEAREST

> Chooses the mipmap that most closely matches the size of the pixel being textured and uses the **GL_LINEAR** criterion (a weighted average of the four texture elements that are closest to the center of the pixel) to produce a texture value.

GL_NEAREST_MIPMAP_LINEAR

> Chooses the two mipmaps that most closely match the size of the pixel being textured and uses the **GL_NEAREST** criterion (the texture element nearest to the center of the pixel) to produce a texture value from each mipmap. The final texture value is a weighted average of those two values.

GL_LINEAR_MIPMAP_LINEAR

> Chooses the two mipmaps that most closely match the size of the pixel being textured and uses the **GL_LINEAR** criterion (a weighted average of the four texture elements that are closest to the center of the pixel) to produce a texture value from each mipmap. The final texture value is a weighted average of those two values.

As more texture elements are sampled in the minification process, fewer aliasing artifacts will be apparent. While the **GL_NEAREST** and **GL_LINEAR** minification functions can be faster than the other four, they sample only one or four texture elements to determine the texture value of the pixel being rendered and can produce moire patterns or ragged transitions. The initial value of **GL_TEXTURE_MIN_FILTER** is **GL_NEAREST_MIPMAP_LINEAR**.

GL_TEXTURE_MAG_FILTER

> The texture magnification function is used when the pixel being textured maps to an area less than or equal to one texture element. It sets the texture magnification function to either **GL_NEAREST** or **GL_LINEAR** (see below). **GL_NEAREST** is generally faster than **GL_LINEAR**, but it can produce textured images with sharper edges because the transition between texture elements is not as smooth. The initial value of **GL_TEXTURE_MAG_FILTER** is **GL_LINEAR**.

GL_NEAREST

Returns the value of the texture element that is nearest (in Manhattan distance) to the center of the pixel being textured.

GL_LINEAR

Returns the weighted average of the four texture elements that are closest to the center of the pixel being textured. These can include border texture elements, depending on the values of **GL_TEXTURE_WRAP_S** and **GL_TEXTURE_WRAP_T**, and on the exact mapping.

GL_TEXTURE_MIN_LOD

Sets the minimum level-of-detail parameter. This floating-point value limits the selection of highest resolution mipmap (lowest mipmap level). The initial value is -1000.

GL_TEXTURE_MAX_LOD

Sets the maximum level-of-detail parameter. This floating-point value limits the selection of the lowest resolution mipmap (highest mipmap level). The initial value is 1000.

GL_TEXTURE_BASE_LEVEL

Specifies the index of the lowest defined mipmap level. This is an integer value. The initial value is 0.

GL_TEXTURE_MAX_LEVEL

Sets the index of the highest defined mipmap level. This is an integer value. The initial value is 1000.

GL_TEXTURE_WRAP_S

Sets the wrap parameter for texture coordinate *s* to either **GL_CLAMP**, **GL_CLAMP_TO_EDGE**, or **GL_REPEAT**. **GL_CLAMP** causes *s* coordinates to be clamped to the range [0,1] and is useful for preventing wrapping artifacts when mapping a single image onto an object. **GL_CLAMP_TO_EDGE** causes *s* coordinates to be clamped to the range $\left[\frac{1}{2N}, 1-\frac{1}{2N}\right]$, where N is the size of the texture in the direction of clamping. **GL_REPEAT** causes the integer part of the *s* coordinate to be ignored; the GL uses only the fractional part, thereby creating a repeating pattern. Border texture elements are accessed only if wrapping is set to **GL_CLAMP**. Initially, **GL_TEXTURE_WRAP_S** is set to **GL_REPEAT**.

GL_TEXTURE_WRAP_T

Sets the wrap parameter for texture coordinate *t* to either **GL_CLAMP**, **GL_CLAMP_TO_EDGE**, or **GL_REPEAT**. See the discussion under **GL_TEXTURE_WRAP_S**. Initially, **GL_TEXTURE_WRAP_T** is set to **GL_REPEAT**.

GL_TEXTURE_WRAP_R

Sets the wrap parameter for texture coordinate *r* to either **GL_CLAMP**, **GL_CLAMP_TO_EDGE**, or **GL_REPEAT**. See the discussion under **GL_TEXTURE_WRAP_S**. Initially, **GL_TEXTURE_WRAP_R** is set to **GL_REPEAT**.

GL_TEXTURE_BORDER_COLOR

Sets a border color. *params* contains four values that comprise the RGBA color of the texture border. Integer color components are interpreted linearly such that the most positive integer maps to 1.0, and the most negative integer maps to -1.0. The values are clamped to the range [0,1] when they are specified. Initially, the border color is (0, 0, 0, 0).

GL_TEXTURE_PRIORITY

Specifies the texture residence priority of the currently bound texture. Permissible values are in the range [0, 1]. See **glPrioritizeTextures** and **glBindTexture** for more information.

NOTES

GL_TEXTURE_3D, GL_TEXTURE_MIN_LOD, GL_TEXTURE_MAX_LOD, **GL_TEXTURE_BASE_LEVEL**, and **GL_TEXTURE_MAX_LEVEL** are available only if the GL version is 1.2 or greater.

Suppose that a program has enabled texturing (by calling **glEnable** with argument **GL_TEXTURE_1D**, **GL_TEXTURE_2D**, or **GL_TEXTURE_3D**) and has set **GL_TEXTURE_MIN_FILTER** to one of the functions that requires a mipmap. If either the dimensions of the texture images currently defined (with previous calls to **glTexImage1D**, **glTexImage2D**, **glTexImage3D**, **glCopyTexImage1D**, or **glCopyTexImage2D**) do not follow the proper sequence for mipmaps (described above), or there are fewer texture images defined than are needed, or the set of texture images have differing numbers of texture components, then it is as if texture mapping were disabled.

Linear filtering accesses the four nearest texture elements only in 2D textures. In 1D textures, linear filtering accesses the two nearest texture elements.

When the **GL_ARB_multitexture** extension is supported, **glTexParameter** specifies the texture parameters for the active texture unit, specified by calling **glActiveTextureARB**.

ERRORS

GL_INVALID_ENUM is generated if *target* or *pname* is not one of the accepted defined values.

GL_INVALID_ENUM is generated if *params* should have a defined constant value (based on the value of *pname*) and does not.

GL_INVALID_OPERATION is generated if **glTexParameter** is executed between the execution of **glBegin** and the corresponding execution of **glEnd**.

ASSOCIATED GETS

glGetTexParameter
glGetTexLevelParameter

SEE ALSO

glActiveTextureARB, glBindTexture, glCopyPixels, glCopyTexImage1D, glCopyTexImage2D, glCopyTexSubImage1D, glCopyTexSubImage2D, glCopyTexSubImage3D, glDrawPixels, glPixelStore, glPixelTransfer, glPrioritizeTextures, glTexEnv, glTexGen, glTexImage1D, glTexImage2D, glTexImage3D, glTexSubImage1D, glTexSubImage2D, glTexSubImage3D

NAME

glTexSubImage1D – specify a one-dimensional texture subimage

C SPECIFICATION

```
void glTexSubImage1D( GLenum target,
                      GLint level,
                      GLint xoffset,
                      GLsizei width,
                      GLenum format,
                      GLenum type,
                      const GLvoid *pixels )
```

PARAMETERS

target Specifies the target texture. Must be **GL_TEXTURE_1D**.

level Specifies the level-of-detail number. Level 0 is the base image level. Level *n* is the *n*th mipmap reduction image.

xoffset Specifies a texel offset in the x direction within the texture array.

width Specifies the width of the texture subimage.

format
    Specifies the format of the pixel data. The following symbolic values are accepted: **GL_COLOR_INDEX**, **GL_RED**, **GL_GREEN**, **GL_BLUE**, **GL_ALPHA**, **GL_RGB**, **GL_BGR**, **GL_RGBA**, **GL_BGRA**, **GL_LUMINANCE**, and **GL_LUMINANCE_ALPHA**.

type Specifies the data type of the pixel data. The following symbolic values are accepted: **GL_UNSIGNED_BYTE**, **GL_BYTE**, **GL_BITMAP**, **GL_UNSIGNED_SHORT**, **GL_SHORT**, **GL_UNSIGNED_INT**, **GL_INT**, **GL_FLOAT**, **GL_UNSIGNED_BYTE_3_3_2**, **GL_UNSIGNED_BYTE_2_3_3_REV**, **GL_UNSIGNED_SHORT_5_6_5**, **GL_UNSIGNED_SHORT_5_6_5_REV**, **GL_UNSIGNED_SHORT_4_4_4_4**, **GL_UNSIGNED_SHORT_4_4_4_4_REV**, **GL_UNSIGNED_SHORT_5_5_5_1**, **GL_UNSIGNED_SHORT_1_5_5_5_REV**, **GL_UNSIGNED_INT_8_8_8_8**, **GL_UNSIGNED_INT_8_8_8_8_REV**, **GL_UNSIGNED_INT_10_10_10_2**, and **GL_UNSIGNED_INT_2_10_10_10_REV**.

pixels Specifies a pointer to the image data in memory.

DESCRIPTION

Texturing maps a portion of a specified texture image onto each graphical primitive for which texturing is enabled. To enable or disable one-dimensional texturing, call **glEnable** and **glDisable** with argument **GL_TEXTURE_1D**.

glTexSubImage1D redefines a contiguous subregion of an existing one-dimensional texture image. The texels referenced by *pixels* replace the portion of the existing texture array with x indices *xoffset* and *xoffset* + *width* − 1,inclusive. This region may not include any texels outside the range of the texture array as it was originally specified. It is not an error to specify a subtexture with width of 0, but such a specification has no effect.

NOTES

glTexSubImage1D is available only if the GL version is 1.1 or greater.

Texturing has no effect in color index mode.

glPixelStore and **glPixelTransfer** modes affect texture images in exactly the way they affect **glDrawPixels**.

Formats **GL_BGR**, and **GL_BGRA** and types **GL_UNSIGNED_BYTE_3_3_2**, **GL_UNSIGNED_BYTE_2_3_3_REV**, **GL_UNSIGNED_SHORT_5_6_5**, **GL_UNSIGNED_SHORT_5_6_5_REV**, **GL_UNSIGNED_SHORT_4_4_4_4**, **GL_UNSIGNED_SHORT_4_4_4_4_REV**, **GL_UNSIGNED_SHORT_5_5_5_1**, **GL_UNSIGNED_SHORT_1_5_5_5_REV**, **GL_UNSIGNED_INT_8_8_8_8**, **GL_UNSIGNED_INT_8_8_8_8_REV**, **GL_UNSIGNED_INT_10_10_10_2**, and **GL_UNSIGNED_INT_2_10_10_10_REV** are available only if the GL version is 1.2 or greater.

When the **GL_ARB_multitexture** extension is supported, **glTexSubImage1D** specifies a one-dimensional sub texture for the current texture unit, specified with **glActiveTextureARB**.

When the **GL_ARB_imaging** extension is supported, the RGBA components specified in *pixels* may be processed by the imaging pipeline. See **glTexImage1D** for specific details.

ERRORS

GL_INVALID_ENUM is generated if *target* is not one of the allowable values.

GL_INVALID_OPERATION is generated if the texture array has not been defined by a previous **glTexImage1D** operation.

GL_INVALID_VALUE is generated if *level* is less than 0.

GL_INVALID_VALUE may be generated if *level* is greater than $\log_2 max$, where *max* is the returned value of **GL_MAX_TEXTURE_SIZE**.

GL_INVALID_VALUE is generated if *xoffset* < −*b*, or if (*xoffset* + *width*) > (*w* − *b*), where *w* is the **GL_TEXTURE_WIDTH**, and *b* is the width of the **GL_TEXTURE_BORDER** of the texture image being modified. Note that *w* includes twice the border width.

GL_INVALID_VALUE is generated if *width* is less than 0.

GL_INVALID_ENUM is generated if *format* is not an accepted format constant.

GL_INVALID_ENUM is generated if *type* is not a type constant.

GL_INVALID_ENUM is generated if *type* is **GL_BITMAP** and *format* is not **GL_COLOR_INDEX**.

GL_INVALID_OPERATION is generated if **glTexSubImage1D** is executed between the execution of **glBegin** and the corresponding execution of **glEnd**.

GL_INVALID_OPERATION is generated if *type* is one of **GL_UNSIGNED_BYTE_3_3_2**, **GL_UNSIGNED_BYTE_2_3_3_REV**, **GL_UNSIGNED_SHORT_5_6_5**, or **GL_UNSIGNED_SHORT_5_6_5_REV** and *format* is not **GL_RGB**.

GL_INVALID_OPERATION is generated if *type* is one of **GL_UNSIGNED_SHORT_4_4_4_4**, **GL_UNSIGNED_SHORT_4_4_4_4_REV**, **GL_UNSIGNED_SHORT_5_5_5_1**, **GL_UNSIGNED_SHORT_1_5_5_5_REV**, **GL_UNSIGNED_INT_8_8_8_8**, **GL_UNSIGNED_INT_8_8_8_8_REV**, **GL_UNSIGNED_INT_10_10_10_2**, or **GL_UNSIGNED_INT_2_10_10_10_REV** and *format* is neither **GL_RGBA** nor **GL_BGRA**.

ASSOCIATED GETS

glGetTexImage
glIsEnabled with argument **GL_TEXTURE_1D**

SEE ALSO

glActiveTextureARB, **glCopyTexImage1D**, **glCopyTexImage2D**, **glCopyTexSubImage1D**, **glCopyTexSubImage2D**, **glCopyTexSubImage3D**, **glDrawPixels**, **glPixelStore**, **glPixelTransfer**, **glTexEnv**, **glTexGen**, **glTexImage1D**, **glTexImage2D**, **glTexImage3D**, **glTexParameter**, **glTexSubImage2D**, **glTexSubImage3D**

NAME

glTexSubImage2D – specify a two-dimensional texture subimage

C SPECIFICATION

void **glTexSubImage2D**(GLenum *target*,
                         GLint *level*,
                         GLint *xoffset*,
                         GLint *yoffset*,
                         GLsizei *width*,
                         GLsizei *height*,
                         GLenum *format*,
                         GLenum *type*,
                         const GLvoid **pixels*)

PARAMETERS

target Specifies the target texture. Must be **GL_TEXTURE_2D**.

level Specifies the level-of-detail number. Level 0 is the base image level. Level *n* is the *n*th mipmap reduction image.

xoffset Specifies a texel offset in the x direction within the texture array.

yoffset Specifies a texel offset in the y direction within the texture array.

width Specifies the width of the texture subimage.

height Specifies the height of the texture subimage.

format

Specifies the format of the pixel data. The following symbolic values are accepted: **GL_COLOR_INDEX**, **GL_RED**, **GL_GREEN**, **GL_BLUE**, **GL_ALPHA**, **GL_RGB**, **GL_BGR**, **GL_RGBA**, **GL_BGRA**, **GL_LUMINANCE**, and **GL_LUMINANCE_ALPHA**.

type Specifies the data type of the pixel data. The following symbolic values are accepted: **GL_UNSIGNED_BYTE**, **GL_BYTE**, **GL_BITMAP**, **GL_UNSIGNED_SHORT**, **GL_SHORT**, **GL_UNSIGNED_INT**, **GL_INT**, **GL_FLOAT**, **GL_UNSIGNED_BYTE_3_3_2**, **GL_UNSIGNED_BYTE_2_3_3_REV**, **GL_UNSIGNED_SHORT_5_6_5**, **GL_UNSIGNED_SHORT_5_6_5_REV**, **GL_UNSIGNED_SHORT_4_4_4_4**, **GL_UNSIGNED_SHORT_4_4_4_4_REV**, **GL_UNSIGNED_SHORT_5_5_5_1**, **GL_UNSIGNED_SHORT_1_5_5_5_REV**, **GL_UNSIGNED_INT_8_8_8_8**, **GL_UNSIGNED_INT_8_8_8_8_REV**, **GL_UNSIGNED_INT_10_10_10_2**, and **GL_UNSIGNED_INT_2_10_10_10_REV**.

pixels Specifies a pointer to the image data in memory.

DESCRIPTION

Texturing maps a portion of a specified texture image onto each graphical primitive for which texturing is enabled. To enable and disable two-dimensional texturing, call **glEnable** and **glDisable** with argument GL_TEXTURE_2D.

glTexSubImage2D redefines a contiguous subregion of an existing two-dimensional texture image. The texels referenced by *pixels* replace the portion of the existing texture array with x indices *xoffset* and *xoffset* + *width* − 1, inclusive, and y indices *yoffset* and *yoffset* + *height* − 1, inclusive. This region may not include any texels outside the range of the texture array as it was originally specified. It is not an error to specify a subtexture with zero width or height, but such a specification has no effect.

NOTES

glTexSubImage2D is available only if the GL version is 1.1 or greater.

Texturing has no effect in color index mode.

glPixelStore and **glPixelTransfer** modes affect texture images in exactly the way they affect **glDrawPixels**.

Formats GL_BGR, and GL_BGRA and types GL_UNSIGNED_BYTE_3_3_2, GL_UNSIGNED_BYTE_2_3_3_REV, GL_UNSIGNED_SHORT_5_6_5, GL_UNSIGNED_SHORT_5_6_5_REV, GL_UNSIGNED_SHORT_4_4_4_4, GL_UNSIGNED_SHORT_4_4_4_4_REV, GL_UNSIGNED_SHORT_5_5_5_1, GL_UNSIGNED_SHORT_1_5_5_5_REV, GL_UNSIGNED_INT_8_8_8_8, GL_UNSIGNED_INT_8_8_8_8_REV, GL_UNSIGNED_INT_10_10_10_2, and GL_UNSIGNED_INT_2_10_10_10_REV are available only if the GL version is 1.2 or greater.

When the **GL_ARB_multitexture** extension is supported, **glTexSubImage2D** specifies a two-dimensional sub texture for the current texture unit, specified with **glActiveTextureARB**.

When the **GL_ARB_imaging** extension is supported, the RGBA components specified in *pixels* may be processed by the imaging pipeline. See **glTexImage1D** for specific details.

ERRORS

GL_INVALID_ENUM is generated if *target* is not GL_TEXTURE_2D.

GL_INVALID_OPERATION is generated if the texture array has not been defined by a previous **glTexImage2D** operation.

GL_INVALID_VALUE is generated if *level* is less than 0.

GL_INVALID_VALUE may be generated if *level* is greater than $\log_2 max$, where *max* is the returned value of **GL_MAX_TEXTURE_SIZE**.

GL_INVALID_VALUE is generated if *xoffset* $< -b$, (*xoffset* + *width*) $> (w - b)$, *yoffset* $< -b$, or (*yoffset* + *height*) $> (h - b)$, where *w* is the **GL_TEXTURE_WIDTH**, *h* is the **GL_TEXTURE_HEIGHT**, and *b* is the border width of the texture image being modified. Note that *w* and *h* include twice the border width.

GL_INVALID_VALUE is generated if *width* or *height* is less than 0.

GL_INVALID_ENUM is generated if *format* is not an accepted format constant.

GL_INVALID_ENUM is generated if *type* is not a type constant.

GL_INVALID_ENUM is generated if *type* is **GL_BITMAP** and *format* is not **GL_COLOR_INDEX**.

GL_INVALID_OPERATION is generated if **glTexSubImage2D** is executed between the execution of **glBegin** and the corresponding execution of **glEnd**.

GL_INVALID_OPERATION is generated if *type* is one of **GL_UNSIGNED_BYTE_3_3_2**, **GL_UNSIGNED_BYTE_2_3_3_REV**, **GL_UNSIGNED_SHORT_5_6_5**, or **GL_UNSIGNED_SHORT_5_6_5_REV** and *format* is not **GL_RGB**.

GL_INVALID_OPERATION is generated if *type* is one of **GL_UNSIGNED_SHORT_4_4_4_4**, **GL_UNSIGNED_SHORT_4_4_4_4_REV**, **GL_UNSIGNED_SHORT_5_5_5_1**, **GL_UNSIGNED_SHORT_1_5_5_5_REV**, **GL_UNSIGNED_INT_8_8_8_8**, **GL_UNSIGNED_INT_8_8_8_8_REV**, **GL_UNSIGNED_INT_10_10_10_2**, or **GL_UNSIGNED_INT_2_10_10_10_REV** and *format* is neither **GL_RGBA** nor **GL_BGRA**.

ASSOCIATED GETS

glGetTexImage
glIsEnabled with argument **GL_TEXTURE_2D**

SEE ALSO

glActiveTextureARB, glCopyTexImage1D, glCopyTexImage2D, glCopyTexSubImage1D, glCopyTexSubImage2D, glCopyTexSubImage3D, glDrawPixels, glPixelStore, glPixelTransfer, glTexEnv, glTexGen, glTexImage1D, glTexImage2D, glTexImage3D, glTexSubImage1D, glTexSubImage3D, glTexParameter

NAME

glTexSubImage3D – specify a three-dimensional texture subimage

C SPECIFICATION

void **glTexSubImage3D**(GLenum *target*,
                       GLint *level*,
                       GLint *xoffset*,
                       GLint *yoffset*,
                       GLint *zoffset*,
                       GLsizei *width*,
                       GLsizei *height*,
                       GLsizei *depth*,
                       GLenum *format*,
                       GLenum *type*,
                       const GLvoid **pixels*)

PARAMETERS

target Specifies the target texture. Must be **GL_TEXTURE_3D**.

level Specifies the level-of-detail number. Level 0 is the base image level. Level *n* is the *n*th mipmap reduction image.

xoffset Specifies a texel offset in the x direction within the texture array.

yoffset Specifies a texel offset in the y direction within the texture array.

zoffset Specifies a texel offset in the z direction within the texture array.

width Specifies the width of the texture subimage.

height Specifies the height of the texture subimage.

depth Specifies the depth of the texture subimage.

format
Specifies the format of the pixel data. The following symbolic values are accepted: **GL_COLOR_INDEX**, **GL_RED**, **GL_GREEN**, **GL_BLUE**, **GL_ALPHA**, **GL_RGB**, **GL_BGR**, **GL_RGBA**, **GL_BGRA**, **GL_LUMINANCE**, and **GL_LUMINANCE_ALPHA**.

type Specifies the data type of the pixel data. The following symbolic values are accepted: **GL_UNSIGNED_BYTE**, **GL_BYTE**, **GL_BITMAP**, **GL_UNSIGNED_SHORT**, **GL_SHORT**, **GL_UNSIGNED_INT**, **GL_INT**, **GL_FLOAT**, **GL_UNSIGNED_BYTE_3_3_2**, **GL_UNSIGNED_BYTE_2_3_3_REV**, **GL_UNSIGNED_SHORT_5_6_5**, **GL_UNSIGNED_SHORT_5_6_5_REV**, **GL_UNSIGNED_SHORT_4_4_4_4**, **GL_UNSIGNED_SHORT_4_4_4_4_REV**, **GL_UNSIGNED_SHORT_5_5_5_1**, **GL_UNSIGNED_SHORT_1_5_5_5_REV**, **GL_UNSIGNED_INT_8_8_8_8**,

GL_UNSIGNED_INT_8_8_8_8_REV, GL_UNSIGNED_INT_10_10_10_2, and GL_UNSIGNED_INT_2_10_10_10_REV.

pixels   Specifies a pointer to the image data in memory.

DESCRIPTION

Texturing maps a portion of a specified texture image onto each graphical primitive for which texturing is enabled. To enable and disable three-dimensional texturing, call **glEnable** and **glDisable** with argument **GL_TEXTURE_3D**.

glTexSubImage3D redefines a contiguous subregion of an existing three-dimensional texture image. The texels referenced by *pixels* replace the portion of the existing texture array with x indices *xoffset* and *xoffset* + *width* − 1, inclusive, y indices *yoffset* and *yoffset* + *height* − 1, inclusive, and z indices *zoffset* and *zoffset* + *depth* − 1, inclusive. This region may not include any texels outside the range of the texture array as it was originally specified. It is not an error to specify a subtexture with zero width, height, or depth but such a specification has no effect.

NOTES

glTexSubImage3D is available only if the GL version is 1.2 or greater.

Texturing has no effect in color index mode.

glPixelStore and **glPixelTransfer** modes affect texture images in exactly the way they affect **glDrawPixels**.

Formats **GL_BGR**, and **GL_BGRA** and types **GL_UNSIGNED_BYTE_3_3_2**, **GL_UNSIGNED_BYTE_2_3_3_REV**, **GL_UNSIGNED_SHORT_5_6_5**, **GL_UNSIGNED_SHORT_5_6_5_REV**, **GL_UNSIGNED_SHORT_4_4_4_4**, **GL_UNSIGNED_SHORT_4_4_4_4_REV**, **GL_UNSIGNED_SHORT_5_5_5_1**, **GL_UNSIGNED_SHORT_1_5_5_5_REV**, **GL_UNSIGNED_INT_8_8_8_8**, **GL_UNSIGNED_INT_8_8_8_8_REV**, **GL_UNSIGNED_INT_10_10_10_2**, and **GL_UNSIGNED_INT_2_10_10_10_REV** are available only if the GL version is 1.2 or greater.

When the **GL_ARB_multitexture** extension is supported, **glTexSubImage3D** specifies a three-dimensional sub texture for the current texture unit, specified with **glActiveTextureARB**.

When the **GL_ARB_imaging** extension is supported, the RGBA components specified in *pixels* may be processed by the imaging pipeline. See **glTexImage3D** for specific details.

ERRORS

GL_INVALID_ENUM is generated if *target* is not **GL_TEXTURE_3D**.

GL_INVALID_OPERATION is generated if the texture array has not been defined by a previous **glTexImage3D** operation.

GL_INVALID_VALUE is generated if *level* is less than 0.

GL_INVALID_VALUE may be generated if *level* is greater than $\log_2 max$, where *max* is the returned value of **GL_MAX_TEXTURE_SIZE**.

GL_INVALID_VALUE is generated if *xoffset* $< -b$, (*xoffset* + *width*) $> (w - b)$, *yoffset* $< -b$, or (*yoffset* + *height*) $> (h - b)$, or *zoffset* $< -b$, or (*zoffset* + *depth*) $> (d - b)$, where *w* is the **GL_TEXTURE_WIDTH**, *h* is the **GL_TEXTURE_HEIGHT**, *d* is the **GL_TEXTURE_DEPTH** and *b* is the border width of the texture image being modified. Note that *w*, *h*, and *d* include twice the border width.

GL_INVALID_VALUE is generated if *width*, *height*, or *depth* is less than 0.

GL_INVALID_ENUM is generated if *format* is not an accepted format constant.

GL_INVALID_ENUM is generated if *type* is not a type constant.

GL_INVALID_ENUM is generated if *type* is **GL_BITMAP** and *format* is not **GL_COLOR_INDEX**.

GL_INVALID_OPERATION is generated if **glTexSubImage3D** is executed between the execution of **glBegin** and the corresponding execution of **glEnd**.

GL_INVALID_OPERATION is generated if *type* is one of **GL_UNSIGNED_BYTE_3_3_2**, **GL_UNSIGNED_BYTE_2_3_3_REV**, **GL_UNSIGNED_SHORT_5_6_5**, or **GL_UNSIGNED_SHORT_5_6_5_REV** and *format* is not **GL_RGB**.

GL_INVALID_OPERATION is generated if *type* is one of **GL_UNSIGNED_SHORT_4_4_4_4**, **GL_UNSIGNED_SHORT_4_4_4_4_REV**, **GL_UNSIGNED_SHORT_5_5_5_1**, **GL_UNSIGNED_SHORT_1_5_5_5_REV**, **GL_UNSIGNED_INT_8_8_8_8**, **GL_UNSIGNED_INT_8_8_8_8_REV**, **GL_UNSIGNED_INT_10_10_10_2**, or **GL_UNSIGNED_INT_2_10_10_10_REV** and *format* is neither **GL_RGBA** nor **GL_BGRA**.

ASSOCIATED GETS

glGetTexImage
glIsEnabled with argument GL_TEXTURE_3D

SEE ALSO

glActiveTextureARB, glCopyTexImage1D, glCopyTexImage2D, glCopyTexSubImage1D, glCopyTexSubImage2D, glCopyTexSubImage3D, glDrawPixels, glPixelStore, glPixelTransfer, glTexEnv, glTexGen, glTexImage1D, glTexImage2D, glTexImage3D, glTexSubImage1D, glTexSubImage2D, glTexParameter

NAME

glTranslated, glTranslatef – multiply the current matrix by a translation matrix

C SPECIFICATION

void **glTranslated**(GLdouble x,
            GLdouble y,
            GLdouble z)
void **glTranslatef**(GLfloat x,
            GLfloat y,
            GLfloat z)

PARAMETERS

x, y, z
      Specify the x, y, and z coordinates of a translation vector.

DESCRIPTION

glTranslate produces a translation by (x, y, z). The current matrix (see **glMatrixMode**) is multiplied by this translation matrix, with the product replacing the current matrix, as if **glMultMatrix** were called with the following matrix for its argument:

$$
\begin{matrix}
1 & 0 & 0 & x \\
0 & 1 & 0 & y \\
0 & 0 & 1 & z \\
0 & 0 & 0 & 1
\end{matrix}
$$

If the matrix mode is either **GL_MODELVIEW** or **GL_PROJECTION**, all objects drawn after a call to **glTranslate** are translated.

Use **glPushMatrix** and **glPopMatrix** to save and restore the untranslated coordinate system.

ERRORS

GL_INVALID_OPERATION is generated if **glTranslate** is executed between the execution of **glBegin** and the corresponding execution of **glEnd**.

ASSOCIATED GETS

glGet with argument **GL_MATRIX_MODE**
glGet with argument **GL_COLOR_MATRIX**
glGet with argument **GL_MODELVIEW_MATRIX**
glGet with argument **GL_PROJECTION_MATRIX**
glGet with argument **GL_TEXTURE_MATRIX**

SEE ALSO

glMatrixMode, **glMultMatrix**, **glPushMatrix**, **glRotate**, **glScale**

NAME

glVertex2d, glVertex2f, glVertex2i, glVertex2s, glVertex3d, glVertex3f, glVertex3i, glVertex3s, glVertex4d, glVertex4f, glVertex4i, glVertex4s, glVertex2dv, glVertex2fv, glVertex2iv, glVertex2sv, glVertex3dv, glVertex3fv, glVertex3iv, glVertex3sv, glVertex4dv, glVertex4fv, glVertex4iv, glVertex4sv – specify a vertex

C SPECIFICATION

```
void glVertex2d( GLdouble x,
                 GLdouble y )
void glVertex2f( GLfloat x,
                 GLfloat y )
void glVertex2i( GLint x,
                 GLint y )
void glVertex2s( GLshort x,
                 GLshort y )
void glVertex3d( GLdouble x,
                 GLdouble y,
                 GLdouble z )
void glVertex3f( GLfloat x,
                 GLfloat y,
                 GLfloat z )
void glVertex3i( GLint x,
                 GLint y,
                 GLint z )
void glVertex3s( GLshort x,
                 GLshort y,
                 GLshort z )
void glVertex4d( GLdouble x,
                 GLdouble y,
                 GLdouble z,
                 GLdouble w )
void glVertex4f( GLfloat x,
                 GLfloat y,
                 GLfloat z,
                 GLfloat w )
void glVertex4i( GLint x,
                 GLint y,
                 GLint z,
                 GLint w )
void glVertex4s( GLshort x,
                 GLshort y,
                 GLshort z,
```

GLshort *w*)

PARAMETERS

x, y, z, w

 Specify *x, y, z,* and *w* coordinates of a vertex. Not all parameters are present in all forms of the command.

C SPECIFICATION

 void **glVertex2dv**(const GLdouble **v*)
 void **glVertex2fv**(const GLfloat **v*)
 void **glVertex2iv**(const GLint **v*)
 void **glVertex2sv**(const GLshort **v*)
 void **glVertex3dv**(const GLdouble **v*)
 void **glVertex3fv**(const GLfloat **v*)
 void **glVertex3iv**(const GLint **v*)
 void **glVertex3sv**(const GLshort **v*)
 void **glVertex4dv**(const GLdouble **v*)
 void **glVertex4fv**(const GLfloat **v*)
 void **glVertex4iv**(const GLint **v*)
 void **glVertex4sv**(const GLshort **v*)

PARAMETERS

v Specifies a pointer to an array of two, three, or four elements. The elements of a two-element array are *x* and *y*; of a three-element array, *x, y,* and *z*; and of a four-element array, *x, y, z,* and *w*.

DESCRIPTION

 glVertex commands are used within **glBegin/glEnd** pairs to specify point, line, and polygon vertices. The current color, normal, and texture coordinates are associated with the vertex when **glVertex** is called.

 When only *x* and *y* are specified, *z* defaults to 0 and *w* defaults to 1. When *x, y,* and *z* are specified, *w* defaults to 1.

NOTES

 Invoking **glVertex** outside of a **glBegin/glEnd** pair results in undefined behavior.

SEE ALSO

 glBegin, glCallList, glColor, glEdgeFlag, glEvalCoord, glIndex, glMaterial, glNormal, glRect, glTexCoord, glVertexPointer

NAME

glVertexPointer – define an array of vertex data

C SPECIFICATION

void **glVertexPointer**(GLint *size*,
 GLenum *type*,
 GLsizei *stride*,
 const GLvoid **pointer*)

PARAMETERS

size   Specifies the number of coordinates per vertex; must be 2, 3, or 4. The initial value is 4.

type   Specifies the data type of each coordinate in the array. Symbolic constants **GL_SHORT**, **GL_INT**, **GL_FLOAT**, and **GL_DOUBLE** are accepted. The initial value is **GL_FLOAT**.

stride   Specifies the byte offset between consecutive vertices. If *stride* is 0, the vertices are understood to be tightly packed in the array. The initial value is 0.

pointer Specifies a pointer to the first coordinate of the first vertex in the array. The initial value is 0.

DESCRIPTION

glVertexPointer specifies the location and data format of an array of vertex coordinates to use when rendering. *size* specifies the number of coordinates per vertex and *type* the data type of the coordinates. *stride* specifies the byte stride from one vertex to the next allowing vertices and attributes to be packed into a single array or stored in separate arrays. (Single-array storage may be more efficient on some implementations; see **glInterleavedArrays**.) When a vertex array is specified, *size*, *type*, *stride*, and *pointer* are saved as client-side state.

To enable and disable the vertex array, call **glEnableClientState** and **glDisableClientState** with the argument **GL_VERTEX_ARRAY**. If enabled, the vertex array is used when **glDrawArrays**, **glDrawElements**, or **glArrayElement** is called.

Use **glDrawArrays** to construct a sequence of primitives (all of the same type) from prespecified vertex and vertex attribute arrays. Use **glArrayElement** to specify primitives by indexing vertices and vertex attributes and **glDrawElements** to construct a sequence of primitives by indexing vertices and vertex attributes.

NOTES

glVertexPointer is available only if the GL version is 1.1 or greater.

NOTES

glVertexPointer is available only if the GL version is 1.1 or greater.

The vertex array is initially disabled and isn't accessed when **glArrayElement**, **glDrawElements** or **glDrawArrays** is called.

Execution of **glVertexPointer** is not allowed between the execution of **glBegin** and the corresponding execution of **glEnd**, but an error may or may not be generated. If no error is generated, the operation is undefined.

glVertexPointer is typically implemented on the client side.

Vertex array parameters are client-side state and are therefore not saved or restored by **glPushAttrib** and **glPopAttrib**. Use **glPushClientAttrib** and **glPopClientAttrib** instead.

ERRORS

GL_INVALID_VALUE is generated if *size* is not 2, 3, or 4.

GL_INVALID_ENUM is generated if *type* is is not an accepted value.

GL_INVALID_VALUE is generated if *stride* is negative.

ASSOCIATED GETS

glIsEnabled with argument **GL_VERTEX_ARRAY**
glGet with argument **GL_VERTEX_ARRAY_SIZE**
glGet with argument **GL_VERTEX_ARRAY_TYPE**
glGet with argument **GL_VERTEX_ARRAY_STRIDE**
glGetPointerv with argument **GL_VERTEX_ARRAY_POINTER**

SEE ALSO

glArrayElement, glColorPointer, glDrawArrays, glDrawElements, glDrawRangeElements, glEdgeFlagPointer, glEnable, glGetPointerv, glIndexPointer, glInterleavedArrays, glNormalPointer, glPopClientAttrib, glPushClientAttrib, glTexCoordPointer

NAME

glViewport – set the viewport

C SPECIFICATION

void **glViewport**(GLint *x*,
  GLint *y*,
  GLsizei *width*,
  GLsizei *height*)

PARAMETERS

x, y

Specify the lower left corner of the viewport rectangle, in pixels. The initial value is (0,0).

width, height

Specify the width and height of the viewport. When a GL context is first attached to a window, *width* and *height* are set to the dimensions of that window.

DESCRIPTION

glViewport specifies the affine transformation of *x* and *y* from normalized device coordinates to window coordinates. Let (x_{nd}, y_{nd}) be normalized device coordinates. Then the window coordinates (x_w, y_w) are computed as follows:

$$x_w = (x_{nd} + 1) \; \frac{width}{2} \; + x$$

$$y_w = (y_{nd} + 1) \; \frac{height}{2} \; + y$$

Viewport width and height are silently clamped to a range that depends on the implementation. To query this range, call **glGet** with argument **GL_MAX_VIEWPORT_DIMS**.

ERRORS

GL_INVALID_VALUE is generated if either *width* or *height* is negative.

GL_INVALID_OPERATION is generated if **glViewport** is executed between the execution of **glBegin** and the corresponding execution of **glEnd**.

ASSOCIATED GETS

glGet with argument **GL_VIEWPORT**
glGet with argument **GL_MAX_VIEWPORT_DIMS**

SEE ALSO

glDepthRange

Chapter 6

GLU Reference Pages

This chapter contains the reference pages for the routines in the
OpenGL Utility Library (GLU) in alphabetical order:

The following commands are deprecated in GLU 1.2 and are included for completeness at the end of the chapter:

gluBeginPolygon,   gluNextContour
gluEndPolygon

NAME

gluBeginCurve, **gluEndCurve** – delimit a NURBS curve definition

C SPECIFICATION

void **gluBeginCurve**(GLUnurbs* *nurb*)

void **gluEndCurve**(GLUnurbs* *nurb*)

PARAMETERS

nurb Specifies the NURBS object (created with **gluNewNurbsRenderer**).

DESCRIPTION

Use **gluBeginCurve** to mark the beginning of a NURBS curve definition. After calling **gluBeginCurve**, make one or more calls to **gluNurbsCurve** to define the attributes of the curve. Exactly one of the calls to **gluNurbsCurve** must have a curve type of **GL_MAP1_VERTEX_3** or **GL_MAP1_VERTEX_4**. To mark the end of the NURBS curve definition, call **gluEndCurve**.

GL evaluators are used to render the NURBS curve as a series of line segments. Evaluator state is preserved during rendering with **glPushAttrib**(GL_EVAL_BIT) and **glPopAttrib**(). See the **glPushAttrib** reference page for details on exactly what state these calls preserve.

EXAMPLE

The following commands render a textured NURBS curve with normals; texture coordinates and normals are also specified as NURBS curves:

```
gluBeginCurve(nobj);
    gluNurbsCurve(nobj,  ..., GL_MAP1_TEXTURE_COORD_2);
    gluNurbsCurve(nobj,  ..., GL_MAP1_NORMAL);
    gluNurbsCurve(nobj,  ..., GL_MAP1_VERTEX_4);
gluEndCurve(nobj);
```

SEE ALSO

gluBeginSurface, **gluBeginTrim**, **gluNewNurbsRenderer**, **gluNurbsCurve**, **glPopAttrib**, **glPushAttrib**

NAME

gluBeginSurface, gluEndSurface – delimit a NURBS surface definition

C SPECIFICATION

void **gluBeginSurface**(GLUnurbs* *nurb*)

void **gluEndSurface**(GLUnurbs* *nurb*)

PARAMETERS

nurb Specifies the NURBS object (created with **gluNewNurbsRenderer**).

DESCRIPTION

Use **gluBeginSurface** to mark the beginning of a NURBS surface definition. After calling **gluBeginSurface**, make one or more calls to **gluNurbsSurface** to define the attributes of the surface. Exactly one of these calls to **gluNurbsSurface** must have a surface type of **GL_MAP2_VERTEX_3** or **GL_MAP2_VERTEX_4**. To mark the end of the NURBS surface definition, call **gluEndSurface**.

Trimming of NURBS surfaces is supported with **gluBeginTrim**, **gluPwlCurve**, **gluNurbsCurve**, and **gluEndTrim**. See the **gluBeginTrim** reference page for details.

GL evaluators are used to render the NURBS surface as a set of polygons. Evaluator state is preserved during rendering with **glPushAttrib**(GL_EVAL_BIT) and **glPopAttrib**(). See the **glPushAttrib** reference page for details on exactly what state these calls preserve.

EXAMPLE

The following commands render a textured NURBS surface with normals; the texture coordinates and normals are also described as NURBS surfaces:

```
gluBeginSurface(nobj);
    gluNurbsSurface(nobj, ..., GL_MAP2_TEXTURE_COORD_2);
    gluNurbsSurface(nobj, ..., GL_MAP2_NORMAL);
    gluNurbsSurface(nobj, ..., GL_MAP2_VERTEX_4);
gluEndSurface(nobj);
```

SEE ALSO

gluBeginCurve, **gluBeginTrim**, **gluNewNurbsRenderer**, **gluNurbsCurve**, **gluNurbsSurface**, **gluPwlCurve**

NAME

gluBeginTrim, gluEndTrim – delimit a NURBS trimming loop definition

C SPECIFICATION

void **gluBeginTrim**(GLUnurbs* *nurb*)

void **gluEndTrim**(GLUnurbs* *nurb*)

PARAMETERS

nurb Specifies the NURBS object (created with **gluNewNurbsRenderer**).

DESCRIPTION

Use **gluBeginTrim** to mark the beginning of a trimming loop, and **gluEndTrim** to mark the end of a trimming loop. A trimming loop is a set of oriented curve segments (forming a closed curve) that define boundaries of a NURBS surface. You include these trimming loops in the definition of a NURBS surface, between calls to **gluBeginSurface** and **gluEndSurface**.

The definition for a NURBS surface can contain many trimming loops. For example, if you wrote a definition for a NURBS surface that resembled a rectangle with a hole punched out, the definition would contain two trimming loops. One loop would define the outer edge of the rectangle; the other would define the hole punched out of the rectangle. The definitions of each of these trimming loops would be bracketed by a **gluBeginTrim/gluEndTrim** pair.

The definition of a single closed trimming loop can consist of multiple curve segments, each described as a piecewise linear curve (see **gluPwlCurve**) or as a single NURBS curve (see **gluNurbsCurve**), or as a combination of both in any order. The only library calls that can appear in a trimming loop definition (between the calls to **gluBeginTrim** and **gluEndTrim**) are **gluPwlCurve** and **gluNurbsCurve**.

The area of the NURBS surface that is displayed is the region in the domain to the left of the trimming curve as the curve parameter increases. Thus, the retained region of the NURBS surface is inside a counterclockwise trimming loop and outside a clockwise trimming loop. For the rectangle mentioned earlier, the trimming loop for the outer edge of the rectangle runs counterclockwise, while the trimming loop for the punched-out hole runs clockwise.

If you use more than one curve to define a single trimming loop, the curve segments must form a closed loop (that is, the endpoint of each curve must be the starting point of the next curve, and the endpoint of the final curve must be the starting point of the first curve). If the endpoints of the curve are sufficiently close together but not exactly coincident, they will be coerced to match. If the endpoints are not sufficiently close, an error results (see **gluNurbsCallback**).

If a trimming loop definition contains multiple curves, the direction of the curves must be consistent (that is, the inside must be to the left of all of the curves). Nested trimming loops are legal as long as the curve orientations alternate correctly. If trimming curves are self-intersecting, or intersect one another, an error results.

If no trimming information is given for a NURBS surface, the entire surface is drawn.

EXAMPLE

This code fragment defines a trimming loop that consists of one piecewise linear curve, and two NURBS curves:

```
gluBeginTrim(nobj);
    gluPwlCurve(..., GLU_MAP1_TRIM_2);
    gluNurbsCurve(..., GLU_MAP1_TRIM_2);
    gluNurbsCurve(..., GLU_MAP1_TRIM_3);
gluEndTrim(nobj);
```

SEE ALSO

gluBeginSurface, **gluNewNurbsRenderer**, **gluNurbsCallback**, **gluNurbsCurve**, **gluPwlCurve**

NAME

> **gluBuild1DMipmapLevels** – builds a subset of one-dimensional mipmap levels

C SPECIFICATION

> GLint **gluBuild1DMipmapLevels**(GLenum *target*,
>   GLint *internalFormat*,
>   GLsizei *width*,
>   GLenum *format*,
>   GLenum *type*,
>   GLint *level*,
>   GLint *base*,
>   GLint *max*,
>   const void **data*)

PARAMETERS

target	Specifies the target texture. Must be **GL_TEXTURE_1D**.
internalFormat	

Requests the internal storage format of the texture image. Must be 1, 2, 3, or 4 or one of the following symbolic constants: **GL_ALPHA, GL_ALPHA4, GL_ALPHA8, GL_ALPHA12, GL_ALPHA16, GL_LUMINANCE, GL_LUMINANCE4, GL_LUMINANCE8, GL_LUMINANCE12, GL_LUMINANCE16, GL_LUMINANCE_ALPHA, GL_LUMINANCE4_ALPHA4, GL_LUMINANCE6_ALPHA2, GL_LUMINANCE8_ALPHA8, GL_LUMINANCE12_ALPHA4, GL_LUMINANCE12_ALPHA12, GL_LUMINANCE16_ALPHA16, GL_INTENSITY, GL_INTENSITY4, GL_INTENSITY8, GL_INTENSITY12, GL_INTENSITY16, GL_RGB, GL_R3_G3_B2, GL_RGB4, GL_RGB5, GL_RGB8, GL_RGB10, GL_RGB12, GL_RGB16, GL_RGBA, GL_RGBA2, GL_RGBA4, GL_RGB5_A1, GL_RGBA8, GL_RGB10_A2, GL_RGBA12** or **GL_RGBA16**.

width	Specifies the width in pixels of the texture image. This should be a power of 2.
format	Specifies the format of the pixel data. Must be one of: **GL_COLOR_INDEX, GL_DEPTH_COMPONENT, GL_RED, GL_GREEN, GL_BLUE, GL_ALPHA, GL_RGB, GL_RGBA, GL_BGR, GL_BGRA, GL_LUMINANCE,** or **GL_LUMINANCE_ALPHA**.
type	Specifies the data type for *data*. Must be one of: **GL_UNSIGNED_BYTE, GL_BYTE, GL_BITMAP, GL_UNSIGNED_SHORT, GL_SHORT, GL_UNSIGNED_INT, GL_INT, GL_FLOAT, GL_UNSIGNED_BYTE_3_3_2,**

GL_UNSIGNED_BYTE_2_3_3_REV, GL_UNSIGNED_SHORT_5_6_5,
GL_UNSIGNED_SHORT_5_6_5_REV,
GL_UNSIGNED_SHORT_4_4_4_4,
GL_UNSIGNED_SHORT_4_4_4_4_REV,
GL_UNSIGNED_SHORT_5_5_5_1,
GL_UNSIGNED_SHORT_1_5_5_5_REV,
GL_UNSIGNED_INT_8_8_8_8, GL_UNSIGNED_INT_8_8_8_8_REV,
GL_UNSIGNED_INT_10_10_10_2, or
GL_UNSIGNED_INT_2_10_10_10_REV.

level   Specifies the mipmap level of the image data.

base   Specifies the minimum mipmap level to pass to **glTexImage1D**.

max   Specifies the maximum mipmap level to pass to **glTexImage1D**.

data   Specifies a pointer to the image data in memory.

DESCRIPTION

gluBuild1DMipmapLevels builds a subset of prefiltered one-dimensional texture maps of decreasing resolutions called a mipmap. This is used for the antialiasing of texture mapped primitives.

A return value of zero indicates success, otherwise a GLU error code is returned (see **gluErrorString**).

A series of mipmap levels from *base* to *max* is built by decimating *data* in half until size 1×1 is reached. At each level, each texel in the halved mipmap level is an average of the corresponding two texels in the larger mipmap level. **glTexImage1D** is called to load these mipmap levels from *base* to *max*. If *max* is larger than the highest mipmap level for the texture of the specified size, then a GLU error code is returned (see **gluErrorString**) and nothing is loaded.

For example, if *level* is 2 and *width* is 16, the following levels are possible: 16×1, 8×1, 4×1, 2×1, 1×1. These correspond to levels 2 through 6 respectively. If *base* is 3 and *max* is 5, then only mipmap levels 8×1, 4×1 and 2×1 are loaded. However, if *max* is 7 then an error is returned and nothing is loaded since *max* is larger than the highest mipmap level which is, in this case, 6.

The highest mipmap level can be derived from the formula $\log_2(width\ 2^{level})$.

See the **glTexImage1D** reference page for a description of the acceptable values for *type* parameter. See the **glDrawPixels** reference page for a description of the acceptable values for *level* parameter.

NOTES

gluBuild1DMipmapLevels is only available if the GLU version is 1.3 or greater.

Formats **GL_BGR**, and **GL_BGRA**, and types **GL_UNSIGNED_BYTE_3_3_2**, **GL_UNSIGNED_BYTE_2_3_3_REV**, **GL_UNSIGNED_SHORT_5_6_5**, **GL_UNSIGNED_SHORT_5_6_5_REV**, **GL_UNSIGNED_SHORT_4_4_4_4**, **GL_UNSIGNED_SHORT_4_4_4_4_REV**, **GL_UNSIGNED_SHORT_5_5_5_1**, **GL_UNSIGNED_SHORT_1_5_5_5_REV**, **GL_UNSIGNED_INT_8_8_8_8**, **GL_UNSIGNED_INT_8_8_8_8_REV**, **GL_UNSIGNED_INT_10_10_10_2**, and **GL_UNSIGNED_INT_2_10_10_10_REV** are only available if the GL version is 1.2 or greater.

ERRORS

GLU_INVALID_VALUE is returned if *level* > *base*, *base* < 0, *max* < *base* or *max* is > the highest mipmap level for *data*.

GLU_INVALID_VALUE is returned if *width* is < 1.

GLU_INVALID_ENUM is returned if *internalFormat*, *format*, or *type* are not legal.

GLU_INVALID_OPERATION is returned if *type* is **GL_UNSIGNED_BYTE_3_3_2** or **GL_UNSIGNED_BYTE_2_3_3_REV** and *format* is not **GL_RGB**.

GLU_INVALID_OPERATION is returned if *type* is **GL_UNSIGNED_SHORT_5_6_5** or **GL_UNSIGNED_SHORT_5_6_5_REV** and *format* is not **GL_RGB**.

GLU_INVALID_OPERATION is returned if *type* is **GL_UNSIGNED_SHORT_4_4_4_4** or **GL_UNSIGNED_SHORT_4_4_4_4_REV** and *format* is neither **GL_RGBA** nor **GL_BGRA**.

GLU_INVALID_OPERATION is returned if *type* is **GL_UNSIGNED_SHORT_5_5_5_1** or **GL_UNSIGNED_SHORT_1_5_5_5_REV** and *format* is neither **GL_RGBA** nor **GL_BGRA**.

GLU_INVALID_OPERATION is returned if *type* is **GL_UNSIGNED_INT_8_8_8_8** or **GL_UNSIGNED_INT_8_8_8_8_REV** and *format* is neither **GL_RGBA** nor **GL_BGRA**.

GLU_INVALID_OPERATION is returned if *type* is **GL_UNSIGNED_INT_10_10_10_2** or **GL_UNSIGNED_INT_2_10_10_10_REV** and *format* is neither **GL_RGBA** nor **GL_BGRA**.

SEE ALSO

glDrawPixels, **glTexImage1D**, **glTexImage2D**, **glTexImage3D**, **gluBuild1DMipmaps**, **gluBuild2DMipmaps**, **gluBuild3DMipmaps**, **gluErrorString**, **glGetTexImage**, **glGetTexLevelParameter**, **gluBuild2DMipmapLevels**, **gluBuild3DMipmapLevels**

NAME

gluBuild1DMipmaps – builds a one-dimensional mipmap

C SPECIFICATION

GLint **gluBuild1DMipmaps**(GLenum *target*,
GLint *internalFormat*,
GLsizei *width*,
GLenum *format*,
GLenum *type*,
const void **data*)

PARAMETERS

target   Specifies the target texture. Must be **GL_TEXTURE_1D**.

internalFormat

Requests the internal storage format of the texture image. Must be 1, 2, 3, 4, or one of the following symbolic constants: **GL_ALPHA**, **GL_ALPHA4**, **GL_ALPHA8**, **GL_ALPHA12**, **GL_ALPHA16**, **GL_LUMINANCE**, **GL_LUMINANCE4**, **GL_LUMINANCE8**, **GL_LUMINANCE12**, **GL_LUMINANCE16**, **GL_LUMINANCE_ALPHA**, **GL_LUMINANCE4_ALPHA4**, **GL_LUMINANCE6_ALPHA2**, **GL_LUMINANCE8_ALPHA8**, **GL_LUMINANCE12_ALPHA4**, **GL_LUMINANCE12_ALPHA12**, **GL_LUMINANCE16_ALPHA16**, **GL_INTENSITY**, **GL_INTENSITY4**, **GL_INTENSITY8**, **GL_INTENSITY12**, **GL_INTENSITY16**, **GL_RGB**, **GL_R3_G3_B2**, **GL_RGB4**, **GL_RGB5**, **GL_RGB8**, **GL_RGB10**, **GL_RGB12**, **GL_RGB16**, **GL_RGBA**, **GL_RGBA2**, **GL_RGBA4**, **GL_RGB5_A1**, **GL_RGBA8**, **GL_RGB10_A2**, **GL_RGBA12**, or **GL_RGBA16**.

width   Specifies the width, in pixels, of the texture image.

format   Specifies the format of the pixel data. Must be one of **GL_COLOR_INDEX**, **GL_DEPTH_COMPONENT**, **GL_RED**, **GL_GREEN**, **GL_BLUE**, **GL_ALPHA**, **GL_RGB**, **GL_RGBA**, **GL_BGR**, **GL_BGRA**, **GL_LUMINANCE**, **GL_LUMINANCE_ALPHA**.

type   Specifies the data type for *data*. Must be one of **GL_UNSIGNED_BYTE**, **GL_BYTE**, **GL_BITMAP**, **GL_UNSIGNED_SHORT**, **GL_SHORT**, **GL_UNSIGNED_INT**, **GL_INT**, **GL_FLOAT**, **GL_UNSIGNED_BYTE_3_3_2**, **GL_UNSIGNED_BYTE_2_3_3_REV**, **GL_UNSIGNED_SHORT_5_6_5**, **GL_UNSIGNED_SHORT_5_6_5_REV**, **GL_UNSIGNED_SHORT_4_4_4_4**, **GL_UNSIGNED_SHORT_4_4_4_4_REV**,

GL_UNSIGNED_SHORT_5_5_5_1,
GL_UNSIGNED_SHORT_1_5_5_5_REV,
GL_UNSIGNED_INT_8_8_8_8, GL_UNSIGNED_INT_8_8_8_8_REV,
GL_UNSIGNED_INT_10_10_10_2, or
GL_UNSIGNED_INT_2_10_10_10_REV.

data   Specifies a pointer to the image data in memory.

DESCRIPTION

gluBuild1DMipmaps builds a series of prefiltered one-dimensional texture maps of decreasing resolutions called a mipmap. This is used for the antialiasing of texture mapped primitives.

A return value of zero indicates success, otherwise a GLU error code is returned (see **gluErrorString**).

Initially, the *width* of *data* is checked to see if it is a power of 2. If not, a copy of *data* is scaled up or down to the nearest power of 2. (If *width* is exactly between powers of 2, then the copy of *data* will scale upwards.) This copy will be used for subsequent mipmapping operations described below. For example, if *width* is 57 then a copy of *data* will scale up to 64 before mipmapping takes place.

Then, proxy textures (see **glTexImage1D**) are used to determine if the implementation can fit the requested texture. If not, *width* is continually halved until it fits.

Next, a series of mipmap levels is built by decimating a copy of *data* in half until size 1×1 is reached. At each level, each texel in the halved mipmap level is an average of the corresponding two texels in the larger mipmap level.

glTexImage1D is called to load each of these mipmap levels. Level 0 is a copy of *data*. The highest level is $\log_2(width)$. *For example, if width is 64 and the implementation can store a texture of this size, the following mipmap levels are built:* 64×1, 32×1, 16×1, 8×1, 4×1, 2×1 *and* 1×1. *These correspond to levels 0 through 6, respectively.*

See the **glTexImage1D** reference page for a description of the acceptable values for the *type* parameter. See the **glDrawPixels** reference page for a description of the acceptable values for the *data* parameter.

NOTES

Note that there is no direct way of querying the maximum level. This can be derived indirectly via **glGetTexLevelParameter**. First, query for the width actually used at level 0. (The width may not be equal to *width* since proxy textures might have scaled it to fit the implementation.) Then the maximum level can be derived from the formula $\log_2(width)$.

Formats **GL_BGR**, and **GL_BGRA**, and types **GL_UNSIGNED_BYTE_3_3_2**, **GL_UNSIGNED_BYTE_2_3_3_REV**, **GL_UNSIGNED_SHORT_5_6_5**, **GL_UNSIGNED_SHORT_5_6_5_REV**, **GL_UNSIGNED_SHORT_4_4_4_4**, **GL_UNSIGNED_SHORT_4_4_4_4_REV**, **GL_UNSIGNED_SHORT_5_5_5_1**, **GL_UNSIGNED_SHORT_1_5_5_5_REV**, **GL_UNSIGNED_INT_8_8_8_8**, **GL_UNSIGNED_INT_8_8_8_8_REV**, **GL_UNSIGNED_INT_10_10_10_2**, and **GL_UNSIGNED_INT_2_10_10_10_REV** are only available if the GL version is 1.2 or greater, and if the GLU version is 1.3 or greater.

ERRORS

GLU_INVALID_VALUE is returned if *width* is < 1.

GLU_INVALID_ENUM is returned if *format* or *type* are not legal.

GLU_INVALID_OPERATION is returned if *type* is **GL_UNSIGNED_BYTE_3_3_2** or **GL_UNSIGNED_BYTE_2_3_3_REV** and *format* is not **GL_RGB**.

GLU_INVALID_OPERATION is returned if *type* is **GL_UNSIGNED_SHORT_5_6_5** or **GL_UNSIGNED_SHORT_5_6_5_REV** and *format* is not **GL_RGB**.

GLU_INVALID_OPERATION is returned if *type* is **GL_UNSIGNED_SHORT_4_4_4_4** or **GL_UNSIGNED_SHORT_4_4_4_4_REV** and *format* is neither **GL_RGBA** nor **GL_BGRA**.

GLU_INVALID_OPERATION is returned if *type* is **GL_UNSIGNED_SHORT_5_5_5_1** or **GL_UNSIGNED_SHORT_1_5_5_5_REV** and *format* is neither **GL_RGBA** nor **GL_BGRA**.

GLU_INVALID_OPERATION is returned if *type* is **GL_UNSIGNED_INT_8_8_8_8** or **GL_UNSIGNED_INT_8_8_8_8_REV** and *format* is neither **GL_RGBA** nor **GL_BGRA**.

GLU_INVALID_OPERATION is returned if *type* is **GL_UNSIGNED_INT_10_10_10_2** or **GL_UNSIGNED_INT_2_10_10_10_REV** and *format* is neither **GL_RGBA** nor **GL_BGRA**.

SEE ALSO

glDrawPixels, **glTexImage1D**, **glTexImage2D**, **glTexImage3D**, **gluBuild2DMipmaps**, **gluBuild3DMipmaps**, **gluErrorString**, **glGetTexImage**, **glGetTexLevelParameter**, **gluBuild1DMipmapLevels**, **gluBuild2DMipmapLevels**, **gluBuild3DMipmapLevels**

NAME

gluBuild2DMipmapLevels – builds a subset of two-dimensional mipmap levels

C SPECIFICATION

GLint **gluBuild2DMipmapLevels**(GLenum *target*,
GLint *internalFormat*,
GLsizei *width*,
GLsizei *height*,
GLenum *format*,
GLenum *type*,
GLint *level*,
GLint *base*,
GLint *max*,
const void **data*)

PARAMETERS

target　　Specifies the target texture. Must be **GL_TEXTURE_2D**.

internalFormat

Requests the internal storage format of the texture image. Must be 1, 2, 3, 4, or one of the following symbolic constants: **GL_ALPHA**, **GL_ALPHA4**, **GL_ALPHA8**, **GL_ALPHA12**, **GL_ALPHA16**, **GL_LUMINANCE**, **GL_LUMINANCE4**, **GL_LUMINANCE8**, **GL_LUMINANCE12**, **GL_LUMINANCE16**, **GL_LUMINANCE_ALPHA**, **GL_LUMINANCE4_ALPHA4**, **GL_LUMINANCE6_ALPHA2**, **GL_LUMINANCE8_ALPHA8**, **GL_LUMINANCE12_ALPHA4**, **GL_LUMINANCE12_ALPHA12**, **GL_LUMINANCE16_ALPHA16**, **GL_INTENSITY**, **GL_INTENSITY4**, **GL_INTENSITY8**, **GL_INTENSITY12**, **GL_INTENSITY16**, **GL_RGB**, **GL_R3_G3_B2**, **GL_RGB4**, **GL_RGB5**, **GL_RGB8**, **GL_RGB10**, **GL_RGB12**, **GL_RGB16**, **GL_RGBA**, **GL_RGBA2**, **GL_RGBA4**, **GL_RGB5_A1**, **GL_RGBA8**, **GL_RGB10_A2**, **GL_RGBA12** or **GL_RGBA16**.

width, height　Specifies the width and height, respectively, in pixels of the texture image. These should be a power of 2.

format　　Specifies the format of the pixel data. Must be one of **GL_COLOR_INDEX**, **GL_DEPTH_COMPONENT**, **GL_RED**, **GL_GREEN**, **GL_BLUE**, **GL_ALPHA**, **GL_RGB**, **GL_RGBA**, **GL_BGR**, **GL_BGRA**, **GL_LUMINANCE**, or **GL_LUMINANCE_ALPHA**.

type	Specifies the data type for *data*. Must be one of GL_UNSIGNED_BYTE, GL_BYTE, GL_BITMAP, GL_UNSIGNED_SHORT, GL_SHORT, GL_UNSIGNED_INT, GL_INT, GL_FLOAT, GL_UNSIGNED_BYTE_3_3_2, GL_UNSIGNED_BYTE_2_3_3_REV, GL_UNSIGNED_SHORT_5_6_5, GL_UNSIGNED_SHORT_5_6_5_REV, GL_UNSIGNED_SHORT_4_4_4_4, GL_UNSIGNED_SHORT_4_4_4_4_REV, GL_UNSIGNED_SHORT_5_5_5_1, GL_UNSIGNED_SHORT_1_5_5_5_REV, GL_UNSIGNED_INT_8_8_8_8, GL_UNSIGNED_INT_8_8_8_8_REV, GL_UNSIGNED_INT_10_10_10_2 or GL_UNSIGNED_INT_2_10_10_10_REV.
level	Specifies the mipmap level of the image data.
base	Specifies the minimum mipmap level to pass to **glTexImage2D**.
max	Specifies the maximum mipmap level to pass to **glTexImage2D**.
data	Specifies a pointer to the image data in memory.

DESCRIPTION

gluBuild2DMipmapLevels builds a subset of prefiltered two-dimensional texture maps of decreasing resolutions called a mipmap. This is used for the antialiasing of texture mapped primitives.

A return value of zero indicates success, otherwise a GLU error code is returned (see **gluErrorString**).

A series of mipmap levels from *base* to *max* is built by decimating *data* in half along both dimensions until size 1×1 is reached. At each level, each texel in the halved mipmap level is an average of the corresponding four texels in the larger mipmap level. (In the case of rectangular images, the decimation will ultimately reach an $N \times 1$ or $1 \times N$ configuration. Here, two texels are averaged instead.) **glTexImage2D** is called to load these mipmap levels from *base* to *max*. If *max* is larger than the highest mipmap level for the texture of the specified size, then a GLU error code is returned (see **gluErrorString**) and nothing is loaded.

For example, if *level* is 2 and *width* is 16 and *height* is 8, the following levels are possible: 16×8, 8×4, 4×2, 2×1, 1×1. These correspond to levels 2 through 6 respectively. If *base* is 3 and *max* is 5, then only mipmap levels 8×4, 4×2 and 2×1 are loaded. However, if *max* is 7 then an error is returned and nothing is loaded since *max* is larger than the highest mipmap level which is, in this case, 6.

The highest mipmap level can be derived from the formula $\log2(\max(width,height)*(2^{level}))$.

See the **glTexImage1D** reference page for a description of the acceptable values for *format* parameter. See the **glDrawPixels** reference page for a description of the acceptable values for *type* parameter.

NOTES

gluBuild2DMipmapLevels is only available if the GLU version is 1.3 or greater.

Formats **GL_BGR**, and **GL_BGRA**, and types **GL_UNSIGNED_BYTE_3_3_2**, **GL_UNSIGNED_BYTE_2_3_3_REV**, **GL_UNSIGNED_SHORT_5_6_5**, **GL_UNSIGNED_SHORT_5_6_5_REV**, **GL_UNSIGNED_SHORT_4_4_4_4**, **GL_UNSIGNED_SHORT_4_4_4_4_REV**, **GL_UNSIGNED_SHORT_5_5_5_1**, **GL_UNSIGNED_SHORT_1_5_5_5_REV**, **GL_UNSIGNED_INT_8_8_8_8**, **GL_UNSIGNED_INT_8_8_8_8_REV**, **GL_UNSIGNED_INT_10_10_10_2**, and **GL_UNSIGNED_INT_2_10_10_10_REV** are only available if the GL version is 1.2 or greater.

ERRORS

GLU_INVALID_VALUE is returned if *level* > *base*, *base* < 0, *max* < *base* or *max* is > the highest mipmap level for *data*.

GLU_INVALID_VALUE is returned if *width* or *height* is < 1.

GLU_INVALID_ENUM is returned if *internalFormat*, *format*, or *type* is not legal.

GLU_INVALID_OPERATION is returned if *type* is **GL_UNSIGNED_BYTE_3_3_2** or **GL_UNSIGNED_BYTE_2_3_3_REV** and *format* is not **GL_RGB**.

GLU_INVALID_OPERATION is returned if *type* is **GL_UNSIGNED_SHORT_5_6_5** or **GL_UNSIGNED_SHORT_5_6_5_REV** and *format* is not **GL_RGB**.

GLU_INVALID_OPERATION is returned if *type* is **GL_UNSIGNED_SHORT_4_4_4_4** or **GL_UNSIGNED_SHORT_4_4_4_4_REV** and *format* is neither **GL_RGBA** nor **GL_BGRA**.

GLU_INVALID_OPERATION is returned if *type* is **GL_UNSIGNED_SHORT_5_5_5_1** or **GL_UNSIGNED_SHORT_1_5_5_5_REV** and *format* is neither **GL_RGBA** nor **GL_BGRA**.

GLU_INVALID_OPERATION is returned if *type* is **GL_UNSIGNED_INT_8_8_8_8** or **GL_UNSIGNED_INT_8_8_8_8_REV** and *format* is neither **GL_RGBA** nor **GL_BGRA**.

GLU_INVALID_OPERATION is returned if *type* is **GL_UNSIGNED_INT_10_10_10_2** or **GL_UNSIGNED_INT_2_10_10_10_REV** and *format* is neither **GL_RGBA** nor **GL_BGRA**.

SEE ALSO

glDrawPixels, **glTexImage1D**, **glTexImage2D**, glTexImage3D,
gluBuild1DMipmaps, **gluBuild2DMipmaps**, **gluBuild3DMipmaps**,
gluErrorString, glGetTexImage, glGetTexLevelParameter,
gluBuild1DMipmapLevels, **gluBuild3DMipmapLevels**

NAME

gluBuild2DMipmaps – builds a two-dimensional mipmap

C SPECIFICATION

GLint **gluBuild2DMipmaps**(GLenum *target*,
GLint *internalFormat*,
GLsizei *width*,
GLsizei *height*,
GLenum *format*,
GLenum *type*,
const void **data*)

PARAMETERS

target Specifies the target texture. Must be **GL_TEXTURE_2D**.

internalFormat

Requests the internal storage format of the texture image. Must be 1, 2, 3, 4, or one of the following symbolic constants: **GL_ALPHA, GL_ALPHA4, GL_ALPHA8, GL_ALPHA12, GL_ALPHA16, GL_LUMINANCE, GL_LUMINANCE4, GL_LUMINANCE8, GL_LUMINANCE12, GL_LUMINANCE16, GL_LUMINANCE_ALPHA, GL_LUMINANCE4_ALPHA4, GL_LUMINANCE6_ALPHA2, GL_LUMINANCE8_ALPHA8, GL_LUMINANCE12_ALPHA4, GL_LUMINANCE12_ALPHA12, GL_LUMINANCE16_ALPHA16, GL_INTENSITY, GL_INTENSITY4, GL_INTENSITY8, GL_INTENSITY12, GL_INTENSITY16, GL_RGB, GL_R3_G3_B2, GL_RGB4, GL_RGB5, GL_RGB8, GL_RGB10, GL_RGB12, GL_RGB16, GL_RGBA, GL_RGBA2, GL_RGBA4, GL_RGB5_A1, GL_RGBA8, GL_RGB10_A2, GL_RGBA12** or **GL_RGBA16**.

width, height Specifies in pixels the width and height, respectively, of the texture image.

format Specifies the format of the pixel data. Must be one of **GL_COLOR_INDEX, GL_DEPTH_COMPONENT, GL_RED, GL_GREEN, GL_BLUE, GL_ALPHA, GL_RGB, GL_RGBA, GL_BGR, GL_BGRA, GL_LUMINANCE,** or **GL_LUMINANCE_ALPHA**.

type Specifies the data type for *data*. Must be one of **GL_UNSIGNED_BYTE, GL_BYTE, GL_BITMAP, GL_UNSIGNED_SHORT, GL_SHORT, GL_UNSIGNED_INT, GL_INT, GL_FLOAT, GL_UNSIGNED_BYTE_3_3_2, GL_UNSIGNED_BYTE_2_3_3_REV, GL_UNSIGNED_SHORT_5_6_5, GL_UNSIGNED_SHORT_5_6_5_REV,**

GL_UNSIGNED_SHORT_4_4_4_4,
GL_UNSIGNED_SHORT_4_4_4_4_REV,
GL_UNSIGNED_SHORT_5_5_5_1,
GL_UNSIGNED_SHORT_1_5_5_5_REV,
GL_UNSIGNED_INT_8_8_8_8, GL_UNSIGNED_INT_8_8_8_8_REV,
GL_UNSIGNED_INT_10_10_10_2, or
GL_UNSIGNED_INT_2_10_10_10_REV.

data   Specifies a pointer to the image data in memory.

DESCRIPTION

gluBuild2DMipmaps builds a series of prefiltered two-dimensional texture maps of decreasing resolutions called a mipmap. This is used for the antialiasing of texture-mapped primitives.

A return value of zero indicates success, otherwise a GLU error code is returned (see **gluErrorString**).

Initially, the *width* and *height* of *data* are checked to see if they are a power of 2. If not, a copy of *data* (not *data*), is scaled up or down to the nearest power of 2. This copy will be used for subsequent mipmapping operations described below. (If *width* or *height* is exactly between powers of 2, then the copy of *data* will scale upwards.) For example, if *width* is 57 and *height* is 23 then a copy of *data* will scale up to 64 in *width* and down to 16 in depth, before mipmapping takes place.

Then, proxy textures (see **glTexImage2D**) are used to determine if the implementation can fit the requested texture. If not, both dimensions are continually halved until it fits. (If the OpenGL version is ≤ 1.0, both maximum texture dimensions are clamped to the value returned by **glGetIntegerv** with the argument **GL_MAX_TEXTURE_SIZE**.)

Next, a series of mipmap levels is built by decimating a copy of *data* in half along both dimensions until size 1×1 is reached. At each level, each texel in the halved mipmap level is an average of the corresponding four texels in the larger mipmap level. (In the case of rectangular images, the decimation will ultimately reach an $N \times 1$ or $1 \times N$ configuration. Here, two texels are averaged instead.)

glTexImage2D is called to load each of these mipmap levels. Level 0 is a copy of *data*. The highest level is $\log_2 (\max(width, height))$. For example, if *width* is 64 and *height* is 16 and the implementation can store a texture of this size, the following mipmap levels are built: 64×16, 32×8, 16×4, 8×2, 4×1, 2×1 and 1×1. These correspond to levels 0 through 6, respectively.

See the **glTexImage1D** reference page for a description of the acceptable values for *format* parameter. See the **glDrawPixels** reference page for a description of the acceptable values for *type* parameter.

NOTES

Note that there is no direct way of querying the maximum level. This can be derived indirectly via **glGetTexLevelParameter**. First, query for the width and height actually used at level 0. (The width and height may not be equal to *width* and *height* respectively since proxy textures might have scaled them to fit the implementation.) Then the maximum level can be derived from the formula $\log_2(\max(width, height))$.

NOTES

Formats **GL_BGR**, and **GL_BGRA**, and types **GL_UNSIGNED_BYTE_3_3_2**, **GL_UNSIGNED_BYTE_2_3_3_REV**, **GL_UNSIGNED_SHORT_5_6_5**, **GL_UNSIGNED_SHORT_5_6_5_REV**, **GL_UNSIGNED_SHORT_4_4_4_4**, **GL_UNSIGNED_SHORT_4_4_4_4_REV**, **GL_UNSIGNED_SHORT_5_5_5_1**, **GL_UNSIGNED_SHORT_1_5_5_5_REV**, **GL_UNSIGNED_INT_8_8_8_8**, **GL_UNSIGNED_INT_8_8_8_8_REV**, **GL_UNSIGNED_INT_10_10_10_2**, and **GL_UNSIGNED_INT_2_10_10_10_REV** are only available if the GL version is 1.2 or greater and if the GLU version is 1.3 or greater.

ERRORS

GLU_INVALID_VALUE is returned if *width*, or *height* is < 1.

GLU_INVALID_ENUM is returned if *internalFormat*, *format*, or *type* is not legal.

GLU_INVALID_OPERATION is returned if *type* is **GL_UNSIGNED_BYTE_3_3_2** or **GL_UNSIGNED_BYTE_2_3_3_REV** and *format* is not **GL_RGB**.

GLU_INVALID_OPERATION is returned if *type* is **GL_UNSIGNED_SHORT_5_6_5** or **GL_UNSIGNED_SHORT_5_6_5_REV** and *format* is not **GL_RGB**.

GLU_INVALID_OPERATION is returned if *type* is **GL_UNSIGNED_SHORT_4_4_4_4** or **GL_UNSIGNED_SHORT_4_4_4_4_REV** and *format* is neither **GL_RGBA** nor **GL_BGRA**.

GLU_INVALID_OPERATION is returned if *type* is **GL_UNSIGNED_SHORT_5_5_5_1** or **GL_UNSIGNED_SHORT_1_5_5_5_REV** and *format* is neither **GL_RGBA** nor **GL_BGRA**.

GLU_INVALID_OPERATION is returned if *type* is **GL_UNSIGNED_INT_8_8_8_8** or **GL_UNSIGNED_INT_8_8_8_8_REV** and *format* is neither **GL_RGBA** nor **GL_BGRA**.

GLU_INVALID_OPERATION is returned if *type* is **GL_UNSIGNED_INT_10_10_10_2** or **GL_UNSIGNED_INT_2_10_10_10_REV** and *format* is neither **GL_RGBA** nor **GL_BGRA**.

SEE ALSO

glDrawPixels, glTexImage1D, glTexImage2D, glTexImage3D,
gluBuild1DMipmaps, gluBuild3DMipmaps, gluErrorString, glGetTexImage,
glGetTexLevelParameter, gluBuild1DMipmapLevels, gluBuild2DMipmapLevels,
gluBuild3DMipmapLevels

NAME

   gluBuild3DMipmapLevels – builds a subset of three-dimensional mipmap levels

C SPECIFICATION

   GLint **gluBuild3DMipmapLevels**(GLenum *target*,

   GLint *internalFormat*,
   GLsizei *width*,
   GLsizei *height*,
   GLsizei *depth*,
   GLenum *format*,
   GLenum *type*,
   GLint *level*,
   GLint *base*,
   GLint *max*,
   const void *data*)

PARAMETERS

   target   Specifies the target texture. Must be **GL_TEXTURE_3D**.

   internalFormat

   Requests the internal storage format of the texture image. Must be 1, 2, 3, 4, or one of the following symbolic constants: **GL_ALPHA**, **GL_ALPHA4**, **GL_ALPHA8**, **GL_ALPHA12**, **GL_ALPHA16**, **GL_LUMINANCE**, **GL_LUMINANCE4**, **GL_LUMINANCE8**, **GL_LUMINANCE12**, **GL_LUMINANCE16**, **GL_LUMINANCE_ALPHA**, **GL_LUMINANCE4_ALPHA4**, **GL_LUMINANCE6_ALPHA2**, **GL_LUMINANCE8_ALPHA8**, **GL_LUMINANCE12_ALPHA4**, **GL_LUMINANCE12_ALPHA12**, **GL_LUMINANCE16_ALPHA16**, **GL_INTENSITY**, **GL_INTENSITY4**, **GL_INTENSITY8**, **GL_INTENSITY12**, **GL_INTENSITY16**, **GL_RGB**, **GL_R3_G3_B2**, **GL_RGB4**, **GL_RGB5**, **GL_RGB8**, **GL_RGB10**, **GL_RGB12**, **GL_RGB16**, **GL_RGBA**, **GL_RGBA2**, **GL_RGBA4**, **GL_RGB5_A1**, **GL_RGBA8**, **GL_RGB10_A2**, **GL_RGBA12**, or **GL_RGBA16**.

   width, *height*, *depth*

   Specifies in pixels the width, height and depth respectively, of the texture image. These should be a power of 2.

   format   Specifies the format of the pixel data. Must be one of **GL_COLOR_INDEX**, **GL_DEPTH_COMPONENT**, **GL_RED**, **GL_GREEN**, **GL_BLUE**, **GL_ALPHA**, **GL_RGB**, **GL_RGBA**, **GL_BGR**, **GL_BGRA**, **GL_LUMINANCE**, or **GL_LUMINANCE_ALPHA**.

type	Specifies the data type for *data*. Must be one of **GL_UNSIGNED_BYTE**, **GL_BYTE**, **GL_BITMAP**, **GL_UNSIGNED_SHORT**, **GL_SHORT**, **GL_UNSIGNED_INT**, **GL_INT**, **GL_FLOAT**, **GL_UNSIGNED_BYTE_3_3_2**, **GL_UNSIGNED_BYTE_2_3_3_REV**, **GL_UNSIGNED_SHORT_5_6_5**, **GL_UNSIGNED_SHORT_5_6_5_REV**, **GL_UNSIGNED_SHORT_4_4_4_4**, **GL_UNSIGNED_SHORT_4_4_4_4_REV**, **GL_UNSIGNED_SHORT_5_5_5_1**, **GL_UNSIGNED_SHORT_1_5_5_5_REV**, **GL_UNSIGNED_INT_8_8_8_8**, **GL_UNSIGNED_INT_8_8_8_8_REV**, **GL_UNSIGNED_INT_10_10_10_2**, or **GL_UNSIGNED_INT_2_10_10_10_REV**.
level	Specifies the mipmap level of the image data.
base	Specifies the minimum mipmap level to pass to **glTexImage3D**.
max	Specifies the maximum mipmap level to pass to **glTexImage3D**.
data	Specifies a pointer to the image data in memory.

DESCRIPTION

gluBuild3DMipmapLevels builds a subset of prefiltered three-dimensional texture maps of decreasing resolutions called a mipmap. This is used for the antialiasing of texture mapped primitives.

A return value of zero indicates success, otherwise a GLU error code is returned (see **gluErrorString**).

A series of mipmap levels from *base* to *max* is built by decimating *data* in half along both dimensions until size $1 \times 1 \times 1$ is reached. At each level, each texel in the halved mipmap level is an average of the corresponding eight texels in the larger mipmap level. (If exactly one of the dimensions is 1, four texels are averaged. If exactly two of the dimensions are 1, two texels are averaged.) **glTexImage3D** is called to load these mipmap levels from *base* to *max*. If *max* is larger than the highest mipmap level for the texture of the specified size, then a GLU error code is returned (see **gluErrorString**) and nothing is loaded.

For example, if *level* is 2 and *width* is 16, *height* is 8 and *depth* is 4, the following levels are possible: $16 \times 8 \times 4$, $8 \times 4 \times 2$, $4 \times 2 \times 1$, $2 \times 1 \times 1$, $1 \times 1 \times 1$. These correspond to levels 2 through 6 respectively. If *base* is 3 and *max* is 5, then only mipmap levels $8 \times 4 \times 2$, $4 \times 2 \times 1$ and $2 \times 1 \times 1$ are loaded. However, if *max* is 7 then an error is returned and nothing is loaded, since *max* is larger than the highest mipmap level which is, in this case, 6.

The highest mipmap level can be derived from the formula
$\log_2 (\max(width, height, depth)\ 2^{level})$.

See the **glTexImage1D** reference page for a description of the acceptable values for *format* parameter. See the **glDrawPixels** reference page for a description of the acceptable values for *type* parameter.

NOTES

gluBuild3DMipmapLevels is only available if the GLU version is 1.3 or greater.

Formats **GL_BGR**, and **GL_BGRA**, and types **GL_UNSIGNED_BYTE_3_3_2**, **GL_UNSIGNED_BYTE_2_3_3_REV**, **GL_UNSIGNED_SHORT_5_6_5**, **GL_UNSIGNED_SHORT_5_6_5_REV**, **GL_UNSIGNED_SHORT_4_4_4_4**, **GL_UNSIGNED_SHORT_4_4_4_4_REV**, **GL_UNSIGNED_SHORT_5_5_5_1**, **GL_UNSIGNED_SHORT_1_5_5_5_REV**, **GL_UNSIGNED_INT_8_8_8_8**, **GL_UNSIGNED_INT_8_8_8_8_REV**, **GL_UNSIGNED_INT_10_10_10_2**, and **GL_UNSIGNED_INT_2_10_10_10_REV** are only available if the GL version is 1.2 or greater.

ERRORS

GLU_INVALID_VALUE is returned if *level* > *base*, *base* < 0, *max* < *base* or *max* is > the highest mipmap level for *data*.

GLU_INVALID_VALUE is returned if *width*, *height*, or *depth* is < 1.

GLU_INVALID_ENUM is returned if *internalFormat*, *format*, or *type* is not legal.

GLU_INVALID_OPERATION is returned if *type* is **GL_UNSIGNED_BYTE_3_3_2** or **GL_UNSIGNED_BYTE_2_3_3_REV** and *format* is not **GL_RGB**.

GLU_INVALID_OPERATION is returned if *type* is **GL_UNSIGNED_SHORT_5_6_5** or **GL_UNSIGNED_SHORT_5_6_5_REV** and *format* is not **GL_RGB**.

GLU_INVALID_OPERATION is returned if *type* is **GL_UNSIGNED_SHORT_4_4_4_4** or **GL_UNSIGNED_SHORT_4_4_4_4_REV** and *format* is neither **GL_RGBA** nor **GL_BGRA**.

GLU_INVALID_OPERATION is returned if *type* is **GL_UNSIGNED_SHORT_5_5_5_1** or **GL_UNSIGNED_SHORT_1_5_5_5_REV** and *format* is neither **GL_RGBA** nor **GL_BGRA**.

GLU_INVALID_OPERATION is returned if *type* is **GL_UNSIGNED_INT_8_8_8_8** or **GL_UNSIGNED_INT_8_8_8_8_REV** and *format* is neither **GL_RGBA** nor **GL_BGRA**.

GLU_INVALID_OPERATION is returned if *type* is **GL_UNSIGNED_INT_10_10_10_2** or **GL_UNSIGNED_INT_2_10_10_10_REV** and *format* is neither **GL_RGBA** nor **GL_BGRA**.

SEE ALSO

glDrawPixels, glTexImage1D, glTexImage2D, glTexImage3D,
gluBuild1DMipmaps, gluBuild2DMipmaps, gluBuild3DMipmaps,
gluErrorString, glGetTexImage, glGetTexLevelParameter,
gluBuild1DMipmapLevels, gluBuild2DMipmapLevels

NAME

gluBuild3DMipmaps – builds a three-dimensional mipmap

C SPECIFICATION

GLint **gluBuild3DMipmaps**(GLenum *target*,
                            GLint *internalFormat*,
                            GLsizei *width*,
                            GLsizei *height*,
                            GLsizei *depth*,
                            GLenum *format*,
                            GLenum *type*,
                            const void **data*)

PARAMETERS

target   Specifies the target texture. Must be **GL_TEXTURE_3D**.

internalFormat

                 Requests the internal storage format of the texture image. Must be 1, 2, 3, 4, or one of the following symbolic constants: **GL_ALPHA**, **GL_ALPHA4**, **GL_ALPHA8**, **GL_ALPHA12**, **GL_ALPHA16**, **GL_LUMINANCE**, **GL_LUMINANCE4**, **GL_LUMINANCE8**, **GL_LUMINANCE12**, **GL_LUMINANCE16**, **GL_LUMINANCE_ALPHA**, **GL_LUMINANCE4_ALPHA4**, **GL_LUMINANCE6_ALPHA2**, **GL_LUMINANCE8_ALPHA8**, **GL_LUMINANCE12_ALPHA4**, **GL_LUMINANCE12_ALPHA12**, **GL_LUMINANCE16_ALPHA16**, **GL_INTENSITY**, **GL_INTENSITY4**, **GL_INTENSITY8**, **GL_INTENSITY12**, **GL_INTENSITY16**, **GL_RGB**, **GL_R3_G3_B2**, **GL_RGB4**, **GL_RGB5**, **GL_RGB8**, **GL_RGB10**, **GL_RGB12**, **GL_RGB16**, **GL_RGBA**, **GL_RGBA2**, **GL_RGBA4**, **GL_RGB5_A1**, **GL_RGBA8**, **GL_RGB10_A2**, **GL_RGBA12**, or **GL_RGBA16**.

width, height, depth
                 Specifies in pixels the width, height and depth respectively, in pixels of the texture image.

format   Specifies the format of the pixel data. Must be one of **GL_COLOR_INDEX**, **GL_DEPTH_COMPONENT**, **GL_RED**, **GL_GREEN**, **GL_BLUE**, **GL_ALPHA**, **GL_RGB**, **GL_RGBA**, **GL_BGR**, **GL_BGRA**, **GL_LUMINANCE**, or **GL_LUMINANCE_ALPHA**.

type   Specifies the data type for *data*. Must be one of: **GL_UNSIGNED_BYTE**, **GL_BYTE**, **GL_BITMAP**, **GL_UNSIGNED_SHORT**, **GL_SHORT**, **GL_UNSIGNED_INT**, **GL_INT**, **GL_FLOAT**, **GL_UNSIGNED_BYTE_3_3_2**,

GL_UNSIGNED_BYTE_2_3_3_REV, GL_UNSIGNED_SHORT_5_6_5,
GL_UNSIGNED_SHORT_5_6_5_REV,
GL_UNSIGNED_SHORT_4_4_4_4,
GL_UNSIGNED_SHORT_4_4_4_4_REV,
GL_UNSIGNED_SHORT_5_5_5_1,
GL_UNSIGNED_SHORT_1_5_5_5_REV,
GL_UNSIGNED_INT_8_8_8_8, GL_UNSIGNED_INT_8_8_8_8_REV,
GL_UNSIGNED_INT_10_10_10_2, or
GL_UNSIGNED_INT_2_10_10_10_REV.

data   Specifies a pointer to the image data in memory.

DESCRIPTION

gluBuild3DMipmaps builds a series of prefiltered three-dimensional texture maps of decreasing resolutions called a mipmap. This is used for the antialiasing of texture-mapped primitives.

A return value of zero indicates success, otherwise a GLU error code is returned (see **gluErrorString**).

Initially, the *width*, *height* and *depth* of *data* are checked to see if they are a power of 2. If not, a copy of *data* (not *data*), is scaled up or down to the nearest power of 2. (If *width*, *height* or *depth* is exactly between powers of 2, then the copy of *data* will scale upwards.) This copy will be used for subsequent mipmapping operations described below. For example, if *width* is 57, *height* is 23 and *depth* is 24 then a copy of *data* will scale up to 64 in width, down to 16 in height and up to 32 in depth, before mipmapping takes place.

Then, proxy textures (see **glTexImage3D**) are used to determine if the implementation can fit the requested texture. If not, all three dimensions are continually halved until it fits.

Next, a series of mipmap levels is built by decimating a copy of *data* in half along all three dimensions until size $1 \times 1 \times 1$ is reached. At each level, each texel in the halved mipmap level is an average of the corresponding eight texels in the larger mipmap level. (If exactly one of the dimensions is 1, four texels are averaged. If exactly two of the dimensions are 1, two texels are averaged.)

glTexImage3D is called to load each of these mipmap levels. Level 0 is a copy of *data*. The highest level is $\log_2(\max(width, height, depth))$. For example, if *width* is 64, *height* is 16 and *depth* is 32, and the implementation can store a texture of this size, the following mipmap levels are built: $64 \times 16 \times 32$, $32 \times 8 \times 16$, $16 \times 4 \times 8$, $8 \times 2 \times 4$, $4 \times 1 \times 2$, $2 \times 1 \times 1$ and $1 \times 1 \times 1$. These correspond to levels 0 through 6, respectively.

See the **glTexImage1D** reference page for a description of the acceptable values for *format* parameter. See the **glDrawPixels** reference page for a description of the acceptable values for *type* parameter.

NOTES

Note that there is no direct way of querying the maximum level. This can be derived indirectly via **glGetTexLevelParameter**. First, query for the width, height and depth actually used at level 0. (The width, height and depth may not be equal to *width*, *height* and *depth* respectively since proxy textures might have scaled them to fit the implementation.) Then the maximum level can be derived from the formula $\log_2(\max(width, height, depth))$.

gluBuild3DMipmaps is only available if the GLU version is 1.3 or greater.

Formats **GL_BGR**, and **GL_BGRA**, and types **GL_UNSIGNED_BYTE_3_3_2**, **GL_UNSIGNED_BYTE_2_3_3_REV**, **GL_UNSIGNED_SHORT_5_6_5**, **GL_UNSIGNED_SHORT_5_6_5_REV**, **GL_UNSIGNED_SHORT_4_4_4_4**, **GL_UNSIGNED_SHORT_4_4_4_4_REV**, **GL_UNSIGNED_SHORT_5_5_5_1**, **GL_UNSIGNED_SHORT_1_5_5_5_REV**, **GL_UNSIGNED_INT_8_8_8_8**, **GL_UNSIGNED_INT_8_8_8_8_REV**, **GL_UNSIGNED_INT_10_10_10_2**, and **GL_UNSIGNED_INT_2_10_10_10_REV** are only available if the GL version is 1.2 or greater.

ERRORS

GLU_INVALID_VALUE is returned if *width*, *height*, or *depth* is < 1.

GLU_INVALID_ENUM is returned if *internalFormat*, *format*, or *type* is not legal.

GLU_INVALID_OPERATION is returned if *type* is **GL_UNSIGNED_BYTE_3_3_2** or **GL_UNSIGNED_BYTE_2_3_3_REV** and *format* is not **GL_RGB**.

GLU_INVALID_OPERATION is returned if *type* is **GL_UNSIGNED_SHORT_5_6_5** or **GL_UNSIGNED_SHORT_5_6_5_REV** and *format* is not **GL_RGB**.

GLU_INVALID_OPERATION is returned if *type* is **GL_UNSIGNED_SHORT_4_4_4_4** or **GL_UNSIGNED_SHORT_4_4_4_4_REV** and *format* is neither **GL_RGBA** nor **GL_BGRA**.

GLU_INVALID_OPERATION is returned if *type* is **GL_UNSIGNED_SHORT_5_5_5_1** or **GL_UNSIGNED_SHORT_1_5_5_5_REV** and *format* is neither **GL_RGBA** nor **GL_BGRA**.

GLU_INVALID_OPERATION is returned if *type* is **GL_UNSIGNED_INT_8_8_8_8** or **GL_UNSIGNED_INT_8_8_8_8_REV** and *format* is neither **GL_RGBA** nor **GL_BGRA**.

GLU_INVALID_OPERATION is returned if *type* is **GL_UNSIGNED_INT_10_10_10_2** or **GL_UNSIGNED_INT_2_10_10_10_REV** and *format* is neither **GL_RGBA** nor **GL_BGRA**.

SEE ALSO

glDrawPixels, glTexImage1D, glTexImage2D, glTexImage3D, gluBuild1DMipmaps, gluBuild3DMipmaps, gluErrorString, glGetTexImage, glGetTexLevelParameter, gluBuild1DMipmapLevels, gluBuild2DMipmapLevels, gluBuild3DMipmapLevels

NAME

gluCheckExtension – determines if an extension name is supported

C SPECIFICATION

GLboolean **gluCheckExtension**(const GLubyte *extName,
const GLubyte *extString)

PARAMETERS

extName Specifies an extension name.

extString Specifies a space-separated list of extension names supported.

DESCRIPTION

gluCheckExtension returns **GL_TRUE** if *extName* is supported otherwise **GL_FALSE** is returned.

This is used to check for the presence for OpenGL, GLU or GLX extension names by passing the extension strings returned by **glGetString**, **gluGetString**, **glXGetClientString**, **glXQueryExtensionsString**, or **glXQueryServerString**, respectively, as *extString*.

NOTES

Cases where one extension name is a substring of another are correctly handled.

There may or may not be leading or trailing blanks in *extString*.

Extension names should not contain embedded spaces.

All strings are null-terminated.

SEE ALSO

glGetString, **gluGetString**, **glXGetClientString**, **glXQueryExtensionsString**,

NAME

gluCylinder – draw a cylinder

C SPECIFICATION

void **gluCylinder**(GLUquadric* *quad*,
                    GLdouble *base*,
                    GLdouble *top*,
                    GLdouble *height*,
                    GLint *slices*,
                    GLint *stacks*)

PARAMETERS

quad   Specifies the quadrics object (created with **gluNewQuadric**).

base   Specifies the radius of the cylinder at $z = 0$.

top   Specifies the radius of the cylinder at $z = height$.

height Specifies the height of the cylinder.

slices Specifies the number of subdivisions around the z axis.

stacks Specifies the number of subdivisions along the z axis.

DESCRIPTION

gluCylinder draws a cylinder oriented along the z axis. The base of the cylinder is placed at $z = 0$, and the top at $z = height$. Like a sphere, a cylinder is subdivided around the z axis into slices, and along the z axis into stacks.

Note that if *top* is set to 0.0, this routine generates a cone.

If the orientation is set to **GLU_OUTSIDE** (with **gluQuadricOrientation**), then any generated normals point away from the z axis. Otherwise, they point toward the z axis.

If texturing is turned on (with **gluQuadricTexture**), then texture coordinates are generated so that t ranges linearly from 0.0 at $z = 0$ to 1.0 at $z = height$, and s ranges from 0.0 at the $+y$ axis, to 0.25 at the $+x$ axis, to 0.5 at the $-y$ axis, to 0.75 at the $-x$ axis, and back to 1.0 at the $+y$ axis.

SEE ALSO

gluDisk, **gluNewQuadric**, **gluPartialDisk**, **gluQuadricTexture**, **gluSphere**

NAME

gluDeleteNurbsRenderer – destroy a NURBS object

C SPECIFICATION

void **gluDeleteNurbsRenderer**(GLUnurbs* *nurb*)

PARAMETERS

nurb Specifies the NURBS object to be destroyed.

DESCRIPTION

gluDeleteNurbsRenderer destroys the NURBS object (which was created with **gluNewNurbsRenderer**) and frees any memory it uses. Once **gluDeleteNurbsRenderer** has been called, *nurb* cannot be used again.

SEE ALSO

gluNewNurbsRenderer

NAME

gluDeleteQuadric – destroy a quadrics object

C SPECIFICATION

void **gluDeleteQuadric**(GLUquadric* *quad*)

PARAMETERS

quad Specifies the quadrics object to be destroyed.

DESCRIPTION

gluDeleteQuadric destroys the quadrics object (created with **gluNewQuadric**) and frees any memory it uses. Once **gluDeleteQuadric** has been called, *quad* cannot be used again.

SEE ALSO

gluNewQuadric

NAME

gluDeleteTess – destroy a tessellation object

C SPECIFICATION

void **gluDeleteTess**(GLUtesselator* *tess*)

PARAMETERS

tess Specifies the tessellation object to destroy.

DESCRIPTION

gluDeleteTess destroys the indicated tessellation object (which was created with **gluNewTess**) and frees any memory that it used.

SEE ALSO

gluBeginPolygon, **gluNewTess**, **gluTessCallback**

NAME

gluDisk – draw a disk

C SPECIFICATION

void **gluDisk**(GLUquadric* *quad*,
GLdouble *inner*,
GLdouble *outer*,
GLint *slices*,
GLint *loops*)

PARAMETERS

quad   Specifies the quadrics object (created with **gluNewQuadric**).

inner   Specifies the inner radius of the disk (may be 0).

outer   Specifies the outer radius of the disk.

slices   Specifies the number of subdivisions around the z axis.

loops   Specifies the number of concentric rings about the origin into which the disk is subdivided.

DESCRIPTION

gluDisk renders a disk on the $z = 0$ plane. The disk has a radius of *outer*, and contains a concentric circular hole with a radius of *inner*. If *inner* is 0, then no hole is generated. The disk is subdivided around the z axis into slices (like pizza slices), and also about the z axis into rings (as specified by *slices* and *loops*, respectively).

With respect to orientation, the +z side of the disk is considered to be "outside" (see **gluQuadricOrientation**). This means that if the orientation is set to GLU_OUTSIDE, then any normals generated point along the +z axis. Otherwise, they point along the –z axis.

If texturing has been turned on (with **gluQuadricTexture**), texture coordinates are generated linearly such that where $r = outer$, the value at $(r, 0, 0)$ is $(1, 0.5)$, at $(0, r, 0)$ it is $(0.5, 1)$, at $(-r, 0, 0)$ it is $(0, 0.5)$, and at $(0, -r, 0)$ it is $(0.5, 0)$.

SEE ALSO

gluCylinder, **gluNewQuadric**, **gluPartialDisk**, **gluQuadricOrientation**, **gluQuadricTexture**, **gluSphere**

NAME

gluErrorString – produce an error string from a GL or GLU error code

C SPECIFICATION

const GLubyte * **gluErrorString**(GLenum *error*)

PARAMETERS

error Specifies a GL or GLU error code.

DESCRIPTION

gluErrorString produces an error string from a GL or GLU error code. The string is in ISO Latin 1 format. For example, **gluErrorString**(GL_OUT_OF_MEMORY) returns the string *out of memory*.

The standard GLU error codes are **GLU_INVALID_ENUM**, **GLU_INVALID_VALUE**, and **GLU_OUT_OF_MEMORY**. Certain other GLU functions can return specialized error codes through callbacks. See the **glGetError** reference page for the list of GL error codes.

ERRORS

NULL is returned if *error* is not a valid GL or GLU error code.

SEE ALSO

glGetError, **gluNurbsCallback**, **gluQuadricCallback**, **gluTessCallback**

NAME

gluGetNurbsProperty – get a NURBS property

C SPECIFICATION

void **gluGetNurbsProperty**(GLUnurbs* *nurb*,
                            GLenum *property*,
                            GLfloat* *data*)

PARAMETERS

nurb   Specifies the NURBS object (created with **gluNewNurbsRenderer**).

property Specifies the property whose value is to be fetched. Valid values are **GLU_CULLING, GLU_SAMPLING_TOLERANCE, GLU_DISPLAY_MODE, GLU_AUTO_LOAD_MATRIX, GLU_PARAMETRIC_TOLERANCE, GLU_SAMPLING_METHOD, GLU_U_STEP, GLU_V_STEP** and **GLU_NURBS_MODE**.

data   Specifies a pointer to the location into which the value of the named property is written.

DESCRIPTION

gluGetNurbsProperty retrieves properties stored in a NURBS object. These properties affect the way that NURBS curves and surfaces are rendered. See the **gluNurbsProperty** reference page for information about what the properties are and what they do.

SEE ALSO

gluNewNurbsRenderer, gluNurbsProperty

NAME

    gluGetString – return a string describing the GLU version or GLU extensions

C SPECIFICATION

    const GLubyte * **gluGetString**(GLenum *name*)

PARAMETERS

    name Specifies a symbolic constant, one of **GLU_VERSION**, or **GLU_EXTENSIONS**.

DESCRIPTION

    gluGetString returns a pointer to a static string describing the GLU version or the GLU extensions that are supported.

    The version number is one of the following forms:

major_number.minor_number
major_number.minor_number.release_number.

    The version string is of the following form:

version number<space>vendor-specific information

    Vendor-specific information is optional. Its format and contents depend on the implementation.

    The standard GLU contains a basic set of features and capabilities. If a company or group of companies wish to support other features, these may be included as extensions to the GLU. If *name* is **GLU_EXTENSIONS**, then **gluGetString** returns a space-separated list of names of supported GLU extensions. (Extension names never contain spaces.)

    All strings are null-terminated.

NOTES

    gluGetString only returns information about GLU extensions. Call **glGetString** to get a list of GL extensions.

    gluGetString is an initialization routine. Calling it after a **glNewList** results in undefined behavior.

ERRORS

    NULL is returned if *name* is not **GLU_VERSION** or **GLU_EXTENSIONS**.

SEE ALSO

    glGetString

NAME

gluGetTessProperty – get a tessellation object property

C SPECIFICATION

void **gluGetTessProperty**(GLUtesselator* *tess*,
                            GLenum *which*,
                            GLdouble* *data*)

PARAMETERS

tess   Specifies the tessellation object (created with **gluNewTess**).

which Specifies the property whose value is to be fetched. Valid values are **GLU_TESS_WINDING_RULE**, **GLU_TESS_BOUNDARY_ONLY**, and **GLU_TESS_TOLERANCE**.

data   Specifies a pointer to the location into which the value of the named property is written.

DESCRIPTION

gluGetTessProperty retrieves properties stored in a tessellation object. These properties affect the way that tessellation objects are interpreted and rendered. See the **gluTessProperty** reference page for information about the properties and what they do.

SEE ALSO

gluNewTess, **gluTessProperty**

NAME

gluLoadSamplingMatrices – load NURBS sampling and culling matrices

C SPECIFICATION

void **gluLoadSamplingMatrices**(GLUnurbs* *nurb*,
const GLfloat **model*,
const GLfloat **perspective*,
const GLint **view*)

PARAMETERS

nurb   Specifies the NURBS object (created with **gluNewNurbsRenderer**).

model   Specifies a modelview matrix (as from a **glGetFloatv** call).

perspective Specifies a projection matrix (as from a **glGetFloatv** call).

view   Specifies a viewport (as from a **glGetIntegerv** call).

DESCRIPTION

gluLoadSamplingMatrices uses *model*, *perspective*, and *view* to recompute the sampling and culling matrices stored in *nurb*. The sampling matrix determines how finely a NURBS curve or surface must be tessellated to satisfy the sampling tolerance (as determined by the **GLU_SAMPLING_TOLERANCE** property). The culling matrix is used in deciding if a NURBS curve or surface should be culled before rendering (when the **GLU_CULLING** property is turned on).

gluLoadSamplingMatrices is necessary only if the **GLU_AUTO_LOAD_MATRIX** property is turned off (see **gluNurbsProperty**). Although it can be convenient to leave the **GLU_AUTO_LOAD_MATRIX** property turned on, there can be a performance penalty for doing so. (A round trip to the GL server is needed to fetch the current values of the modelview matrix, projection matrix, and viewport.)

SEE ALSO

gluGetNurbsProperty, **gluNewNurbsRenderer**, **gluNurbsProperty**

NAME

gluLookAt – define a viewing transformation

C SPECIFICATION

void **gluLookAt**(GLdouble *eyeX*,
  GLdouble *eyeY*,
  GLdouble *eyeZ*,
  GLdouble *centerX*,
  GLdouble *centerY*,
  GLdouble *centerZ*,
  GLdouble *upX*,
  GLdouble *upY*,
  GLdouble *upZ*)

PARAMETERS

eyeX, eyeY, eyeZ

Specifies the position of the eye point.

centerX, centerY, centerZ

Specifies the position of the reference point.

upX, upY, upZ Specifies the direction of the *up* vector.

DESCRIPTION

gluLookAt creates a viewing matrix derived from an eye point, a reference point indicating the center of the scene, and an *UP* vector.

The matrix maps the reference point to the negative *z* axis and the eye point to the origin. When a typical projection matrix is used, the center of the scene therefore maps to the center of the viewport. Similarly, the direction described by the *UP* vector projected onto the viewing plane is mapped to the positive *y* axis so that it points upward in the viewport. The *UP* vector must not be parallel to the line of sight from the eye point to the reference point.

Let

$$F = \begin{matrix} centerX & - & eyeX \\ centerY & - & eyeY \\ centerZ & - & eyeZ \end{matrix}$$

Let *UP* be the vector (upX, upY, upZ).

Then normalize as follows: $f = \dfrac{F}{||F||}$

$UP' = \dfrac{UP}{||UP||}$

Finally, let $s = f \times UP'$, and $u = s \times f$.

M is then constructed as follows: $M = \begin{matrix} s[0] & s[1] & s[2] & 0 \\ u[0] & u[1] & u[2] & 0 \\ -f[0] & -f[1] & -f[2] & 0 \\ 0 & 0 & 0 & 1 \end{matrix}$

and **gluLookAt** is equivalent to

```
glMultMatrixf(M);
glTranslated (-eyex, -eyey, -eyez);
```

SEE ALSO

glFrustum, **gluPerspective**

NAME

gluNewNurbsRenderer – create a NURBS object

C SPECIFICATION

GLUnurbs* **gluNewNurbsRenderer**(void)

DESCRIPTION

gluNewNurbsRenderer creates and returns a pointer to a new NURBS object. This object must be referred to when calling NURBS rendering and control functions. A return value of 0 means that there is not enough memory to allocate the object.

SEE ALSO

gluBeginCurve, **gluBeginSurface**, **gluBeginTrim**, **gluDeleteNurbsRenderer**, **gluNurbsCallback**, **gluNurbsProperty**

NAME

    gluNewQuadric – create a quadrics object

C SPECIFICATION

    GLUquadric* **gluNewQuadric**(void)

DESCRIPTION

    gluNewQuadric creates and returns a pointer to a new quadrics object. This object must be referred to when calling quadrics rendering and control functions. A return value of 0 means that there is not enough memory to allocate the object.

SEE ALSO

    gluCylinder, **gluDeleteQuadric**, **gluDisk**, **gluPartialDisk**, **gluQuadricCallback**, **gluQuadricDrawStyle**, **gluQuadricNormals**, **gluQuadricOrientation**, **gluQuadricTexture**, **gluSphere**

NAME

gluNewTess – create a tessellation object

C SPECIFICATION

GLUtesselator* **gluNewTess**(void)

DESCRIPTION

gluNewTess creates and returns a pointer to a new tessellation object. This object must be referred to when calling tessellation functions. A return value of 0 means that there is not enough memory to allocate the object.

SEE ALSO

gluTessBeginPolygon, **gluDeleteTess**, **gluTessCallback**

NAME

gluNurbsCallback – define a callback for a NURBS object

C SPECIFICATION

void **gluNurbsCallback**(GLUnurbs* *nurb*,
GLenum *which*,
GLvoid *(*CallBackFunc)( )*

PARAMETERS

nurb   Specifies the NURBS object (created with **gluNewNurbsRenderer**).

which   Specifies the callback being defined. Valid values are
**GLU_NURBS_BEGIN, GLU_NURBS_VERTEX,
GLU_NURBS_NORMAL, GLU_NURBS_COLOR,
GLU_NURBS_TEXTURE_COORD, GLU_NURBS_END,
GLU_NURBS_BEGIN_DATA, GLU_NURBS_VERTEX_DATA,
GLU_NURBS_NORMAL_DATA, GLU_NURBS_COLOR_DATA,
GLU_NURBS_TEXTURE_COORD_DATA, GLU_NURBS_END_DATA,**
and **GLU_NURBS_ERROR.**

CallBackFunc Specifies the function that the callback calls.

DESCRIPTION

gluNurbsCallback is used to define a callback to be used by a NURBS object. If the specified callback is already defined, then it is replaced. If *CallBackFunc* is NULL, then this callback will not get invoked and the related data, if any, will be lost.

Except the error callback, these callbacks are used by NURBS tessellator (when **GLU_NURBS_MODE** is set to be **GLU_NURBS_TESSELLATOR**) to return back the OpenGL polygon primitives resulting from the tessellation. Note that there are two versions of each callback: one with a user data pointer and one without. If both versions for a particular callback are specified then the callback with the user data pointer will be used. Note that "userData" is a copy of the pointer that was specified at the last call to **gluNurbsCallbackData**.

The error callback function is effective no matter which value that **GLU_NURBS_MODE** is set to. All other callback functions are effective only when **GLU_NURBS_MODE** is set to **GLU_NURBS_TESSELLATOR**.

The legal callbacks are as follows:

GLU_NURBS_BEGIN

The begin callback indicates the start of a primitive. The function takes a single argument of type GLenum, which can be one of **GL_LINES, GL_LINE_STRIP, GL_TRIANGLE_FAN, GL_TRIANGLE_STRIP, GL_TRIANGLES,** or **GL_QUAD_STRIP.** The default begin callback function is NULL. The function prototype for this callback looks like:

```
void begin ( GLenum type );
```

GLU_NURBS_BEGIN_DATA

The same as the **GLU_NURBS_BEGIN** callback except that it takes an additional pointer argument. This pointer is a copy of the pointer that was specified at the last call to **gluNurbsCallbackData**. The default callback function is NULL. The function prototype for this callback function looks like:

```
void beginData (GLenum type, void *userData);
```

GLU_NURBS_VERTEX

The vertex callback indicates a vertex of the primitive. The coordinates of the vertex are stored in the parameter "vertex". All the generated vertices have dimension 3, that is, homogeneous coordinates have been transformed into affine coordinates. The default vertex callback function is NULL. The function prototype for this callback function looks like:

```
void vertex ( GLfloat *vertex );
```

GLU_NURBS_VERTEX_DATA

This is the same as the **GLU_NURBS_VERTEX** callback, except that it takes an additional pointer argument. This pointer is a copy of the pointer that was specified at the last call to **gluNurbsCallbackData**. The default callback function is NULL. The function prototype for this callback function looks like:

```
void vertexData ( GLfloat *vertex, void *userData );
```

GLU_NURBS_NORMAL

The normal callback is invoked as the vertex normal is generated. The components of the normal are stored in the parameter "normal". In the case of a NURBS curve, the callback function is effective only when the user provides a normal map (**GL_MAP1_NORMAL**). In the case of a NURBS surface, if a normal map (**GL_MAP2_NORMAL**) is provided, then the generated normal is computed from the normal map. If a normal map is not provided then a surface normal is computed in a manner similar to that described for evaluators when **GL_AUTO_NORMAL** is enabled.

The default normal callback function is NULL. The function prototype for this callback function looks like:

```
void normal ( GLfloat *normal );
```

GLU_NURBS_NORMAL_DATA

The same as the **GLU_NURBS_NORMAL** callback except that it takes an additional pointer argument. This pointer is a copy of the pointer that was specified at the last call to **gluNurbsCallbackData**. The default callback function is NULL. The function prototype for this callback function looks like:

```
void normalData ( GLfloat *normal, void *userData );
```

GLU_NURBS_COLOR

The color callback is invoked as the color of a vertex is generated. The components of the color are stored in the parameter "color". This callback is effective only when the user provides a color map (-**GL_MAP1_COLOR_4** or **GL_MAP2_COLOR_4**). "color" contains four components: R,G,B,A. The default color callback function is NULL. The prototype for this callback function looks like:

```
void color ( GLfloat *color );
```

GLU_NURBS_COLOR_DATA

The same as the **GLU_NURBS_COLOR** callback except that it takes an additional pointer argument. This pointer is a copy of the pointer that was specified at the last call to **gluNurbsCallbackData**. The default callback function is NULL. The function prototype for this callback function looks like:

```
void colorData ( GLfloat *color, void *userData );
```

GLU_NURBS_TEXTURE_COORD

The texture callback is invoked as the texture coordinates of a vertex are generated. These coordinates are stored in the parameter "texCoord". The number of texture coordinates can be 1, 2, 3, or 4 depending on which type of texture map is specified (**GL_MAP1_TEXTURE_COORD_1**, **GL_MAP1_TEXTURE_COORD_2**, **GL_MAP1_TEXTURE_COORD_3**, **GL_MAP1_TEXTURE_COORD_4**, **GL_MAP2_TEXTURE_COORD_1**, **GL_MAP2_TEXTURE_COORD_2**, **GL_MAP2_TEXTURE_COORD_3**, **GL_MAP2_TEXTURE_COORD_4**). If no texture map is specified, this callback function will not be called.

The default texture callback function is NULL. The function prototype for this callback function looks like:

```
void texCoord ( GLfloat *texCoord );
```

GLU_NURBS_TEXTURE_COORD_DATA

This is the same as the **GLU_NURBS_TEXTURE_COORD** callback, except that it takes an additional pointer argument. This pointer is a copy of the pointer that was specified at the last call to **gluNurbsCallbackData**. The default callback function is NULL. The function prototype for this callback function looks like:

```
void texCoordData (GLfloat *texCoord, void *userData);
```

GLU_NURBS_END

The end callback is invoked at the end of a primitive. The default end callback function is NULL. The function prototype for this callback function looks like:

```
void end ( void );
```

GLU_NURBS_END_DATA

This is the same as the **GLU_NURBS_END** callback, except that it takes an additional pointer argument. This pointer is a copy of the pointer that was specified at the last call to **gluNurbsCallbackData**. The default callback function is NULL. The function prototype for this callback function looks like:

```
void endData ( void  *userData );
```

GLU_NURBS_ERROR

The error function is called when an error is encountered. Its single argument is of type GLenum, and it indicates the specific error that occurred. There are 37 errors unique to NURBS named **GLU_NURBS_ERROR1** through **GLU_NURBS_ERROR37**. Character strings describing these errors can be retrieved with **gluErrorString**.

NOTES

gluNurbsCallback is available only if the GLU version is 1.2 or greater.

GLU version 1.2 supports only the **GLU_ERROR** parameter for *which*. The **GLU_ERROR** value is deprecated in GLU version 1.3 in favor of **GLU_NURBS_ERROR**. All other accepted values for *CallBackFunc* are available only if the GLU version is 1.3 or greater.

SEE ALSO

gluErrorString, **gluNewNurbsRenderer**, **gluNurbsCallbackData**, **gluNurbsProperty**

NAME

gluNurbsCallbackData – set a user data pointer

C SPECIFICATION

void **gluNurbsCallbackData**(GLUnurbs* *nurb*,
                                            GLvoid* *userData*)

PARAMETERS

nurb   Specifies the NURBS object (created with **gluNewNurbsRenderer**).

userData Specifies a pointer to the user's data.

DESCRIPTION

gluNurbsCallbackData is used to pass a pointer to the application's data to NURBS tessellator. A copy of this pointer will be passed by the tessellator in the NURBS callback functions (set by **gluNurbsCallback**).

NOTES

gluNurbsCallbackData is available only if the GLU version is 1.3 or greater.

SEE ALSO

gluNewNurbsRenderer, **gluNurbsCallback**

NAME

gluNurbsCallbackDataEXT – set a user data pointer

C SPECIFICATION

void **gluNurbsCallbackDataEXT**(GLUnurbs* *nurb,*
GLvoid* *userData*)

PARAMETERS

nurb   Specifies the NURBS object (created with **gluNewNurbsRenderer**).

userData Specifies a pointer to the user's data.

DESCRIPTION

gluNurbsCallbackDataEXT is used to pass a pointer to the application's data to NURBS tessellator. A copy of this pointer will be passed by the tessellator in the NURBS callback functions (set by **gluNurbsCallback**).

SEE ALSO

gluNurbsCallback

NAME

gluNurbsCurve – define the shape of a NURBS curve

C SPECIFICATION

void **gluNurbsCurve**(GLUnurbs* *nurb*,
                         GLint *knotCount*,
                         GLfloat **knots*,
                         GLint *stride*,
                         GLfloat **control*,
                         GLint *order*,
                         GLenum *type*)

PARAMETERS

nurb   Specifies the NURBS object (created with **gluNewNurbsRenderer**).

knotCount
            Specifies the number of knots in *knots*. *knotCount* equals the number of control points plus the order.

knots   Specifies an array of *knotCount* nondecreasing knot values.

stride   Specifies the offset (as a number of single-precision floating-point values) between successive curve control points.

control Specifies a pointer to an array of control points. The coordinates must agree with *type*, specified below.

order   Specifies the order of the NURBS curve. *order* equals degree + 1, hence a cubic curve has an order of 4.

type   Specifies the type of the curve. If this curve is defined within a **gluBeginCurve**/**gluEndCurve** pair, then the type can be any of the valid one-dimensional evaluator types (such as **GL_MAP1_VERTEX_3** or **GL_MAP1_COLOR_4**). Between a **gluBeginTrim**/**gluEndTrim** pair, the only valid types are **GLU_MAP1_TRIM_2** and **GLU_MAP1_TRIM_3**.

DESCRIPTION

Use **gluNurbsCurve** to describe a NURBS curve.

When **gluNurbsCurve** appears between a **gluBeginCurve**/**gluEndCurve** pair, it is used to describe a curve to be rendered. Positional, texture, and color coordinates are associated by presenting each as a separate **gluNurbsCurve** between a **gluBeginCurve**/**gluEndCurve** pair. No more than one call to **gluNurbsCurve** for each of color, position, and texture data can be made within a single **gluBeginCurve**/**gluEndCurve** pair. Exactly one call must be made to describe the position of the curve (a *type* of **GL_MAP1_VERTEX_3** or **GL_MAP1_VERTEX_4**).

When **gluNurbsCurve** appears between a **gluBeginTrim**/**gluEndTrim** pair, it is used to describe a trimming curve on a NURBS surface. If *type* is **GLU_MAP1_TRIM_2**, then it describes a curve in two-dimensional (*u* and *v*) parameter space. If it is **GLU_MAP1_TRIM_3**, then it describes a curve in two-dimensional homogeneous (*u*, *v*, and *w*) parameter space. See the **gluBeginTrim** reference page for more discussion about trimming curves.

EXAMPLE

The following commands render a textured NURBS curve with normals:

```
gluBeginCurve(nobj);
    gluNurbsCurve(nobj, ..., GL_MAP1_TEXTURE_COORD_2);
    gluNurbsCurve(nobj, ..., GL_MAP1_NORMAL);
    gluNurbsCurve(nobj, ..., GL_MAP1_VERTEX_4);
gluEndCurve(nobj);
```

NOTES

To define trim curves which stitch well, use **gluPwlCurve**.

SEE ALSO

gluBeginCurve, **gluBeginTrim**, **gluNewNurbsRenderer**, **gluPwlCurve**

NAME

gluNurbsProperty – set a NURBS property

C SPECIFICATION

void **gluNurbsProperty**(GLUnurbs* *nurb*,
GLenum *property*,
GLfloat *value*)

PARAMETERS

nurb   Specifies the NURBS object (created with **gluNewNurbsRenderer**).

property Specifies the property to be set. Valid values are
**GLU_SAMPLING_TOLERANCE, GLU_DISPLAY_MODE, GLU_CULLING,
GLU_AUTO_LOAD_MATRIX, GLU_PARAMETRIC_TOLERANCE,
GLU_SAMPLING_METHOD, GLU_U_STEP, GLU_V_STEP,** or
GLU_NURBS_MODE.

value   Specifies the value of the indicated property. It may be a numeric value, or
one of **GLU_OUTLINE_POLYGON, GLU_FILL, GLU_OUTLINE_PATCH,
GL_TRUE, GL_FALSE, GLU_PATH_LENGTH,
GLU_PARAMETRIC_ERROR, GLU_DOMAIN_DISTANCE,
GLU_NURBS_RENDERER,** or **GLU_NURBS_TESSELLATOR.**

DESCRIPTION

gluNurbsProperty is used to control properties stored in a NURBS object. These properties affect the way that a NURBS curve is rendered. The accepted values for *property* are as follows:

GLU_NURBS_MODE

value should be set to be either **GLU_NURBS_RENDERER** or
GLU_NURBS_TESSELLATOR. When set to
GLU_NURBS_RENDERER, NURBS objects are tessellated into
OpenGL primitives and sent to the pipeline for rendering. When set
to **GLU_NURBS_TESSELLATOR,** NURBS objects are tessellated into
OpenGL primitives but the vertices, normals, colors, and/or textures
are retrieved back through a callback interface (see
gluNurbsCallback). This allows the user to cache the tessellated
results for further processing. The initial value is
GLU_NURBS_RENDERER.

GLU_SAMPLING_METHOD

Specifies how a NURBS surface should be tessellated. *value* may be
one of **GLU_PATH_LENGTH, GLU_PARAMETRIC_ERROR,
GLU_DOMAIN_DISTANCE, GLU_OBJECT_PATH_LENGTH,** or
GLU_OBJECT_PARAMETRIC_ERROR. When set to

GLU_PATH_LENGTH, the surface is rendered so that the maximum length, in pixels, of the edges of the tessellation polygons is no greater than what is specified by **GLU_SAMPLING_TOLERANCE**.

GLU_PARAMETRIC_ERROR specifies that the surface is rendered in such a way that the value specified by **GLU_PARAMETRIC_TOLERANCE** describes the maximum distance, in pixels, between the tessellation polygons and the surfaces they approximate.

GLU_DOMAIN_DISTANCE allows users to specify, in parametric coordinates, how many sample points per unit length are taken in *u, v* direction.

GLU_OBJECT_PATH_LENGTH is similar to **GLU_PATH_LENGTH** except that it is view independent, that is, the surface is rendered so that the maximum length, in object space, of edges of the tessellation polygons is no greater than what is specified by **GLU_SAMPLING_TOLERANCE**.

GLU_OBJECT_PARAMETRIC_ERROR is similar to **GLU_PARAMETRIC_ERROR** except that it is view independent, that is, the surface is rendered in such a way that the value specified by **GLU_PARAMETRIC_TOLERANCE** describes the maximum distance, in object space, between the tessellation polygons and the surfaces they approximate.

The initial value of **GLU_SAMPLING_METHOD** is **GLU_PATH_LENGTH**.

GLU_SAMPLING_TOLERANCE

Specifies the maximum length, in pixels or in object space length unit, to use when the sampling method is set to **GLU_PATH_LENGTH** or **GLU_OBJECT_PATH_LENGTH**. The NURBS code is conservative when rendering a curve or surface, so the actual length can be somewhat shorter. The initial value is 50.0 pixels.

GLU_PARAMETRIC_TOLERANCE

Specifies the maximum distance, in pixels or in object space length unit, to use when the sampling method is **GLU_PARAMETRIC_ERROR** or **GLU_OBJECT_PARAMETRIC_ERROR**. The initial value is 0.5.

GLU_U_STEP Specifies the number of sample points per unit length taken along the *u* axis in parametric coordinates. It is needed when **GLU_SAMPLING_METHOD** is set to **GLU_DOMAIN_DISTANCE**. The initial value is 100.

GLU_V_STEP   Specifies the number of sample points per unit length taken along the *v* axis in parametric coordinate. It is needed when **GLU_SAMPLING_METHOD** is set to **GLU_DOMAIN_DISTANCE**. The initial value is 100.

GLU_DISPLAY_MODE

value can be set to **GLU_OUTLINE_POLYGON**, **GLU_FILL**, or **GLU_OUTLINE_PATCH**. When **GLU_NURBS_MODE** is set to be **GLU_NURBS_RENDERER**, *value* defines how a NURBS surface should be rendered. When *value* is set to **GLU_FILL**, the surface is rendered as a set of polygons. When *value* is set to **GLU_OUTLINE_POLYGON**, the NURBS library draws only the outlines of the polygons created by tessellation. When *value* is set to **GLU_OUTLINE_PATCH** just the outlines of patches and trim curves defined by the user are drawn.

When **GLU_NURBS_MODE** is set to be **GLU_NURBS_TESSELLATOR**, *value* defines how a NURBS surface should be tessellated. When **GLU_DISPLAY_MODE** is set to **GLU_FILL** or **GLU_OUTLINE_POLYGON**, the NURBS surface is tessellated into OpenGL triangle primitives which can be retrieved back through callback functions. If **GLU_DISPLAY_MODE** is set to **GLU_OUTLINE_PATCH**, only the outlines of the patches and trim curves are generated as a sequence of line strips which can be retrieved back through callback functions.

The initial value is **GLU_FILL**.

GLU_CULLING

value is a boolean value that, when set to **GL_TRUE**, indicates that a NURBS curve should be discarded prior to tessellation if its control points lie outside the current viewport. The initial value is **GL_FALSE**.

GLU_AUTO_LOAD_MATRIX

value is a boolean value. When set to **GL_TRUE**, the NURBS code downloads the projection matrix, the modelview matrix, and the viewport from the GL server to compute sampling and culling matrices for each NURBS curve that is rendered. Sampling and culling matrices are required to determine the tessellation of a NURBS surface into line segments or polygons and to cull a NURBS surface if it lies outside the viewport.

If this mode is set to **GL_FALSE**, then the program needs to provide a projection matrix, a modelview matrix, and a viewport for the NURBS renderer to use to construct sampling and culling matrices. This can be done with the **gluLoadSamplingMatrices** function.

This mode is initially set to **GL_TRUE**. Changing it from **GL_TRUE** to **GL_FALSE** does not affect the sampling and culling matrices until **gluLoadSamplingMatrices** is called.

NOTES

If **GLU_AUTO_LOAD_MATRIX** is true, sampling and culling may be executed incorrectly if NURBS routines are compiled into a display list.

A *property* of **GLU_PARAMETRIC_TOLERANCE**, **GLU_SAMPLING_METHOD**, **GLU_U_STEP**, or **GLU_V_STEP**, or a *value* of **GLU_PATH_LENGTH**, **GLU_PARAMETRIC_ERROR**, **GLU_DOMAIN_DISTANCE** are only available if the GLU version is 1.1 or greater. They are not valid parameters in GLU 1.0.

gluGetString can be used to determine the GLU version.

GLU_NURBS_MODE is only availble if the GLU version is 1.3 or greater.

The **GLU_OBJECT_PATH_LENGTH** and **GLU_OBJECT_PARAMETRIC_ERROR** values for the **GLU_SAMPLING_METHOD** property are only available if the GLU version is 1.3 or greater.

SEE ALSO

gluGetNurbsProperty, **gluLoadSamplingMatrices**, **gluNewNurbsRenderer**, **gluGetString**, **gluNurbsCallback**

NAME

gluNurbsSurface – define the shape of a NURBS surface

C SPECIFICATION

void **gluNurbsSurface**(GLUnurbs* *nurb*,
GLint *sKnotCount*,
GLfloat* *sKnots*,
GLint *tKnotCount*,
GLfloat* *tKnots*,
GLint *sStride*,
GLint *tStride*,
GLfloat* *control*,
GLint *sOrder*,
GLint *tOrder*,
GLenum *type*)

PARAMETERS

nurb   Specifies the NURBS object (created with **gluNewNurbsRenderer**).

sKnotCount
                Specifies the number of knots in the parametric *u* direction.

sKnots   Specifies an array of *sKnotCount* nondecreasing knot values in the parametric *u* direction.

tKnotCount
                Specifies the number of knots in the parametric *v* direction.

tKnots   Specifies an array of *tKnotCount* nondecreasing knot values in the parametric *v* direction.

sStride   Specifies the offset (as a number of single-precision floating point values) between successive control points in the parametric *u* direction in *control*.

tStride   Specifies the offset (in single-precision floating-point values) between successive control points in the parametric *v* direction in *control*.

control   Specifies an array containing control points for the NURBS surface. The offsets between successive control points in the parametric *u* and *v* directions are given by *sStride* and *tStride*.

sOrder   Specifies the order of the NURBS surface in the parametric *u* direction. The order is one more than the degree, hence a surface that is cubic in *u* has a *u* order of 4.

tOrder   Specifies the order of the NURBS surface in the parametric *v* direction. The order is one more than the degree, hence a surface that is cubic in *v* has a *v* order of 4.

type   Specifies type of the surface. *type* can be any of the valid two-dimensional evaluator types (such as **GL_MAP2_VERTEX_3** or **GL_MAP2_COLOR_4**).

DESCRIPTION

Use **gluNurbsSurface** within a NURBS (Non-Uniform Rational B-Spline) surface definition to describe the shape of a NURBS surface (before any trimming). To mark the beginning of a NURBS surface definition, use the **gluBeginSurface** command. To mark the end of a NURBS surface definition, use the **gluEndSurface** command. Call **gluNurbsSurface** within a NURBS surface definition only.

Positional, texture, and color coordinates are associated with a surface by presenting each as a separate **gluNurbsSurface** between a **gluBeginSurface/gluEndSurface** pair. No more than one call to **gluNurbsSurface** for each of color, position, and texture data can be made within a single **gluBeginSurface/gluEndSurface** pair. Exactly one call must be made to describe the position of the surface (a *type* of **GL_MAP2_VERTEX_3** or **GL_MAP2_VERTEX_4**).

A NURBS surface can be trimmed by using the commands **gluNurbsCurve** and **gluPwlCurve** between calls to **gluBeginTrim** and **gluEndTrim**.

Note that a **gluNurbsSurface** with *sKnotCount* knots in the *u* direction and *tKnotCount* knots in the *v* direction with orders *sOrder* and *tOrder* must have (*sKnotCount* - *sOrder*) × (*tKnotCount* - *tOrder*) control points.

EXAMPLE

The following commands render a textured NURBS surface with normals; the texture coordinates and normals are also NURBS surfaces:

```
gluBeginSurface(nobj);
    gluNurbsSurface(nobj, ..., GL_MAP2_TEXTURE_COORD_2);
    gluNurbsSurface(nobj, ..., GL_MAP2_NORMAL);
    gluNurbsSurface(nobj, ..., GL_MAP2_VERTEX_4);
gluEndSurface(nobj);
```

SEE ALSO

gluBeginSurface, **gluBeginTrim**, **gluNewNurbsRenderer**, **gluNurbsCurve**, **gluPwlCurve**

NAME

gluOrtho2D – define a 2D orthographic projection matrix

C SPECIFICATION

void **gluOrtho2D**(GLdouble *left*,
                    GLdouble *right*,
                    GLdouble *bottom*,
                    GLdouble *top*)

PARAMETERS

left, right

> Specify the coordinates for the left and right vertical clipping planes.

bottom, top

> Specify the coordinates for the bottom and top horizontal clipping planes.

DESCRIPTION

gluOrtho2D sets up a two-dimensional orthographic viewing region. This is equivalent to calling **glOrtho** with *near* = -1 and *far* = 1.

SEE ALSO

glOrtho, **gluPerspective**

NAME

gluPartialDisk – draw an arc of a disk

C SPECIFICATION

void **gluPartialDisk**(GLUquadric* *quad*,
GLdouble *inner*,
GLdouble *outer*,
GLint *slices*,
GLint *loops*,
GLdouble *start*,
GLdouble *sweep*)

PARAMETERS

quad   Specifies a quadrics object (created with **gluNewQuadric**).

inner   Specifies the inner radius of the partial disk (can be 0).

outer   Specifies the outer radius of the partial disk.

slices   Specifies the number of subdivisions around the z axis.

loops   Specifies the number of concentric rings about the origin into which the partial disk is subdivided.

start   Specifies the starting angle, in degrees, of the disk portion.

sweep
Specifies the sweep angle, in degrees, of the disk portion.

DESCRIPTION

gluPartialDisk renders a partial disk on the $z = 0$ plane. A partial disk is similar to a full disk, except that only the subset of the disk from *start* through *start* + *sweep* is included (where 0 degrees is along the $+y$ axis, 90 degrees along the $+x$ axis, 180 degrees along the $-y$ axis, and 270 degrees along the $-x$ axis).

The partial disk has a radius of *outer*, and contains a concentric circular hole with a radius of *inner*. If *inner* is 0, then no hole is generated. The partial disk is subdivided around the z axis into slices (like pizza slices), and also about the z axis into rings (as specified by *slices* and *loops*, respectively).

With respect to orientation, the $+z$ side of the partial disk is considered to be outside (see **gluQuadricOrientation**). This means that if the orientation is set to **GLU_OUTSIDE**, then any normals generated point along the $+z$ axis. Otherwise, they point along the $-z$ axis.

If texturing is turned on (with **gluQuadricTexture**), texture coordinates are generated linearly such that where $r = outer$, the value at $(r, 0, 0)$ is $(1.0, 0.5)$, at $(0, r, 0)$ it is $(0.5, 1.0)$, at $(-r, 0, 0)$ it is $(0.0, 0.5)$, and at $(0, -r, 0)$ it is $(0.5, 0.0)$.

SEE ALSO

gluCylinder, gluDisk, gluNewQuadric, gluQuadricOrientation, gluQuadricTexture, gluSphere

NAME

gluPerspective – set up a perspective projection matrix

C SPECIFICATION

void **gluPerspective**(GLdouble *fovy*,
  GLdouble *aspect*,
  GLdouble *zNear*,
  GLdouble *zFar*)

PARAMETERS

fovy   Specifies the field of view angle, in degrees, in the *y* direction.

aspect Specifies the aspect ratio that determines the field of view in the *x* direction. The aspect ratio is the ratio of *x* (width) to *y* (height).

zNear   Specifies the distance from the viewer to the near clipping plane (always positive).

zFar   Specifies the distance from the viewer to the far clipping plane (always positive).

DESCRIPTION

gluPerspective specifies a viewing frustum into the world coordinate system. In general, the aspect ratio in **gluPerspective** should match the aspect ratio of the associated viewport. For example, *aspect* = 2.0 means the viewer's angle of view is twice as wide in *x* as it is in *y*. If the viewport is twice as wide as it is tall, it displays the image without distortion.

The matrix generated by **gluPerspective** is multipled by the current matrix, just as if **glMultMatrix** were called with the generated matrix. To load the perspective matrix onto the current matrix stack instead, precede the call to **gluPerspective** with a call to **glLoadIdentity**.

Given *f* defined as follows:

$$f = cotangent\left(\frac{fovy}{2}\right)$$

The generated matrix is

$$
\begin{pmatrix}
\dfrac{f}{aspect} & 0 & 0 & 0 \\[1em]
0 & f & 0 & 0 \\[1em]
0 & 0 & \dfrac{zFar+zNear}{zNear-zFar} & \dfrac{2*zFar*zNear}{zNear-zFar} \\[1em]
0 & 0 & -1 & 0
\end{pmatrix}
$$

NOTES

Depth buffer precision is affected by the values specified for *zNear* and *zFar*. The greater the ratio of *zFar* to *zNear* is, the less effective the depth buffer will be at distinguishing between surfaces that are near each other. If

$$
r = \frac{zFar}{zNear}
$$

roughly $\log_2 r$ bits of depth buffer precision are lost. Because *r* approaches infinity as *zNear* approaches 0, *zNear* must never be set to 0.

SEE ALSO

glFrustum, **glLoadIdentity**, **glMultMatrix**, **gluOrtho2D**

NAME

gluPickMatrix – define a picking region

C SPECIFICATION

void **gluPickMatrix**(GLdouble *x*,
                       GLdouble *y*,
                       GLdouble *delX*,
                       GLdouble *delY*,
                       GLint **viewport*)

PARAMETERS

x, y
> Specify the center of a picking region in window coordinates.

delX, delY
> Specify the width and height, respectively, of the picking region in window coordinates.

viewport
> Specifies the current viewport (as from a **glGetIntegerv** call).

DESCRIPTION

gluPickMatrix creates a projection matrix that can be used to restrict drawing to a small region of the viewport. This is typically useful to determine what objects are being drawn near the cursor. Use **gluPickMatrix** to restrict drawing to a small region around the cursor. Then, enter selection mode (with **glRenderMode**) and rerender the scene. All primitives that would have been drawn near the cursor are identified and stored in the selection buffer.

The matrix created by **gluPickMatrix** is multiplied by the current matrix just as if **glMultMatrix** is called with the generated matrix. To effectively use the generated pick matrix for picking, first call **glLoadIdentity** to load an identity matrix onto the perspective matrix stack. Then call **gluPickMatrix**, and finally, call a command (such as **gluPerspective**) to multiply the perspective matrix by the pick matrix.

When using **gluPickMatrix** to pick NURBS, be careful to turn off the NURBS property **GLU_AUTO_LOAD_MATRIX**. If **GLU_AUTO_LOAD_MATRIX** is not turned off, then any NURBS surface rendered is subdivided differently with the pick matrix than the way it was subdivided without the pick matrix.

EXAMPLE

When rendering a scene as follows:

```
glMatrixMode(GL_PROJECTION);
glLoadIdentity();
gluPerspective(...);
glMatrixMode(GL_MODELVIEW);
/* Draw the scene */
```

a portion of the viewport can be selected as a pick region like this:

```
glMatrixMode(GL_PROJECTION);
glLoadIdentity();
gluPickMatrix(x, y, width, height, viewport);
gluPerspective(...);
glMatrixMode(GL_MODELVIEW);
/* Draw the scene */
```

SEE ALSO

glGet, **glLoadIndentity**, **glMultMatrix**, **glRenderMode**, **gluPerspective**

NAME

gluProject – map object coordinates to window coordinates

C SPECIFICATION

GLint **gluProject**(GLdouble *objX*,
         GLdouble *objY*,
         GLdouble *objZ*,
         const GLdouble **model*,
         const GLdouble **proj*,
         const GLint **view*,
         GLdouble* *winX*,
         GLdouble* *winY*,
         GLdouble* *winZ*)

PARAMETERS

objX, *objY*, *objZ*
     Specify the object coordinates.

model   Specifies the current modelview matrix (as from a **glGetDoublev** call).

proj   Specifies the current projection matrix (as from a **glGetDoublev** call).

view   Specifies the current viewport (as from a **glGetIntegerv** call).

winX, *winY*, *winZ*
     Return the computed window coordinates.

DESCRIPTION

gluProject transforms the specified object coordinates into window coordinates using *model*, *proj*, and *view*. The result is stored in *winX*, *winY*, and *winZ*. A return value of **GL_TRUE** indicates success, a return value of **GL_FALSE** indicates failure.

To compute the coordinates, let $v = (objX, objY, objZ, 1.0)$ represented as a matrix with 4 rows and 1 column. Then **gluProject** computes v' as follows:

$$v' = P \times M \times v$$

where P is the current projection matrix *proj*, M is the current modelview matrix *model* (both represented as 4×4 matrices in column-major order) and '×' represents matrix multiplication.

The window coordinates are then computed as follows:

$winX = view(0) + view(2) * (v'(0) + 1) / 2$

$winY = view(1) + view(3) * (v'(1) + 1) / 2$

$winZ = (v'(2) + 1) / 2$

SEE ALSO
    glGet, **gluUnProject**

NAME

gluPwlCurve – describe a piecewise linear NURBS trimming curve

C SPECIFICATION

void **gluPwlCurve**(GLUnurbs* *nurb*,
 GLint *count*,
 GLfloat* *data*,
 GLint *stride*,
 GLenum *type*)

PARAMETERS

nurb Specifies the NURBS object (created with **gluNewNurbsRenderer**).

count Specifies the number of points on the curve.

data Specifies an array containing the curve points.

stride Specifies the offset (a number of single-precision floating-point values) between points on the curve.

type Specifies the type of curve. Must be either **GLU_MAP1_TRIM_2** or **GLU_MAP1_TRIM_3**.

DESCRIPTION

gluPwlCurve describes a piecewise linear trimming curve for a NURBS surface. A piecewise linear curve consists of a list of coordinates of points in the parameter space for the NURBS surface to be trimmed. These points are connected with line segments to form a curve. If the curve is an approximation to a curve that is not piecewise linear, the points should be close enough in parameter space that the resulting path appears curved at the resolution used in the application.

If *type* is **GLU_MAP1_TRIM_2**, then it describes a curve in two-dimensional (*u* and *v*) parameter space. If it is **GLU_MAP1_TRIM_3**, then it describes a curve in two-dimensional homogeneous (*u*, *v*, and *w*) parameter space. See the **gluBeginTrim** reference page for more information about trimming curves.

NOTES

To describe a trim curve that closely follows the contours of a NURBS surface, call **gluNurbsCurve**.

SEE ALSO

gluBeginCurve, **gluBeginTrim**, **gluNewNurbsRenderer**, **gluNurbsCurve**

gluQuadricCallback

NAME

gluQuadricCallback – define a callback for a quadrics object

C SPECIFICATION

void **gluQuadricCallback**(GLUquadric* *quad,*
                            GLenum *which,*
                            GLvoid *(*CallBackFunc)( )*

PARAMETERS

quad   Specifies the quadrics object (created with **gluNewQuadric**).

which   Specifies the callback being defined. The only valid value is
                GLU_ERROR.

CallBackFunc Specifies the function to be called.

DESCRIPTION

gluQuadricCallback is used to define a new callback to be used by a quadrics
object. If the specified callback is already defined, then it is replaced. If *CallBackFunc*
is NULL, then any existing callback is erased.

The one legal callback is **GLU_ERROR**:

GLU_ERROR   The function is called when an error is encountered. Its single argu-
                ment is of type GLenum, and it indicates the specific error that
                occurred. Character strings describing these errors can be retrieved
                with the **gluErrorString** call.

SEE ALSO

gluErrorString, **gluNewQuadric**

NAME

gluQuadricDrawStyle – specify the draw style desired for quadrics

C SPECIFICATION

void **gluQuadricDrawStyle**(GLUquadric* *quad,*
GLenum *draw*)

PARAMETERS

quad Specifies the quadrics object (created with **gluNewQuadric**).

draw Specifies the desired draw style. Valid values are **GLU_FILL**, **GLU_LINE**,
GLU_SILHOUETTE, and **GLU_POINT**.

DESCRIPTION

gluQuadricDrawStyle specifies the draw style for quadrics rendered with *quad*. The
legal values are as follows:

GLU_FILL Quadrics are rendered with polygon primitives. The polygons are
drawn in a counterclockwise fashion with respect to their normals
(as defined with **gluQuadricOrientation**).

GLU_LINE Quadrics are rendered as a set of lines.

GLU_SILHOUETTE

Quadrics are rendered as a set of lines, except that edges separating
coplanar faces will not be drawn.

GLU_POINT Quadrics are rendered as a set of points.

SEE ALSO

gluNewQuadric, **gluQuadricNormals**, **gluQuadricOrientation**,
gluQuadricTexture

NAME

gluQuadricNormals – specify what kind of normals are desired for quadrics

C SPECIFICATION

void **gluQuadricNormals**(GLUquadric* *quad*,
                                            GLenum *normal*)

PARAMETERS

quad   Specifes the quadrics object (created with **gluNewQuadric**).

normal Specifies the desired type of normals. Valid values are **GLU_NONE**, **GLU_FLAT**, and **GLU_SMOOTH**.

DESCRIPTION

gluQuadricNormals specifies what kind of normals are desired for quadrics rendered with *quad*. The legal values are as follows:

GLU_NONE   No normals are generated.

GLU_FLAT   One normal is generated for every facet of a quadric.

GLU_SMOOTH

One normal is generated for every vertex of a quadric. This is the initial value.

SEE ALSO

gluNewQuadric, **gluQuadricDrawStyle**, **gluQuadricOrientation**, **gluQuadricTexture**

NAME

gluQuadricOrientation – specify inside/outside orientation for quadrics

C SPECIFICATION

void **gluQuadricOrientation**(GLUquadric* *quad*,
                                                 GLenum *orientation*)

PARAMETERS

quad   Specifies the quadrics object (created with **gluNewQuadric**).

orientation
                    Specifies the desired orientation. Valid values are **GLU_OUTSIDE** and **GLU_INSIDE**.

DESCRIPTION

gluQuadricOrientation specifies what kind of orientation is desired for quadrics rendered with *quad*. The *orientation* values are as follows:

GLU_OUTSIDE

                    Quadrics are drawn with normals pointing outward (the initial value).

GLU_INSIDE   Quadrics are drawn with normals pointing inward.

Note that the interpretation of *outward* and *inward* depends on the quadric being drawn.

SEE ALSO

gluNewQuadric, **gluQuadricDrawStyle**, **gluQuadricNormals**, **gluQuadricTexture**

NAME

gluQuadricTexture – specify if texturing is desired for quadrics

C SPECIFICATION

void **gluQuadricTexture**(GLUquadric* *quad*,
                                         GLboolean *texture*)

PARAMETERS

quad   Specifies the quadrics object (created with **gluNewQuadric**).

texture Specifies a flag indicating if texture coordinates should be generated.

DESCRIPTION

gluQuadricTexture specifies if texture coordinates should be generated for quadrics rendered with *quad*. If the value of *texture* is **GL_TRUE**, then texture coordinates are generated, and if *texture* is **GL_FALSE**, they are not. The initial value is **GL_FALSE**.

The manner in which texture coordinates are generated depends upon the specific quadric rendered.

SEE ALSO

gluNewQuadric, **gluQuadricDrawStyle**, **gluQuadricNormals**, **gluQuadricOrientation**

NAME

gluScaleImage – scale an image to an arbitrary size

C SPECIFICATION

GLint **gluScaleImage**(GLenum *format*,
                      GLsizei *wIn*,
                      GLsizei *hIn*,
                      GLenum *typeIn*,
                      const void **dataIn*,
                      GLsizei *wOut*,
                      GLsizei *hOut*,
                      GLenum *typeOut*,
                      GLvoid* *dataOut*)

PARAMETERS

format   Specifies the format of the pixel data. The following symbolic values are valid: **GL_COLOR_INDEX**, **GL_STENCIL_INDEX**, **GL_DEPTH_COMPONENT**, **GL_RED**, **GL_GREEN**, **GL_BLUE**, **GL_ALPHA**, **GL_RGB**, **GL_RGBA**, **GL_BGR**, **GL_BGRA**, **GL_LUMINANCE**, and **GL_LUMINANCE_ALPHA**.

wIn, hIn
      Specify in pixels the width and height, respectively, of the source image.

typeIn   Specifies the data type for *dataIn*. Must be one of **GL_UNSIGNED_BYTE**, **GL_BYTE**, **GL_BITMAP**, **GL_UNSIGNED_SHORT**, **GL_SHORT**, **GL_UNSIGNED_INT**, **GL_INT**, **GL_FLOAT**, **GL_UNSIGNED_BYTE_3_3_2**, **GL_UNSIGNED_BYTE_2_3_3_REV**, **GL_UNSIGNED_SHORT_5_6_5**, **GL_UNSIGNED_SHORT_5_6_5_REV**, **GL_UNSIGNED_SHORT_4_4_4_4**, **GL_UNSIGNED_SHORT_4_4_4_4_REV**, **GL_UNSIGNED_SHORT_5_5_5_1**, **GL_UNSIGNED_SHORT_1_5_5_5_REV**, **GL_UNSIGNED_INT_8_8_8_8**, **GL_UNSIGNED_INT_8_8_8_8_REV**, **GL_UNSIGNED_INT_10_10_10_2**, and **GL_UNSIGNED_INT_2_10_10_10_REV**.

dataIn   Specifies a pointer to the source image.

wOut, hOut
      Specify the width and height, respectively, in pixels of the destination image.

typeOut Specifies the data type for *dataOut*. Must be one of **GL_UNSIGNED_BYTE**, **GL_BYTE**, **GL_BITMAP**, **GL_UNSIGNED_SHORT**, **GL_SHORT**, **GL_UNSIGNED_INT**, **GL_INT**, **GL_FLOAT**, **GL_UNSIGNED_BYTE_3_3_2**, **GL_UNSIGNED_BYTE_2_3_3_REV**, **GL_UNSIGNED_SHORT_5_6_5**, **GL_UNSIGNED_SHORT_5_6_5_REV**, **GL_UNSIGNED_SHORT_4_4_4_4**,

GL_UNSIGNED_SHORT_4_4_4_4_REV, GL_UNSIGNED_SHORT_5_5_5_1, GL_UNSIGNED_SHORT_1_5_5_5_REV, GL_UNSIGNED_INT_8_8_8_8, GL_UNSIGNED_INT_8_8_8_8_REV, GL_UNSIGNED_INT_10_10_10_2, or GL_UNSIGNED_INT_2_10_10_10_REV.

dataOut
Specifies a pointer to the destination image.

DESCRIPTION

gluScaleImage scales a pixel image using the appropriate pixel store modes to unpack data from the source image and pack data into the destination image.

When shrinking an image, **gluScaleImage** uses a box filter to sample the source image and create pixels for the destination image. When magnifying an image, the pixels from the source image are linearly interpolated to create the destination image.

A return value of zero indicates success, otherwise a GLU error code is returned (see **gluErrorString**).

See the **glReadPixels** reference page for a description of the acceptable values for the *format*, *typeIn*, and *typeOut* parameters.

NOTES

Formats **GL_BGR**, and **GL_BGRA**, and types **GL_UNSIGNED_BYTE_3_3_2**, **GL_UNSIGNED_BYTE_2_3_3_REV**, **GL_UNSIGNED_SHORT_5_6_5**, **GL_UNSIGNED_SHORT_5_6_5_REV**, **GL_UNSIGNED_SHORT_4_4_4_4**, **GL_UNSIGNED_SHORT_4_4_4_4_REV**, **GL_UNSIGNED_SHORT_5_5_5_1**, **GL_UNSIGNED_SHORT_1_5_5_5_REV**, **GL_UNSIGNED_INT_8_8_8_8**, **GL_UNSIGNED_INT_8_8_8_8_REV**, **GL_UNSIGNED_INT_10_10_10_2**, and **GL_UNSIGNED_INT_2_10_10_10_REV** are only available if the GL version is 1.2 or greater.

ERRORS

GLU_INVALID_VALUE is returned if *wIn*, *hIn*, *wOut*, or *hOut* is negative.

GLU_INVALID_ENUM is returned if *format*, *typeIn*, or *typeOut* is not legal.

GLU_INVALID_OPERATION is returned if *typeIn* or *typeOut* is **GL_UNSIGNED_BYTE_3_3_2** or **GL_UNSIGNED_BYTE_2_3_3_REV** and *format* is not **GL_RGB**.

GLU_INVALID_OPERATION is returned if *typeIn* or *typeOut* is **GL_UNSIGNED_SHORT_5_6_5** or **GL_UNSIGNED_SHORT_5_6_5_REV** and *format* is not **GL_RGB**.

GLU_INVALID_OPERATION is returned if *typeIn* or *typeOut* is **GL_UNSIGNED_SHORT_4_4_4_4** or **GL_UNSIGNED_SHORT_4_4_4_4_REV** and *format* is neither **GL_RGBA** nor **GL_BGRA**.

GLU_INVALID_OPERATION is returned if *typeIn* or *typeOut* is
GL_UNSIGNED_SHORT_5_5_5_1 or GL_UNSIGNED_SHORT_1_5_5_5_REV and
format is neither GL_RGBA nor GL_BGRA.

GLU_INVALID_OPERATION is returned if *typeIn* or *typeOut* is
GL_UNSIGNED_INT_8_8_8_8 or GL_UNSIGNED_INT_8_8_8_8_REV and *format* is
neither GL_RGBA nor GL_BGRA.

GLU_INVALID_OPERATION is returned if *typeIn* or *typeOut* is
GL_UNSIGNED_INT_10_10_10_2 or GL_UNSIGNED_INT_2_10_10_10_REV and
format is neither GL_RGBA nor GL_BGRA.

SEE ALSO

glDrawPixels, glReadPixels, gluBuild1DMipmaps, gluBuild2DMipmaps,
gluBuild3DMipmaps, gluErrorString

NAME

gluSphere – draw a sphere

C SPECIFICATION

void **gluSphere**(GLUquadric* *quad*,
                     GLdouble *radius*,
                     GLint *slices*,
                     GLint *stacks*)

PARAMETERS

quad   Specifies the quadrics object (created with **gluNewQuadric**).

radius Specifies the radius of the sphere.

slices Specifies the number of subdivisions around the z axis (similar to lines of longitude).

stacks Specifies the number of subdivisions along the z axis (similar to lines of latitude).

DESCRIPTION

gluSphere draws a sphere of the given radius centered around the origin. The sphere is subdivided around the z axis into slices and along the z axis into stacks (similar to lines of longitude and latitude).

If the orientation is set to **GLU_OUTSIDE** (with **gluQuadricOrientation**), then any normals generated point away from the center of the sphere. Otherwise, they point toward the center of the sphere.

If texturing is turned on (with **gluQuadricTexture**), then texture coordinates are generated so that t ranges from 0.0 at $z = -radius$ to 1.0 at $z = radius$ (t increases linearly along longitudinal lines), and s ranges from 0.0 at the $+y$ axis, to 0.25 at the $+x$ axis, to 0.5 at the $-y$ axis, to 0.75 at the $-x$ axis, and back to 1.0 at the $+y$ axis.

SEE ALSO

gluCylinder, **gluDisk**, **gluNewQuadric**, **gluPartialDisk**, **gluQuadricOrientation**, **gluQuadricTexture**

NAME

gluTessBeginContour, gluTessEndContour – delimit a contour description

C SPECIFICATION

void **gluTessBeginContour**(GLUtesselator* *tess*)

void **gluTessEndContour**(GLUtesselator* *tess*)

PARAMETERS

tess Specifies the tessellation object (created with **gluNewTess**).

DESCRIPTION

gluTessBeginContour and **gluTessEndContour** delimit the definition of a polygon contour. Within each **gluTessBeginContour/gluTessEndContour** pair, there can be zero or more calls to **gluTessVertex**. The vertices specify a closed contour (the last vertex of each contour is automatically linked to the first). See the **gluTessVertex** reference page for more details. **gluTessBeginContour** can only be called between **gluTessBeginPolygon** and **gluTessEndPolygon**.

SEE ALSO

gluNewTess, gluTessBeginPolygon, gluTessVertex, gluTessCallback, gluTessProperty, gluTessNormal, gluTessEndPolygon

NAME

gluTessBeginPolygon – delimit a polygon description

C SPECIFICATION

void **gluTessBeginPolygon**(GLUtesselator* *tess*,
GLvoid* *data*)

PARAMETERS

tess Specifies the tessellation object (created with **gluNewTess**).

data
Specifies a pointer to user polygon data.

DESCRIPTION

gluTessBeginPolygon and **gluTessEndPolygon** delimit the definition of a convex, concave or self-intersecting polygon. Within each **gluTessBeginPolygon**/**gluTessEndPolygon** pair, there must be one or more calls to **gluTessBeginContour**/**gluTessEndContour**. Within each contour, there are zero or more calls to **gluTessVertex**. The vertices specify a closed contour (the last vertex of each contour is automatically linked to the first). See the **gluTessVertex**, **gluTessBeginContour**, and **gluTessEndContour** reference pages for more details.

data is a pointer to a user-defined data structure. If the appropriate callback(s) are specified (see **gluTessCallback**), then this pointer is returned to the callback function(s). Thus, it is a convenient way to store per-polygon information.

Once **gluTessEndPolygon** is called, the polygon is tessellated, and the resulting triangles are described through callbacks. See **gluTessCallback** for descriptions of the callback functions.

EXAMPLE

A quadrilateral with a triangular hole in it can be described as follows:

```
gluTessBeginPolygon(tobj, NULL);
 gluTessBeginContour(tobj);
   gluTessVertex(tobj, v1, v1);
   gluTessVertex(tobj, v2, v2);
   gluTessVertex(tobj, v3, v3);
   gluTessVertex(tobj, v4, v4);
 gluTessEndContour(tobj);
```

```
gluTessBeginContour(tobj);
   gluTessVertex(tobj, v5, v5);
   gluTessVertex(tobj, v6, v6);
   gluTessVertex(tobj, v7, v7);
 gluTessEndContour(tobj);
gluTessEndPolygon(tobj);
```

SEE ALSO

gluNewTess, **gluTessBeginContour**, **gluTessVertex**, **gluTessCallback**, **gluTessProperty**, **gluTessNormal**, **gluTessEndPolygon**

NAME

gluTessCallback – define a callback for a tessellation object

C SPECIFICATION

void **gluTessCallback**(GLUtesselator* *tess*,
                    GLenum *which*,
                    GLvoid *(*CallBackFunc)( )*

PARAMETERS

tess   Specifies the tessellation object (created with **gluNewTess**).

which   Specifies the callback being defined. The following values are valid:
GLU_TESS_BEGIN, GLU_TESS_BEGIN_DATA,
GLU_TESS_EDGE_FLAG, GLU_TESS_EDGE_FLAG_DATA,
GLU_TESS_VERTEX, GLU_TESS_VERTEX_DATA, GLU_TESS_END,
GLU_TESS_END_DATA, GLU_TESS_COMBINE,
GLU_TESS_COMBINE_DATA, GLU_TESS_ERROR, and
GLU_TESS_ERROR_DATA.

CallBackFunc Specifies the function to be called.

DESCRIPTION

gluTessCallback is used to indicate a callback to be used by a tessellation object. If the specified callback is already defined, then it is replaced. If *CallBackFunc* is NULL, then the existing callback becomes undefined.

These callbacks are used by the tessellation object to describe how a polygon specified by the user is broken into triangles. Note that there are two versions of each callback: one with user-specified polygon data and one without. If both versions of a particular callback are specified, then the callback with user-specified polygon data will be used. Note that the *polygon_data* parameter used by some of the functions is a copy of the pointer that was specified when **gluTessBeginPolygon** was called. The legal callbacks are as follows:

GLU_TESS_BEGIN

The begin callback is invoked like **glBegin** to indicate the start of a (triangle) primitive. The function takes a single argument of type GLenum. If the **GLU_TESS_BOUNDARY_ONLY** property is set to **GL_FALSE**, then the argument is set to either **GL_TRIANGLE_FAN**, **GL_TRIANGLE_STRIP**, or **GL_TRIANGLES**. If the **GLU_TESS_BOUNDARY_ONLY** property is set to **GL_TRUE**, then the argument will be set to **GL_LINE_LOOP**. The function prototype for this callback is:

```
void begin ( GLenum type );
```

GLU_TESS_BEGIN_DATA

The same as the **GLU_TESS_BEGIN** callback except that it takes an additional pointer argument. This pointer is identical to the opaque pointer provided when **gluTessBeginPolygon** was called. The function prototype for this callback is:

```
void beginData ( GLenum type, void *polygon_data );
```

GLU_TESS_EDGE_FLAG

The edge flag callback is similar to **glEdgeFlag**. The function takes a single boolean flag that indicates which edges lie on the polygon boundary. If the flag is **GL_TRUE**, then each vertex that follows begins an edge that lies on the polygon boundary, that is, an edge that separates an interior region from an exterior one. If the flag is **GL_FALSE**, then each vertex that follows begins an edge that lies in the polygon interior. The edge flag callback (if defined) is invoked before the first vertex callback.

Since triangle fans and triangle strips do not support edge flags, the begin callback is not called with **GL_TRIANGLE_FAN** or **GL_TRIANGLE_STRIP** if a non-NULL edge flag callback is provided. (If the callback is initialized to NULL, there is no impact on performance). Instead, the fans and strips are converted to independent triangles. The function prototype for this callback is:

```
void edgeFlag ( GLboolean flag );
```

GLU_TESS_EDGE_FLAG_DATA

The same as the **GLU_TESS_EDGE_FLAG** callback except that it takes an additional pointer argument. This pointer is identical to the opaque pointer provided when **gluTessBeginPolygon** was called. The function prototype for this callback is:

```
void edgeFlagData ( GLboolean flag, void *polygon_data );
```

GLU_TESS_VERTEX

The vertex callback is invoked between the begin and end callbacks. It is similar to **glVertex**, and it defines the vertices of the triangles created by the tessellation process. The function takes a pointer as its only argument. This pointer is identical to the opaque pointer provided by the user when the vertex was described (see **gluTessVertex**). The function prototype for this callback is:

```
        void vertex ( void *vertex_data );
```

GLU_TESS_VERTEX_DATA

The same as the **GLU_TESS_VERTEX** callback except that it takes an additional pointer argument. This pointer is identical to the opaque pointer provided when **gluTessBeginPolygon** was called. The function prototype for this callback is:

```
        void vertexData ( void *vertex_data, void *polygon_data );
```

GLU_TESS_END

The end callback serves the same purpose as **glEnd**. It indicates the end of a primitive and it takes no arguments. The function prototype for this callback is:

```
        void end ( void );
```

GLU_TESS_END_DATA

The same as the **GLU_TESS_END** callback except that it takes an additional pointer argument. This pointer is identical to the opaque pointer provided when **gluTessBeginPolygon** was called. The function prototype for this callback is:

```
        void endData ( void *polygon_data);
```

GLU_TESS_COMBINE

The combine callback is called to create a new vertex when the tessellation detects an intersection, or wishes to merge features. The function takes four arguments: an array of three elements each of type GLdouble, an array of four pointers, an array of four elements each of type GLfloat, and a pointer to a pointer. The prototype is:

```
        void combine( GLdouble coords[3], void *vertex_data[4],
                 GLfloat weight[4], void **outData );
```

The vertex is defined as a linear combination of up to four existing vertices, stored in *vertex_data*. The coefficients of the linear combination are given by *weight*; these weights always add up to 1. All vertex pointers are valid even when some of the weights are 0. *coords* gives the location of the new vertex.

The user must allocate another vertex, interpolate parameters using *vertex_data* and *weight*, and return the new vertex pointer in *outData*. This handle is supplied during rendering callbacks. The user is responsible for freeing the memory some time after **gluTessEndPolygon** is called.

For example, if the polygon lies in an arbitrary plane in 3-space, and a color is associated with each vertex, the **GLU_TESS_COMBINE** callback might look like this:

```
void myCombine( GLdouble coords[3], VERTEX *d[4],
                GLfloat w[4], VERTEX **dataOut )
{
    VERTEX *new = new_vertex();

    new->x = coords[0];
    new->y = coords[1];
    new->z = coords[2];
    new->r = w[0]*d[0]->r + w[1]*d[1]->r + w[2]*d[2]->r + w[3]*d[3]->r;
    new->g = w[0]*d[0]->g + w[1]*d[1]->g + w[2]*d[2]->g + w[3]*d[3]->g;
    new->b = w[0]*d[0]->b + w[1]*d[1]->b + w[2]*d[2]->b + w[3]*d[3]->b;
    new->a = w[0]*d[0]->a + w[1]*d[1]->a + w[2]*d[2]->a + w[3]*d[3]->a;
    *dataOut = new;
}
```

If the tessellation detects an intersection, then the **GLU_TESS_COMBINE** or **GLU_TESS_COMBINE_DATA** callback (see below) must be defined, and it must write a non-NULL pointer into *dataOut*. Otherwise the **GLU_TESS_NEED_COMBINE_CALLBACK** error occurs, and no output is generated.

GLU_TESS_COMBINE_DATA

The same as the **GLU_TESS_COMBINE** callback except that it takes an additional pointer argument. This pointer is identical to the opaque pointer provided when **gluTessBeginPolygon** was called. The function prototype for this callback is:

```
void combineData ( GLdouble coords[3], void *vertex_data[4],
                   GLfloat weight[4], void **outData,
                   void *polygon_data );
```

GLU_TESS_ERROR

The error callback is called when an error is encountered. The one argument is of type GLenum; it indicates the specific error that occurred and will be set to one of **GLU_TESS_MISSING_BEGIN_POLYGON**, **GLU_TESS_MISSING_END_POLYGON**, **GLU_TESS_MISSING_BEGIN_CONTOUR**, **GLU_TESS_MISSING_END_CONTOUR**, **GLU_TESS_COORD_TOO_LARGE**, **GLU_TESS_NEED_COMBINE_CALLBACK** or **GLU_OUT_OF_MEMORY**. Character strings describing these errors can be retrieved with the

gluErrorString call. The function prototype for this callback is:

```
void error ( GLenum errno );
```

The GLU library will recover from the first four errors by inserting the missing call(s). **GLU_TESS_COORD_TOO_LARGE** indicates that some vertex coordinate exceeded the predefined constant **GLU_TESS_MAX_COORD** in absolute value, and that the value has been clamped. (Coordinate values must be small enough so that two can be multiplied together without overflow.) **GLU_TESS_NEED_COMBINE_CALLBACK** indicates that the tessellation detected an intersection between two edges in the input data, and the **GLU_TESS_COMBINE** or **GLU_TESS_COMBINE_DATA** callback was not provided. No output is generated. **GLU_OUT_OF_MEMORY** indicates that there is not enough memory so no output is generated.

GLU_TESS_ERROR_DATA

The same as the **GLU_TESS_ERROR** callback except that it takes an additional pointer argument. This pointer is identical to the opaque pointer provided when **gluTessBeginPolygon** was called. The function prototype for this callback is:

```
void errorData ( GLenum errno, void *polygon_data );
```

EXAMPLE

Polygons tessellated can be rendered directly like this:

```
gluTessCallback(tobj, GLU_TESS_BEGIN, glBegin);
gluTessCallback(tobj, GLU_TESS_VERTEX, glVertex3dv);
gluTessCallback(tobj, GLU_TESS_END, glEnd);
gluTessCallback(tobj, GLU_TESS_COMBINE, myCombine);
gluTessBeginPolygon(tobj, NULL);
  gluTessBeginContour(tobj);
    gluTessVertex(tobj, v, v);
    ...
  gluTessEndContour(tobj);
gluTessEndPolygon(tobj);
```

Typically, the tessellated polygon should be stored in a display list so that it does not need to be retessellated every time it is rendered.

SEE ALSO

glBegin, **glEdgeFlag**, **glVertex**, **gluNewTess**, **gluErrorString**, **gluTessVertex**, **gluTessBeginPolygon**, **gluTessBeginContour**, **gluTessProperty**, **gluTessNormal**

NAME

gluTessEndPolygon – delimit a polygon description

C SPECIFICATION

void **gluTessEndPolygon**(GLUtesselator* *tess*)

PARAMETERS

tess   Specifies the tessellation object (created with **gluNewTess**).

DESCRIPTION

gluTessBeginPolygon and **gluTessEndPolygon** delimit the definition of a convex, concave or self-intersecting polygon. Within each **gluTessBeginPolygon/gluTessEndPolygon** pair, there must be one or more calls to **gluTessBeginContour/gluTessEndContour**. Within each contour, there are zero or more calls to **gluTessVertex**. The vertices specify a closed contour (the last vertex of each contour is automatically linked to the first). See the **gluTessVertex**, **gluTessBeginContour** and **gluTessEndContour** reference pages for more details.

Once **gluTessEndPolygon** is called, the polygon is tessellated, and the resulting triangles are described through callbacks. See **gluTessCallback** for descriptions of the callback functions.

EXAMPLE

A quadrilateral with a triangular hole in it can be described like this:

```
gluTessBeginPolygon(tobj, NULL);
 gluTessBeginContour(tobj);
   gluTessVertex(tobj, v1, v1);
   gluTessVertex(tobj, v2, v2);
   gluTessVertex(tobj, v3, v3);
   gluTessVertex(tobj, v4, v4);
 gluTessEndContour(tobj);
 gluTessBeginContour(tobj);
   gluTessVertex(tobj, v5, v5);
   gluTessVertex(tobj, v6, v6);
   gluTessVertex(tobj, v7, v7);
 gluTessEndContour(tobj);
gluTessEndPolygon(tobj);
```

In the above example the pointers, $v1$ through $v7$, should point to different addresses, since the values stored at these addresses will not be read by the tesselator until **gluTessEndPolygon** is called.

SEE ALSO

gluNewTess, **gluTessBeginContour**, **gluTessVertex**, **gluTessCallback**, **gluTessProperty**, **gluTessNormal**, **gluTessBeginPolygon**

NAME

gluTessNormal – specify a normal for a polygon

C SPECIFICATION

void **gluTessNormal**(GLUtesselator* *tess*,
                        GLdouble *valueX*,
                        GLdouble *valueY*,
                        GLdouble *valueZ*)

PARAMETERS

tess   Specifies the tessellation object (created with **gluNewTess**).

valueX Specifies the first component of the normal.

valueY Specifies the second component of the normal.

valueZ Specifies the third component of the normal.

DESCRIPTION

gluTessNormal describes a normal for a polygon that the program is defining. All input data will be projected onto a plane perpendicular to one of the three coordinate axes before tessellation and all output triangles will be oriented CCW with respect to the normal (CW orientation can be obtained by reversing the sign of the supplied normal). For example, if you know that all polygons lie in the x-y plane, call **gluTessNormal**(tess, 0.0, 0.0, 1.0) before rendering any polygons.

If the supplied normal is (0.0, 0.0, 0.0) (the initial value), the normal is determined as follows. The direction of the normal, up to its sign, is found by fitting a plane to the vertices, without regard to how the vertices are connected. It is expected that the input data lies approximately in the plane; otherwise, projection perpendicular to one of the three coordinate axes may substantially change the geometry. The sign of the normal is chosen so that the sum of the signed areas of all input contours is nonnegative (where a CCW contour has positive area).

The supplied normal persists until it is changed by another call to **gluTessNormal**.

SEE ALSO

gluTessBeginPolygon, **gluTessEndPolygon**

NAME

gluTessProperty – set a tessellation object property

C SPECIFICATION

void **gluTessProperty**(GLUtesselator* *tess*,
                         GLenum *which*,
                         GLdouble *data*)

PARAMETERS

tess   Specifies the tessellation object (created with **gluNewTess**).

which Specifies the property to be set. Valid values are **GLU_TESS_WINDING_RULE**, **GLU_TESS_BOUNDARY_ONLY**, **GLU_TESS_TOLERANCE**.

data   Specifies the value of the indicated property.

DESCRIPTION

gluTessProperty is used to control properties stored in a tessellation object. These properties affect the way that the polygons are interpreted and rendered. The legal values for *which* are as follows:

GLU_TESS_WINDING_RULE

Determines which parts of the polygon are on the "interior". *data* may be set to one of **GLU_TESS_WINDING_ODD**, **GLU_TESS_WINDING_NONZERO**, **GLU_TESS_WINDING_POSITIVE**, or **GLU_TESS_WINDING_NEGATIVE**, or **GLU_TESS_WINDING_ABS_GEQ_TWO**.

To understand how the winding rule works, consider that the input contours partition the plane into regions. The winding rule determines which of these regions are inside the polygon.

For a single contour C, the winding number of a point x is simply the signed number of revolutions we make around x as we travel once around C (where CCW is positive). When there are several contours, the individual winding numbers are summed. This procedure associates a signed integer value with each point x in the plane. Note that the winding number is the same for all points in a single region.

The winding rule classifies a region as "inside" if its winding number belongs to the chosen category (odd, nonzero, positive, negative, or absolute value of at least two). The previous GLU tessellator (prior to GLU 1.2) used the "odd" rule. The "nonzero" rule is another common way to define the interior. The other three rules are useful for polygon CSG operations.

GLU_TESS_BOUNDARY_ONLY

Is a boolean value ("value" should be set to GL_TRUE or GL_FALSE). When set to GL_TRUE, a set of closed contours separating the polygon interior and exterior are returned instead of a tessellation. Exterior contours are oriented CCW with respect to the normal; interior contours are oriented CW. The **GLU_TESS_BEGIN** and **GLU_TESS_BEGIN_DATA** callbacks use the type GL_LINE_LOOP for each contour.

GLU_TESS_TOLERANCE

Specifies a tolerance for merging features to reduce the size of the output. For example, two vertices that are very close to each other might be replaced by a single vertex. The tolerance is multiplied by the largest coordinate magnitude of any input vertex; this specifies the maximum distance that any feature can move as the result of a single merge operation. If a single feature takes part in several merge operations, the total distance moved could be larger.

Feature merging is completely optional; the tolerance is only a hint. The implementation is free to merge in some cases and not in others, or to never merge features at all. The initial tolerance is 0.

The current implementation merges vertices only if they are exactly coincident, regardless of the current tolerance. A vertex is spliced into an edge only if the implementation is unable to distinguish which side of the edge the vertex lies on. Two edges are merged only when both endpoints are identical.

SEE ALSO

gluGetTessProperty, **gluNewTess**

NAME

gluTessVertex – specify a vertex on a polygon

C SPECIFICATION

void **gluTessVertex**(GLUtesselator* *tess*,
                        GLdouble **location*,
                        GLvoid* *data*)

PARAMETERS

tess   Specifies the tessellation object (created with **gluNewTess**).

location Specifies the location of the vertex.

data   Specifies an opaque pointer passed back to the program with the vertex callback (as specified by **gluTessCallback**).

DESCRIPTION

gluTessVertex describes a vertex on a polygon that the program defines. Successive **gluTessVertex** calls describe a closed contour. For example, to describe a quadrilateral **gluTessVertex** should be called four times. **gluTessVertex** can only be called between **gluTessBeginContour** and **gluTessEndContour**.

data normally points to a structure containing the vertex location, as well as other per-vertex attributes such as color and normal. This pointer is passed back to the user through the **GLU_TESS_VERTEX** or **GLU_TESS_VERTEX_DATA** callback after tessellation (see the **gluTessCallback** reference page).

EXAMPLE

A quadrilateral with a triangular hole in it can be described as follows:

```
gluTessBeginPolygon(tobj, NULL);
 gluTessBeginContour(tobj);
   gluTessVertex(tobj, v1, v1);
   gluTessVertex(tobj, v2, v2);
   gluTessVertex(tobj, v3, v3);
   gluTessVertex(tobj, v4, v4);
 gluTessEndContour(tobj);
 gluTessBeginContour(tobj);
   gluTessVertex(tobj, v5, v5);
   gluTessVertex(tobj, v6, v6);
   gluTessVertex(tobj, v7, v7);
 gluTessEndContour(tobj);
gluTessEndPolygon(tobj);
```

NOTES

It is a common error to use a local variable for *location* or *data* and store values into it as part of a loop. For example:

```
for (i = 0; i < NVERTICES; ++i) {
  GLdouble data[3];
  data[0] = vertex[i][0];
  data[1] = vertex[i][1];
  data[2] = vertex[i][2];
  gluTessVertex(tobj, data, data);
}
```

This doesn't work. Because the pointers specified by *location* and *data* might not be dereferenced until **gluTessEndPolygon** is executed, all the vertex coordinates but the very last set could be overwritten before tessellation begins.

Two common symptoms of this problem are consists of a single point (when a local variable is used for *data*) and a **GLU_TESS_NEED_COMBINE_CALLBACK** error (when a local variable is used for *location*).

SEE ALSO

gluTessBeginPolygon, **gluNewTess**, **gluTessBeginContour**, **gluTessCallback**, **gluTessProperty**, **gluTessNormal**, **gluTessEndPolygon**

NAME

gluUnProject – map window coordinates to object coordinates

C SPECIFICATION

GLint **gluUnProject**(GLdouble *winX*,
        GLdouble *winY*,
        GLdouble *winZ*,
        const GLdouble **model*,
        const GLdouble **proj*,
        const GLint **view*,
        GLdouble* *objX*,
        GLdouble* *objY*,
        GLdouble* *objZ*)

PARAMETERS

winX, *winY*, *winZ*
       Specify the window coordinates to be mapped.

model   Specifies the modelview matrix (as from a **glGetDoublev** call).

proj   Specifies the projection matrix (as from a **glGetDoublev** call).

view   Specifies the viewport (as from a **glGetIntegerv** call).

objX, *objY*, *objZ* Returns the computed object coordinates.

DESCRIPTION

gluUnProject maps the specified window coordinates into object coordinates using *model*, *proj*, and *view*. The result is stored in *objX*, *objY*, and *objZ*. A return value of **GL_TRUE** indicates success; a return value of **GL_FALSE** indicates failure.

To compute the coordinates (*objX*, *objY*, and *objZ*), **gluUnProject** multiplies the normalized device coordinates by the inverse of *model**proj as follows:

$$
\begin{bmatrix} objX \\ objY \\ objZ \\ W \end{bmatrix} = INV(PM) \begin{bmatrix} \dfrac{2(winX - view[0])}{view[2]} - 1 \\ \dfrac{2(winY - view[1])}{view[3]} - 1 \\ 2(winZ) - 1 \\ 1 \end{bmatrix}
$$

INV() denotes matrix inversion. W is an unused variable, included for consistent matrix notation.

SEE ALSO
    glGet, **gluProject**

NAME

gluUnProject4 – map window and clip coordinates to object coordinates

C SPECIFICATION

GLint **gluUnProject4**(GLdouble *winX*,
                    GLdouble *winY*,
                    GLdouble *winZ*,
                    GLdouble *clipW*,
                    const GLdouble **model*,
                    const GLdouble **proj*,
                    const GLint **view*,
                    GLdouble *near*,
                    GLdouble *far*,
                    GLdouble* *objX*,
                    GLdouble* *objY*,
                    GLdouble* *objZ*,
                    GLdouble* *objW*)

PARAMETERS

winX, winY, winZ

    Specify the window coordinates to be mapped.

clipW   Specify the clip w coordinate to be mapped.

model   Specifies the modelview matrix (as from a **glGetDoublev** call).

proj   Specifies the projection matrix (as from a **glGetDoublev** call).

view   Specifies the viewport (as from a **glGetIntegerv** call).

near, far   Specifies the near and far planes (as from a **glGetDoublev** call).

objX, objY, objZ, objW

    Returns the computed object coordinates.

DESCRIPTION

gluUnProject4 maps the specified window coordinates *winX*, *winY* and *winZ* and its clip w coordinate *clipW* into object coordinates (*objX*, *objY*, *objZ*, *objW*) using *model*, *proj* and *view*. *clipW* can be other than 1 as for vertices in **glFeedbackBuffer** when data type **GL_4D_COLOR_TEXTURE** is returned. This also handles the case where the *near* and *far* planes are different from the default, 0 and 1, respectively. A return value of **GL_TRUE** indicates success; a return value of **GL_FALSE** indicates failure.

To compute the coordinates (*objX*, *objY*, *objZ* and *objW*), **gluUnProject4** multiplies the normalized device coordinates by the inverse of *model**proj as follows:

$$
\begin{matrix}
objX \\
objY \\
objZ \\
objW
\end{matrix}
= INV(PM)
\begin{matrix}
\dfrac{2(winX - view[0])}{view[2]} - 1 \\[2mm]
\dfrac{2(winY - view[1])}{view[3]} - 1 \\[2mm]
\dfrac{2(winZ - near)}{(far - near)} - 1 \\[2mm]
clipW
\end{matrix}
$$

$INV()$ denotes matrix inversion.

gluUnProject4 is equivalent to **gluUnProject** when $clipW$ is 1, $near$ is 0 and far is 1.

NOTES

gluUnProject4 is available only if the GLU version is 1.3 or greater.

SEE ALSO

glGet, **glFeedbackBuffer**, **gluProject**, **gluUnProject**

NAME

gluBeginPolygon, gluEndPolygon – delimit a polygon description

C SPECIFICATION

void **gluBeginPolygon**(GLUtesselator* *tess*)

void **gluEndPolygon**(GLUtesselator* *tess*)

PARAMETERS

tess   Specifies the tessellation object (created with **gluNewTess**).

DESCRIPTION

gluBeginPolygon and **gluEndPolygon** delimit the definition of a nonconvex polygon. To define such a polygon, first call **gluBeginPolygon**. Then define the contours of the polygon by calling **gluTessVertex** for each vertex and **gluNextContour** to start each new contour. Finally, call **gluEndPolygon** to signal the end of the definition. See the **gluTessVertex** and **gluNextContour** reference pages for more details.

Once **gluEndPolygon** is called, the polygon is tessellated, and the resulting triangles are described through callbacks. See **gluTessCallback** for descriptions of the callback functions.

NOTES

This command is obsolete and is provided for backward compatibility only. Calls to **gluBeginPolygon** are mapped to **gluTessBeginPolygon** followed by **gluTessBeginContour**. Calls to **gluEndPolygon** are mapped to **gluTessEndContour** followed by **gluTessEndPolygon**.

EXAMPLE

A quadrilateral with a triangular hole in it can be described like this:

```
gluBeginPolygon(tobj);
   gluTessVertex(tobj, v1, v1);
   gluTessVertex(tobj, v2, v2);
   gluTessVertex(tobj, v3, v3);
   gluTessVertex(tobj, v4, v4);
gluNextContour(tobj, GLU_INTERIOR);
   gluTessVertex(tobj, v5, v5);
   gluTessVertex(tobj, v6, v6);
   gluTessVertex(tobj, v7, v7);
gluEndPolygon(tobj);
```

SEE ALSO

gluNewTess, gluNextContour, gluTessCallback, gluTessVertex, gluTessBeginPolygon, gluTessBeginContour

NAME

gluNextContour – mark the beginning of another contour

C SPECIFICATION

void **gluNextContour**(GLUtesselator* *tess*,
                        GLenum *type*)

PARAMETERS

tess Specifies the tessellation object (created with **gluNewTess**).

type Specifies the type of the contour being defined. Valid values are
GLU_EXTERIOR, **GLU_INTERIOR**, **GLU_UNKNOWN**, **GLU_CCW**, and
GLU_CW.

DESCRIPTION

gluNextContour is used in describing polygons with multiple contours. After the
first contour has been described through a series of **gluTessVertex** calls, a
gluNextContour call indicates that the previous contour is complete and that the
next contour is about to begin. Another series of **gluTessVertex** calls is then used to
describe the new contour. This process can be repeated until all contours have been
described.

type defines what type of contour follows. The legal contour types are as follows:

GLU_EXTERIOR   An exterior contour defines an exterior boundary of the polygon.

GLU_INTERIOR   An interior contour defines an interior boundary of the polygon
(such as a hole).

GLU_UNKNOWN An unknown contour is analyzed by the library to determine if it
is interior or exterior.

GLU_CCW,

GLU_CW   The first **GLU_CCW** or **GLU_CW** contour defined is considered
to be exterior. All other contours are considered to be exterior if
they are oriented in the same direction (clockwise or counterclockwise) as the first contour, and interior if they are not.

If one contour is of type **GLU_CCW** or **GLU_CW**, then all contours must be of the
same type (if they are not, then all **GLU_CCW** and **GLU_CW** contours will be
changed to **GLU_UNKNOWN**).

Note that there is no real difference between the **GLU_CCW** and **GLU_CW** contour
types.

Before the first contour is described, **gluNextContour** can be called to define the type of the first contour. If **gluNextContour** is not called before the first contour, then the first contour is marked **GLU_EXTERIOR**.

This command is obsolete and is provided for backward compatibility only. Calls to **gluNextContour** are mapped to **gluTessEndContour** followed by **gluTessBeginContour**.

EXAMPLE

A quadrilateral with a triangular hole in it can be described as follows:

```
gluBeginPolygon(tobj);
    gluTessVertex(tobj, v1, v1);
    gluTessVertex(tobj, v2, v2);
    gluTessVertex(tobj, v3, v3);
    gluTessVertex(tobj, v4, v4);
gluNextContour(tobj, GLU_INTERIOR);
    gluTessVertex(tobj, v5, v5);
    gluTessVertex(tobj, v6, v6);
    gluTessVertex(tobj, v7, v7);
gluEndPolygon(tobj);
```

SEE ALSO

gluBeginPolygon, **gluNewTess**, **gluTessCallback**, **gluTessVertex**, **gluTessBeginContour**

Chapter 7

GLX Reference Pages

This chapter contains the reference pages for all routines in the OpenGL extension to X (GLX) in alphabetical order. Consider starting with the **glXIntro** page, which provides an overview of OpenGL in the X Window System. The following pages are provided in this chapter:

The following commands' functionality was superseded by new GLX 1.3 routines. Their manual pages are included at the end of the chapter. Their use is still supported, but not recommended for new application development.

glXChooseVisual	glXCreateGLXPixmap	glXGetConfig
glXCreateContext	glXDestroyGLXPixmap	

NAME

glXChooseFBConfig – return a list of GLX frame buffer configurations that match the specified attributes

C SPECIFICATION

GLXFBConfig * **glXChooseFBConfig**(Display *dpy*,
                    int *screen*,
                    const int *attrib_list*,
                    int *nelements*)

PARAMETERS

dpy   Specifies the connection to the X server.

screen   Specifies the screen number.

attrib_list

    Specifies a list of attribute/value pairs. The last attribute must be **None**.

nelements

    Returns the number of elements in the list returned by **glXChooseFBConfig**.

DESCRIPTION

glXChooseFBConfig returns GLX frame buffer configurations that match the attributes specified in *attrib_list*, or **NULL**, if no matches are found. If *attrib_list* is **NULL** then **glXChooseFBConfig** returns an array of GLX frame buffer configurations that are available on the specified screen. If an error occurs, no frame buffer configurations exist on the specified screen, or if no frame buffer configurations match the specified attributes, then **NULL** is returned. Use **XFree** to free the memory returned by **glXChooseFBConfig**.

All attributes in *attrib_list*, including boolean attributes, are immediately followed by the corresponding desired value. The list is terminated with **None**. If an attribute is not specified in *attrib_list* then the default value (see below) is used (and the attribute is said to be specified implicitly). For example, if **GLX_STEREO** is not specified then it is assumed to be **False**. For some attributes, the default is **GLX_DONT_CARE** meaning that any value is OK for this attribute, so the attribute will not be checked.

Attributes are matched in an attribute-specific manner. Some of the attributes, such as **GLX_LEVEL**, must match the specified value exactly; others, such as, **GLX_RED_SIZE** must meet or exceed the specified minimum values. If more than one GLX frame buffer configuration is found, then a list of configurations, sorted according to the "best" match criteria, is returned. The match criteria for each attribute and the exact sorting order is defined below.

The interpretations of the various GLX visual attributes are as follows:

GLX_FBCONFIG_ID   Must be followed by a valid XID that indicates the desired GLX frame buffer configuration. When a **GLX_FBCONFIG_ID** is specified, all attributes are ignored. The default value is **GLX_DONT_CARE**.

GLX_BUFFER_SIZE   Must be followed by a nonnegative integer that indicates the desired color index buffer size. The smallest index buffer of at least the specified size is preferred. This attribute is gnored if **GLX_COLOR_INDEX_BIT** is not set in **GLX_RENDER_TYPE**. The default value is 0.

GLX_LEVEL   Must be followed by an integer buffer-level specification. This specification is honored exactly. Buffer level 0 corresponds to the default frame buffer of the display. Buffer level 1 is the first overlay frame buffer, level two the second overlay frame buffer, and so on. Negative buffer levels correspond to underlay frame buffers. The default value is 0.

GLX_DOUBLEBUFFER   Must be followed by **True** or **False**. If **True** is specified, then only double-buffered frame buffer configurations are considered; if **False** is specified, then only single-buffered frame buffer configurations are considered. The default value is **GLX_DONT_CARE**.

GLX_STEREO   Must be followed by **True** or **False**. If **True** is specified, then only stereo frame buffer configurations are considered; if **False** is specified, then only monoscopic frame buffer configurations are considered. The default value is **False**.

GLX_AUX_BUFFERS   Must be followed by a nonnegative integer that indicates the desired number of auxiliary buffers. Configurations with the smallest number of auxiliary buffers that meet or exceed the specified number are preferred. The default value is 0.

GLX_RED_SIZE   Must be followed by a nonnegative minimum size specification. If this value is zero, the smallest available red buffer is preferred. Otherwise, the largest available red buffer of at least the minimum size is preferred. The default value is 0.

GLX_GREEN_SIZE Must be followed by a nonnegative minimum size specification. If this value is zero, the smallest available green buffer is preferred. Otherwise, the largest available green buffer of at least the minimum size is preferred. The default value is 0.

GLX_BLUE_SIZE Must be followed by a nonnegative minimum size specification. If this value is zero, the smallest available blue buffer is preferred. Otherwise, the largest available blue buffer of at least the minimum size is preferred. The default value is 0.

GLX_ALPHA_SIZE Must be followed by a nonnegative minimum size specification. If this value is zero, the smallest available alpha buffer is preferred. Otherwise, the largest available alpha buffer of at least the minimum size is preferred. The default value is 0.

GLX_DEPTH_SIZE Must be followed by a nonnegative minimum size specification. If this value is zero, frame buffer configurations with no depth buffer are preferred. Otherwise, the largest available depth buffer of at least the minimum size is preferred. The default value is 0.

GLX_STENCIL_SIZE Must be followed by a nonnegative integer that indicates the desired number of stencil bitplanes. The smallest stencil buffer of at least the specified size is preferred. If the desired value is zero, frame buffer configurations with no stencil buffer are preferred. The default value is 0.

GLX_ACCUM_RED_SIZE Must be followed by a nonnegative minimum size specification. If this value is zero, frame buffer configurations with no red accumulation buffer are preferred. Otherwise, the largest possible red accumulation buffer of at least the minimum size is preferred. The default value is 0.

GLX_ACCUM_GREEN_SIZE

Must be followed by a nonnegative minimum size specification. If this value is zero, frame buffer configurations with no green accumulation buffer are preferred. Otherwise, the largest possible green accumulation buffer of at least the minimum size is preferred. The default value is 0.

GLX_ACCUM_BLUE_SIZE

Must be followed by a nonnegative minimum size specification. If this value is zero, frame buffer configurations with no blue accumulation buffer are preferred. Otherwise, the largest possible blue accumulation buffer of at least the minimum size is preferred. The default value is 0.

GLX_ACCUM_ALPHA_SIZE

Must be followed by a nonnegative minimum size specification. If this value is zero, frame buffer configurations with no alpha accumulation buffer are preferred. Otherwise, the largest possible alpha accumulation buffer of at least the minimum size is preferred. The default value is 0.

GLX_RENDER_TYPE Must be followed by a mask indicating which OpenGL rendering modes the frame buffer configuration must support. Valid bits are **GLX_RGBA_BIT** and **GLX_COLOR_INDEX_BIT**. If the mask is set to **GLX_RGBA_BIT | GLX_COLOR_INDEX_BIT** then only frame buffer configurations that can be bound to both RGBA contexts and color index contexts will be considered. The default value is **GLX_RGBA_BIT**.

GLX_DRAWABLE_TYPE Must be followed by a mask indicating which GLX drawable types the frame buffer configuration must support. Valid bits are **GLX_WINDOW_BIT**, **GLX_PIXMAP_BIT** and **GLX_PBUFFER_BIT**. For example, if mask is set to **GLX_WINDOW_BIT | GLX_PIXMAP_BIT**, only frame buffer configurations that support both windows and GLX pixmaps will be considered. The default value is **GLX_WINDOW_BIT**.

GLX_X_RENDERABLE Must be followed by **True** or **False**. If **True** is specified, then only frame buffer configurations that have associated X visuals (and can be used to render to Windows and/or GLX pixmaps) will be considered. The default value is **GLX_DONT_CARE**.

GLX_X_VISUAL_TYPE Must be followed by one of **GLX_TRUE_COLOR**, **GLX_DIRECT_COLOR**, **GLX_PSEUDO_COLOR**, **GLX_STATIC_COLOR**, **GLX_GRAY_SCALE**, **GLX_STATIC_GRAY**, indicating the desired X visual type. Not all frame buffer configurations have an associated X visual. If **GLX_DRAWABLE_TYPE** is specified in *attrib_list* and the mask that follows does not have **GLX_WINDOW_BIT** set, then this value is ignored. It is also ignored if **GLX_X_RENDERABLE** is specified as **False**.

RGBA rendering may be supported for visuals of type **GLX_TRUE_COLOR**, **GLX_DIRECT_COLOR**, **GLX_PSEUDO_COLOR**, or **GLX_STATIC_COLOR**, but color index rendering is only supported for visuals of type **GLX_PSEUDO_COLOR** or **GLX_STATIC_COLOR** (i.e., single-channel visuals).

The tokens **GLX_GRAY_SCALE** and **GLX_STATIC_GRAY** will not match current OpenGL enabled visuals, but are included for future use.

The default value for **GLX_X_VISUAL_TYPE** is **GLX_DONT_CARE**.

GLX_CONFIG_CAVEAT   Must be followed by one of **GLX_NONE**, **GLX_SLOW_CONFIG**, **GLX_NON_CONFORMANT_CONFIG**. If **GLX_NONE** is specified, then only frame buffer configurations with no caveats will be considered; if **GLX_SLOW_CONFIG** is specified, then only slow frame buffer configurations will be considered; if **GLX_NON_CONFORMANT_CONFIG** is specified, then only non-conformant frame buffer configurations will be considered. The default value is **GLX_DONT_CARE**.

GLX_TRANSPARENT_TYPE

Must be followed by one of **GLX_NONE**, **GLX_TRANSPARENT_RGB**, **GLX_TRANSPARENT_INDEX**. If **GLX_NONE** is specified, then only opaque frame buffer configurations will be considered; if **GLX_TRANSPARENT_RGB** is specified, then only transparent frame buffer configurations that support RGBA rendering will be considered; if **GLX_TRANSPARENT_INDEX** is specified, then only transparent frame buffer configurations that support color index rendering will be considered. The default value is **GLX_NONE**.

GLX_TRANSPARENT_INDEX_VALUE

Must be followed by an integer value indicating the transparent index value; the value must be between 0 and the maximum framebuffer value for indices. Only frame buffer configurations that use the specified transparent index value will be considered. The default value is **GLX_DONT_CARE**.

This attribute is ignored unless **GLX_TRANSPARENT_TYPE** is included in *attrib_list* and specified as **GLX_TRANSPARENT_INDEX**.

GLX_TRANSPARENT_RED_VALUE

Must be followed by an integer value indicating the transparent red value; the value must be between 0 and the maximum framebuffer value for red. Only frame buffer configurations that use the specified transparent red value will be considered. The default value is **GLX_DONT_CARE**.

This attribute is ignored unless **GLX_TRANSPARENT_TYPE** is included in *attrib_list* and specified as **GLX_TRANSPARENT_RGB**.

GLX_TRANSPARENT_GREEN_VALUE

Must be followed by an integer value indicating the transparent green value; the value must be between 0 and the maximum framebuffer value for green. Only frame buffer configurations that use the specified transparent green value will be considered. The default value is **GLX_DONT_CARE**.

This attribute is ignored unless **GLX_TRANSPARENT_TYPE** is included in *attrib_list* and specified as **GLX_TRANSPARENT_RGB**.

GLX_TRANSPARENT_BLUE_VALUE

Must be followed by an integer value indicating the transparent blue value; the value must be between 0 and the maximum framebuffer value for blue. Only frame buffer configurations that use the specified transparent blue value will be considered. The default value is **GLX_DONT_CARE**.

This attribute is ignored unless

GLX_TRANSPARENT_TYPE is included in *attrib_list* and specified as **GLX_TRANSPARENT_RGB**.

GLX_TRANSPARENT_ALPHA_VALUE
Must be followed by an integer value indicating the transparent alpha value; the value must be between 0 and the maximum framebuffer value for alpha. Only frame buffer configurations that use the specified transparent alpha value will be considered. The default value is **GLX_DONT_CARE**.

When more than one GLX frame buffer configuration matches the specified attributes, a list of matching configurations is returned. The list is sorted according to the following precedence rules, which are applied in ascending order (i.e., configurations that are considered equal by a lower numbered rule are sorted by the higher numbered rule):

1. By **GLX_CONFIG_CAVEAT** where the precedence is **GL_NONE**, **GLX_SLOW_CONFIG**, and **GLX_NON_CONFORMANT_CONFIG**.

2. Larger total number of RGBA color components (**GLX_RED_SIZE**, **GLX_GREEN_SIZE**, **GLX_BLUE_SIZE**, plus **GLX_ALPHA_SIZE**) that have higher number of bits. If the requested number of bits in *attrib_list* is zero or **GLX_DONT_CARE** for a particular color component, then the number of bits for that component is not considered.

3. Smaller **GLX_BUFFER_SIZE**.

4. Single buffered configuration (**GLX_DOUBLEBUFFER** being **False** precedes a double buffered one.

5. Smaller **GLX_AUX_BUFFERS**.

6. Larger **GLX_DEPTH_SIZE**.

7. Smaller **GLX_STENCIL_SIZE**.

8. Larger total number of accumulation buffer color components (-**GLX_ACCUM_RED_SIZE**, **GLX_ACCUM_GREEN_SIZE**, **GLX_ACCUM_BLUE_SIZE**, plus **GLX_ACCUM_ALPHA_SIZE**) that have higher number of bits. If the requested number of bits in *attrib_list* is zero or **GLX_DONT_CARE** for a particular color component, then the number of bits for that component is not considered.

9. By **GLX_X_VISUAL_TYPE** where the precedence order is **GLX_TRUE_COLOR**, **GLX_DIRECT_COLOR**, **GLX_PSEUDO_COLOR**, **GLX_STATIC_COLOR**, **GLX_GRAY_SCALE**, **GLX_STATIC_GRAY**.

EXAMPLES

    attrib_list = {**GLX_RENDER_TYPE**, **GLX_RGBA_BIT**, **GLX_RED_SIZE**, 4,
                    GLX_GREEN_SIZE, 4, **GLX_BLUE_SIZE**, 4, **None**};

Specifies a frame buffer configuration that supports RGBA rendering and exists in the normal frame buffer, not an overlay or underlay buffer. The returned visual supports at least four bits each of red, green, and blue, and possibly no bits of alpha. It does not support stereo display. It may or may not have one or more auxiliary color buffers, a back buffer, a depth buffer, a stencil buffer, or an accumulation buffer.

NOTES

glXChooseFBConfig is available only if the GLX version is 1.3 or greater.

If the GLX version is 1.1 or 1.0, the GL version must be 1.0. If the GLX version is 1.2, then the GL version must be 1.1. If the GLX version is 1.3, then the GL version must be 1.2.

glXGetFBConfigs and **glXGetFBConfigAttrib** can be used to implement selection algorithms other than the generic one implemented by **glXChooseFBConfig**. Call **glXChooseFBConfig** to retrieve all the frame buffer configurations on a particular screen or, alternatively, all the frame buffer configurations with a particular set of attributes. Next call **glGetFBConfigAttrib** to retrieve additional attributes for the frame buffer configurations and then select between them.

GLX implementers are strongly discouraged, but not proscribed, from changing the selection algorithm used by **glXChooseFBConfig**. Therefore, selections may change from release to release of the client-side library.

ERRORS

NULL is returned if an undefined GLX attribute is encountered in *attrib_list*, if *screen* is invalid or if *dpy* does not support the GLX extension.

SEE ALSO

glXGetFBConfigAttrib, **glXGetFBConfigs**, **glXGetVisualFromFBConfig**

NAME

glXCopyContext – copy state from one rendering context to another

C SPECIFICATION

void **glXCopyContext**(Display *dpy,
                        GLXContext src,
                        GLXContext dst,
                        unsigned long mask)

PARAMETERS

dpy   Specifies the connection to the X server.

src   Specifies the source context.

dst   Specifies the destination context.

mask Specifies which portions of src state are to be copied to dst.

DESCRIPTION

glXCopyContext copies selected groups of state variables from src to dst. mask indicates which groups of state variables are to be copied. mask contains the bitwise OR of the same symbolic names that are passed to the GL command **glPushAttrib**. The single symbolic constant **GL_ALL_ATTRIB_BITS** can be used to copy the maximum possible portion of rendering state.

The copy can be done only if the renderers named by src and dst share an address space. Two rendering contexts share an address space if both are nondirect using the same server, or if both are direct and owned by a single process. Note that in the nondirect case it is not necessary for the calling threads to share an address space, only for their related rendering contexts to share an address space.

Not all values for GL state can be copied. For example, pixel pack and unpack state, render mode state, and select and feedback state are not copied. The state that can be copied is exactly the state that is manipulated by the GL command **glPushAttrib**.

An implicit **glFlush** is done by **glXCopyContext** if src is the current context for the calling thread.

NOTES

A *process* is a single execution environment, implemented in a single address space, consisting of one or more threads.

A *thread* is one of a set of subprocesses that share a single address space, but maintain separate program counters, stack spaces, and other related global data. A *thread* that is the only member of its subprocess group is equivalent to a *process*.

ERRORS

BadMatch is generated if rendering contexts *src* and *dst* do not share an address space or were not created with respect to the same screen.

BadAccess is generated if *dst* is current to any thread (including the calling thread) at the time **glXCopyContext** is called.

GLXBadCurrentWindow is generated if *src* is the current context and the current drawable is a window that is no longer valid.

GLXBadContext is generated if either *src* or *dst* is not a valid GLX context.

SEE ALSO

glPushAttrib, **glXCreateContext**, **glXIsDirect**

NAME

glXCreateNewContext – create a new GLX rendering context

C SPECIFICATION

GLXContext **glXCreateNewContext**(Display **dpy*,
                              GLXFBConfig *config*,
                              int *render_type*,
                              GLXContext *share_list*,
                              Bool *direct*)

PARAMETERS

dpy   Specifies the connection to the X server.

config   Specifies the GLXFBConfig structure with the desired attributes for the context.

render_type Specifies the type of the context to be created. Must be one of **GLX_RGBA_TYPE** or **GLX_COLOR_INDEX_TYPE**.

share_list   Specifies the context with which to share display lists. **NULL** indicates that no sharing is to take place.

share_list   Specifies whether rendering is to be done with a direct connection to the graphics system if possible (**True**) or through the X server (**False**).

DESCRIPTION

glXCreateNewContext creates a GLX rendering context and returns its handle. This context can be used to render into GLX windows, pixmaps, or pixel buffers. If **glXCreateNewContext** fails to create a rendering context, **NULL** is returned.

If *render_type* is **GLX_RGBA_TYPE**, then a context that supports RGBA rendering is created. If *config* is **GLX_COLOR_INDEX_TYPE**, then context supporting color-index rendering is created.

If *render_type* is not **NULL**, then all display-list indexes and definitions are shared by context *render_type* and by the newly created context. An arbitrary number of contexts can share a single display-list space. However, all rendering contexts that share a single display-list space must themselves exist in the same address space. Two rendering contexts share an address space if both are nondirect using the same server, or if both are direct and owned by a single process. Note that in the non-direct case, it is not necessary for the calling threads to share an address space, only for their related rendering contexts to share an address space.

If *share_list* is **True**, then a direct rendering context is created if the implementation supports direct rendering, if the connection is to an X server that is local, and if a direct rendering context is available. (An implementation may return an indirect context when *share_list* is **True**.) If *share_list* is **False**, then a rendering context that

633

renders through the X server is always created. Direct rendering provides a performance advantage in some implementations. However, direct rendering contexts cannot be shared outside a single process, and they may be unable to render to GLX pixmaps.

NOTES

glXCreateNewContext is available only if the GLX version is 1.3 or greater.

If the GLX version is 1.1 or 1.0, the GL version must be 1.0. If the GLX version is 1.2, then the GL version must be 1.1. If the GLX version is 1.3, then the GL version must be 1.2.

ERRORS

NULL is returned if execution fails on the client side.

GLXBadContext is generated if *render_type* is not a GLX context and is not **NULL**.

GLXBadFBConfig is generated if *config* is not a valid GLXFBConfig.

BadMatch is generated if the context to be created would not share the address space or the screen of the context specified by *render_type*.

BadAlloc is generated if the server does not have enough resources to allocate the new context.

BadValue is generated if *config* is not a valid visual (for example, if a particular GLX implementation does not support it).

SEE ALSO

glXChooseFBConfig, **glXCreateContext**, **glXDestroyContext**, **glXGetFBConfigs**, **glXGetFBConfigAttrib**, **glXIsDirect**, **glXMakeContextCurrent**

NAME

glXCreatePbuffer – create an off-screen rendering area

C SPECIFICATION

GLXPbuffer **glXCreatePbuffer**(Display **dpy*,
                              GLXFBConfig *config*,
                              const int **attrib_list*)

PARAMETERS

dpy   Specifies the connection to the X server.

config   Specifies a GLXFBConfig structure with the desired attributes for the window.

attrib_list
            Specifies a list of attribute value pairs, which must be terminated with **None**, or **NULL**. Accepted attributes are **GLX_PBUFFER_WIDTH**, **GLX_PBUFFER_HEIGHT**, **GLX_PRESERVED_CONTENTS**, and **GLX_LARGEST_PBUFFER**.

DESCRIPTION

glXCreatePbuffer creates an off-screen rendering area and returns its XID. Any GLX rendering context that was created with respect to *config* can be used to render into this window. Use **glXMakeContextCurrent** to associate the rendering area with a GLX rendering context.

The accepted attributes for a GLXPbuffer are:

GLX_PBUFFER_WIDTH
            Specify the pixel width of the requested GLXPbuffer. The default value is 0.

GLX_PBUFFER_HEIGHT
            Specify the pixel height of the requested GLXPbuffer. The default value is 0.

GLX_LARGEST_PBUFFER
            Specify to obtain the largest available pixel buffer, if the requested allocation would have failed. The width and height of the allocated pixel buffer will never exceed the specified **GLX_PBUFFER_WIDTH** or **GLX_PBUFFER_HEIGHT**, respectively. Use **glXQueryDrawable** to retrieve the dimensions of the allocated pixel buffer. The default value is **False**.

GLX_PRESERVED_CONTENTS
Specify if the contents of the pixel buffer should be preserved when a resource conflict occurs. If set to **False**, the contents of the pixel buffer may be lost at any time. If set to **True**, or not specified in *attrib_list*, then the contents of the pixel buffer will be preserved (most likely by copying the contents into main system memory from the frame buffer). In either case, the client can register (using **glXSelectEvent**, to receive pixel buffer clobber events which are generated when the pbuffer contents have been preserved or damaged.

GLXPbuffers contain the color and ancillary buffers specified by *config*. It is possible to create a pixel buffer with back buffers, and swap those buffers using **glXSwapBuffers**.

NOTES

glXCreatePbuffer is available only if the GLX version is 1.3 or greater.

If the GLX version is 1.1 or 1.0, the GL version must be 1.0. If the GLX version is 1.2, then the GL version must be 1.1. If the GLX version is 1.3, then the GL version must be 1.2.

GLXPbuffers are allocated from frame buffer resources; applications should consider deallocating them when they are not in use.

ERRORS

BadAlloc is generated if there are insufficient resources to allocate the requested GLXPbuffer.

GLXBadFBConfig is generated if *config* is not a valid GLXFBConfig.

BadMatch is generated if *config* does not support rendering to pixel buffers. (e.g., **GLX_DRAWABLE_TYPE** does not contain **GLX_PBUFFER_BIT**).

SEE ALSO

glXChooseFBConfig, glXCreatePbuffer, glXMakeContextCurrent, glXSelectEvent

NAME

glXCreatePixmap – create an off-screen rendering area

C SPECIFICATION

GLXPixmap **glXCreatePixmap**(Display **dpy*,
                              GLXFBConfig *config*,
                              Pixmap *pixmap*,
                              const int **attrib_list*)

PARAMETERS

dpy   Specifies the connection to the X server.

config   Specifies a GLXFBConfig structure with the desired attributes for the window.

pixmap   Specifies the X pixmap to be used as the rendering area.

attrib_list
             Currently unused. This must be set to **NULL**, or be an empty list (i.e., one in which the first element is **None**).

DESCRIPTION

glXCreatePixmap creates an off-screen rendering area and returns its XID. Any GLX rendering context that was created with respect to *config* can be used to render into this window. Use **glXMakeCurrent** to associate the rendering area with a GLX rendering context.

NOTES

glXCreatePixmap is available only if the GLX version is 1.3 or greater.

If the GLX version is 1.1 or 1.0, the GL version must be 1.0. If the GLX version is 1.2, then the GL version must be 1.1. If the GLX version is 1.3, then the GL version must be 1.2.

ERRORS

BadMatch is generated if *pixmap* was not created with a visual that corresponds to *config*.

BadMatch is generated if *config* does not support rendering to windows (e.g., **GLX_DRAWABLE_TYPE** does not contain **GLX_WINDOW_BIT**).

BadWindow is generated if *pixmap* is not a valid window XID.

BadAlloc is generated if there is already a GLXFBConfig associated with *pixmap*.

BadAlloc is generated if the X server cannot allocate a new GLX window.

GLXBadFBConfig is generated if *config* is not a valid GLXFBConfig.

SEE ALSO

glXChooseFBConfig, glXCreateGLXPixmap, glXDestoryWindow, glXMakeContextCurrent

NAME

      glXCreatePixmap – create an off-screen rendering area

C SPECIFICATION

      GLXPixmap **glXCreatePixmap**(Display **dpy*,
                                GLXFBConfig *config*,
                                Pixmap *pixmap*,
                                const int **attrib_list*)

PARAMETERS

      dpy   Specifies the connection to the X server.

      config   Specifies a GLXFBConfig structure with the desired attributes for the window.

      pixmap Specifies the X window to be used as the rendering area.

      attrib_list
                 Currently unused. This must be set to **NULL**, or be an empty list (i.e. one in which the first element is **None**).

DESCRIPTION

      glXCreatePixmap creates an on-screen rendering area from an existing X window which was created with a visual which matches *config*. the XID of the GLXWindow is returned. Any GLX rendering context that was created with respect to *config* can be used to render into this window. Use **glXMakeContextCurrent** to associate the rendering area with a GLX rendering context.

NOTES

      glXCreatePixmap is available only if the GLX version is 1.3 or greater.

      If the GLX version is 1.1 or 1.0, the GL version must be 1.0. If the GLX version is 1.2, then the GL version must be 1.1. If the GLX version is 1.3, then the GL version must be 1.2.

ERRORS

      BadMatch is generated if *pixmap* was not created with a visual that corresponds to *config*.

      BadMatch is generated if *config* does not support rendering to windows (i.e. **GLX_DRAWABLE_TYPE** does not contain **GLX_WINDOW_BIT**).

      BadWindow is generated if *pixmap* is not a valid pixmap XID.

      BadAlloc is generated if there is already a GLXFBConfig associated with *pixmap*.

BadAlloc is generated if the X server cannot allocate a new GLX window.

GLXBadFBConfig is generated if *config* is not a valid GLXFBConfig.

SEE ALSO

glXChooseFBConfig, **glXDestroyPixmap**,

NAME

glXDestroyContext – destroy a GLX context

C SPECIFICATION

void **glXDestroyContext**(Display *dpy,
GLXContext ctx)

PARAMETERS

dpy Specifies the connection to the X server.

ctx Specifies the GLX context to be destroyed.

DESCRIPTION

If the GLX rendering context *ctx* is not current to any thread, **glXDestroyContext** destroys it immediately. Otherwise, *ctx* is destroyed when it becomes not current to any thread. In either case, the resource ID referenced by *ctx* is freed immediately.

ERRORS

GLXBadContext is generated if *ctx* is not a valid GLX context.

SEE ALSO

glXCreateContext, **glXCreateNewContext**, **glXMakeCurrent**

NAME

glXDestroyPbuffer – destroy an off-screen rendering area

C SPECIFICATION

void **glXDestroyPbuffer**(Display *dpy*,
                        GLXPbuffer *pbuf*)

PARAMETERS

dpy   Specifies the connection to the X server.

pbuf Specifies the GLXPbuffer to be destroyed.

DESCRIPTION

glXDestroyPbuffer destroys a GLXPbuffer created by **glXCreatePbuffer**.

NOTES

glXDestroyPbuffer is available only if the GLX version is 1.3 or greater.

If the GLX version is 1.1 or 1.0, the GL version must be 1.0. If the GLX version is 1.2, then the GL version must be 1.1. If the GLX version is 1.3, then the GL version must be 1.2.

ERRORS

GLXBadPbuffer is generated if *pbuf* is not a valid GLXPbuffer.

SEE ALSO

glXChooseFBConfig, **glXCreatePbuffer**,

NAME

glXDestroyPixmap – destroy an off-screen rendering area

C SPECIFICATION

void **glXDestroyPixmap**(Display *dpy,
                          GLXPixmap *pixmap*)

PARAMETERS

dpy   Specifies the connection to the X server.

pixmap
           Specifies the GLXPixmap to be destroyed.

DESCRIPTION

glXDestroyPixmap destroys a GLXPixmap created by **glXCreatePixmap**.

NOTES

glXDestroyPixmap is available only if the GLX version is 1.3 or greater.

If the GLX version is 1.1 or 1.0, the GL version must be 1.0. If the GLX version is
1.2, then the GL version must be 1.1. If the GLX version is 1.3, then the GL version
must be 1.2.

ERRORS

GLXBadPixmap is generated if *pixmap* is not a valid GLXPixmap.

SEE ALSO

glXChooseFBConfig, **glXCreatePixmap**, **glXDestroyGLXPixmap**,

NAME

glXDestroyWindow – destroy an on-screen rendering area

C SPECIFICATION

void **glXDestroyWindow**(Display *dpy,
                    GLXWindow win)

PARAMETERS

dpy Specifies the connection to the X server.

win Specifies the GLXWindow to be destroyed.

DESCRIPTION

glXDestroyWindow destroys a GLXWindow created by **glXCreateWindow**.

NOTES

glXDestroyWindow is available only if the GLX version is 1.3 or greater.

If the GLX version is 1.1 or 1.0, the GL version must be 1.0. If the GLX version is 1.2, then the GL version must be 1.1. If the GLX version is 1.3, then the GL version must be 1.2.

ERRORS

GLXBadWindow is generated if *win* is not a valid GLXPixmap.

SEE ALSO

glXChooseFBConfig, **glXCreateWindow**,

NAME

glXGetClientString – return a string describing the client

C SPECIFICATION

const char * **glXGetClientString**(Display *dpy*,
int *name*)

PARAMETERS

dpy   Specifies the connection to the X server.

name Specifies which string is returned. One of **GLX_VENDOR**, **GLX_VERSION**, or **GLX_EXTENSIONS**.

DESCRIPTION

glXGetClientString returns a string describing some aspect of the client library. The possible values for *name* are **GLX_VENDOR**, **GLX_VERSION**, and **GLX_EXTENSIONS**. If *name* is not set to one of these values, **glXGetClientString** returns **NULL**. The format and contents of the vendor string is implementation dependent.

The extensions string is null-terminated and contains a space-separated list of extension names. (The extension names never contain spaces.) If there are no extensions to GLX, then the empty string is returned.

The version string is laid out as follows:

<major_version.minor_version><space><vendor-specific info>

Both the major and minor portions of the version number are of arbitrary length. The vendor-specific information is optional. However, if it is present, the format and contents are implementation specific.

NOTES

glXGetClientString is available only if the GLX version is 1.1 or greater.

If the GLX version is 1.1 or 1.0, the GL version must be 1.0. If the GLX version is 1.2, then the GL version must be 1.1. If the GLX version is 1.3, then the GL version must be 1.2.

glXGetClientString only returns information about GLX extensions supported by the client. Call **glGetString** to get a list of GL extensions supported by the server.

SEE ALSO

glXQueryVersion, **glXQueryExtensionsString**, **glXQueryServerString**

NAME

glXGetCurrentContext – return the current context

C SPECIFICATION

GLXContext **glXGetCurrentContext**(void)

DESCRIPTION

glXGetCurrentContext returns the current context, as specified by **glXMakeCurrent**. If there is no current context, **NULL** is returned.

glXGetCurrentContext returns client-side information. It does not make a round trip to the server.

SEE ALSO

glXCreateContext, **glXGetCurrentDisplay**, **glXGetCurrentDrawable**, **glXMakeCurrent**

NAME

glXGetCurrentDisplay – get display for current context

C SPECIFICATION

Display * **glXGetCurrentDisplay**(void)

DESCRIPTION

glXGetCurrentDisplay returns the display for the current context. If no context is current, **NULL** is returned.

glXGetCurrentDisplay returns client-side information. It does not make a round-trip to the server, and therefore does not flush any pending events.

NOTES

glXGetCurrentDisplay is only supported if the GLX version is 1.2 or greater.

SEE ALSO

glXGetCurrentContext, **glXGetCurrentDrawable**, **glXQueryVersion**, **glXQueryExtensionsString**

NAME

glXGetCurrentDrawable – return the current drawable

C SPECIFICATION

GLXDrawable **glXGetCurrentDrawable**(void)

DESCRIPTION

glXGetCurrentDrawable returns the current drawable, as specified by **glXMakeCurrent**. If there is no current drawable, **None** is returned.

glXGetCurrentDrawable returns client-side information. It does not make a round trip to the server.

SEE ALSO

glXCreateGLXPixmap, **glXGetCurrentContext**, **glXGetCurrentDisplay**, **glXGetCurrentReadDrawable**, **glXMakeCurrent**

NAME

glXGetCurrentReadDrawable – return the current drawable

C SPECIFICATION

GLXDrawable **glXGetCurrentReadDrawable**(void)

DESCRIPTION

glXGetCurrentReadDrawable returns the current read drawable, as specified by **read** parameter of **glXMakeContextCurrent**. If there is no current drawable, **None** is returned.

glXGetCurrentReadDrawable returns client-side information. It does not make a round-trip to the server.

NOTES

glXGetCurrentReadDrawable is only supported if the GLX version is 1.3 or greater.

SEE ALSO

glXGetCurrentContext, **glXGetCurrentDisplay**, **glXGetCurrentDrawable**, **glXMakeContextCurrent**

NAME

glXGetFBConfigAttrib – return information about a GLX frame buffer configuraton

C SPECIFICATION

int **glXGetFBConfigAttrib**(Display **dpy*,
                                GLXFBConfig *config*,
                                int *attribute*,
                                int **value*)

PARAMETERS

dpy   Specifies the connection to the X server.

config   Specifies the GLX frame buffer configuration to be queried.

attribute
           Specifies the attribute to be returned.

value   Returns the requested value.

DESCRIPTION

glXGetFBConfigAttrib sets *value* to the *attribute* value of GLX drawables created with respect to *config*. **glXGetFBConfigAttrib** returns an error code if it fails for any reason. Otherwise, **Success** is returned.

attribute is one of the following:

GLX_FBCONFIG_ID   XID of the given GLXFBConfig.

GLX_BUFFER_SIZE   Number of bits per color buffer. If the frame buffer configuration supports RGBA contexts, then **GLX_BUFFER_SIZE** is the sum of **GLX_RED_SIZE**, **GLX_GREEN_SIZE**, **GLX_BLUE_SIZE**, and **GLX_ALPHA_SIZE**. If the frame buffer configuration supports only color index contexts, **GLX_BUFFER_SIZE** is the size of the color indexes.

GLX_LEVEL   Frame buffer level of the configuration. Level zero is the default frame buffer. Positive levels correspond to frame buffers that overlay the default buffer, and negative levels correspond to frame buffers that underlie the default buffer.

GLX_DOUBLEBUFFER
           True if color buffers exist in front/back pairs that can be swapped, **False** otherwise.

GLX_STEREO   **True** if color buffers exist in left/right pairs, **False** otherwise.

GLX_AUX_BUFFERS   Number of auxiliary color buffers that are available. Zero indicates that no auxiliary color buffers exist.

GLX_RED_SIZE   Number of bits of red stored in each color buffer. Undefined if RGBA contexts are not supported by the frame buffer configuration.

GLX_GREEN_SIZE   Number of bits of green stored in each color buffer. Undefined if RGBA contexts are not supported by the frame buffer configuration.

GLX_BLUE_SIZE   Number of bits of blue stored in each color buffer. Undefined if RGBA contexts are not supported by the frame buffer configuration.

GLX_ALPHA_SIZE   Number of bits of alpha stored in each color buffer. Undefined if RGBA contexts are not supported by the frame buffer configuration.

GLX_DEPTH_SIZE   Number of bits in the depth buffer.

GLX_STENCIL_SIZE Number of bits in the stencil buffer.

GLX_ACCUM_RED_SIZE
    Number of bits of red stored in the accumulation buffer.

GLX_ACCUM_GREEN_SIZE
    Number of bits of green stored in the accumulation buffer.

GLX_ACCUM_BLUE_SIZE
    Number of bits of blue stored in the accumulation buffer.

GLX_ACCUM_ALPHA_SIZE
    Number of bits of alpha stored in the accumulation buffer.

GLX_RENDER_TYPE   Mask indicating what type of GLX contexts can be made current to the frame buffer configuration. Valid bits are **GLX_RGBA_BIT** and **GLX_COLOR_INDEX_BIT**.

GLX_DRAWABLE_TYPE
    Mask indicating what drawable types the frame buffer configuration supports. Valid bits are **GLX_WINDOW_BIT**, **GLX_PIXMAP_BIT**, and **GLX_PBUFFER_BIT**.

GLX_X_RENDERABLE
    True if drawables created with the frame buffer configuration can be rendered to by X.

GLX_VISUAL_ID XID of the corresponding visual, or zero if there is no associated visual (i.e., if **GLX_X_RENDERABLE** is **False** or **GLX_DRAWABLE_TYPE** does not have the **GLX_WINDOW_BIT** bit set.)

GLX_X_VISUAL_TYPE

Visual type of associated visual. The returned value will be one of: **GLX_TRUE_COLOR**, **GLX_DIRECT_COLOR**, **GLX_PSEUDO_COLOR**, **GLX_STATIC_COLOR**, **GLX_GRAY_SCALE**, **GLX_STATIC_GRAY**, or **GLX_NONE**, if there is no associated visual (i.e., if **GLX_X_RENDERABLE** is **False** or **GLX_DRAWABLE_TYPE** does not have the **GLX_WINDOW_BIT** bit set.)

GLX_CONFIG_CAVEAT

One of **GLX_NONE**, **GLX_SLOW_CONFIG**, or **GLX_NON_CONFORMANT_CONFIG**, indicating that the frame buffer configuration has no caveats, some aspect of the frame buffer configuration runs slower than other frame buffer configurations, or some aspect of the frame buffer configuration is nonconformant, respectively.

GLX_TRANSPARENT_TYPE

One of **GLX_NONE**, **GLX_TRANSPARENT_RGB**, **GLX_TRANSPARENT_INDEX**, indicating that the frame buffer configuration is opaque, is transparent for particular values of red, green, and blue or is transparent for particular index values, respectively.

GLX_TRANSPARENT_INDEX_VALUE

Integer value between 0 and the maximum frame buffer value for indices, indicating the transparent index value for the frame buffer configuration. Undefined if **GLX_TRANSPARENT_TYPE** is not **GLX_TRANSPARENT_INDEX**.

GLX_TRANSPARENT_RED_VALUE

Integer value between 0 and the maximum frame buffer value for red, indicating the transparent red value for the frame buffer configuration. Undefined if **GLX_TRANSPARENT_TYPE** is not **GLX_TRANSPARENT_RGB**.

GLX_TRANSPARENT_GREEN_VALUE

Integer value between 0 and the maximum frame buffer value for green, indicating the transparent green value for the frame buffer configuration. Undefined if

GLX_TRANSPARENT_TYPE is not
GLX_TRANSPARENT_RGB.

GLX_TRANSPARENT_BLUE_VALUE

Integer value between 0 and the maximum frame buffer
value for blue, indicating the transparent blue value for the
frame buffer configuration. Undefined if
GLX_TRANSPARENT_TYPE is not
GLX_TRANSPARENT_RGB.

GLX_TRANSPARENT_ALPHA_VALUE

Integer value between 0 and the maximum frame buffer
value for alpha, indicating the transparent blue value for the
frame buffer configuration. Undefined if
GLX_TRANSPARENT_TYPE is not
GLX_TRANSPARENT_RGB.

GLX_MAX_PBUFFER_WIDTH

The maximum width that can be specified to
glCreateGLXPbuffer.

GLX_MAX_PBUFFER_HEIGHT

The maximum height that can be specified to
glCreateGLXPbuffer.

GLX_MAX_PBUFFER_PIXELS

The maximum number of pixels (width times height) for a
pixel buffer. Note that this value may be less than
GLX_MAX_PBUFFER_WIDTH times
GLX_MAX_PBUFFER_HEIGHT. Also, this value is static and
assumes that no other pixel buffers or X resources are con-
tending for the frame buffer memory. As a result, it may not
be possible to allocate a pixel buffer of the size given by
GLX_MAX_PBUFFER_PIXELS.

Applications should choose the frame buffer configuration that most closely meets
their requirements. Creating windows, GLX pixmaps, or GLX pixel buffers with
unnecessary buffers can result in reduced rendering performance as well as poor
resource allocation.

NOTES

glXGetFBConfigAttrib is available only if the GLX version is 1.3 or greater.

If the GLX version is 1.1 or 1.0, the GL version must be 1.0. If the GLX version is
1.2, then the GL version must be 1.1. If the GLX version is 1.3, then the GL version
must be 1.2.

ERRORS

> **GLX_NO_EXTENSION** is returned if *dpy* does not support the GLX extension.
> **GLX_BAD_ATTRIBUTE** is returned if *attribute* is not a valid GLX attribute.

SEE ALSO

> glXGetFBConfigs, glXChooseFBConfig, glXGetVisualFromFBConfig,
> glXGetConfig

NAME

glXGetFBConfigs – list all GLX frame buffer configurations for a given screen

C SPECIFICATION

GLXFBConfig * **glXGetFBConfigs**(Display *dpy*,
int *screen*,
int *nelements*)

PARAMETERS

dpy   Specifies the connection to the X server.

screen   Specifies the screen number.

nelements
              Returns the number of GLXFBConfigs returned.

DESCRIPTION

glXGetFBConfigs returns a list of all GLXFBConfigs available on the screen specified by *screen*. Use **glXGetFBConfigAttrib** to obtain attribute values from a specific GLXFBConfig.

NOTES

glXGetFBConfigs is available only if the GLX version is 1.3 or greater.

If the GLX version is 1.1 or 1.0, the GL version must be 1.0. If the GLX version is 1.2, then the GL version must be 1.1. If the GLX version is 1.3, then the GL version must be 1.2.

SEE ALSO

glXGetFBConfigAttrib, **glXGetVisualFromFBConfig** **glXChooseFBConfig**

NAME

glXGetSelectedEvent – returns GLX events that are selected for a window or a GLX pixel buffer

C SPECIFICATION

void **glXGetSelectedEvent**(Display **dpy*,
                                                GLXDrawable *draw*,
                                                unsigned long **event_mask*)

PARAMETERS

dpy   Specifies the connection to the X server.

draw   Specifies a GLX drawable. Must be a GLX pixel buffer or a window.

event_mask
               Returns the events that are selected for *draw*.

DESCRIPTION

glXGetSelectedEvent returns in *event_mask* the events selected for *draw*.

NOTES

glXGetSelectedEvent is available only if the GLX version is 1.3 or greater.

If the GLX version is 1.1 or 1.0, the GL version must be 1.0. If the GLX version is 1.2, then the GL version must be 1.1. If the GLX version is 1.3, then the GL version must be 1.2.

ERRORS

GLXBadDrawable is generated if *draw* is not a valid window or a valid GLX pixel buffer.

SEE ALSO

glXSelectEvent, **glXCreatePbuffer**

NAME

glXGetVisualFromFBConfig – return visual that is associated with the frame buffer configuration

C SPECIFICATION

XVisualInfo * **glXGetVisualFromFBConfig**(Display *dpy*,

GLXFBConfig *config*)

PARAMETERS

dpy   Specifies the connection to the X server.

config Specifies the GLX frame buffer configuration.

DESCRIPTION

If *config* is a valid GLX frame buffer configuration and it has an associated X Visual then information describing that visual is returned; otherwise **NULL** is returned. Use **XFree** to free the data returned.

NOTES

glXGetVisualFromFBConfig is available only if the GLX version is 1.3 or greater.

If the GLX version is 1.1 or 1.0, the GL version must be 1.0. If the GLX version is 1.2, then the GL version must be 1.1. If the GLX version is 1.3, then the GL version must be 1.2.

XVisualInfo is defined in *Xutil.h*. It is a structure that includes *visual*, *visualID*, *screen*, and *depth* elements.

ERRORS

Returns **NULL** if *config* is not a valid GLXFBConfig.

SEE ALSO

glXGetFBConfigAttrib, **glXChooseFBConfig**, **glXChooseVisual**, **glXGetConfig**

NAME

glXIntro – Introduction to OpenGL in the X window system

OVERVIEW

OpenGL (called GL in other pages) is a high-performance 3D-oriented renderer. It is available in the X window system through the GLX extension. To determine whether the GLX extension is supported by an X server, and if so, what version is supported, call **glXQueryExtension** and **glXQueryVersion**.

GLX extended X servers make a subset of their visuals available for OpenGL rendering. Drawables created with these visual can also be rendered into using the core X renderer and or any other X extension that is compatible with all core X visuals.

GLX extends a drawable's standard color buffer with additional buffers. These buffers include back and auxiliary color buffers, a depth buffer, a stencil buffer, and a color accumulation buffer. Some or all of the buffers listed are included in each X visual that supports OpenGL.

GLX supports rendering into three types of drawables: windows, pixmaps and pbuffers (pixel buffers). GLX windows and pixmaps are X resources, and capable of accepting core X rendering as well as OpenGL rendering. GLX pbuffers are GLX only resources, and might not accept core X rendering.

To render using OpenGL into a GLX drawable, you must determine the appropriate GLXFBConfig which supports the rendering features your application requires. **glXChooseFBConfig** returns a GLXFBConfig matching the required attributes, or **NULL** if no match is found. A complete list of GLXFBConfigs supported by a server can be obtained by calling **glXGetFBConfigs**. Attributes of a particular GLXFBConfig can be queried by calling **glXGetFBConfigAttrib**.

For GLX windows and pixmaps, a suitable X drawable (using either **XCreateWindow** or **XCreatePixmap**, respectively) with a matching visual must be created first. Call **glXGetVisualFromFBConfig** to obtain the necessary XVisualInfo structure for creating the X drawable. For pbuffers, no underlying X drawable is required.

To create a GLX window from an X window, call **glXCreateWindow**. Likewise, to create a GLX pixmap, call **glXCreatePixmap**. Pbuffers are created by calling **glXCreatePbuffer**. Use **glXDestroyWindow**, **glXDestroyPixmap**, and **glXDestroyPbuffer** to release previously allocated resources.

A GLX context is required to bind OpenGL rendering to a GLX resource. A GLX resource and rendering context must have compatible GLXFBConfigs. To create a GLX context, call **glXCreateNewContext**. A context may be bound to a GLX drawable by using **glXMakeContextCurrent**. This context/drawable pair becomes the current context and current drawable, and is used by all OpenGL rendering commands until **glXMakeContextCurrent** is called with different arguments.

Both core X and OpenGL commands can be used to operate on drawables, however, the X and OpenGL command streams are not synchronized. Synchronization can be explicitly specified using by calling **glXWaitGL**, **glXWaitX**, **XSync**, and **XFlush**.

EXAMPLES

Below is a minimal example of creating an RGBA-format, X window that's compatible with OpenGL using GLX 1.3 commands. The window is cleared to yellow when the program runs. The program does minimal error checking; all return values should be checked.

```
#include <stdio.h>
#include <stdlib.h>
#include <GL/gl.h>
#include <GL/glx.h>

int singleBufferAttributess[] = {
    GLX_DRAWABLE_TYPE, GLX_WINDOW_BIT,
    GLX_RENDER_TYPE,   GLX_RGBA_BIT,
    GLX_RED_SIZE,      1,   /* Request a single buffered color buffer */
    GLX_GREEN_SIZE,    1,   /* with the maximum number of color bits  */
    GLX_BLUE_SIZE,     1,   /* for each component                     */
    None
};

int doubleBufferAttributes[] = {
    GLX_DRAWABLE_TYPE, GLX_WINDOW_BIT,
    GLX_RENDER_TYPE,   GLX_RGBA_BIT,
    GLX_DOUBLEBUFFER,  True,  /* Request a double-buffered color buffer with */
    GLX_RED_SIZE,      1,     /* the maximum number of bits per component    */
    GLX_GREEN_SIZE,    1,
    GLX_BLUE_SIZE,     1,
    None
};


static Bool WaitForNotify( Display *dpy, XEvent *event, XPointer arg ) {
    return (event->type == MapNotify) && (event->xmap.window == (Window) arg);
}
```

```
int main( int argc, char *argv[] )
{
    Display              *dpy;
    Window                xWin;
    XEvent                event;
    XVisualInfo          *vInfo;
    XSetWindowAttributes  swa;
    GLXFBConfig          *fbConfigs;
    GLXContext            context;
    GLXWindow             glxWin;
    int                   swaMask;
    int                   numReturned;
    int                   swapFlag = True;

    /* Open a connection to the X server */
    dpy = XOpenDisplay( NULL );
    if ( dpy == NULL ) {
        printf( "Unable to open a connection to the X server0 );
        exit( EXIT_FAILURE );
    }

    /* Request a suitable framebuffer configuration - try for a double
    ** buffered configuration first */
    fbConfigs = glXChooseFBConfig( dpy, DefaultScreen(dpy),
                                   doubleBufferAttributes, &numReturned );

    if ( fbConfigs == NULL ) {  /* no double buffered configs available */
      fbConfigs = glXChooseFBConfig( dpy, DefaultScreen(dpy),
                                     singleBufferAttributess, &numReturned );
      swapFlag = False;
    }

    /* Create an X colormap and window with a visual matching the first
    ** returned framebuffer config */
    vInfo = glXGetVisualFromFBConfig( dpy, fbConfigs[0] );

    swa.border_pixel = 0;
    swa.event_mask = StructureNotifyMask;
    swa.colormap = XCreateColormap( dpy, RootWindow(dpy, vInfo->screen),
                                    vInfo->visual, AllocNone );

    swaMask = CWBorderPixel | CWColormap | CWEventMask;
```

```
xWin = XCreateWindow( dpy, RootWindow(dpy, vInfo->screen), 0, 0, 256, 256,
                      0, vInfo->depth, InputOutput, vInfo->visual,
                      swaMask, &swa );

/* Create a GLX context for OpenGL rendering */
context = glXCreateNewContext( dpy, fbConfigs[0], GLX_RGBA_TYPE,
                      NULL, True );

/* Create a GLX window to associate the frame buffer configuration
** with the created X window */
glxWin = glXCreateWindow( dpy, fbConfigs[0], xWin, NULL );

/* Map the window to the screen, and wait for it to appear */
XMapWindow( dpy, xWin );
XIfEvent( dpy, &event, WaitForNotify, (XPointer) xWin );

/* Bind the GLX context to the Window */
glXMakeContextCurrent( dpy, glxWin, glxWin, context );

/* OpenGL rendering ... */
glClearColor( 1.0, 1.0, 0.0, 1.0 );
glClear( GL_COLOR_BUFFER_BIT );

glFlush();

if ( swapFlag )
    glXSwapBuffers( dpy, glxWin );

sleep( 10 );
exit( EXIT_SUCCESS );
}
```

NOTES

An X color map must be created and passed to **XCreateWindow**.

A GLX context must be created and bound to a GLX drawable before OpenGL commands can be executed. OpenGL commands executed while no context/drawable pair is current result in undefined behavior.

Exposure events indicate that *all* buffers associated with the specified window may be damaged and should be repainted. Although certain buffers of some visuals on some systems may never require repainting (the depth buffer, for example), it is incorrect to write a program assuming that these buffers will not be damaged.

GLX commands utilize XVisualInfo structures rather than pointers to visuals or visualIDs directly. XVisualInfo structures contain *visual*, *visualID*, *screen*, and *depth* elements, as well as other X-specific information.

USING GLX EXTENSIONS

All supported GLX extensions will have a corresponding definition in glx.h and a token in the extension string returned by **glXQueryExtensionsString**. For example, if the **EXT_visual_info** extension is supported, then this token will be defined in glx.h and **EXT_visual_info** will appear in the extension string returned by **glXQueryExtensionsString**. The definitions in glx.h can be used at compile time to determine if procedure calls corresponding to an extension exist in the library.

OpenGL itself is capable of being extended. Refer to **glIntro** for more information.

GLX 1.1, GLX 1.2, and GLX

GLX 1.3 is now supported, and is backward compatible with GLX 1.1 and GLX 1.2. It introduces new functionality (namely GLXFBConfigs) that supersedes the GLX 1.2 functionality. GLX 1.2 commands are supported, but their use in new application development is not recommended.

GLX 1.3 corresponds to OpenGL versions 1.2, and introduces the following new calls: **glXGetFBConfigs, glXGetFBConfigAttrib, glXGetVisualFromFBConfig, glXCreateWindow, glXDestroyWindow, glXCreatePixmap, glXDestroyPixmap, glXCreatePbuffer, glXDestroyPbuffer, glXQueryDrawable, glXCreateNewContext, glXMakeContextCurrent, glXGetCurrentReadDrawable, glXGetCurrentDisplay, glXQueryContext, glXSelectEvent, glXGetSelectedEvent**.

GLX 1.2 corresponds to OpenGL version 1.1 and introduced the following new call: **glGetCurrentDisplay**.

GLX 1.1 corresponds to OpenGL version 1.0 and introduces the following new calls: **glXQueryExtensionsString, glXQueryServerString**, and **glXGetClientString**.

Call **glQueryVersion** to determine at runtime what version of GLX is available. **glQueryVersion** returns the version that is supported on the connection. Thus if 1.3 is returned, both the client and server support GLX 1.3. You can also check the GLX version at compile time: GLX_VERSION_1_1 will be defined in glx.h if GLX 1.1 calls are supported, GLX_VERSION_1_2 will be defined if GLX 1.2 calls are supported, and GLX_VERSION_1_3 will be defined if GLX 1.3 calls are supported.

SEE ALSO

glIntro, glFinish, glFlush, glXChooseVisual, glXCopyContext, glXCreateContext, glXCreateGLXPixmap, glXDestroyContext, glXGetClientString, glXGetConfig, glXIsDirect, glXMakeCurrent, glXQueryExtension, glXQueryExtensionsString, glXQueryServerString, glXQueryVersion, glXSwapBuffers, glXUseXFont, glXWaitGL, glXWaitX, glXGetFBConfigs, glXGetFBConfigAttrib, glXGetVisualFromFBConfig, glXCreateWindow, glXDestroyWindow, glXCreatePixmap, glXDestroyPixmap,

glXCreatePbuffer, glXDestroyPbuffer, glXQueryDrawable,
glXCreateNewContext, glXMakeContextCurrent, glXGetCurrentReadDrawable,
glXGetCurrentDisplay, glXQueryContext, glXSelectEvent, glXGetSelectedEvent.
XCreateColormap, XCreateWindow, XSync

NAME

glXIsDirect – indicate whether direct rendering is enabled

C SPECIFICATION

Bool **glXIsDirect**(Display **dpy*,
                                    GLXContext *ctx*)

PARAMETERS

dpy Specifies the connection to the X server.

ctx Specifies the GLX context that is being queried.

DESCRIPTION

glXIsDirect returns **True** if *ctx* is a direct rendering context, **False** otherwise. Direct rendering contexts pass rendering commands directly from the calling process's address space to the rendering system, bypassing the X server. Nondirect rendering contexts pass all rendering commands to the X server.

ERRORS

GLXBadContext is generated if *ctx* is not a valid GLX context.

SEE ALSO

glXCreateContext,

NAME

glXMakeContextCurrent – attach a GLX context to a GLX drawable

C SPECIFICATION

Bool **glXMakeContextCurrent**(Display **display*,
          GLXDrawable *draw*,
          GLXDrawable *read*,
          GLXContext *ctx*)

PARAMETERS

display   Specifies the connection to the X server.

draw   Specifies a GLX drawable that to render into. Must be an XID representing a GLXWindow, GLXPixmap, or GLXPbuffer.

read   Specifies a GLX drawable that to read from. Must be an XID representing a GLXWindow, GLXPixmap, or GLXPbuffer.

ctx   Specifies the GLX context to be bound to *read* and *ctx*.

DESCRIPTION

glXMakeContextCurrent binds *ctx* to the current rendering thread and to the *draw* and *read* GLX drawables. *draw* and *read* may be the same.

draw is used for all OpenGL operations except:

Any pixel data that are read based on the value of **GL_READ_BUFFER**. Note that accumulation operations use the value of **GL_READ_BUFFER**, but are not allowed unless *draw* is identical to *read*.

Any depth values that are retrieved by **glReadPixels** or **glCopyPixels**.

Any stencil values that are retrieved by **glReadPixels** or **glCopyPixels**.

Frame buffer values are taken from *draw*.

If the current rendering thread has a current rendering context, that context is flushed and replaced by *ctx*.

The first time that *ctx* is made current, the viewport and scissor dimensions are set to the size of the *draw* drawable. The viewport and scissor are not modified when *ctx* is subsequently made current.

To release the current context without assigning a new one, call **glXMakeContextCurrent** with *draw* and *read* set to **None** and *ctx* set to **NULL**.

glXMakeContextCurrent returns **True** if it is successful, **False** otherwise. If **False** is returned, the previously current rendering context and drawable (if any) remain unchanged.

NOTES

glXMakeContextCurrent is available only if the GLX version is 1.3 or greater.

If the GLX version is 1.1 or 1.0, the GL version must be 1.0. If the GLX version is 1.2, then the GL version must be 1.1. If the GLX version is 1.3, then the GL version must be 1.2.

ERRORS

BadMatch is generated if *draw* and *read* are not compatible.

BadAccess is generated if *ctx* is current to some other thread.

GLXContextState is generated if there is a current rendering context and its render mode is either **GL_FEEDBACK** or **GL_SELECT**.

GLXBadContext is generated if *ctx* is not a valid GLX rendering context.

GLXBadDrawable is generated if *draw* or *read* is not a valid GLX drawable.

GLXBadWindow is generated if the underlying X window for either *draw* or *read* is no longer valid.

GLXBadCurrentDrawable is generated if the previous context of the calling thread has unflushed commands, and the previous drawable is no longer valid.

BadAlloc is generated if the X server does not have enough resources to allocate the buffers.

BadMatch is generated if:

> *draw* and *read* cannot fit into frame buffer memory simultaneously.

> *draw* or *read* is a GLXPixmap and *ctx* is a direct rendering context.

> *draw* or *read* is a GLXPixmap and *ctx* was previously bound to a GLXWindow or GLXPbuffer.

> *draw* or *read* is a GLXWindow or GLXPbuffer and *ctx* was previously bound to a GLXPixmap.

SEE ALSO

glXCreateNewContext, **glXCreateWindow**, **glXCreatePixmap**, **glXCreatePbuffer**, **glXDestroyContext**, **glXGetCurrentContext**, **glXGetCurrentDisplay**, **glXGetCurrentDrawable**, **glXGetCurrentReadDrawable**, **glXMakeCurrent**

NAME

glXMakeCurrent – attach a GLX context to a window or a GLX pixmap

C SPECIFICATION

Bool **glXMakeCurrent**(Display *dpy,
                        GLXDrawable drawable,
                        GLXContext ctx)

PARAMETERS

dpy   Specifies the connection to the X server.

drawable Specifies a GLX drawable. Must be either an X window ID or a GLX pixmap ID.

ctx   Specifies a GLX rendering context that is to be attached to drawable.

DESCRIPTION

glXMakeCurrent does two things: It makes ctx the current GLX rendering context of the calling thread, replacing the previously current context if there was one, and it attaches ctx to a GLX drawable, either a window or a GLX pixmap. As a result of these two actions, subsequent GL rendering calls use rendering context ctx to modify GLX drawable drawable (for reading and writing). Because **glXMakeCurrent** always replaces the current rendering context with ctx, there can be only one current context per thread.

Pending commands to the previous context, if any, are flushed before it is released.

The first time ctx is made current to any thread, its viewport is set to the full size of drawable. Subsequent calls by any thread to **glXMakeCurrent** with ctx have no effect on its viewport.

To release the current context without assigning a new one, call **glXMakeCurrent** with drawable set **None** and ctx set to **NULL**

glXMakeCurrent returns **True** if it is successful, **False** otherwise. If **False** is returned, the previously current rendering context and drawable (if any) remain unchanged.

NOTES

A process is a single-execution environment, implemented in a single address space, consisting of one or more threads.

A thread is one of a set of subprocesses that share a single address space, but maintain separate program counters, stack spaces, and other related global data. A thread that is the only member of its subprocess group is equivalent to a process.

ERRORS

BadMatch is generated if *drawable* was not created with the same X screen and visual as *ctx*. It is also generated if *drawable* is **None** and *ctx* is not **NULL**.

BadAccess is generated if *ctx* was current to another thread at the time **glXMakeCurrent** was called.

GLXBadDrawable is generated if *drawable* is not a valid GLX drawable.

GLXBadContext is generated if *ctx* is not a valid GLX context.

GLXBadContextState is generated if **glXMakeCurrent** is executed between the execution of **glBegin** and the corresponding execution of **glEnd**.

GLXBadContextState is also generated if the rendering context current to the calling thread has GL renderer state **GL_FEEDBACK** or **GL_SELECT**.

GLXBadCurrentWindow is generated if there are pending GL commands for the previous context and the current drawable is a window that is no longer valid.

BadAlloc may be generated if the server has delayed allocation of ancillary buffers until **glXMakeCurrent** is called, only to find that it has insufficient resources to complete the allocation.

SEE ALSO

glXCreateContext, **glXCreateGLXPixmap glXGetCurrentContext**, **glXGetCurrentDisplay**, **glXGetCurrentDrawable**, **glXGetCurrentReadDrawable**, **glXMakeContextCurrent**

NAME

glXQueryContext – query context information

C SPECIFICATION

int **glXQueryContext**(Display *dpy,
                        GLXContext ctx,
                        int attribute,
                        int *value)

PARAMETERS

dpy   Specifies the connection to the X server.

ctx   Specifies a GLX rendering context.

attribute
            Specifies that a context parameter should be retrieved. Must be one of
            GLX_FBCONFIG_ID, **GLX_RENDER_TYPE**, or **GLX_SCREEN**.

value   Contains the return value for *attribute*.

DESCRIPTION

glXQueryContext sets *value* to the value of *attribute* with respect to *ctx*. *attribute*
may be one of the following:

GLX_FBCONFIG_ID   Returns the XID of the GLXFBConfig associated with *ctx*.

GLX_RENDER_TYPE   Returns the rendering type supported by *ctx*.

GLX_SCREEN   Returns the screen number associated with *ctx*.

Success is returned unless *attribute* is not a valid GLX context attribute, in which
case **GLX_BAD_ATTRIBUTE** is returned.

This call may cause a round-trip to the server.

NOTES

glXQueryContext is available only if the GLX version is 1.3 or greater.

If the GLX version is 1.1 or 1.0, the GL version must be 1.0. If the GLX version is
1.2, then the GL version must be 1.1. If the GLX version is 1.3, then the GL version
must be 1.2.

ERRORS

GLXBadContext is generated if *ctx* does not refer to a valid context.

SEE ALSO

glXCreateNewContext, **glXGetCurrentContext**, **glXQueryVersion**,
glXQueryExtensionsString

NAME

glXQueryExtension – indicate whether the GLX extension is supported

C SPECIFICATION

Bool **glXQueryExtension**(Display *dpy*,
                        int *errorBase*,
                        int *eventBase*)

PARAMETERS

dpy   Specifies the connection to the X server.

errorBase Returns the base error code of the GLX server extension.

eventBase Returns the base event code of the GLX server extension.

DESCRIPTION

glXQueryExtension returns **True** if the X server of connection *dpy* supports the GLX extension, **False** otherwise. If **True** is returned, then *errorBase* and *eventBase* return the error base and event base of the GLX extension. These values should be added to the constant error and event values to determine the actual event or error values. Otherwise, *errorBase* and *eventBase* are unchanged.

errorBase and *eventBase* do not return values if they are specified as **NULL**.

SEE ALSO

glXQueryVersion

NAME

glXQueryExtensionsString – return list of supported extensions

C SPECIFICATION

const char * **glXQueryExtensionsString**(Display *dpy*,
                                                                          int *screen*)

PARAMETERS

dpy   Specifies the connection to the X server.

screen Specifies the screen number.

DESCRIPTION

glXQueryExtensionsString returns a pointer to a string describing which GLX extensions are supported on the connection. The string is null-terminated and contains a space-separated list of extension names. (The extension names themselves never contain spaces.) If there are no extensions to GLX, then the empty string is returned.

NOTES

glXQueryExtensionsString is available only if the GLX version is 1.1 or greater.

glXQueryExtensionsString only returns information about GLX extensions. Call **glGetString** to get a list of GL extensions.

SEE ALSO

glGetString, **glXQueryVersion**, **glXQueryServerString**, **glXGetClientString**

NAME

glXQueryServerString – return string describing the server

C SPECIFICATION

const char * **glXQueryServerString**(Display *dpy*,
int *screen*,
int *name*)

PARAMETERS

dpy   Specifies the connection to the X server.

screen Specifies the screen number.

name   Specifies which string is returned: one of **GLX_VENDOR**, **GLX_VERSION**, or **GLX_EXTENSIONS**.

DESCRIPTION

glXQueryServerString returns a pointer to a static, null-terminated string describing some aspect of the server's GLX extension. The possible values for *name* and the format of the strings is the same as for **glXGetClientString**. If *name* is not set to a recognized value, **NULL** is returned.

NOTES

glXQueryServerString is available only if the GLX version is 1.1 or greater.

If the GLX version is 1.1 or 1.0, the GL version must be 1.0. If the GLX version is 1.2, the GL version must be 1.1. If the GLX version is 1.3, the GL version must be 1.2.

glXQueryServerString only returns information about GLX extensions supported by the server. Call **glGetString** to get a list of GL extensions. Call **glXGetClientString** to get a list of GLX extensions supported by the client.

SEE ALSO

glXQueryVersion, **glXGetClientString**, **glXQueryExtensionsString**

NAME

glXQueryVersion – return the version numbers of the GLX extension

C SPECIFICATION

Bool **glXQueryVersion**(Display **dpy*,
                          int **major*,
                          int **minor*)

PARAMETERS

dpy   Specifies the connection to the X server.

major Returns the major version number of the GLX server extension.

minor Returns the minor version number of the GLX server extension.

DESCRIPTION

glXQueryVersion returns the major and minor version numbers of the GLX extension implemented by the server associated with connection *dpy*. Implementations with the same major version number are upward compatible, meaning that the implementation with the higher minor number is a superset of the version with the lower minor number.

major and *minor* do not return values if they are specified as **NULL**.

ERRORS

glXQueryVersion returns **False** if it fails, **True** otherwise.

major and *minor* are not updated when **False** is returned.

SEE ALSO

glXQueryExtension

NAME

glXSelectEvent – select GLX events for a window or a GLX pixel buffer

C SPECIFICATION

void **glXSelectEvent**(Display **dpy*,
                        GLXDrawable *draw*,
                        unsigned long *event_mask*)

PARAMETERS

dpy   Specifies the connection to the X server.

draw   Specifies a GLX drawable. Must be a GLX pixel buffer or a window.

event_mask
              Specifies the events to be returned for *draw*.

DESCRIPTION

glXSelectEvent sets the GLX event mask for a GLX pixel buffer or a window. Calling **glXSelectEvent** overrides any previous event mask that was set by the client for *draw*. Note that it does not affect the event masks that other clients may have specified for *draw* since each client rendering to *draw* has a separate event mask for it.

Currently, only one GLX event, **GLX_PBUFFER_CLOBBER_MASK**, can be selected. The following data is returned to the client when a **GLX_PBUFFER_CLOBBER_MASK** event occurs:

```
typdef struct {11.
    int event_type;     /* GLX_DAMAGED or GLX_SAVED */
    int draw_type;      /* GLX_WINDOW or GLX_PBUFFER */
    unsigned long serial;/* # of last request processed by server */
    Bool send_event;    /* true if this came for SendEvent request */
    Display *display;   /* display the event was read from */
    GLXDrawable drawable;/* i.d. of Drawable */
    unsigned int buffer_mask;/* mask indicating affectedbuffers */
    int x, y;
    int width, height;
    int count;          /* if nonzero, at least this many more */
} GLXPbufferClobberEvent;
```

The valid bit masks used in *buffer_mask* are:

center; lb lb l l. _ Bitmask   Corresponding Buffer _

GLX_FRONT_LEFT_BUFFER_BIT Front left color buffer

GLX_FRONT_RIGHT_BUFFER_BIT Front right color buffer

GLX_BACK_LEFT_BUFFER_BIT Back left color buffer

GLX_BACK_RIGHT_BUFFER_BIT Back right color buffer

GLX_AUX_BUFFERS_BIT Auxillary buffer **GLX_DEPTH_BUFFER_BIT**Depth buffer

GLX_STENCIL_BUFFER_BIT Stencil buffer

GLX_ACCUM_BUFFER_BIT Accumulation buffer _

A single X server operation can cause several buffer clobber events to be sent. (e.g., a single GLX pixel buffer may be damaged and cause multiple buffer clobber events to be generated). Each event specifies one region of the GLX drawable that was affected by the X Server operation. The *buffer_mask* field indicates which color buffers and ancillary buffers were affected. All the buffer clobber events generated by a single X server action are guaranteed to be contiguous in the event queue. The conditions under which this event is generated and the *event_type* varies, depending on the type of the GLX drawable.

When the **GLX_AUX_BUFFERS_BIT** is set in *buffer_mask*, then *aux_buffer* is set to indicate which buffer was affected. If more than one aux buffer was affected, then additional events are generated as part of the same contiguous event group. Each additional event will have only the **GLX_AUX_BUFFERS_BIT** set in *buffer_mask*, and the *aux_buffer* field will be set appropriately. For nonstereo drawables, **GLX_FRONT_LEFT_BUFFER_BIT** and **GLX_BACK_LEFT_BUFFER_BIT** are used to specify the front and back color buffers.

For preserved GLX pixel buffers, a buffer clobber event with type **GLX_SAVED** is generated whenever the contents of the GLX pixel buffer is moved out of offscreen memory. The event(s) describes which portions of the GLX pixel buffer were affected. Clients who receive many buffer clobber events, referring to different save actions, should consider freeing the GLX pixel buffer resource in order to prevent the system from thrashing due to insufficient resources.

For an unpreserved GLXPbuffer, a buffer clobber event, with type **GLX_DAMAGED**, is generated whenever a portion of the GLX pixel buffer becomes invalid. The client may wish to regenerate the invalid portions of the GLX pixel buffer.

For Windows, buffer clobber events, with type **GLX_SAVED**, occur whenever an ancillary buffer, associated with the window, gets clobbered or moved out of offscreen memory. The event contains information indicating which color buffers and ancillary buffers-and which portions of those buffers-were affected.

NOTES

glXSelectEvent is available only if the GLX version is 1.3 or greater.

If the GLX version is 1.1 or 1.0, the GL version must be 1.0. If the GLX version is 1.2, then the GL version must be 1.1. If the GLX version is 1.3, then the GL version must be 1.2.

ERRORS

GLXBadDrawable is generated if *draw* is not a valid window or a valid GLX pixel buffer.

ASSOCIATED GETS

glXGetSelectedEvent

SEE ALSO

glXCreatePbuffer

NAME

glXSwapBuffers – exchange front and back buffers

C SPECIFICATION

void **glXSwapBuffers**(Display *dpy,
                        GLXDrawable *drawable*)

PARAMETERS

dpy   Specifies the connection to the X server.

drawable Specifies the drawable whose buffers are to be swapped.

DESCRIPTION

glXSwapBuffers promotes the contents of the back buffer of *drawable* to become the contents of the front buffer of *drawable*. The contents of the back buffer then become undefined. The update typically takes place during the vertical retrace of the monitor, rather than immediately after **glXSwapBuffers** is called.

glXSwapBuffers performs an implicit **glFlush** before it returns. Subsequent OpenGL commands may be issued immediately after calling **glXSwapBuffers**, but are not executed until the buffer exchange is completed.

If *drawable* was not created with respect to a double-buffered visual, **glXSwapBuffers** has no effect, and no error is generated.

NOTES

The contents of the back buffer become undefined after a swap. Note that this applies to pixel buffers as well as windows.

All GLX rendering contexts share the same notion of which are front buffers and which are back buffers. One consequence is that when multiple clients are rendering to the same double-buffered window, all of them should finish rendering before one of them issues the command to swap buffers. The clients are responsible for implementing this synchronization. Typically this is accomplished by executing **glFinish** and then using a semaphore in shared memory to rendezvous before swapping.

ERRORS

GLXBadDrawable is generated if *drawable* is not a valid GLX drawable.

GLXBadCurrentWindow is generated if *dpy* and *drawable* are respectively the display and drawable associated with the current context of the calling thread, and *drawable* identifies a window that is no longer valid.

SEE ALSO

glFlush

NAME

glXUseXFont – create bitmap display lists from an X font

C SPECIFICATION

void **glXUseXFont**(Font *font*,
                       int *first*,
                       int *count*,
                       int *listBase*)

PARAMETERS

font   Specifies the font from which character glyphs are to be taken.

first   Specifies the index of the first glyph to be taken.

count   Specifies the number of glyphs to be taken.

listBase Specifies the index of the first display list to be generated.

DESCRIPTION

glXUseXFont generates *count* display lists, named *listBase* through *listBase+count–1*, each containing a single **glBitmap** command. The parameters of the **glBitmap** command of display list *listBase+i* are derived from glyph *first+i*. Bitmap parameters *xorig, yorig, width,* and *height* are computed from font metrics as *descent–1, –lbearing, rbearing–lbearing,* and *ascent+descent,* respectively. *xmove* is taken from the glyph's *width* metric, and *ymove* is set to zero. Finally, the glyph's image is converted to the appropriate format for **glBitmap**.

Using **glXUseXFont** may be more efficient than accessing the X font and generating the display lists explicitly, both because the display lists are created on the server without requiring a round trip of the glyph data, and because the server may choose to delay the creation of each bitmap until it is accessed.

Empty display lists are created for all glyphs that are requested and are not defined in *font*. **glXUseXFont** is ignored if there is no current GLX context.

ERRORS

BadFont is generated if *font* is not a valid font.

GLXBadContextState is generated if the current GLX context is in display-list construction mode.

GLXBadCurrentWindow is generated if the drawable associated with the current context of the calling thread is a window, and that window is no longer valid.

SEE ALSO

glBitmap, **glXMakeCurrent**

NAME

glXWaitGL – complete GL execution prior to subsequent X calls

C SPECIFICATION

void **glXWaitGL**(void)

DESCRIPTION

GL rendering calls made prior to **glXWaitGL** are guaranteed to be executed before X rendering calls made after **glXWaitGL**. Although this same result can be achieved using **glFinish**, **glXWaitGL** does not require a round trip to the server, and it is therefore more efficient in cases where client and server are on separate machines.

glXWaitGL is ignored if there is no current GLX context.

NOTES

glXWaitGL may or may not flush the X stream.

ERRORS

GLXBadCurrentWindow is generated if the drawable associated with the current context of the calling thread is a window, and that window is no longer valid.

SEE ALSO

glFinish, **glFlush**, **glXWaitX**, **XSync**

NAME

glXWaitX – complete X execution prior to subsequent GL calls

C SPECIFICATION

void **glXWaitX**(void)

DESCRIPTION

X rendering calls made prior to **glXWaitX** are guaranteed to be executed before GL rendering calls made after **glXWaitX**. Although the same result can be achieved using **XSync**, **glXWaitX** does not require a round trip to the server, and it is therefore more efficient in cases where client and server are on separate machines.

glXWaitX is ignored if there is no current GLX context.

NOTES

glXWaitX may or may not flush the GL stream.

ERRORS

GLXBadCurrentWindow is generated if the drawable associated with the current context of the calling thread is a window, and that window is no longer valid.

SEE ALSO

glFinish, **glFlush**, **glXWaitGL**, **XSync**

NAME

glXChooseVisual – return a visual that matches specified attributes

C SPECIFICATION

XVisualInfo* **glXChooseVisual**(Display **dpy*,
                                                     int *screen*,
                                                     int **attribList*)

PARAMETERS

dpy   Specifies the connection to the X server.

screen   Specifies the screen number.

attribList
             Specifies a list of boolean attributes and integer attribute/value pairs. The
             last attribute must be **None**.

DESCRIPTION

glXChooseVisual returns a pointer to an XVisualInfo structure describing the visual
that best meets a minimum specification. The boolean GLX attributes of the visual
that is returned will match the specified values, and the integer GLX attributes will
meet or exceed the specified minimum values. If all other attributes are equivalent,
then TrueColor and PseudoColor visuals have priority over DirectColor and StaticColor visuals, respectively. If no conforming visual exists, **NULL** is returned. To
free the data returned by this function, use **XFree**.

All boolean GLX attributes default to **False** except **GLX_USE_GL**, which defaults to
True. All integer GLX attributes default to zero. Default specifications are superseded by attributes included in *attribList*. Boolean attributes included in *attribList*
are understood to be **True**. Integer attributes and enumerated type attributes are
followed immediately by the corresponding desired or minimum value. The list
must be terminated with **None**.

The interpretations of the various GLX visual attributes are as follows:

GLX_USE_GL   Ignored. Only visuals that can be rendered with GLX are
                                considered.

GLX_BUFFER_SIZE Must be followed by a nonnegative integer that indicates the
                                desired color index buffer size. The smallest index buffer of
                                at least the specified size is preferred. Ignored if **GLX_RGBA**
                                is asserted.

GLX_LEVEL   Must be followed by an integer buffer-level specification.
                                This specification is honored exactly. Buffer level zero
                                corresponds to the main frame buffer of the display. Buffer
                                level one is the first overlay frame buffer, level two the

second overlay frame buffer, and so on. Negative buffer levels correspond to underlay frame buffers.

GLX_RGBA   If present, only TrueColor and DirectColor visuals are considered. Otherwise, only PseudoColor and StaticColor visuals are considered.

GLX_DOUBLEBUFFER

If present, only double-buffered visuals are considered. Otherwise, only single-buffered visuals are considered.

GLX_STEREO   If present, only stereo visuals are considered. Otherwise, only monoscopic visuals are considered.

GLX_AUX_BUFFERS   Must be followed by a nonnegative integer that indicates the desired number of auxiliary buffers. Visuals with the smallest number of auxiliary buffers that meets or exceeds the specified number are preferred.

GLX_RED_SIZE   Must be followed by a nonnegative minimum size specification. If this value is zero, the smallest available red buffer is preferred. Otherwise, the largest available red buffer of at least the minimum size is preferred.

GLX_GREEN_SIZE   Must be followed by a nonnegative minimum size specification. If this value is zero, the smallest available green buffer is preferred. Otherwise, the largest available green buffer of at least the minimum size is preferred.

GLX_BLUE_SIZE   Must be followed by a nonnegative minimum size specification. If this value is zero, the smallest available blue buffer is preferred. Otherwise, the largest available blue buffer of at least the minimum size is preferred.

GLX_ALPHA_SIZE   Must be followed by a nonnegative minimum size specification. If this value is zero, the smallest available alpha buffer is preferred. Otherwise, the largest available alpha buffer of at least the minimum size is preferred.

GLX_DEPTH_SIZE   Must be followed by a nonnegative minimum size specification. If this value is zero, visuals with no depth buffer are preferred. Otherwise, the largest available depth buffer of at least the minimum size is preferred.

GLX_STENCIL_SIZE   Must be followed by a nonnegative integer that indicates the desired number of stencil bitplanes. The smallest stencil buffer of at least the specified size is preferred. If the desired value is zero, visuals with no stencil buffer are preferred.

GLX_ACCUM_RED_SIZE
Must be followed by a nonnegative minimum size specification. If this value is zero, visuals with no red accumulation buffer are preferred. Otherwise, the largest possible red accumulation buffer of at least the minimum size is preferred.

GLX_ACCUM_GREEN_SIZE
Must be followed by a nonnegative minimum size specification. If this value is zero, visuals with no green accumulation buffer are preferred. Otherwise, the largest possible green accumulation buffer of at least the minimum size is preferred.

GLX_ACCUM_BLUE_SIZE
Must be followed by a nonnegative minimum size specification. If this value is zero, visuals with no blue accumulation buffer are preferred. Otherwise, the largest possible blue accumulation buffer of at least the minimum size is preferred.

GLX_ACCUM_ALPHA_SIZE
Must be followed by a nonnegative minimum size specification. If this value is zero, visuals with no alpha accumulation buffer are preferred. Otherwise, the largest possible alpha accumulation buffer of at least the minimum size is preferred.

EXAMPLES

attribList = {**GLX_RGBA**, **GLX_RED_SIZE**, 4, **GLX_GREEN_SIZE**, 4, **GLX_BLUE_SIZE**, 4, **None**};

Specifies a single-buffered RGB visual in the normal frame buffer, not an overlay or underlay buffer. The returned visual supports at least four bits each of red, green, and blue, and possibly no bits of alpha. It does not support color index mode, double-buffering, or stereo display. It may or may not have one or more auxiliary color buffers, a depth buffer, a stencil buffer, or an accumulation buffer.

NOTES

XVisualInfo is defined in *Xutil.h*. It is a structure that includes *visual*, *visualID*, *screen*, and *depth* elements.

glXChooseVisual is implemented as a client-side utility using only **XGetVisualInfo** and **glXGetConfig**. Calls to these two routines can be used to implement selection algorithms other than the generic one implemented by **glXChooseVisual**.

GLX implementers are strongly discouraged, but not proscribed, from changing the selection algorithm used by **glXChooseVisual**. Therefore, selections may change from release to release of the client-side library.

There is no direct filter for picking only visuals that support GLXPixmaps. GLXPixmaps are supported for visuals whose **GLX_BUFFER_SIZE** is one of the pixmap depths supported by the X server.

ERRORS

NULL is returned if an undefined GLX attribute is encountered in *attribList*.

SEE ALSO

glXCreateContext, **glXGetConfig**

NAME

glXCreateContext – create a new GLX rendering context

C SPECIFICATION

GLXContext **glXCreateContext**(Display **dpy*,
XVisualInfo **vis*,
GLXContext *shareList*,
Bool *direct*)

PARAMETERS

dpy   Specifies the connection to the X server.

vis   Specifies the visual that defines the frame buffer resources available to the rendering context. It is a pointer to an **XVisualInfo** structure, not a visual ID or a pointer to a **Visual**.

shareList Specifies the context with which to share display lists. **NULL** indicates that no sharing is to take place.

direct Specifies whether rendering is to be done with a direct connection to the graphics system if possible (**True**) or through the X server (**False**).

DESCRIPTION

glXCreateContext creates a GLX rendering context and returns its handle. This context can be used to render into both windows and GLX pixmaps. If **glXCreateContext** fails to create a rendering context, **NULL** is returned.

If *direct* is **True**, then a direct rendering context is created if the implementation supports direct rendering, if the connection is to an X server that is local, and if a direct rendering context is available. (An implementation may return an indirect context when *direct* is **True**). If *direct* is **False**, then a rendering context that renders through the X server is always created. Direct rendering provides a performance advantage in some implementations. However, direct rendering contexts cannot be shared outside a single process, and they may be unable to render to GLX pixmaps.

If *shareList* is not **NULL**, then all display-list indexes and definitions are shared by context *shareList* and by the newly created context. An arbitrary number of contexts can share a single display-list space. However, all rendering contexts that share a single display-list space must themselves exist in the same address space. Two rendering contexts share an address space if both are nondirect using the same server, or if both are direct and owned by a single process. Note that in the nondirect case, it is not necessary for the calling threads to share an address space, only for their related rendering contexts to share an address space.

If the GL version is 1.1 or greater, then all texture objects except object 0, are shared by any contexts that share display lists.

NOTES

XVisualInfo is defined in *Xutil.h*. It is a structure that includes *visual*, *visualID*, *screen*, and *depth* elements.

A *process* is a single execution environment, implemented in a single address space, consisting of one or more threads.

A *thread* is one of a set of subprocesses that share a single address space, but maintain separate program counters, stack spaces, and other related global data. A *thread* that is the only member of its subprocess group is equivalent to a *process*.

It may not be possible to render to a GLX pixmap with a direct rendering context.

ERRORS

NULL is returned if execution fails on the client side.

BadMatch is generated if the context to be created would not share the address space or the screen of the context specified by *shareList*.

BadValue is generated if *vis* is not a valid visual (for example, if a particular GLX implementation does not support it).

GLXBadContext is generated if *shareList* is not a GLX context and is not **NULL**.

BadAlloc is generated if the server does not have enough resources to allocate the new context.

SEE ALSO

glXDestroyContext, **glXGetConfig**, **glXIsDirect**, **glXMakeCurrent**

NAME

glXCreateGLXPixmap – create an off-screen GLX rendering area

C SPECIFICATION

GLXPixmap **glXCreateGLXPixmap**(Display *dpy*,
                                                            XVisualInfo *vis*,
                                                            Pixmap *pixmap*)

PARAMETERS

dpy   Specifies the connection to the X server.

vis   Specifies the visual that defines the structure of the rendering area. It is a pointer to an **XVisualInfo** structure, not a visual ID or a pointer to a **Visual**.

pixmap
              Specifies the X pixmap that will be used as the front left color buffer of the off-screen rendering area.

DESCRIPTION

glXCreateGLXPixmap creates an off-screen rendering area and returns its XID. Any GLX rendering context that was created with respect to *vis* can be used to render into this off-screen area. Use **glXMakeCurrent** to associate the rendering area with a GLX rendering context.

The X pixmap identified by *pixmap* is used as the front left buffer of the resulting off-screen rendering area. All other buffers specified by *vis*, including color buffers other than the front left buffer, are created without externally visible names. GLX pixmaps with double-buffering are supported. However, **glXSwapBuffers** is ignored by these pixmaps.

Some implementations may not support GLX pixmaps with direct rendering contexts.

NOTES

XVisualInfo is defined in *Xutil.h*. It is a structure that includes *visual*, *visualID*, *screen*, and *depth* elements.

ERRORS

BadMatch is generated if the depth of *pixmap* does not match the depth value reported by core X11 for *vis*, or if *pixmap* was not created with respect to the same screen as *vis*.

BadValue is generated if *vis* is not a valid XVisualInfo pointer (for example, if a particular GLX implementation does not support this visual).

BadPixmap is generated if *pixmap* is not a valid pixmap.

BadAlloc is generated if the server cannot allocate the GLX pixmap.

SEE ALSO

glXCreateContext, **glXCreatePixmap**, **glXDestoryGLXPixmap**, **glXIsDirect**, **glXMakeCurrent**

NAME

glXDestroyGLXPixmap – destroy a GLX pixmap

C SPECIFICATION

void **glXDestroyGLXPixmap**(Display *dpy,
                              GLXPixmap pix)

PARAMETERS

dpy Specifies the connection to the X server.

pix Specifies the GLX pixmap to be destroyed.

DESCRIPTION

If the GLX pixmap *pix* is not current to any client, **glXDestroyGLXPixmap** destroys it immediately. Otherwise, *pix* is destroyed when it becomes not current to any client. In either case, the resource ID is freed immediately.

ERRORS

GLXBadPixmap is generated if *pix* is not a valid GLX pixmap.

SEE ALSO

glXCreateGLXPixmap, **glXDestroyPixmap**, **glXMakeCurrent**

NAME

glXGetConfig – return information about GLX visuals

C SPECIFICATION

int **glXGetConfig**(Display *dpy,
                      XVisualInfo *vis,
                      int attrib,
                      int *value)

PARAMETERS

dpy   Specifies the connection to the X server.

vis   Specifies the visual to be queried. It is a pointer to an **XVisualInfo** structure, not a visual ID or a pointer to a **Visual**.

attrib Specifies the visual attribute to be returned.

value Returns the requested value.

DESCRIPTION

glXGetConfig sets *value* to the *attrib* value of windows or GLX pixmaps created with respect to *vis*. **glXGetConfig** returns an error code if it fails for any reason. Otherwise, zero is returned.

attrib is one of the following:

GLX_USE_GL   **True** if OpenGL rendering is supported by this visual, **False** otherwise.

GLX_BUFFER_SIZE   Number of bits per color buffer. For RGBA visuals, **GLX_BUFFER_SIZE** is the sum of **GLX_RED_SIZE**, **GLX_GREEN_SIZE**, **GLX_BLUE_SIZE**, and **GLX_ALPHA_SIZE**. For color index visuals, **GLX_BUFFER_SIZE** is the size of the color indexes.

GLX_LEVEL   Frame buffer level of the visual. Level zero is the default frame buffer. Positive levels correspond to frame buffers that overlay the default buffer, and negative levels correspond to frame buffers that underlay the default buffer.

GLX_RGBA   **True** if color buffers store red, green, blue, and alpha values. **False** if they store color indexes.

GLX_DOUBLEBUFFER
                      True if color buffers exist in front/back pairs that can be swapped, **False** otherwise.

GLX_STEREO   **True** if color buffers exist in left/right pairs, **False** otherwise.

GLX_AUX_BUFFERS   Number of auxiliary color buffers that are available. Zero indicates that no auxiliary color buffers exist.

GLX_RED_SIZE   Number of bits of red stored in each color buffer. Undefined if **GLX_RGBA** is **False**.

GLX_GREEN_SIZE   Number of bits of green stored in each color buffer. Undefined if **GLX_RGBA** is **False**.

GLX_BLUE_SIZE   Number of bits of blue stored in each color buffer. Undefined if **GLX_RGBA** is **False**.

GLX_ALPHA_SIZE   Number of bits of alpha stored in each color buffer. Undefined if **GLX_RGBA** is **False**.

GLX_DEPTH_SIZE   Number of bits in the depth buffer.

GLX_STENCIL_SIZE   Number of bits in the stencil buffer.

GLX_ACCUM_RED_SIZE
Number of bits of red stored in the accumulation buffer.

GLX_ACCUM_GREEN_SIZE
Number of bits of green stored in the accumulation buffer.

GLX_ACCUM_BLUE_SIZE
Number of bits of blue stored in the accumulation buffer.

GLX_ACCUM_ALPHA_SIZE
Number of bits of alpha stored in the accumulation buffer.

The X protocol allows a single visual ID to be instantiated with different numbers of bits per pixel. Windows or GLX pixmaps that will be rendered with OpenGL, however, must be instantiated with a color buffer depth of **GLX_BUFFER_SIZE**.

Although a GLX implementation can export many visuals that support GL rendering, it must support at least one RGBA visual. This visual must have at least one color buffer, a stencil buffer of at least 1 bit, a depth buffer of at least 12 bits, and an accumulation buffer. Alpha bitplanes are optional in this visual. However, its color buffer size must be as great as that of the deepest **TrueColor**, **DirectColor**, **PseudoColor**, or **StaticColor** visual supported on level zero, and it must itself be made available on level zero.

In addition, if the X server exports a **PseudoColor** or **StaticColor** visual on framebuffer level 0, a color index visual is also required on that level. It must have at least one color buffer, a stencil buffer of at least 1 bit, and a depth buffer of at least 12 bits. This visual must have as many color bitplanes as the deepest **PseudoColor** or **StaticColor** visual supported on level 0.

Applications are best written to select the visual that most closely meets their requirements. Creating windows or GLX pixmaps with unnecessary buffers can result in reduced rendering performance as well as poor resource allocation.

NOTES

XVisualInfo is defined in *Xutil.h.* It is a structure that includes *visual, visualID, screen,* and *depth* elements.

ERRORS

GLX_NO_EXTENSION is returned if *dpy* does not support the GLX extension.

GLX_BAD_SCREEN is returned if the screen of *vis* does not correspond to a screen.

GLX_BAD_ATTRIBUTE is returned if *attrib* is not a valid GLX attribute.

GLX_BAD_VISUAL is returned if *vis* doesn't support GLX and an attribute other than **GLX_USE_GL** is requested.

SEE ALSO

glXChooseVisual, **glXCreateContext**